PRINCIPLES OF
MICROECONOMICS

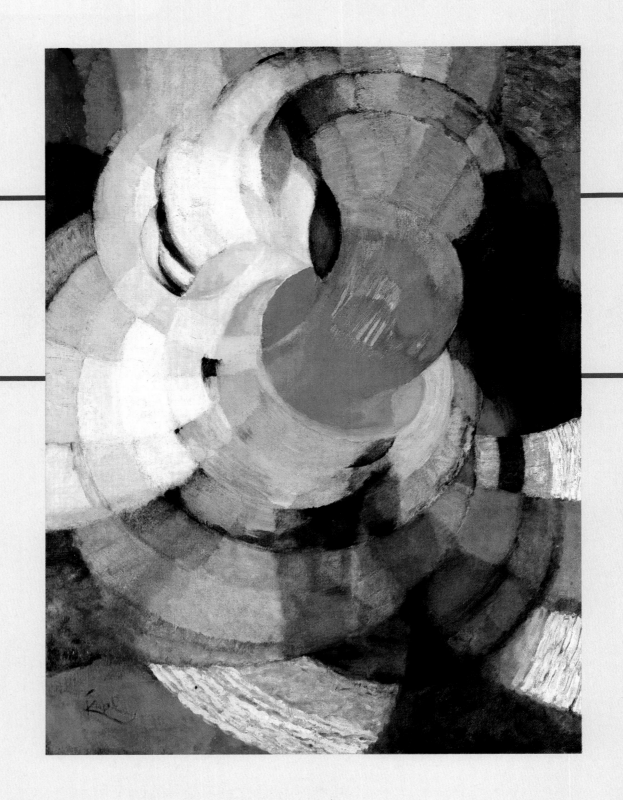

PRINCIPLES OF
MICROECONOMICS

Karl E. Case
Wellesley College

Ray C. Fair
Yale University

Prentice Hall, Englewood Cliffs, New Jersey 07632

Library of Congress Cataloging-in-Publication Data

Case, Karl E.
Principles of microeconomics/Karl E. Case, Ray C. Fair.
    p.   cm.
Includes index.
ISBN 0-13-710310-7
1. Microeconomics.   I. Fair, Ray C.   II. Title.
HB172.C36   1989
338.5—dc19   88-25425
                                  CIP

Development editor: Cheryl Kupper
Editorial production supervision: Susan Fisher
Interior and cover design: Suzanne Behnke
Manufacturing buyer: Margaret Rizzi
Page layout: Richard Dombrowski
Cover painting:
Kupka, F., Discs of Newton
Philadelphia Museum of Art:
The Louise and Walter Arensberg Collection.

Principles of Microeconomics
Karl E. Case and Ray C. Fair

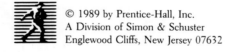

Printed in the United States of America
10 9 8 7 6 5 4 3 2 1

ISBN 0-13-710310-7

Prentice-Hall International (UK) Limited, *London*
Prentice-Hall of Australia Pty. Limited, *Sydney*
Prentice-Hall Canada Inc., *Toronto*
Prentice-Hall Hispanoamericana, S.A., *Mexico*
Prentice-Hall of India Private Limited, *New Delhi*
Prentice-Hall of Japan, Inc., *Tokyo*
Simon & Schuster Asia Pte. Ltd., *Singapore*
Editora Prentice-Hall do Brasil, Ltda., *Rio de Janeiro*

Brief Table of Contents

Contents

2

Scarcity and Choice: The Economic Problem   29

3

The Basic Structure of the U.S. Economy: The Private and Public Sectors   49

4

Markets and Prices: The Basic Forces of Supply and Demand   77

5

Supply and Demand: The Nature of the System, Applications, and Elasticity   105

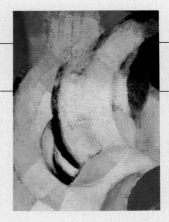

PART TWO
MICROECONOMICS

6

Household Behavior and Consumer Choice   133

7

The Firm: Organization, Profits, and Production   163

8

The Firm: Short-Run Costs and Competitive Output Decisions   181

9

The Firm: Costs and Competitive Supply in the Long Run   203

10

The Firm: Demand in Competitive Input Markets   227

11

Capital Markets and Land Markets: Profit, Interest, and Rent   253

12

General Equilibrium, the Efficiency of Competition, and Sources of Market Failure   279

13

Imperfect Competition: Monopoly Markets   303

14

Imperfect Competition: Monopolistic Competition and Oligopoly   333

15

Imperfect Markets and Public Policy: Antitrust and Regulation   357

16

Government in the Economy: Externalities, Public Goods, and Public Choice   379

17

Income Distribution and Poverty   407

18

Public Finance: The Economics of Taxation 433

19

The Economics of Labor Markets and Labor Unions 463

20

The Location of Economic Activity: Cities and Regions   489

PART THREE
INTERNATIONAL ECONOMICS

21

International Trade and the Theory of Comparative Advantage   515

22

Economic Growth in Developing Nations   541

23

Alternative Economic Systems   563

Preface

This textbook contains the first five introductory chapters, fifteen microeconomics chapters, and selected international chapters from our hardbound *Principles of Economics* textbook. It has been specially prepared for microeconomics courses where professors prefer to assign a paperback "split" rather than a single volume containing coverage of both microeconomics and macroeconomics.

So that users of this book and its companion volume, *Principles of Macroeconomics*, can fully understand our rationale in writing our new principles of economics text, what follows is an adaptation of the preface as it appears in our single hardbound volume.

We hope that this book will have an important impact on the teaching of introductory economics. The main goal of any introductory economics text, we believe, is to get students to "think like economists." In order to do that, they first need a structure within which economic issues can be discussed and debated. The foundation of such a structure is the set of key concepts that all economists, regardless of ideological bent, understand and use in conversation and analysis. Concepts such as opportunity cost, capital, efficiency, and general equilibrium must be taught almost like a foreign language, with repetition and practice.

In our view, introductory texts have become too detailed. They try to teach *too much*. In this book, we have chosen to pay careful attention to the key concepts of economics and to its basic structure. Without a clear framework, details have nothing to hang on, and they are soon forgotten.

Lack of clear structure seems a particularly acute problem in the macro part of introductory texts. Topics come and go, with few unifying themes. This lack of unity to the macro material runs counter to the trend in macroeconomic research during the last decade or so, which has sought better theoretical foundations for the subject. Although general agreement is still rare in macroeconomics, the field has changed substantially since the 1960s, and it has much more structure now, even after adjusting for differing views.

We also find that much of the basic framework of microeconomics has become obscured by detail in more recent editions of leading texts. We think that the best way to unify the micro material is to begin with a complete development of the competitive model—household and firm behavior in both output *and* input markets. With the competitive model in place, students have seen all the pieces of a complete simple economy, they have derived important welfare conclusions, and they are ready to relax assumptions and deal with critical material.

In the interest of coherence, we put more emphasis on structure and connections in laying out both the micro and macro material than other texts do. The aim is to present the key concepts slowly and carefully. New topics are not introduced until students are ready and until they know where the topic fits in the overall scheme of the book. Each chapter builds on the one before it, and there is a common thread that runs through the entire book.

THE PLAN OF THE MICROECONOMICS SPLIT

As we were writing this text, we spent many hours talking with each other and with our colleagues about our purpose. We feel that the book's final form will ensure a fulfilling learning experience for the student. After we introduce basic concepts in the first five chapters (where we hope to capture the student's attention), we lay out the perfectly competitive model in Chapters 6 through 12. Chapter 6 describes household behavior, including both demand for goods and supply of factors (including labor). Chapters 7 through 10 discuss the behavior of perfectly competitive firms. Chapters 10 and 11 emphasize the links between households and firms and between decision making in output and input markets. When we take up capital markets in Chapter 11, we describe the various institutional mechanisms through which household saving is channeled into productive investment projects on the firm side of the market.

Chapter 12 is a transitional chapter that closes out our treatment of perfect competition and analyzes the strengths and weaknesses of market systems. The core of the chapter is a discussion of the efficiency of competition. It focuses on the critical role of prices in input and output markets, prices that determine the tradeoffs facing households and firms. It shows how individual decisions lead to efficient choices from society's viewpoint *when all the assumptions of perfect competition hold*. The chapter then begins the process of relaxing these assumptions and exposing problems, a task that takes the next five chapters. The topics covered in these subsequent chapters include monopoly, monopolistic competition, oligopoly, public goods, externalities, and income distribution.

Three applied chapters follow the microeconomic core: public finance, labor economics, and urban economics. The microeconomics split closes with three chapters on international issues.

THE PLAN OF THE MACROECONOMICS SPLIT

The macroeconomics split is a renumbered version of the macro material found in our combined volume. It, too, begins with the first five chapters found in the combined volume. We then present three additional chapters to introduce macroeconomics. Although inflation and unemployment are covered in the last of these chapters (Chapter 8), we keep the coverage descriptive rather than analytical. At this point, clearly, we are not ready for any analysis. We then build our macro model in Chapters 9 through 17. Chapters 9 and 10 develop a simple model of the goods market (the multiplier model), first without, and then with, a government. This discussion introduces the tools of fiscal policy. Chapters 11 and 12 introduce the Federal Reserve and build a simple model of the money market. This material introduces the tools of monetary policy.

Chapter 13 brings together the lessons of the previous four chapters. It combines the model of the goods market with the model of the money market in a construct we call the "income/interest rate model." (This, in essence, is the *IS-LM* model, but we do *not* use the *IS* and *LM* curves.) At the end of Chapter 13 we introduce the price level and derive the aggregate demand (*AD*) curve. Note that we have spent five chapters (9–13) leading up to the *AD* curve. The reasoning behind the *AD* curve is actually quite complicated, and we have taken particular care not to present it until enough preparatory material, namely the income/interest rate model, has been presented. The *AD* curve must not be confused with market demand curves, a common problem, and we are careful to stress the differences.

Chapter 14 presents a more complete discussion of household behavior as it relates to macroeconomics, and Chapters 15 and 16 present a more complete discussion of firm behavior. In Chapter 16 we derive the aggregate supply (*AS*) curve under the assumption of perfect competition.

Chapter 17 brings everything together. It first takes the *AD* curve from Chapter 13 and the *AS* curve from Chapter 16 (assuming that the *AS* curve exists) and puts them together. This *AS-AD* model determines income, the interest rate, and the price level. The analysis is then expanded to include the imperfectly competitive case, where the *AS* curve does not exist. Then the chapter takes the more realistic discussion of household and firm behavior from Chapters 14 through 16 and incorporates it into the analysis. This is our "complete" macro model. The rest of the chapter analyzes the complete model. Chapters 18 and 19, which are intended to get students thinking like macroeconomists, use the complete model to analyze various macro issues.

The macroeconomics core ends with a chapter on alternative macroeconomic theories (theories that differ from those behind the complete model) and a chapter on growth.

The final four chapters open up the text to the rest of the world. Chapter 22 is on international trade, Chapter 23 on open-economy macroeconomics, Chapter 24 on developing countries, and Chapter 25 on comparative systems.

One important feature of the macroeconomics chapters is that many of them close with a brief section describing the data relevant to the chapter. Various macro time series are plotted quarterly for the period since 1970 and then discussed. We have found it useful to tie the theoretical discussion to real world data.

We do microeconomics first in the combined volume, and we feel strongly that it should come first. Most of the key concepts in economics are microeconomic ones. The structure of the discipline is really its microeconomic structure. One does not see, for example, research whose goal is to build firmer *macro*economic foundations for *micro*economics. We realize, however, that many institutions require or allow macroeconomics to be taken first, and so we have written the combined text and the macro split to allow this to be done. When we take up macroeconomics, we do *not* assume that students have had micro. Where we need to use micro concepts in the macroeconomics, we present them and teach them there. For those who have had micro these sections serve as a good review. Thus anyone can study macroeconomics first using this textbook.

In writing this book, we have made an effort not to expose our own ideological preferences. Although we choose orthodox neoclassical micro theory (with some Keynesian theory in the macro part) as the core model of the book, we use critical material (both from the left and right) to show both the strengths and weaknesses of market allocation. The book presents a number of debates, without resolving them. Many are left for the student to resolve, with the warning that there are no easy answers—just trade-offs.

HOW THIS TEXT WAS DEVELOPED

This text is the culmination of nearly four years of writing, careful market research to confirm our approach, intensive editorial development, in-depth reviewing, and wide-ranging class testing. From the beginning our goal was to develop a principles of economics text that would set the standard for the 1990s and beyond.

Market Research

Early in the development of the text, we and the publisher prepared a detailed questionnaire that sought to determine what our colleagues wanted in the next generation of economics texts. That survey confirmed our original conception of the book.

Development Editing

As each chapter of each draft was written, it was extensively analyzed and carefully edited by a skilled development editor. Drawing on a background that included the development of dozens of introductory college textbooks, this editor worked to ensure that, sentence by sentence and paragraph by paragraph, we had laid out for the reader, in the clearest possible way, the fundamental principles of economics. This process was repeated for each new draft, and many chapters went through four drafts.

Reviewing

As the manuscript was being edited by the development editor, it was simultaneously being reviewed by dozens of academic experts to ensure its technical accuracy and pedagogical effectiveness. While the editor viewed the manuscript from the perspective of the student, the reviewers took the perspective of an instructor using the text.

Class Testing

Based on the development editor's work and the reviews, we prepared draft after draft until we felt that the manuscript was ready for testing in the classroom. That draft was then used by hundreds of students at six schools.

Reviewer Conference

When the reviews and the class testing were complete, we met with reviewers, editors, and the Prentice Hall marketing staff for an intensive reviewer conference. There the entire manuscript was gone over line by line in order to create final draft that would be a superior teaching tool for tomorrow's students. Based on the input from the class testing, the final reviews, the reviewer conference, and the editors' suggestions, we made our final revisions.

We feel that the long process of development and the many resources that the publisher provided have helped us to reach our goal of writing an economics text that will meet the needs of today's students and instructors.

THE TEACHING/LEARNING PACKAGE

Each component of the teaching and learning package has been carefully crafted to ensure that the principles of economics course is a rewarding experience for both instructors and students. A number of innovative supplements have been created by the authors and the publisher. They are available in a comprehensive *Instructor's Resource Package*.

The Annotated Instructor's Edition

The *Annotated Instructor's Edition*, by Professor Chris Waller of Indiana University and Professor Thomas Beveridge of the University of North Carolina, is a special printing of the textbook created for instructors. Preceding the student text are chapter outlines, summaries, learning objectives, lecture suggestions, and discussion questions. In the text itself, marginal notes enhance the teaching of economics by providing suggestions for classroom discussion. Sections of the text that might require special attention on the part of the instructor are highlighted. Where possible, the marginal notes make reference to other parts of the teaching and learning package for a comprehensive, integrated teaching and learning experience.

Testing

Over three thousand questions, written by Professor Joseph Sulock of the University of North Carolina at Asheville, Jay Sultan of Arizona State University, and Dereka Rushbrook of the University of Texas at Austin, are provided in the *Microeconomics Test Item File* and the *Macroeconomics Test Item File*. An average of eighty multiple-choice and true-false questions have been written for each chapter.

Both test item files are available for use on the highly successful DIPLOMA Classroom Management and Testing System, which consists of four computer programs that operate on IBM, Apple IIc and IIe, and compatible microcomputers.

EXAM provides question creation and editing features for use in developing, maintaining, and altering test banks. Unlimited questions can be accommodated in each format: multiple-choice, true/false, matching, and short answer/essay.

GRADEBOOK addresses the task of grade management. It automatically tracks running averages for both students and tests and can display letter grades, percentage averages, GPA, or points earned.

PROCTOR allows students to take tests generated by EXAM at a computer. While testing, students can browse, skip hard questions, alter answers, and review responses, as if the test were being taken on paper. Automatic grading.

CALENDAR is a free-form scheduling tool that allows you to enter up to eleven events or messages for any particular day. A transfer feature permits recurring events to be entered for several dates without retyping. Messages can be easily entered, edited, saved, displayed, or printed.

For those with limited access to computers or secretarial support, Prentice Hall's *Telephone Testing Service* allows professors to order customized tests by calling a toll-free telephone number a few days before a test is to be administered. Additional information about the various forms of testing service can be obtained by contacting your local Prentice Hall representative.

Color Transparencies and Transparency/Handout Masters

There are over four hundred charts, graphs, and tables in this textbook. One hundred and fifty graphs have been carefully selected and reproduced as 8 1/2 x 11 color transparencies for classroom use. These color transparencies are available from the publisher upon adoption of the textbook. In addition, every chart, table, and graph in the textbook has been reproduced in 8 1/2 x 11″ format in a special booklet called *Transparency and Handout Masters*, which is intended for use in classroom demonstration and discussion.

Electronic Transparencies

Some instructors have found it helpful to use the personal computer to demonstrate economic graphing. A series of electronic simulations designed for classroom use has been developed by Darryl Ward is available to professors who adopt this text. These simulations can be previewed on a special demonstration diskette, which is included in the *Instructor's Resource Package*.

Study Guide with Practice Tests

A special *Study Guide* containing practice tests has been prepared by Professors David Hoaas and Harold Christensen of Centenary College. This study aid reinforces the textbook and provides motivated students with applications and exercises. Each chapter of the *Study Guide* contains the following features:

Learning Objectives The first section of each chapter provides an overview of the important ideas and issues discussed in the textbook.

Chapter Review This section provides a written summary of the important issues in the chapter. It is intended as a review for students who have already read the appropriate chapter and wish to remind themselves of the key ideas.

Glossary This section helps the student learn the new terms and phrases used in economics. Together with the "Key Concepts" section found at the end of each chapter of the textbook, the glossary helps students to look up and review major ideas.

Study Tips Tips are provided to make the student's study time more efficient. This section also points out common errors or potential sources of confusion that often arise as students attempt to learn and remember important economic principles.

"Where We've Been/Where We're Going" This section of the *Study Guide* has a two-fold purpose. First, it relates the material presented in the current text chapter to the material presented in previous chapters. It describes how the new theory being explained grows out of ideas already developed. Second, it foreshadows lessons to come, describing where and how ideas presented in the current chapter will reappear for development in later chapters. This underscores the importance, relevance, and "fit" of the models and diagrams under current consideration.

Multiple-Choice Questions This section provides the first testing of the concepts learned. Eight to 20 multiple-choice questions are designed to test a student's knowledge of the terms and concepts presented in the chapter. The level of difficulty of these questions is comparable to the Test Item File.

Analytic Exercises The tools of mathematical analysis have become increasingly useful in the study of economics. This portion of the study guide contains exercises that often require the use of algebra or geometry to solve for a specific economic value. As the student will quickly learn, graphs are one of the primary tools used by economists to convey information.

Essay Questions These questions require time and thought by the student to determine an answer. We suggest that students write out answers to these problems and compare these answers with those of their fellow students. In many cases, these questions have more than one answer and no single right or wrong one.

Answers This section provides correct answers to the multiple-choice questions as well as abbreviated answers to several of the analytic exercises. Students should consult this portion of the chapter only after they have attempted to work the questions and exercises.

It should be clear by now that the development of the supplements was considered as important as the development of the text itself, and this promises an unparalleled teaching package.

ACKNOWLEDGMENTS

No textbook can be written without the help of many people. One of our greatest debts is to Peter Siegelman, who made numerous contributions to the early drafts of the macro chapters. Kathryn Dominguez also played an important role at the same stage of development. Robert Moore was an especially helpful reviewer of the early drafts of the micro chapters. Sharon Oster read most of the chapters, many more than once, and made invaluable comments. David Lindauer wrote the first draft of Chapter 39, and Sanford Sloan wrote the first draft of the accounting appendix in Chapter 3. Ann Royalty read and corrected the entire manuscript in galleys.

Chris Waller encouraged us to keep the micro foundations correct and clear in the macro discussion, in particular regarding the nonexistence of the AS curve in imperfect competition. Lynn Gillette and Rick McIntyre were instrumental in helping us to keep a balanced ideological view. Chris Waller, Lynn Gillette, and Rick McIntyre, along with Jean Shackleford and James Aylesworth, commented on the entire manuscript at the reviewers' conference. We cannot overstate the importance of this conference to the final development of the book.

Others whose comments were extremely helpful include Carolyn Shaw Bell, Dutch Leonard, and Len Nichols.

The following individuals were of immense help in reviewing all or part of this manuscript in various stages of its development:

Jack Adams, The University of Maryland
Doulas Agbetsiafa, Indiana University at South Bend
Sam Alapati, Rutgers University
Polly Allen, The University of Connecticut
Stuart Allen, The University of North Carolina at Greensboro
James Aylesworth, Lakeland Community College
Bruce Bolnick, Northeastern University
G.E. Breger, The University of South Carolina
Dennis Brennan, William Rainey Harper Junior College
Daniel Christiansen, Albion College
David Colander, Middlebury College
Jay Egger, Towson State University
Mosin Farminesh, Temple University
Dan Feaster, Miami University of Ohio
Susan Feiner, Virginia Commonwealth University
William Field, DePauw University
Gary Gigliotti, Rutgers University
Lynn Gillette, Texas A&M University
Roger Goldberg, Ohio Northern University
Douglas Greenley, Moorhead State University

A.R. Gutowsky, California State University at Sacramento
Stephen Happel, Arizona State University
Mitchell Harwitz, State University of New York at Buffalo
Harry Holzer, Michigan State University
Janet Hunt, The University of Georgia
Hirshel Kasper, Oberlin College
Bruce Kaufman, Georgia State University
Dominique Khactu, The University of North Dakota
Phillip King, San Francisco State University
Barbara Kneeshaw, Wayne County Community College
Jane Lillydahl, The University of Colorado at Boulder
Al Link, The University of North Carolina at Greensboro
Gerald Lynch, Purdue University
Michael Magura, The University of Toledo
Don Maxwell, Central State University
Rick McIntyre, The University of Rhode Island
Robert Moore, Occidental College
David Nickerson, The University of British Columbia
Kent Olson, Oklahoma State University
Carl Parker, Fort Hays State University
Michael Rendich, Westchester Community College
Richard Rosenberg, Pennsylvania State University
Jean Shackleford, Bucknell University
Linda Shaffer, California State University at Fresno
Alden Shiers, California Polytechnic State University
Ernst Stromsdorfer, Washington State University
Michael Taussig, Rutgers University
Norman Vancott, Ball State University
Chris Waller, Indiana University at Bloomington
Walter Wessels, North Carolina State University

We also thank Kathy Simpson for typing and Ed Lyon, Carrie Portis, and Sue White for helping with preliminary versions of art work. Catherine Christensen, Maura Doyle, Lynn Blais, and Pam Matthews provided valuable research assistance and moral support.

Cheryl Kupper, the development editor, went over every chapter many times and enormously improved the writing. Ray Mullaney, editor in chief of Prentice Hall's text development group, has been the guiding force for this project since its inception. Susan Fisher, the production editor, did a superb job in producing the book. Bill Webber, economics editor, Jim Edwards, marketing manager, and Ellen Greenberg, supplements editor, applied their varied talents to the creation of the overall teaching/learning package.

Case thanks Susan and Kristen for their love and patience over the years, the economics majors in the Wellesley class of 1985 for inspiration, and the Federal Reserve Bank of Boston for a wonderful environment in which to work. Fair owes much to Emily, Stephen, and John, who are enthusiastic about selling this book to the neighbors.

Karl E. Case
Ray C. Fair

About the Authors

Karl E. Case is Professor of Economics at Wellesley College. He also lectures on Economics and Tax Policy in the International Tax Program at Harvard Law School and is a Visiting Scholar at the Federal Reserve Bank of Boston. He received his B.A. from Miami University in 1968, spent three years in the Army and received the M.A. and Ph.D. from Harvard University. In 1980-81 he was a Liberal Arts Fellow in Law and Economics at Harvard Law School.

Professor Case's research has been in the areas of public finance, taxation and housing. He is the author of four other books including *Economics and Tax Policy* and *Property Taxation: The Need for Reform* as well as numerous articles in professional journals.

Undergraduate teaching has always been one focal point of Professor Case's professional life. For the past 12 years he has taught at Wellesley where he was Department Chair from 1982-85. Before coming to Wellesley, he spent two years as Head Tutor (director of undergraduate studies) at Harvard where he won the Allyn Young Teaching Prize. He has been a member of the AEA's Committee on Economic Education and was Associate Editor of the *Journal of Economic Education* responsible for the section on innovations in teaching. Professor Case has taught at least one section of the Principles course every year since 1972.

Ray C. Fair is Professor of Economics at Yale University. He is a member of the Cowles Foundation at Yale, a Research Associate of the National Bureau of Economic Research, and a Fellow of the Econometric Society. He received a B.A. in economics from Fresno State College in 1964 and a Ph.D. in economics from M.I.T. in 1968. He taught at Princeton University from 1968 to 1974 and has been at Yale since 1974.

Professor Fair's research has primarily been in the areas of macroeconomics and econometrics, with particular emphasis on macroeconometric model building. He is the author of five other books, including *Specification, Estimation, and Analysis of Macroeconometric Models*, Harvard University Press, 1984, and numerous journal articles.

Professor Fair has taught introductory and intermediate economics at Yale. He has also taught graduate courses in macroeconomic theory and macroeconometrics.

I INTRODUCTION

1 The Scope and Method of Economics

The study of economics should begin with a sense of wonder.

Pause for a moment and consider a typical day in your life. You eat. For breakfast you might have bread made in a local bakery with flour produced in Minnesota from wheat grown in Kansas and bacon from pigs raised in Ohio packaged in plastic made in New Jersey. You spill coffee from Colombia on your shirt made in Texas from textiles shipped from South Carolina.

After class you drive with a friend in a Japanese car on an interstate highway system that took 20 years and billions of dollars worth of resources to build. You stop for gasoline refined in Louisiana from Saudi Arabian crude oil brought here on a supertanker that took three years to build at a shipyard in Maine.

At night you call your brother in Mexico City. The call travels over newly laid fiber-optic cable to a powerful antenna that sends it to a transponder on one of over 1000 communications satellites orbiting the earth.

You use or consume tens of thousands of things, both tangible and intangible, every day: buildings, the music of a rock band, the compact disc it is recorded on, telephone services, staples, paper, toothpaste, tweezers, soap, a digital watch, fire protection, antacid tablets, beer, banks, electricity, eggs, insurance, football fields, computers, busses, rugs, subways, health services, sidewalks, and so forth. Somebody made all of these things. Somebody decided to organize men and women and materials to produce them and distribute them. Thousands of decisions went into their completion. Somehow they got to you.

One hundred sixteen million people in the United States—almost half the total population—work at hundreds of thousands of different kinds of jobs producing over four trillion dollars worth of goods and services every year. Some cannot find work; some choose not to work for pay. Some are rich; others are poor.

We import 50 billion dollars worth of petroleum and petroleum products each year, and we export 30 billion dollars worth of food. High-rise office buildings go up in central cities. Condominiums and homes are built in the suburbs. In other places homes are abandoned and boarded up.

Some countries are wealthy. Others are impoverished. Some are growing. Some are stagnating. Some businesses are doing well. Others are going bankrupt.

At any moment in time every society faces constraints imposed by nature and by previous generations. Some societies are handsomely endowed by nature with fertile land, water, sunshine, natural resources, and so forth. Others have deserts and few mineral resources. Some societies receive much from previous generations—art, music, technical knowledge, beautiful buildings, and productive factories. Others are left with over-grazed, eroded land, cities leveled by war, or polluted natural environments. *All* societies face limits.

Economics   The study of how human beings and societies choose to use the scarce resources that nature and previous generations have provided.

Economics *is the study of how human beings and societies choose to use the scarce resources that nature and previous generations have provided.* What is produced? How is it produced? Who gets it? Why? Is the result good or bad? Can it be improved?

WHY STUDY ECONOMICS?

To Learn a Way of Thinking

Probably the most important reason for studying economics is to *learn a particular way of thinking.* A good way to introduce economics is to review three of its most fundamental concepts—*opportunity cost, marginalism,* and *efficient markets.* If this book is successful, you will find yourself using these concepts every day in making decisions, both on economic matters and on matters that have nothing to do with economics.

Opportunity cost   That which we forgo, or give up, when we make a choice or a decision.

Opportunity Cost   What happens in an economy is the outcome of thousands of individual decisions. Households must decide how to divide up their incomes over all the goods and services available in the marketplace. Individuals must decide whether to work or not to work, whether to go to school, and how much to save. Businesses must decide what to produce, how much to produce, how much to charge and where to locate. It is not surprising that economic analysis focuses on the process of decision making.

Nearly all decisions involve **trade-offs**: there are advantages and disadvantages, costs and benefits, associated with every action and every choice. A key concept that recurs again and again in analyzing the decision-making process is the notion of *opportunity cost.* The full "cost" of making a specific choice includes what we give up by not making the alternative choice. That which we forgo when we make a choice or a decision is called the **opportunity cost** of that decision.

The concept applies to individuals, businesses, and entire societies. The opportunity cost of going to a movie is the value of the other things you could have done with the same money and time. If you decide to take time off in lieu of working, the opportunity cost of your leisure is the forgone pay that you would have earned had you worked. Part of the cost of a college education is the income you could have earned by working full time. If a firm purchases a new piece of modern equipment for $3000, it does so because it expects that equipment to generate more profit. There is an opportunity cost, however, since that $3000 could have been deposited in an interest-earning account. To a society, the opportunity cost of using resources for military hardware is the value of the private/civilian goods that could have been produced with the same resources.

The reason that opportunity costs arise is that resources are *scarce*. Consider time. There are only 24 hours in a day, and we must live our lives under this constraint. Many things in life are scarce, and much of economics is concerned with behavior in the face of **scarcity.** People are forced to make choices in the face of scarcity. If your neighbor mows his lawn today, he won't have time to take his children to the zoo, and this is an opportunity cost of mowing the lawn. This fundamental observation that decisions have opportunity costs is the reason that economics is sometimes called the "dismal science."

Marginalism and Sunk Costs   A second key concept used in analyzing choices is the notion of **marginalism.** In weighing the costs and benefits of a decision, it is important to weigh only the costs and benefits that are contingent upon the decision. Suppose, for example, that you lived in New Orleans and that you were weighing the costs and benefits of visiting your mother in Iowa. If business required that you travel to Kansas City, the cost of visiting Mom would be only the additional, or *marginal*, time and money cost of getting to Iowa from Kansas City.

Consider the cost of producing this book. Assume that 10,000 copies are produced. The total cost of producing the copies includes the cost of the authors' time in writing the book, the cost of editing, the cost of making the plates for printing, and the cost of the paper and ink. If the total cost were $300,000, then the average cost of one copy would be $30, which is simply $300,000 divided by 10,000.

Although average cost is an important concept, there are times when a book publisher must know more than simply the average cost of a book. For example, suppose a second printing is being debated. That is, should another 10,000 copies be produced? In deciding whether to proceed, the costs of writing, editing, making plates, and so forth are irrelevant. Why? Because they have already been incurred—they are *sunk costs*. **Sunk costs** are costs that cannot be avoided, regardless of what is done in the future, because they have already taken place. All that matters now are the costs associated with the additional, or *marginal*, books to be printed. Technically, as you will see later in the book, *marginal cost* is the cost of producing one more unit of output.

There are numerous examples in which the concept of marginal cost is useful. For an airplane that is about to take off with empty seats, the marginal cost of an extra passenger is essentially zero; the total cost of the trip is essentially unchanged by the addition of an extra passenger. Thus, setting aside a few seats to be sold at big discounts can be profitable even if the fare for those seats is far below the average cost per seat of making the trip. As long as it succeeds in filling seats that would otherwise have been empty, it is a profitable thing to do—the added revenue is greater than marginal cost.

Another area where marginal analysis is helpful is the study of the effects of tax rates on people's behavior. The tax system in the United States is progressive, which means that people with higher incomes pay higher tax rates. (We are ignoring here tax loopholes, which result in some high-income people paying lower effective tax rates than low- and middle-income people.) Suppose the tax system is such that you pay no tax on the first $10,000 that you make, 20 percent on the amount you make between $10,001 and $20,000, and 30 percent on any amount over $20,000. Now suppose that you make $25,000. You pay total taxes of $3500, which is .2 times $10,000 plus .3 times $5000. Your *average tax rate* is the total tax that you pay divided by your total income. In this example your average tax rate is .14, which is $3500 divided by $25,000.

Your *marginal tax rate* is the rate you have to pay on any additional, or marginal, income that you earn; in this example your marginal tax rate is .3. You are making more than $20,000, and any income over $20,000 is taxed at 30 percent. The marginal tax rate is 20 percent for anyone earning between $10,001 and $20,000, and it is zero for anyone earning less than $10,000.

Suppose you are considering doing some part-time work after hours. Which tax rate is relevant for this decision? The answer is fairly obvious. Your marginal tax rate determines how much you get to keep out of the added income you earn. Even though you pay on average only 14 percent of your income in taxes, you pay 30 cents on each *extra* dollar earned. In short, marginal tax rates, not average tax rates, affect decisions.

Efficient Markets—No Free Lunch   Suppose you are driving on a highway with three lanes going in your direction and you come upon a toll plaza with six toll booths. Three toll booths are straight ahead in the three lanes of traffic, and the three other booths are off to the right. Which lane should you choose? It is usually the case that the wait time is approximately the same no matter what you do. There are usually enough people searching for the shortest line so as to make all the lines about the same length. If one line is much shorter than the others, cars will quickly move into it until the lines are equalized. There are usually enough drivers searching for the fastest line to equalize the average wait time.

Economists sometimes talk about *profit opportunities*. In the toll booth example a profit opportunity exists if one line is shorter than the others. The general view of economics is that profit opportunities are rare. At any one time there are many people searching for such opportunities, and as a consequence few exist. In the toll booth example it is seldom the case that one line is substantially shorter than the others.

Another example of a possible profit opportunity is the following. At major banks in big cities, you can buy foreign currencies. The prices are essentially determined in world money markets. Let's concentrate on the U.S. dollar, the German mark, and the French franc. Prices are posted for marks in terms of dollars, francs in terms of marks, and dollars in terms of francs, among other possible combinations. With dollars we can buy marks; with these marks we can buy francs; and with these francs we can buy back dollars. Can we make money on this transaction? In other words, can the prices be such that we end up with more dollars at the end than we started with? If this is possible, we say that there are profit opportunities in the market. There are in fact almost never any profit opportunities of this kind in foreign currency markets. There are hundreds or thousands of individuals looking for such opportunities each minute, and if any opportunity does arise it is quickly eliminated.

If, for example, the mark-franc price is too low given the other prices, there is an immediate rush to buy marks and sell francs, not by ordinary citizens at bank windows, but by a few large currency traders in Tokyo, London, or Zurich who watch prices every minute. Such a rush drives up the mark-franc price to the no-profit-opportunity point. Markets like this, where any profit opportunities are eliminated almost instantaneously, are said to be **efficient markets**.

In order for a market to be efficient, it is not necessary that everyone trading in the market be a super calculator of profit opportunities. It usually takes only a few. A multinational corporation, for example, can enter the foreign currency market without being concerned about possible discrepancies in the various currency prices. It knows that there are essentially no discrepancies. In the toll booth example, a quick glance usually reveals that the choice makes little difference. It is generally a safe assumption that others will have already equalized wait times. Of course, if too many drivers feel this way, there *will* be profit opportunities.

The common language way of expressing the efficient markets hypothesis is "there's no such thing as a free lunch." How should one react when a stockbroker calls up with a hot tip on the stock market? With skepticism. There are thousands of individuals each day looking for hot tips in the market, and if a particular tip about a stock is valid there will be an immediate rush to buy the stock, which will quickly drive its price up. By the time the tip gets to your broker and then to you, the profit opportunity that arose from the tip (assuming that there was one) is likely to have been eliminated. Similar arguments can be made for bond markets and commodity markets. There are many "experts" in these markets, who take quick advantage of any news that affects prices. Again, the number of experts need not necessarily be large to have the markets be efficient.

This view of economists that there are very limited profit opportunities around can, of course, be carried too far. There is a story about two people walking along, one an economist and one not. The noneconomist sees a twenty dollar bill on the sidewalk and says, "There's a twenty dollar bill on the sidewalk." The economist replies, "That is not possible. If there were, somebody would already have picked it up."

There are clearly times when profit opportunities exist. Someone has to be first to get the news, and some people have quicker insights than others. Nevertheless, news does get disseminated quickly, and there are thousands of people with quick insights. The general view that profit opportunities are rare is close to the mark.

The kinds of profit opportunities we have been talking about are *riskless* opportunities. If the three currency prices are out of line there is an opportunity to make a profit *with no risk of losing anything*. Although there may be few riskless profit opportunities, there are clearly opportunities of making profits if one is willing to bear some risk. Someone with an idea who is willing to take some risk may be rewarded handsomely if the idea turns out to be a good one. If you think IBM stock will rise in price in the future and buy some today, you will make a profit if the stock does in fact rise. You do bear risk, however, because the stock may in fact fall in price. In short, profits are clearly there to be made, but usually not without some risk.

To Understand Society

Another reason for studying economics is to understand society better. You cannot hope to understand how a society functions without a basic knowledge of its economy, and you cannot understand a society's economy without knowing its economic history. Clearly, past and present economic decisions have an enormous influence on the character of life in a society. The current state of the physical environment, the level of wealth and material well-being, and the nature and number of jobs are all, in part, products of the economic system.

To get a sense of the ways in which economic decisions have shaped our environment imagine that you are looking out of a window on the top floor of a high-rise office building in any of the thirty metropolitan areas in the United States with populations of over a million. All around you are other tall glass and steel buildings full of workers. In the distance you see the smoke of factories. Looking down, if it's morning, you see thousands of commuters pouring off trains and busses, and cars backed up on freeway exit ramps. You see trucks carrying goods from one place to another. You also see the face of urban poverty: just beyond the freeway is a large public housing project and beyond that, perhaps, burned-out and boarded-up buildings.

What you see before you is the product of millions of economic decisions made over hundreds of years. People at some point decided to spend time and money building those buildings and factories. Somebody cleared the land, laid the tracks, built the roads, and produced the cars and busses.

Not only have economic decisions shaped our physical environment, they have determined the character of society as well. At no time has the impact of economic change on the character of a society been more evident than in England during the late eighteenth and early nineteenth centuries, a period that we now call the **Industrial Revolution**. Increases in the productivity of agriculture, new manufacturing technologies, and the development of more efficient forms of transportation led to a massive movement of the population from the countryside to the city. In the early 1700s approximately three out of four people in Great Britain were engaged in agriculture; it was largely a rural peasant society. By 1812 only one in four remained in agriculture, and by 1900 the figure was less than one in ten. People jammed into overcrowded cities and worked long hours in factories. The world had changed completely in two centuries, a period that, in the run of history, was nothing more than the blink of an eye.

It is not surprising that the discipline of economics really began during this period. Social critics and philosophers looked around them and knew that their philosophies must expand to accommodate the changes. Adam Smith's *Wealth of Nations* appeared in 1776. It was followed by the writings of David Ricardo, Karl Marx, Thomas Malthus, and others. Each tried to make sense out of what was happening. Who was building the factories? Why? What determined the level of wages paid to workers or the price of food? What would happen in the future, and what *should* happen? These people were the first economists.

Similar changes continue to affect the character of life today. As late as 1950 approximately one out of six people in the United States lived on farms. In 1987 the figure was a little over one in fifty. The tremendous productivity of modern corporate farms using new agricultural technologies, combined with the very high borrowing costs of the early 1980s, made survival on small, less efficient family farms very difficult; thousands of farmers went bankrupt, defaulted on loans, and lost their farms at auctions.

The plight of small farmers across the United States has important political and social dimensions. But at its roots it is an economic problem: the price paid for agricultural products today does not cover what it costs many farmers to produce them. They lose money and are forced out of business. Why? What determines the price of corn? Of wheat? What determines the interest rates that farmers must pay on loans to buy equipment and seed?

The study of economics is an essential part of the study of society.

To Understand World Affairs

Two enormous tensions exist in the world today: (1) the dangerous mutual distrust between the United States and its allies on the one hand and the Soviet Union and its allies on the other, and (2) the growing gap between the rich developed countries and the poor countries. Although historical and cultural differences play their part, both of these tensions are, at their roots, *economic* tensions.

At the center of the ideological struggle between the two superpowers lie the differences between *two economic systems*. Both nations have similar primary problems to solve, but they set about solving them on the basis of entirely different assumptions. The U.S. economy is basically *capitalist*. This means that most economic decisions are made by private citizens in search of personal economic gain. Private citizens build and own the factories, decide what to produce, hire the workers, and so forth. Private profit is viewed as

Industrial revolution *The period in Europe, and chiefly in England, during the late eighteenth and early nineteenth centuries in which new manufacturing technologies and improved transportation gave rise to the modern factory system, enormous increases in productivity, and a massive movement of the population from the countryside to the cities.*

a just reward for taking risks and organizing production. Those who believe in capitalism point to the remarkable productivity and efficiency of the free enterprise system.

The *socialist* system of the Soviets is quite different. Factories, most farms, and all other industries are owned collectively by the people, and the state makes most decisions about what to produce, when, and how to distribute. The Soviet economy is managed by long-term planning on the part of the central government. The Soviet system is at least partly anchored in the writings of Karl Marx, who looked at conditions in the early nineteenth century and concluded that capitalism necessarily leads to the exploitation of labor and the repression of the people.

These issues are certainly far more complex than a few paragraphs can indicate, and this, indeed, is the point. To understand what it is that stands between the Americans and the Soviets, you must understand the fundamental differences between the two economic systems. Of course, differences in economic philosophy do not explain everything, but they are clearly an important part of the conflict.

The second major tension in the world is the widening gap between rich nations and poor nations. In 1986 world population was just under 5 billion. Of that number, 3.8 billion lived in less-developed countries and 1.2 billion lived in more-developed countries.[1] The 75 percent of the world's population that lives in the less-developed countries receives less than 20 percent of the world's income. In dozens of countries per capita income is a few hundred dollars a year.

The United Nations projects that within 35 years there will be 8.2 billion people in the world, 6.8 billion of them, 83 percent of the world's population, in less-developed countries. To make things worse, the economies of most less-developed countries are growing more slowly than those of the more-developed countries. This is clearly a major economic problem that the world will face in the future, a problem for which an understanding of economics is essential.

To Be an Informed Voter

During the last fifteen years, the U.S. economy has been on a roller coaster. In 1973–1974, the Organization of Petroleum Exporting Countries (OPEC) stopped shipping oil to the United States and at the same time succeeded in raising the price of crude oil in world markets by 400 percent. Simultaneously, a sequence of events in the world food market drove food prices up by 25 percent. By mid–1974, prices in the United States were rising across the board at a very rapid rate. Partially as a result of government policy to fight runaway inflation, the economy went into a recession in 1975. The recession succeeded in slowing price increases, but in the process millions found themselves unemployed and there was a great deal of economic hardship.

From 1979 through 1983, it happened all over again. Prices rose rapidly, the government reacted with more policies designed to stop prices from rising, and we ended up with an even worse recession in 1982. By the end of that year, 10.7% of the work force was unemployed.

These were serious problems that deserved and got a tremendous amount of debate in the political arena. In the last three presidential elections, economic issues were absolutely central.

---

[1]The more-developed nations are the United States, Japan, Australia, New Zealand, the Soviet Union, Canada, and the countries of Europe. Source: U.S. Department of Commerce, Bureau of the Census, *Statistical Abstract of the United States*, 1987, section 32, Comparative International Statistics.

In the last few years, many major political issues have been essentially economic issues. Should we restrict imports to protect our own textile, steel, and automobile industries? Should we drastically restructure our tax system? What should be done about the enormous federal deficits that have pushed the national debt to well over two trillion dollars? What can be done to help small family farmers survive?

When we participate in the political process, we are voting on issues that require a basic understanding of economics. Unfortunately, the level at which the public press, as well as our politicians, can or will discuss economic issues is sadly inadequate. Although more and more people are getting some basic economic education, there is a long way to go.

A SURPRISINGLY BROAD SUBJECT

Most students taking economics for the first time are surprised by the breadth of what they study. Some think that economics will teach them about the stock market, say, or what to do with their money. Others think that it deals exclusively with economic problems like inflation and unemployment. In fact, it deals with all these subjects, but they are pieces of a much larger puzzle.

Economics has deep roots in, and close ties to, social philosophy. An issue of great importance to philosophers, for example, is distributional justice. Why are some people rich and others poor, and whatever the answer, is this fair? A number of nineteenth century social philosophers wrestled with these questions, and out of their musings economics as a separate discipline was born.

The easiest way to get a feel for the breadth and depth of what you will be studying is to explore briefly the way economics is organized. First of all there are two major divisions of economics: microeconomics and macroeconomics.

Microeconomics and Macroeconomics

Microeconomics *The branch of economics that deals with the functioning of individual industries and the behavior of individual decision-making units, that is, single businesses and households.*

Microeconomics deals with the functioning of individual industries and the behavior of individual economic decision-making units: single business firms and households. The choices of firms about what to produce and how much to charge and the choices of households about what to buy and how much of it to buy help to explain why the economy produces the things it does.

Another big question that microeconomics addresses is who gets the things that are produced. Those households with higher incomes or more wealth get more, and the forces that determine this distribution of income and wealth are the province of microeconomics. Why do we have poverty? Who is poor? Why do some jobs pay more than others? Why do teachers or plumbers or baseball pitchers get paid what they do?

Think again about all the things you consume in a day, and then think back to that view out over a big city. Somebody decided to build those factories. Somebody decided to construct the roads, build the housing, produce the cars, knit the T-shirts, and smoke the bacon. Why? What is going on in all those buildings? It is easy to see that understanding individual micro decisions is very important to any understanding of your society.

Macroeconomics   The branch of economics that examines the economic behavior of aggregates—income, employment, output, and so on—on a national scale.

Macroeconomics adds it all up and looks at the economy as a whole. Instead of trying to understand what determines the output of a single firm or industry or the consumption patterns of a single household or group of households, we turn to the factors that determine national output, or national product. Macroeconomics turns from *household* income to *national* income.

While microeconomics focuses on individual product prices and relative prices, macroeconomics looks at the price level and the general rate of inflation. Microeconomics questions how many people will be hired (or fired) this year in the steel industry or in the high-tech firms around San Jose, California—what factors determine how much labor a firm or an industry will hire. Macroeconomics deals with *aggregate* employment and unemployment: how many jobs exist in the economy, and how many people who are willing to work will not be able to find work.

Microeconomics, then, looks at the individual unit—the household, the firm, the industry. It sees and examines the "trees." Macroeconomics looks at the whole, the aggregate. It sees and analyzes the "forest." Table 1.1 summarizes these divisions and some of the subjects with which they are concerned.

TABLE 1.1
Examples of Microeconomics and Macroeconomics

MICROECONOMICS	MACROECONOMICS
Production	
Production/output in individual industries and businesses	*National production/output*
How much steel	Total industrial output
How much office space	Gross National Product
How many cars	Growth of output
	Decline during recessions
Prices	
Price of individual goods and services	*Aggregate price level*
Price of medical care	Consumer prices
Price of gasoline	Producer prices
Food prices	Rate of inflation
Apartment rents	
Income	
Distribution of income and wealth	*National income*
Wages in the auto industry	Total wages and salaries
Minimum wage	Total corporate profits
Executive salaries	
Poverty	
Discrimination	
Employment	
Employment by individual businesses and industries	*Employment and unemployment in the economy*
Jobs in the steel industry	Total number of jobs
Number of employees in a firm	Unemployment rate
Number of accountants	Discouraged workers
Number of doctors	

The Special Fields of Economics

Perhaps the best way to convey the diversity of economics is to introduce some of the major special fields of study within it. If you decide to major in economics, you may take advanced courses in these or other areas. This is by no means meant to be an exhaustive list. The specific topics taught in an economics department at a major university would fill many pages, but this list should give you a sense of the kinds of issues that economists address.

Comparative economic systems examines the ways alternative economic systems function. What are the advantages and disadvantages of different systems? How do capitalist economies differ from socialist economies? Most courses specifically compare the Soviet Union and the United States; many also look at China, Japan, and Yugoslavia.

Industrial organization looks carefully at the structure and performance of industries and firms. How and why do monopolies behave differently from firms in more competitive industries? Why do we have antitrust laws? What have been the effects of events like the breakup of the American Telephone and Telegraph Company in 1983? When there is a small number of large firms competing in an industry, they often develop complicated strategies to outdo each other. How do those strategies work? Who gains and who loses?

Urban and regional economics studies the spatial arrangement of economic activity. Why do we have cities? Why are manufacturing firms locating farther and farther from the center of urban areas? What leads to abandonment and decline in some neighborhoods? Why does the center of the city attract firms such as banks, insurance companies, and law firms? Why are some regions growing rapidly while others are declining? Why do blacks and whites live where they do?

Econometrics applies statistical techniques and data to economic problems. The computer age has transformed the field of economics. It is much easier now than it was thirty years ago to collect and analyze data in an effort to test hypotheses and theoretical models of how the economy works. Most departments require majors to take at least one course in statistics or econometrics.

Economic development focuses on the problems of poor countries. Most courses analyze the process of economic growth and barriers to it in Third World nations. What can they do to promote development? What are their prospects? Topics usually include population growth and control, provision for basic needs, and possible strategies for international trade, among others.

Labor economics deals with the factors that determine wage rates, employment, and unemployment. How do people decide whether to work, how much to work, and at what kind of a job? Why and how do people get training? Why are some skills in plentiful supply and others scarce? What determines the number of jobs that will be created in a particular industry or in the economy as a whole? What role do unions play? How have the roles of unions and management changed in recent years? Is there a link between wages (or fees) and the value of what is produced?

International trade and *international monetary economics* study trade flows among countries and international financial institutions. What are the advantages and disadvantages for a country that allows its citizens to buy and sell freely in world markets? Should countries impose restrictions on imports to protect their own industries? What determines exchange rates? Can exchange rates be manipulated? Why is the dollar strong or weak? What is the function of gold in the world economy?

Public finance examines the role of government in the economy. What are the economic functions of government, and what should they be? How should the government finance the services that it provides? What effects do taxes have on the behavior of individual businesses and households and on the economy? What kinds of government programs should we have to deal with poverty, unemployment, air and water pollution, and other general problems? Do government programs such as social security change people's behavior?

Economic history traces the development of the modern industrial economy. What economic and political events and scientific advances caused the Industrial Revolution that began in eighteenth century Great Britain? What explains the tremendous growth and progress of post-World-War-II Japan? What was the Great Depression of the 1930s all about? What was the role of slavery in the American economy, and how far-reaching was it?

Law and economics analyzes the economic function of legal rules and institutions. How does a network of legal rules and regulations change the behavior of individuals and businesses? Do different liability rules make accidents and injuries more, or less, likely? Do rules that enforce contracts make people more likely to take risks? What is the economic role of the institution of private property? What are the economic costs of crime?

The history of economic thought is grounded in philosophy. It studies the development of economic ideas and theories over time. Most courses start with Adam Smith in the eighteenth century and discuss the works of economic thinkers such as Thomas Malthus, Karl Marx, John Stuart Mill, Jeremy Bentham, Stanley Jevons, Leon Walras, Alfred Marshall, John R. Hicks, and John Maynard Keynes. Economic theory is constantly developing and changing—what is accepted and orthodox today may not be accepted tomorrow. As we learn more and more about how different economies function under changing conditions, new theories emerge and old ones die out. Studying the history of ideas helps give meaning to modern theory and puts it in perspective.

THE METHOD OF ECONOMICS

Positive and Normative Economics

Positive economics   An approach to economics that seeks to understand behavior and the operation of systems without making judgments. It describes what is and how it works.

Normative economics   An approach to economics that analyzes outcomes of economic behavior, evaluates them as good or bad, and may suggest improvements.

Economics asks and attempts to answer two kinds of questions, positive and normative. **Positive economics** attempts to understand behavior and the operation of economic systems *without making judgments* about whether the outcomes are good or bad. It strives to describe what exists and how it works. What determines the wage rate for unskilled workers? What would happen if we abolished the corporate income tax? Who would benefit? Who would lose? The answers to such questions are the subject of positive economics.

Normative economics, on the other hand, looks at the outcomes of economic behavior and asks if they are good or bad and whether the outcomes can be made better. Normative economics, then, involves judgments and prescriptions for preferred courses of action. Should the government be involved in regulating the price of gasoline? Should the income tax be changed to reduce or increase the burden on upper income families? Should AT&T have been broken up into a set of smaller companies? Should we protect the automobile industry from foreign competition? Often normative economics is called policy economics.

Of course most normative questions involve positive questions. To know whether the government *should* take a particular action, we must know first if it *can* and second what the consequences are likely to be. (For example, if AT&T is broken up will there be more competition and lower prices?)

Some claim that positive, value free economic analysis is impossible. They argue that analysts come to problems with biases that cannot help but influence their work. Furthermore, even in choosing what questions to ask or what problems to analyze, economists are influenced by political, ideological, and moral views.

While this argument has some merit, it is nevertheless important to distinguish between analyses that attempt to be positive and those that are intentionally and explicitly normative. Economists who ask explicitly normative questions should be forced to specify their grounds for judging one outcome superior to another. What does it mean to be better? The criteria for such evaluations must be clearly spelled out and thoroughly understood for conclusions to have meaning.

Positive economics is often divided into descriptive economics and economic theory. **Descriptive economics** is simply the compilation of data that describe phenomena and facts. Examples of such data appear in the *Statistical Abstract of the United States*, a large volume of data published by the Department of Commerce every year that describes many features of the U.S. economy.

Where do all these data come from? The Census Bureau produces an enormous amount of raw data every year, as do the Bureau of Labor Statistics, the Bureau of Economic Analysis, and private agencies such as the University of Michigan Survey Research Center. One important study now published annually is the *Survey of Consumer Expenditure*, which asks individual households to keep careful records of all their expenditures over a long period of time. Another is the *National Longitudinal Survey of Labor Force Behavior*, conducted over many years by the center for human resource development at Ohio State University.

Industry studies by industrial organization economists usually begin with pure descriptive economics. Most have chapters that describe in detail the industry to be analyzed. How many firms are there? How large are they? Do they produce the exact same product, or do they each produce a slight variation? How do they sell or market their products?

Economic theory   A general statement or set of statements about cause and effect in economic life.

Economic theory attempts to generalize about data and interpret them. An **economic theory** is a statement or set of related statements about cause and effect, action and reaction. One of the first theories you will encounter in this text is the *law of demand*, which was most clearly stated by Alfred Marshall in 1890: when the price of a product rises, people tend to buy less of it; when the price of a product falls, they tend to buy more.

The process of observing regular patterns from raw data and drawing generalizations from them is called **inductive reasoning**. In all sciences, theories begin with inductive reasoning and observed regularities. Physical scientists have, for centuries, observed and described the motion of the sun, moon, and planets and proposed theories about how and why they behave as they do. Nearly two thousand years ago the astronomer Ptolemy (127–151A.D.) developed an elaborate theory that explained the movement of the planets based on the assumption that the earth was the center of the cosmos. In the sixteenth century the Polish astronomer Nicholas Copernicus, having observed celestial motions, proposed an alternative theory that placed the sun at the center. Over time, as techniques of observation and measurement became more refined, the Copernican theory became generally accepted.

Social scientists, including economists, study human behavior—they develop and test theories of how human beings, institutions, and societies behave. The behavior of human beings is by its nature not as regular or predictable as the behavior of electrons, molecules, or planets, but there are patterns, regularities, and tendencies.

Theories do not always arise out of formal numerical data. All of us have been collecting observations of people's behavior and their responses to economic stimuli for most of our lives. We may have observed our parents' reaction to a sudden increase—or decrease—in income or to the loss of a job or the acquisition of a new one. We have all seen people standing in line waiting for a bargain. Of course, our own actions and reactions are another important source of data. When we read a theory about behavior that is inconsistent with our own experience, we question it.

Theories and Models

Model The formal statement of a theory. Usually a mathematical statement, or series of such statements, of a relationship between two or more variables.

In many disciplines, including physics, chemistry, meteorology, political science, and economics, theorists build formal models of behavior. A **model** is simply a formal statement of a theory. It is usually a mathematical statement of a presumed relationship between two or more variables.

A **variable** is a magnitude or measure that can change from time to time or from observation to observation. Income is a variable—it has different values for different people, and it has different values for the same person at different times. The rental price of a movie on a video cassette is a variable; it has different values at different stores and at different times. Competition has pushed prices down in recent years, for example. There are countless other examples.

Because all models simplify reality by stripping part of it away, they are abstractions. Critics of economics often point to abstraction as a weakness. Most economists, however, see abstraction as a real strength.

The easiest way to see how abstraction can be helpful is to think of a map. A map, like a model, substitutes for the real thing. It is a representation of reality that is simplified and also abstract. A city or state appears on a piece of paper as a series of lines. The amount of reality that the map maker can strip away before the map loses something essential depends upon what it is going to be used for. If I want to drive from St. Louis to Phoenix, I only need to know the major interstate highways and roads. I lose absolutely nothing and gain clarity by cutting out the local streets and roads. If, on the other hand, I need to get around in Phoenix, I may need to see every street and alley.

Most maps are two-dimensional representations of a three-dimensional world; they show where roads and highways go but do not show hills and valleys along the way. Trail maps for hikers, however, have "contour lines" that represent changes in elevation. When you are in a car, changes in elevation matter very little; they would make a map needlessly complex and much more difficult to read. But if you are on foot carrying a 60-pound pack, elevation is crucial.

All this can be said about models as well. Models are abstractions that strip away detail to expose only those aspects of behavior that are important to the question being asked. The principle that irrelevant detail should be cut away is called the principle of *Occam's razor* after the fourteenth century philosopher William Occam.

But be careful. Although abstraction is a powerful tool for exposing and analyzing specific aspects of behavior, it is possible to oversimplify. Economic models and the theories that give rise to them strip away a good deal of social and political reality to get at underlying concepts. When an economic theory is used to help formulate actual government or institutional policy, political and social reality must often be reintroduced if the policy is to have a chance of working.

The key here is that the appropriate amount of simplification and abstraction depends upon the use to which the model will be put. To return to the map for a minute, you don't want to walk around San Francisco with a map made for drivers—there are too many very steep hills!

All Else Equal: Ceteris Paribus   It is almost always true that whatever you want to explain with a model depends on more than one factor. Suppose, for example, that you want to explain the total number of miles driven by owners of automobiles in the United States. The number of miles driven will change from year to year or month to month; it is a variable. The issue, if we want to understand and explain changes that occur, is what factors cause those changes.

Obviously, many things might have an impact on total distance driven. First of all, more or fewer people may be driving. This, in turn, can be affected by changes in the number of people of driving age, by population growth, or by changes in state laws. Some states have increased the legal driving age, for example, decreasing the number of drivers on the road and therefore decreasing the total number of miles driven.

Factors that might affect the amount that an individual household drives include the price of gasoline, the household's income, the number and age of children in the household, the distance from home to work, the location of shopping facilities, and the availability and quality of public transport, among many other factors. When any of these variables change, the household may drive more or less. If changes in any of these variables affect large numbers of households across the country, the total number of miles driven will change.

Very often we need to isolate or separate out these effects. For example, suppose that we want to know the impact on driving of a higher tax on gasoline. This change would raise the price of gasoline at the pump, but would not, at least in the near term, affect income, work place location, number of children, and so forth.

Ceteris paribus   *Literally, "all else being equal." Used to analyze the relationship between two variables while the values of other variables are held unchanged.*

To isolate the impact of one single factor, we use the device of **ceteris paribus**, or "**all else equal.**" We ask, What is the impact of a change in gasoline price on driving behavior, ceteris paribus, or assuming that nothing else changes? If gasoline prices rise by 10 percent, we ask how much less driving there will be, assuming no simultaneous change in anything else—that is, assuming that income, number of children, population, laws, and so on all remain constant.

Using the device of ceteris paribus is one part of the process of abstraction. In formulating economic theory, the concept helps us simplify reality in order to focus on the relationships that we are interested in. We can then think about the relationship between two variables by simply assuming that all else is equal.

Empirical economics   *An approach to economics that uses observation to test theories.*

Later on we will discuss **empirical economics**, which involves the observation and measurement of behavior. Isolating and *measuring* separate effects is more difficult because many things change at the same time in the real world. Physical scientists, such as physicists, chemists, and geologists, can often deal with these problems by imposing the condition of ceteris paribus in controlled experiments. They can, for example, observe and measure the effect of one chemical on another while literally holding all else constant in an environment that they totally control. Social scientists very rarely have this luxury, our subjects being people rather than chemicals.

While controlled experiments are difficult in economics and the other social sciences, we can and do attempt to isolate and measure the effects of single factors and of changes in single factors. There are a number of ways to do this. One of the easiest is to observe the behavior of groups of similar people under different circumstances. To separate the impact of changes in gasoline prices from changes in income, for example, you might observe the reactions to changes in gasoline prices of a number of households that have the *same* income during the time they are observed.

Sometimes the effects of separate factors can also be identified statistically. If, for example, you have data on the miles driven by a large number of households, as well as information on their incomes, the number of children they have, and the price they pay for gasoline, you can apply widely used statistical techniques to the analysis of your data.

These techniques look at the variation in driving across families and estimate the portion of that variation that can be "explained" by observed differences in number of children, income, the price of gasoline, and so forth.

Expressing Models in Words, Graphs, and Equations   Models can be expressed in several ways. Most modeling begins with a simple description of each of the variables and their hypothesized relationships. Suppose, for example, that you are considering opening a store that rents movies on video cassettes and that you need to estimate how many cassettes you will rent per week. It would be nice to have a model of *demand* for video cassettes.

Expressing the model in words, you might say that the number of rentals per week will depend on the price per rental, the number of videos available (the choice you offer), the number of families with video cassette recorders in your town, and the weather. You can safely assume that you will rent more video cassettes if you charge a low rental fee and fewer video cassettes if you charge a higher rental fee. You might also guess that a wide choice will attract more customers. Clearly, the more families that have VCRs, the more potential customers you will have. Finally, people are more likely to stay home and watch a video movie when it rains. Using more precise language, economists would say that the number of rentals per week is a function of, or depends on, price, number of movies available, number of VCRs, and the weather.

Assuming ceteris paribus, or all else equal, we can express the relationship between price and quantity graphically. Table 1.2 shows rentals per week at several different prices. These data might have come from the records kept by a store in the next town: 500 titles were available and about the same number of households in that town have VCRs. The store owner tried lowering her price from $4.00 to $1.00 over four weeks. Figure 1.1 expresses the same data graphically. The two variables, quantity rented and price per rental, are measured along the axes of the graph. Then a line is drawn through the four points. The relationship is a *negative* one: as price rises quantity rented falls.[2]

TABLE 1.2
Video Cassettes
Rented per Week
at Various Prices

Price	Quantity
$4.00	40
$3.00	155
$2.00	270
$1.00	385

FIGURE 1.1
Video Rentals per Week

A two-dimensional graph shows the relationship between two variables *ceteris paribus*. In this graph, a decrease in the price of video rentals causes an increase in the quantity of rentals per week, all else being equal. Thus we say that quantity of video rentals is a function of price.

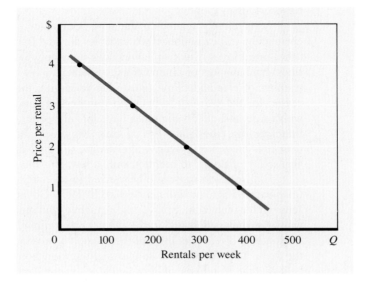

[2]For simplicity the four points in Figure 1.1 have been chosen to lie on a straight line. In practice, economic relationships are not this precise. By the use of econometric techniques, one can find a line that "best fits" a series of points, but in general the points will not all lie exactly on the line.

Models or theories are also often expressed as equations. For example, the straight line in Figure 1.1 can be expressed as follows:

$$Q^d = 500 - 115P.$$

where Q^d is the quantity demanded and P is the price per rental. Notice that if price were zero, the quantity demanded would be 500 rentals. At a price of $4.00, on the other hand, the equation shows that rentals would fall to just 40. For every dollar increase in price, the quantity demanded falls by 115 units.

(Appendix A to this chapter presents a careful review of graphing. Graphical techniques are used extensively in economics, so it is important that you read graphs with ease. Study the concept of "slope" until it becomes automatic.)

Cautions and Pitfalls

Post hoc, ergo propter hoc Literally, "after this (in time), therefore because of this." A common error made in thinking about causation: if Event A happens before Event B happens, you cannot infer that A caused B.

THE POST HOC FALLACY   Theories often make statements, or sets of statements, about *cause and effect*. It can be quite tempting to look at two events that happen in sequence and assume that the first caused the second to happen. Clearly, that is not always the case. This common error is called the **post hoc ergo propter hoc** (or "after this, therefore because of this") fallacy.

There are thousands of examples. Last night I watched a basketball game on television. When I turned it on the score was 21 to four in favor of my team. Five minutes later, the score was 27 all. I must have "jinxed" them. They played poorly *because* I turned on the game.

Stock market analysts indulge in what is perhaps the most striking example of the post hoc fallacy in action. Every day the stock market goes up or down, and every day some analyst on some national news program singles out one or two of the day's events as the *cause* of some change in the market: "Today the Dow Jones industrial average rose five points on heavy trading; analysts say that the increase was due to progress at the arms negotiations in Geneva."

Very closely related to the post hoc fallacy is the often erroneous link between correlation and causation. Two variables are said to be *correlated* if one moves when the other one moves. But correlation does not imply causation. Cities that have high crime rates also have lots of automobiles, so there is a very high degree of correlation between number of cars and crime rates. Can we argue, then, that cars *cause* crime? No. The reason for the correlation between numbers of cars and crime may have nothing to do with cause and effect. Big cities have lots of people, lots of people have lots of cars, and therefore big cities have lots of cars. Big cities also have high crime rates for lots of reasons—crowding, poverty, anonymity, unequal distribution of wealth, and the ready availability of drugs, to mention only a few. But the presence of cars is not one of them.

This caution must also be viewed in reverse. Sometimes events that seem entirely unconnected actually *are* connected. In 1978 Governor Michael Dukakis of Massachusetts ran for reelection. Still young, attractive, and quite popular most of the time, Dukakis was nevertheless defeated in the Democratic primary that year. The weekend before, the Boston Red Sox, in the thick of the division championship race, had been badly beaten by the New York Yankees in four straight games. Some very respectable political analysts believe that hundreds of thousands of Boston sports fans vented their anger on the incumbent governor the following Tuesday.

THE FALLACY OF COMPOSITION   To conclude that what is true for a part is necessarily true for the whole is to fall into the **fallacy of composition**. Often what holds for an individual does not hold for a group or for society as a whole. One classic example is that of the farmer who knows he will be better off if he produces more wheat. His income is essentially the number of bushels of wheat he produces multiplied by the price he gets per bushel. Individual farmers cannot control the market price of wheat; all they can control is the amount they produce. Thus, producing more means more income. But if *all* farmers produce more, the price of wheat falls and farmers may, in fact, be worse off.

A large group of cattle ranchers graze their cattle on the same range. To an individual rancher, more cattle and more grazing mean a higher income. But the land can support only so many cattle: its capacity is limited. If every cattle rancher increased the number of cattle sent out to graze, the land would become over-grazed and barren, and everyone's income would fall. This example of the fallacy of composition is called the *tragedy of commons*.

Theories that seem to work well when applied to individuals or households often break down when they are applied to the whole.

Testing Theories and Models: Empirical Economics   In science a theory is rejected when it fails to explain what is observed or when another theory explains what is observed better. Prior to the sixteenth century almost everyone believed that the earth was the center of the universe and that the sun and stars rotated around it. As we said earlier, Ptolemy actually built a model that explained and predicted the movements of the heavenly bodies in a geocentric universe. Early in the sixteenth century, however, Copernicus found himself dissatisfied with the Ptolemaic model and proposed an alternative theory or model, placing the sun at the center of the known universe and relegating the earth to the status of one planet among many. The battle between the competing models was waged, at least in part, with data based on observations—actual measurements of the movements of the planets. The new model ultimately predicted much better than the old, and in time it came to be accepted.

In the seventeenth century, building on the works of Copernicus and others, Sir Isaac Newton constructed yet another body of theory that seemed to predict with more accuracy still. Newtonian physics became the accepted body of theory, relied on for almost three hundred years. Then Albert Einstein did his work. The theory of relativity replaced Newtonian physics because it predicted even better. Relativity was able to explain some things that earlier theories could not.

Economic theories are also confronted with new and often conflicting data from time to time. The use of observation to test economic theory is called *empirical economics*. The ability of the computer to manipulate huge amounts of data has made it easier to test even the most complicated theories against observation. For example, economists studying the labor market can now test behavioral theories against the actual working experiences of thousands of randomly selected people who have been surveyed continuously since the 1960s by economists at Ohio State University. Macroeconomists continuously monitoring and studying the behavior of the national economy pass thousands of items of data, collected by both government agencies and private companies, back and forth on floppy disks and over telephone lines. Housing market analysts analyze data tapes containing observations recorded in connection with millions of home sales.

Economic Policy

Economic theory helps us understand how the world works, but the formulation of *economic policy* requires a second step: we must have objectives. What do we want to change? Why? What is good and what is bad about the way the system is operating? Can we make it better?

Such questions force us to be specific about the grounds for judging one outcome superior to another. What does it mean to be better? Four criteria are frequently applied in making these judgments:

1. Efficiency
2. Equity
3. Growth
4. Stability

Efficiency When applied to economics, the condition in which the system is producing what people want at the least cost. More formally, a condition in which no one can be made better off without making someone else worse off.

Efficiency   The term **efficiency** has a number of meanings. In physics it refers to the ratio of useful energy delivered by a system to the energy supplied to it. An efficient automobile engine, for example, is one that uses up a small amount of fuel per mile for a given level of power.

In economics we speak of *allocative efficiency*. An *efficient economy is one that produces what people want and does so at the least cost.* If the system allocates resources to the production of things that nobody wants, it is inefficient. When steel beams lie in the rain and rust because somebody fouled up a shipping schedule, this is inefficient. If a firm could produce its product using 25 percent less labor and energy without sacrificing quality, it too is inefficient.

To use the term more technically, *an efficient change in the allocation of resources is one that at least potentially makes some people better off without making others worse off.* The clearest example of an efficient change is a voluntary exchange. If you and I each want something that the other has and we agree to exchange, we are both better off, and no one loses. If a company reorganizes its production or adopts a new technology that enables it to produce more of its product with fewer inputs, without sacrificing quality, this is an efficient change; at least potentially, the inputs saved could be used to produce *more* of something. Sometimes a single firm gains control of a market and is able to exclude competitors. When this happens it can be shown that the system is not producing the combination of things that the people want. Regulating such market power may be justified on efficiency grounds.

While we shall deal with the concept of efficiency in much more detail later, it is important to understand two things about it. First, it assumes that the ultimate purpose of an economic system is to produce what people want. When we say a change makes people better off, it is the people themselves who define what "better off" means. For example, by engaging in a voluntary exchange, you and I reveal that we are better off afterwards than before. A voluntary exchange is efficient because it improves the well-being of the participants *as they themselves define it.*

Second, since most changes that can be made in an economy will leave some people better off and others worse off, we must have a way of comparing the gains and losses that may result from any given change. Most often we simply compare their sizes in dollar terms. A change is at least potentially efficient if the value of the resulting gains exceeds the value of the resulting losses.

Equity   "Fairness." One criterion for judging the final distribution of what society produces.

Equity   While efficiency has a fairly precise definition that can be applied with some degree of rigor, **equity** lies in the eye of the beholder. Few people agree on what is fair and what is unfair. To many, fairness implies a more equal distribution of income and wealth. Fairness may imply alleviating poverty, but the extent to which poverty should be reduced is the subject of enormous disagreement. For thousands of years philosophers have wrestled with the principles of justice that should guide social decisions. They will probably wrestle with such questions for thousands of years to come.

Despite the impossibility of defining equity or fairness universally, public policy makers judge the fairness of economic outcomes all the time. Rent control laws were passed because some legislators thought that landlords treated low income tenants unfairly. Certainly most social welfare programs are created in the name of equity.

Growth   As the result of technological change, the building of capital, and the acquisition of knowledge, societies learn to produce new things and to produce old things better. In the early days of the American economy, it took nearly half the population to produce the required food supply. Today less than three percent of the country's population is engaged in agriculture.

Economic growth   An increase in the total output of an economy. Often the term is used to refer to increases in output per capita.

When we devise new and better ways of producing the things we use now and develop new products and services to satisfy our wants, the standard of living rises. One very rough measure of this increase is the total amount of production per person in an economy. **Economic growth** is a rise in total output per capita. When an economy grows, there is more of what people want and standards of living generally rise. Poor, rural, agrarian societies become modern industrial societies as a result of economic growth.

Some policies discourage economic growth and others encourage it. Tax laws, for example, can be designed to encourage the development and application of new production techniques. Research and development in some societies is subsidized by the government. Building roads, highways, bridges, and transport systems in developing countries may speed up the process of economic growth. If businesses and wealthy people invest their wealth outside a country rather than in its own industries, growth may be slowed.

Stability   A condition in which output is steady or growing with low inflation and full employment of resources. Refers to stability of output and prices.

Stability   An economy may at times be unstable. During the 1950s and 1960s, the U.S. economy experienced a long period of relatively steady growth, stable prices, and low unemployment. Between 1951 and 1969, consumer prices never rose more than 5 percent in a single year, and in only two years did the number of unemployed exceed 6 percent of the labor force. The decades of the 1970s and 1980s, however, have been unstable. We have experienced two periods of rapid price inflation (over 10 percent) and two periods of severe unemployment. In 1982, for example, 12 million people (10.7% of the workforce) were looking for work. When we get to macroeconomics, we discuss various ways that governments try to lessen these kinds of fluctuations and promote **stability.**

AN INVITATION

This chapter is meant to prepare you for what is to come. The first part of the chapter invites you into an exciting discipline that deals with important issues and questions. You cannot begin to understand how a society functions without knowing something about its economic history and its economic system.

The second part of the chapter introduces, in a very rough way, the method of reasoning that economics requires. We believe that learning to think in this very powerful way will help you better understand the world.

SUMMARY

1. All societies at all times face constraints imposed by nature and previous generations; resources are *scarce*.
2. Economics is the study of how human beings and societies choose to use the scarce resources that nature and previous generations have provided.
3. There are many reasons to study economics, including (a) to learn a way of thinking, (b) to understand society, (c) to understand world affairs, (d) to be an informed voter.
4. That which we forgo when we make a choice or a decision is called the opportunity cost of that decision.
5. Economics is a surprisingly broad discipline. It has deep roots in social philosophy and deals with important societal issues.
6. Microeconomics deals with the functioning of individual markets and industries and with the behavior of individual decision making units: firms and households.
7. Macroeconomics adds it all up and looks at the economy as a whole. It deals with national output, national income, and overall price movements.
8. One way to learn about the subject matter of economics is to look at the contents of the major subfields of study within it, such as comparative economic systems and industrial organization.
9. Economics asks and attempts to answer two kinds of questions: positive and normative. *Positive economics* attempts to understand behavior and the operating economies without making judgments about whether the outcomes are good or bad. *Normative economics* looks at the results or outcomes of economic behavior and asks if they are good or bad and whether they can be improved.
10. Positive economics is often divided into two parts, descriptive economics and economic theory. *Descriptive economics* involves the compilation of data that accurately describe economic facts and events. *Economic theory* attempts to generalize and explain what is observed. It involves statements of cause and effect—of action and reaction.
11. An economic model is a formal statement of an economic theory. Models simplify and abstract from reality.
12. It is often useful to isolate the effects of one variable or another while holding "all else constant." This is the device of ceteris paribus.
13. Models and theories can be expressed in many ways. The most common ways are in words, in graphs, and in equations.
14. Because one event happened before another, it did not necessarily happen *as a result* of the first event. To assume that "after" implies "because" is to commit the fallacy of post hoc ergo propter hoc.
15. To conclude that what is true for a part is necessarily true for the whole is called the fallacy of composition.
16. Empirical economics involves the testing of economic theories with data. In principle, the best model is the one that yields the most accurate predictions.
17. To make policy, one must be careful to specify criteria for making judgments. Four specific criteria are used most often in economics: efficiency, equity, growth, and stability.

REVIEW CONCEPTS

economics   4
trade-offs   4
opportunity cost   4
marginalism   5
sunk costs   5
efficient markets   6
Industrial Revolution   8
microeconomics   10
macroeconomics   11
positive economics   13
normative economics   13
descriptive economics   14

economic theory   14
inductive reasoning   14
model   15
variable   15
ceteris paribus   16
empirical economics   16
post hoc ergo propter hoc   18
fallacy of composition   18
efficiency   20
equity   20
economic growth   21
stability   21

REVIEW QUESTIONS

1. Most people using this book decided to attend college or take a course in economics. What is the "cost" of attending college? Specifically, what are the opportunity costs? What is the "cost" of taking this particular course? What are the opportunity costs?
2. Give three examples of the fallacy of composition.
3. One of the scarce resources that constrain our behavior is time. Each of us has only 24 hours in a day. How do you go about allocating your time in a given day among competing alternatives? How do you go about weighing the alternatives? Once you choose a most important use of time, why not spend all your time on it? Use the notion of opportunity cost in your answer.
4. Define positive economics. In what ways does economics as a science differ from the physical sciences? What problems do economists face in attempting to avoid value judgments that chemists, for example, may not?

5. Suppose that a city is considering building a bridge across a river. The bridge will be paid for out of tax dollars, and the city gets its revenues from a sales tax imposed on things sold in the city. The bridge would provide more direct access for commuters and shoppers and would alleviate the huge traffic jam that occurs every morning at the bridge down the river. Who would gain if the bridge were built? Do you think those gains could be measured? How? Who, on balance, would be hurt? Could those costs be measured? How would you determine if it were efficient to build the bridge?
6. Define equity. How would you decide if building the bridge described in question 5 was fair/equitable?
7. Define economic growth. What changes is economic growth likely to bring to a poor country like Haiti? What changes is economic growth likely to bring to the U.S.? Be bold in your speculation, and give specific examples.

APPENDIX TO CHAPTER 1
How to Read and Understand Graphs

It is frequently useful in economics to display quantitative material graphically. A graph is simply a two-dimensional geometric representation of data. Displaying data graphically often reveals things that are difficult to see when looking at sets or tables of numbers.

Table 1A.1 presents some data that were collected by the Bureau of Labor Statistics (BLS). In 1980 and 1981 the bureau did a survey of over 48,000 households. (See footnote to table 1A.1) Each household was asked to keep careful track of all its expenditures. The table shows average income and average spending for those households that were surveyed, ranked by income. For example, if you take only the top fifth (20 percent) of the households, their average income was $44,616, and their average spending was $30,563.

TABLE 1A.1

Consumption Expenditures and Income*

*Income and consumption data are for "consumer units." Consumer units are defined as (1) all members of a particular household related by blood, marriage, adoption, or other legal arrangements. (2) a person living alone or sharing a household with others, but who is financially independent, or (3) two or more persons living together who pool their incomes.

	Average Income	Average consumption expenditures
Bottom fifth	$ 3,473	$ 7,852
2nd fifth	9,791	11,570
3rd fifth	16,809	15,736
4th fifth	25,128	20,714
Top fifth	44,616	30,563

Source: U.S. Bureau of Labor Statistics, *Consumer Expenditure Survey, 1980–81*, BLS Bulletin 2225 (April 1985), table pp. 10, 11.

Figure 1A.1 presents the same numbers graphically. Every graph has two scales. Along the horizontal scale in Figure 1A.1 (called the X axis), we measure income. Along the vertical scale (called the Y axis), we measure consumption spending. Each point in the space between the axes represents a pair of numbers. The point where the two axes intersect is the point of zero income and zero spending; it is called the *origin*. The five pairs of numbers from Table 1A.1 are represented by circles; a line is drawn connecting them.

To help read this particular graph a dotted line is drawn connecting all the points where consumption and income would be equal. Be sure that you understand that this 45° line does not represent any data. The heavy black line traces out the BLS data; the dotted line is only to help you read the graph.

There are several things to look for in reading a graph. The first thing you should notice is whether it slopes upward or downward as you move to the right. This particular graph slopes upward, indicating that there seems to be a positive relationship between income and spending; as we look at higher income households they tend to consume more. If we had graphed the percentage of each group receiving welfare payments along the Y axis, it would presumably slope downward, indicating lower percentages at higher income levels.

The *slope* of a line or curve is a measure that indicates whether the relationship is positive or negative and how much of a response there seems to be in Y (the variable on the vertical axis) when X (the variable on the horizontal axis) changes. The slope of a *line* between two points is the change in the quantity being measured on the Y axis divided by the change in the quantity being measured on the X axis. We will normally use Δ (the Greek letter delta) to refer to a change in a variable. In Figure 1A.2, the slope of the line between points A and B is ΔY divided by ΔX. Sometimes it's easy to remember slope as "the rise over the run," indicating the vertical change over the horizontal change.

Moving from A to B in Figure 1A.2a, both X and Y are increasing; thus, the slope is a positive number. On the other hand, moving from A to B in Figure 1A.2b, X is

FIGURE 1A.1
Graph of Household Consumption and Income

A graph is a simple two dimensional geometric representation of data. This graph displays the data from Table 1A.1. Along the horizontal scale (X axis), we measure household income. Along the vertical scale (Y axis), we measure household expenditure.

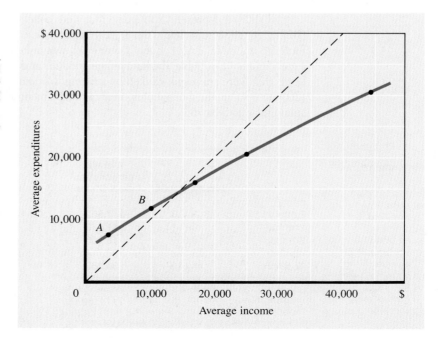

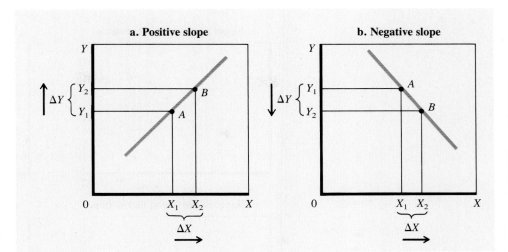

FIGURE 1A.2
A Curve with a Positive Slope (a)
and a Curve with a Negative
Slope (b)

A *positive* slope indicates that increases in X are associated with increases in Y and that decreases in X are associated with decreases in Y. A *negative* slope indicates the opposite—when X increases, Y decreases and when X decreases, Y increases.

increasing [$(X_2 - X_1)$ is a positive number], but Y is decreasing [$(Y_2 - Y_1)$ is a negative number]; thus, the slope is a negative number, since a negative number divided by a positive one gives a negative quotient.

Returning to Figure 1A.1, to calculate the slope between points A and B, we need to calculate ΔY and ΔX. Since consumption is measured on the Y axis, ΔY is 3718 (11,570 minus 7852). Since income is measured along the X axis, ΔX is 6318 (9791 minus 3473). The slope between A and B is $3718/6318 = +.588$.

Another interesting thing to note about the BLS data graphed in Figure 1A.1 is that all the points lie roughly along a straight line. A straight line has a constant slope. That is, if you pick any two points along it and calculate the slope, you will get the same number. Notice that a horizontal line has a zero slope (ΔY is zero); a vertical line has an "infinite" slope, since ΔY is too big to be measured.

A slope along a *curve* is continuously changing. Consider the curves in Figure 1A.3. Figure 1A.3a is a curve with a positive slope, but the slope is decreasing as X increases; in 1A.3b, the slope is positive, but it increases as X increases. Figure 1A.3c shows a curve with a negative slope that is increasing (in absolute value)[3] as X increases; in 1A.3d the slope is negative, but its absolute value decreases as we move to the right.

In Figure 1A.3e the slope goes from positive to negative as X increases. In 1A.3f the slope goes from negative to positive. At point A in both, the slope is zero.

When you read a graph, it is important to think carefully about what the points in the space defined by the axes represent. Table 1A.2 and Figure 1A.4 present another graph of consumption and income that is very different from the one in Table 1A.1 and Figure 1A.1. First, each point represents a different year; in the first graph each point represented a different group of households at the *same* point in time (1980–1981). Second, the points now represent *aggregate* consumption and income for the whole nation measured in billions of dollars; in the first graph, the points represented average *household* income and consumption. The numbers were measured in thousands of dollars.

---

[3]The *absolute value* of a number is its value disregarding its sign, that is, disregarding whether it is positive or negative: -7 is bigger in absolute value than -4; -9 is bigger in absolute value than $+8$.

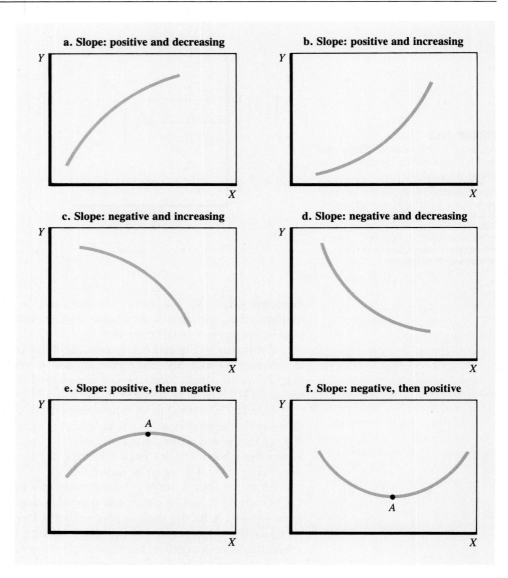

FIGURE 1A.3
Changing Slopes Along Curves

TABLE 1A.2
Aggregate Income and
Consumption for the Entire
United States

	Aggregate national income (billions of dollars)	Aggregate consumption (billions of dollars)
1930	73.8	69.9
1940	79.7	71.0
1950	237.6	192.0
1960	415.7	324.9
1970	810.7	621.7
1980	2117.1	1667.2

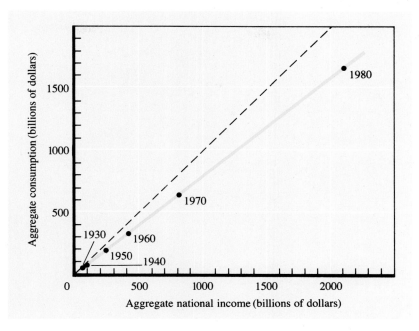

FIGURE 1A.4

National Income and
Consumption

It is important to think carefully about
what is represented by the points in
the space defined by the axes of a
graph. In this graph, we have income
graphed with consumption expenditure, as was the case in Figure 1A.1,
but here each observation point is
national income and aggregate consumption in *different years,* measured
in billions of dollars.

It is interesting to compare these two graphs. All points on the aggregate
consumption curve in Figure 1A.4 lie below the 45-degree line, which means that
aggregate consumption is always less than aggregate income. On the other hand, the
graph of average household income and consumption in Figure 1A.1 crosses the
45-degree line. Why do you think these graphs are different? This question has been the
subject of much discussion.

2 Scarcity and Choice: The Economic Problem

THREE FUNDAMENTAL QUESTIONS
  Scarcity, Choice, and Opportunity Cost
  The Production Possibility Frontier
THE THREE FUNDAMENTAL QUESTIONS
  IN MORE COMPLEX ECONOMIES
  Many Possible Systems
A LOOK AHEAD
SUMMARY

The previous chapter began with a broad definition of economics. As you saw there, every society has some system or mechanism that transforms what nature and previous generations provide into useful form. Economics is the study of that process and its outcomes. Economists attempt to answer the questions: What gets produced? How is it produced? Who gets it? Why? Is it good or bad? Can it be improved?

This chapter explores these questions further. In a sense, the entire chapter *is* the definition of economics. It lays out the central problems addressed by the discipline of economics and provides the framework that will guide you through the rest of the book.

Human wants are unlimited, but resources are not. Limited, or *scarce*, resources force individuals and societies to *choose*. The central function of any economy, no matter how simple or how complex, is to transform resources into useful form in accordance with those choices. The process by which this transformation takes place is called **production**.

The term **resources** is very broad. Some resources are the product of nature: natural resources include land, wildlife, minerals, timber, energy, even the rain and the wind. At any given time, the resources available to a society also include those things that have been produced by previous generations, such as buildings and equipment. Things that are produced and then used to produce other valuable goods or services later on are called *capital resources*, or simply **capital**. Buildings, machinery, equipment, tables, roads, bridges, desks, and so forth are part of the nation's *capital stock. Human resources*—labor, skills and knowledge—are also, of course, an important part of a nation's resources.

Producers are those who take resources and transform them into usable products, or *outputs*. Private manufacturing firms purchase resources and produce products for the market. Governments do so as well. National defense, the justice system, police and fire protection, and sewer services are all examples of outputs produced by the government, sometimes called the *public sector*.

Individual households often produce products for themselves. A household that owns its own home is in essence using land and a structure (capital) to produce "housing

Production   The process by which resources are transformed into useful forms.

Resources   Anything provided by nature or previous generations that can be used directly or indirectly to satisfy human wants.

Capital   Things that have already been produced that are in turn used to produce other usable goods and services over time.

Producers   Any person or group of people, whether private or public, who transform resources into usable output.

29

services" that it consumes itself. The Boston Symphony Orchestra is no less a producer than General Motors. An orchestra takes capital resources—a building, musical instruments, lighting fixtures, musical scores, and so on—and combines them with land and highly skilled labor to produce performances.

THREE FUNDAMENTAL QUESTIONS

The three basic questions The *questions that all societies answer by means of their economic organization: (1) What gets produced? (2) How does it get produced? (3) Who gets what is produced?*

All societies must answer **three basic questions**:

What will be produced?
How will it be produced?
Who will get it?

Stated a slightly different way, the system must determine the **allocation of resources** among producers, the **mix of output**, and the **distribution of that output** (see Figure 2.1).

Scarcity and Choice in a One-Person Economy   The simplest of all economies is one in which a single person exists alone on an island where no one has ever been before. Consider Bill, the survivor of a plane crash over open ocean, who finds himself cast ashore in such a place. Here, of course, individual and society are one; there is no distinction between social and private. *Nonetheless, nearly all of the basic decisions that characterize complex economies must be made.* Bill must decide how to allocate the resources of the island, what to produce, how to produce it, and when to produce it.

First, he must decide *what* he wants, what to produce. Notice that the word "needs" does not appear here. Needs are absolute requirements, and, beyond just enough water, basic nutrition, and shelter to survive, those are very difficult to define. What is an

FIGURE 2.1
The Economic Problem

All societies are endowed by nature and by previous generations with limited—or scarce—resources. Every society must decide how to use them to satisfy human wants. Specifically, resources must be divided up among producers who transform them into useful things—*products* or *outputs*—that must somehow then be divided up among households or members of society.

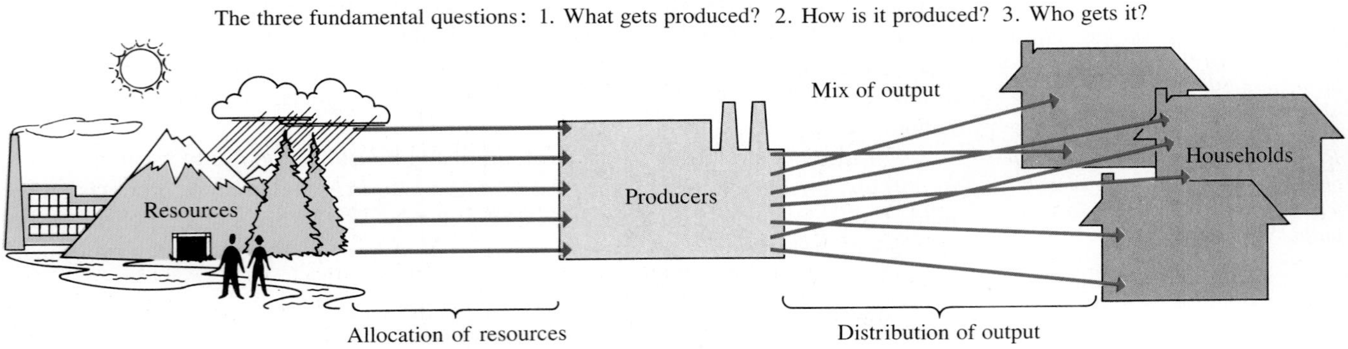

The three fundamental questions: 1. What gets produced? 2. How is it produced? 3. Who gets it?

Resources — Producers — Mix of output — Households

Allocation of resources   Distribution of output "absolute necessity" for one may not be for another. In any case, Bill must put his wants in some order of priority and make some choices.

Next he must look around at the *possibilities*. What can he do to satisfy those wants, given the limits of the island? In every society, no matter how simple or complex, *no matter how rich or poor*, wants are constrained in some way. In this society of one, Bill's wants are constrained by time, his physical condition, his knowledge, his skills, and the resources and climate of the island.

Given that resources are limited, or scarce, Bill must decide *how* to use them best to satisfy his hierarchy of wants. Probably food would come close to the top of his list. Should he spend his time simply gathering natural fruits and berries? Should he hunt for game? Should he clear a field and plant seeds? Notice that the planting option involves more time than the other two. If he takes time away from gathering food today, he will have less to eat today, but he may have more to eat tomorrow.

Clearly the answers to these questions depend on the character of the island, its climate, its flora and fauna (*are* there any fruits and berries?); the extent of his skills and knowledge (does he know anything about farming technology?), and his preferences (he may be a vegetarian).

Scarcity and Choice in an Economy of Two or More   Now, suppose that another survivor of the crash, First Officer Colleen, appears on the island. Now that Bill is not alone things are more complex, and some new decisions must be made. Clearly Bill's and Colleen's preferences about what things to produce are likely to be different. They will probably not have the same knowledge or skills, and that may lead to some division of labor and specialization. How should they split the work that needs to be done? Once things are produced, they must somehow decide how to divide them up. How should their products be *distributed*?

The mechanism for answering these fundamental questions is clear when Bill alone is on the island. The "central plan" is his; he simply decides what he wants and what to do about it. The minute someone else appears, however, a number of decision-making arrangements immediately become possible. One or the other may take charge, in which case that person will decide for the two of them. The two may agree to cooperate, with each having an equal say, and come up with a joint plan. Or they may agree to split the planning, as well as the production duties. Finally, they may go off to live alone at opposite ends of the island. Even if they live apart, however, they may take advantage of each other's presence by specializing and trading.

Modern industrial societies must answer exactly the same questions, but the mechanics of larger economies are naturally more complex. Instead of two people living together, we have 240 million in the United States. Still we must decide what to produce, how to produce it, and who gets it.

Scarcity, Choice, and Opportunity Cost

The concepts of *constrained choice* and *scarcity* are absolutely central to the discipline of economics. They can be applied when discussing the behavior of individuals like Bill, or Bill and Colleen together, and when analyzing the behavior of large groups of people in complex societies.

Given the scarcity of time and resources, if Bill chooses to hunt, he has less time to gather—he trades more meat for less fruit. There is a trade-off between food and shelter, too. If Bill likes to be comfortable he may work on building a nice place to live, but that

Opportunity cost   What we give up, or forgo, when we choose one thing over another.

requires giving up the food he might have produced. As we said in Chapter 1, we call that which we forego when we make a choice the **opportunity cost** of the choice.

Bill and Colleen may occasionally decide to rest, to lie on the beach and enjoy the sun. In one sense that benefit is free—they don't have to pay for the privilege. In reality, however, it does have a cost, an opportunity cost. Lying in the sun means using time that otherwise could have been spent doing something else. The true cost of that leisure is the value to Bill and Colleen of the other things they could have produced, but did not, during that time.

In the 1960s, the United States decided to put a man on the moon. To do so required devoting enormous resources to the space program, resources that could have been used to produce other things. The opportunity cost of placing a man on the moon was the total value of all the other things that those resources could have produced. Among other possibilities, taxes might have been lower. That would have meant more income for all of us to spend on goods and services that would have contributed to our personal pleasure. On the other hand, those resources could have been used for medical research, for aid to education, to build a bridge, or to support the arts.

In making everyday decisions it is sometimes helpful to think about opportunity costs. Should I go to the dorm party or not? First, it costs $4.00 to get in. When I pay out money for anything, I give up the other things that I could have bought with that money. Second, it costs two or three hours. Clearly time is a valuable commodity for a college student. I have exams next week and I need to study. I could go to a movie. I could go to another party. I could sleep. Just as Bill and Colleen must weigh the value of sunning on the beach against more food or better housing, so I must weigh the value of the fun I may have at the dorm party against everything else I might otherwise do with the time and money.

Weighing Present and Expected Future Costs and Benefits   Very often we find ourselves weighing benefits available today against benefits available tomorrow. Here too the notion of opportunity cost is helpful.

Bill had to choose between cultivating a field and just gathering wild nuts and berries. Gathering nuts and berries provides food now; gathering seeds and clearing a field for planting will yield food tomorrow, if all goes well. Using today's time to farm may well be worth it if the effort will yield more food than he would otherwise have in the future. By planting Bill is trading present value for future values. Working to gather seeds and clear a field has an opportunity cost—the present leisure he might consume and the value of the berries he might gather if he did not work the field.

The simplest example of trading present for future benefits is the common act of saving. When I put income aside today for use in the future, I give up some things that I could have had today in exchange for something tomorrow. The saver must weigh the value of what that income can buy today against what it might be expected to buy later. Since nothing is certain, some judgment about future events and *expected values* must be made. What are interest rates likely to be? What will my income be in ten years? How long am I likely to live?

We trade off present and future benefits in small ways all the time. If you decide to study rather than go to the dorm party, you are trading present fun for the expected future benefits of higher grades. If you decide to go outside on a very cold day and run five miles, you are trading discomfort in the present for being in better shape later on.

Capital Goods and Consumer Goods   A society trades present for expected future benefits when it devotes a portion of its resources to research and development or to investment in capital. As we said earlier, in its broadest definition capital is anything that is produced that will be used to produce other valuable goods or services over time.

Thus, building capital means trading present benefits for future ones. Bill and Colleen might trade lying in the sun for a nicer house in the future, or for a boat. In a modern society resources used to produce capital goods could have been used to produce *consumer* goods for present consumption. Heavy industrial machinery does not directly satisfy the wants of anyone, but producing it requires resources that could instead have gone into producing food, clothing, disco music, toys, golf clubs, and so forth.

Capital is everywhere. A road is capital. Once built, we can drive on it or transport goods and services over it for many years to come. The benefits of producing it will be realized over many years. A house is also capital. When it is built, the builder presumes that it will provide shelter and valuable services for a long time. Before a new manufacturing firm can start up, it must put some capital in place. The buildings, equipment, and inventories that it owns are its capital. As it contributes to the production process, this capital yields valuable services through time.

Capital does not have to be tangible. When you spend time and resources developing skills or getting an education, you are investing in human capital, your own human capital, that will continue to exist and yield benefits to you for years to come. A computer program produced by a software company may come on a tangible disk that costs $.75 to make, but its true intangible value comes from the ideas embodied in the program itself, which will continue to drive computers to do valuable tasks over time. It too is capital.

Investment   The process of using resources to produce new capital.

The process of using resources to produce new capital is called **investment**. (In everyday language, the term "investment" is often used to refer to the act of buying a share of stock or a bond, as in "I invested in some Treasury bonds." In economics, however, "investment" *always* refers to the creation of capital: the purchase or putting in place of buildings, equipment, roads, houses, and the like.) A wise investment in capital is one that yields future benefits that are more valuable than the present cost. When you spend money for a house, for example, presumably you value its future benefits; that is, you expect to gain more from living in it than you would from the things you could buy today with the same money.

Capital is also able to generate future benefits in excess of cost by increasing the *productivity of labor*. A person who has to dig a hole can dig a bigger hole with a shovel than without a shovel and an even bigger hole with a backhoe. A computer can do in several seconds what it took hundreds of bookkeepers hours to do fifteen years ago. This increased productivity makes it less costly to produce products.

In Chapter 1 we talked about the enormous amount of capital—buildings, roads, factories, housing, cars, trucks, telephone lines, and so forth—that you might see from a window high in a skyscraper. Much of it was put in place by previous generations, yet it continues to provide valuable services today; it is part of this generation's endowment of resources. In order to build every building, every road, every factory, every house, every car or truck, society must forgo using resources to produce consumer goods today. To get an education, I pay tuition and drop out of the work force for awhile. Because resources are scarce, *the opportunity cost of every investment in capital is foregone present consumption*.

The Production Possibility Frontier

Production possibility frontier (ppf)   A graph that shows all the combinations of goods and services that can be produced given the resources of a society and the existing state of technology.

A simple graphical device called the **production possibility frontier (ppf)** illustrates the principle of constrained choice and scarcity. The ppf is a graph that shows all the combinations of goods and services that can be produced if all of society's resources are used efficiently. Figure 2.2 shows a ppf for a hypothetical economy.

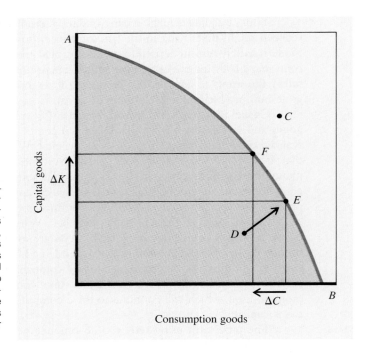

FIGURE 2.2
Production Possibility Frontier

The production possibility frontier illustrates a number of economic concepts. One of the most important is *opportunity cost*. Moving from E to F, society produces more capital goods and fewer consumption goods. Δ*K* is the change in the number of capital goods; here it shows an increase. To produce more capital goods, resources must be transferred from the production of consumer goods. Δ*C* is the change in number of consumer goods; here it shows a decrease.

On the *Y* axis we measure the quantity of capital goods produced, and on the *X* axis, the quantity of consumption goods. All points below and to the left of the curve (the shaded area) represent combinations of capital and consumption goods that are possible for the society given the resources available and existing technology. Points above and to the right of the curve, such as point *C*, represent combinations that cannot be reached. If an economy were to end up at point A on the graph, it would be producing no consumption goods at all; all resources would be used for the production of capital. On the other hand, if an economy were to end up at point *B* it would be devoting none of its resources to the formation of capital.

While all economies produce some of each kind of good, different economics emphasize different things. About 19 percent of gross output in the United States each year is new "fixed capital." In Japan, capital accounts for 32 percent of gross output, while in Ethiopia the figure is only around 10 percent. Japan is closer to point A on its curve, Ethiopia closer to *B*, and the United States is somewhere in between.

Points that are actually on the production possibility frontier can be thought of as points of both full employment and "production efficiency." Resources are not going unused, and there is no waste. Points that lie within the shaded area, but that are not on the frontier, represent either unemployment or production inefficiency. At point *D* in Figure 2.2 an economy can produce more capital goods and more consumption goods, for example, by moving to *E*. This is only possible if (1) resources were initially not fully employed or (2) they were not being used efficiently.

Unemployment   During the Great Depression of the 1930s, the U.S. economy experienced prolonged unemployment. Millions of workers who were willing to work found themselves without jobs. In 1933 a full 25 percent of the civilian labor force was unemployed, and the figure stayed above 14 percent until 1940, when our entry into World War II created millions of jobs. In 1975, and again in 1982, the economy experienced high levels of unemployment. In June of 1975, the unemployment rate went over 9 percent for the first time since the 1930s. In December of 1982, the rate hit 10.7%—nearly 12 million were out looking for work.

In addition to the hardship that falls on the unemployed themselves, unemployment of labor means unemployment of capital. During the downturn of 1982, industrial plants were running at less than 66 percent of their total capacity. That meant that a considerable fraction of the nation's industrial capital was sitting idle and, in effect, being wasted. Clearly, when there is unemployment we are not producing all that we can.

Periods of unemployment thus correspond to points inside the production possibility frontier, points like D in Figure 2.2. Moving to the frontier from a point like D means moving up and to the right, achieving full employment and increasing production of both capital goods and consumer goods.

Inefficiency   Recall that an "efficient" economy is one that produces the things that people want, and does so at the least cost. Although production inefficiency occurs when a country is producing inside its production possibility frontier, an economy is also inefficient when it is producing at the wrong point on the ppf—that is, when it is producing a combination of goods and services that does not match the wants of its people.

Certainly, if an economy is managed badly it will not produce up to potential and will be inside the ppf. Suppose, for example, that the land and climate in Ohio were best suited for corn production and that the land and climate in Kansas were best suited for wheat production. If Congress passes a law forcing farmers in Ohio to plant 50 percent of their acreage in wheat and farmers in Kansas to plant 50 percent in corn, neither corn nor wheat production will be up to potential. The economy will be at a point like A in Figure 2.3—inside the production possibility frontier. Allowing each state to specialize in producing the crop that it produces best increases the production of both corn and wheat and moves the economy to a point like B in Figure 2.3.

We've seen that inefficiency can lead to a point *inside* the ppf or to the *wrong* point on the ppf, as when society produces an output mix that does not match the tastes and preferences of its members. In an extreme case, a wrong output mix is obvious. Suppose,

FIGURE 2.3
Inefficiency from Misallocation of Land in Farming

Society can end up inside its production possibility frontier at a point like *A* by using its resources inefficiently. If, for example, Ohio's climate and soil were best suited for corn production and those of Kansas were best suited for wheat production, a law that forced Kansas farmers to produce corn and Ohio farmers to produce wheat would result in less of both. In such a case society might be at point *A* rather than point *B* on the graph.

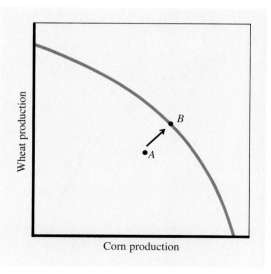

for example, that a society uses all of its resources to produce beef efficiently, but everyone in the society is a vegetarian. The result is a total waste of resources (assuming that the society cannot trade beef for vegetables with another society).

A wrong mix of output can be less obvious, however. Beef production is a highly competitive industry in the United States. Hundreds of thousands of farmers sell millions of cattle each year to hundreds of meat packing firms. Most grocery stores have plentiful stocks at reasonable prices because there are many suppliers competing for business.

Suppose instead that the government granted a monopoly on beef production —that is, the sole right to produce beef—to a single company. Later you will see more formally that an unregulated monopoly can increase profit if it cuts production and raises price. Even if all resources remained fully and efficiently employed, the monopoly would push the economy to a less desirable point on the ppf, that is, a point at which beef is underproduced and other goods are overproduced, a point such as *B* instead of *A* in Figure 2.4. In the absence of the monopoly, the society can move back to point *A*, which more closely matches the preferences of its people.

Scarcity and Negative Slope   Points that lie on the production possibility frontier, then, represent points of full employment and efficiency of production. Society can choose only one point on the curve, however. Because a society's choices are constrained by available resources and existing technology, when those resources are fully and efficiently employed it can produce more capital goods only by reducing production of consumption goods. The United States might be represented by a point such as *E* in Figure 2.2. A movement to point *F*, which is more like the allocation in Japan, would involve giving up consumption to create capital.

Recall that the slope of a curve between two points can be approximated by the change between the points on the *Y* axis (ΔY) divided by the change on the *X* axis (ΔX). Moving from point *E* to point *F* involves increasing capital production by ΔK units and decreasing production of consumption goods by ΔC units. Capital production increases (ΔK is a positive number) and consumption goods production decreases (ΔC is a negative number). Thus the numerical value of the slope, $\Delta K/\Delta C$, is a negative number.

FIGURE 2.4
Inefficient Mix of Output
Resulting from a Monopoly

Even if resources are combined efficiently in production, the result is inefficient if the economy is not producing the combination of goods and services that people want. This can occur if a monopoly controls an industry.

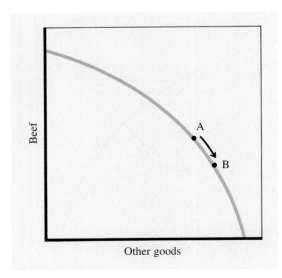

Marginal rate of transformation (MRT)   The numerical value of the slope of the production possibilities frontier. The number of units of one kind of good you can get by giving up one unit of another kind of good.

The numerical value of the slope of the production possibility frontier is called a society's **marginal rate of transformation** (**MRT**). The MRT is the number of units of capital goods you can get from giving up each unit of consumer goods. If in moving from E to F in Figure 2.2 we gained 100 units of capital goods and gave up 50 units of consumer goods, the marginal rate of transformation would be -2. We can transform consumer goods into capital goods at a rate of 2 to 1 — two units of capital goods for every one unit of consumer goods. As you will see, the MRT is likely to change as we move along the ppf.

Negative Slope and Opportunity Cost   An attractive feature of the production possibility frontier is that it forces you to think of opportunity cost. With no resource costs or money costs in the diagram, the only cost of producing more capital goods is the loss of consumer goods. If we want more consumer goods, the cost is a sacrifice of capital goods. The marginal rate of transformation is actually a way of stating the opportunity cost. If the marginal rate of transformation of capital goods into consumption goods is currently -2, the opportunity cost of a unit of consumption goods is the two units of capital goods that must be foregone.

The Shape of the Production Possibility Frontier   We have suggested that the slope of the ppf indicates the trade-off that a society faces between two goods that it produces. We can learn something further about the shape of the frontier—or the terms of this trade-off. Let us look at the trade-off between corn and wheat production in Kansas and Ohio. In a recent year Kansas and Ohio together produced about 510 million bushels of corn and about 380 million bushels of wheat. Table 2.1 presents these two numbers plus some hypothetical combinations of corn and wheat production that might exist for Kansas and Ohio together. Figure 2.5 graphs the data from Table 2.1

Now suppose that the demand for corn dramatically increased. If this happened, farmers would probably shift some of their acreage from wheat to corn. Such a shift is represented by a move up and to the left along the ppf toward points A and B in Figure 2.5. As this happens, it becomes more and more difficult to produce additional corn.

The best land for corn production was presumably in corn, and the best land for wheat production in wheat. As we try to produce more and more corn, the land is less and less well suited to that crop. And as we take more and more land out of wheat production, we will be taking increasingly better wheat-producing land. All of this is to say that the opportunity cost of more corn, measured in terms of wheat, increases.

Moving from E to D, we can get 100 million bushels of corn by sacrificing only 50 million bushels of wheat—that is, we get two bushels of corn for every bushel of wheat. The marginal rate of transformation is thus -2. However, when we are already taxing the

TABLE 2.1
Production Possibility Schedule for Total Wheat and Corn Production in Ohio and Kansas

	Total corn production (millions of bushels per year)	Total wheat production (millions of bushels per year)
	700	100
	650	200
Actual production	510	380
	400	500
	300	550

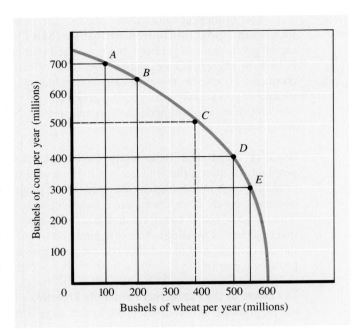

FIGURE 2.5

Corn and Wheat Production in Ohio and Kansas

The ppf illustrates that as we shift resources from wheat production to corn production the opportunity cost increases. Moving from *E* to *D*, we get an additional 100 million bushels of corn at a cost of 50 million bushels of wheat. Moving from *B* to *A*, we get only 50 million bushels of corn at a cost of 100 million bushels of wheat. The cost *per bushel* of corn —measured in lost or forgone wheat —has increased by a factor of four.

ability of the land to produce corn, it becomes more difficult, and the opportunity cost goes up. Moving from *B* to *A*, we can get only 50 million bushels of corn by sacrificing 100 million bushels of wheat. For every bushel of wheat, we get only a half bushel of corn. Now the marginal rate of transformation has dropped to −.5. On the other hand, if the demand for *wheat* were to increase substantially and we were to move down and to the right along the production possibility frontier, it would become increasingly difficult to produce wheat, and the opportunity cost of wheat, in terms of corn, would rise.

It is important to remember that the graph represents choices available within the constraints imposed by the current state of agricultural technology. In the long run technology may change, and when that happens we have *growth*.

Economic growth   An increase in the total output of an economy. It occurs when a society acquires or puts to use new resources or when it learns to produce more using existing resources.

Economic Growth   **Economic growth** occurs when a society acquires new resources or when society learns to produce more with existing resources. New resources may mean a larger labor force or an increased capital stock. The production and use of new machinery and equipment (capital) increases the productivity of workers. Improved productivity also comes from technological change and innovation: the discovery and application of new, efficient techniques of production. Figure 2.6 shows how growth shifts the ppf.

The last 30 years have seen dramatic increases in the productivity of American agriculture. Based on data compiled by the Department of Agriculture, Table 2.2 shows that yield per acre in corn production has more than doubled—increased 142 percent—since the late 1950s, while the labor required to produce it has dropped by 85 percent. Productivity in wheat production has also increased, at only a slightly less remarkable rate: output per acre is up 70 percent, while labor requirements are down nearly 60 percent. These increases are the result of more efficient farming techniques and

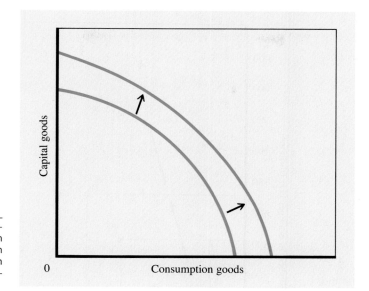

FIGURE 2.6
Shift of a Production Possibility
Frontier Due to Economic
Growth

Economic growth occurs when a society acquires more resources, or when
a society learns to produce more with
existing resources. Economic growth
shifts a society's production possibility frontier up and to the right.

TABLE 2.2
Increasing Productivity in Corn
and Wheat Production in the
United States, 1955–1985

	CORN		**WHEAT**	
	Yield per acre (bushels)	Labor hours per 100 bushels	Yield per acre (bushels)	Labor hours per 100 bushels
1955–1959	48.7	20	22.3	17
1960–1964	62.2	11	25.2	12
1965–1969	78.5	7	27.5	11
1970–1974	84.0	5	31.0	9
1975–1979	95.3	4	31.3	9
1980–1984	101.4	3	36.2	7
1985	118.0	NA	38.0	NA

Source: U.S. Department of Agriculture, Economic Research Service, *Agricultural Statistics*.

more and better capital (tractors, combines, and other equipment), backed up by advances
in scientific knowledge and technological change (hybrid seeds, fertilizers, and so forth).
As you can see in Figure 2.7, increases such as these shift the possibilities and constraints
that we face as a society up and out to the right on the graph. The figures for 1969, 1981,
and 1985 are actual production figures for Ohio and Kansas.

Sources of Growth and the Dilemma of the Poor Countries   Economic growth arises
from many sources, the two most important of which, over the years, have been the
accumulation of capital and technological change. For poor countries, capital is essential;
they must build the communication networks and transportation systems necessary to
develop industries that function efficiently. They also need capital goods in order to
develop their agricultural sectors.

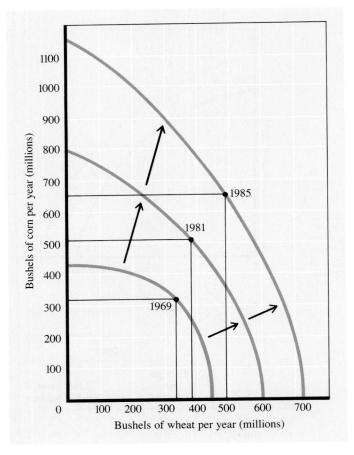

FIGURE 2.7
Increasing Productivity Shifts the PPF Up and to the Right

Productivity increases enhanced the ability of Kansas and Ohio to produce both corn and wheat. As Table 2.2 shows, productivity increases were more dramatic for corn than for wheat. The shift was thus not parallel.

Note: The ppf also shifts if the amount of land or labor in corn and wheat production changes. Although we emphasize productivity increases here, part of the actual shifts between years is due to land and labor changes.

Recall that capital goods are produced only at a sacrifice of consumption goods. The same can be said for technological change. Technological change comes from research and development that uses resources, and thus it too must be paid for. The resources used to produce capital goods—to build a road, a tractor, or a manufacturing plant—*and* to develop new technologies could have been used to produce consumption goods.

When a large part of the population is very poor, taking resources out of the production of consumption goods such as food and clothing is very difficult to do. In some countries, those with wealth to invest in domestic industries may instead invest abroad because of constant political turmoil at home. It often falls to the government to generate revenues for capital production and research out of tax collections.

This means that the gap between rich and poor nations is continually growing. Figure 2.8 graphs the result, using production possibility frontiers. On the left, the rich country devotes a larger portion of its production to capital, while the poor country produces mostly consumption goods. On the right, you see the result: the ppf of the rich country shifts up and out farther and faster.

Although it exists only as an abstraction, the production possibility frontier points up a number of very important concepts that we shall use throughout the rest of the book: scarcity, unemployment, inefficiency, opportunity cost, the law of increasing opportunity cost, and growth.

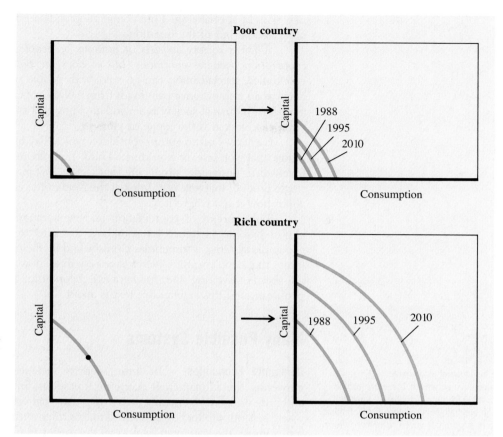

FIGURE 2.8
Capital Goods and Growth in
Poor and Rich Countries

Rich countries find it easier to devote
resources to the production of capital
than poor countries do. But the more
resources that flow into capital production, the faster the rate of economic growth. Thus the gap between poor
and rich countries has grown over
time.

THE THREE FUNDAMENTAL QUESTIONS IN MORE COMPLEX ECONOMIES

Recall that the three basic questions facing all economic systems are (1) What will be produced? (2) How will it be produced? (3) Who will get it?

When Bill was alone on the island, the mechanism for answering these questions was simple: He thought about his own wants and preferences, looked at the constraints and limits imposed by the resources of the island and his own skills and time, and made his decisions. As he set about his work, he allocated available resources quite simply, more or less by dividing up his available time. Distribution of the output was irrelevant. Because Bill was the society, he got it all.

Introducing even one more person changes all that. Resource allocation now involves deciding not only how each person spends time but also who does what. Labor has to be allocated across the various tasks. And now there are two sets of wants and preferences to worry about. The question of distribution, which did not matter before, suddenly becomes central. Even after two people decide what to produce, they have to decide how to divide it up. If Bill and Colleen go off on their own and form two completely separate self-sufficient economies, there will be *lost potential*. Clearly, two people can do many more things than one person can do alone. They may even develop new skills by specializing. Thus cooperation and coordination give rise to gains that would otherwise be out of the question.

When a society consists of millions of people, the problem of coordination and cooperation becomes enormous, but so does the potential for gain. In large, complex economies, specialization can go wild, with people working in jobs as different in their detail as an impressionist painting is from a blank page. The range of products available in a modern industrial society is beyond anything that could have been imagined a hundred years ago, and so is the range of jobs.

Earlier we asked you to consider a typical day in your life and to think about all the things that you use or consume. Think now about the number of people that were involved in designing, producing, packaging, shipping, wholesaling, and retailing every single product that you use. Look at the food in the cafeteria line, for example, and think about how it got where it is.

The amount of coordination and cooperation in a modern industrial society is almost hard to imagine, yet somehow it seems to work. Something seems to drive economic systems, if sometimes clumsily and inefficiently, toward producing many of the things that people want. Given scarce resources, how, exactly, do large, complex societies go about answering the fundamental economic questions? This is the **economic problem**, and this is what this text is about.

Many Possible Systems

Command economy An economy in which the state makes most economic decisions. That is, the central government decides what gets produced, when, and for whom.

Command Economies   In some modern societies government plays a big role in answering the fundamental economic questions. In **command economies,** a central authority or agency generally draws up a plan that establishes what will be produced and when, sets out production goals, and makes rules for its distribution. In the Soviet Union, for example, the state owns almost all the means of production, including factories, land, and equipment. Since the 1920s the Soviets have produced "five-year plans" that set very specific output targets.

Not only does the central government decide what to produce in such systems, it decides how to produce it and *how to distribute* it as well. Planners use complex computer programs to determine the materials, labor, and energy required to produce a variety of output targets. The final output targets are then set with an eye toward the same constraint that the single manager of a one-person economy faces—limited resources. Centrally determined income policies then establish how much compensation workers and managers are to receive for their labors.

Even in planned economies, people do exercise some choice. Commodities are sold at prices set by the government, and to the extent that they are able to pay those prices people are free to buy what is available. Sometimes more is demanded than is produced; sometimes goods are left on the shelves. These signals are used in the next plan to adjust output targets.

Central planning and command economies are examined in much more detail later. This brief sketch, however, should give you an impression of how differently complex systems can address the same basic questions.

Laissez-faire economy Literally from the French: "allow them to do." An economy in which individual people and firms pursue their own self-interests without any interference or direction by government. The free market operates entirely without restraint.

Laissez-Faire Economies: The Free Market   At the opposite end of the spectrum from the command economy is the **laissez-faire economy.** The term *laissez-faire*, which, translated literally from French, means "allow [them] to do," implies a complete lack of government involvement. In such an economy individual people pursue their own self-interest without any central direction or regulation; the sum total of millions of individual decisions ultimately determines all basic economic outcomes. The central institution through which a laissez-faire system answers the basic questions is the **market**, a term that is used in economics to signify an institution through which buyers and sellers interact and engage in exchange.

Market *The institution through which buyers and sellers interact and engage in exchange.*

The interactions between buyers and sellers in any market may be very simple, or they may be quite complex. Early explorers of the North American Midwest who wished to exchange with Native Americans did so simply by bringing their goods to a central place and trading them. Today suppliers and demanders interact through market institutions that are much more complex. Take the Federal Funds market, for example. Banks must keep a specific percentage of their deposits on hand as a "reserve" for anyone who may want to make withdrawals. Any money beyond this can be loaned out or put to work earning interest. Among the many ways that banks with extra reserves do this is to seek out other banks in need of cash in the Federal Funds market. The banks never communicate directly, and no money ever really moves, because all communications and transactions are done electronically through a desk in New York. Nonetheless, buyers and sellers exchange in this market.

Even more traditional shopping now takes place electronically. A jewelry maker in Maine may sell gold necklaces to a buyer through the Home Shopping Network that shows the product on television—customers call in orders and pay with a credit card. Ultimately funds are transferred through a complicated chain of financial transactions. The result is that a buyer in Oakland, California, buys a necklace from an unseen jewelry producer in Maine and pays for it out of income made working as an account executive for an advertising firm specializing in marketing toothpaste. With a home computer, you can use your telephone to gain access to shopping services that do a computer search to find the lowest available price for the item you want to buy. You can then enter your credit card number, and the item will be on your doorstep in four days.

As you can see, some markets are simple and others are complex, but they all involve buyers and sellers engaging in exchange. The behavior of buyers and sellers in a laissez-faire economy determines what gets produced, how it is produced, and who gets it. The following chapters explore market systems in great depth. A quick preview is worthwhile here, however.

In a free, unregulated market, wares are produced and sold only if the supplier can make a **profit**. In simple terms, making a profit means selling goods or services for more than it costs to produce them. Now clearly you can't make a profit unless someone wants the product that you are selling. This logic, in turn, leads to the notion of **consumer sovereignty**. The mix of output found in any free-market system is dictated ultimately by the tastes and preferences of consumers who "vote" by buying or not buying. Businesses rise and fall in response to consumer demands.

Consumer sovereignty *The idea that consumers ultimately dictate what will be produced (or not produced) by choosing what to purchase (and what not to purchase).*

In a free market economy, producers may be small or large. One person who hand paints eggshells may start to sell them as a business; a woman who has been showing her poodle may start handling other people's dogs in the show ring. On a larger scale a group of furniture designers may put together a large portfolio of sketches, several million dollars, and start a bigger business. At the ultimate extreme are huge corporations like IBM, General Motors, and Exxon that individually sell tens of billions of dollars worth of products every year.

In a free market system a business may be started by anyone who sees an opportunity. The incentive for business ventures is profit. Private energies are devoted to production because people want the product, they are willing to pay for it, and it can be produced for less than what it will sell for in the market. Thus, under free enterprise it is the *expectation of profit* that determines whether something gets produced. No central directive or plan is necessary.

Next, individual producers must figure out how to organize and coordinate the actual production of their products. The owner of a small shoe repair shop must buy the equipment and tools that she needs, hang signs, set prices, and so forth by herself. In a big corporation, so many people are involved in planning the production process that in many ways corporate planning resembles the planning in a command economy. Whether the firms are large or small, however, production decisions are made by separate private organizations acting in what they perceive to be their own interests.

Decision making that is structured in this way, it is argued, leads to more efficient production. If a producer produces inefficiently, competitors will come along, fight for the business, and eventually take it away. Thus in a free market economy competition forces producers to use efficient techniques of production. It is competition, then, that ultimately dictates how outputs are produced.

In a free market system, the distribution of output—who gets what—is also determined in a decentralized way. The amount that any one household gets depends on its *income* and *wealth*. Wealth may be inherited or accumulated by saving. Income depends on decisions made by individual people and by conditions in the market.

To the extent that income comes from working for a wage, it is at least in part determined by individual choice. You will work for the wages available in the market only if these wages (and the things they can buy) are sufficient to compensate you for what you give up by working. If you don't work your leisure certainly has a value. You may also discover that you can increase your income by getting more training. You *can't* increase your income, however, if you acquire a skill that no one wants. Again, it's like profit: if acquiring a skill will bring you more income or job satisfaction than it costs you to get that skill, you will probably go for it. You need no central directive to tell you that this is so.

While income determines how much of society's output you can buy and consume, not all income comes from working. Individuals may also earn income by owning all or part of a business for which they do not work. Those who risk their wealth by buying shares in companies or by loaning it out to be used for business investments earn a return on their wealth. Returns may come directly, as profit, or indirectly, as interest or dividends on stock. In a free market economy, people make independent decisions about what to do with wealth that they own.

In a free market system, then, the basic economic questions find answers without the necessity of a central government plan or directives. This is what the "free" in free market means—the system is left to operate according to its own terms, with no outside interference. Individuals pursuing their own self-interest will go into business and produce the products that people want; others will decide whether to acquire skills or not, whether to work or not to work, and whether to buy, sell, invest, or save the income that they earn.

The basic coordinating mechanism in a free market system is price. A **price** is the amount that a product sells for per unit, and it reflects what society is willing to pay. Prices of inputs—labor, land, capital, and so on—determine how much it costs to produce a product. Prices of various kinds of labor, *or wage rates*, determine the rewards for working in different jobs and professions. Many of the independent decisions made in a market economy involve the weighing of prices and costs, so it is not surprising that much of economic theory focuses on the factors that influence and determine prices. This is why microeconomic theory is often simply called **price theory**.

Mixed Systems, Markets, and Governments   The differences between command economies and laissez-faire economies in their pure forms are enormous. But in fact these pure forms do not exist in the world; all real systems are in some sense "mixed." That is, individual enterprise exists and independent choice is exercised even in the economy of the Soviet Union; at the same time, government is by necessity significantly involved in all economies, including that of the United States.

In the Soviet Union about 30 percent of all agricultural output is produced for the market *on private farms*. A system of decentralized, quasi-market-based decision making has existed in Yugoslavia since 1948. Individual plant managers set production revenue and cost targets and are rewarded with higher incomes when revenues exceed costs.

As you will see in Chapter 40, both the Soviet Union and China are currently undertaking major economic reforms. Many decisions previously made centrally are being delegated to the marketplace, and private enterprise is being encouraged. Experience with central planning has led many in those countries to conclude that in its pure form it results in waste, inefficiency, and poor rates of economic growth.

Conversely, no market economies exist without government involvement and government regulation. In the United States we have basically a free market economy, but government purchases account for about 20 percent of our total production. The government directly employs about 18 percent of all workers, and taxes are about a quarter of national income. The government also redistributes income by means of taxation and social welfare expenditures, and it regulates many economic activities.

One of the major themes in this book, and indeed in economics, is the tension between the advantages of free, unregulated markets and the need for government involvement in the economy. Advocates of markets argue that they work best when left to themselves. They produce only what people want; without buyers, sellers go out of business. Competition forces firms to adopt efficient production techniques. Wage differentials lead people to acquire needed skills. Competition also leads to innovation in both production techniques and products—we get quality and variety.

But even staunch defenders of the free enterprise system recognize that market systems are not perfect. Before we go on we will briefly outline some of the problems that free market systems naturally encounter: (1) they do not always produce what people want at lowest cost—there are inefficiencies; (2) rewards (income) may be unevenly distributed, leaving some groups out; and (3) periods of unemployment and inflation recur with some regularity.

Many people point to these problems as reasons for government involvement. Indeed, for some problems government involvement may be the only solution. But government decisions are made by people who presumably, like the rest of us, act in their own self-interest. While governments may indeed be called upon to improve the functioning of the economy, there is no guarantee that they will do so. Just as markets may fail to produce an allocation of resources that is perfectly efficient and fair, governments may fail to improve matters.

INEFFICIENCIES   Free markets may not produce all the goods that people want at prices that cover the costs of producing them. There are some goods and services whose benefits are social, or *collective*, such as national defense, open park areas, a system of justice, and police protection. Because these goods, once produced, provide benefits to everyone, whether or not people pay for them, private firms in a free market economy find it impossible to make a profit producing them. Thus, the members of society get together collectively, through government, to arrange for their production. The result is that governments collect taxes and produce **public goods and services**.

Government intervention may also be necessary because private decision makers, seeking profits, can make bad decisions from society's point of view if they fail to weigh all the costs and benefits of their decisions. The market system provides an incentive to produce a product if, and only if, people are willing to pay more for it than the cost of the resources needed to produce it. That works to society's advantage as long as the resource costs reflect the full cost to society of producing the product. If the environment is damaged, however, and producers do not factor in those costs, their profit-producing activities may not, on balance, work to society's advantage. Governments involve themselves in free markets to make sure that decision makers consider all the benefits and costs of their decisions. That is why we have the Environmental Protection Agency, the National Forest Service, and similar agencies.

Markets work best when they are competitive. Recall that competition seems to drive producers to choose the most efficient methods of production. Inefficient producers are driven out of business by the forces of competition. Competition also leads to innovation and new products. Sometimes, however, powerful firms in free markets can gain control of their markets and block competition. A firm that monopolizes a market may stifle innovation, charge higher prices than necessary, and generally cause a misallocation of resources. Since the turn of the century, noncompetitive behavior and the exercise of monopoly power has been illegal in the United States.

REDISTRIBUTION OF INCOME   Governments may also get involved in a basically decentralized market system because the final distribution of income and thus of output is considered to be inequitable. Free market systems are based on the principle of individual self-interest and enterprise: our rewards are supposed to be commensurate with how well we compete and how lucky we are. But some people are not well equipped to compete—some are physically unable to work, some are mentally unable to deal with a job. Whatever the cause, thousands of people find that they are unable to get along economically. Sometimes this is their fault, and sometimes it is not. In all cases, however, society must decide what, if anything, to do about it.

Every government redistributes income to a certain extent. In the United States we have welfare, unemployment compensation, and a host of other programs designed to be of some help to the poor. In recent years government has substantially reduced its role in income redistribution. The budget cuts and tax reductions of the Reagan years have moved us back toward a distribution of income determined by the market rather than by government policy.

This is, of course, a subject of endless debate. Some claim that taxes on the rich and programs for the poor destroy the incentives that the market provides for hard work, enterprise, and risk taking. Others argue that because many of the poor, particularly children, are in the position they are in through no fault of their own, such cuts are cruel and unfair.

STABILIZATION   When we turn to macroeconomics, we will explore the causes and consequences of unemployment and price inflation. In market economies, the level of unemployment is not planned, and prices are set freely by the forces of supply and demand. But governments can, through taxing and spending policies and by regulating the banking system, exert some influence over prices and over the general level of output and employment.

As with distribution, the desirability and the character of government involvement in the macroeconomy are hotly debated. This debate fills about a quarter of this book.

A LOOK AHEAD

This chapter has described the economic problem in broad terms. We have outlined the questions that all economic systems must answer. We also discussed very broadly two kinds of economic system and some of the advantages and disadvantages of each. In the next chapter we turn from the general to the specific. There we discuss in some detail the institutions of American capitalism: how the private sector is organized, and what the government actually does. Chapters 4 and 5 then begin the task of analyzing the way market systems operate.

SUMMARY

1. Every society has some system or mechanism for transforming what nature and previous generations have provided into useful form. Economics is the study of that process and its outcomes.
2. *Producers* are those who take resources and transform them into usable products, or outputs. Private firms, households, and governments all produce something.
3. All societies must answer three questions: What will be produced? How will it be produced? Who will get it?
4. One person alone on an island must make the same basic decisions that complex societies make.
5. When society consists of more than one person, questions of distribution, cooperation, and specialization arise.
6. In large complex societies the potential gains from cooperation and specialization are enormous, but so are the problems.
7. Because resources are scarce relative to human wants in all societies, using resources to produce one good or service implies *not* using them to produce something else. The concept of opportunity cost is central to an understanding of economics.
8. Using resources to produce capital that will in turn produce benefits in the future implies *not* using those resources to produce consumer goods that provide benefits in the present.
9. A production possibility frontier is a graph that shows all of the combinations of goods and services that can be produced if all of society's resources are used efficiently.
10. The production possibility frontier illustrates a number of important economic concepts: scarcity, unemployment, inefficiency, increasing opportunity cost, and economic growth.
11. Economic growth occurs when a society acquires more resources, or when a society learns to produce more with existing resources. Improved productivity may come from additional capital, or from the discovery and application of new, more efficient, techniques of production.
12. In some modern societies government plays a big role in answering the fundamental questions. In command economies, a central authority generally draws up a plan that determines what will be produced, how it will be produced, and who will get it.
13. A *market* is an institution through which buyers and sellers interact and engage in exchange. Some markets involve simple face-to-face exchange; others involve a complex series of transactions, often over great distance or over wires.
14. A laissez-faire economy is one in which individuals independently pursuing their own self-interest, without any central direction or regulation, ultimately determine all basic economic outcomes.
15. There are no purely planned economies and no pure laissez-faire economies; all economies are mixed. On the one hand individual enterprise, independent choice, and relatively free markets exist in centrally planned economies such as that of the Soviet Union. On the other hand there is, of necessity, significant government involvement in market economies such as that of the United States.

REVIEW CONCEPTS

REVIEW QUESTIONS

1. In a recent national contest, the first prize is a town. The winner receives a furnished house, a general store and gasoline station, a pick-up truck, and 100 acres of land. The store comes fully stocked with everything you might find in a country general store. The town is located 100 miles from a small city. It is the shopping center for about a thousand families who live in the countryside. In addition, the road through the town is fairly well traveled. Suppose you win the contest and decide to try running the town as a business for at least a year.
   a. Describe the resources available to the "economy" of your town. Use your imagination. Specifically, what is the potential labor force? What are the natural resources?
   b. Describe the capital stock of your town.
   c. Your income will depend on some factors beyond your control, but it may also be affected by decisions that you make. List some of the factors that are beyond your control that will affect your income.
   d. List some of the decisions you must make that could affect your income, and explain what their effects might be.
   e. Without doubt, you will have to make some decisions about present versus future consumption and income. Define investment. List some capital investments you might make in your town. How will you pay for them? What are the opportunity costs of your investments?
   f. At the end of the first year, you must decide whether to stay or go back to college. How will you decide? What factors will you weigh in making your decision? What role do your expectations play? Thinking of a college education as an investment in human capital, how do you decide whether it is worthwhile?

2. Suppose that a simple society has an economy with only one resource, labor. Labor can be used to produce only two commodities X, a necessity good (food) and Y, a luxury good (music and merriment). Suppose that the labor force consists of 100 workers. One laborer can produce either at a rate of five units of necessity per month (by hunting and gathering) or at a rate of 10 units of luxury per month (by writing songs, playing the guitar, dancing, and so on).
   a. On a graph, draw the economy's economic production possibility frontier. Where does the ppf intersect the Y axis? Where does it intersect the X axis? What meaning do those point have?
   b. What is the marginal rate of transformation?
   c. Suppose the economy ended up producing at a point *inside* the ppf. Give at least two reasons that this could occur. If you were the president of the society that had this economy, what would, or could, you do about that?
   d. Suppose you succeeded in lifting your economy until it was producing at a point *on* its ppf. What point would you choose? How might your small society decide at which point it wanted to be? If you were a dictator, how would *you* decide? If you wanted to let the "free market" decide, describe how that might work.
   e. Once you have chosen a point on the ppf, you still need to decide how your society's product will be divided up. If you were a dictator, how would you decide? What would happen if you left it to the "free market?"

3 The Basic Structure of the U.S. Economy: The Private and Public Sectors

The previous chapter described the economic problem. All societies are endowed by nature and by previous generations with scarce resources. These resources are combined and transformed by a process called "production" into goods and services that are, if things go right, demanded by the members of society. At the end of Chapter 2, we briefly described the kinds of alternative economic systems that exist in the world today. In some systems, such as that of the Soviet Union, most production decisions are made by the government, and resources are allocated according to a centrally developed plan. In others, like those of Japan and the United States, most production decisions are made by private individuals and organizations pursuing their own interests in markets. Resources get allocated through millions of independent private decisions.

This chapter describes the basic institutional structure of the U.S. economy in more detail. Because most production is undertaken by private individuals and organizations, we first look at the private sector. The **private sector** is made up of independently owned firms that exist to make a profit, of nonprofit organizations, and of individual households. It includes General Motors, Occidental College, the Catholic Church, soybean farms in Iowa, the corner drug store, and the baby sitter down the street. What defines the private sector is independent ownership and control. In essence it includes all the decision-making units within the economy that are not part of the government.

The **public sector** is the government—federal, state, and local. Government employees—tax assessors, public school teachers, post office workers, colonels in the army, and the President—work in the public sector. Just as the Ford Motor Company uses land, labor, and capital to produce automobiles, the public sector uses land, labor, and

Private sector *Includes all independently owned profit-making firms, nonprofit organizations, and households; all the decision-making units in the economy that are* not *the government.*

Public sector *Includes all agencies at all levels of government—federal, state, and local.*

capital to produce, among other things, public services such as police and fire protection, education, national defense, and a system of justice. The public sector in the United States also produces some things that are simultaneously produced by the private sector. The post office provides overnight express-mail service that competes directly with similar services provided by private firms such as Federal Express and United Parcel. The University of Michigan, part of the public sector, directly competes for "buyers" of its "product" with private sector colleges and universities such as Northwestern and Colorado College.

Recall the distinction drawn in Chapter 1 between descriptive economics and economic theory, and then notice what this chapter is not. We do not analyze behavior or build models in this chapter. Here we only describe institutions as they exist. Neither do we discuss whether the institutions that we describe are good. In fact, we try very hard to avoid any normative distinctions. We do not talk about proper or improper roles of government in the economy, for example, or the things that governments might do to make the economy more or less efficient or fair.

In Chapter 4 we begin to analyze behavior. Chapters 4 through 12 build a complete model, or theory, of a market system in which all decisions are made either by small private business firms or by households—there is no government or government regulation in the model. In this part of the text we describe some of the virtues of the market mechanism and of *private sector* decision making. Chapters 13 through 17 then focus on problems that occur in unregulated market systems. In these chapters the focus is on the potential role of the *public sector* in improving the allocation of resources. Can the government actually increase the efficiency of the economy or the fairness of its operation? We also discuss some of the problems of government. For example, how might collective action through government lead to inefficiency or inequity?

Before we begin the analysis in Chapter 4, however, it is important to have some sense of the institutional landscape. As we said in Chapter 1, models are abstract representations of reality. One purpose for studying economics, however, is to understand the world and what people actually do. This chapter provides some important facts that describe the realities of the U.S. economy.

It is also important to have some knowledge of accounting in studying economics. How do firms keep their books, and how do we know if a firm is doing well or poorly? The appendix to this chapter provides a brief introduction to financial accounting.

THE PRIVATE SECTOR: BUSINESS AND INDUSTRIAL ORGANIZATION IN THE UNITED STATES

How is business actually organized in the United States? Let us see first how the law permits *individual firms* to be organized. Then we can talk about the different ways that *industries* have come to be structured. An individual firm's behavior depends on both its own legal structure and its relationship to other firms in its industry.

The Legal Organization of Firms

Most private sector activity takes place within business firms that exist to make a profit. Some other private sector organizations that exist for reasons other than profit—clubs, cooperatives, and nonprofit organizations, for example—do produce goods or services.

Because these organizations repesent a small fraction of private sector activity, however, we focus here on profit-making firms.

If you or a group of your associates decide to form a business in order to make profits, you may organize it according to one of three basic legal forms: you can set up (1) a *proprietorship,* (2) a *partnership,* or (3) a *corporation.* A single business may pass through more than one of these forms of organization during its development.

The Proprietorship   The least complex and most common form a business can take is the simple **proprietorship.** With a proprietorship, there is no legal process to go through before you start a business. You simply start operating. For tax purposes, you must keep records of revenues and costs, of course, and if you make a profit you must add it to your other personal income and pay taxes on it.

Proprietorship   A form of business organization in which a person simply sets up to provide goods or services at a profit. In a proprietorship, the proprietor, or owner, is the firm. The assets and liabilities of the firm are the owner's assets and liabilities without limit.

A professor who does consulting on the side, for example, receives fees and has costs (computer expenses, data, research materials, and so forth). This consulting business is a proprietorship, even though the proprietor is the only employee and the business is very limited. A large restaurant that employs hundreds of people and serves thousands of meals may also be a proprietorship if it is owned by a single person. Most doctors and lawyers in private practice report their incomes and expenses as proprietors.

What distinguishes a proprietorship is that one person owns the firm, and, in a sense, that person *is* the firm. If the firm owes money, the proprietor owes the money; if the firm earns a profit, it goes to the proprietor, who pays whatever taxes are due on it. There is no limit to the responsibility of the owner. If the business gets into financial trouble, the proprietor alone is liable. That is, if a business does poorly or ends up in debt, those debts are the proprietor's personal responsibility. There is no wall of protection between a proprietor and her business, as we will see there is between corporations and their owners.

The Internal Revenue Service estimates that nearly 11 million proprietorships exist in the United States. That is one for every 13 adults in the country. Needless to say, most of these proprietorships are small; while they make up over 70 percent of all businesses, they account for under 6 percent of total sales (see Table 3.1).

Partnership   A form of business organization in which there is more than one proprietor. The owners are responsible jointly and separately for the firm's obligations.

The Partnership   A **partnership** is a proprietorship with more than one proprietor. When two or more people agree to share the responsibility for a business, they form a partnership. While no formal legal process is required to start this kind of business, most partnerships are based on agreements, signed by all the partners, that detail who pays what part of the costs and how profits shall be carved up. Profits from partnerships are taxable

TABLE 3.1
Number of Firms and Sales by Type of Business, 1983

	Number of firms (thousands)	Percent of total firms	Total sales ($ billions)	Percent of total sales
Proprietorships	10,704	70.2	465	5.9
Partnerships	1,542	10.1	291	3.7
Corporations	2,999	19.7	7,135	90.4
Total		100.0		100.0

Source: U.S. Internal Revenue Service, *Statistics of Income, 1983.* Based on number of tax returns filed for 1983.

income. Therefore accurate records of receipts and expenditures must be kept and each party's profits must be reported to the IRS.

As with a proprietorship, there is no limit to the liability of the owners, that is, the partners, for the debts of the firm. But with a partnership it can be worse. If you own one third of a partnership that goes out of business with a debt of $300,000, you owe the creditors $100,000, and so does each of your partners. But if they skip town, you owe the whole $300,000. Thus each partner is both jointly and separately liable for all the debts of the partnership.

Just over 10 percent of all firms in the United States are partnerships, and they account for only 3.7% of total sales (see again Table 3.1).

Corporation   A form of business organization resting on a legal charter that establishes the corporation as an entity separate from its owners. Owners hold shares and are liable for the firm's debts only up to the limit of their investment, or share in the firm.

The Corporation   A **corporation** is a formally established legal entity that exists separately from those who establish it and those who own it. To establish a corporation, a corporate charter must be obtained from a state government. In most states this is quite easy to do. A lawyer simply fills out the appropriate paper work and files it with the right state agency, along with certain fees. When a corporation is formed, shares of stock are issued and either sold or assigned. A corporation is actually owned by its shareholders, who are in a sense partners in the success or failure of the firm. Shareholders differ from simple partners, however, in two important ways.

For one thing, the liability of shareholders is limited to the amount they paid for the stock. If the company goes out of business or bankrupt, the shareholders may lose what they have invested, but no more than that. They are *not* liable for the debts of the corporation beyond the amount they invested. For another thing, the federal government and all but four states levy special taxes on corporations. The federal corporate income tax is a tax on the **net income**, or profits, of corporations. Since 1987 the tax has been 15 percent of net income on the first $50,000, but it rises to 34 percent after income exceeds that amount. Actually, 99 percent of all corporate net income is taxed at the 34 percent rate.[1] In essence, this means that tax is paid twice on corporate net income: once by the corporation when it pays tax on its profits, and again by the shareholders when they pay tax on their **dividends**, that is, the share of profits they receive from the corporation.

Net income   That which is left after costs are deducted from revenues; the profits of a firm.

Dividends   The profits of a corporation that the firm pays out each period to shareholders. Also called "distributed profits."

The special privilege granted to corporations limiting their liability is often called a *franchise*. Some view the corporate tax as a payment to the government in exchange for this grant of limited liability status. In New York State, for example, the state corporation tax is actually called the franchise tax.

Corporate net income, or profit, is usually divided up into three pieces. Some of it, of course, goes to federal and state governments in *taxes*. Some of it is paid out to shareholders as *dividends*, which are sometimes called *distributed profits*. And some of it usually stays within the corporation to be used for the purchase of capital assets or simply to accumulate. This part of corporate profits is called **retained earnings**, or *undistributed profits*.

Retained earnings   The profits that a corporation keeps, usually for investment purposes, rather than paying them out to shareholders. Also called "undistributed profits."

In 1987 corporations in the United States earned total profits of $274.1 billion. Out of this, they paid $136.3 billion in taxes, leaving $137.8 billion in after-tax profits. Of this amount, $93.8 billion was paid out to shareholders and the rest, $43.9 billion, was retained. In percentage terms, taxes accounted for 49.7 percent, while shareholders received 34.2 percent of total profits (see Table 3.2).

Turning again to Table 3.1, in 1983 there were three million corporations, just under 20 percent of all firms. But these three million firms accounted for over 90 percent

[1]Department of Commerce, Bureau of the Census, *Statistical Abstract of the United States*, 1984, table 891, p. 533 and authors' projections for 1987.

TABLE 3.2
The Distribution of Corporate
Profits in 1987

	Billions of dollars	Percent of before-tax profit
Profits before tax	274.1	100.0
Minus profits tax liability*	− 136.3	−49.7
Profits after tax	137.8	50.3
Minus dividends paid	− 93.8	−34.2
Undistributed profits	43.9	16.1

Source: U.S. Department of Commerce
*Federal, state, and local

of total sales. Needless to say, many corporations are very large. Each year *Fortune Magazine* publishes a list of the 500 largest industrial corporations in the United States. Topping the *Fortune* 500 in 1987 was General Motors. GM's total sales in 1986 were nearly $103 billion. The company made profits of almost $3 billion and employed 660,000 people!

The internal organization of a firm, whether it is a proprietorship, a partnership, or a corporation, affects its behavior and the behavior of potential investors. For example, protected by the limited liability status of a corporation, potential investors may be more likely to back high-risk but potentially high-payoff ventures. Further, most shareholders in corporations are not involved in managing the firm.

While the internal structure of a firm is important, it is less important to an understanding of a firm's behavior than is the organization of the industry or the market in which the firm competes. For example, whether it is a proprietorship or a corporation, a firm with little or no competition is likely to behave differently from a firm facing stiff competition from many rivals. With this in mind, we now expand our focus from the individual firm to the industry that encompasses many firms.

The Organization of Industries

Industry   *All the firms that produce a similar product. The boundaries of a "product" can be drawn very widely—"agricultural products"—less widely—"dairy products"—or very narrowly—"cheese." The term "industry" can be used interchangeably with the term "market."*

The term **industry** is used loosely to refer to groups of firms that produce similar products. Industries can be defined narrowly or more broadly, depending on the issue being discussed. For example, a company that produces and packages cheese is a part of the cheese industry, the dairy products industry, the food products industry, and the agricultural products industry.[2]

But whether we define industries broadly or narrowly, how firms within any industry behave depends on how that industry is organized—whether there are many competitors or few, whether they are large firms or small, whether the products of competing firms are perfect substitutes or very imperfect substitutes.

Market organization   *The way an industry is structured. Structure is defined by how many firms there are in an industry, whether products are differentiated or are virtually the same, whether or not firms in the industry can control prices or wages, and whether or not competing firms can enter and leave the industry freely.*

The kind of industry—or *market*—in which a firm operates thus determines, in large part, how it will behave. The four main kinds of **market organization** in the United States are summarized in Figure 3.1.

The following industry categories are the ones that we will use later in the book to analyze the behavior of firms. In the economic theory presented, the categories are assumed to be precise. That is, we analyze industries as if their structures fit the definitions precisely. In reality, industries are not always easy to categorize. Some industries have

[2]The Department of Commerce has devised a code system, the Standard Industrial Classification (S.I.C.) System, which defines industries at various levels of detail. That system is discussed at length in Chapter 14.

	Number of firms	Products differentiated or homogeneous	Price a decision variable	Free entry	Distinguished by	Examples
Perfect competition	Many	Homogeneous	No	Yes	Price competition only	Wheat farmer Textile firm
Monopoly	One	A single, unique product	Yes	No	Still constrained by market demand	Public utility Beer in Taiwan
Monopolistic competition	Many	Differentiated	Yes, but limited	Yes	Price and quality competition	Restaurants Hand soap
Oligopoly	Few	Either	Yes	Limited	Strategic behavior	Automobiles Aluminum

FIGURE 3.1
Characteristics of Different
Market Organizations

characteristics generally associated with one form of organization and other characteristics associated with a different form of organization. Nonetheless, the categories as described in theory provide a useful and convenient framework for thinking about the organization of industries in the U.S. economy.

Perfect competition *An industry structure (or market organization) in which there are many firms, each small relative to the industry, producing virtually identical products and in which no firm has any control over prices but takes price as given. In perfectly competitive industries, new competitors can freely enter and exit the market.*

Homogeneous products *Undifferentiated outputs: products that are identical to, or indistinguishable from, one another and perfectly substitutable for each other—such as wheat from two different farms.*

Perfect Competition   At one end of the spectrum is the competitive industry in which many relatively small firms produce nearly identical products. **Perfect competition** is a very precisely defined form of industry structure. (The word "perfect" here does not refer to virtue. It simply means "total," or "complete.") The most important point about perfect competition is that within such an industry *no single firm has any control over prices*—no single firm can affect the market price of its product or the price of the inputs that it buys. This crucial observation follows from two characteristics of competitive industries. First, a competitive industry is composed of many firms, each small relative to the size of the industry. Second, every firm in a perfectly competitive industry produces exactly the same product—the output of one firm cannot be distinguished from the output of the others. Thus all products in the industry are said to be **homogeneous**.

These characteristics limit the decisions open to competitive firms and simplify the analysis of competitive behavior. The formal discussion of perfectly competitive behavior begins in Chapter 7. Firms in perfectly competitive industries do not "differentiate" their products, nor do they have any control over the prices at which they sell their output. Taking prices as a given, then, each firm can decide only how much output to produce and how to produce it.

Consider agriculture, the classic example of a perfectly competitive industry. A wheat farmer in Kansas has absolutely no control over the price of wheat because, as you will see in the next few chapters, prices are determined by the interaction of many suppliers and many demanders. The only decisions left to the wheat farmer are how much wheat to plant and when and how to produce the crop.

Another mark of perfectly competitive industries is that new firms can, and do, frequently enter industries in search of profits, while others go out of business when they suffer losses. *Ease of entry* means that if firms in an industry earn high profits, new firms seeking to do the same thing are likely to spring up. No barriers exist to prevent a start-up firm from competing. For example, a few firms did very well producing and marketing personal and home computers in the late 1970s. Within a few years, dozens of new firms producing nearly identical computers were marketing products in hopes of doing likewise. Or if wheat prices were to rise sharply, nothing would prevent farmers from shifting their land out of other crops into wheat, and this is probably what they would do.

When a firm *exits* an industry, it simply stops producing a product. Sometimes an exiting firm goes out of business altogether. During the last ten years, thousands of small farmers have gone out of business, sold off their assets, paid what bills they could, and disappeared. Sometimes exiting means simply dropping a product line. The Digital Equipment Corporation decided, for example, to exit the personal computer market in 1985. The corporation remained a healthy, going concern; it simply moved out of one market.

To summarize, perfectly competitive industries are made up of many firms, each small relative to the size of the total market. In these industries, individual firms do not distinguish or differentiate their products from those of their competitors. Prices are determined by the forces of supply and demand and are virtually unaffected by decisions of any single firm. Entry and exit are relatively easy.

Monopoly   An industry structure (or market organization) in which there is only one large firm that produces a product for which there are no close substitutes. Monopolists can set prices although they are subject to some market discipline. For a monopoly to continue to exist something must prevent potential competitors from entering and competing for profits.

Monopoly   At the other end of the spectrum is **monopoly**, a market or industry in which only one firm produces a product for which there are no close substitutes.

Common sense tells us that if there is only one firm in a market, that firm sets the price of its product. This does not mean, however, that monopolies can set any price they please. Even monopolies face the constraint of the market. What good would it do, for example, to monopolize the production of celluloid frizzles if no one would pay your price for celluloid frizzles? Even if a firm produces a good that everyone likes, the firm gains nothing if it charges a price so high that no one buys it. Clearly, the price a monopolist chooses determines the quantity of its good or service it will be able to sell. Although price is a "decision variable," it is still subject to some discipline imposed by the market.

Barrier to entry   One of a number of ways to prevent new firms from entering and competing in monopolistic industries: Barriers include licensing or other explicit government policies, patents, huge start-up costs, hostile actions, etc.

In order for a monopoly to remain a monopoly, there must be some **barrier to entry**, some way to keep other firms from entering its market. Often governments erect these barriers themselves. Sometimes they grant an exclusive license to one producer. In Taiwan, for example, the national government licensed only one company to produce beer and excluded imports until 1987. There are also less formal government protections. In the United States, public utilities—electric power and gas companies, for example, most of which are privately owned—have traditionally been shielded by the government from competition. For many years the American Telephone and Telegraph Company was the exclusive producer of telephone services, both local and long-distance. Dramatic changes in the telecommunications industry in the last few years, including the break-up of AT&T by the courts in 1983, however, have made that market much more competitive.

Many other factors may bar entry into a monopolistic industry. A private company may hold a monopoly by virtue of a patent. The Polaroid Corporation, for instance, was the only producer of instant cameras for many years because it developed and patented the technology.

A monopoly, then, is a one-firm industry that produces a product for which there are no close substitutes. By virtue of its monopoly power, which is normally protected from competition by barriers to entry, such a firm can set price. Its pricing behavior is still constrained, however, by its market—it can only sell a product if people are willing to buy it.

Monopolistic competition   An industry structure (or market organization) in which many firms compete, producing similar but slightly differentiated products. There are close substitutes for the product of any given firm. Monopolistic competitors have some control over price. Price and quality competition follow from product differentiation. Entry and exit are relatively easy, and success invites new competitors.

Monopolistic Competition   Somewhere on the spectrum in between monopoly and competition, but much closer to competition, is a very common hybrid market organization called **monopolistic competition**. A monopolistically competitive industry is one in which many firms compete for essentially the same customers, but each firm produces a slightly different product. If these firms can **"differentiate" their products**

successfully, they establish a *brand loyalty* that in a small way allows them to enjoy the benefits of a monopoly. Procter & Gamble is the only producer of Ivory Soap—it "monopolizes" the market for Ivory—but the soap business is still very competitive because many close substitutes are available. Prentice Hall is the only company that can sell this book, but there are many substitutes.

While individual wheat farmers, in their perfectly competitive markets, have no control over the price they will get for their wheat, monopolistic competitors do exercise some price-setting power. That control is quite limited, however, because of the many close substitutes available—monopolistically competitive firms are subject to a great deal of "market discipline." Procter & Gamble can charge slightly more for Ivory Soap and continue to sell it because some people simply like Ivory Soap, but some Ivory users will switch to other brands.

In monopolistically competitive industries, there is both *price and quality competition*. Firms often enter these industries because they have an idea for a new product that represents a slight variation or improvement on an old one. Perhaps the purest example of a monopolistically competitive market is the restaurant industry. Every major city in the world contains hundreds upon hundreds of restaurants, each producing a slightly differentiated product in a highly competitive way. The cosmetics and clothing industries are also monopolistically competitive. Firms in such industries must decide on output, price, and quality of product.

Free, or at least *relatively easy, entry and exit* characterize monopolistic competition. When a firm enjoys success in one of its product lines, its profits invite new firms to come into its market with new brands or styles that are similar. Many new restaurants are born every year and many unsuccessful ones quietly expire.

To summarize, monopolistically competitive firms contain large numbers of relatively small firms. What distinguishes monopolistic competition from perfect competition is that firms differentiate their products. Individual firms produce unique products and thus, despite their small size, exercise some control over price. Entry and exit are relatively easy.

Oligopoly   An industry in which there are only a small number of firms is called an **oligopoly**. The automobile industry in the United States, for example, has only three major competitors and a very few smaller ones. Except for the fact that each contains only a few competitors, however, oligopolistic industries have little in common. In some, products are highly differentiated (automobiles, for example); in others, they are standardized (cement, steel, and aluminum, for example). In some, the industry is dominated by one very large firm; in others, the participating firms have roughly equal size and power.

Oligopoly   *An industry structure (or market organization) with a small number of (usually) large firms producing products that range from highly differentiated (automobiles) to standardized (steel). One huge firm may dominate or a few large firms may share market power. Firm behavior in an oligopoly varies from monopolistic to highly competitive. In general, entry of new firms into an oligopolistic industry is difficult but possible.*

Oligopolies behave somewhat unpredictably. In markets where two or three large rivals compete head-on, the competing firms often execute strategies that anticipate counter strategies. In setting price, for example, one firm must take into account how its competitors in the oligopoly are likely to react. One firm's action usually triggers a reaction from another, which in turn triggers still another reaction, and so on. The strategies and counter strategies that these firms employ determine who gets the sales. As a result, oligopolies are characterized by a great deal of uncertainty, and it is very difficult to generalize about their behavior.

Entry into an oligopolistic industry is usually possible, but difficult. Firms in oligopolies are generally large, and thus a large initial investment is usually required to break in.

To summarize, oligopolies are industries with a few large firms, but beyond that it is hard to generalize. In some oligopolies, firms differentiate their products; in others, they do not. Individual firms do exercise control over prices and generally behave "strategically" with respect to one another.

How Competitive Is the U.S. Economy?   In an article published early in the 1980s, William G. Shepherd provides some evidence on the extent of competition in the U.S. economy.[3] Shepherd defines four market types that correspond roughly to the categories we have just defined: (1) pure monopolies, (2) industries with dominant firms, (3) tight oligopolies, and (4) effectively competitive industries.

In Shepherd's classification scheme, monopolies are just as we described them. One firm accounts for 100 percent (or nearly 100 percent) of total sales. No close substitutes for its product exist and entry to the market is blocked. Industries with dominant firms are near-monopolies. In such industries, the dominant firm accounts for 50 to 90 percent of total industry sales, no close rivals exist, and entry to the market is difficult. Tight oligopolies are defined as industries in which the top four firms account for over 60 percent of total sales, and, again, entry barriers are high. Finally, Shepherd lumps everything else together under "effectively competitive."

The classification "effectively competitive" signifies more than just perfect competition. It certainly includes all of what we described as monopolistic competition. In Shepherd's "effectively competitive" group, the top four firms control less than 40 percent of the market, and entry barriers are low.

Table 3.3 shows what happened, according to Shepherd's estimates, to the level of competition in the U.S. economy between 1939 and 1980. Pure monopolies, a category that includes most public utilities and some patented goods, accounted for only 2.5% of total national income in 1980, down from 6.2% in 1939. In fact, purely monopolistic and dominant-firm industries together accounted for just a little over 5 percent of national income in 1980. On the other hand, 76.7% of national income originates in sectors that Shepherd classifies as effectively competitive, up from 52.4% in 1939. The estimates indicate that the percentage of national income originating in tight oligopolies has been cut in half since 1958.

The U.S. economy has apparently become significantly more competitive over the years. As later chapters show, a number of factors may have contributed to the change. Without going into detail here, these factors include increased competition from imports,

TABLE 3.3
Trends in Competition in the U.S. Economy 1939–1980: Percentage Share of National Income by Industry Category

	1939	1958	1980
Pure monopoly	6.2	3.1	2.5
Dominant firm	5.0	5.0	2.8
Tight oligopoly	36.4	35.6	18.0
Effectively competitive firm	52.4	56.3	76.7
Total	100.00	100.0	100.0

Source: William G. Shepherd, "Causes of Increased Competition in the U.S. Economy, 1939–1980," Review of Economics and Statistics, LXIV (November 1982), 613–626.

[3]William G. Shepherd, "Causes of Increased Competition in the U.S. Economy, 1939–1980," Review of Economics and Statistics, LXIV (November 1982), 613–626.

deregulation (particularly in the trucking, airline, and telecommunications industries), and enforcement of anti-monopoly laws.

Structural Change Since 1970   Table 3.4 gives a breakdown of national income by major product type or industry. These data point up a number of important changes. First, the percent of total national income accounted for by manufacturing has been continuously shrinking for fifteen years. In 1970 more than a quarter of our national income originated in the manufacturing sector. The decline since then has been due in part to increased competition from abroad: we buy a tremendous number of products, including automobiles, textiles, televisions, VCRs, cameras, and machine tools from the Koreans, the Japanese, and the Taiwanese. By 1985 the portion of total U.S. income originating in the manufacturing sector had dropped to only 21.1%, barely over one fifth of national income.

The fastest growing sector has been the service sector. We eat at restaurants, stay at hotels, and consume recreation, entertainment, and personal services at a far greater rate than ever before. The other sector that seems to have grown in relative terms between 1970 and 1985 is finance, insurance, and real estate. There are increasing numbers of people working for banks, financial services companies, stockbrokers, and the like.

One frequently voiced concern is that we are losing "good" jobs and replacing them with "bad" ones. Manufacturing in the United States is a high-wage sector. Most people who work in plants get substantial hourly wages. As manufacturing has declined, more and more jobs have opened up in the expanding service sector, where hourly wages are low relative to those in manufacturing.

While some people are deeply concerned over this change in the structure of the American economy, others see it as a natural consequence of continued economic growth and progress. Looking back at Table 3.4, notice that the first category, "agriculture, forestry, and fisheries," is also declining in relative importance. Once agriculture alone accounted for 50 percent of national income. But as farmers learned more and more productive farming methods, the need for farm labor declined, and so did food prices. With lower food prices, people could spend their incomes on other things —manufactured goods and services. Since agriculture needed fewer workers, labor was available to be employed in the new expanding sectors. Thus as the American economy grew and developed, some sectors, such as agriculture, shrank in relative importance and others, such as manufacturing and services, grew in relative importance.

TABLE 3.4
Percentage Share of National Income by Major Sector, 1970, 1980, and 1985

	1970	1980	1985
Agriculture, forestry, fisheries	3.1	2.7	2.4
Mining and construction	6.7	7.5	6.6
Manufacturing	25.8	23.5	21.1
Transportation	3.8	3.8	3.6
Communications and utilities	3.9	4.0	4.5
Wholesale and retail trade	15.3	14.7	15.0
Finance, insurance, real estate	11.5	12.3	12.9
Services	13.1	15.1	17.9
Government	15.9	14.2	14.8
Other	.9	2.1	1.3
Total	100.0	100.0	100.0

Source: Statistical Abstract of the United States, 1987, table 704.

Modern economies are in a continuous state of change. Resources are always moving. Literally thousands of new firms are started every year, and old, tired firms—not to mention young, inefficient ones—go out of business every day. Some firms grow rapidly in size, while others shrink. In the process, the basic industrial structure changes. In a very real sense, the purpose of this book is to help you understand this process. Why do new firms get formed? Why do others go out of business? Why are some sectors expanding while others are contracting?

The focus of Chapters 6–12 is on the private sector. We look first at the sets of decisions facing small, independent, private firms. By the end of Chapter 12, we will have developed a model of resource allocation that offers an explanation for observed changes in industrial structure. But that is only part of the story. While the U.S. economy is basically a market economy, we also have a public sector that plays a major role in determining the allocation of resources, the mix of output, and the distribution of rewards. To understand the workings of any economic system, it is necessary to understand the role of government—the public sector.

THE PUBLIC SECTOR: TAXES AND GOVERNMENT SPENDING IN THE UNITED STATES

Government in the United States operates on three different levels—federal, state, and local. Each of these levels has assumed a different set of functions and responsibilities over the years, and although there is some overlap, each level derives its main revenues from different sources. How big is this public sector? What does it spend its money on, and where does it get its money?

The Size of the Public Sector

Gross national product (GNP)   *The total value of all final goods and services produced by a national economy within a given time period.*

The **gross national product, or GNP,** is the total value of all final goods and services produced in the economy in a given period of time, say, a year. The concept of GNP is used extensively in macroeconomics. Here it is enough to say that the GNP is used as a measure of the total annual "output" of a nation. As you can see from Figure 3.2, public expenditure at all levels, as a percentage of GNP, increased from 18.4% in 1940 to 34.9% in 1985. The federal portion of total expenditures increased more rapidly, nearly doubling since 1940, while the state and local share only grew from 8.4% of GNP to 10.4%.[4]

Government purchases of goods and services   *A category of government spending that includes the portion of national output that the government buys within a given period—F14s for the Navy, memo pads for the FBI, salaries for mail sorters.*

Government spending can be broken into three major categories: *purchases of goods and services, transfer payments to households,* and *interest payments.* **Purchases of goods and services** make up that portion of national output that government actually uses, or "consumes," directly. They include the airplanes purchased from McDonnell Douglas by the Air Force, the new Senate office building (in the year that it was built), and the paper, books, and pens, produced by private companies, that are used by government employees. This category also includes the wages and salaries paid for the services of government employees.

[4]Notice that federal grants to state and local governments are included as a federal expenditure, and are not counted among state and local expenditures, because they are paid for out of federal tax revenues. Federal grants in 1985 amounted to about $100 billion. Including that figure with state and local expenditures would push state and local expenditures to 12.9% of GNP.

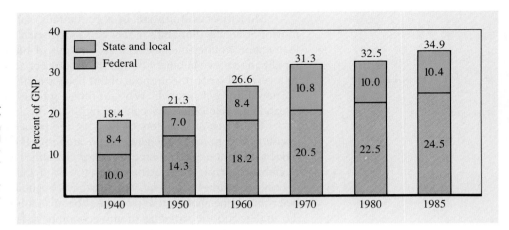

FIGURE 3.2

Total Government Expenditure as a Percentage of GNP

Total government expenditures grew from 18.4% of GNP in 1940 to 34.9% in 1985. While the share of state and local governments grew only two percent, the federal share more than doubled.
Source: U.S. Department of Commerce (Grants to states and localities included in federal.)

Table 3.5 shows that government purchases of goods and services have not increased as dramatically as total government expenditures. In fact, government purchases of goods and services have stayed at roughly the same percentage of GNP for the last 25 years.

Transfer payments are cash payments made directly to households—social security benefits, unemployment compensation payments, welfare payments, and so forth. **Interest payments** are also cash payments, but they are paid to those who own government bonds. Taken together, transfer payments and interest payments account for nearly the entire increase in government expenditure since 1960.

As Table 3.5 shows, interest payments in 1985 doubled as a percentage of GNP over the 1980 level. This is because of the huge deficits run up during the early 1980s. When the government spends more than it taxes, it must borrow. It does so by issuing bonds, and it must pay interest on the bonds. The increase in the size of the social security system accounts for much of the increase in transfer payments. Social security is a

TABLE 3.5

The Size of the Public Sector, 1940–1985

Total government expenditure has grown as a percentage of GNP, but government purchases of goods and services, that part of the national output "consumed" by the government, has grown little since 1960. Government employment did not grow as a percent of the total between 1970 and 1985.

Government Expenditure as a percentage of GNP	1940	1950	1960	1970	1980	1985
Total	18.4	21.3	26.6	31.3	32.5	34.9
Purchases of goods and services, nondefense	11.9	8.5	10.7	14.0	14.2	14.0
Purchases of goods and services, defense	2.2	5.0	8.8	7.6	5.2	6.4
Transfer payments	2.7	6.2	5.7	8.3	11.7	11.9
Interest payments (net)	1.2	1.6	1.3	1.2	1.2	2.4
Subsidies	0.4	0.0	0.1	0.2	0.2	0.2

Government employment as a percentage of total employment in the economy	1940	1950	1960	1970	1980	1985
Total	13.1	13.3	15.6	17.6	18.0	16.7
Federal	3.1	4.2	4.3	3.8	3.2	2.9
State and local	10.0	9.1	11.3	13.8	14.8	13.7

Source: U.S. Department of Commerce.

self-financing system in which benefits are paid out of taxes contributed by workers and their employers. Some have argued that because workers who have contributed will ultimately be entitled to benefits, the system should be separated from other federal receipts and expenditures for accounting purposes, but this has not been done so far.

Another way to look at the relative size of the public sector is to look at government employment as a percentage of total employment (see again Table 3.5). The numbers may surprise you. In 1985 the federal government employed only 2.9% of the total work force. In addition, federal employment as a fraction of total employment in the United States has fallen steadily since 1950, and it is actually lower than it was in 1940. State and local government employment did grow steadily as a fraction of total employment in the economy through 1980. Since 1980, however, it has dropped back to the same level as in 1970. Total government employment in 1985 was 16.7% of total employment in the economy, only one point higher than the 15.6% it had been 25 years earlier.

How big is the public sector in the United States relative to the public sectors in other countries? Good statistics on employment and spending are not easy to find, but Figure 3.3 presents some international comparisons based on taxes collected. The figure shows total national and local taxes as a percentage of **gross domestic product (GDP)**. GDP is similar to GNP. Briefly, it is the value of all final goods and services produced in a country by the factors of production *located in the country*. GNP is the same thing for the factors of production owned by the citizens of the country. For most countries GNP and GDP are quite close.

FIGURE 3.3

Taxes (National and Local) as a Percentage of Gross Domestic Product, 1975 and 1984
Source: Statistical Abstract of the U.S. 1987, Table 1452

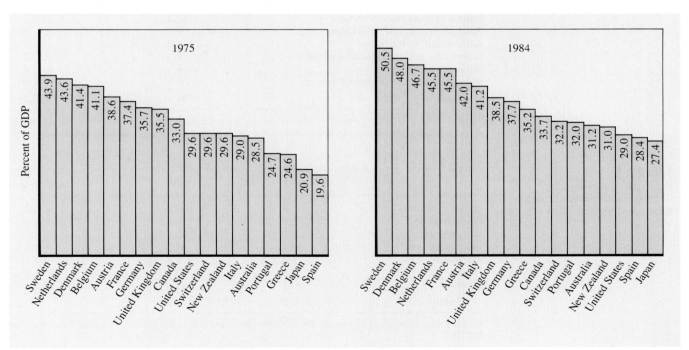

In 1975 U.S. federal, state, and local taxes amounted to 29.6% of GDP. This placed the United States in a tie for eighth place among the 18 countries in the comparison. Between 1975 and 1984, taxes as a percentage of GDP increased in every one of the 18 countries except the United States. In the United States, taxes fell from 29.6% to 29 percent. Only Spain and Japan had lower taxes per dollar of GDP in 1984.

What the Government Spends Money On

The detailed breakdown of the federal budget for fiscal year 1987 in Table 3.6 shows that the top six categories account for over 87 percent of the total. National defense and social security alone account for about half of federal spending. Table 3.7 compares the same categories for 1987 and 1978. National defense and net interest have increased sharply.

TABLE 3.6
Federal Expenditures by Function, 1987

	Billions of dollars	Percentage of total
National defense	282.2	28.4
Social security	212.2	21.3
Net interest	148.0	14.9
Income security	118.4	11.9
Medicare	70.2	7.1
Health	35.0	3.5
Education, training, employment	27.4	2.8
Veterans benefits	26.4	2.7
Transportation	25.5	2.6
Agriculture	19.5	2.0
International affairs	18.6	1.9
Natural resources environment	12.0	1.2
Science, space, and technology	9.2	.9
Administration of justice	6.9	.7
Community and regional development	6.5	.7
General governments	6.1	.6
Miscellaneous and offsetting receipts	−30.1	−3.0
Total	994.0	100.0

Source: Executive Office of the President, Office of Management and Budget, *The U.S. Budget in Brief, Fiscal Year 1987*.

TABLE 3.7
Federal Expenditures by Function: Percentage shares of total compared for 1978 and 1987

	1978	1987	Change in share
National defense	22.8	28.4	+ 5.6
Social security	20.4	21.3	+ .9
Net interest	7.7	14.9	+ 7.2
Income security	13.4	11.9	− 1.5
Medicare	5.0	7.1	+ 2.1
Health	4.0	3.5	− .5
All other	26.7	12.9	−13.8
Total	100.0	100.0	0

Source: Executive Office of the President, Office of Management and Budget, *The U.S. Budget in Brief, Fiscal Years 1978 and 1987*.

TABLE 3.8
State and Local Expenditures by
Function

	Billions of dollars, 1984	Percentage of total, 1984	Percentage of total, 1975
Education	176.1	35.0	38.2
Public welfare	6 .7	12.9	11.8
Health and Hospitals	46.4	92	8.2
Highways	39.4	7.8	9.8
Interest on debt	28.7	5.7	3.8
Police and fire	27.5	5.5	5.2
General administration	22.5	4.5	3.8
Other*	98.1	19.4	19.2
Total	503.4	100.0	100.0

*Includes parks, sanitation, and housing, among other areas.

Source: Statistical Abstract of the United States, 1987, table 438.

Medicare and social security have increased somewhat less. It is especially interesting that the share of "everything else" has dropped from 26.7% of the budget to less than 13 percent.

Table 3.8 shows state and local government spending by category in 1984.[5] In that year 35 percent of state and local spending went for education, most of it public elementary and secondary education, although all states spend money on higher education as well. Since 1975 education and highways have contracted as a portion of the total budget, while interest on debt and general administration have assumed a larger share. The overall distribution of state and local government spending during the decade did not change very much, however.

Sources of Government Revenue

A breakdown of the sources of federal tax revenues appears in Table 3.9. The biggest single source of tax revenue is the **individual income tax**, which accounted for 45.4% of the total in 1987. Federal income tax is withheld from most people's pay each month by

TABLE 3.9
Federal Receipts by Source,
1977 and 1987

	FISCAL YEAR 1977		FISCAL YEAR 1987	
	Billions of dollars	Percent	Billions of dollars	Percent
Individual income taxes	157.6	44.3	386.0	45.4
Corporation income taxes	54.9	15.4	86.7	10.2
Social insurance taxes	106.5	29.9	302.8	35.6
Excise taxes	17.5	4.9	35.2	4.1
Estate and gift taxes	7.3	2.1	5.7	0.7
Customs duties	5.2	1.5	12.9	1.5
Miscellaneous	6.5	1.8	21.1	2.5
Total	355.6	100.0	850.4	100.0

Source: Executive Office of the President, Office of Managment and Budget, The U.S. Budget in Brief, Fiscal Year 1987.

[5]More recent figures are not available.

Social insurance, or payroll tax   Assessments figured as a percentage of wages and salaries levied on employees and employers. Proceeds support various government-administered social-benefit programs. The largest of these is the social security system, which issues various cash and health benefits to retirees, the disabled, and survivors of workers who paid into the system; another program is the unemployment compensation system administered by the states.

Corporate income tax Assessments levied on the profits (or net incomes) of corporations. (Profits from proprietorships and partnerships are taxed as ordinary personal income of the owners.)

their employers, who send it to the Internal Revenue Service. Self-employed people are responsible for sending in their own estimated taxes four times per year. Each spring we add up our total income, subtract the items we are allowed to exclude or deduct, and figure out the total tax that we should have paid for the previous year. If we owe more than we have prepaid, we send the rest by April 15. If we have prepaid more than we owe, we get a refund.

Social insurance taxes are levied at a flat rate on wages and salaries, up to a maximum amount. Because these taxes are figured as a percentage of wages and salaries, they are also known as **payroll taxes**. The largest of the payroll taxes supports the social security system. In 1987 employers contributed at the rate of 7.15%, and employees contributed an additional 7.15%, from their wages and salaries, up to a maximum of $43,800. Self-employed people paid at a rate of 12.3% in 1987, subject to the same maximum income level. These taxes go into one of several trust funds that pay social security cash and health benefits to retirees, the disabled, and the survivors of workers who paid into the system. Social insurance taxes on payrolls also fund the unemployment compensation system. The unemployment tax is paid by employers at a rate of 6.2% on the first $7000 of the wages of each covered employee.

Social insurance, or payroll, taxes now account for a much larger portion of federal revenues than they have in the past. In 1987 they brought in 35.6% of total federal revenues, which is up from 29.9% ten years earlier. In 1965 they brought in only 19% of total revenues. The tax rate has been increased steadily because of worries about the future solvency of the system. A huge number of people will reach retirement age soon after the year 2000. At the same time, the labor force will be smaller. Because the tax rate required to support the increasing number of elderly then would be intolerable, the rate was sharply increased during the 1970s, and it continues to increase now, in order to generate a surplus in the social security trust funds that should prevent the collapse of the system in the future.

Corporation income taxes are levied on the profits, or net income, of corporations only, not on the profits of other forms of business organization, such as proprietorships or partnerships. The profits from the latter two are taxed directly as ordinary personal income to the owners. While payroll taxes have been increasing as a share of total tax revenues, corporate income taxes were shrinking until 1987. In 1960 they accounted for nearly 25 percent of federal revenues. Table 3.9 shows that they accounted for 15.4% in 1977 and only 10.2% in 1987. Big cuts came in 1981 when the Congress enacted the Economic Recovery Tax Act that was designed to stimulate business investment. The Tax Reform Act of 1986 reversed this trend. Estimates are that by the time it is fully in effect the reformed corporate tax will generate about the same portion of total federal revenue as it did in the 1970s.

All other tax revenues make up less than 10 percent of the federal total. Taxes on estates, except for those on very large estates, and taxes on gifts have virtually gone out of existence. A number of federal excise taxes are levied—on cigarettes, alcoholic beverages, gasoline, tires and tubes, telephone service, and a few other things. Customs duties have remained at 1.5 percent of revenues since 1977.

The sources of *state and local revenues* in 1987 appear in Table 3.10. Indirect business taxes except for property taxes account for 34.9% of the total. These taxes are primarily sales taxes levied by states. Property taxes account for 22.4% of the total. These taxes are primarily levied by local governments such as counties, cities, and towns. They are levied on the estimated, or "assessed," value of commercial, industrial, and residential property. Personal income taxes account for 29.4% of state and local revenues, while social insurance taxes account for 8.4% and corporate taxes account for 4.9%.

TABLE 3.10
State and Local Tax Receipts, 1987

	Billions of dollars	Percent of total taxes
Indirect business taxes except property taxes	191.1	34.9
Property taxes	122.6	22.4
Personal income taxes	161.1	29.4
Social insurance taxes	46.1	8.4
Corporate taxes	26.9	4.9
Total	547.8	100.0

Source: U.S. Department of Commerce

FROM INSTITUTIONS TO THEORY

This chapter has sketched out the institutional structure of the U.S. economy. As we turn to economic theory, both positive and normative, you should reflect on the basic realities of economic life in the United States presented here. Why is the service sector expanding and the manufacturing sector contracting? Why is the public sector as large as it is? What economic functions does it perform? Why does the government, rather than the private sector, provide roads, national defense, and social security? To some extent, the theory we are about to develop explains how the structure of the U.S. economy came about.

One of the great questions we will ultimately explore concerns the relative merits of public sector involvement in the economy. Should the government be involved in the economy at all or should the market be left to its own devices? Before we can deal with such large issues, we need to establish a theoretical framework. Our study of the economy and its operation begins with the behavior of suppliers and demanders in private markets.

SUMMARY

1. This chapter simply describes the basic institutional structure of the U.S. economy. It does not present economic theory, analyze behavior, build models, or make any judgments about whether the current structure is good or bad.
2. The private sector is made up of privately owned firms that exist to make a profit, nonprofit organizations, and individual households. The public sector is the government—federal, state, and local.
3. A proprietorship is a firm with a single owner. A partnership has two or more owners. Proprietors and partners are fully liable for all the debts of the business. A corporation is a formally established legal entity that limits the liability of the owners. The owners are not responsible for the debts of the firm beyond what they invest.
4. The term "industry" is used loosely to refer to groups of firms that produce similar products. Industries can be broadly or narrowly defined. A company that produces cheese belongs to the cheese industry, the dairy industry, the food products industry, and the agricultural products industry.

5. In perfect competition, no single firm has any control over prices. This follows from two characteristics of this industry structure: (1) perfectly competitive industries are composed of many firms, each small relative to the size of the industry, and (2) each firm in a perfectly competitive industry produces exactly the same product—that is, products are said to be homogeneous.
6. A monopoly is a market, or industry, in which there is only one firm producing a product, for which there are no close substitutes. To remain a monopoly in a profitable industry, a firm must be able to block the entry of competing firms.
7. Monopolistic competition is an industry structure in which many firms compete, but each firm produces a slightly different product. Although each firm's product is unique, however, there are many close substitutes.
8. An oligopoly is an industry with a small number of firms.
9. Public expenditures at all levels increased from 18.4% of GNP in 1940 to 34.9% in 1985. The federal portion of total expenditures grew more rapidly than the state and local portions, nearly doubling since 1940.

10. Other measures of the size of the public sector have not increased as rapidly. Government employment increased from 15.6% of total employment in 1960 to 16.7% in 1985. Transfer payments, especially social security, and interest payments on government debt, account for nearly the entire increase in government spending since 1960. The portion of total national output actually purchased by the government has increased only slightly since 1960.

11. National defense and social security account for over half of federal spending. The top four categories of state and local spending are education, public welfare, health and hospitals, and highways.

12. Individual income taxes and social insurance taxes together accounted for over 80% of federal revenues in 1987. Over the last quarter century, social insurance taxes have increased dramatically as a portion of total federal revenues. Sales taxes and property taxes accounted for about 57% of state and local revenues in 1987.

REVIEW CONCEPTS

private sector   49
public sector   49
proprietorship   51
partnership   51
corporation   52
net income   52
dividends   52
retained earnings   52
industry   53
market organization   53
perfect competition   54
homogeneous products   54
monopoly   55

barrier to entry   55
monopolistic competition   55
product differentiation   55
oligopoly   56
gross national product (GNP)   59
government purchases of goods and services   59
government transfer payments   60
government interest payments   60
gross domestic product (GDP)   61
individual income tax   63
social insurance, or payroll, tax   64
corporation income tax   64

REVIEW QUESTIONS

1. The chapter contains conflicting evidence on whether the public sector has expanded relative to the rest of the economy in the last 10 to 15 years. Discuss.

2. What are the differences between a proprietorship and a corporation? If you were going to start a small business, which form of organization would you choose? What are the advantages and disadvantages of the two forms of organization?

3. "Most firms are corporations, but they account for a relatively small portion of total output in the U.S." Do you agree or disagree with this statement? Explain your answer.

4. In 1985 shareholders received only 36.6% of total corporate profits. What happened to the rest?

5. Perfectly competitive industries are made up of large numbers of firms, each small relative to the size of the industry and each producing homogeneous products. What does this imply about an individual firm's ability to influence price? Explain your answer.

6. How is a monopolistically competitive industry like a monopoly? In what ways is it like a perfectly competitive industry?

7. What is the difference between government purchases of goods and services and government expenditures? Explain precisely.

8. How is it possible for government spending to increase as a percentage of GNP while taxes and government employment are both decreasing?

9. Why does the federal government seem to be spending much more on interest payments now than it was a decade ago? Explain.

APPENDIX TO CHAPTER 3
Concepts of Financial Accounting

Accounting is called the language of business, and it is a uniform and widely used language. But like any language, accounting can be very intimidating to those not versed in its complexities. Owners, managers, and investors use accounting statements regularly. In fact, without their accounting and financial reports, the owners and managers of a company could not determine their firm's financial health and profitability. For their part, investors could not judge the soundness of their investment decisions without in-depth and careful analysis of an organization's financial statements.

This appendix focuses on the two basic statements found in all annual reports published by U.S. corporations: the *balance sheet* and the *income statement*. These two statements contain most of the accounting data needed to determine the financial health of an organization. (We do not discuss the mechanics of accounting here. All basic financial accounting textbooks describe how to record individual financial events —making a sale, purchasing inventory, and selling stock for instance.)

Before we get to the balance sheet and the income statement, however, we need to talk about some fundamental concepts of accounting. After a detailed look at the two statements, we describe how an economist might view and rewrite them. Finally, we show how owners, managers, and investors use financial statements to set financial goals and to set values on corporations.

Basic Accounting Concepts

The task of accounting is to measure and report the flow of resources into and out of an organization. These resources include (1) the initial investment by the owners of the organization; (2) other investments, often through stock sales, and loans, such as bank notes and bonds, from outside parties; (3) the purchase and use of the organization's capital, its property, plant, and equipment; (4) and the gains or losses from operations.

Generally accepted accounting principles (GAAP)   The rules established by precedent or current authoritative ruling that govern the measurement and reporting of the flow of resources throughout the economy.

The rules governing the measurement and reporting of the flow of resources are known as **generally accepted accounting principles (GAAP)**. These rules can be the result either of a pronouncement by an authoritative accounting rule-making body or of a historically accepted procedure. While all public organizations must follow GAAP, there are often a number of different ways to report the same economic event legitimately. (We describe two examples of this in detail when we discuss inventory and depreciation.)

Historical cost   Cost at the time of purchase; establishes the value of an asset on the books of a firm.

When an asset is purchased by an organization, it is recorded at its **historical cost**, or cost at time of purchase. The asset remains on the books at its historical cost even if it increases in value. This practice provides an objective and verifiable, if not perfectly accurate, way to value all the assets of an organization.

Accrual basis   A way of reporting revenues and expenses in which revenues are recognized when they are earned (not when actually received) and obligations are recognized when they are incurred (not when actually paid).

The reporting of revenues, that is, the resources generated from the sale of inventory, and expenses, that is, the resources used by an organization, is done on an **accrual basis**. This means that revenue is recognized when it is earned, instead of when the cash is actually collected, and expenses are recognized when they are incurred, rather than when they are actually paid. Revenues that have been earned but not yet collected are called **receivables**, and expenses that are incurred but not yet paid are called **payables**. There are many payable accounts, the most common being accounts payable (money owed for inventory), wages payable, taxes payable, and interest payable.

Receivables and payables   Receivables are revenues earned but not yet collected; payables are obligations incurred but not yet paid.

Matching principle   An accountant's practice of recognizing expenses and the revenues they generate at the same time in order to match the two.

An added complication when recognizing (recording) expenses is that accountants attempt to match expenses with the revenue these expenses will generate. They recognize the expense at the same time that the revenue is recognized. This is known as the **matching principle**.

We said earlier that financial statements reflect the flow of resources in and out of an organization, based on generally accepted accounting principles. The rules governing the measurement and reporting of resources for tax purposes often differ from GAAP, however. Therefore the expenses and profits reported on an organization's financial statement might differ significantly from the expenses and profit reported to federal, state, and local governments. These differences will become clearer when we examine depreciation. For now let us move on to the two basic financial statements, the balance sheet and the income statement.

The Balance Sheet

Balance sheet   An overall account of an organization's financial status, showing what it has, what it owes, and what it is worth at any given point in time.

The **balance sheet** is a financial snapshot of an organization. It reports the economic status of an organization at a specific point in time.

The balance sheet is built on the **fundamental accounting identity**:

$$\text{assets} = \text{liabilities} + \text{owners' equity}.$$

Fundamental accounting identity   The basic equation around which the balance sheet is organized:
assets = liabilities + owner's equity, or
owner's equity = assets − liabilities.

This equation simply says that the total assets of an organization are equal to all outstanding debts, or liabilities, plus all residual claims by the owners.

Rearranging the terms, we see that

$$\text{owners' equity} = \text{assets} - \text{liabilities}.$$

This equation says that the owners' claims on the total value of the organization equal the organization's total assets less all outstanding debts.

The balance sheet is always presented in two sections, with assets in one section and liabilities and owners' equity in the other. The two sections must always add to the same value, that is, they must be in balance. As we describe each section, it will be helpful to follow along with the balance sheet of ABC Corporation, a small start-up company, presented in Table 3A.1.

Assets   The **assets** of an organization are all the resources available to carry out the economic activity of the organization. The assets can be **tangible**—physical assets such

TABLE 3A.1
Balance Sheet for ABC Corporation at December 31, 1990

Assets		Liabilities	
Current assets:		*Current liabilities:*	
Cash	$100,000	Accounts payable	$100,000
Inventory	100,000		
	200,000		100,000
Long-term assets:		*Long-term liabilities:*	
Land	100,000	Bank note payable	200,000
Plant and equipment	200,000	Owners' equity	200,000
Total assets	$500,000	Total liabilities and equities	$500,000

Assets   All the property of a firm or organization. Tangible *assets* have a physical reality: cash, land, equipment, buildings. Intangible *assets exist only in law or in people's minds: patents, franchises, copyrights, good will, trademarks. Current *assets* are cash or can be converted into cash within one year. Long-term *assets* are not easily converted into cash: property, buildings, plant equipment, intangible assets and so forth.*

as cash, inventory, land, buildings, and equipment—or **intangible**—legal assets such as patents, copyrights, franchises, goodwill, and trademarks. Some nonphysical assets, that is, assets you cannot physically touch, such as accounts receivable and bank deposits, are considered by accountants to be tangible assets.

On the balance sheet, assets are divided into two categories, current and long-term assets. **Current assets** are cash and assets that can be converted into cash within one year. These include bank deposits, accounts receivable, inventory, and prepaid expenses—prepaid rent or a prepaid insurance plan, for example. **Long-term assets** include all assets that are not easily turned into cash, including property, plant, equipment, long-term investments (usually in other organizations), and intangible assets.

Now look again at the balance sheet of ABC Corporation (Table 3A.1). The first thing to notice is that the date of the balance sheet is December 31, 1990. This statement describes the company at a time before any sales have taken place.

Next, look at the assets column. ABC started with $500,000 in assets, consisting of current assets of $100,000 in cash and $100,000 in inventory, and long-term assets including land purchased for $100,000 and plant and equipment purchased for $200,000. To understand where the money to purchase all these assets came from, we must turn to the other half of the balance sheet.

Liabilities   All the short- and long-term debts of an organization. Current *liabilities are owed within one year. Long-term *liabilities are debts that are owed in more than one year.*

Liabilities

The **liabilities** of an organization are all the short- and long-term debts of the organization. Like assets, these debts are separated into **current liabilities**, or debts owed within one year, and **long-term liabilities**, or debts owed over more than one year.

The current liabilities of the ABC Corporation include the total amounts ABC owes on its inventory purchases and the amount ABC owes on its loans within the next year. In this example, there is a direct link between the current liabilities and the current assets: ABC has purchased $100,000 worth of inventory (the asset) and has not yet paid the bill for it (the liability).

The long-term liabilities show all the long-term debts of an organization, less any part of the principal that will be paid within the next year. Typical entries under long-term liabilities include bank notes payable, mortgages payable, and bonds payable.

The ABC Corporation was started with only one long-term liability, a $200,000 loan from a local bank at a 10 percent interest rate. The loan will be due in full in five years, and interest of $20,000 must be paid annually. For simplicity, we will assume that no interest has accrued on the loan prior to January 1, 1991.

Owners' Equity

Now let's turn to owners' equity. By definition, **owners' equity** is the value of the assets owners would have left if they paid off all the organization's debts. It is not necessarily equal to the amount of cash investors put into the business, nor is it equal to the true market value or resale value of the firm. It is merely equal to assets less liabilities. Once again, let's turn to ABC Corporation for an example.

ABC was started with $200,000 in cash put up by the owners and a bank loan for $200,000. From this initial cash supply of $400,000, ABC purchased land, a building, and manufacturing equipment for $300,000. This left the owners with $100,000 in cash. Because of their excellent standing in the community, they were able to purchase inventory for later sale without putting cash up-front. (This is what created the accounts payable account.) Owners' equity is equal to assets ($500,000) less liabilities ($300,000), or $200,000. Notice that the fundamental accounting identity holds here: total assets equal total liabilities plus owners' equity on the balance sheet. This will always be true, no matter how complex the individual transactions become.

The Income Statement

Income statement, statement of earnings *A statement of an organization's revenues and costs from its activities over an operating cycle, usually a year.*

The second financial statement appearing in all annual reports is the **income statement,** or **statement of earnings.** This is the statement that shows the gains or losses from an organization's activities over a period of time. Unlike the balance sheet, which is a snapshot at a specific date, the income statement shows the total gains or losses over an operating cycle, usually one year. The income statement shows the *flows* of importance to the firm, while the balance sheet shows the *stocks.* Like the balance sheet, the income statement is commonly subdivided into sections, each of which is described below.

The income statement shows the total revenues of the organization less the total expenses of the organization. The income statement has three major subdivisions:

Gross margin, or gross profit *Net sales revenues minus the cost of goods sold.*

1. The calculation of **gross margin,** or gross profit—

$$\text{Gross margin} = \text{Net sales revenue} - \text{Cost of goods sold.}$$

Net operating income *The gross margin minus other operating expenses.*

2. The calculation of **net operating income**—

$$\text{Net operating income} = \text{Gross margin} - \text{Other operating expenses.}$$

Net income *Net operating income minus other expenses but plus other revenues.*

3. The calculation of **net income**—

$$\text{Net income} = \text{Net operating income} - \text{Other expenses} + \text{Other revenues.}$$

Sales Revenue   We said earlier that sales revenue is recognized (recorded) when it is earned. Sales revenue is usually shown after deductions for sales discounts, allowances for returnable items, and actual returns. As shown in Table 3A.2, sales revenue for the ABC Corporation during 1991 was $600,000.

Cost of Goods Sold   *Cost of goods sold* is the sum of all costs directly associated with the production and sale of the firm's product. These include materials, labor, transportation, and other costs associated with the production process. The most complex issue associated with cost of goods sold is how to value the inventory sold over the year.

There are two primary ways to evaluate inventory, the first-in, first-out (FIFO) method, and the last-in, first-out (LIFO) method.

FIFO versus LIFO   The method a firm chooses to value its inventory can have a profound impact on the firm's reported profitability and cash flow. If the cost of materials and labor used in the production of inventory were constant over time, either valuation

TABLE 3A.2
Income Statement for ABC Corporation for the Year Ending December 31, 1991

Sales revenue		$600,000
Cost of goods sold		400,000
Gross margin		200,000
Selling, general, and administration		80,000
Net operating income		120,000
Other expenses:		
Interest expense	20,000	
Tax expense	40,000	
Total other expenses		60,000
Net income		$ 60,000

method would produce the same result. But if prices are rising or falling, the cost of producing a unit of inventory at the beginning of the year may differ significantly from the cost of producing a unit of inventory at the end of the year.

Accountants try to match the expense associated with a product with the revenue generated by the sale of that product. Although a firm could track the exact cost associated with each of its products sold, this would not be practical, cost effective, or even particularly useful. Instead, the firm's accountant may choose to assign the cost of either the oldest product in the warehouse or the newest product in the warehouse to units as they are sold. **FIFO** uses the first-in, or oldest, product value, and **LIFO** uses the last-in, or most recent, product value to determine the cost of goods sold.

If prices are rising rapidly, as they were in the 1970s and early 1980s, the difference between the cost of goods sold using FIFO or LIFO can be substantial. Firms choose to use the FIFO method if they want their reported net income to be as high as possible; they may be about to borrow money or issue bonds or stocks, and they may want to show high profits to encourage lenders and potential investors. On the other hand, during an era of rising prices, firms might choose the LIFO method in order to increase their cost of goods sold, reduce their pre-tax income, and so reduce their tax expense. Cash flow is a very important consideration for a manager, and the choice of inventory valuation method can have a dramatic effect on an organization's tax expense and thus on cash flow.

We said earlier that tax reporting and GAAP reporting often differ. A major exception to this rule is inventory valuation. The Internal Revenue Service (IRS) has decided that if a firm selects LIFO for tax purposes, it must be consistent in its use of LIFO for financial statement reporting.

Depreciation   The process of allocating the cost of a long-term asset over the life of the asset. In this scheme, the asset loses value, or is "used up," beginning in the first year of its use and continues to lose value for a given number of years until its value is zero. Straight-line depreciation takes the cost of the asset, deducts salvage value, and spreads the cost evenly over the years of the asset's useful life. Accelerated depreciation takes the cost, deducts salvage value, and front loads the cost of the asset in the early years according to various formulas.

DEPRECIATION   Another major component of cost of goods sold is depreciation. In accounting, **depreciation** is defined as the process of allocating the cost of a long-term asset over the life of the asset. For example, if a new truck cost a firm $15,000, had a useful life of five years, and had no resale value at the end of five years, then the typical depreciation expense on that truck would be $3,000 per year ($15,000 divided by 5 years).

Depreciation arises from the matching principle. The revenue generated from an asset is assumed to be spread over the life of the asset. In order to match the expense with the revenue, then, accountants must spread the expense over the life of the asset as well.

A number of depreciation methods are acceptable to accountants and to the IRS. The most common method used in financial statements is the straight-line method, which we used to describe the depreciation of the truck. **Straight-line depreciation** takes the cost of the asset, minus the salvage value, and spreads that cost out evenly over the asset's useful life. All other acceptable depreciation methods accelerate the cost recovery of fixed assets. There are several formulas for **accelerated depreciation**. For example, the *double-declining balance method* doubles the rate at which cost recovery can take place: instead of depreciating the cost of the truck by one fifth in the first year, two fifths of the cost would be depreciated in the first year. This method offsets larger expenses in the early years. But, of course, depreciation expenses in the later years are far less than they would be using the straight-line method.

As you may have guessed, depreciation is an area where financial reporting and tax reporting can differ substantially. The U.S. Congress creates all tax legislation, and it has specifically created accelerated depreciation, reported for tax purposes, as a means of stimulating investment in plant and equipment. When Congress passed the 1981 Economic Recovery Tax Act (ERTA), it created the accelerated cost recovery system (ACRS), which not only accelerated the depreciation rate per year but also shortened the number of years over which an asset could be depreciated. Congress repealed the ACRS in 1984 but instituted double-declining balance in its place as the acceptable depreciation method for tax reporting. In 1986 we got yet another method of depreciation for tax purposes (see Chapter 18).

Although most firms take advantage of accelerated depreciation when filing their tax returns, by and large they use straight-line depreciation for financial statement reporting.

Gross Margin   Total cost of goods sold is the sum of materials, labor, transportation, and depreciation associated with the production process. (Depreciation for corporations also includes some depreciation of assets not directly related to production— for example, office buildings. This part of depreciation appears in the selling, general, and administrative account rather than the cost of goods sold account.) The *gross margin* is the firm's net revenues minus the cost of goods sold. As you can see in Table 3A.2, the cost of goods sold for ABC Corporation is $400,000 and its gross margin is $200,000.

Net Operating Income   *Net operating income* is the income from product-related activities, that is, the gross margin minus operating expenses that are not directly product related. These operating expenses usually appear on the income statement as selling, general, and administrative expense, and they include both marketing costs and general overhead costs.

Selling, general, and administrative expense for ABC Corporation totaled $80,000 in 1991 (again see Table 3A.2), which we assume includes a $20,000 depreciation expense for the year. Its net operating income, that is, its pre-tax income associated with the ongoing economic activity of the firm, was $120,000.

Net Income   *Net income*, or *net earnings*, the firm's so-called "bottom line," includes all income from operations, less all nonoperating revenue and expenses. Nonoperating revenues include dividends from common stock that the organization holds. Nonoperating expenses include financing expenses, particularly interest costs, and taxes. Other entries in this section of the income statement include the gains or losses from the sale of assets, and the gains or losses from paying off debts early. The ABC Corporation had a net income of $60,000 after deducting $20,000 in interest expense and $40,000 in taxes (see Table 3A.2).

The Balance Sheet Revisited

The ABC Corporation has completed its first year of operations and the income statement for the year has been prepared. The firm can now create a new balance sheet, updating the previous year's to include all the economic activity of the past year. As before, the balance sheet is prepared at a single point in time, in this case at December 31, 1991.

Assets   Now let us examine the new balance sheet in Table 3A.3. The first obvious change is the inclusion of a new account, *accounts receivable*. This says that ABC Corporation is owed $50,000 by its customers for sales during 1991. In addition, note that the cash account has increased by $20,000 and that inventory has increased by $50,000.

Another new account appears under *long-term assets*. Accumulated depreciation is the sum of all the previous year's depreciation expenses, included either in the cost of goods sold account or (as we assumed for the ABC Corporation) in the selling, general, and administrative account on the income statement. Because this is ABC's first year of operation, only one year's depreciation expense has been accumulated. At the end of the

TABLE 3A.3

Balance Sheet for ABC Corporation at December 31, 1991

Assets		Liabilities	
Current assets:		*Current liabilities:*	
Cash	$120,000	Accounts payable	$ 80,000
Accounts receivable	50,000	Taxes payable	40,000
Inventory	150,000	Interest payable	20,000
	320,000		140,000
Long-term assets:		*Long-term liabilities:*	
Land	100,000	Bank note payable	200,000
Plant and equipment 200,000			
less accumulated depreciation (20,000)			
Net plant and equipment	180,000		
		Shareholder equity:	
		Common stock	200,000
		Retained earnings	60,000
Total assets	$600,000	Total liabilities and equity	$600,000

coming year, the accumulated depreciation account should be $40,000, the year after that $60,000, and so on. Net plant and equipment is defined as the historical cost of the plant and equipment minus accumulated depreciation.

The original cost of ABC's plant and equipment was $200,000. The net plant and equipment at December 31, 1991, was $200,000 less the accumulated depreciation of $20,000, or $180,000.

Liabilities and Shareholders' Equity   The liabilities and shareholders' equity side of the balance sheet shows three new accounts. The first is *taxes payable*, that is, simply the taxes accrued but not yet paid by ABC Corporation. The second new account is **common stock**. During 1991 the owners of ABC Corporation decided that they would have an easier time raising capital if they were able to issue stock. Therefore, they issued stock to themselves and this appears in the "shareholders' equity" section of the balance sheet (the name has been changed from "owners' equity"). For simplicity, we have made the issue value of the stock exactly equal to the previous value of owners' equity.

The third new account is **retained earnings**. The value of retained earnings is the sum of all the previous year's undistributed net income. If cash **dividends** are paid to shareholders, their total value reduces retained earnings. In the case of ABC Corporation, the firm showed net income for 1991 of $60,000 and paid no dividends. Therefore, retained earnings increased by $60,000. If the owners had decided to pay themselves a cash dividend of, say, $20,000, then the retained earnings on the balance sheet would have been only $40,000, and the cash account under current assets would have been $20,000 lower.

Retained earnings is a very important account on the balance sheet. It is through retained earnings that the income statement and the balance sheet communicate. Every year a firm's profit or loss is posted to retained earnings. As we shall see, however, retained earnings is not a surrogate for the cash value or market value of a firm.

Book Value versus Economic Book Value

The **book value** of an organization is the value in the equity section of the balance sheet, or the difference between the assets and liabilities on the "books." The **economic value** of a firm is the amount owners would get if they decided to sell the firm or sell off the assets and pay off the liabilities. Book value is commonly quoted as a measure of an organization's value, but as we have seen throughout this appendix, many of the accounting conventions distort the value of an asset. Both depreciation and inventory valuation methods are merely rough estimates of the true market cost of the expenses.

Economists also have other concerns when they speak of the value of a firm. They need to think about the opportunity cost associated with the use of capital. Accountants, as you have seen, are concerned only with historical cost. They have no interest in how funds used for the purchase of inventory might have been otherwise employed.

Accounting and the Manager

Managers are very much interested in the financial statements of their organizations. Although the accounts and the accountants provide the information required to make informed managerial decisions, financial statements alone can be deceiving. Firms can show positive net income every year, pay large dividends to their shareholders, and show assets well in excess of their liabilities, and still be forced into bankruptcy. How can this happen? Very simply, an organization needs cash to remain in business. Having a warehouse full of goods and large amounts of accounts receivable is useless if the firm cannot sell its product or collect its accounts receivable.

Financial analysts and managers very carefully manage the **cash flow**—the actual money available to make purchases and pay bills—of their organizations. Accountants regularly convert a firm's financial statements into statements that show the flow of cash into and out of an organization. Such analyses are called *statements of changes in financial position* or *funds flow statements*, and they are included in most annual reports. No thorough financial analysis of an organization can be complete without the careful, accurate analysis of cash flow.

REVIEW CONCEPTS

generally accepted accounting principles (GAAP)   67
historical cost   67
accrual basis   67
receivables and payables   67
matching principle   68
balance sheet   68
fundamental accounting identity   68
assets   68
tangible and intangible assets   68–69
current and long-term assets   69
liabilities   69

current and long-term liabilities   69
owners' equity   69
income statement, or statement of earnings   70
gross margin, net operating income, and net income   70
FIFO vs. LIFO   71
depreciation   71
straight-line depreciation vs. accelerated depreciation   71
common stock, retained earnings, and dividends   73
book value vs. economic value   73
cash flow   74

REVIEW QUESTIONS

1. What accounts appear as assets on the balance sheet? As liabilities? As equities? What is the fundamental accounting identity?

2. What is a tangible asset? An intangible asset? How would you classify a bank deposit? Accounts receivable?

3. The ABC Corporation has current assets that exceed current liabilities. Why is this information useful to an ABC manager? To an outside investor?

4. The ABC Corporation sells $100,000 in additional stock in 1992. It uses half of the investment to purchase more land and half to purchase a new building. What amounts will appear in the land, plant and equipment account, and in the common stock account at the time of purchase? (Ignore depreciation for now.)

5. The ABC Corporation has net income of $100,000 for 1992. The depreciation expense for the year is $25,000 (including the additional depreciation from question 4). Current assets and current liabilities have not changed. Including the data from question 4, prepare a new balance sheet dated December 31, 1992.

6. Review the ABC Corporation income statement in Table 3A.2. By changing its inventory valuation system from FIFO to LIFO, ABC Corporation increases its inventory expense (cost of goods sold) from $400,000 to $450,000. The annual tax rate is 40 percent. Prepare a new income statement for 1991. What is the new net income? What is the tax savings to ABC Corporation from this change? The cash savings?

7. An internationally known takeover artist is interested in acquiring ABC Corporation, and you have been hired as her advisor. How would you approach the problem? What accounts would you examine? What additional information would you like to have before you turned in your recommendations?

4 Markets and Prices: The Basic Forces of Supply and Demand

Chapters 1 and 2 introduced the discipline and methodology of economics and its subject matter. Chapter 3 described the institutional landscape of the U. S. economy, both private and public sectors. We now begin the task of analyzing how the economy actually works. Chapters 4 through 12 will build a complete theory, or model, of a simple market economy with no government, in which all decisions are made by private business firms and households. As we introduce the government into this system in Chapters 13 through 20, we will relax some of the strict assumptions made in earlier chapters.

As we proceed to define terms and make assumptions, it is important to keep in mind what we are doing. In Chapter 1 we were very careful to explain what economic theory attempts to do. Theories are abstract representations of reality, like a map that represents a city. We believe that the model presented here will help you understand the workings of the economy just as a map helps you get where you want to go in a city. But just as a map presents one view of the world, so too does any given theory or model of the economy. Alternatives exist to the model that we present, and it does not explain all economic events. Needless to say, however, if we did not think it was a useful representation of reality, we would not have devoted 17 chapters to developing it.

The Economic Problem Revisited

In the simple society of Colleen and Bill discussed in Chapter 2, the economic problem was solved directly. The two of them allocated their time and used the resources of the island to satisfy their wants. He might be a farmer, she a hunter and carpenter. He might be a civil engineer, she a doctor. There was exchange, but no need for complex markets.

In societies of many people, however, production must satisfy wide-ranging tastes and preferences, and producers therefore specialize. Farmers produce more food than they can eat in order to sell it to buy manufactured goods. Physicians are paid for specialized services, and with their incomes they buy food, cars, and other goods. When there is specialization, there must be exchange, and exchange takes place in markets.

This chapter begins to explore the basic forces at work in market systems. The purpose of the model we will build is to explain how the individual decisions of households and firms together, without any central planning or direction, answer the three fundamental questions that must be answered by all economies: what will be produced, how will it be produced, and for whom will it be produced? We begin with some basic definitions.

FIRMS AND HOUSEHOLDS: THE BASIC DECISION-MAKING UNITS

Throughout the book, we discuss and analyze the behavior of two fundamental decision-making units: *firms* and *households*. Both are made up of people performing different functions and playing different roles, and therefore what we are developing is essentially a theory of human behavior.

Firm   An organization that comes into being when someone or some group decides to transform resources (inputs) into products (outputs) for sale in the market. Firms are the primary producing units in a market economy.

A **firm** exists when someone or some group decides to produce a product or products by transforming *inputs*, that is, resources in the broadest sense, into *outputs*, the products that are sold in the market. Some firms produce goods, others produce services. Some are large, some are small, and some are in between. But all firms exist to transform resources into things that people want. The Boston Symphony Orchestra takes labor, land, a building, musically talented people, electricity, and other inputs and combines them to produce concerts. The production process can be extremely complicated. The first flutist in the orchestra, for example, takes training, talent, previous performance experience, a score, an instrument, the conductor's interpretation, and her own feelings about the music to produce just one contribution to an overall performance.

Most firms exist to make a profit for their owners, but some do not. The University of North Carolina, for example, fits the description of a firm: it takes inputs in the form of labor, land, skills, books, buildings, and so forth and produces a service that we call education. Although it sells that service for a price, it does not *exist* to make a profit, but rather to provide education of the highest quality possible at the most reasonable cost possible.

Still, most firms do exist for profit. They engage in production because they can sell their product for more than it costs to produce it. The analysis of firm behavior that follows rests on the assumption that *firms make decisions in order to maximize profits*.

Household   The consuming units in the economy.

The consuming units in an economy are *households*. A **household** may consist of any number of people: a single person living alone, a married couple with four children, or fifteen unrelated people sharing a house. Household decisions are presumably based on the individual tastes and preferences of the consuming unit—the household buys what it wants and can afford. In a large, heterogeneous, and open society such as the United States, wildly different tastes find expression in the marketplace. A six-block walk in any direction on any street in Manhattan or a drive from the Chicago Loop south into rural Illinois should be enough to convince anyone that it is difficult to generalize about what people like and do not like.

Even though households have wide ranging preferences, they also have some things in common. All—even the very rich—have ultimately limited incomes, and all must pay one way or another for the things they consume. While households may have some control over their incomes—they can work more or less—they are constrained by the availability of jobs, current wages, their own abilities, and their accumulated and inherited wealth or lack of it.

INPUT MARKETS AND OUTPUT MARKETS

Product, or output, markets
The markets in which final goods and services are exchanged.

Input markets   *The markets in which the resources used to produce products are demanded by firms and supplied by households.*

Households and firms interact in two basic kinds of markets: **product, or output, markets** and **input markets** (see Figure 4.1). Final goods and services that are intended for use by households are exchanged in *output* markets. Here competing firms *supply* and competing households *demand*.

In order to produce final goods and services, however, firms must buy resources in *input markets*. Here competing firms *demand*. When a firm decides how much to produce (supply) in output markets, it must simultaneously decide how much of each input it needs. To produce automobiles, Chrysler Corporation must use many inputs, including tires, steel, complicated machinery, and many different kinds of skilled labor.

Firms also generally choose among alternative methods or technologies of production, that is, their outputs can be produced using different kinds of inputs in different combinations. Automobiles can be produced using human workers or robots along an assembly line. In digging the foundation for a new building, a contractor can use many workers with shovels or a single worker with a steam shovel.

FIGURE 4.1
The Market Allocation
Mechanism

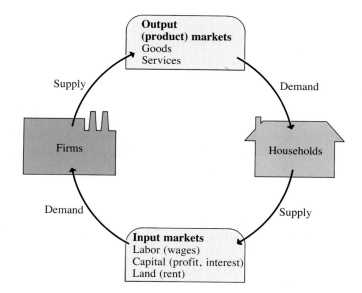

Labor markets   *The input, or resource, markets in which households supply work for wages to firms that demand labor.*

Capital markets   *The input, or resource, markets in which households supply their savings, for interest or for claims to future profits, to firms who demand funds in order to invest in capital.*

In *input markets*, households *supply* resources. The amount that a household is able to buy (demand) in output markets depends at least in part on its income. Most households earn their incomes by working—they supply their labor in the **labor market** and are paid a wage. Households may also loan their accumulated or inherited savings to firms for interest or exchange those savings for claims to future profits, as when a household buys shares of stock in a corporation. In the **capital market**, households supply the funds that firms use to buy capital goods. Households may also supply land or other real property in exchange for rent.

The supply of inputs and their prices ultimately determine incomes. The amount of income earned by a household thus depends at least in part on the decisions it makes. Whether to stay in school, how much and what kind of training to get, whether to start a business, how many hours to work, whether to work at all, and how to invest savings are all household decisions that affect income.

As you can see, input and output markets are connected through the behavior of both firms and households. Firms determine the quantities and character of outputs produced, the types and quantities of inputs demanded, and the technologies used in production. Households determine the types and quantities of products demanded and the quantities and types of inputs supplied.[1]

DEMAND IN PRODUCT (OUTPUT) MARKETS

In real life, households make many decisions at the same time. To see how the forces of demand and supply work, however, let us focus first on the amount of a single product that an individual household decides to consume within some given period of time, such as a month or a year. As we might expect, the household choice depends upon a number of factors:

The *income available* to the household.

The *amount of accumulated wealth* of the household.

The *price of the product* in question.

The *prices of other products* available to the household.

The *tastes or preferences* of the household.

The *expectations* of the household about future income, wealth, and prices.

Quantity demanded   *The amount of a product that a household would buy in a given period if it could buy all it wanted at the current price.*

Quantity demanded is the amount of a product that a household would buy each period *if it could buy all it wanted at the current market price*. It is important to see demand as distinct from supply. When asked to list the factors that determine demand, students often include "the amount available." Of course, the amount of a product that households finally purchase depends on the amount of product actually available in the market. But the quantity demanded at any moment may exceed or fall short of the

[1]Our description of markets begins with the behavior of firms and households. Modern orthodox economic theory essentially combines two distinct but closely related theories of behavior. The "theory of household behavior," or "consumer behavior," has its roots in the works of nineteenth-century utilitarians such as Jeremy Bentham, William Jevons, Carl Menger, Leon Walras, Vilfredo Pareto, and F. Y. Edgeworth. The "theory of the firm" developed out of the earlier classical political economy of Adam Smith, David Ricardo, and Thomas Malthus. In 1890 Alfred Marshall published the first of many editions of his *Principles of Economics*. That volume pulled together the main themes of both the classical economists and the utilitarians into what is now called "neoclassical economics." While there have been many changes over the years, the basic structure of the model that we build in the next several chapters can be found in Marshall's work.

quantity supplied. These differences between the quantity demanded and the quantity supplied turn out to be very important, and in analyzing markets it is essential to separate the supply decision from the demand decision. Thus the phrase *"if it could buy all it wanted"* is critical because it allows for the possibility that quantity supplied and quantity demanded may be unequal.

Our analysis of demand and supply is leading up to a theory of how market *prices* are determined. Prices are determined by interaction between demanders and suppliers, and to understand that interaction, we first need to know how product prices influence the behavior of both suppliers and demanders separately. On the demand side of output markets, therefore, we begin by focusing on the relationship between quantity demanded by an individual household and the price of the commodity or product in question, ceteris paribus (all else being equal). That is, we will discuss changes in quantity demanded in response to changes in price, holding income, wealth, other prices, preferences, and expectations constant.

Price and Quantity Demanded: The Law of Demand

Demand schedule   A table showing how much of a given product households will buy at different prices.

A **demand schedule** shows the quantities of a product that a household would buy at alternative prices. Table 4.1 presents a hypothetical demand schedule for a student, let's call her Anna, who went off to college to study economics while her boyfriend went to art school. If telephone calls were free (a price of zero), she would call him every day, or 30 times a month. At a price of $.50, she cuts back to 25 calls a month, and when the price hits $3.50, she cuts back to 7 calls a month. When this same information is presented graphically, we call it a **demand curve**. Anna's demand curve is presented in Figure 4.2.[2]

Demand curve   A graph illustrating the data in a demand schedule—that is, how much households will buy of a good or service at different prices.

Demand Curves Slope Downward   Our data show that at lower prices, Anna calls more frequently; at higher prices, she calls less frequently. Thus, there is a *negative, or inverse, relationship between the quantity demanded and price.* When price rises, quantity demanded falls, and vice versa. When the line that connects the points, that is, the

TABLE 4.1

Anna's Demand Schedule for Telephone Calls

A demand schedule shows the quantities of a product that a household would buy at alternative prices. If phone calls were free, this student would call her boyfriend 30 times per month. A price of $15.00 would discourage her from calling altogether.

Price (per call)	Quantity demanded (calls per month)
$ 0	30
.50	25
3.50	7
7.00	3
10.00	1
15.00	0

[2]Drawing a smooth curve, as we do in Figure 4.2, suggests that Anna can make a quarter of a phone call or half of a phone call. For example, according to the graph, at a price of $12.00 per call, Anna would make half of a call and at $8.00 per call, about a call and a half. While this may be reasonable for goods that are *divisible*, such as phone calls—you might talk for one minute instead of two minutes—or products sold by weight, it is unreasonable for large purchases, such as automobiles. We use the term *lumpy* to describe such goods. You would not draw a smooth downward sloping curve of a household's demand for automobiles; for example, because there might be only one, or at most two, points, and any points in between would be meaningless. Whenever we draw a smooth demand curve, we are *assuming divisibility*.

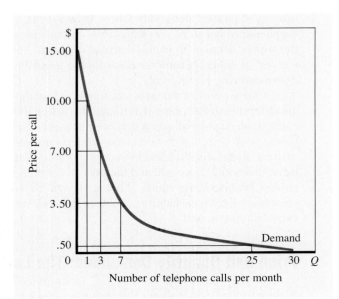

FIGURE 4.2

Anna's Demand Curve

When the relationship between price and quantity demanded is presented graphically, it is called a *demand curve*. Demand curves have a negative slope indicating that lower prices (−) cause quantity demanded to increase (+).

demand curve, slopes downward, it is said to have a *negative slope*. This negative relationship between price and quantity demanded is often referred to as the "**law of demand**," a term first used by Alfred Marshall in 1890.

Many people are put off by the abstractness of demand curves. Of course, we don't actually draw our own demand curves for products. When we want to make a purchase, we usually face only a single price, and how much we would buy at other prices is irrelevant. But demand curves help us as analysts to understand the kind of behavior that households are *likely* to exhibit if they are actually faced with a higher or lower price. We know, for example, that if the price of a good rises enough, the quantity demanded must ultimately drop to zero. The demand curve is thus a tool that helps us explain economic behavior and predict reactions to possible price changes.

Marshall's definition of a social "law" captures the idea:

> The term "law" means nothing more than a general proposition or statement of tendencies, more or less certain, more or less definite . . . a *social law* is a statement of social tendencies; that is, that a certain course of action may be expected from the members of a social group under certain conditions.[3]

It seems reasonable to expect consumers to demand more of a product at a lower price and less of it at a higher price. Households must divide their incomes up over a wide range of goods and services. If the price of beef rises while income and the prices of all other products remain the same, the household must sacrifice more of something in order to buy each pound of beef. If I spend $4.50 for a pound of prime beef, I am sacrificing the other things that I might have bought with that $4.50. If prime beef were to jump to $7.00 per pound, while chicken breasts remained at $1.99, (remember ceteris paribus —we are holding all else constant), I would have to give up more chicken and/or other items in order to buy that pound of beef. So I would probably eat more chicken and less

[3]Alfred Marshall, *Principles of Economics*, 8th ed., (New York: Macmillan, 1948,) p. 33. (The first edition of this text was published in 1890.)

beef. Anna calls home three times when phone calls cost $7.00 each. A fourth call would mean sacrificing $7.00 worth of other purchases. At a price of $3.50, however, the opportunity cost of each call is lower, and she calls more frequently.

Another reason that demand curves are likely to slope downward introduces the notion of *utility*. Presumably we consume goods and services because they yield satisfaction, or utility. But as we consume more of a product within a given period of time, it is likely that each additional unit consumed will yield successively less satisfaction. The utility I gain from a second ice cream cone is likely to be less than the utility I gained from the first; the third is worth even less, and so forth. This law of *diminishing marginal utility* is developed more fully in Chapter 6. If each successive unit of a good is worth less subjectively, I am not going to be willing to pay as much for it. Thus, it is reasonable to expect a downward slope in the demand curve for that good.

The idea of diminishing marginal utility also helps to explain Anna's behavior. The demand curve is a way of representing what she is willing to pay per phone call. At a price of $7.00, she calls her boyfriend three times. A fourth call, however, is worth less than the third, that is, it is worth something less than $7.00 to her, so she stops at three. If the price were only $3.50, however, she would keep right on calling. But even at $3.50, she would stop at seven calls. This behavior reveals that the eighth call has less value to Anna than the seventh.

An even more formal argument supporting the law of demand involves what are called *income effects* and *substitution effects*. Let's consider the ways that consumers are affected by a decline in price, using beef again as our example. If the price of beef goes down and people continue to buy the exact same quantities of every good, including beef, that they did before the price of beef fell, *they will have money left over*. They are better off and can afford more of all goods, *including beef*. This is called the **income effect** of a price decline.

At the same time, the price decline implies that beef is cheaper relative to potential substitutes. A decline in the price of beef means that relative to chicken it is more attractive. This is called the **substitution effect** of a price decline.

Returning to our hypothetical student, Anna, consider her response to an increase in price from $3.50 to $7.00 per telephone call. First, these calls to her boyfriend are now more expensive relative to alternative ways of communicating, such as writing letters. Thus, she is likely to substitute letter writing and call less frequently (substitution effect). Second, she is worse off overall because of the higher price—if she calls the same number of times at the higher price, she will have less income to spend on other things. Her income will no longer buy everything that it did before, and she must cut something. One of the things she is likely to cut is telephone calls (income effect).

In general, then, it is reasonable to expect quantity demanded to fall when price rises, ceteris paribus, and to expect quantity demanded to rise when price falls, ceteris paribus. Therefore, demand curves have a negative slope.

Other Properties of Demand Curves   Two additional things are notable about Anna's demand curve. First, it intersects the Y, or price, axis. This means that there is a price above which no calls will be made. In this case, when the price reaches $15.00 per call, Anna simply stops calling. A*s long as households have limited incomes and wealth, all demand curves will hit the price axis*. For any commodity, there is always a price above which a household will not, or cannot, pay. Even if the good or service is very important, all households are ultimately "constrained," or limited, by income and wealth.

Second, Anna's demand curve intersects the X, or quantity, axis. Even at a zero price, there is some limit to the number of phone calls Anna will make. If telephone calls were free, she would call 30 times a month, but not more. That demand curves hit the quantity axis is a matter of common sense. Demands for most goods are limited, if only by time, even at a zero price.

Other Determinants of Household Demand

Of the many factors likely to influence a household's demand for a specific product, we have considered only the price of the product itself. Other determining factors include household income and wealth, the prices of other goods, and, of course, tastes and preferences.

Income and Wealth   Before we can proceed, we need to define two terms that are often confused, *income* and *wealth*. A household's **income** is the sum of all the wages, salaries, profits, interest payments, rents, and other forms of earnings received by the household *in a given period of time*. Income is thus a *flow* measure: we must specify a time period for it—income *per month* or *per year*. You can spend or consume more or less than your income in any given period. If you consume less than the amount of your income, you save. In order to consume more than your income in a period, you either have to borrow or to draw down some savings accumulated from previous periods.

Wealth is the total value of what we own less what we owe. Another word for wealth is **net worth**—the amount a household would have left if it sold off all its possessions and paid off all its debts. Wealth is a *stock* measure: it is measured at a given moment, or point, in time. If, in a given period, you spend less than your income, you save; the amount that you save is added to your wealth. Saving is the flow that affects the stock of wealth. When you spend more than your income you dissave—you reduce your wealth.

Clearly households with higher incomes and higher accumulated savings or inherited wealth can afford to buy more things. In general, then, we would expect higher demand at higher levels of income/wealth and lower demand at lower levels of income/wealth. When this relationship holds true for a product, the good is called a **normal good**.

Normal good   *A good for which demand goes up when income is higher and for which demand goes down when income is lower.*

But generalization in economics can be hazardous. Sometimes demand for a good falls when household income rises. Consider, for example, the various qualities of meat available. When a household's income rises, it is likely to buy higher quality meats—its demand for filet mignon is likely to rise—but its demand for lower quality meats—chuck steak, for example—is likely to fall. Transportation is another example. At higher incomes, people can afford to fly. People who can afford to fly are less likely to take the bus. Thus higher income may reduce the number of times someone takes a bus. When an increase in income causes demand for a good to fall, the good is called an **inferior good**.

Inferior good   *A good for which demand goes down when income goes up.*

Prices of Other Goods and Services   No consumer decides in isolation on the amount of any one commodity to buy. The decision is only part of a larger set of decisions that are made simultaneously. Obviously households must apportion their incomes over many different goods and services. As a result, the price of any one good can and does affect the demand for other goods.

This is most obviously the case when there is a relationship such as the goods being substitutes for each other. To return to our lonesome first-year student, Anna, if the price of a telephone call rises to $10.00, she will call her boyfriend at art school only once a month. But of course she can get in touch with him in other ways. Presumably she substitutes some other, less costly, form of communication, such as writing more letters.

There is currently much discussion about the relative merits of cars produced in the United States and cars produced in Japan. Recently, American consumers have faced a sharp rise in the price of Japanese cars. As a result we would expect to see consumers substitute American-made cars for Japanese-made cars. The demand for U.S. cars should rise and the demand for Japanese cars should fall.

To be substitutes, two products need not be identical. If they are identical, we call them perfect substitutes. Japanese cars are not identical to American cars. Nonetheless, both have four wheels, are capable of carrying people, and run on gasoline. Thus, significant changes in the price of one can be expected to influence demand for the other. Compact disks are substitutes for records and tapes, restaurant meals are substitutes for meals eaten at home, and flying from New York to Washington is a substitute for taking the train.

Substitutes   *Goods that can serve as a replacement one for the other; when the price of one increases, demand for the other goes up.*

In general, when an *increase* in the price of one good causes demand for another good to *increase* (a positive relationship) we say that the goods are **substitutes**. Similarly, a *fall* in the price of a good causes a *decline* in demand for its substitutes.

Often, on the other hand, two products "go together"—that is, they complement each other. Our lonesome letter writer, for example, will find her demand for stamps and stationery rising. Bacon and eggs are **complementary goods**, as are cars and gasoline, and cameras and film. During the big price war among the airlines in 1986, when travel became less expensive, the demand for taxi service to and from airports, and for luggage, increased across the country. In general, if two goods are complements, an *increase* in the price of one results in a *decline* in demand for the other.

Complements, complementary goods   *Goods that "go together"; when the demand for one goes up, the demand for the other also goes up.*

Since any one good may have many potential substitutes and complements at the same time, a single price change may affect a household's demands for many goods simultaneously; some may rise while others may fall. In the last few years, it became quite inexpensive to rent video tapes of movies. As this happened, the demand for video cassette recorders/players (VCRs) increased dramatically. Clearly, video tapes and video players are complements. At the same time, however, fewer people are going to see movies at the theater. Movies at home and movies in the theater are substitutes.

Tastes and Preferences   Income, wealth, and the prices of things available are the three factors that determine the combinations of things that a household is *able* to buy. You know that you cannot afford to rent an apartment at $1200 per month if your monthly income is only $400. But within those constraints, you are more or less free to *choose* what to buy. Your final choice depends upon your own individual tastes and preferences.

Changes in preferences can and do manifest themselves in market behavior. As the medical consequences of smoking have become more and more clear, fewer and fewer people smoke, and the demand for cigarettes has fallen off significantly. Fifteen years ago the major big-city marathons drew only a few hundred runners. Now tens of thousands enter and run. The demand for running shoes, running suits, stop watches, and other such paraphernalia has exploded.

Within the constraints of prices and incomes, it is preference that shapes the demand curve, and it is always difficult to generalize about tastes and preferences. First of all, they are volatile: five years ago, more people smoked cigarettes, few people had VCRs, and very few teenaged boys had pierced ears. Second, they are idiosyncratic: some people like to talk on the telephone, while others prefer the written word; some people prefer dogs, while others are crazy about cats; some people like chicken wings, while others prefer legs. The diversity of individual demands is almost infinite.

Expectations   Certainly what you decide to buy today depends importantly on today's prices and your current income and wealth, but you also have expectations about what your position will be in the future. You may have expectations about future changes in prices, too, and these may affect your decisions today.

Examples of the ways in which expectations affect demand abound. Often when people buy a house or a car, they must borrow the money and pay it back over a number of years. In deciding what kind of house or car to buy, they presumably must think about their income today, as well as what their income is likely to be in the future. As another example, consider a student in her final year of medical school living on an income of $10,000 from a scholarship. Compare her with an older person earning $5.00 an hour at a full-time job, with no expectation of a significant change in income in the future. The two have virtually identical incomes, and even if they had the same tastes, the medical student is likely to demand different things, simply because she expects a major increase in income later on. You also might be tempted to buy some good today if you expected that it would cost you a lot more in the future—that is, if you expected its price to rise.

Increasingly, economic theory has come to recognize the importance of expectations. We will devote a good deal of time, particularly in macroeconomics, to discussing how expectations affect more than just demand. For the time being, however, it is important to understand that demand depends on more than just *current* incomes, prices, and tastes.

Shift of Demand Versus Movements Along a Demand Curve

Recall that a demand curve shows the relationship between quantity demanded and the price of a good. Such demand curves are *derived while holding income, tastes, and other prices constant*. If this condition of *ceteris paribus* were relaxed, however, we would have to derive an entirely new relationship between price and quantity. To put this statement another way, *the demand curve would shift*.

Let us return one more time to Anna (Table 4.1 and Figure 4.2). Suppose that when we derived the demand schedule in Table 4.1, Anna had a part-time job that paid $200.00 per month. Now suppose that her parents inherited some money and began sending her an additional $200.00 per month. Assuming she keeps the job, her income is now $400.00 per month.[4]

With her higher income, Anna would probably call home more frequently, whatever the price of a call. Table 4.2 and Figure 4.3 present such a change. At $.50 per call, the frequency of her calls (or the quantity she demands) increases from 25 to 33 calls per month; at $3.50 per call, frequency increases from 7 to 18 calls per month; at $10.00 per call, frequency increases from 1 to 7 calls per month.[5]

Such a change is referred to as a **shift in the demand curve**. What is really happening is that the conditions that were in place at the time the original demand curve was derived have now changed. In other words, the world has changed, and we now have a new relationship between price and quantity demanded.

Shift of a demand curve   What happens when a new relationship between quantity demanded of a good and the price of that good is brought about by a change in something that had previously been held constant, like tastes or income.

[4]The income from home may affect the amount of time she spends working. Of course in the extreme, she may quit her job and her income will remain at $200.00. In essence, she would be spending the entire $200.00 on leisure. Here we assume that she keeps the job and her income is higher. The point is that since labor supply decisions affect income, they are closely tied to output demand decisions. In a sense, they are made simultaneously.

[5]Notice in Figure 4.3 that even if calls are free, her income matters; at zero price, her demand increases in the diagram. With a higher income, she may travel more, for example, and more visits might mean more phone calls to organize and plan.

TABLE 4.2
Shift of Anna's Demand
Schedule Due to Increase in
Income

At a higher income, Anna would probably call home more frequently, for a
given price of a call. Such a change is
called a *shift* of the demand schedule
(or the demand curve). We now have a
new relationship between price and
quantity demanded.

Price (per call)	Quantity demanded (calls per month at an income of $200.00 per month)	Quantity demanded (calls per month) at an income of $400.00 per month)
$ 0	30	35
.50	25	33
3.50	7	18
7.00	3	12
10.00	1	7
15.00	0	2

FIGURE 4.3
Shift of a Demand Curve
Following a Rise in Income

When the price of a good changes we
move *along* the demand curve for that
good. When any other factor that influences demand changes (income,
tastes, etc.), the *relationship* between
price and quantity is different; there is
a *shift* of the demand curve.

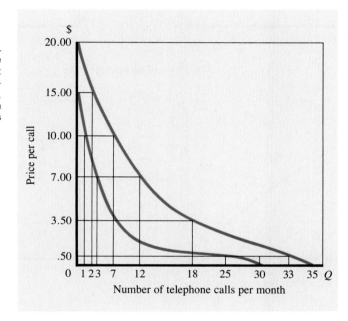

*Movement along a demand
curve   What happens when a
change in price, up or down, causes
quantity demanded to change.*

It is very important to distinguish between a *change in quantity demanded*, that is,
some movement along a demand curve, and a *shift of demand*. Demand schedules and
demand curves show the relationship between the price of a good or service and the
quantity demanded per period, ceteris paribus. If price changes, quantity demanded will
change—that is a **movement along the demand curve**. When any of the other factors
that influence demand change, however, this sets up a new relationship between price
and quantity demanded—*the demand curve shifts*. What we really have is a new demand
curve. Changes in income, preferences, or prices of *other* goods may cause such a change
in demand.

Change in *own price*
  └──→ Change in *quantity demanded*
      └──→ *Movement along* the demand curve.

Change in *income, preferences,* or *other prices*
  └──→ Change in *demand*
      └──→ *Shift of* demand curve.

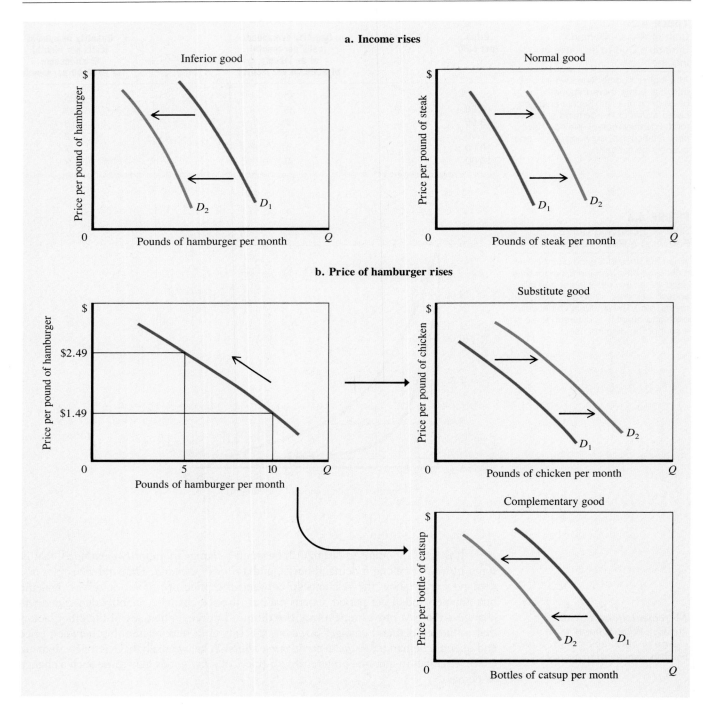

FIGURE 4.4
Shifts versus Movements Along a Demand Curve

a. When income increases, the demand for normal goods *shifts up* (to the *right*) and the demand for inferior goods *shifts down* (to the *left*). b. If the price of hamburger rises, the quantity of hamburger demanded declines—a movement along the demand curve. The same price rise would *shift* the demand for chicken (a *substitute* for hamburger) up—to the right, and it would *shift* the demand for catsup (a *complement* to hamburger) down—to the left.

Figure 4.4 illustrates the point. In 4.4a an increase in household income causes demand for hamburger (an inferior good) to decline, or *shift* to the left. (Remember that quantity is measured on the horizontal axis so that down, or decrease, means to the left). Demand for steak (a normal good), on the other hand, increases, or shifts to the right.

In 4.4b an increase in the price of hamburger causes a household to buy less hamburger each month, that is, the *quantity demanded* declines. This change represents a movement along the demand curve for hamburger. In place of hamburger, households buy more chicken. The household's demand for chicken (a substitute) rises—the demand curve shifts to the right. The demand for catsup (a good that complements hamburger) declines—its demand curve shifts to the left.

From Household Demand to Market Demand

Market demand   The sum of all the quantities of a good or service demanded by all the households buying in the market for that good or service.

Market demand is simply the sum of all the amounts demanded each period by all the households that are shopping in a particular market. Figure 4.5 shows the derivation of a market demand curve from three individual demand curves. (Although this curve is derived from the behavior of only three people, most markets have thousands of

FIGURE 4.5

Deriving Market Demand from Individual Demand Curves

Total demand in the marketplace is nothing more or less than the sum of the demands of all the households shopping in the market. It is the horizontal sum of all the individual demand curves.

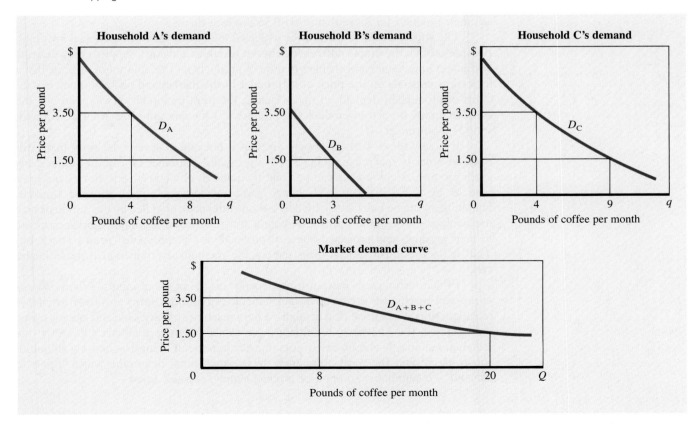

demanders.) When the price of a pound of coffee is $3.50, both A and C would purchase four pounds of coffee per month, while B would buy none; at that price, presumably, he drinks tea. Market demand at $3.50 would thus be a total of four plus four, or eight pounds. At a price of $1.50 per pound, however, A would purchase eight pounds per month, B three pounds, and C nine pounds. Thus at $1.50 per pound, market demand would be eight plus three plus nine, or 20 pounds of coffee per month.

The total quantity demanded in the marketplace at a given price is nothing more than the sum of all the quantities demanded by all the individual households shopping in the market at that price. A market demand curve shows the total amount of a product that would be sold at each price if households could buy all they wanted at that price. As you can see from the diagram, the market demand curve is the horizontal sum of all the individual demand curves. The market demand curve thus takes its shape and position from the shapes, positions, and *number* of individual demand curves. If more people decide to shop in this market, more demand curves must be added, and the *market* demand curve will move, or shift, to the right. Market demand curves may shift as a result of preference changes, income changes, or changes in the number of demanders.

SUPPLY IN PRODUCT (OUTPUT) MARKETS

Microeconomic theory also deals with the behavior of business firms, which supply in product markets and demand in input markets (see again Figure 4.1). Firms engage in production, and we assume that they do so for profit. Profit is, in very simple terms, the difference between *revenues* and *costs*. To make a profit, then, successful firms are able to sell their products for more than it costs to produce them.

The supply decision can thus be expected to depend upon the potential for profit. Because profit is the simple difference between revenues and costs, supply is likely to react to changes in revenues and changes in costs of production. The amount of revenue that a firm earns depends on the price of its product in the market and on how much it sells. Costs of production depend on many factors, the most important of which are (1) the kinds of inputs needed to produce the product, (2) the amount of each input required, and (3) input prices.

It is easy to see that the supply decision is but one of several decisions that firms make in order to maximize profit. There are usually a number of ways to produce any given product. A golf course can be built by hundreds of workers with shovels and grass seed or by a few workers with heavy earth moving equipment and sod blankets. Hamburgers can be individually fried by a short-order cook or grilled by the hundreds on a mechanized moving grill. Firms must choose that production technique most appropriate to their products and projected levels of production. ("Appropriate" means least cost.) That is, to maximize profits, firms choose the method of production that minimizes cost.

Which technique is best, in turn, depends on the prices of inputs. Where labor is cheap and machinery is expensive and difficult to transport, firms are likely to choose techniques that use a great deal of labor. Where machines are available and labor is scarce or expensive, they are likely to choose more capital-intensive methods. Obviously, the technique ultimately chosen determines input requirements. Thus by choosing an output supply target and the most appropriate technology, firms determine which inputs to *demand*. To summarize, output, or product supply, depends upon

1. Revenues
   a. Price of output
   b. Quantity sold
2. Costs of production
   a. Quantity of each input needed
   b. Prices of inputs

With the caution that no single decision exists in a vacuum, then, let us begin our examination of firm behavior by focusing on the output supply decision and the relationship between quantity supplied and output price, *ceteris paribus.*

Price and Quantity Supplied: The Law of Supply

Supply schedule   A table showing how much of a product firms will supply at different prices.

A **supply schedule** shows how much of a product a firm will supply at alternative prices. Table 4.3 itemizes the quantities of soybeans that an individual farmer such as Clarence Brown might supply at various prices. If the market paid only $1.00 a bushel for soybeans, Brown would not supply any soybeans. For one thing, it costs more than $1.00 to produce a bushel of soybeans, and for another, he can use his land more profitably to produce something else. At $1.75 per bushel, however, at least some soybean production takes place, and a price increase from $1.75 to $2.25 per bushel causes the quantity supplied to rise from 10,000 to 20,000 bushels per year. The higher price may justify shifting land from wheat to soybean production or putting marginal, previously fallow land into soybeans. Or it may lead to more intensive farming of land already in soybeans, using expensive fertilizer or equipment which was not cost-justified at the lower price.

In general, then, we can reasonably expect an increase in market price to lead to an increase in quantity supplied. In other words, there is a *positive relationship between the quantity of a good supplied and price.* This statement is sometimes referred to as the **law of supply.** Presented graphically, such information is called a **supply curve,** and *supply curves slope upward.* The upward, or positive, slope of Brown's curve in Figure 4.6, for example, reflects just such a positive relationship between price and quantity supplied.

Supply curve   A graph illustrating the data in a supply schedule—that is, the quantity of a product that firms will supply at different prices.

You probably noticed on this supply schedule, however, that when price rises above $4.00 to $5.00, quantity supplied no longer increases. Often the ability of an individual firm to respond to an increase in price is limited, or constrained, by its existing scale of operations, or capacity, *in the short run.* For example, Clarence Brown's ability to produce more soybeans obviously depends upon the size of his farm, the fertility of his soil, and the equipment he has. The fact that output seems to stay constant at 45,000 bushels per year suggests that he is running up against the limits imposed by the size of his farm and his existing technology.

TABLE 4.3

Clarence Brown's Supply
Schedule for Soybeans

A supply schedule shows how much of a product a firm will supply at each of a number of alternative prices. Clarence Brown would produce no soybeans at all at $1.00 a bushel but would push his farm to capacity, 45,000 bushels, if prices jumped to $4.00 per bushel.

Price (per bushel)	Quantity supplied (bushels per year)
$1.00	0
1.75	10,000
2.25	20,000
3.00	30,000
4.00	45,000
5.00	45,000

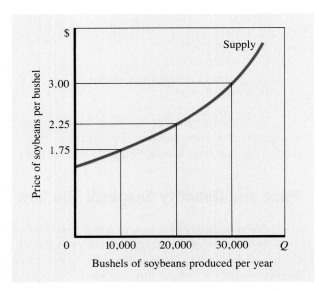

FIGURE 4.6
Clarence Brown's Individual
Supply Curve

A producer will supply more when the
price of output is higher. The slope of
the supply curve is positive.

In the longer run, however, Brown may acquire more land, or technology may
change, allowing for more soybean production. The terms "short run" and "long run"
are defined very precisely in Chapter 7. Here it is important only to understand that time
plays a critical role in supply decisions. When prices change, firms' immediate response
may be different from what they are able to do after a month or a year; short run and long
run supply curves are often different.

Shift of Supply Versus Movement Along a Supply Curve

A supply curve shows the relationship between the quantity of a good or service supplied
by a firm and the price it brings. Higher prices are likely to lead to an increase in quantity
supplied, ceteris paribus—that is, the supply curve is derived holding everything constant
except price. But supply decisions are also influenced by factors other than price. Just as
with demand, when we allow other factors that influence supply to change, we have new
relationships between price and quantity supplied, that is, we have a new supply curve. To
state this another way, we say that the supply curve *shifts*. Any number of factors might
cause supply schedules to shift, but perhaps the most important are those factors that
influence costs of production.

Recall that cost of production depends upon the price of inputs and the
technologies of production available. Now suppose that a major breakthrough in the
production of soybeans has occurred—genetic engineering has produced a superstrain of
disease- and pest-resistant seed, for example. Such a *technological change* would enable
individual farmers to supply more soybeans at *any* market price. Table 4.4 and Figure 4.7
describe this change. At $3.00 a bushel, farmers would have produced 30,000 bushels
from the old seed; instead, with the lower cost of production and higher yield resulting
from the new seed, they produce 40,000 bushels. At $1.75 per bushel, they would have
produced 10,000 bushels, but with the lower costs and higher yields, output rises to
23,000 bushels.

TABLE 4.4

Shift of Supply Schedule for Soybeans Following Development of a New Disease-Resistant Seed Strain

The development of a new disease-resistant seed strain that increases potential yield will encourage Brown to increase output for a given market price. Such a change causes a *shift* of the supply schedule, or supply curve; we now have a new relationship between price and quantity supplied.

Price (per bushel)	Quantity supplied (bushels per year using old seed)	Quantity supplied (bushels per year using new seed)
$1.00	0	5,000
1.75	10,000	23,000
2.25	20,000	33,000
3.00	30,000	40,000
4.00	45,000	54,000
5.00	45,000	54,000

FIGURE 4.7

Shift of Supply Curve for Soybeans Following Development of a New Seed Strain

When the price of output changes, we move *along* the supply curve for that product. When any other factor affecting supply changes, the supply curve *shifts*.

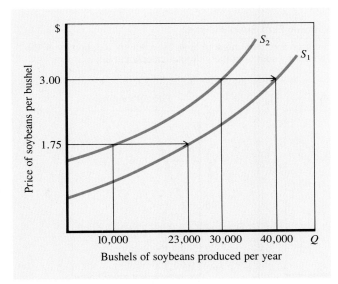

Bushels of soybeans produced per year

Indirect costs may also affect supply decisions. During the 1970s, farm productivity rose rapidly as new technologies came into use. At the same time, however, a number of things caused farm costs to rise. Improved fertilizers were made from petrochemical products, and their production required energy. Oil and energy prices rose dramatically during the mid 1970s. Vastly increased crop plantings required the use of huge new machines that were expensive to buy and used increasingly expensive fuel. Such increases in cost of production shift the supply curve back to the left—that is, less is produced at any given market price. If our soybean supply curve shifted far enough to the left, it would hit the price axis at a higher point, meaning that it would take a higher market price to induce our farmer to produce any soybeans at all.

As with demand, it is very important to distinguish between *movements along* supply curves (changes in quantity supplied) and *shifts in* supply curves (changes in supply):

Change in *own price*
  └→Change in *quantity supplied*
      └→Movement *along* a supply curve.
Change in *costs, input prices,* and *technology*
  └→ Change in *supply*
      └→ *Shift* of supply curve.

From Individual Firm Supply to Market Supply

Market supply The sum of all the quantities of a good or service supplied by all the firms producing in the market for that good.

Market supply is constructed in the same fashion as *market demand*. It is simply the sum of all that is supplied each period by all producers of a single product. Figure 4.8 derives a market supply curve from the supply curves of three individual firms. (For more firms, total market supply would be the sum of the amounts produced by each of them.) At a price of $3.00, farm A supplies 30,000 bushels of soybeans, farm B supplies 10,000 bushels, and farm C supplies 25,000 bushels. At this price, the total amount supplied in the market is 30,000 plus 10,000 plus 25,000, or 65,000 bushels. At a price of $1.75, however, the total amount supplied is only 25,000 bushels. Thus, the market supply

FIGURE 4.8
Deriving Market Supply from Individual Firm Supply Curves

Total supply in the marketplace is nothing more than the sum of all the amounts supplied by all the firms selling in the market; it is the horizontal sum of all the individual supply curves.

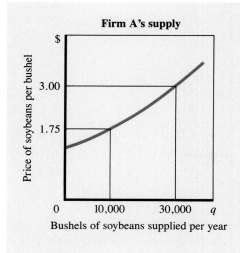
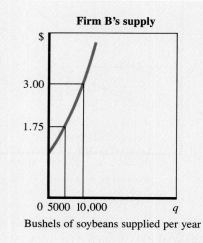
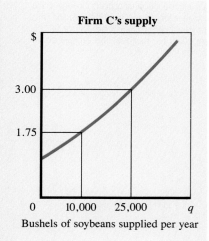

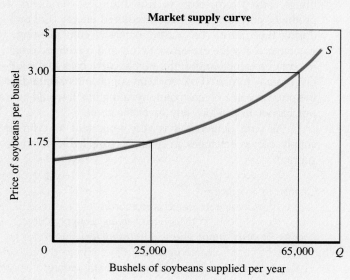

schedule is nothing more or less than the simple horizontal addition of the supply schedules of all the individual firms in a particular market.

The position and shape of the market supply curve depends upon the positions and shapes of the individual firms' supply curves from which it is derived. But it also depends on the *number of firms* that produce in that market. If firms that produce for a particular market are earning high profits, other firms may be tempted to go into that business. When the technology to produce computers for home use became available, literally hundreds of new firms got into the act. The popularity and profitability of professional football has twice led to the formation of a new league. When new firms enter an industry, the supply curve shifts to the right. When firms go out of business, or "exit" the market, the supply curve shifts to the left.

So far we have identified a number of factors that influence the amount that households demand and firms supply in product, or output, markets. The discussion has emphasized the role of market price as a determinant both of quantity demanded and of quantity supplied. We are now ready to see how supply and demand in the market interact to *determine* the final market price.

THE NATURE OF MARKET EQUILIBRIUM

Equilibrium   The condition in which quantity supplied and quantity demanded are equal. The price at which this happens is the equilibrium price.

So far we have been very careful to separate household decisions about how much to demand from firm decisions about how much to supply. The operation of the market, however, clearly depends on the interaction between suppliers and demanders. At any moment, one of three conditions prevails in every market: (1) the quantity demanded exceeds the quantity supplied at the current price, a situation called *excess demand*; (2) the quantity supplied exceeds the quantity demanded at the current price, a situation called *excess supply*; or (3) the quantity supplied equals the quantity demanded at the current price, a situation called **equilibrium**.

Excess Demand

Excess demand   The condition in which quantity demanded exceeds quantity supplied at the current price.

Excess demand exists when quantity demanded is greater than quantity supplied at the current price. Figure 4.9 illustrates such a situation. As you can see, market demand at $1.75 per bushel exceeds the amount that farmers are currently producing.

When excess demand occurs in an unregulated market, there is a *tendency for price to rise* as demanders bid against each other for the limited supply. The adjustment mechanisms may differ, but the outcome is always the same. In an auction, items are simply sold directly to the highest bidder. When the auctioneer starts the bidding at a low price, many people bid for the item, creating excess demand: quantity demanded exceeds quantity supplied. As would-be buyers offer higher and higher prices, bidders drop out, until the one who offers the most ends up with the item being auctioned. *Price rises until quantity demanded and quantity supplied are equal.*

At a price of $1.75 (see Figure 4.9), farmers produce soybeans at a rate of 25,000 bushels per year, but at that price the demand is for 50,000 bushels. Most farm products are sold to local dealers who in turn sell large quantities in major market centers, where bidding would push prices up if quantity demanded exceeded quantity supplied. As price rises above $1.75, two things happen: (1) the quantity demanded falls as buyers drop out of the market and perhaps choose a substitute, and (2) the quantity supplied increases as

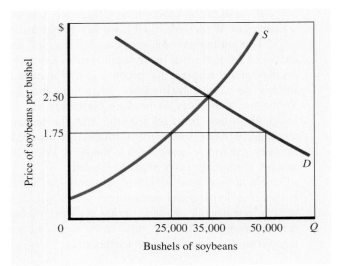

FIGURE 4.9
Excess Demand

At a price of $1.75 per bushel, quantity demanded exceeds quantity supplied. When an *excess demand* occurs, there is a tendency for price to rise. As price rises from $1.75 to $2.50, quantity demanded falls and quantity supplied rises until they are equal and the excess demand is eliminated.

farmers find themselves receiving a higher price for their product and shift additional acres into soybeans.[6]

This process continues until the excess demand is eliminated. In Figure 4.9, this occurs at $2.50, where quantity demanded has fallen from 50,000 bushels per year to 35,000 and quantity supplied has increased from 25,000 bushels per year to 35,000. When quantity demanded and quantity supplied are equal, and there is no further bidding, the process has achieved an *equilibrium*, a situation in which there is no natural tendency for further adjustment.

The process through which excess demand leads to higher prices is different in different markets. Consider the market for houses in Boomville, a small town in the Midwest with a population of 25,000 people, most of whom live in single-family homes. Real estate agents list the properties for sale and introduce prospective buyers to sellers. Normally about 75 homes are sold in the Boomville market each year. But last year, a major business opened a plant in town, creating 1500 new jobs that pay good wages. This attracted new residents to the area, and real estate agents now have more buyers than there are properties for sale: quantity demanded now exceeds quantity supplied. In other words, there is excess demand.

Auctions are not unheard of in the housing market, but they are rare. This market usually works more subtly, but the outcome is the same. Properties are sold very quickly as housing prices begin to rise. Boomville sellers soon learn that there are more buyers than usual, however, and they begin to "hold out" for higher offers. As prices for houses in Boomville rise, quantity demanded eventually drops off and quantity supplied increases. Supply increases in at least two ways: (1) encouraged by the high prices, builders begin constructing new houses, and (2) some people may think of moving—retiring to Florida, for example, because they find the higher prices attractive—and put their houses on the

[6]Once farmers have produced in any given season, they cannot change their minds and produce more, of course. When we derived Clarence Brown's supply schedule in Table 4.3, we imagined him reacting to prices that existed at the time he decided how much land to plant in soybeans. Here, the upward slope shows that higher prices justify shifting land from other crops. Final price may not be determined until final production figures are in. For our purposes here, however, we have ignored this timing problem. Perhaps the best way to think about it is that demand and supply are *flows*, or *rates*, of production—that is, we are talking about the number of bushels produced *per production period*. Adjustments in the rate of production take place over a number of production periods.

Supply and Demand in the Market for Rare Works of Art

One of the easiest and yet most complex of all markets to analyse is the market for works of art. The easy part is supply. For a specific piece of existing art, supply is fixed. There is only one *Mona Lisa* and only one *American Gothic*. When supply in any market is strictly limited, market price depends exclusively on what demanders are willing to pay. Since each painting is unique and can have only one owner, the painting goes to *the* person willing to pay the most.

That makes market price or value very difficult to determine. There are enormous differences in tastes and preferences that express themselves in market choices. The preferences of people who buy rare works of art are as widely variant as those of anyone else—perhaps more so!

When the bidding at an art auction reached $41 million, the people in the audience applauded. When it hit $48 million, they gasped. When the auction ended with a bid of $49 million, they cheered. What was being auctioned? *Irises*, an 1889 painting by the Dutch artist Vincent van Gogh, that in late 1987 brought its owner the highest sum ever paid at auction for a work of art. The seller was John Whitney Payson, whose mother had bought *Irises* for $47,000 forty years earlier.

The price paid for *Irises* broke the record that another of van Gogh's works had set earlier that year. His painting *Sunflowers* had sold for $39.9 million, three times more than any work of art before it. Although these sky-high price tags are unusual, the scarcity of good art is pushing up the price of works by many lesser-known artists as well. *Out the Window*, a painting by living American artist Jasper Johns, sold in the fall of 1986 for $3.6 million.

In the eighteenth and nineteenth centuries, a small circle of aristocrats did all the buying and kept art prices fairly stable. They were joined in the mid-nineteenth century by industrialists eager to span the social gap and buy their way into society. In the twentieth century, American collectors entered the market, upping the art world's ante. In 1921, Henry E. Huntington paid $620,000 for Thomas Gainsborough's *The Blue Boy* (1771).

In those days, dealers offered valuable art to the moneyed few in private transactions. This all changed in 1958 when the British auction house Sotheby's, flaunting tradition, decided to publicly auction off six rare paintings. At that auction, Paul Mellon bid roughly half a million dollars for Paul Cezanne's *Boy in the Red Waistcoat*. The recordbreaking prices brought in by these paintings showed the auctioneers that art was big business.

Art prices have continued to rise, and so have the fortunes of Sotheby's and Christie's. The two largest auction houses together tallied up sales of over $2 billion in 1987—up sixfold from the $330 million they earned a decade earlier. This increase stems only in part from inflation; the price of artwork has appreciated fourfold over the last ten years.

The new art market with its upscale prices has brought with it a new set of collectors. The traditional art connoisseur who bought for beauty's sake is being outbid by wealthy businesspeople with a more recent interest in fine art. This new demand bids up the price of the limited supply of great art. A Japanese real-estate tycoon recently spent $6 million during a two-day shopping spree at Sotheby's.

Collectors, whatever their motivation in buying the art, have one thing in common: an appreciation of a rare commodity that may increase in value with time. Which of today's artists will bring in tomorrow's million-dollar price tag? No one can be sure. After all, van Gogh never considered his own work to be worth much. He was once heard to say, "It is *absolutely* certain that I shall never do important things." One thing we can be sure of is that the principle of supply and demand will continue to affect the world of fine art.

Sources: "What Price Art?", *Barrons*, June 29, 1987; "Tracking Prices in the Global Gallery," *Forbes*, November 2, 1987; and "The Picture Is Still Pretty in the Art World—So Far," *Business Week*, December 28, 1987.

market. Discouraged by higher prices, potential buyers (demanders) may also begin to look for housing in neighboring towns and settle on commuting.

While the mechanics of price adjustment in the housing market differ from the mechanics of an auction, the outcome is exactly the same. *When quantity demanded exceeds quantity supplied, price tends to rise. When the price in a market rises, quantity demanded falls and quantity supplied rises until an equilibrium is reached at which quantity demanded and quantity supplied are equal.*

What is happening in this process is called *price rationing*. When there is excess demand, some people will be satisfied and some will not. When the market operates without interference, price increases distribute what is available to those who are willing and able to pay the most. As long as there is a way for buyers and sellers to interact, those who are willing to pay more will make that known somehow. (The nature of the price system as a rationing device is discussed in great detail in Chapter 5.)

Excess Supply

Excess supply *The condition in which quantity supplied exceeds quantity demanded at the current price.*

Excess supply exists when the quantity supplied exceeds the quantity demanded at the current price. Figure 4.10 illustrates such a situation. At $3.00 a bushel, farmers supply soybeans well in excess of the quantity demanded. When there is excess supply, price tends to fall as competing suppliers attempt to sell their product by lowering the price.

As with excess demand, the mechanics of price adjustment in the face of excess supply can differ from market to market. When there is a surplus, the product remains unsold. If automobile dealers find themselves with unsold cars in the fall when the new models are coming in, you can expect to see price cuts. Sometimes dealers offer discounts to encourage buyers, sometimes buyers themselves simply offer less than the price initially asked. In any event, products do no one any good sitting in dealers' lots or on warehouse shelves. In an auction, if the initial asking price is too high, no one bids, and the auctioneer tries a lower price. In 1984, when stores found themselves with large inventories and weak sales at Christmas, most retailers held big sales a week or two before the holiday. Quantities supplied exceeded quantities demanded at the current prices, and so stores cut prices.

Across the state from Boomville is Bustville, where last year a manufacturer of drugs shut down its operations and 1500 people found themselves out of work. With no other prospects for work, many residents decided to pack up and move. They put their houses up for sale, but there were few buyers. Here there was an excess supply of houses: the quantity of houses supplied exceeded the quantity demanded at the current prices.

As houses sit unsold on the market for months, sellers start to cut their asking prices. Real estate agents suggest to potential buyers that they offer considerably less than sellers are asking. As prices fall, two things are likely to happen. First, the low housing prices may attract new buyers. People who might have bought in a neighboring town see that there are housing bargains to be had in Bustville. In other words, quantity demanded rises in response to price decline. Second, some of those who put their houses on the market may be discouraged by the lower prices and decide to stay. Developers are certainly not likely to be building new housing in town. This suggests that lower prices lead to a decline in quantity supplied, as potential movers pull their houses from the market.

To return to soybean production as shown in Figure 4.10, at a price of $3.00 farmers are supplying soybeans at a rate of 65,000 bushels per year, but buyers demand

FIGURE 4.10
Excess Supply

At a price of $3.00, quantity supplied exceeds quantity demanded; there is excess supply and price will fall.

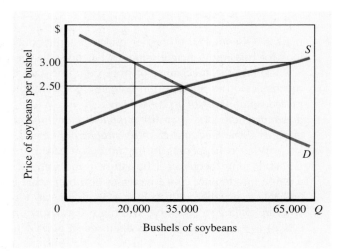

only 20,000. With 45,000 bushels of soybeans going unsold, the market price falls. As price falls from $3.00 to $2.50, quantity supplied decreases from 65,000 bushels per year to 35,000 as farmers shift land out of soybeans into other crops. The lower price causes quantity demanded to rise from 20,000 to 35,000. At $2.50, quantity demanded and quantity supplied are equal. For the data shown here, then, $2.50 and 35,000 bushels are the equilibrium price and quantity.

During 1985 and 1986, crude oil production worldwide exceeded the quantity demanded, and prices fell significantly as competing producer countries tried to maintain their share of world markets. Although the mechanism by which price is adjusted is different for automobiles, housing, soybeans, and crude oil, the outcome is the same. *When quantity supplied exceeds quantity demanded at the current price, the price tends to fall. When price falls, quantity supplied is likely to decrease and quantity demanded is likely to increase until an equilibrium price is reached where quantity supplied and quantity demanded are equal.*

Changes in Equilibrium

When demand or supply curves shift, the equilibrium price and quantity change. In the spring of 1985, those concerned with the coffee market were paying close attention to the weather in Brazil. Brazil is a major producer of coffee beans. A cold snap there can reduce the coffee harvest enough to affect the world price of coffee beans. In the mid 1970s, a major freeze in South America drove the price of coffee in grocery stores in the United States from around $1.50 per pound to $4.50.

Figure 4.11 illustrates a shift in the coffee supply that initially resulted in excess demand. At $1.50 a pound, the quantity demanded (Q_D) was greater than the quantity supplied (Q_S). The price of coffee began to rise in this unregulated market, and as it did two things occurred. First, quantity demanded declined as people shifted to substitute

FIGURE 4.11
A Shift of Supply and Subsequent Price Adjustment

Initially supply shifts up from *S* to *S'*. At $1.50 per pound, quantity demanded (Q_D) exceeds quantity supplied (Q_s). Price will rise to $4.50 where quantity supplied and quantity demanded are equal at Q^*.

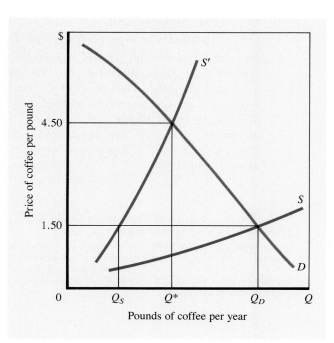

products such as tea. Second, the quantity supplied began to increase, but within the limits imposed by the damage from the freeze.[7] That is, the quantity supplied increased in response to the higher price, *along* the new supply curve, which lies to the left of the old. The final result was a higher price, a smaller quantity exchanged in the market, and coffee going only to those who were willing to pay $4.50 per pound.

DEMAND AND SUPPLY IN PRODUCT MARKETS: A QUICK REVIEW

As you continue your study of economics, you will discover that it is a discipline full of controversy and debate. There is, however, very little disagreement about the basic way that the forces of supply and demand operate in free markets. If you hear that a freeze in Florida has destroyed a good portion of the citrus crop, you can bet that the price of oranges will rise.[8] If you read that the weather in the Midwest has been good and a record corn crop is expected, you can bet that corn prices will fall. When fishermen in Massachusetts go on strike and stop bringing in the daily catch, you can bet that the price of fish will go up.

Here are some of the important points to remember about the mechanics of supply and demand in product, or output, markets.

1. Demand is determined by household preferences, household income and wealth, prices, and expectations.
2. Supply is determined by costs of production and prices. Costs of production are determined by input prices and available technologies of production.
3. On the demand side, the question is, how much would the household buy if it could buy *all it wanted* at the given price? On the supply side, the question is, how much would be produced if a firm could sell *all it wanted* at the given price?
4. Price is always *price per unit*.
5. Quantity demanded is always *per time period*, that is, per day, per month, or per year.
6. Be careful to distinguish between *movements along* supply and demand curves and *shifts of* those curves. When the price of a good changes, the quantity of that good demanded, or supplied, changes—that is, a movement occurs along the curve. Because supply and demand curves are derived, ceteris paribus, when any of the other determining factors change, the curves shift, or change position. For example, an increase in income will shift the demand curve to the right; an increase in cost of production will shift the supply curve to the left. Such changes, in effect, force us to derive another curve.

---

[7]It might also be that some countries or areas with high costs of production, previously unprofitable, come into production and ship to the world market at the higher price.

[8]In economics you have to think twice, however, even about a "safe" bet. If you bet that the price of *frozen orange juice* will rise after a freeze, you will lose your money. It turns out that much of the crop that is damaged by a freeze can be used, but for only one thing—to make frozen orange juice. Thus, a freeze actually *increases* the supply of frozen juice on the national market. Following the last two hard freezes in Florida, the price of oranges shot up, but the price of juice fell sharply!

Supply and Demand and Odd Yellow Fruit

Before the beginning of World War II nearly 50 years ago, this oblong yellow fruit was considered to be an exotic product of the tropics. It had to be peeled and had a white, sweet, pulpy interior. Today this fruit sells for about 50 cents a pound in your local supermarket. In the same supermarket you can probably find another oblong yellow fruit, also an exotic product of the tropics, that sports five fins, does not need to be peeled, and can be sliced into tangy star-shaped segments. This fruit will cost you about $5.99 a pound. The first fruit is a banana, the second a carambola.

The reason why carambolas cost twelve times as much as bananas has a lot to do with supply and demand. Whenever a popular new product that is in short supply appears on the market, it generally commands a high price. This is what has happened recently in the case of carambolas and other exotic tropical fruits—kiwifruit, passion fruit, sweetsop (sugar apples), breadfruit, to name a few.

Exotic tropical fruits are now widely available at produce counters of supermarkets and even in neighborhood groceries because consumer demand for these fruits has skyrocketed. For example, J.R. Brooks & Son, a Florida fruit grower, shipped 50,000 pounds of carambolas in 1983 but expects to ship 6 million pounds in 1989. The current trend toward healthier diets and physical fitness was made for these tasty, nourishing, and low-calorie exotics. What better than a passion fruit following a brisk morning run? Diet conscious consumers can watch their waistlines, enjoy a wide variety of tasty tropical fruits, and get good nutrition, all at the same time.

Large numbers of immigrants from the Caribbean, Latin America, and Asia have also fueled the demand for fruits that were common in their homelands but are just gaining popularity in the United States. For example, Marc and Kiki Ellenby supply the growing Cuban and Asian populations in Dade County, Florida, with sugar apples. This fruit looks like a gray-green pine cone on the outside, but inside it's a slurpy mass of sweet white pulp.

On the supply side, potentially high profits prompt growers to enter the market. A single exotic fruit tree can yield nearly $1,000 in fruit. Purplish, wrinkled passion fruits sell for 98 cents each, and carambolas also sell for about $1. A South Florida tomato grower who had a single carambola tree in his backyard offered its production to a wholesaler. He was so pleasantly surprised at the price he got that he now has 50 acres of carambola trees.

Kiwifruits, one of the earliest and most popular exotics, are about the size of an egg, have a furry brown exterior, and a white and bright green interior. They sell for about 50 cents each and are imported mainly from New Zealand. Driven by demand for kiwifruits (named after the flightless kiwi bird in the 1950s), New Zealand's farmers devote thousands of new acres to kiwifruit production each year. A typical 100-acre kiwi orchard can bring in $1 million per year, whereas a traditional dairy farm of the same size might earn only about $30,000. The kiwifruit growers can toast their profits with a newly developed kiwi wine.

High prices for the new tropical fruits are due to their relative scarcity. Currently, there are a limited number of tropical fruit growers in the United States, and almost all these are located in South Florida, where the subtropical growing conditions that these crops demand are found.

Prices could decline, however, as more sellers attracted by high profit margins enter the industry. The profit on exotic fruits is seven times higher than that on citrus fruits, and acres now planted in oranges and lemons could be turned over to carambola and mango. Homeowners will soon realize that a tropical fruit tree or two in the back yard can mean extra income. The product cycle for exotic fruits is just beginning. As more farmers grow these products, the supply curve will shift to the right, and prices could drop sharply.

Many tropical fruit growers are diversifying to cover possible price drops and resulting losses. The Ellenbys plant lychee, longan, sugar apples, and passion fruits, among others. They figure that if the lychee market fails, they still have the sugar apple, and if the passion for passion fruit falls flat, the longan might still be highly prized. The Ellenbys are experimenting with the atemoya, a relative of the sugar apple. They are trying to develop an atemoya that is less perishable than the sugar apple in order to decrease shipping and handling costs. They hope to find a variety that will appeal to the American consumer as a whole—not just to Cubans and Latin Americans in the Miami area. Greater demand will mean higher prices for the atemoya—and the sugar apple.

The demand for exotic fruits is clearly a matter of consumer tastes and preferences. As prices for these items drop, the quantity demanded could expand, and new crops could attract larger numbers of customers. Growers hope that this type of demand curve shift will help them to make up for lost revenues from falling prices by increased sales volume.

Tropical fruits could follow the pattern of alfalfa sprouts, fresh mushrooms, and avocados. Only 15 years ago these items were a relatively oddity in grocery stores. Today grocers sell them by the trailerload. Who knows? Passion fruit sorbet and kiwi tarts could become staples of the American diet.

Consumer tastes and preferences, however, can be fickle. The success of the kiwifruit may not be matched by the passion fruit or the carambola.

Sources: Noel D. Vietmeyer, "The Captivating Kiwifruit," *National Geographic*, May 1987; Laura Shapiro, "New Rx: Try an Atemoya a Day," *Newsweek*, November 23, 1987; Carolyn Lockhead, "Tilling a Market for Exotic Produce," *Insight*, February 8, 1988.

MARKETS AND THE ALLOCATION OF RESOURCES

You can already begin to see how markets answer the fundamental economic questions of what is produced, how it is produced, and for whom. Firms will produce what is profitable to produce. If a product can be sold at a price that is sufficient to leave a profit after production costs are paid, the product will in all likelihood be produced. Resources will flow in the direction of profit opportunities.

Demand curves reflect what people are willing and able to pay for products—they depend on incomes, wealth, and preferences. Because product prices are determined by the interaction of supply and demand, prices reflect what people are willing to pay. If people's preferences or incomes change, the allocation of resources will respond. Consider, for example, an increase in demand—a shift in the market demand curve. Beginning at an equilibrium, households simply begin buying more. At the equilibrium price, quantity demanded is now greater than quantity supplied. When there is excess demand, prices will rise, and higher prices mean higher profits for firms in the industry. Higher profits, in turn, provide existing firms with an incentive to expand and new firms an incentive to enter the industry. Thus the decisions of independent private firms responding to prices and potential profits determine *what* will be produced, with no central direction.

Firms in business to make a profit have a good reason to pick the best available technology—lower costs mean higher profits. Thus individual firms determine *how* to produce their products, again with no central direction.

So far we have barely touched on the question of distribution—*who* gets what is produced? But part of the answer can be seen in the simple supply and demand diagrams. When a good is in short supply, price rises. As it does, those who are willing and able to continue buying do so; others drop out. Willingness and ability to pay depend on preferences, income, and wealth, which are in part determined in input markets—wage rates, for example, determine how much workers earn.

The next chapter begins with a more detailed discussion of these questions. How, exactly, is the final allocation of resources, the mix of output and the distribution of output, determined in a market system?

SUMMARY

1. In societies with many people, production must satisfy wide ranging tastes and preferences, and producers must therefore specialize.
2. A firm exists when someone or some group decides to produce a product or products by transforming resources, or *inputs*, into *outputs*—the products that are sold in the market.
3. We assume that firms make decisions to maximize profits.
4. The incomes of households are ultimately limited. They are constrained by wages, the availability of jobs, their own abilities, and their accumulated and inherited wealth or lack of it.

5. Quantity demanded by an individual household is likely to depend upon (1) income, (2) wealth, (3) the price of the product, (4) the prices of other products, and (5) tastes and preferences.
6. For an individual household, quantity demanded is the amount of a product that it would buy if it could buy all it wanted at the current price.
7. A demand schedule shows the quantities of a product that a household would buy at alternative prices. The same information presented graphically is called a demand curve.
8. Demand curves slope downward. There are several reasons this is so. For one thing, higher price means

greater opportunity cost. Another reason is that marginal utility diminishes with additional consumption. Income and substitution effects can also be used to explain the shape of demand curves.

9. When an increase in income causes demand for a good to rise, that good is a normal good. When an increase in income causes demand for a good to fall, that good is an inferior good.

10. If a rise in the price of good X causes demand for good Y to increase, the goods are substitutes. If a rise in the price of X causes demand for Y to fall, the goods are complements.

11. It is very important to distinguish between movements along demand and supply curves and shifts of demand and supply curves. The demand curve shows the relationship between price and quantity demanded. Thus a change in price is a movement along the curve. Changes in tastes, income, wealth, or expectations cause demand curves to shift.

12. A market demand curve is simply the horizontal sum of all the individual household demand curves for the product in question. It takes its shape from the shapes and positions of the number of individual demand curves it represents.

13. A supply schedule shows the quantities of output that an individual firm would supply at alternative prices. The same information presented graphically is a supply curve.

14. A market supply curve is simply the horizontal sum of all the individual firm supply curves for the product in question. It takes its shape from the shapes and positions of the number of individual supply curves it represents.

15. When quantity demanded exceeds quantity supplied at the current price, the price tends to rise. When prices in a market rise, quantity demanded falls and quantity supplied rises until an equilibrium is reached at which quantity supplied and quantity demanded are equal.

16. When quantity supplied exceeds quantity demanded at the current price, the price tends to fall. When price falls, quantity supplied is likely to decrease and quantity demanded is likely to increase until an equilibrium price is reached where quantity supplied and quantity demanded are equal.

REVIEW CONCEPTS

firms   78
households   78
product, or output, markets   79
input markets   79
labor market   80
capital market   80
quantity demanded   80
demand schedule   81
demand curve   81
law of demand   82
income effect   83
substitution effect   83
income   84
wealth or net worth   84

normal good   84
inferior good   84
substitute   85
complement, complementary goods   85
shift of a demand curve   86
movement along a demand curve   87
market demand   89
supply schedule   91
law of supply   91
supply curve   91
market supply   94
equilibrium   95
excess demand   95
excess supply   98

REVIEW QUESTIONS

1. Think of some commodity that you like (try to avoid "lumpy" things, like cars or houses, and pick something like coffee, movies, trips to a frequently visited place, records, long distance phone calls, and so on).
   a. Roughly sketch your demand curve for that commodity. Does it hit the price axis? Where? How much would you buy at a zero price?
   b. Are there substitutes for this commodity? How does the availability of substitutes affect the shape of your curve?
   c. How would your demand curve change in response to the change in the price of some substitute?
   d. How would it change if you won the lottery and were to receive $2000 per week for life?

2. The United States government administers two programs that

affect the market for cigarettes. Media campaigns and labeling requirements are aimed at making the public aware of the dangers of cigarettes. At the same time, the Department of Agriculture maintains a program of price supports for tobacco. Under this program, the supported price is above the market equilibrium price, and the government limits the amount of land that can be devoted to tobacco production. Are these two programs at odds with respect to the goal of reducing cigarette consumption? Explain carefully. As a part of your answer, illustrate graphically the effects of both policies on the market for cigarettes.

3. In the 1960s, a good deal of evidence revealed that the urban housing market was in fact a "dual" market divided along racial lines. That is, there were completely separate supply and demand forces at work in black and white "submarkets." Blacks could buy housing only in certain areas, and the supply of housing in these areas was relatively fixed. The empirical evidence also indicated that the price of housing in the black submarket was higher than in the white submarket, that is, houses in the black areas were selling for more than identical houses in white areas. Urban economists attributed this differential to "demand pressure" because demand trends showed that blacks had been moving from the rural South to the urban North in large numbers.

   A recent economic study of discrimination in the rural South found the same sort of "dual" housing market. Rural black populations have been declining, both relatively and absolutely, and the researchers had anticipated finding a price differential favoring blacks. In other words, they expected to find blacks paying a lower price for housing. Instead, despite the decline in black population, the price of housing in black neighborhoods was in fact higher than the price of identical housing in white neighborhoods.

   Give at least two possible explanations for this seeming paradox. Use simple supply and demand graphs in your explanation.

4. Assume that the Boston Red Sox baseball team charges $5.00 per ticket for all seats at all regular season games. Assume also that the capacity of their stadium, Fenway Park, is 35,000. In August the Red Sox played games against the New York Yankees (a great rival) and the Cleveland Indians (a team in last place) on consecutive Sundays. All tickets to the Yankee game were sold out a month in advance, and many people who wanted tickets could not get them. At the Cleveland game, there were 15,000 vacant seats.

   a. Draw two imaginary supply and demand curves (two graphs), one for tickets to each of the two games.

   b. Is there a pricing policy that would fill the stadium for the Cleveland game? Would such a policy bring the Red Sox more, or less, revenue?

   c. Because a price rationing system is not necessary for tickets to the Yankee game, how might they be rationed?

5 Supply and Demand: The Nature of the System, Applications, and Elasticity

Every society has a system of institutions that determines what gets produced, how it gets produced, and for whom it gets produced. While in many societies the decisions that determine economic outcomes are made centrally, through planning agencies or by government directive, in every society many decisions are made in a decentralized way, through the operation of markets.

Markets exist in all societies, and Chapter 4 provided a bare-bones description of how all markets operate. This chapter reflects briefly on the outcomes of supply and demand in operation and then applies supply and demand analysis to a real problem. The second half of the chapter introduces the important concept of elasticity. A knowledge of the market allocation mechanism is essential to understanding both microeconomics and macroeconomics.

THE PRICE SYSTEM: RATIONING AND ALLOCATION OF RESOURCES

The price system performs two important and closely related functions for a society with unregulated markets. First, it provides an automatic mechanism for distributing scarce goods and services—it serves as a "**price rationing**" device for dividing up goods and services whenever the quantity demanded exceeds the quantity supplied. Second, the price system ultimately determines how resources are allocated among producers and what the final mix of outputs will be.

Price Rationing

Consider first the simple process by which the price system eliminates excess demand. Figure 5.1 illustrates the situation that existed when the South American coffee crop was partially destroyed by frost in 1985. With much less coffee available, significant excess demand still existed at a price of $2.49 per pound. There simply was not enough coffee around to meet the quantity demanded at that price.

As price rose, however, excess demand was quickly eliminated. Look carefully at what occurred as price went up from $2.49 to $4.50. While coffee output increased somewhat as the higher price attracted producers, the most significant factor was the reduction in the quantity demanded. Households wanted to purchase fewer and fewer pounds of coffee as prices rose. Some switched to substitutes, such as tea or hot chocolate. But the important point here is that *those who were willing and able to pay the higher price were the ones who ended up getting the coffee.*

Willingness is, of course, always constrained by ability. One's ability to purchase a commodity at a higher price depends on income and wealth, and that is exactly why some people object to the price rationing system—it allocates goods and services, in some large measure, according to income and wealth. But it is easy to oversimplify this. Do only the rich drink coffee? Of course not. As price rises, many people, some of them rich and some of them poor, decide to go right on drinking coffee. Ultimately, income and wealth constrain demand, but within those constraints, people exercise choice. Some of the poor continue to drink coffee and some of the rich switch to tea. The idea of "willingness to pay" is central, and willingness depends both on desire, or preferences, and on income/wealth.

There is some price that will clear any market you can think of. Consider the market for a famous painting such as van Gogh's "Irises." Figure 5.2 illustrates the operation of such a market. At a low price, there would be an enormous excess demand for such an important painting. The price would be bid up until there was only one remaining demander. The demander who got the painting would be the one who was willing and able

FIGURE 5.1

Price Rationing in the Coffee Market

After the freeze in 1985, the supply of coffee declined sharply. Only those who were willing and able to pay the new higher price drank coffee in 1986. Coffee was *rationed* to those willing to pay the most. Willingness to buy, in turn, depends on strength of preferences and ability to pay.

In this diagram, Q_D is the quantity demanded at the price of $2.49 and Q_s is the quantity supplied in 1986 at this price. The equilibrium price in 1986 is $4.50.

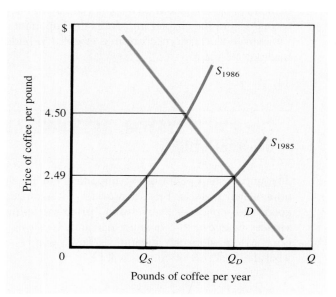

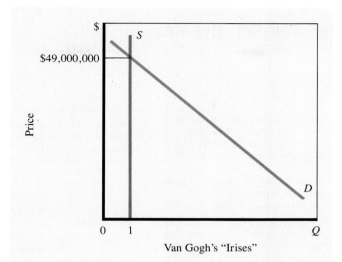

FIGURE 5.2
Market for a Single Copy of a
Rare Painting

There is some price that will clear any
market even if supply is strictly limited. In an auction for a unique painting,
price will rise until only one bidder
remains.

to pay the most. Presumably, that price would be very high. In fact, van Gogh's "Irises" sold for $49 million in 1987. If the product is in strictly scarce supply, as a single paint- ing is, its price is said to be *demand determined*, that is, its price is determined solely and exclusively by the amount that the highest bidder, or highest bidders, are willing to pay.

One might interpret the statement that "there is some price that will clear any market," to mean "everything has its price." That is not exactly what it means. Suppose you own a small silver bracelet that has been in your family for many generations. It is quite possible that you wouldn't sell it for *any* amount of money. Does this mean that the market is not working, or that quantity supplied and quantity demanded are not equal? Not at all. It means simply that *you* are the highest bidder. By turning down all bids, you are setting your own price, revealing that the bracelet is worth more to you than to those who bid on it. In order to keep the bracelet, *you must be willing to forgo what anybody offers for it.*

Constraints on the Market and Alternative Rationing Mechanisms

On occasion, both governments and private firms decide to use some mechanism other than the market system alone to ration an item for which there is excess demand at the current price. Policies designed to stop price rationing are commonly justified in a number of ways.

The rationale most often voiced is "fairness." It is not "fair" to let landlords charge high rents, not "fair" for oil companies to run up the price of gasoline, or for insurance companies to charge enormous premiums, and so on. After all, the argument goes, we have no choice but to pay—housing and insurance are necessary, and one needs gasoline to get to work. While it is not precisely true that price rationing allocates goods and services on the basis of income and wealth, income and wealth do constrain willingness to pay. Why should all the gasoline or all the tickets to the World Series go just to the rich? it is asked.

Various schemes to keep price from rising to equilibrium are based on several perceptions of injustice, among them (1) that price-gouging monopolists are bad, (2) that

Excess Demand for Housing in China

The following article appeared in the *China Daily* in the People's Republic of China on March 21, 1987:

A severe housing shortage has been a headache for Chinese urban dwellers for many years, nevertheless, they have not realized until recently that their extremely low rents were one of the factors very much responsible for the shortage and poor housing conditions.

For the past 30 years or so, house building in China has been carried on under the State centralized management. Houses are built with State funds and allotted to people as welfare items. . . .

Over the past several years, the cost of living has risen considerably and people's incomes have also increased. But low rents have remained, by and large, unchanged. This has further reduced the proportion of rent a family must pay in relation to its income. According to a survey published in the newspaper World Economic Herald in 1978, a family in Beijing spent about 2.3 per cent of its total income on housing; but in 1985, the figure had dwindled to 1.25 per cent.

The State-subsidized rent makes houses a great bargain. Some people try every means to get as much housing as they can, and some use it to corrupt government officials to gain personal favours. Meanwhile, large numbers of city inhabitants, who have

no way of getting housing, make do with tiny living quarters. . . . the present housing shortage will not be eased unless changes are made in China's housing system. The key is to make houses a commodity and to let people buy their own apartments.

Having come to this conclusion, many Chinese cities have started reforming the old system. In 1985, 4.8 million square metres of housing were sold to individuals. A popular practice is "subsidized sales." To buy a flat, an individual pays one-third of the price, and the difference is made up by the State and his or her work unit. Although the State still has to subsidize individual buyers, it receives much more than it could by collecting rents. . . .

At the same time, rents will rise in a bid to urge people to buy their own homes. . . .

The biggest difficulty facing the commercialization of housing is the comparatively low income of the average Chinese family and the shortage of funds in most units that wish to buy houses for their employees.

Here, banks may lend a helping hand. Banks could collect funds from different units—funds that have been earmarked for house purchase or construction—for the development of urban commercialized housing. If units that have joined the fund want to build their own housing, they could receive bank loans.

Source: Zhong Hua, "Too Low Rents Cause Housing Shortage," *China Daily*, March 21, 1987.

income is unfairly distributed, and (3) that some items are necessities, and everyone should be able to buy them at a "reasonable" price. Regardless of the rationale, the following examples should make two things clear. First, attempts to bypass the market and to use alternative rationing devices are much more difficult and costly than they would seem at first glance. Second, the replacement schemes are often less "fair" than the free market.

Oil, Gasoline, and OPEC   In 1973 and 1974, the Organization of Petroleum Exporting Countries (OPEC) imposed an embargo on shipments of crude oil to the United States. What followed was a drastic reduction in the quantity of gasoline available at local gas pumps.

Had the market system been allowed to operate, refined gasoline prices would have increased very dramatically until quantity supplied was equal to quantity demanded. Those who were willing and able to pay a very high price, probably over $2.00 per gallon, would have been the ones to get the gasoline. But the government decided that rationing gasoline to only those who were willing and able to pay the most was unfair, and Congress imposed a **price ceiling**, or maximum price, on gasoline at the pump. That price ceiling was intended to keep gasoline "affordable," but it also perpetuated the *shortage*: at the restricted price, quantity demanded remained greater than quantity supplied, and the available gasoline had to be divided up somehow among all potential demanders.

Several devices were found. The most common of all **nonprice rationing** systems is **queuing**, a term that simply means waiting in line. During 1974 very long lines began to appear at gas stations, starting as early as 5:00 in the morning. Often people waited for

Price ceiling   A *maximum price usually set by government often in the name of fairness.*

Queuing   A *nonprice-rationing mechanism which uses waiting in line as a means of allocating goods and services.*

hours. Under this system, gasoline went to those who were willing to pay the most, but the sacrifice was measured in hours and aggravation, rather than in dollars.[1]

A second nonprice rationing device used during the gasoline shortage was that of the **favored customer**. Many gas station owners decided not to sell gasoline to the general public at all but to reserve their scarce supplies for friends and favored customers. Not surprisingly, many customers tried to become "favored" by offering side payments to gas station owners. Owners also charged high prices for service. By tying the gasoline to service, they increased the real price of gasoline but hid it in service overcharges to get around the ceiling.

Yet another method of dividing up a shortage is to use **ration coupons**. It was suggested both in 1974 and later in 1979 that families be given ration tickets, or coupons, that would entitle them to purchase a certain number of gallons of gasoline each month; that way everyone would get the same amount, regardless of income. Such a system was employed in the United States during the 1940s, when wartime price ceilings on meat, sugar, butter, tires, nylon stockings, and many other items had been imposed.

When ration coupons are used with no prohibition against trading them, however, the result is almost identical to a system of price rationing. Those who are willing and able to pay the most simply *buy up the coupons* and use them to purchase gasoline, chocolate, fresh eggs, or anything else that is sold at a restricted price.[2] Even when trading coupons is declared illegal, it is virtually impossible to stop "black markets" from developing.

Super Bowl XX, 1986   Important sporting events such as the World Cup for soccer and the Super Bowl for American football are held in stadiums that have finite seating capacities. In most cases many, many fans, far more than can fit into the largest stadium, want to attend those events, even at high ticket prices. A classic example was Super Bowl XX in which the Chicago Bears played the New England Patriots at the Super Dome in New Orleans on January 26, 1986. Neither of those teams had ever been in a Super Bowl, and the fans in Chicago and those in Boston became very enthusiastic.

The Super Dome contains just over 73,000 seats, and for the Super Bowl, the National Football League had to decide how to divide up those seats and how much to charge for them. If the NFL's only objective had been to maximize current revenues from ticket sales, it could have put them up for sale in Boston and Chicago at a *very* high price.

The NFL had other objectives, however. One important one was *fairness*. Selling the tickets at the market clearing price would have brought cries of "price gouging." According to some estimates, if all the tickets had been put on the market at $400.00 each, the stadium would have sold out. (As it happened, individual tickets did trade on the black market for over $1000.) But at $400.00 a ticket only the rich or those willing to

---

[1]You can also show formally that the result is inefficient—that there is a resulting net loss of total value to society. First, there is the cost of waiting in line. As you will see in great detail later on, time has a value. With price rationing, no one has to wait in line and the value of that time is saved. Second, there may be additional lost value if the gasoline ends up in the hands of someone who places a lower value on it than someone else who gets no gas. Suppose, for example, that the market price of gasoline if unconstrained would rise to $2.00, but that the government has it fixed at $1.00. There will be long lines to get gas. Imagine that to motorist A, 10 gallons of gas is worth $35.00 but she fails to get it because her time is too valuable to wait in line. To motorist B, 10 gallons is worth only $15.00, but his time is worth much less, so he gets the gas. Clearly at the end, A could pay B for the gas and both could be better off. If A pays B $30.00 for the gas, A is $5.00 better off and B is $15.00 better off. In addition, B doesn't have to wait in line. Thus, the allocation that results from nonprice rationing involves a net loss of value. Such losses are called *"dead weight losses."*

[2]Of course, if you are assigned a number of tickets, and you sell them, you are better off than you would be with price rationing. Ration tickets thus serve as a way of redistributing income.

make big sacrifices could go. The less affluent fans who had supported the Bears and the Patriots through many lean years would be either frozen out or forced to sacrifice a lot to go.

So one quarter of the tickets—18,000 of them—went to each of the two teams to distribute to its fans. The price at $75.00 was high, but not ridiculous. At that point, each team had to decide how to distribute the tickets among the thousands of fans who wanted to go. At $75.00 per ticket there was an enormous excess demand to deal with in both cities. As it turned out, both teams rewarded their loyal fans: Super Bowl tickets went to season ticket holders. In Chicago, there was a random drawing, even among the season ticket holders. As the following newspaper story the week before the game described it,

> Yesterday marked the big day for Bears fans who were seeking tickets. The Bears placed a full-page advertisement in the *Chicago Tribune* listing the more than 4000 winners of a lottery to get seats for Super Bowl XX. The team listed code numbers for the winning season ticket-holders rather than their names. Season ticket-holders will get one, two, four or six tickets for the game. 'We didn't want to get into listing people's names for obvious reasons,' explains Bears general manager Jerry Vainisi.[3]

Initially, then, the market did not play a big role. The NFL and the two teams involved distributed the tickets at a price far below equilibrium, using what they felt was a more fair system. Then the fun began. On January 16, the *Boston Globe* ran dozens of advertisements that read: "Super Bowl Tickets wanted: Top $$$$ Paid in Cash . . . call 24 hours." Many listed toll free 800 numbers to call. Within a very short time, a national market had been established, and those who were willing and able to pay the top dollar were communicating their desires to those who were lucky enough to have the tickets. Price offers ranged from $500.00 to $1000.00 *per ticket*! Many of the offers came from travel agents, who resold the tickets at even higher prices.

Now consider the people who got to buy their tickets for $75.00. The moment the market appeared, the price of those tickets went up. Going to the game now meant giving up over $500.00—the opportunity cost of the ticket. Even though they didn't have to reach in their pockets and pull out the $500.00, they had to reveal that the tickets were worth that much. It was exactly as if each ticket holder had been awarded enough cash to buy a ticket at its market price less $75.00.

The New York Marathon   Recently, running has become something of a national obsession in the United States. Fifteen years ago only a handful of people ran marathons; in 1987 over 20,000 ran the New York City Marathon. In order to run in that marathon, you need a number. The numbers are sold for a small entry fee, and at that fee there are far more runners than there are available numbers. (The number of participants is limited to about 20,000.) The excess demand at the price of entry is quite large.

Instead of raising the fee, the sponsors of the New York City Marathon settled on a complex series of hoops for potential runners to jump through to get numbers. The essential feature of the system is that numbers are mailed out on a first-come, first-served basis. The applications are handled in the order that they are received, but they cannot be postmarked before a certain date. There are a number of time-consuming procedures that runners can follow to increase their chances of getting in.

What would you expect to happen in a situation like this? Where there is "willingness to pay" for an available product, you expect to see enterprise. Agencies grew up that would, for a price substantially above the entry fee, promise to get a number for

[3]*Boston Globe*, January 19, 1986.

you. These agencies got to know the system well and spent the time necessary to insure that runners got their numbers. What these agencies were really doing was allowing the price system to allocate at least some of the numbers.

These examples describe the nature of the price rationing system and suggest some alternatives to it. The problem is that no matter how well intentioned private organizations and governments are, it is very difficult to prevent the price system from operating and to stop *willingness to pay* from asserting itself. Every time an alternative is tried, the price system seems to sneak in the back door. With favored customers and black markets, the final distribution may be even more unfair than that which would result from simple price rationing.

Prices and the Allocation of Resources

Thinking of the market system as a mechanism for allocating scarce goods and services among competing demanders reveals much about its nature. But the market determines much more than just the distribution of final outputs. It also determines what gets produced and how resources are allocated among competing uses.

You can see how this works when you consider a change in consumer preferences that leads to an increase, or shift, in demand for a specific good or service. During the 1970s, people began going to restaurants much more frequently than before. Researchers think that this trend, which still continues, is partially the result of social changes that include a dramatic rise in the number of two-earner families and partially the result of rising incomes. The market responded to this change in demand by shifting resources, both capital and labor, into more and better restaurants.

With the increase in demand, the price of eating out rose, and the restaurant business became more profitable. The higher profits attracted new businesses and provided old restaurants with an incentive to expand. As new capital, seeking profits, flowed into the restaurant business, so too did labor. New restaurants need chefs. Chefs need training, and the higher wages that came with increased demand provided an incentive for them to get it. In response to the increase in demand for training, new cooking schools opened up and existing schools began to offer courses in the culinary arts.

This story could run on and on, but the point is already clear. Price changes resulting from shifts of demand in output markets cause profits to rise and fall. Profits attract capital; losses lead to disinvestment. Higher wages attract labor and encourage workers to acquire skills. At the core of the system we see supply, demand, and prices in input and output markets determining the allocation of resources and the ultimate combinations of things produced.

SUPPLY AND DEMAND ANALYSIS: THE INCIDENCE OF AN EXCISE TAX IN THE SHORT RUN

The incidence of a tax *Refers to the ultimate distribution of the burden of the tax among households.*

The basic logic of supply and demand is very powerful. Because it explains much of the behavior that we observe in the market, it helps us understand the nature of the "system" that is functioning around us. In addition, it is a powerful tool of analysis. It provides a way to structure our thinking in order to answer difficult questions of policy.

Public policy makers often find themselves asking "what if?" questions. What if we stopped regulating air travel? What if we allowed telephone rates to be set in the market? What if we increased the corporate profits tax? To answer these questions, we need to know how the people that are affected by a change will react. Our analysis of supply and demand is nothing more than an analysis of the behavior of households and firms. The behavior of households and firms in the marketplace, in turn, determines the ultimate impact of a policy change. To illustrate this, we now examine the arena of tax policy.

It doesn't take a great deal of thought to see that the person or institution that initially pays a tax does not necessarily bear its burden. To take a classic example, the corporate income tax is paid initially by corporations. Corporations are separate entities, but they are also extensions of individuals, and the question is, *which individuals* ultimately end up paying the tax? There are several candidates: stockholders, i.e., corporation owners, who may earn lower after-tax profits; consumers, who may pay more for what the corporation produces; and employees, who may receive lower salaries and benefits from the corporation. The ultimate distribution of any tax burden depends on how markets react to it.

Tax shifting   What happens when the person or institution on which a tax is initially levied does not bear its entire burden. The burden of a tax can be shifted when markets and prices adjust to its presence.

What follows is an analysis designed to show how **tax shifting** takes place as a result of supply and demand adjustment. The tax we consider is an excise tax, that is, a tax imposed on the sale or production of a good or service. In the United States, we have excise taxes on a number of products including gasoline, tobacco, alcohol, telephone service, and tires. Most often these taxes are initially paid by producers.

Figure 5.3 shows equilibrium in a market with no tax. The quantity supplied by firms in a market depends upon the price they receive for the product. The quantity demanded by households in a market depends on the price they must pay to obtain the product. When the item in question is not taxed, the amount that consumers pay is exactly the same as the amount that producers receive, and as the price adjusts, the market clears.

The presence of a tax, however, whether imposed on producers or on consumers directly, means that producers receive a different amount from the amount consumers pay. If the tax is imposed directly on *consumers*, they pay it in addition to the net price of the product, and thus the total price includes the tax. If the price is imposed on *producers*, they must deduct the tax from their receipts, and the net price they receive is lower than that paid by consumers.

When a tax is present, we can draw the supply curve in two ways. In Figure 5.4, we graph supply as a function of what producers receive, a standard supply curve that reflects the direct response of firms to changing prices. In the diagram, if producers receive $5.00

FIGURE 5.3
Equilibrium in a Market with No Tax

Quantity *demanded* depends upon the price actually paid by consumers for a good; quantity *supplied* depends on the price that firms receive per unit of product. When there are *no taxes,* those two prices are the same.

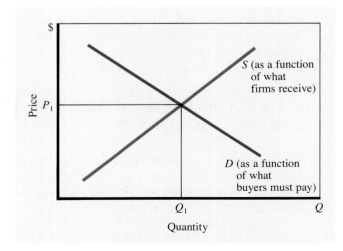

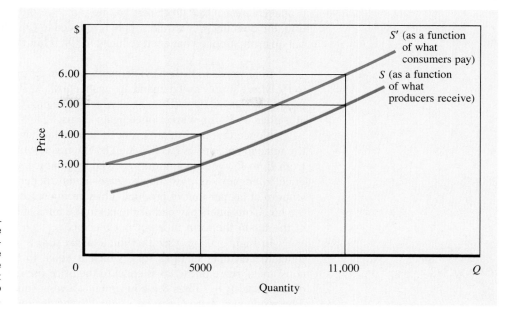

FIGURE 5.4

Two Supply Curves when a Tax Is Levied on Producers

When a tax is imposed, whether the burden falls on consumers or producers, there is a difference between the price consumers pay and the price producers receive. Thus, we must draw different supply schedules to describe these two aspects of supply.

per unit, they will supply 11,000 units per period; if they receive $3.00 per unit, however, they will supply only 5000 units per period. In the same figure, we also show the same supply curve as a function of what consumers pay assuming there is a tax of $1.00 per unit. In order for producers to receive $5.00 per unit, consumers must pay $6.00 whether consumers pay the tax or producers pay the tax. If consumers pay $6.00 per unit, producers will receive $5.00 and supply 11,000 units per period. For producers to receive $3.00 per unit, households must pay $4.00. If households pay $4.00, producers will receive $3.00 per unit and supply 5000 units per period.

Now suppose that an excise tax of T dollars per unit is imposed directly on producers. Figure 5.5 shows the adjustment that would take place in response. Initially, the market is in equilibrium with a price of P_1 and a quantity of Q_1. Imposing a tax of T on

FIGURE 5.5

An Excise Tax in the Short Run

The price consumers pay and the quantity supplied should be read off the S' curve, while the price producers receive should be read off the S curve. The new equilibrium quantity is Q_2, and although the consumer's price is P_2, producers receive only $P_3 = (P_2 - T)$ per unit.

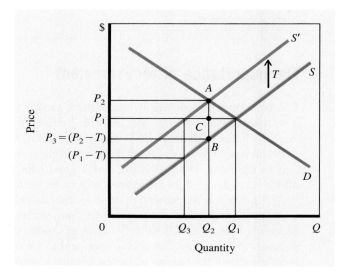

producers means that producers will now receive only $(P_1 - T)$. If that is all they get per unit, the quantity they would supply is reduced to Q_3. Quantity demanded remains at Q_1, but quantity supplied has been reduced to Q_3. Thus there is excess demand at the original price.

In response to the excess demand, the market price begins to rise. It rises all the way to P_2, where supply and demand are again equal. At P_2 the quantity demanded is Q_2. At P_2 producers receive $P_3 = (P_2 - T)$, at which price producers also produce quantity Q_2. Thus at a price of P_2 the market once again clears.

Notice that the imposition of the excise tax has resulted in a price increase, but that the price to consumers has not risen by the full amount of the tax. Equilibrium price rises from P_1 to P_2, but the amount received by producers falls from P_1 to P_3. The increase in price to consumers plus the decrease in return per unit to producers equals the total amount of tax per unit of product. Thus producers and consumers share the "burden" of the tax. Consumers pay part of the tax in the form of higher prices; producers pay the rest of the tax in the form of lower net receipts.

In Figure 5.5 you see that the total tax paid is equal to $T \times Q_2$, or the tax per unit times the number of units sold, which is equal to the area of rectangle P_2P_3BA. The consumers' share of the tax is equal to the price rise per unit $(P_2 - P_1)$ times the number of units sold (Q_2). Thus the consumers' share is equal to the area of rectangle P_1P_2AC. The producers' share of the tax is equal to the decline in the return to producers per unit $(P_1 - P_3)$ times the number of units sold (Q_2). Thus, the producers' share is equal to the area of rectangle P_1P_3BC.

The relative size of the consumers' share of the burden and the producers' share depends upon the shape of the demand curve and the shape of the supply curve. As Figure 5.6a illustrates, when demand is relatively unresponsive to price, which means that the quantity demanded does not change very much when the price changes, consumers bear the lion's share of the burden. As Figure 5.6b illustrates, when demand is responsive to price, which means that the quantity demanded changes a lot when the price changes, quantity demanded drops off sharply, and producers bear the lion's share of the burden. The responsiveness of the quantity demanded or the quantity supplied to a price change is measured by *elasticity*, and it is to this concept that we now turn.

ELASTICITY

The Importance of Measurement

Elasticity   Responsiveness. Used to quantify the response in one variable when another variable changes. The elasticity of A with respect to B is the percentage change in A divided by the percentage change in B.

The basic principles of supply and demand enable us to make certain predictions about how households and firms are likely to behave. When the price of a good rises, for example, households are likely to purchase less of it, and firms are likely to supply more of it. When costs of production fall, firms are likely to supply more—supply will increase, or shift to the right. When the price of a good falls, households are likely to buy fewer substitutes—demand for substitutes is likely to decrease, or shift to the left.

The *size*, or *magnitude*, of these reactions can be very important. You have already seen that during the oil embargo of the early 1970s by the Organization of Petroleum Exporting Countries (OPEC), the price of crude oil increased substantially. This raised revenues to the oil producing countries, and so we might expect this strategy to work for everyone. But if the banana exporting countries, which we will call OBEC, had done the same thing, the strategy would not have worked.

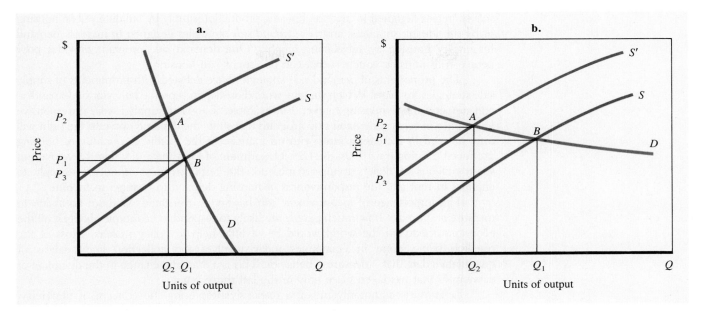

FIGURE 5.6

An Excise Tax Under Two Different Demand Conditions

In the presence of an excise tax, when demand is relatively *elastic,* consumers are able to avoid the tax by buying substitutes. As a result, producers bear the bulk of the tax burden. When demand is relatively *inelastic,* consumers do not avoid the tax by switching to substitutes, and, as a result, consumers bear most of the burden of the tax through an increase in price.

Why not? Suppose the banana exporting countries decide to cut production by 30 percent to drive up the world price. At first, when the quantity supplied declines, the quantity demanded is greater than the quantity supplied and the world price rises. The issue for OBEC is how far. Unless the percentage increase in price is greater than the percentage decrease in output, they will lose revenues. The news is not good. As the price of bananas rises, people simply eat fewer bananas and eat more pineapples or oranges. There are many reasonable substitutes for bananas. The quantity demanded declines 30 percent—to the new quantity supplied—after only a modest price rise, and OBEC fails in its mission.

The quantity of oil demanded is not nearly as responsive to a change in price as is the quantity of bananas demanded, however, because no substitutes for oil are readily available. When the price of crude oil went up in the early 1970s, 130 million motor vehicles, getting an average of 12 miles per gallon and consuming over 100 billion gallons of gasoline each year, were on the road in the United States. Millions of homes were heated with oil, and industry ran on equipment that used petroleum products. When OPEC cut production, price rose sharply. Quantity demanded fell, but nonetheless the price increased over 400 percent. What makes these two cases different is the *magnitude* of the response in the quantity demanded to a change of price.

An ability to measure and predict responsiveness is also important for formulating rational domestic policy. For example, being able to quantify responsiveness is important in many areas of public policy—designing effective housing policy, for example. Since the Housing Act of 1946, the federal government has been committed, at least on paper, to a policy of insuring that all Americans have decent homes to live in. To improve the quality of housing for the poor, the government has tried two basic strategies: (1) *supply side* strategies designed to increase housing production simply by building public housing or by subsidizing suppliers, and (2) *demand side* strategies designed to increase demand for quality housing by subsidizing tenants. One demand side program provides poor people with housing vouchers that can be "spent" on housing.

The proponents of demand side strategies have debated with proponents of supply side strategies for years. Which strategy works best depends on the behavior of demanders and suppliers in the housing market. For example, if housing supply is very unresponsive to changes in rents, a demand side program that shifts the demand curve to the right will only succeed in increasing rents with no increase in the quality or quantity of housing produced. During the 1970s, the U.S. Department of Housing and Urban Development spent millions of dollars trying to measure the responsiveness of housing supply to changes in rent and the responsiveness of housing demand to changes in income.

The importance of *measurement* can hardly be overstated. Without an ability to measure and predict how much people are likely to respond to economic changes, all the economic theory in the world would be of little help to policy makers. Most of the research being done in economics today involves the collection and analysis of quantitative data that "measures" behavior. This is a dramatic change in the discipline of economics that has taken place only in the last thirty years.

Economists commonly measure responsiveness using the concept of **elasticity**. Elasticity is a perfectly general measure that can be used to quantify many different relationships. If some variable, A, changes in response to changes in another variable, B, the elasticity of A with respect to B is equal to the percentage change in A divided by the percentage change in B, that is,

$$\text{the elasticity of } A \text{ with respect to } B = \%\Delta A / \%\Delta B.$$

We may speak of the elasticity of demand or supply with respect to price, of the elasticity of investment with respect to the interest rate, or of the elasticity of tax payments with respect to income. We begin with a discussion of price elasticity of demand.

Price Elasticity of Demand

You have already been exposed to the law of demand. As you recall, when prices rise, quantity demanded can be expected to decline, ceteris paribus, and when prices fall, quantity demanded can be expected to rise. The normal negative relationship between price and quantity demanded is reflected in the downward slope of demand curves.

Slope and Elasticity   The slope of a demand curve may in a rough way reveal the responsiveness of the quantity demanded to price changes, but slope can be quite misleading. In fact, it is not a good formal measure.

Consider the two identical demand curves in Figure 5.7. The only difference between the two is that on the left quantity demanded is measured in pounds and on the right quantity demanded is measured in ounces. When we calculate the numerical value of each slope, however, we get very different answers. The curve on the left has a slope of $-1/5$, and the curve on the right has a slope of $-1/80$, yet they represent the *exact same behavior*. If we had changed dollars to cents on the Y axis, the two slopes would be -20 and -1.25 respectively. (Review the Appendix to Chapter 1 if you don't understand how these numbers are calculated.)

Our problem is that the numerical value of the slope of a line or curve depends upon the units used to measure the variables on the axes. To correct this problem, we

FIGURE 5.7
Slope Is not a Useful Measure of
Responsiveness of Demand

Changing the unit of measure from
pounds to ounces changes the measured slope of the demand curve dramatically. But the behavior of buyers
in the two diagrams is identical. Since
it depends on the unit of measure on
both X and Y axes, slope is a poor
measure of "responsiveness."

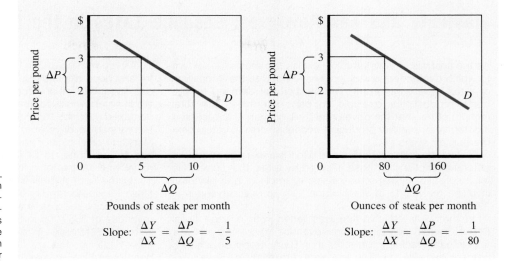

Slope: $\dfrac{\Delta Y}{\Delta X} = \dfrac{\Delta P}{\Delta Q} = -\dfrac{1}{5}$ Slope: $\dfrac{\Delta Y}{\Delta X} = \dfrac{\Delta P}{\Delta Q} = -\dfrac{1}{80}$

convert the changes in price and quantity to *percentages*. The price increase in Figure 5.7
leads to a decline of five pounds, or 80 ounces, in the quantity of steak demanded, a
decline of 50 percent from the initial 10 pounds, or 160 ounces, *whether we measure it in
pounds or ounces.*

We define

$$\text{price elasticity of demand} = \frac{\%\ \text{change in quantity demanded}}{\%\ \text{change in price}} = \frac{\%\ \Delta\ Q^d}{\%\ \Delta\ P}$$

Price elasticity of demand *The
ratio of the percentage change in
quantity demanded to the
percentage change in price.*

Price elasticity of demand, then, is simply the ratio of the percentage change in
quantity demanded to the percentage change in price. Percentage changes should always
carry the sign (plus or minus) of the change—positive changes, or increases, take a $(+)$;
negative changes, or decreases, take a $(-)$. *The law of demand implies that price elasticity
of demand is nearly always a negative number*: price increases $(+)$ will lead to decreases
in quantity demanded $(-)$, and vice versa. Thus, the numerator and denominator should
have opposite signs, resulting in a negative ratio.

Table 5.1 gives the hypothetical responses of demanders to a 10-percent price
increase in four markets. Insulin is absolutely necessary to a diabetic, and the quantity
demanded is unlikely to respond to an increase in price. If the quantity demanded does
not respond at all, the percent change in quantity demanded is zero, and the elasticity is
zero. Thus we say that the demand for insulin is **perfectly inelastic**. Basic telephone
service, however, is generally considered a necessity, but not an absolute necessity. If a
10-percent increase in telephone rates results in a one-percent decline in the quantity of
service demanded, demand elasticity is $-.1$. If the percentage change in quantity

TABLE 5.1
Hypothetical Demand Elasticities
for Four Products

Product	% Δ price	% Δ quantity demanded	Elasticity	
Insulin	+ 10%	0%	0	Perfectly inelastic
Basic telephone service	+ 10%	− 1%	−.1	Inelastic
Beef	+ 10%	− 10%	−1.0	Unitary elastic
Bananas	+ 10%	− 30%	−3.0	Elastic

Elasticity and Tax Revenues: Gasoline Taxes in the Nation's Capital

As the analysis of a hypothetical excise tax shows, the extent to which demanders and suppliers respond to the imposition of a tax is very important. The elasticity of demand for the taxed product, for example, in part determines the total amount of tax that the government will ultimately collect, and it determines whether producers or consumers ultimately bear the burden of the tax.

Unless tax administrators and fiscal planners consider the potential reactions of those affected by a tax, they may be in for a surprise. Perhaps the classic example of bad planning involved the efforts of Washington, DC, to raise revenues in 1980.

In that year, Washington was faced with a huge fiscal deficit. The city needed to raise revenues quickly. As part of a tax-increase package, Mayor Marion Barry proposed a new 6 percent gasoline tax. The tax went into effect on August 6, 1980. It was imposed on top of an existing 10-cents-per-gallon tax, and it had the effect of raising the price of gasoline about 8 additional cents per gallon.

This was the second highest local gasoline tax in the nation (second to Chicago). It pushed the price of unleaded gasoline in the District to $1.32–$1.35 per gallon, while in Maryland the same gasoline sold for $1.25. While city officials predicted some drop in sales, they expected to raise a substantial amount of revenue with the tax.

As you will see later in the chapter, the elasticity of demand for any good depends upon the ease with which consumers can substitute other goods for the taxed good. Anybody in Washington who lived near a border had an easily accessible, nontaxed, perfect substitute available for DC gasoline; they merely had to drive across the border and buy their gas in Maryland or Virginia. Those who commuted into the city only had to remember to fill up before they came to town. The result was catastrophic for the district.

By the end of the first month, gasoline sales in DC had fallen 27.5 percent! Since the tax raised prices by 6 percent, the elasticity of demand was over 4.0. The city had predicted revenues of $960,000 in the first month, but actual revenues were just $750,000. While data are hard to come by, one survey claims that by October sales had dropped by 40 percent and 242 workers had been laid off by gasoline stations in the District. While no hard data exist on the number of gasoline stations that closed as a result, it is clear that some did.

On Monday, November 24, Mayor Barry admitted defeat, and the tax was officially lifted on December 1 of the same year.

The story of the District's gasoline tax is extreme, but it highlights problems that governments have in trying to forecast the amount of revenue that they will collect.

demanded is smaller in absolute size than the percentage change in price, then elasticity is less than one in absolute size. Thus we say that the demand for basic telephone service is *inelastic*[4].

To be precise, *demand is inelastic if it has an elasticity between zero and minus one*. But you must be very careful about signs. Because it is generally understood that demand elasticities are negative, they are often reported and discussed without the negative sign. For example, a technical paper might report that the price elasticity of demand for housing "appears to be inelastic, or less than one (.6)." What the writer means is that the estimated elasticity is −.6, which is between zero and minus one.

To return to Table 5.1, those who demand beef can find substitutes, but they are not perfect substitutes. If a 10-percent increase in beef prices drives down the quantity of beef demanded by 10 percent, demand elasticity is −1. We say that the demand for beef has a **unitary elasticity**. If the decrease in quantity demanded turns out to be larger than the increase in price in absolute size, we say that demand is **elastic**. The demand for bananas, for example, is likely to be quite elastic. If a 10-percent increase in price leads to a 30-percent decrease in quantity demanded, elasticity is −3.0.

Calculating Elasticities   Calculating elasticities from numerical data must be done cautiously. Consider the demand schedule in Table 5.2 and the demand curve in Figure 5.8. Herb works about 20 days per month in a downtown San Francisco office tower. On

Elastic; unitary elasticity
Elastic *describes a demand relationship in which the percentage change in quantity demanded is larger in absolute value than the percentage change in price.* Unitary elasticity *describes a demand relationship in which the percentage change in quantity of a product demanded is the same as the percentage change in price (a demand elasticity of -1).*

[4]Note that the term "absolute size" or "absolute value" means ignoring the sign. The absolute value of −4 is 4; the absolute value of −3.8 is greater than the absolute value of 2.

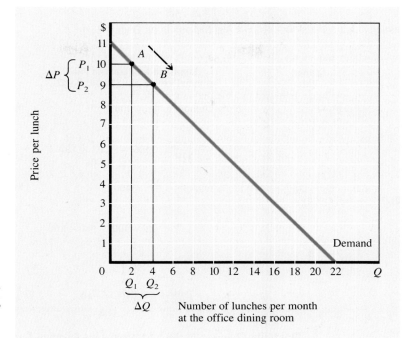

FIGURE 5.8

Demand for Lunch at the Office Dining Room

To calculate elasticity, the first step is to convert the changes ΔQ and ΔP into percentage changes.

TABLE 5.2

Demand Schedule for Office Lunches

Price (per lunch)	Quantity demanded (lunches per month)
$11.00	0
10.00	2
9.00	4
8.00	6
7.00	8
6.00	10
5.00	12
4.00	14
3.00	16
2.00	18
1.00	20
0	22

the top floor of the building is a beautiful dining room; on the street is a hot dog stand where an edible lunch costs $2.00. If lunch in the dining room costs $10.00, Herb would only eat there twice a month. If the price of a lunch fell to $9.00, however, he would eat there twice as often, or four times a month. Figure 5.8 calculates Herb's demand elasticity between points A and B on his demand curve.

Demand elasticity calculated between two points on a demand curve is called *arc elasticity*. As you will shortly see, elasticity is actually different at every *point* along a demand curve. Elasticity calculated at a given point is called *point elasticity* (see the Appendix to this chapter). The first step in calculating an arc elasticity is to turn the changes in price and quantity into percentage changes. When the price of Herb's lunch, for example, falls from $10.00 to $9.00, the change in price is −$1.00. When quantity demanded increases from two to four, the change in quantity demanded is +2 lunches per month. But these are not percentage changes.

To convert the change in price of −$1.00 to a percentage, we must decide on a *base*. Often the initial value serves as the base for the calculation. The initial price was $10.00, and so $1.00 (the change) is one tenth, or 10 percent, of that base. Thus price has fallen 10 percent. Using the initial quantity of 2 lunches demanded as the base, a change of 2 lunches (up from 2 to 4) is an increase of 100 percent. Finally, the price of Herb's lunch *fell* by 10 percent, so the percentage change is −10; quantity demanded *increased* by 100 percent so the percentage change is +100. Elasticity, that is, the ratio of the percentage change in quantity to the percentage change in price, between points A and B is +100/−10 or −10.

A preferred alternative base for calculating percentage changes is the arc midpoint. The midpoint of the arc between A and B is $9.50 and 3 lunches [$(P_2 + P_1)/2 = \$9.50$ and $(Q_2 + Q_1)/2 = 3$ lunches]. The change in quantity (2 lunches) is 2/3, or 66.7%, of the new base quantity; the change in price (−$1) is 1/9.50 = .105 or 10.5% of the new base. If we take the arc midpoint as a basis for calculation, elasticity is −6.4 (see the calculations in Table 5.3).

TABLE 5.3
Calculating Arc Elasticity Using Initial Values and Arc Midpoints as Base

	Change (Δ)	Expressed as a fraction (%) of initial values (P_1=$10.00, Q_1=2)	Expressed as a fraction (%) of arc midpoint (P=$9.50, Q=3)
Change in price (P)	$\Delta P = (P_2 - P_1)$ $= (9 - 10) = -\$1.00$	% change $= \frac{\Delta P}{P_1} \times 100$	% change $= \frac{\Delta P}{(P_2 + P_1)/2} \times 100 =$
		$= \frac{-\$1.00}{\$10} \times 100 = -.10 \times 100$ $= -10\%$	$\frac{-\$1.00}{(10+9)/2} \times 100 = \frac{-\$1.00}{\$9.50} \times 100$ $= -10.5\%$
Change in quantity demanded (Q)	$\Delta Q = (Q_2 - Q_1)$ $= (4 - 2) = +2$	% change $= \frac{\Delta Q}{Q_1} \times 100$	% change $= \frac{\Delta Q}{(Q_1 + Q_2)/2} \times 100$
		$= \frac{+2}{2} \times 100 = +1 \times 100$	$= \frac{+2}{(4+2)/2} \times 100$
		$= +100\%$	$= +66.7\%$
Elasticity		$\frac{\%\Delta Q}{\%\Delta P} = \frac{+100\%}{-10\%} = -10$	$\frac{\%\Delta Q}{\%\Delta P} = \frac{+66.7\%}{-10.5\%} = -6.4$

Elasticity Changes Along a Straight-Line Demand Curve   An interesting and important point is that elasticity actually changes from point to point and arc to arc along a demand curve even if the slope of that demand curve does not change—that is, even along a straight-line demand curve. Indeed, the differences can be quite large.

Returning to Herb's lunch, at a price of $3.00, he eats in the office dining room 16 times per month; if price drops to $2.00, he eats there 18 times per month (see Figure 5.9). These changes expressed in numerical terms are exactly the same as the price and quantity changes between points A and B in Figure 5.8—price falls $1.00, and quantity demanded increases by 2 meals. Expressed in percentage terms, however, these changes are very different.

Using the arc midpoints as the base, the $1.00 price decline is only a 10.5% reduction when price is up around $9.50. The same $1.00 price decline is a 40-percent reduction when price is down around $2.50. The two-meal increase in quantity demanded is a 66.7% increase when Herb averages only two and a half meals per month, but it is only an 11.8% increase when he averages 17 meals per month. The elasticity of demand between points C and D is thus 11.8% divided by −40 percent, or −.295 (see the calculations in Table 5.4).

The percentage changes between A and B are very different from those between C and D, and so are the elasticities. Herb's demand is quite elastic (−6.4) between points A and B; a 10.5% reduction in price caused a 66.7% increase in quantity. But his demand is inelastic (−.295) between points C and D; a 40-percent decrease in price caused only an 11.8% increase in quantity. (This whole point is developed more formally in the appendix to this chapter.)

Elasticity and Total Revenue   You have seen that OPEC was successful in the early 1970s in increasing its flow of revenues by restricting supply and pushing up the market price of crude oil. On the other hand, we argued that a similar strategy by OBEC, the Organization of Banana Exporting Countries, would likely fail. The reason that OBEC was likely to fail while OPEC succeeded, we said, was that demand for oil is inelastic, while the demand for bananas is not.

FIGURE 5.9

Demand for Lunch at the Office
Dining Room

Between *A* and *B*, demand is *elastic*; a
$1.00 decrease in price is a small
percentage change and a two meal
increase in quantity is a large *percentage* change. Between *C* and *D*, demand is *inelastic*; the same $1.00 decrease in price is a large percentage
change, and the same two meal increase in quantity is a small percentage change.

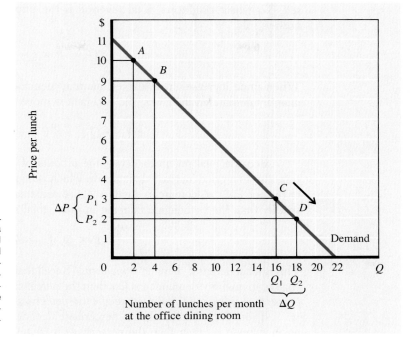

Number of lunches per month
at the office dining room

TABLE 5.4

Calculating Arc Elasticity Using
Arc Midpoint as Base

	Change (Δ)	Expressed as a fraction (%) of arc midpoint ($P = \$2.50$, $Q = 17$)
Change in price (P)	$\Delta P = (P_2 - P_1)$	% change $= \dfrac{\Delta P}{(P_2 + P_1)/2} \times 100$
	$= (2 - 3) = -\$1.00$	$= \dfrac{-\$1.00}{(2 + 3)/2} \times 100 = -\dfrac{\$1.00}{\$2.50} \times 100$
		$= -40\%$
Change in quantity demanded (Q)	$\Delta Q = (Q_2 - Q_1)$	% change $= \dfrac{\Delta Q}{(Q_2 + Q_1)/2} \times 100$
	$= (18 - 16) = +2$	$= \dfrac{+2}{(18 + 16)/2} \times 100 = \dfrac{+2}{17} \times 100$
		$= +11.8\%$
Elasticity		$\dfrac{\%\Delta Q}{\%\Delta P} = \dfrac{+11.8\%}{-40\%} = -.295$

We can now use the more formal definition of elasticity to make the argument
more precise. We begin by simplifying the story. Let's assume that there is only one
producer in a market, and that that producer is free to *set* his price, subject to the
limitations of market demand. That is, once the price is set, people can buy all they want.

In any market, $P \times Q$ is total revenue (*TR*) received by producers. OPEC's total
revenue is the price per barrel of oil times the number of barrels its participant countries

sell. To wheat producers, total revenue is the price per bushel times the number of bushels sold:

$$TR = P \times Q.$$

When price increases in a market, quantity demanded declines. When price declines, quantity demanded increases; the two factors move in opposite directions:

$$P \uparrow \; \rightarrow Q \downarrow \; \text{and} \; P \downarrow \; \rightarrow Q \uparrow.$$

Because total revenue (TR) is the *product* of P and Q, whether it rises or falls in response to a price increase depends on which is bigger, the percentage increase in price or the percentage decrease in quantity. If the percentage decrease in quantity demanded is *smaller* than the percentage increase in price, total revenue will *rise*:

$$\uparrow \; P \times Q \downarrow \; = TR \uparrow.$$

This is what occurs if demand is *inelastic*. (Recall that *inelastic* means that the percentage change in quantity demanded is *less* than the percentage change in price.) In this case, the percentage price rise simply outweighs the percentage quantity decline, and $P \times Q$ rises.

If, on the other hand, the percentage decline in quantity demanded following a price increase is *larger* than the percentage increase in price, total revenue will *fall*:

$$\uparrow P \times Q \downarrow \; = TR \downarrow.$$

This occurs if demand is *elastic*. (*Elastic* means that the percentage change in quantity demanded is *greater* than the percentage change in price.) The percentage price increase is outweighed by the percentage quantity decline.

The opposite is true for a price *cut*. If demand is *elastic*, a cut in price *increases* total revenues:

$$\downarrow P \times Q \uparrow \; = TR \uparrow.$$

and if demand is *inelastic*, a cut in price *reduces* total revenues:

$$\downarrow \; P \times Q \uparrow \; = TR \downarrow.$$

(Review the logic of these equations to make sure you understand the reasoning thoroughly. Table 5.5 also summarizes the relationship between total revenue and elasticity.)

The Determinants of Demand Elasticity   Elasticity of demand is a way of measuring quantitatively the responsiveness of consumers' demand to changes in price. As a measure of behavior, it can be applied to individual households or to market demand as a whole. I love peaches and I would hate to give them up. My demand for peaches is therefore inelastic. But not everyone is crazy about peaches, and, in fact, their market demand is relatively elastic. Because no two people have exactly the same preferences, reactions to price changes will be different for different people, and this makes generalizations hazardous. Nonetheless, a few principles do seem to hold.

TABLE 5.5
Changes in Total Revenues in
Response to Price Change
Note: Total revenue equals
P × Q.

	VALUE OF E_D*			
	Elasticity ($E_D>1$)	Unitary elasticity ($E_D=1$)	Inelasticity ($1>E_D>0$)	Perfect inelasticity $E_D=0$
	$\frac{\Delta Q}{Q} > \frac{\Delta P}{P}$	$\frac{\Delta Q}{Q} = \frac{\Delta P}{P}$	$\frac{\Delta Q}{Q} < \frac{\Delta P}{P}$	$\Delta Q=0$
Effect of a fall in P on revenue ($P \times Q$)	Increase	Constant	Decrease	Fall in ($P \times Q$) is proportional to fall in P
Effect of a rise in P on revenue ($P \times Q$)	Decrease	Constant	Increase	Rise in ($P \times Q$) is proportional to rise in P

*Where E_D = absolute value of demand elasticity.

AVAILABILITY OF SUBSTITUTES   Perhaps the most obvious circumstance that affects demand elasticity is the availability of substitutes. When substitute products are easy to obtain, the quantity demanded is likely to respond quite readily to changes in price. Consider a number of farm stands lined up along a country road. If every stand sells fresh corn of roughly the same quality, Mom's Green Thumb will find it very difficult to charge a price much higher than the competition charges; a nearly perfect substitute is available just down the road. The quantity of Mom's corn demanded is thus likely to be very elastic: an increase in price will lead to a rapid decline in the quantity demanded of Mom's corn.

When substitutes are not readily available, demand is likely to be less elastic. In Table 5.1, we considered two products that have no readily available substitutes, local telephone service and insulin for diabetics, and there are many others. Demand for these products is likely to be quite inelastic.

THE IMPORTANCE OF BEING UNIMPORTANT   When an item represents a relatively small part of our total budget, we probably pay little attention to its price. For example, if I pick up a pack of mints once in a while when I go to the supermarket and simply add it on to my total purchases, I might not even notice an increase in price from $.25 to $.35, yet that is a 40-percent increase in price. In cases such as these, we are not likely to respond very much to changes in price, and demand is likely to be inelastic.

THE TIME DIMENSION   When oil-producing nations cut output and succeeded in pushing up the price of crude oil in the early 1970s, few substitutes were immediately available. Demand was relatively inelastic, and prices rose substantially. During the last fifteen years, however, we have had time to adjust our behavior in response to the higher price, and the quantity demanded has fallen dramatically. Automobiles manufactured today get more miles per gallon, and some drivers have cut down on their driving. Millions have insulated their homes, most have turned down their thermostats, and some have explored alternative energy sources such as solar and wind. We have all become more energy conscious.

All this illustrates a very important point. The elasticity of demand in the short run may be very different from the elasticity of demand in the long run. In the longer run, demand is likely to become *more* elastic, or responsive, simply because households make adjustments over time and producers develop substitute goods.

Other Important Elasticities

So far we have been discussing price elasticity of demand, which measures the responsiveness of quantity demanded to changes in price. Elasticity, however, is a perfectly general concept. If A causes a change in B and we can measure the change in both, we can calculate the elasticity of A with respect to B. Let us look briefly at three other important types of elasticity: (1) income elasticity of demand, (2) cross-price elasticity, and (3) elasticity of supply.

Income elasticity of demand
Measures the responsiveness of quantity demanded to a change in income.

Income Elasticity of Demand   **Income elasticity of demand**, which measures the responsiveness of demand to income, is defined as

$$\text{income elasticity of demand} = \frac{\% \text{ change in quantity demanded}}{\% \text{ change in income}} = \frac{\% \, \Delta \, Q^d}{\% \, \Delta \, I}.$$

Calculating and measuring income elasticities is important for many reasons. We have already mentioned the time and money that housing policy makers spent during the 1970s weighing the relative merits of different policies that could improve the quality of housing in the United States. One alternative to subsidizing housing production was to give poor people added income or housing vouchers that they could use to buy housing. This "income strategy" would work to improve housing quality only if people actually spent much of the added income on housing. If the income elasticity of demand for housing were very low, however, the strategy would fail.

During the 1970s, the Department of Housing and Urban Development conducted a huge experiment in four cities. In the "housing allowance demand experiment," low-income families received housing vouchers over an extended period of time, and researchers watched their housing consumption for several years. HUD spent over $300 million to estimate the income elasticity of housing demand. Most estimates, including the ones from the HUD study, put the income elasticity of housing demand between .5 and .8. That is, a 10-percent increase in income can be expected to raise a household's housing demand by between five and eight percent.

Normal goods   *Goods for which income elasticity is positive.*

As you recall from Chapter 4, for **normal goods** consumption rises as income increases. Now we can say more formally that for normal goods, income elasticity is *positive*. Because an increase in income leads to an increase in demand and a decrease in income leads to a decrease in demand, both numerator and denominator have the same sign. For **inferior goods**, income elasticity is *negative*. Because an increase in income leads to a decrease in demand and a decrease in income leads to an increase in demand, the numerator and denominator have opposite signs. For a third category of goods, **luxury goods**, income elasticity is *positive and greater than one*—that is, demand goes up *faster* than income as income rises, and the percentage change in demand is larger than the percentage change in income.

Inferior goods   *Goods for which income elasticity is negative.*

Luxury goods   *Goods for which income elasticity is positive and greater than one.*

Cross-price elasticity of demand
A measure of the response in demand for one good to a change in the price of another good.

Cross-Price Elasticity of Demand   **Cross-price elasticity of demand**, which measures the response of quantity of one good demanded to a change in the price of another, is defined as

$$\text{cross-price elasticity of demand} = \frac{\% \text{ change in quantity of } Y \text{ demanded}}{\% \text{ change in price of } X} = \frac{\% \Delta Q_Y^d}{\% \Delta P_X}.$$

Like income elasticity, cross-price elasticity can be either positive or negative. If it turns out to be *positive*, it says that an increase in the price of X causes the demand for Y

Measuring Elasticity: Can Public Policy Change Behavior?

As we pointed out from the very beginning there are circumstances when government is called upon to intervene in free markets. One such circumstance is when the choices made by consumers or producers inflict harm on other members of society. These third party effects are called "externalities," and for the economy to function efficiently, decision makers should have an incentive to consider them.

Clearly, cigarette smoking is an activity that has external effects. Smoke annoys nonsmokers, and it may be hazardous to their health. In addition, even if the health damage is confined to the smoking population, health insurance premiums and Medicaid and Medicare costs borne by nonsmoking taxpayers are higher because of smoking.

The government has relied primarily on direct regulation and education to discourage smoking. In 1964 the U.S. Surgeon General declared that smoking causes lung cancer, heart disease, and other respiratory illnesses. Cigarette packages began carrying health warnings, ads were pulled from radio and TV, and states and cities began passing laws restricting smoking in businesses and restaurants. In April 1986 smoking was linked to cancer and respiratory disease in *nonsmokers*. In April 1988 smoking was banned on all airline flights of under two hours.

There is another approach used by federal, state, and local governments that impose excise taxes on cigarettes, and by the Senate Finance Committee which voted in favor of doubling the federal excise tax on a pack of cigarettes to 32 cents in 1988.

What are the effects of such an increase likely to be? How much of the proposed increase will be passed on to consumers of cigarettes in higher cigarette prices? How much will smoking decline as a result? As you now know, the answer depends on the price elasticity of demand for cigarettes. Only if demand is perfectly inelastic will each 1 cent of tax mean a 1 cent increase in cigarette prices. Also, the higher the absolute value of the elasticity of demand, the larger the impact on cigarette smoking.

A recent study done at the National Bureau of Economic Research* estimates these elasticities by looking at smoking behavior across states where smokers face different cigarette prices. The study, which was done when the Government was contemplating raising the tax to 16 cents in 1981, reached the following conclusion:

> In this paper, we have attempted to assess the potential for using excise taxes to reduce smoking by measuring the price elasticity of demand for cigarettes. Excise tax increases will discourage smoking to the extent that excise tax increases are passed on to smokers in the form of higher retail cigarette prices . . .
>
> Our empirical results have indicated (1) that the price elasticity of demand for cigarettes is −.42; (2) that price impacts cigarette demand primarily by affecting the decision to begin smoking regularly among members of the population less than 25 years; and (3) that price effects are much larger for males than females —in fact our estimates show a price elasticity near zero for females over 20 years old.
>
> The results have implications for any future Federal government attempts to influence cigarette demand through excise tax policy. The short-run impact of an excise tax increase would be small. For example, if the federal excise tax was doubled to 16 cents a pack, and if the tax increase was completely passed on to the consumer, then the average retail price would increase by about 13% (using the average 1979 average retail price as a reference). Accordingly, applying our estimated price elasticity of -.42, cigarette consumption would fall by about 5.5%. The fall-off in demand would result from approximately a 3.9% decline in smoking participation and a 1.3% decline in the quantity of cigarettes smoked by smokers. In the long run, however, the impact of such a tax increase would be much more substantial.

Sources: " 'No Smoking' Sweeps America," *Business Week*, July 27, 1987; and "Where Cigarettes and Spirits Are Still Booming," *Business Week*, September 14, 1987.

*Quote from Eugene M. Lewit and Douglas Coate, "The Potential for Using Excise Taxes to Reduce Smoking," National Bureau of Economic Research, September 1981.

Substitutes *Goods for which an increase in the price of one increases the demand for the other.*

Complements *Goods for which an increase in the price of one decreases the demand for the other.*

Elasticity of supply *A measure of the response of quantity of a good supplied to a change in price of that good. Likely to be positive in output markets.*

to rise. That implies that the goods are **substitutes**. If it turns out to be *negative*, an increase in the price of X causes a decrease in the demand for Y. That implies that the goods are **complements**.

Elasticity of Supply **Elasticity of supply**, which measures the response of quantity supplied to a change in price, is defined as

$$\text{elasticity of supply} = \frac{\%\text{ change in quantity supplied}}{\%\text{ change in price}} = \frac{\%\Delta Q^S}{\%\Delta P}.$$

Elasticity of labor supply A *measure of the response of labor supplied to a change in the price of labor. Can be positive or negative.*

In output markets, the elasticity of supply is likely to be a positive number—that is, a higher price leads to an increase in the quantity supplied, ceteris paribus. (As you recall, we have been looking at upward-sloping supply curves in the last two chapters.)

In input markets, however, some interesting problems crop up. Perhaps the most studied elasticity of all is the **elasticity of labor supply**. Economists have examined household labor supply responses to welfare programs, the social security system, the income tax system, need-based student aid, and unemployment insurance, among others. A recent book by Mark Killingsworth synthesizes literally dozens of empirical studies of labor supply behavior.[5]

In simple terms, the elasticity of labor supply is defined as

$$\text{elasticity of labor supply} = \frac{\%\text{ change in quantity of labor supplied}}{\%\text{ change in the wage rate}} = \frac{\%\Delta L^S}{\%\Delta W}.$$

It seems reasonable at first glance to assume that an increase in wages increases the quantity of labor supplied. That would imply an upward-sloping supply curve and a *positive* labor supply elasticity. But this is not necessarily so. An increase in wages makes workers better off: they can work the same amount and have higher incomes. One of the things that they might like to "buy" with that higher income is more *leisure time.* "Buying" leisure simply means working fewer hours, and the "price" of leisure is the lost wages. Thus it is quite possible that an *increase* in wages to some groups will lead to a *reduction* in the quantity of labor supplied. If this happens, the labor supply curve will have a negative slope—that is, it will bend back at some point.

LOOKING AHEAD

We have now examined the basic forces of supply and demand, as well as the nature of a market system. We will use the important concept of elasticity time and time again as we continue our investigation of microeconomics. Behind everything that we have observed so far lies the behavior of individual households and firms. The next several chapters explore the factors that influence their behavior more fully.

We begin with households in Chapter 6. Households demand final goods and services in output markets and supply factors of production in input markets. In Chapters 7, 8, and 9, we turn our attention to the behavior of firms.

SUMMARY

1. The price system performs two important functions for society. It determines who gets the goods and how resources are allocated to produce the goods.
2. Governments, as well as private firms, often decide not to use the market system for rationing an item for which there is an excess demand at current prices. If price is not allowed to rise to equilibrium, other mechanisms must be

found. Examples include queuing, favored customers, ration coupons, and lotteries.
3. The most common rationale for policies or practices designed to avoid price rationing is the concept of "fairness."
4. Attempts to bypass the market and use alternative rationing devices are much more difficult and costly than it

---

[5]Mark Killingsworth, *Labor Supply*, Cambridge Surveys of Economic Literature Series (New York, London, and Sydney: Cambridge University Press, 1983).

would seem at first glance. Schemes that open up opportunities for favored customers, black markets, and side payments often end up less "fair" than the free market.

5. The basic logic of supply and demand is a powerful tool of analysis. For example, supply and demand analysis shows that the response of households and firms to the imposition of a simple excise tax can shift its actual burden off those who are required by law to pay it.

6. The final distribution of the burden of an excise tax depends on the elasticity of supply and the elasticity of demand for the good on which it is imposed.

7. The importance of measuring the actual size of behavioral responses, for prediction and for policy design, cannot be overstated. Most of the research being done in economics today involves the collection and analysis of quantitative data and the "measurement" of behavior.

8. Elasticity is a perfectly general measure that can be used to quantify many different relationships. If one variable, A, changes in response to changes in another variable, B, the elasticity of A with respect to B is equal to the percentage change in A divided by the percentage change in B.

9. The slope of a demand curve is an inadequate measure of responsiveness, because its value depends on the units of measurement used.

10. Elasticity changes from point to point along a straight-line demand curve.

11. If demand is elastic, a price increase will reduce the quantity demanded by a larger percentage than the percentage increase in price, and total revenue ($P \times Q$) will fall. If demand is inelastic, a price increase will increase revenue.

12. Demand elasticity depends on (1) the availability of substitutes, (2) the importance of the item in individual budgets, and (3) the time frame in question.

13. Other important elasticities are income elasticity of demand, cross-price elasticity of demand, and elasticity of supply.

REVIEW CONCEPTS

REVIEW QUESTIONS

1. For the past ten years the price of natural gas sold in interstate commerce has been regulated by the federal government. In 1983 the regulated price was thought to be substantially below equilibrium. For several years the Congress debated those regulations.
   a. If prices had been held at their 1983 levels for a long time, how would we have known that they were not at an equilibrium? What evidence would you have looked for?
   b. Illustrate the situation with supply and demand curves.
   c. Those in favor of deregulation argued that deregulation would increase the supply of natural gas. Those in favor of maintaining the regulations argued that the supply of natural gas is very inelastic. If supply is very inelastic, and thus will not respond to high prices, what will happen if price is deregulated?

2. Taxicab fares in most cities are regulated. In Boston several years ago, taxicab drivers obtained permission to raise their fares 10 percent, and they anticipated that revenues would increase by about 10 percent as a result. They were disappointed, however. When the commissioner granted the 10 percent increase, revenues increased by only about 5 percent.
   a. What can you infer about the elasticity of demand for taxicab rides? What were taxicab drivers assuming about the elasticity of demand?

3. The freeze which destroyed a good portion of the South American coffee crop in the mid-1970s increased the price of tea. Explain, using supply and demand diagrams.
4. Several members of a college faculty were standing in a rather long line at the student cafeteria. One was heard to remark that she wished the cafeteria would increase prices. Can you explain why?
5. Review the section on incidence of an excise tax in the short run.

Notice that the imposition of an excise tax is borne in part by consumers of the product, in the form of higher prices, and in part by producers of the product. Suppose that the lower price received by producers led to lower profits, and as a consequence a number of the firms in the industry went out of business in the longer run. Explain who would bear the burden of the tax in the longer run, using diagrams.

APPENDIX TO CHAPTER 5
Point Elasticity

Two different arc elasticities were calculated along the demand curve in Figure 5.9. Between points A and B we discovered that Herb's demand for lunches in the fancy dining room was very elastic: a price decline of only 10.5% resulted in his eating 66.7% more lunches in the dining room (elasticity = -6.4). Between points C and D, however, on the same demand curve, we discovered that his demand for meals was very inelastic: a price decline of 40 percent resulted in only a modest increase in lunches consumed of 11.8% (elasticity = $-.295$).

Now consider the straight-line demand curve in Figure 5A.1. We can write an expression for elasticity at point C as follows:

$$\text{elasticity} = \frac{\%\Delta Q}{\%\Delta P} = \frac{\frac{\Delta Q}{Q}\cdot 100}{\frac{\Delta P}{P}\cdot 100} = \frac{\frac{\Delta Q}{Q_1}}{\frac{\Delta P}{P_1}} = \frac{\Delta Q}{\Delta P}\cdot\frac{P_1}{Q_1}$$

$\Delta Q/\Delta P$ is the *reciprocal* of the slope of the curve. Slope in the diagram is constant along the curve, and it is negative. To calculate slope, we take *minus* the length of line segment CQ_1 divided by Q_1B or M_1. Thus

$$\frac{\Delta Q}{\Delta P} = \frac{M_1}{CQ_1}.$$

But the length of CQ_1 is equal to P_1. Thus

$$\frac{\Delta Q}{\Delta P} = \frac{M_1}{P_1}.$$

Substituting, we get

$$\text{elasticity} = \frac{M_1}{P_1}\cdot\frac{P_1}{Q_1} = \frac{M_1}{P_1}\cdot\frac{P_1}{M_2} = \frac{M_1}{M_2}.$$

Elasticity at point C is simply the ratio of line segment M_1 to line segment M_2. It is easy to see that if we had chosen a point to the left of Q_1, M_1 would have been larger and M_2 would have been smaller, indicating a higher elasticity. If we had chosen a point to the right of Q_1, M_1 would have been smaller and M_2 would have been larger, indicating a lower elasticity.

In Figure 5A.2, you can see that elasticity is unitary (equal to -1) at the midpoint of the demand curve, Q_3. At points to the right, such as Q_2, segment Q_2C (M_1 from

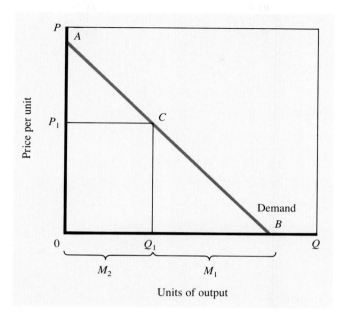

FIGURE 5A.1
Elasticity at a Point Along a
Demand Curve

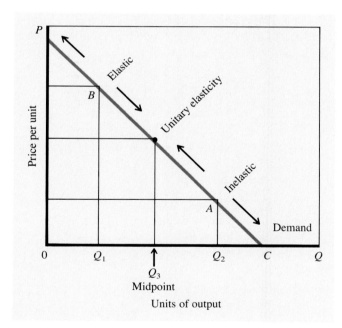

FIGURE 5A.2
Point Elasticity Changes Along a
Demand Curve

Figure 5A.1) is smaller than segment $0Q_2$ (M_2 from Figure 5A.1). This means that the absolute size of the ratio is *less than one*, and demand is *inelastic* at point A. At points to the left, such as Q_1, segment Q_1C (M_1) is larger than segment $0Q_1$ (M_2). This means that the absolute size of the ratio is *greater than one*, and demand is elastic at point B.

Compare the results here with the results of the arc elasticities calculated for Herb in Tables 5.3 and 5.4.

II MICROECONOMICS

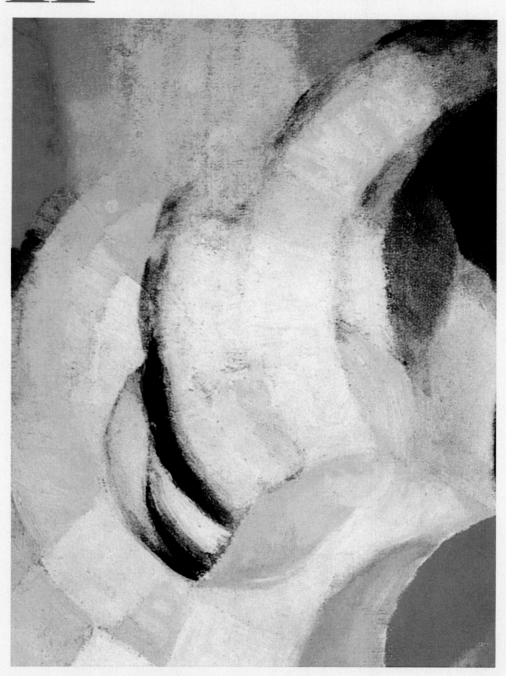

6 Household Behavior and Consumer Choice

Now that we have discussed the basic forces of supply and demand, we can go behind the supply and demand curves and explore the underlying behavior of the two fundamental economic decision-making units, households and firms. This chapter deals with households and the choices they make in both output markets and input markets. Chapters 7 through 10 take up the behavior of firms.

Every household must decide how to allocate limited incomes across a great variety of goods and services—how much of each output to demand. But output demand is just one of several decisions that households must make simultaneously. Income constrains, or limits, the choices a household can make in the market, but that very income depends in part upon other choices that the household makes. Everyone in the household must decide, for example, whether to work and, if so, how much to work. A household may also opt not to spend all of its income but to save some of it.

Every household must make three basic decisions (see Figure 6.1):

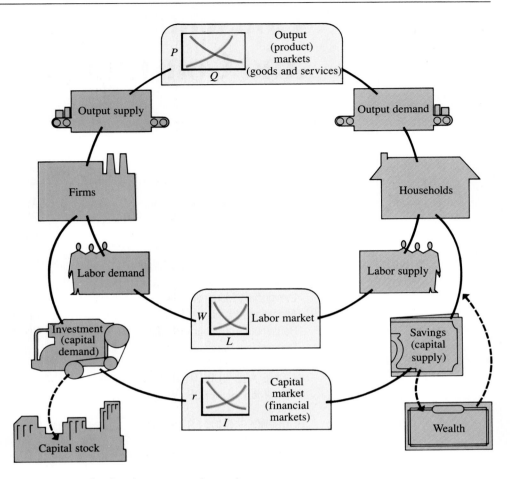

FIGURE 6.1
Firm and Household Decisions

Households demand in output markets and supply labor and capital in input markets

1. How much of each output to demand
2. How much labor to supply
3. How much to spend today, and how much to save for the future

We assume that choice in each of these areas is constrained, or limited, by factors over which households have no control. Looking carefully at the constraints within which households operate can tell us a great deal about the process of household decision making, and therefore the chapter begins by analyzing these constraints. Later we explore the nature of the decision-making process itself. In other words, given our assumption of **constrained choice**, how do people go about selecting from the large number of goods and services that are available to them?

Before we proceed with the discussion of household choice, we need to make yet a few more assumptions. Our basic assumption as we begin to model the behavior of households and firms in chapters 6 through 10 is that *all markets are* **perfectly competitive markets** even though, in fact, many markets are not. In a perfectly competitive market system, both households and firms are considered "price takers" in input and output markets. In other words, no single household or single firm is large enough or powerful enough to influence market price. For our purposes here, we shall assume price to be determined *only* by the interaction of many firms supplying and many households demanding in each market, even though reality is more complicated.

Perfect competition   An *industry structure (or market organization) in which there are many firms, each small relative to the industry, producing virtually identical products and in which no firm has any control over prices but takes price as given. In perfectly competitive industries, new competitors can freely enter and exit the market.*

We also assume that households possess all the information they need to make market choices. Specifically, we assume a knowledge of the qualities and prices of everything available and a knowledge of wage rates. This is often referred to as the assumption of **perfect knowledge**.

In the next five chapters, then, we discuss competitive markets under a set of fairly restrictive assumptions. What we are building is a complete model of a simple competitive economy. In subsequent chapters, we will relax these assumptions one by one and change the model to reflect different aspects of the real world.

BEHIND THE DEMAND CURVE: HOUSEHOLD CHOICE IN OUTPUT MARKETS

Households make economic choices in three arenas: output, labor, and capital markets (see Figure 6.1). As we begin our fairly lengthy look at demand in output markets, you must remember that the choices underlying the demand curve are only part of the larger household choice problem. Closely related decisions about how much to work and how much to save are equally important and must, in a sense, be made simultaneously.

The Determinants of Demand

As we saw in Chapter 4, several factors are likely to influence household demand in a market:

> The price of the product
>
> The income[1] available to the household
>
> The amount of accumulated wealth[1] of the household
>
> The prices of other products available to the household
>
> The tastes and preferences of the household
>
> Expectations about future income, wealth, and prices

Demand schedules and demand curves express the relationship between quantity demanded and price, *ceteris paribus*; changes in income, in other prices, or in preferences *shift* demand curves to the left or right. But the interrelationship among these variables is more complex than the simple exposition in Chapter 4 might lead you to believe.

The Idea of Constrained Choice

Before we examine the choice process itself, we need to discuss exactly what choices are open or not open to households. If you look carefully at the six factors that influence demand, you will see that the first four actually *define* the set of options available. In other

---

[1]Remember that we drew the distinction between income and wealth in Chapter 4. *Income* is the sum of a household's earnings *within* a given period: it is a *flow* variable. *Wealth*, on the other hand, is a *stock* variable: briefly it is what a household owns minus what it owes *at* a given point in time.

words, information on a household's income and wealth and on product prices makes it possible to distinguish those combinations of goods and services that are affordable from those that are not.

Budget constraint   *The limits imposed on household choices by income, wealth, and product prices. A line which separates those bundles of goods that are available to a household from those that are not.*

Income, wealth, and prices thus define what we call a household's **budget constraint**. The budget constraint facing any household results in great part from limits imposed externally by one or more markets. In competitive markets, for example, households cannot control prices; they buy goods and services at market-determined prices. A household has some control over its income: its members can choose to work or not, and they can sometimes decide how many hours to work, and how many jobs to hold. But there are constraints in the labor market too. The amount that household members are paid is limited by current market wage rates; whether they can get a job is determined by the availability of jobs.

While income does in fact depend, at least in part, on the choices that households make, for the time being we will treat it as a given. As we discuss consumer choice in output markets, it helps at first to treat income as a simple limit, or constraint. Later on we will relax this assumption and explore labor supply choices more specifically.

The income, wealth, and price constraints that surround the exercise of choice are best illustrated with an example. Consider Barbara, recent graduate of a top Midwestern university, who takes a job as a junior loan officer in a bank. Let's assume that she receives a salary that gives her $1000 per month after taxes, and that she has no wealth and no credit. Barbara's monthly expenditures are limited to her flow of income. Table 6.1 summarizes some of the choices open to her.

A careful search of the housing market reveals four vacant apartments. The least expensive is a one-room studio with a small kitchenette that rents for $400.00 per month including utilities. If she lived there, Barbara could afford to spend $250.00 per month on food and still have $350.00 left over for other things.

About four blocks away is a one-bedroom apartment with wall-to-wall carpeting and a larger kitchen. It has much more space, but it is 50-per-cent more expensive: the rent is $600.00, again including utilities. If she took this apartment, she might cut her food expenditures by $50.00 per month and have only $200.00 per month left for everything else.

In the same building as the one-bedroom apartment is an identical unit, but it is on the top floor of the building and has a beautiful balcony facing west toward the sunset. The balcony and view add $100.00 to the monthly rent. To live there, Barbara would be left with only $300.00 to split between food and other expenses.

Just because she was curious, Barbara took a look at a beautiful town house in the suburbs which was renting for $1000 per month. Obviously, unless she could get along without eating or doing anything else that costs money, she could not afford it: the combination of the town house and any amount of food is outside her budget constraint.

Notice that what we have done is to use the information that we have on income and prices to identify different combinations of housing, food, and other items that are

TABLE 6.1
Possible Budget Choices of a Person Earning $1000 per Month After Taxes

Income and prices determine which combinations of goods and services are available to a household and which are not.

Bundle	Monthly rent	Food	Other expenses	Total	Available
A	$400	$250	$350	$1000	yes
B	$600	$200	$200	$1000	yes
C	$700	$150	$150	$1000	yes
D	$1000	$100	$100	$1200	no

available to a single-person household with an income of $1000 per month. We have said nothing about the process of choosing. We have carved out what is called a **choice set**, the set of options that is defined and limited by Barbara's budget constraint.

Preferences, Tastes, and Trade-offs So far, all we have done is to set up the *limits* facing consumers. We have identified the combinations of goods and services that are available and those that are not. Within the constraints imposed by limited incomes and fixed prices, however, households are free to choose what they will buy and what they will not buy. Their ultimate choices are governed by their individual preferences and tastes.

It will help you to think of the household-choice process as a process of allocating income over a large number of available goods and services. A household's final demand for any *single* product is just one of many outcomes that result from the decision-making process. Think, for example, of a demand curve that shows a household's reaction to a price change such as the drop in the price of air travel that took place in 1986 when the airlines waged a price war. As special fares flooded the market, many people decided to take trips that they otherwise would not have taken. The decision to travel, however, is a decision not to do or buy something else. If I live in Florida and decide to spend $149.00 to visit my mother in New York, that is $149.00 that I will not be spending on a new outfit, dinners out at a restaurant, or a new set of tires.

Thus a change in the price of a *single* good changes the constraints within which households choose, and this may change the entire allocation—demand for some goods and services may rise while demand for others may fall. As you can see, a complicated set of trade-offs lies behind the shape and position of a household's demand curve for a single good. Whenever a household makes a choice, it is really weighing the good or service it chooses against *all* the other things that the same money could buy.

Consider again our young banker and the options open to her listed in Table 6.1. Her choice of an apartment from among the three alternatives that lie within her budget constraint depends on her own tastes and preferences. She must make a personal, subjective judgment about the relative values that *she* places on housing, food, and other things. If she hates to cook, likes to eat at restaurants, and goes out three nights a week, she will probably trade off some housing for dinners out and money to spend on clothes and other things. She will rent the studio for $400.00. But she may love to spend long evenings at home reading, listening to classical music, and sipping wine while watching the sunset. In that case, she will probably trade off some restaurant meals, evenings out, and travel expenses for the added comfort of the larger apartment with the porch and the view.

Thinking of constraints in this way highlights a very important point: as long as a household faces a limited budget, and all households ultimately do, the real cost of any good or service is the value of the other goods and services that could have been purchased with the same amount of money.

The Budget Constraint More Formally Consider a household with no wealth and a known income (I). Assume that the household purchases only two goods, X and Y. In addition, X and Y sell for known prices, P_X and P_Y. The budget constraint here is quite simple: the household may choose any combination of X and Y as long as the total amount spent on the two does not exceed income. We can write the constraint more formally:

$$P_X{\cdot}X + P_Y{\cdot}Y \leq I,$$

where X is the number of units of good X, and Y is the number of units of good Y. The total amount spent on X (P_X times X) plus the total amount spent on Y (P_Y times Y) must be less than or equal to ($\leq$) income (I).

This same budget constraint is illustrated graphically in Figure 6.2. In the diagram, each point represents a combination of X and Y. Point A, for example, represents X_A units of X and Y_A units of Y. The budget constraint itself, line segment DE, shows all the combinations of X and Y that the household could buy if it spent *all* of its income.

Look at point D. If the household chose point D, it would be spending *all* of its income on Y and buying no X at all. If it did, the number of *units* of Y it could buy would be I/P_Y (I divided by the price of Y). If your allowance is $1.00 a week, gum cost $.05 a pack, and you spend it all on gum, you can buy 20 packs ($1.00 divided by $.05). If the household spent its entire income on X and nothing on Y, the total amount of X it could buy would be I/P_X, indicated by point E in Figure 6.2.

All points below and to the left of the budget constraint, DE, are *available*, and they make up what is called the choice set, or **opportunity set**. It is represented by the shaded area in the figure. Point A is available, but at that point the household does not spend its entire income.[2] Point C is not available; that is, it represents a particular combination of X and Y (X_C and Y_C) that cannot be purchased with an income of I. The household's problem is to pick one of the points in the shaded area—a choice, once again, that depends on it own unique tastes and preferences.

Figure 6.3 illustrates the effect of an increase in the price of X on the household's budget constraint. The point where the constraint DE intersects the X axis, which, you recall, measures the number of *units* of good X, moves in to the left. If the price of gum went up to $.10, you could buy only 10 packs with your dollar instead of 20. The only point on the old budget constraint that remains the same on the new one is point D on the Y axis. At that point, the household buys no X, and so an increase in the price of X has no effect.

Opportunity set or choice set
The options among which a household may choose in the market after considering the limitations imposed by its budget constraint. The set of all commodity bundles available to a household given its income, wealth, and current prices.

FIGURE 6.2
Budget Constraint and Opportunity Set for a Household Consuming Two Goods

A household's budget constraint separates those combinations of goods and services that are available, given its limited income, from those that are not. Those that are available make up the household's opportunity set.

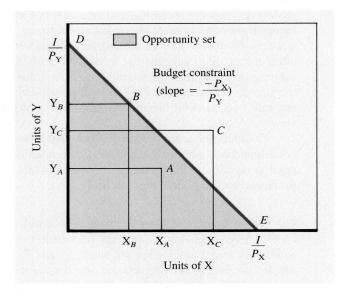

[2]Saving can be thought of in a number of ways, and it will be dealt with in depth later on. The two-dimensional world of X and Y is a representation of a multidimensional world. One dimension that is left out is time. Saving is the way we use income earned today to buy goods in the future. It is often assumed that households consume all their income and thus choose a point on the budget constraint. For now we will make this assumption.

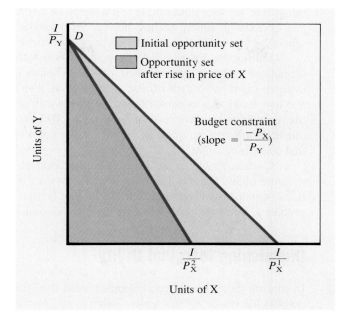

FIGURE 6.3

The Effect of an Increase in the
Price of X on a Household's
Budget Constraint

When the price of a good increases,
the budget constraint swivels, reducing the opportunities available and limiting choice.

This *shift*, or *swivel*, in its budget constraint presents the household with an entirely
new choice set, and presumably the household will pick an entirely new bundle. The
opportunity set is smaller, which means that the household has fewer options.

Figure 6.3 thus illustrates a very important point. We said earlier that when the
price of a single good such as X changes, it affects more than just the quantity of good X
demanded. What happens is that the household is faced with an entirely new
problem—the opportunity set has changed. Opportunity sets get bigger when prices fall
and smaller when prices rise. The opportunities open to the banker, which are described
in Table 6.1, are reduced if rents rise. On the other hand, if you frequently visit your
mother in New York, and you fly to get there, a decline in air fares increases, or opens up,
opportunities—not just opportunities to fly more, but to buy other goods and services as
well.

All this simply shows that behind each household demand curve is a more
complicated constrained-choice problem. The constraint is defined by income, wealth,
and prices. Within those limits, households are free to choose, and the household's
ultimate choice depends on its own likes and dislikes.

Obviously the range of goods and services available in a modern society is as vast as
tastes are variable, and this makes any generalization about the choice process hazardous.
Nonetheless, the theory of household behavior is an attempt to derive some logical
propositions about the way households behave. Now let us look at the choice process
itself.

THE BASIS OF CHOICE: UTILITY

You have seen that individual tastes and preferences ultimately determine the decisions
that households make within the constraints imposed by the market. Somehow, from the
infinite variety of things that are available, each of us manages to sort out a set of goods
and services to buy. In doing so, we make specific judgments about the relative worth of

things that are very different. If you were given $10.00 to spend, you might buy a book, take yourself to lunch, or buy flowers for a friend. Our fresh-from-college bank loan officer had to weigh the relative worth of apartment quality and food.

During the nineteenth century, this notion of the subjective weighing of values was formalized into a concept called utility. Whether one item is preferable to another depends upon how much **utility**, or satisfaction, it yields relative to the alternatives. What is it that enables us to decide on the relative worth of a new puppy or a stereo? A trip to the mountains or a weekend in New York City? Working or not working? As we make our trade-offs and our choices, we are weighing something in our minds. Economists call that something utility.

Certain problems are implicit in the concept of utility. First, it is impossible to measure utility. Second, it is impossible to compare the utilities of different people—that is, one cannot say whether person A or person B has a higher level of utility. Despite these problems, however, the idea of utility helps us understand the process of choice better.

Diminishing Marginal Utility

In making their choices, most people spread their incomes over many different kinds of goods. One reason for this variety is that as we consume more and more of any one good, the *marginal*, or "extra," satisfaction we get out of it declines.

Suppose that you live next to a store that sells wonderful homemade ice cream, and you are crazy about it. Even though you get a great deal of pleasure from eating ice cream and you say that you never get tired of it, you still don't spend your entire income on it. The first cone of the day tastes heavenly. The second is merely delicious. The third is still very good, but it's clear that the glow is fading. The more of any one good we consume in a given period, the less satisfaction, or utility, we get out of each additional, or *marginal*, unit. In 1890 Alfred Marshall called this "familiar and fundamental tendency of human nature" the **law of diminishing marginal utility**.[3]

Take this simple numerical example. Frank loves country music, and a country band is playing seven nights a week at a lively club near his house. Table 6.2 shows how the utility he derives from the band might change as he goes to the club more and more frequently. The first visit generates 12 units of utility—for lack of a better term, we call these units *utils*. If he goes again another night he enjoys it, but not quite as much as the first night. The second night by itself yields 10 additional utils. *Marginal utility* is 10, while the total utils derived from two nights at the club is 22. Three nights per week at the club provide 28 total utils, and the marginal utility of the third night is 6, since utility went

Utility   The basis of choice. The satisfaction, or reward, a product yields. The intangible "worth" we find in things that enables us to compare and rank unlike things.

Marginal utility   The additional satisfaction gained by the consumption or use of one more unit of something.

Diminishing marginal utility   The decrease in satisfaction found in a single unit of a product as more and more of it is consumed.

TABLE 6.2
Total Utility and Marginal Utility of Trips to the Club

Trips to club	Total utility	Marginal utility
1	12	12
2	22	10
3	28	6
4	32	4
5	34	2
6	34	0

[3]Alfred Marshall, *Principles of Economics*, 8th ed., (New York: MacMillan, 1948), p. 93. (First ed., 1890.)

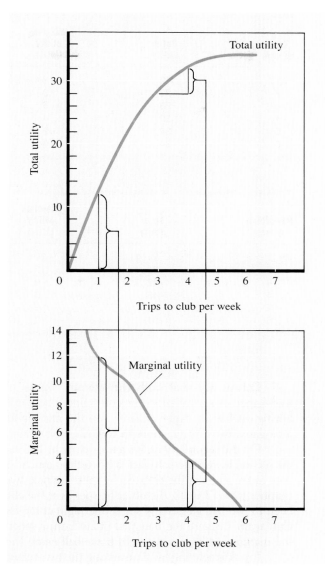

FIGURE 6.4
Graphs of Total and Marginal Utility

Marginal utility is the additional utility gained by consuming one additional unit of a commodity—in this case trips to the club. As long as a good yields positive marginal utility, total utility will increase with output. When marginal utility is zero, total utility stops rising.

up from 22 to 28. Figure 6.4 graphs total and marginal utility: total utility increases up through Frank's fifth trip to the club, but on the sixth night, it levels off. *Marginal* utility, which has declined from the beginning, is now at zero.

Allocating Income to Maximize Utility

How many times would Frank go to the club? That depends on three things: his income, the price of going, and the alternatives available. If the price of going were zero and no alternatives existed, he would probably go five nights a week. (The sixth does not increase his utility, remember.) But Frank is also a basketball fan. His city has many good high school and college teams, and he can go to games six nights a week if he wants to. Table 6.3 gives his total and marginal utilities from attending basketball games.

TABLE 6.3
Allocation of Fixed Expenditure
per Week Between Two
Alternatives

Trips to club	Total utility	Marginal utility (MU_x)	Price (P_x)	$\dfrac{MU_x}{P_x}$
1	12	12	$3.00	4.0
2	22	10	3.00	3.3
3	28	6	3.00	2.0
4	32	4	3.00	1.3
5	34	2	3.00	0.7
6	34	0	3.00	0

Basketball games	Total utility	Marginal utility (MU_y)	Price (P_y)	$\dfrac{MU_y}{P_y}$
1	21	21	$6.00	3.5
2	33	12	6.00	2.0
3	42	9	6.00	1.5
4	48	6	6.00	1.0
5	51	3	6.00	.5
6	51	0	6.00	0

Let us say that both the country music club and the basketball games are free—there is no price/income constraint. There is a time constraint, however, the week having only seven nights. Clearly, on the first night Frank will go to a basketball game. The game is worth far more to him (21 utils) than a trip to the club (12 utils).

On the second night, it's a tossup. As he has been to one basketball game this week, the second is worth less. In fact, it is worth so much less that he is *indifferent* to whether he goes to the game or the club. So he splits the next two nights: one night he sees ball game number two (12 utils), the other he spends at the club (12 utils). At this point, Frank has been to two ball games and spent one night at the club. On evening four, he goes to the club again, because the marginal utility from a second club trip (10 utils) is greater than the marginal utility from a third basketball game (nine utils).

Frank is splitting his time among the two activities in order to maximize total utility. At each successive step, he chooses the activity that yields the most marginal utility. Continuing with this logic, you see that if Frank ends up spending three nights at the club and four nights watching basketball, his total utility is 76 utils each week (28 plus 48). No other combination of games and club trips can produce as much utility.

So far, the only cost of a night listening to country music is a forgone basketball game, and the only cost of a basketball game is a forgone night of country music. Now let's suppose that it costs $3.00 to get into the club and $6.00 to go to a basketball game. Suppose further that after paying rent and taking care of other necessary expenses Frank has only $21.00 left over to spend on entertainment. Typically, consumers allocate limited incomes, or *budgets*, over a large set of goods and services. Here we have a limited income ($21.00) being allocated over only two goods, but the principle is the same. Income ($21.00) and prices ($3.00 and $6.00) define Frank's budget constraint. *Within that constraint*, Frank chooses in order to maximize utility.

Because the two activities now cost different amounts, we need to find the *marginal utility per dollar* spent on each activity. If Frank is to spend his money on the combination of activities lying within his budget constraint that gives him the most total utility, each night he must choose the activity that gives him the *most utility per dollar spent*. As you see from Table 6.3, the first night Frank goes to the club and gets four utils per dollar. On night two he goes to a game and gets three and one half utils per dollar. On night three it's back to the club. Then what happens? When all is said and done—work this out for yourself—Frank ends up going to two games and spending three nights at the club. No other combination of activities that $21.00 will buy yields more utility.

Household Equilibrium Condition

In general, a utility-maximizing consumer spreads out his or her expenditures until the following condition holds:

$$\frac{MU_X}{P_X} = \frac{MU_Y}{P_Y} \text{ for all pairs of goods,}$$

where MU_X is the marginal utility derived from the last unit of X consumed, MU_Y is the marginal utility derived from the last unit of Y consumed, P_X is the price per unit of X, and P_Y is the price per unit of Y.

To see why this is true, think for a moment about what would happen if it were *not* true. For example, suppose MU_X/P_X were greater than MU_Y/P_Y; that is, suppose that the marginal utility from the last dollar spent on X were greater than the marginal utility from the last dollar spent on Y. This would imply that spending a dollar less on Y and spending it on X instead *increases* utility. As a household shifts to buying more X and less Y, it runs into diminishing marginal utility. Buying more units of X decreases the marginal utility derived from consuming additional units of X. Thus, the marginal utility of another dollar spent on X—MU_X/P_X—falls. Now *less* is being spent on Y and that means its *marginal* utility increases. This process continues until $MU_X/P_X = MU_Y/P_Y$.

You can see how it works in the story about Frank's choice between country music and basketball. At each stage, Frank chooses the one that gives him the most utility *per dollar*. If he goes to a game, the utility he will derive from the next game—marginal utility—falls. If he goes to the club, the utility he will derive from his next visit falls, and so forth.

Another way of looking at this condition is to say

$$\frac{MU_X}{MU_Y} = \frac{P_X}{P_Y} \text{ for all pairs of goods.}$$

This is simply another way of writing $MU_X/P_X = MU_Y/P_Y$. All we have done is to multiply both sides by P_X and divide both sides by MU_Y.

Marginal rate of substitution *The rate at which a person is willing to substitute X for Y. More formally, the ratio of the marginal utility derived from consuming good X to the marginal utility derived from consuming good Y.*

The ratio of the marginal utility of X to the marginal utility of Y is called the **marginal rate of substitution (MRS)**. If MU_X/MU_Y is equal to four, it means that a unit of X is four times more valuable to me than a unit of Y—that is, I would be willing to trade four units of Y for one unit of X. The price ratio, P_X/P_Y, tells me the rate at which the market allows me to trade off X for Y. If P_X/P_Y is equal to five, it means that a unit of X sells for five times more than a unit of Y—that is, if I gave up one unit of X, I could buy five units of Y.

If MU_X/MU_Y were four and P_X/P_Y were five, I would, in fact, *buy more* Y. I lose no utility if I trade one unit of X for *four* units of Y, but the market will get me *five*. Thus I gain utility if I consume less X and more Y. The opposite would occur if MU_X/MU_Y were greater than the price ratio. But consuming more Y lowers MU_Y, and buying less X raises MU_X. That pushes the ratio MU_X/MU_Y, the marginal rate of substitution, toward the price ratio. When they are equal, no further adjustment will increase utility.[4]

Diminishing Marginal Utility and Downward-Sloping Demand

The idea of diminishing marginal utility offers us one reason why people spread their incomes over a variety of goods and services rather than spending them all on one or two items. It also leads us to conclude that demand curves slope downward.

If a demand curve shows how much of a product will be purchased either by a single household or by all households in the market at each price, it also tells us about *willingness to pay*. In private markets, we have to pay for what we want in order to get it. Consumption is contingent upon payment. This means that we are *forced* to reveal through our behavior how much each good is worth to us. If the marginal utility of a product declines as we consume more and more of it, the amount that we are willing to pay per unit also declines. That is one reason why individual demand curves that express actual market behavior slope downward.

In conclusion, then, the concept, or general idea, of utility and the specific idea of diminishing marginal utility provide insights into the process of consumer choice—that is, the allocation of limited incomes among available alternatives. Households maximize total utility by spreading income across goods until the marginal utility *per dollar* spent on each item is equal. Diminishing marginal utility also implies that demand curves—reflecting willingness to pay—are very likely to slope downward.

But the concept of utility as we have discussed it here is quite abstract. To many, it seems artificial, first because utility cannot be measured, and second because comparisons cannot be made between individuals. While the idea of utility is, we believe, a helpful way of thinking about the choice process, there is an explanation for downward-sloping demand curves that does not rely on the concept of utility or the assumption of diminishing marginal utility.

INCOME AND SUBSTITUTION EFFECTS

Another way to think about household choices avoids any direct use of the concept of utility. It also leads us to the conclusion that a negative, or downward-sloping, relationship is very likely to exist between quantity demanded and price.

Keeping in mind that consumers face constrained choices, consider the probable response of a household to a decline in the price of some heavily used product, ceteris

---

[4]This condition is an important one. As long as it holds for all consumers, it can be shown that the distribution of final output is *efficient*—that is, there are no trades that can be made to make both parties better off. This is discussed in detail in chapter 12.

paribus. How might a household currently consuming many goods be likely to respond to a fall in the price of one of those goods if its income, its preferences, and all other prices remained unchanged? Clearly the household would then be dealing with a new budget constraint, and its final choice of all goods and services might change. A decline in the price of gasoline, for example, may affect not only how much gasoline you purchase but also the kind of car you buy, when and how much you travel, where you go, and, not so directly, how many movies you see this month and how many projects around the house you get done.

Price changes affect households in two ways. First, if we assume that households confine their choices to products that improve their well-being, then a decline in the price of any product, ceteris paribus, makes the household unequivocally *better off*. In other words, if a household continues to buy the exact same amount of every good and service, it will have income left over. That extra income may be spent on the product whose price has declined, hereafter called good X, or on other products. The change in consumption of X due to this improvement in well-being is called the **income effect of a price change**.

Looking back at Figure 6.2 you can see that a decline in price, ceteris paribus, makes households better off. A decline in the price of X moves point E out to the right and enlarges the opportunity set. Households thus have a larger set of available choices, and they can buy more X, more Y, or more of both. Everything that was available before is still available, but the price decline has added opportunities.

In addition, when a product price falls, that product becomes *relatively* cheaper, that is, it becomes more attractive relative to potential substitutes. Even if a household were *not* made better off by a fall in the price of X, it might shift its purchasing patterns away from substitutes and toward X. Remember that the price ratio, P_X/P_Y, determines the number of units of Y that I must sacrifice to get an added unit of X; the price ratio determines the *opportunity cost* of X. If the price of X falls, it means I can get a unit of X by sacrificing less Y. An increase in the consumption of X because it is now cheaper relative to potential substitutes is called the **substitution effect of a price change**.

Consider again the significant decline in the price of gasoline that actually occurred in the United States after 1980. A lower price of gas makes it less costly to drive; I may travel to see my friends in Montreal *more* frequently and play tennis at the club *less* frequently. This is partly because, with cheaper gasoline, I am better off and can afford to travel more (income effect) and partly because visiting my friends in Montreal is now relatively cheaper than playing tennis (substitution effect).

Everything works in the opposite direction when a price rises, ceteris paribus. A price increase makes households worse off. If income and other prices don't change, spending the same amount of money buys them less—they will be forced to buy less of something. They may purchase less X or cut spending on other things. Again, this is the income effect. In addition, when the price of a product rises, that item becomes more expensive relative to potential substitutes, and the household is likely to substitute other goods for it. This is the substitution effect.

For *normal goods*, where consumption of the good rises with income, both the income and substitution effects imply a negative relationship between price and quantity demanded—in other words, they imply downward-sloping demand. When the price of something *falls*, ceteris paribus, we are better off, and we are likely to buy *more* of that good and other goods (income effect). Lower price also means "less expensive relative to substitutes," and again we are likely to buy *more* of the good (substitution effect). When the price of something *rises*, we are worse off, and we will buy *less* of it (income); higher price also means "more expensive relative to substitutes," and we are likely to buy *less* of it and more of other goods (substitution).[5]

CONSUMER SURPLUS: VALUE VERSUS PRICE

The argument, made several times already, that the market forces us to reveal a great deal about our own personal preferences and values, is an extremely important one, and it bears repeating at least once more here. If you are free to choose within the constraints imposed by prices and your income and you decide to buy, say, a cheeseburger for $2.50, you have "revealed" that a cheeseburger is worth at least $2.50 to you.

A simple market demand curve such as the one in Figure 6.5 illustrates this point quite clearly. If the current market price is P^1_X, the demand curve shows that consumers will purchase Q^1_X. There is only one price in the market, and the demand curve tells us how much X households would buy if they could purchase all they wanted at the posted price. Anyone who values a unit of X higher than P^1_X will buy it; anyone who does not value it that highly will not.

Consumer surplus The *difference between the maximum amount a person is willing to pay for a good and its current market price.*

But notice that some people value X at *more than* P^1_X. If, for example, price were P^2_X, Q^2_X would be sold. If the market price turned out to be P^1_X, the people who would have continued to buy at P^2_X would get a "**consumer surplus.**" They value X at P^2_X or higher, but have to pay only P^1_X. The total value of the consumer surplus suggested by the data in Figure 6.5 is roughly equal to the area of the shaded triangle. To see this, think about offering X to consumers at successively lower prices. If the good were actually sold at a price P^1_X, those near point A on the demand curve would get a large surplus; those near point B would get a smaller surplus. Those at point C would get none.

The idea of consumer surplus helps to explain an old paradox that dates back to Plato. Adam Smith wrote about it in 1776:

> The things which have the greatest value in use have frequently little or no value in exchange; and on the contrary, those which have the greatest value in exchange have frequently little or no value in use. Nothing is more useful than water: but it will purchase scarce any thing; scarce any thing can be had in exchange for it. A diamond, on the contrary, has scarce any value in use; but a very great quantity of other goods may frequently be had in exchange for it.[6]

---

[5]Careful thought should convince you that for some goods the income and substitution effects work in opposite directions. As you recall, when our income rises, we may buy *less* of some goods. In Chapter 4, we called such goods *inferior goods*.

When the price of an inferior good rises, it is, like any other good, more expensive relative to substitutes, and we are likely to buy *less* of it as we replace it with lower-priced substitutes. However, the price increase leaves us worse off, and when we are worse off we *increase* our demand for inferior goods. Thus the income effect could lead us to buy *more* of the good, partially offsetting the substitution effect.

Even if a good is "very inferior," demand curves will slope downward as long as the substitution effect is larger than the income effect. But it is possible, at least in theory, for the income effect to be larger. In such a case, a price increase would actually lead to an increase in demand. This possibility was pointed out by Alfred Marshall in his nineteenth-century text, *Principles of Economics*. Marshall attributes the notion of an upward-sloping demand curve to Sir Robert Giffin, and it is often referred to as *Giffin's paradox*. Fortunately or unfortunately, no one has ever demonstrated that a Giffin good has ever existed.

[6]Adam Smith, *The Wealth of Nations*, Modern Library Edition (New York: Random House, 1937). First edition (1776), p. 28. The cheapness of water is referred to by Plato in *Euthydem.*, 304B.

FIGURE 6.5
Market Demand, Revealed
Preference, and Consumer
Surplus

Market demand can be used to estimate the total value of producing a
good or service. If a good is produced
and sold at a price P^1_X, all those who
value it *less* than P^1_X will not buy it, and
those who value it *more* than P_X^1 will
buy it. Very few of the buyers value it
at exactly P^1_X. Most people who buy X
in fact earn a "surplus." Notice that
some people would have bought X
even at a price of P^2_X. Because the
good is actually sold at P^1_X, those
people earn what is called a consumer
surplus of at least $(P^2_X - P^1_X)$.

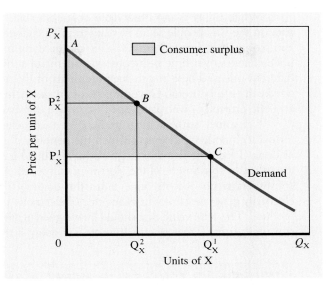

FIGURE 6.6
Consumption Surplus Derived
from the Consumption of Water

Even though nothing is more useful
than water, it commands a very low
price. The reason is that water is plentiful. Since water has such a great use
value, but sells for a low price, we all
receive a large consumer surplus.

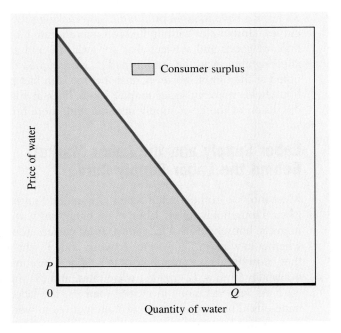

Although diamonds have arguably more than "scarce any value in use" today,
Smith's **"diamond/water paradox"** is still instructive, at least where water is concerned.

The low price of water owes much to the fact that it is in plentiful supply. Each of
us enjoys an enormous consumer surplus when we consume nearly free water. We tend
to take water for granted, but imagine what would happen to its price if there were simply
not enough for everyone. If water were in very short supply, it would command a high
price indeed. (Figure 6.6 shows the relationship between price and value for water.) Thus
we all enjoy a very significant consumer surplus. Although water has enormous use value,
it commands only a low price because it is so plentiful.

While utility is not observable or measurable, behavior certainly is. By collecting data on the way people seem to react to price changes, economists can actually estimate and plot market demand curves. This can be done by observing behavior in response to price changes over time or by observing demand at different locations where people face different prices. These rough measurements of the actual value that society places on a good can be very useful. Governments often use them to decide whether to go ahead with a public project, power plant, road, or bridge, for example.

Consumer surplus measurement is a key element in *cost-benefit analysis*, the formal technique by means of which the benefits of a public project are weighed against its costs. To decide whether to go ahead and build a new power plant, we need to know the value, to consumers, of the electricity that it will produce. Just as the value of water to consumers is not just its price times the quantity that people consume, the value of electricity generated is not just the price of electricity times the quantity the new plant will produce. The total value that should be weighed against the costs of the plant includes the consumer surplus that electricity users will enjoy if the plant is built.

HOUSEHOLD CHOICES IN INPUT MARKETS

So far, we have focused on the decision-making process that lies behind output demand curves. Households with limited incomes allocate those incomes across various combinations of goods and services that are available and affordable. In looking at the factors affecting choices in the output market, we assumed that income was fixed, or given. We noted at the outset, however, that income is in fact partially determined by choices that households make in input markets (look back at Figure 6.1). We shall now turn to a discussion of the labor supply decision and, more briefly, the saving decision.

Labor Supply and the Labor Market: Behind the Labor Supply Curve

Most income in the United States is wage and salary income paid in compensation for labor. Households supply labor in exchange for wages or salaries. As they do in output markets, households also face *constrained choices* in input markets. They must decide (1) whether to work, (2) how much to work, and (3) what kind of a job to work at. In essence, they must decide how much labor to supply. The choices they make are limited by (1) the availability of jobs, (2) market wage rates, and (3) the skills of the household.

As with decisions in output markets, the labor supply decision involves a set of trade-offs. There are basically two alternatives to working for a wage: (1) leisure and (2) nonpaid work. If I don't work, I sacrifice income for the benefits of staying at home and reading, watching TV, going swimming, or sleeping. Another option is to work and produce, but not for a money wage. In this case, I sacrifice money income for the benefits of growing my own food in my garden, bringing up children, or taking care of my house.

As with the trade-offs in output markets, my final choice depends on how I subjectively value the alternatives available. If I work, I earn a wage that I can use to buy things. Thus the trade-off is between the use value of the goods and services I can buy in the market with the wages I earn working and either the value of things I can produce at home—home-grown food, manageable children, clean clothes, and so on—or the value I place on leisure. This choice is shown in Figure 6.7. We can condense this whole thought into the following statement: *the wage rate can be thought of, then, as the price—or the opportunity cost—of either the benefits of unpaid work or of leisure.*

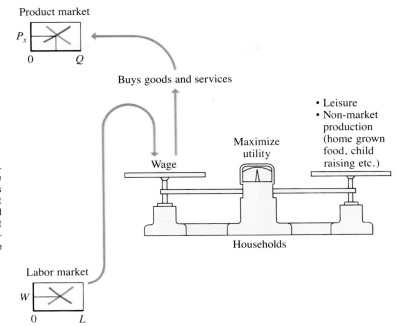

FIGURE 6.7
The Trade-off Facing Households

The decision to enter the work force involves a trade-off between wages (and the goods and services that wages will buy) on the one hand, and leisure and the value of nonmarket production on the other. The opportunity cost of one hour leisure is W, the wage rate per hour.

Leisure as an Option: A New Budget Constraint

Adding the labor supply decision to a household's choices in output markets is almost like adding another good to that household's opportunity set. As we put the problem before, households had to allocate a limited budget across a set of goods and services. Now they must choose among goods, services, and **leisure**.

When we add leisure to this picture, however, we do so with one important difference. Trading off one good for another involves buying less of one and more of another, so households simply reallocate *money* from one thing to the other. "Buying" more leisure, however, means reallocating time between work and nonwork activities.

If we assume that jobs are available, that households have the option of part-time work, that households receive no nonwage income such as interest, dividends, or gifts from Uncle George, and that there are no taxes, we can draw the budget constraint facing a typical household. Figure 6.8 shows the new opportunity set that includes leisure. The quantity of leisure consumed appears on the X axis; on the Y axis is the amount of daily income. Assuming that the primary motive for working is to obtain the things that wages will buy, we can think of the Y axis as a measure of all other goods. Since there is no nonwage income, the only way to get goods and services is by working to earn wages.

If I decide to use all my time for leisure activities, I will earn no income and consume no other goods, the situation indicated by point A on the budget constraint. If I decide to work every hour of the day and night for a wage of $w per hour, I will earn $24w per day and be at point B on the budget constraint. If I take a regular job and work eight hours per day, I will earn $8w per day and consume 16 hours of leisure, point C on the budget constraint. For each hour of leisure that I decide to consume, I give up $w. In other words, $w is the *price of leisure*.[7]

---

[7] The budget constraint in Figure 6.8 is a straight line with a constant slope of −w. For every unit of leisure I consume, income drops by w.

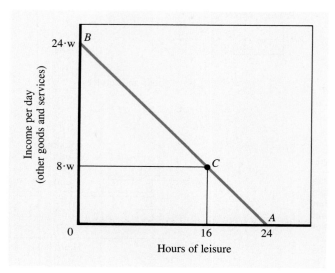

FIGURE 6.8
The Labor-Leisure Choice

By plotting income on the Y axis and hours of leisure on the X axis, the diagram shows all combinations of daily income and leisure available to someone who can choose how many hours to work at wage rate w. If he chose not to work, he would consume 24 hours of leisure and earn no income. If he worked all the time, he would earn $24w per day and have no leisure at all.

Conditions in the labor market, then, determine the budget constraints and final opportunity sets that face households. The availability of jobs and the wage rates of those jobs determine the final combinations of goods and services a household can afford. The final choice within these constraints depends, again, on the unique tastes and preferences of each household. Some people place very little value on leisure, while others place a high value on things like playing tennis or lying on the beach—but everyone needs to put food on the table.

Income and Substitution Effects of a Wage Change

A labor supply curve shows the quantity of labor supplied as a function of the wage rate. The shape of the labor supply curve depends on how households react to changes in the wage rate.

Consider an increase in wages. First of all, an increase in wages makes households better off; if they work the same number of hours, that is, if they supply the same amount of labor, they will earn higher incomes and be able to buy more goods and services. But they can also buy more leisure. If leisure is a normal good, an increase in income will lead to a *higher* demand for leisure and a *lower* labor supply. This is the **income effect of a wage increase**.

There is also, however, a potential **substitution effect of a wage increase**. A higher wage rate means that leisure is more "expensive." If you think of the wage rate as the price of leisure, at a higher wage each individual hour of leisure consumed costs more in forgone wages. As a result, we would expect households to substitute other goods for leisure. This means working more, or a *lower* demand for leisure and a *higher* labor supply.

Note that in the labor market the income and substitution effects work in *opposite* directions when leisure is a normal good. The income effect of a wage increase implies buying more leisure and working less; the substitution effect implies buying less leisure and working more. Whether households will in the aggregate supply more labor or less labor when wages rise depends, then, on the relative strength of both the income and the substitution effects.

Household Choices and Opportunity Costs—Olympic Gold

Chapter 2 described the choices facing Bill and Colleen, the only residents of a small island. Their choices were constrained by the resources of the island, their own skills, and time. Time spent in one activity—for example, gathering food—meant less time spent in other activities—like sleeping on the beach. Time spent building a boat involved trading work today for potentially greater gain tomorrow.

These choices lie at the heart of our economic system, and all of us face them every day. Final allocation of resources in an economy depends ultimately on the choices we make. How much to work, whether to stay in school, what skills to acquire, what goods and services to buy, and so forth.

The trade-offs facing people born with great talent are more dramatic. The bronze medal that Debi Thomas won in figure skating during the 1988 Winter Olympics cost her at least $125,000. Thomas is studying to be an orthopedic surgeon, and that's the sum she can expect to earn annually. Training for the Olympics cost her a year of school and so delayed the time when she'll be practicing medicine instead of skating.

Now consider Midori Ito. The 18-year-old figure skater from Japan dazzled audiences in Calgary with her powerhouse jumping and she placed fifth in overall competition. That honor didn't come easy. For many years before the competition, Ito gave up the opportunity to enjoy any leisure time, choosing instead to live, eat, and dream skating. She begins her days at 5:30 A.M. and spends several hours practicing figures on the ice. After attending school, she hits the ice again to run through her skating program. At 8 P.M., she dines with her coaches, and then they listen to music, searching for scores to fit her Olympic routines. After that, there's homework and, finally, bed at around midnight. Although the 1988 Olympics are over, Ito will continue to incur these substantial opportunity costs because she's considered a strong contender for the 1992 games.

Although he practices the same sport, Canadian figure skater Brian Orser has a somewhat different set of trade-offs. Orser spends his off-rink time meeting with an impressive entourage. He's attended by his coach, his figure coach, a financial adviser, a rolfer (a masseuse who attempts to realign muscles), and a choreographer. He also works regularly with a nutritionist, a costume designer, and a sports psychologist who helps him to envision, practice, and achieve success. Orser skated away from Calgary with the silver medal.

The Olympic gold medal went to Brian Boitano, Orser's U.S. competitor, who nailed the prize with an extraordinary series of complex loops and powerful leaps. The 24-year-old Boitano has been practicing these feats six days a week, five hours a day for the past sixteen years at some rather shabby San Francisco-area rinks. Now that he's won at the Olympics, perhaps Boitano will have the opportunity to pursue yet another dream: that of opening an Italian restaurant in his home town.

Training for the Olympics costs these athletes the ability to lead a normal life—to play other sports, to study different fields, even to spend time with their families. For Bonnie Blair, a speed skater affectionately dubbed "Bonnie the Blur," lack of family time has not been a problem. Blair's father has coached her four siblings into national speed skating champions, and he began training her when she became a "rink rat" at age two. Blair's most significant opportunity cost has been the loss of a school year in her pursuit of a physical education degree.

Is going for the gold worth missing so many opportunities?

One athlete who might say yes is East German figure skater Katarina Witt, who skated away with top honors at the Calgary Olympics. Witt's efforts on the ice have also won her adulation in her country and many perquisites not readily available to East Germans, including a beautiful wardrobe, an apartment, and a sedan. "When you do well, you simply have certain privileges," she says. "That's true everywhere."

Bonnie Blair probably finds the opportunity costs worth paying. She's won a gold and a bronze medal and broken a world record. No doubt Debi Thomas found the experience worthwhile as well; although she iced only the bronze, she came away from Calgary with the Hemingway Award, given to the athlete who reacts with the most grace under pressure.

Sources: "The Soaring, Spinning Battle of the Brians," and "The Word She Uses is 'Invincible,' " *Time*, February 15, 1988; and "Such Amazing Grace," *Time*, March 7, 1988.

If the substitution effect is bigger than the income effect, the wage increase will indeed increase labor supply. This suggests that the labor supply curve slopes upward, or has a positive slope, like the one in Figure 6.9a. If the income effect outweighs the substitution effect, however, a higher wage will lead to added consumption of leisure, and labor supply will decrease. This implies that the labor supply curve "bends back," as the one in Figure 6.9b does.

During the early years of the Industrial Revolution in the late eighteenth century in Great Britain, the textile industry operated under what was called the "putting-out" system. Spinning and weaving were done in small cottages to supplement the family farm income. During that period, wages and household incomes rose considerably. Some

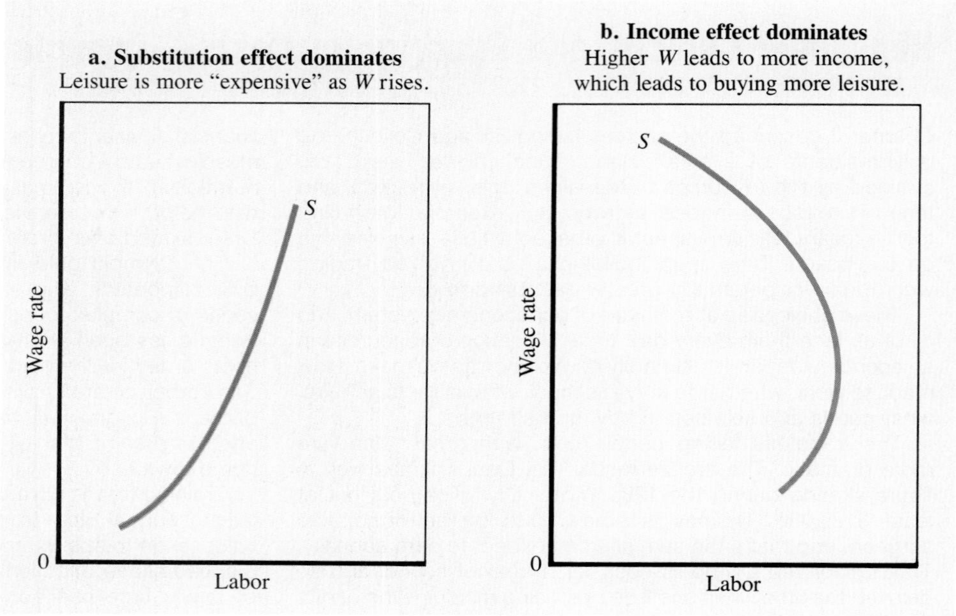

a. Substitution effect dominates
Leisure is more "expensive" as W rises.

b. Income effect dominates
Higher W leads to more income,
which leads to buying more leisure.

FIGURE 6.9
Two Labor Supply Curves

If we think of leisure as a normal good, an increase in wages that increases income may lead to more leisure and less work. This can lead to the intriguing notion of a "backward bending" labor supply curve: lower labor supply at higher wages.

economic historians claim that this higher income actually led many households to take more leisure and work fewer hours; the evidence suggests a backward-bending labor supply curve.

Just as income and substitution effects helped us understand household choices in *output* markets, they now help us understand household choices in *input* markets. The point here is that when leisure is added to the choice set, the line between input and output market decisions becomes blurred. In fact, households decide how much of each good to consume and how much leisure to consume at the same time.

Labor Supply and Taxes

In recent years much has been written and said about the effect of taxes on the incentive to work. Some claim that because taxes take some of what we earn, people work less, and some people may even decide to stay out of the labor force altogether. If we reduce tax rates, they argue, people will work harder, more people will work, and the economy will be more productive. Using the language of economics, the question is, How do tax rates affect the supply of labor?

Let's first look to theory to see if there is an answer. Jennifer does freelance drafting, working mostly on illustrations and graphics for books and magazines. Suppose she works for $10.00 per hour and pays 20 percent of what she earns in taxes. If she works 50 hours per week, she makes $500.00 and pays taxes of $100.00, taking home $400.00. Her tax *rate* is 20 percent, or .20. At those tax and wage rates, each hour of leisure "costs" Jennifer $8.00. If she works an extra hour, she makes $10.00, but $2.00 goes in taxes. Eight dollars, then, is her after-tax wage, and that amount is the *price* of one hour of leisure.

Now suppose the tax rate is suddenly reduced to *10* percent. Will Jennifer work more? Surprisingly, perhaps, the answer to this question is unclear; theory is ambiguous about whether she will work more or less. The reason for this is that the income and substitution effects work in opposite directions. First, the tax cut means that Jennifer's after-tax wage rate is *higher*. By working an additional hour, she now earns $9.00 instead of just $8.00. This means that the price, or opportunity cost, of an added hour of leisure is higher. When the relative price of a good—in this case leisure—rises, households will substitute other goods for it. This substitution effect should push Jennifer in the direction of working *more hours*.

But things are not this simple. Jennifer is also better off. By working 50 hours, she still earns $500.00 before tax, but now she takes home $450.00 instead of $400.00. She may decide to "spend" some of this added "income," or potential income, on *leisure*. This income effect should push Jennifer in the direction of working *less*. Whether, on balance, a tax rate cut increases or decreases the supply of labor depends on the relative size of the income and substitution effects.

Many empirical studies have tried to estimate the actual effect of taxes on labor supply. The evidence available suggests that, in general, the substitution effect is somewhat larger—that is, tax cuts should indeed lead to a larger labor supply. The elasticity, or responsiveness, of labor supply for most groups seems, however, to be fairly low—that is, it is inelastic. (This subject is explored in much more detail in Chapter 19.)

SAVING AND BORROWING: PAST AND FUTURE INCOME

We began this chapter by looking behind the demand curve to examine the process of allocating a fixed income over a large number of available goods and services. We then pointed out that, at least in part, choices made by households determine income levels. Within the constraints imposed by the market, households can decide whether to work and how much to work.

So far, however, we have talked about only the current period—the allocation of current income among alternative uses and the work/leisure choice *today*. But households can also (1) use present income to finance future spending—they can *save*—or (2) use future income to finance present spending—they can *borrow*.

When a household decides not to spend part of its current income but to *save* it, it is using *current* income to finance *future* consumption. That future consumption may come in three years, when you use your savings to buy a car, in 10 years, when you sell stock to put a deposit on a house, or in 45 years, when you retire and begin to receive money out of your pension plan. On the other hand, most people cannot finance large purchases—a home, let us say—out of current income and savings. They almost always borrow money and sign a mortgage. When a household *borrows*, it is, in essence, financing a *current* purchase with *future* income. It pays back the loan out of future income.

Even in simple economies such as the two-person economy of Colleen and Bill on a desert island, people must make decisions about **present versus future consumption**. Colleen and Bill had a number of options: they could (1) produce goods for today's consumption by hunting and gathering, (2) consume leisure by sleeping on the beach, or (3) work on projects to enhance future consumption opportunities. Building a house over a five-year period is, in essence, trading present for future consumption. In complex societies, we make these decisions through a highly developed set of institutions collectively referred to as the *capital market*.

During their earning years, most households are net savers. Most of the time when a household saves, it puts the money into something that will generate a flow of interest, or profit. There is no sense in putting money under your mattress when you can make it work in so many ways—government bonds, savings accounts, money market funds, common stocks, corporate bonds, and so forth—especially when many of them are virtually risk free.

When you put your money in any of these places, you are loaning it out, and the borrower pays you a fee, most often interest, for its use. Business firms borrow most often to finance capital investment projects. Thus the amount of capital investment in an economy is constrained in the long run by the saving rate of that economy.[8] You can think of household **savings** each year, then, as the supply of capital. Look back at Figure 6.1. When a firm borrows to finance a capital acquisition, it is almost as if households have supplied the capital for a fee, a fee we call **interest**.

Just as changes in wage rates affect household behavior in the labor market, so do changes in interest rates affect household behavior in capital markets. When interest rates change, they affect both the cost of borrowing *and* the return to saving. Higher interest rates mean that borrowing is more expensive—required monthly payments on a newly purchased house or car will be higher. Higher interest rates also mean that saving will earn a higher return: $1000 invested in a 5 percent saving account or bond yields $50.00 per year, but if rates rise to 10 percent, the annual flow becomes $100.00.

If we think of saving as future consumption, **interest rates** determine the trade-off between present consumption spending and future consumption. Higher interest rates mean that we sacrifice more future consumption when we spend today because any additional present consumption must be financed either by borrowing or by saving less. Higher interest rates tend to encourage saving and discourage borrowing. Lower interest rates do the opposite. The very complicated process behind all of this involves a huge and complex set of institutions, the **financial capital market**, in which the suppliers of capital (households that save) and the demand for capital (business firms that want to invest) interact, but this is the subject of Chapter 11.

Financial capital markets The complex set of institutions in which borrowers and lenders interact which facilitates the flow of saving into productive capital investment.

HOUSEHOLDS IN OUTPUT AND INPUT MARKETS

In probing the behavior of households in both input and output markets, we went behind the household output demand curve, using the simplifying assumption that income was fixed and given, in order to examine the nature of "constrained choice." Income, wealth, and prices set the limits, or *constraints*, within which households must make their choices in output markets. Within those limits, they make their choices on the basis of personal tastes and preferences.

The notion of *utility* helps to explain the process of choice. The law of *diminishing marginal utility* explains in part why people seem to spread their incomes over many different goods and services and why demand curves have a negative slope. Another important explanation for the negative relationship between price and quantity demanded lies in *income effects and substitution effects*.

As we turned to input markets, we relaxed the assumption that income was fixed and given. In the labor market, households are forced to weigh the value of leisure against

[8]Here we are looking at a country as if it were isolated from the rest of the world—as if it were a *closed* economy. Very often, however, capital investment is financed by funds loaned or provided by foreign citizens or governments. For example, in recent years a huge volume of Japanese savings has poured into the United States to buy stocks, bonds, and other financial instruments. In part, these flows finance capital investment. Also, the United States and other countries that contribute funds to the World Bank and the International Monetary Fund have provided billions in outright grants and loans to help developing countries produce capital.

the value of goods and services that can be bought with wage income. Once again, we found household preferences for goods and leisure operating within a set of constraints imposed by the market. Households also face the problem of allocating income and consumption over more than one period of time. They can finance spending in the future with today's income by saving and earning interest, or they can spend tomorrow's income today by borrowing.

At this point, we have at least a rough sketch of the factors that determine *output demand* and *input supply*. (You can review these in Figure 6.1.) In the next three chapters, we turn to firm behavior and explore in substantial detail the factors that affect *output supply* and *input demand*.

SUMMARY

1. Output demand is just one of several decisions that households must make simultaneously. Every household must make three basic decisions: (1) how much of each product, or output, to demand, (2) how much labor to supply, and (3) how much to spend today and how much to save for the future.

2. In Chapters 6–10, we make the assumption that all markets are perfectly competitive. In such markets, prices are determined by the forces of supply and demand, and no single household or firm has any control over them.

3. We also assume that households possess knowledge of product prices, product availability, product quality, and wage rates.

4. Income, wealth, and prices define a household's budget constraint. The budget constraint separates those combinations of goods and services that are available from those that are not.

5. It is best to think of the household choice problem as one of allocating income over a large number of goods and services. A change in the price of one good may change the entire allocation. Demand for some goods may rise while demand for others may fall.

6. As long as a household faces a limited income, the *real* cost of any single good or service is the value of the *other* goods and services that could have been purchased with the same amount of money.

7. All the points below and to the left of a graph of the budget constraint make up the *choice set*, or *opportunity set*.

8. While prices, income, and wealth constrain household choices, ultimate decisions depend on preferences—likes, dislikes, and tastes.

9. The idea of subjective weighing of values was formalized in the nineteenth century into the concept of utility;

whether one item is preferable to another depends on how much utility, or satisfaction, it yields relative to the alternatives.

10. The law of diminishing marginal utility says that the more of any one good we consume in a given period of time, the less satisfaction, or utility, we get out of each additional, or marginal, unit.

11. We assume that households allocate income among goods and services in order to maximize utility. This implies choosing activities that yield the highest marginal utility per dollar.

12. In a two-good world, households will choose so as to equate the marginal utility per dollar spent on X with the marginal utility per dollar spent on Y.

13. The fact that demand curves slope downward, or have a negative slope, can be explained in two ways: (1) marginal utility diminishes and (2) for most goods, the income and substitution effects of a price decline both lead to more consumption of the good.

14. When any good is sold at a fixed price, households must "reveal" whether it is worth the price being asked. In free markets no one forces you to buy any good. For many people who buy in a given market, the product is worth more than its current price. Those people receive a consumer surplus.

15. In the labor market, the trade-off is between the value of the goods and services that can be bought in the market or produced at home and the value that one places on leisure. The opportunity cost of paid work is leisure and unpaid work. The wage rate is the price, or opportunity cost, of either the benefits of unpaid work or of leisure.

16. The income and substitution effects of a change in the wage rate work in opposite directions. Higher wages mean (1) leisure is more expensive (likely response: work *more*)

and (2) more income is earned in a given number of hours so some time may be spent on leisure (likely response: work *less*).

17. The effect of a tax cut on labor supply cannot be predicted from theory alone.
18. You can think of household saving as the supply of capital.
19. Interest rates determine the trade-off between present

consumption spending and future consumption spending. Higher interest rates imply that the amount of future consumption sacrificed to enjoy more present consumption is higher—borrowing is more expensive and savings will earn a greater return. Higher interest rates thus encourage saving and discourage borrowing, and this shifts resources to the future.

REVIEW CONCEPTS

REVIEW QUESTIONS

1. Assume that as a result of 2 recent outbreak of hijackings and bombings, peoples' desire to fly diminishes significantly. Describe how you might expect the air travel market to react. What might happen to the price of airline tickets? Explain consumers' reactions to any price changes in terms of income and substitution effects.

2. Assume that consumers in Lumpland buy only two goods: X (a necessity) and Y (a luxury). Suppose Ms. A has an income of 1000 nurds per year, the price of X is five nurds and the price of Y is 10 nurds.
   a. Sketch A's budget constraint.
   b. Shade in A's opportunity set.
   c. If A were relatively poor for Lumpland, where on the budget constraint might you expect her choice to lie?
   d. Suppose that the price of Y were to fall from 10 nurds to 5 nurds. Sketch the new budget constraint. What happens to the size and position of the opportunity set?
   e. Suppose that prior to the price decrease a tax of 20 percent had been placed on luxury goods. Assume that the tax is paid by the consumer. Sketch the new budget constraint facing Ms. A.

3. Sketch the income/leisure budget constraint facing a person with
   a. a twenty-four-hour endowment of time daily,
   b. fifty dollars in property income per day (received regardless of work effort),

   c. a job that requires a minimum of eight hours of work per day and that pays a wage of $w per hour, plus time-and-a-half for all work over eight hours (1.5 × $w), and
   d. no other work opportunities.
   Note: all these should be embodied in a *single* budget constraint.

4. In 1981 Congress passed the Economic Recovery Tax Act. This legislation included, among other provisions, a major reduction in individual income tax rates. Proponents of the bill argued that the reduction in taxes would significantly increase the incentive to work, and they predicted that the result would be an increase in labor supply. In fact, evidence suggests that for some groups labor supply has actually declined. Using income and substitution effects, explain how this could be possible.

5. For each of the following events, consider how you might react. What things might you consume more of? What things might you consume less of? Would you work more or less? Would you increase or decrease your saving? Are your responses consistent with the discussion of household behavior in this chapter?
   a. Tuition at your college is cut 25 percent.
   b. You receive an award that pays you $300.00 per month for the next five years.
   c. The price of food doubles (if you are on a meal plan, assume your board charges double).
   d. A new business opens up nearby offering part-time jobs to all comers at $10.00 per hour.

6. Suppose two gourmet ice cream stores sell wonderful ice cream cones in your town. Store A's cones sell for $1.25 and store B's cones sell for $1.00. Suppose further that you love ice cream and have decided to budget $50.00 per month for ice cream cones.
a. Sketch your budget constraint and the opportunity set of combinations of A's cones and B's cones available for $50.00.
b. Suppose that A's cones and B's cones were perfect substitutes in your mind. That is, you are indifferent between cones from store A and store B. What point on your budget constraint will you choose?

APPENDIX TO CHAPTER 6
Indifference Curves

Early in the chapter, you saw how a consumer choosing between two goods is constrained by the prices of those goods and by his or her income. This appendix returns to that example and analyzes the process of choice more formally. (Before we proceed, review carefully the text under the heading "The Budget Constraint More Formally.")

Assumptions

We base the following analysis on four assumptions:
1. We assume that the analysis is restricted to goods that yield positive marginal utility, or, more simply, we assume that "more is better." One way to justify this assumption is to say that if more of something actually makes you worse off, you can simply throw it away at no cost. This is the assumption of *free disposal*.
2. We assume diminishing marginal rate of substitution. That is, as you consume more of X and less of Y, MU_X/MU_Y declines. This is almost, but not precisely, equivalent to assuming diminishing marginal utility. It means that as you consume more of X and less of Y, the rate at which you are willing to substitute X for Y declines—X becomes less valuable in terms of units of Y, or Y becomes more valuable in terms of X.
3. We assume that consumers have the ability to choose among the combinations of goods and services available. Confronted with the choice between two alternative combinations of goods and services, A and B, a consumer will respond in one of three ways: (1) she prefers A over B, (2) she prefers B over A, or (3) she is indifferent between A and B.
4. We assume that consumer choices are consistent with a simple postulate of rationality. If a consumer shows that he prefers A to B and subsequently shows that he prefers B to a third alternative, C, then if confronted with A and C, he should prefer A to C.

Deriving Indifference Curves

If we accept these four assumptions, we can then construct a "map" of a consumer's preferences. These preference maps are made up of indifference curves. An *indifference curve* is a set of points, each point representing a combination of goods X and Y, all of which yield the same total utility.

Figure 6A.1 shows how we might go about deriving an indifference curve for a hypothetical consumer. Each point in the diagram represents some amount of X and some amount of Y. Pick a random point and label it A. Point A in the diagram represents X_A units of X and Y_A units of Y. Now take some amount of Y away from our hypothetical consumer, moving him to A'. At A' he has the same amount of X—that is, X_A units—but less Y; he now has only Y_C units of Y. Since "more is better," he is unequivocally worse off at A' than he was at A.

Now to compensate for the loss of Y, we begin giving him some more X. If you give him just a little, he will still be worse off than he was at A; if you give him lots of X, he will be better off. But there must be some quantity of X that will just compensate for the loss of Y. By giving him that amount, we have put together a bundle, Y_C and X_C, which yields the exact same total utility as bundle A. If confronted with bundles A and C, our consumer will say "Either one; I don't care." In other words, he is *indifferent* between A and C. If confronted with bundles C and B, representing X_B and Y_B units of X and Y, he is also indifferent. The points along the curve labeled i in Figure 6A.1 represent all the combinations of X and Y that yield the same total utility to our consumer. That curve is thus an indifference curve.

Obviously, each consumer has a whole set of indifference curves. To see this, go back to Figure 6A.1. Starting at point A again, imagine giving the consumer a tiny bit more X *and* a tiny bit more Y. Because more is better, we know that the new bundle will yield a higher level of total utility, and the consumer will be better off. Now, just as we constructed the first indifference curve, construct a second one. Notice that what you get is an indifference curve that parallels the first, but it is higher and to the right of it. Because utility along an indifference curve is constant at all points, every point along the new curve represents a higher level of total utility then every point along the first.

Figure 6A.2 shows a set of four indifference curves. The curve labeled i_4 represents the combinations of X and Y that yield the highest level of total utility among the four.

FIGURE 6A.1

An Indifference Curve

An indifference curve is a set of points, each representing a combination of some amount of X and some amount of Y that all yield the same amount of total utility. The consumer depicted here is indifferent between bundles *A* and *B*, *B* and *C*, and *A* and *C*.

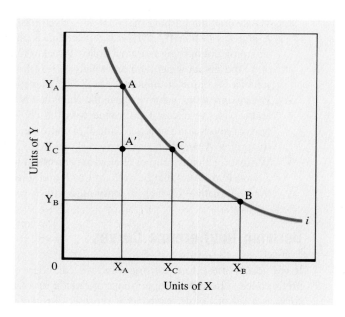

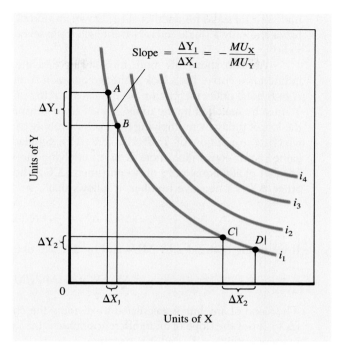

FIGURE 6A.2

A Preference Map: A Family of Indifference Curves

Each consumer has a unique family of indifference curves called a preference map. Higher indifference curves represent higher levels of total utility.

Many other indifference curves exist between those shown on the diagram; in fact, their number is infinite. Notice that as you move up and to the right, utility is increasing. The indifference curves are like contour lines on a map—each indicates a higher elevation.

The shapes of the indifference curves depend upon the preferences of the consumer, and the whole set is called a "preference map." Each consumer has a unique preference map.

Properties of Indifference Curves The indifference curves shown in Figure 6A.2 are drawn bowing out toward the origin, or zero point, on the axes. In other words, the absolute value of the slope decreases, or the curve gets flatter, as we move to the right. Thus we say that they are "convex toward the origin." This shape follows directly from the assumption of diminishing marginal rate of substitution and makes sense if you remember the law of diminishing marginal utility.

To understand the convex shape, compare the segment of curve i_1 between A and B with the segment of the same curve between C and D. Moving from A to B, the consumer is willing to give up a substantial amount of Y to get a small amount of X. (Remember that total utility is constant along an indifference curve, that is, the consumer is indifferent between A and B.) Moving from C to D, however, the consumer is willing to give up only a small amount of Y to get more X. This changing trade-off makes intuitive sense. Notice that between A and B, a lot of Y is consumed, and the *marginal* utility derived from a unit of Y is likely to be small. In addition, only a little bit of X is being consumed, and so the marginal utility derived from consuming a unit of X is likely to be high.

Suppose, for example, that X is pizza and Y is soda. Up around A and B, a thirsty, hungry football player who has 10 sodas in front of him but only one slice of pizza will trade several sodas for another slice. Down around C and D, however, he has 20 slices of pizza and only a single soda. Now he will trade several slices of pizza to get an additional soda.

We can show this more formally by deriving an expression for the slope of an indifference curve. Let's look at the arc between A and B. We know that in moving from A to B, total utility is constant. That means that the utility lost as a result of consuming less Y must be matched by the utility gained from consuming more X. We can approximate the loss of utility by multiplying the marginal utility of Y (MU_Y) by the number of units by which consumption of Y is curtailed (ΔY). Similarly, we can approximate the utility gained from consuming more X by multiplying the marginal utility of X (MU_X) by the number of additional units of X consumed (ΔX). These two must be equal in magnitude. Since ΔY is a negative number, it follows that

$$MU_X \cdot \Delta X = -(MU_Y \cdot \Delta Y).$$

If we divide both sides by MU_Y and by ΔX, we obtain

$$\Delta Y / \Delta X = -(MU_X / MU_Y).$$

The slope of any line is calculated by dividing the change in Y (ΔY) by the change in X (ΔX). Thus the slope of an indifference curve is the ratio of the marginal utility of X to the marginal utility of Y, and it is negative.

Now returning to pizza (X) and soda (Y), as we move down from the A:B area to the C:D area, our football player is consuming less soda and more pizza. The marginal utility of pizza (MU_X) is falling and the marginal utility of soda (MU_Y) is rising. That means that MU_X / MU_Y is falling, and the absolute value of the slope of the indifference curve is declining. And, indeed, it does get flatter.

Consumer Choice   As you recall, demand depends upon income, the prices of goods and services, and preferences or tastes. We are now ready to see how preferences as embodied in indifference curves interact with budget constraints to determine the final quantities of X and Y that will be chosen.

In Figure 6A.3, a set of indifference curves is superimposed on a consumer's budget constraint. Recall that the budget constraint separates those combinations of X and Y that are available to our consumer from those that are not. The constraint simply shows those combinations that can be purchased with an income of $\$I$ at prices P_X and P_Y. The X intercept is $\$I/P_X$, or the number of units of X that can be purchased with $\$I$ if nothing is spent on Y. Similarly, the Y intercept is $\$I/P_Y$, or the number of units of Y that can be purchased with an income of $\$I$ if nothing is spent on X. The shaded area is called the consumer's opportunity set. The slope of a budget constraint is $-P_X/P_Y$.

Consumers will choose from among those combinations of X and Y available the one that maximizes utility. In graphic terms, the consumer will move along the budget constraint until he or she is on the highest possible indifference curve. Utility rises by moving from points such as A or C toward B. Any movement away from point B moves the consumer to a lower indifference curve—a lower level of utility. Thus, utility is maximized when our consumer buys X^* units of X and Y^* units of Y. At point B, the budget constraint is just tangent to indifference curve i_2. As long as indifference curves are convex to the origin, utility maximization will be at such a tangency.

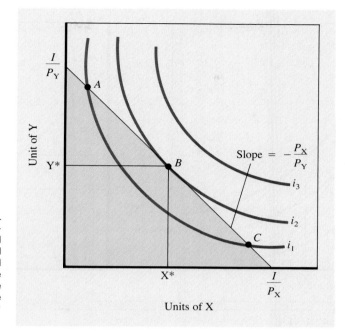

FIGURE 6A.3
Consumer Utility Maximizing
Equilibrium

Consumers will choose that combination of X and Y that maximizes total utility. Graphically, the consumer will move along the budget constraint until the highest possible indifference curve is reached. At that point, the budget constraint and the indifference curve are tangent. This occurs at X^* and Y^*.

The tangency condition has important implications. Where two curves are tangent, they have the same slope, which implies that the slope of the indifference curve is exactly equal to the slope of the budget constraint:

$$MU_X/MU_Y = P_X/P_Y.$$

This same consumer equilibrium condition can be written

$$MU_X/P_X = MU_Y/P_Y.$$

This is the same condition derived in our discussion without using indifference curves. We can describe this condition intuitively by saying that consumers maximize their total utility by equating the marginal utility per dollar spent on X with the marginal utility per dollar spent on Y. If this were not true, utility could be increased by shifting money from one good to the other.

Deriving a Demand Curve from Indifference Curves and Budget Constraints

We now turn to the task of deriving a simple demand curve from indifference curves and budget constraints. A demand curve shows the quantity of a single good, X in this case, that a consumer will demand at various prices. To derive it we want to confront our consumer with several alternative prices for X while keeping other prices, income, and preferences constant.

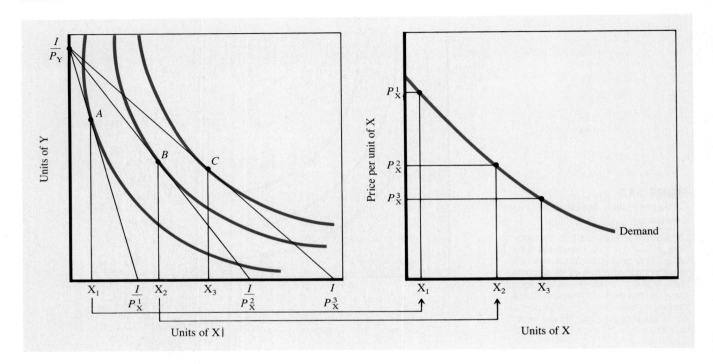

FIGURE 6A.4
Deriving a Demand Curve from Indifference Curves and a Budget Constraint

Lowering the price of X from P^1_X to P^2_X and then to P^3_X swivels the budget constraint out to the right. The Y intercept does not change since at that point nothing is spent on X and the price of Y has not changed. At each price there is a different utility maximizing combination of X and Y. Plotting the three prices against the quantities of X chosen results in a standard demand curve.

Figure 6A.4 shows the derivation. We begin with price P^1_X. At that price, the utility-maximizing point is A, where the consumer demands X_1 units of X. Therefore, in the right hand diagram, we plot P^1_X against X_1. This is the first point on our demand curve.

Now we lower the price of X to P^2_X. Lowering the price expands the opportunity set. The X intercept of the budget constraint shifts out to the right. Because the price of X has fallen, if our consumer spends all of his income on X, he can buy more of it. He is also better off, since he can move to a higher indifference curve. The new utility-maximizing point is B, where the consumer demands X_2 units of X. Back in the right-hand diagram, because the consumer demands X_2 units of X at a price of P^2_X, we plot P^2_X against X_2. A second price cut to P^3_X moves our consumer to point C, where he demands X_3 units of X, and so on. We see then how the demand curve can be derived from knowing a consumer's preference map and budget constraint.

7 The Firm: Organization, Profits, and Production

In Chapter 6, we took an introductory look at household decisions that lie behind supply and demand curves. There we spent some time discussing household choices: how much to work and how to choose among the wide range of goods and services available in the market within the constraints of prices and income. Then we identified some of the factors likely to influence household demand in output markets, as well as some of the factors that affect household supply in input markets such as the labor market.

Now we turn to the other side of the system, the behavior of firms. Business firms purchase inputs in order to produce and sell outputs. In other words, they *demand* factors of production in input markets and they *supply* goods and services in output markets. (Figure 7.1 repeats the circular diagram you first encountered in Chapter 6, and will serve as a road map to guide you through the next several chapters. Chapter 7 looks inside the firm at the process of production that actually transforms inputs into outputs. Chapters 8 and 9 use information on input prices and production technology to derive cost curves from which, in turn, we derive firms' output supply curves. In chapters 10 and 11, we turn to input markets and derive firms' input demand curves.

Firms come in different sizes and internal organizations, but they all take inputs and transform them into things for which there is some demand. An independent accountant, for example, combines labor, paper, telephone service, time, learning, a personal computer, and so forth to provide help to confused taxpayers at tax time. General Motors uses land, buildings, labor of many kinds, robots, steel, rubber, plastic, glass, and so forth to produce automobiles. A rock band combines talent, energy, instruments, costumes, amplifiers, lighting, and labor to produce music.

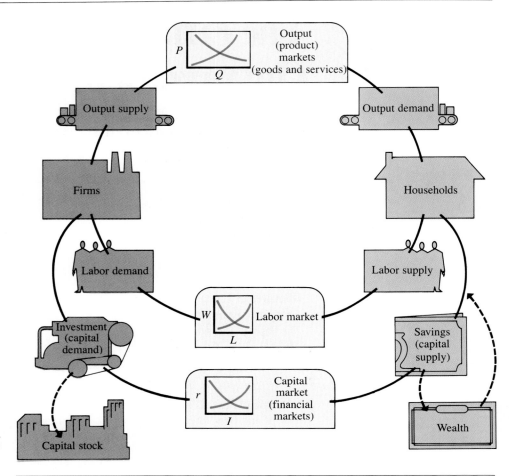

FIGURE 7.1
Firm and Household Decisions

Firms supply output and demand labor and capital in input markets.

SOME BASIC ASSUMPTIONS

Production in Firms, Households, and Government

While our model focuses on profit-making business firms, it is important to understand that production and productive activity are not confined to private business firms. Households also engage in transforming factors of production into useful things. When I work in my garden, I am combining land, labor, fertilizer, seeds, and tools (capital) into the vegetables I eat and the flowers I enjoy. From an economic point of view, the child-rearing activities of a young family transform their unsocialized young into productive human beings. We sometimes refer to the talents and skills that people acquire as they are reared and educated as human capital. The government also combines land, labor, and capital to produce public services for which demand exists—national defense, police and fire protection, and education, to name a few.

What sets private business firms apart from other producers, such as households and government, is their *purpose*. A **firm** exists when someone or some group of people decides to produce a good or service to meet a perceived demand. In most cases firms exist to *make a profit*. They engage in production because they can sell their products for more than it costs to produce them.

Firm *A person or group that transforms inputs or resources into output. The primary producing unit in a market economy.*

Even among firms that exist to make a profit, however, there are many important differences. Their behavior is likely to depend upon how they are organized internally and upon their relationship to the firms with which they compete: How many of them are there? How large are they? How do they compete?

In Chapter 3 we discussed the different ways that a business can organize—as proprietorships, as partnerships, or as corporations. We also discussed different ways that industries are organized in the U.S. economy—perfect competition, monopolistic competition, oligopoly, and monopoly. Before we finish with microeconomics, we will analyze the behavior of all four of these industry types.

But it is logical to start with the simplest. Thus the next three chapters will deal exclusively with the behavior of firms in *perfectly competitive industries*. By the end of Chapter 12, we will have a complete model of an economy based on the assumptions of perfect competition.

Perfect Competition

As we first defined it in Chapter 3, **perfect competition** was said to exist in an industry that contains many relatively small firms producing identical products. The most important characteristic of a perfectly competitive industry is that no single firm has any control over prices—an individual firm can not affect the market price of its product or of the inputs that it buys. This important characteristic follows from two assumptions. First, a competitive industry is composed of many firms, each small relative to the size of the industry. Second, every firm in a perfectly competitive industry produces exactly the same product; the output of one firm cannot be distinguished from the output of the others. The products of a perfectly competitive industry are said to be **homogeneous**.

Homogeneous products
Products that are indistinguishable from one another.

These assumptions limit the decisions open to competitive firms and simplify the analysis of competitive behavior. Firms in perfectly competitive industries do not "differentiate" their products, nor do they make decisions about price. Each firm takes prices as *given*, that is, as determined in the market by the laws of supply and demand, and decides only how much to produce and how to produce it.

The idea that competitive firms are price takers is quite central. Of course, we do not mean by this that firms cannot affix price tags to their merchandise; all firms have this ability. We simply mean that—given availability of perfect substitutes—any product priced over the market price will not be sold. Thus, to sell any goods, competitive firms must adhere to the market price.

Perfectly elastic demand   A horizontal demand curve. If price is increased, quantity demanded drops to zero.

These assumptions also imply that the demand for the product of a competitive firm is **perfectly elastic**. Take for example the Ohio corn farmer shown in Figure 7.2. On the left side of the diagram is the situation in the market. Corn is currently selling for a price of $2.45 per bushel. The right side of the diagram shows the demand for corn as the farmer sees it. If she were to *raise* her price, she would sell no corn at all; because there are perfect substitutes available, demand would drop to zero. To lower her price would be silly because she can sell all she wants at the current price.

Free entry and exit   The condition in which no barriers prevent new firms seeking profits from entering and producing in a market and in which existing firms seeking to cut losses can stop production and leave a market. An assumption of perfect competition.

In addition, in perfect competition we assume that new firms can and do have **free entry and exit** to and from the business. The assumption of *free entry* implies that if firms in an industry are earning excessively high profits, new firms that seek to do the same thing are likely to spring up. There are no barriers that prevent a start-up firm from competing. If soybean prices rise sharply, corn farmers can shift land out of corn production and into soybeans without incurring enormous costs. In essence, this would mean new firms moving into soybean production. Fast food restaurants are quick to spring up when a new shopping area starts operating, and new gas stations appear when a

FIGURE 7.2
Demand Facing a Single Firm in
a Competitive Market

In *perfectly* competitive industries, each firm is small relative to the size of the industry. In addition, the products of one firm cannot be distinguished from the products of others. It follows, therefore, that firms are "price takers." As individual firms, they have no control over market prices. Each firm faces a perfectly elastic demand curve, *d*.

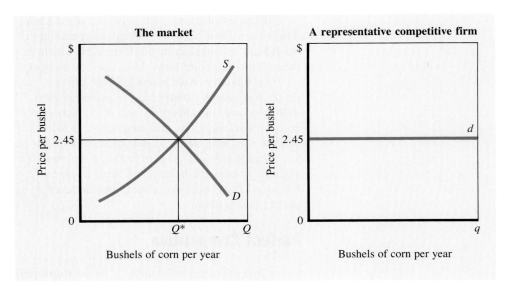

development is built or a new highway opens up. Where profit opportunities present themselves, we assume that firms will enter and compete for them.

When a firm *exits* an industry, it simply stops producing a product. In the 1950s, two dominant industries in the Northeast were textiles and furniture. As time went on and conditions changed, fewer and fewer of those firms remained in business. Generally speaking, when a firm closes down it is because it is suffering losses or because profits are insufficient. New England textile and furniture producers found themselves facing increasing foreign competition, as well as lower production costs in the South. While some firms packed up and moved, others simply got out of the business altogether.

As you saw in Chapter 3, probably the best examples of perfect competition are found in agriculture. There, products are absolutely homogeneous—it is impossible to distinguish one farmer's wheat from another's—and prices are set by the forces of supply and demand in a huge national market.

THE BEHAVIOR OF PERFECTLY COMPETITIVE FIRMS

Firms in perfectly competitive industries must make three basic decisions in order to achieve what we assume to be their primary objective, that is, maximum profits:

1. How much output to supply (quantity of product).
2. How to produce that output (what production technique to use).
3. How much of each input to demand.

The first and last choices are linked by the second choice. Once a firm has decided how much to produce, choosing a production method determines its input requirements. If a sweater company decides to produce 5000 sweaters this month, it knows how many production workers it will need, how much electricity it will use, how much raw yarn to purchase, and how many machines will be working. A grower who sets out to produce and ship 3000 bushels of apples knows how many pickers to hire, how many baskets to have on hand, and so forth.

Similarly, given a technique of production, any set of input quantities determines the amount of output that can be produced. Certainly the number of machines and workers employed in a sweater mill determine how many sweaters can be produced, and the number of trees and pickers determine the number of bushels of apples a grower can ship.

Changing the technology of production, however, will change the relationship between input and output quantities. A fully automated textile mill will turn out more sweaters in a month than one with fewer and less sophisticated machines that more workers are needed to operate. An apple orchard that uses expensive equipment to raise pickers up into the trees will harvest more fruit with fewer workers in a given period of time than an orchard where pickers use simple ladders.

Remember as we proceed that we are discussing and analyzing the behavior of *perfectly competitive* firms. Thus we have said nothing about price-setting behavior, product quality and other characteristics of the product, or choices that lead to product differentiation. In perfect competition, both input and output prices are beyond a firm's control—they are determined in the market and are not the decisions of any individual firm. And remember that all firms in a given industry produce the same exact product. When we come to analyze the behavior of firms in other kinds of markets, the three basic decisions will be expanded to include the setting of prices and the determination of product quality.

Objectives of Firms: Profits

Because we are discussing only firms that are in business to make a profit, we can assume that these firms make the decisions they make in order to *maximize profits*. But what is profit? In simplest terms, **profit** is the difference between revenues and costs:

$$\text{profit} = \text{total revenue} - \text{total cost}.$$

Revenue, total revenue
Receipts from the sale of product.
P x Q.

Economic costs   The full costs of production including (1) a normal rate of return on investment, and (2) the opportunity cost of each factor of production.

Revenues are simply receipts from the sale of the product. *Total revenue* is equal to the number of units produced and sold (Q) times the price received per unit (P). *Costs*, however, are a little more complicated. In economics the definition of costs differs slightly from the costs that an accountant calculates. **Economic costs** include (1) a normal rate of return, or profit, and (2) the opportunity cost of each factor of production.

Normal Rate of Return, or Profit   When someone decides to start a firm, he or she must commit resources. To operate a manufacturing firm, you need a plant and some equipment. To start a restaurant, you need to buy grills, ovens, tables, chairs, and so forth. In other words you invest in *capital*. It takes resources to do that, and those resources stay tied up in the firm as long as it is in operation. Even firms that have been around a long time must continue to invest. Plant and equipment wears out and must be replaced. Firms often decide to expand and put new capital in place. This is as true of proprietorships, where the resources come directly from the proprietor, as it is for corporations, where the resources to make investments come from shareholders.

Whenever resources are used to invest in a business, there is an *opportunity cost*. Instead of opening a candy store, I could always put my funds into a certificate of deposit or a government bond and earn interest. Instead of using its retained earnings to build a new plant, a firm could simply earn interest on those savings by doing likewise.

Why, then, do firms put their funds into the business rather than into the bank? When resources are used to invest in a business, we assume that the decision is based on the expectation of profit. But a firm isn't profitable in a meaningful sense unless it earns more for its investors than what they forgo by not just buying a bond or a certificate of deposit. Using resources to invest in a firm thus has an opportunity cost.

Normal rate of profit, or return
A rate of profit that is just sufficient to keep owners and investors satisfied; for relatively risk-free firms it should be the same as the interest rate on risk-free government bonds.

A **normal rate of profit**, or **return,** is the rate that is just sufficient to keep owners or investors interested in the firm. From the standpoint of a manager, it is the "actual" cost of capital. If the rate of return were to fall below normal, it would be difficult or impossible for managers to raise needed resources. Owners of the firm would be receiving profits that were lower than they could receive elsewhere in the economy.

If the firm has fairly steady revenues and the future looks secure, the normal profit rate should be very close to the interest rate on "safe" bonds. I certainly won't keep investors interested in my firm if I don't pay them a rate of return at least as high as they can get by buying a risk-free government or corporate bond at a fixed interest rate. If my firm is rock solid and the economy is steady, I may not have to pay much more. But if, on the other hand, my firm is in a very speculative industry and the future of the economy is shaky, I may have to pay substantially more to keep my shareholders happy. In exchange for taking such a risk, they will expect a higher return.

A normal profit rate is *added* to other costs in calculating full economic costs. Suppose, for example, that I am running a firm in a relatively safe industry where a 15-percent return on investment is considered normal. That is, if you were a shareholder in my firm and you owned $1000 worth of stock, you would expect to earn a profit of at least $150.00 per year. If the total asset value of my firm were $100,000, the *economic* costs of running my firm would include $15,000 of what an accountant would call *net income,* or profit. Again, we add a normal return as a cost because it represents the opportunity cost of capital in this industry. After all, owners could always sell out and put their money in certificates of deposit or bonds.

Economic profits, or excess profits   *Profits over and above the normal rate of return on investment; anything greater than the normal opportunity cost of investing.*

Adding a normal profit rate to cost means that when a firm earns exactly a normal rate of return or profit, it actually earns zero economic profits. **Economic profits**, or **excess profits** as they are sometimes called, are profits over and above normal. In other words, profits are excessive only if they are greater than the opportunity cost of investing.

When a firm earns *positive* economic profits, it is earning profit at a rate more than sufficient to retain the interest of investors. In fact, economic profits are likely to attract new firms into an industry and cause existing firms to expand.

When a firm suffers *negative* economic profits, that is, when it incurs economic losses, it is earning at a rate below that required to keep investors happy. Such economic losses may or may not be losses as an accountant would measure them. Even if I earn a positive profit of 10 percent on my assets, I am earning below normal profits, or economic losses, if a normal return for my industry is 15 percent. Investors will be looking to bail out of industries in which firms are earning negative economic profits. Some firms may exit the industry; others will contract in size. Certainly new investment will not flow into such an industry.

Opportunity Costs of All Inputs   *Economic costs* include the opportunity costs of all inputs, not just accounting costs. If you open a restaurant and work 40 hours a week helping to run it, the cost of running the restaurant includes the cost of your time, even if you do not formally pay yourself a wage. (If you don't pay yourself a wage, your time does not show up on the restaurant's books). If you could be earning $15 per hour working at a local factory, then the opportunity cost of your time helping run the restaurant is at least $600 per week. In analyzing costs, it is important to include both direct out-of-pocket costs *and* opportunity costs.

Short-Run versus Long-Run Decisions

The decisions that a firm makes—how much to produce, how to produce it, and what inputs to demand—clearly have a time dimension. If a firm decides that it wants to double or triple its output, it may take time to arrange financing, hire architects and contractors, and build a new plant. Planning for a major expansion can take years. In the meantime, the firm must decide how much to produce *within the constraint of its existing plant*. On the other hand, if a firm decides that it wants to get out of a particular business, it may take time to arrange an orderly exit. There may be contract obligations, equipment to sell, and so forth. Once again, the firm must decide what to do in the meantime.

A firm's immediate response to a change in the economic environment may also differ from its response over time. Consider, for example, the response of American industry to the dramatic increases in crude oil prices in 1973 and 1974. Most firms had, in a sense, built the use of inexpensive oil into their operations, and most had no choice but to continue to buy it. Initially, demand for petroleum seemed to be very inelastic with respect to price.

Over a period of years, however, as new plants were built and old ones were modernized, firms adopted more energy-efficient techniques. Households, too, responded over time by buying more fuel-efficient automobiles and by insulating their homes. Ultimately, the quantity of petroleum demanded went down significantly. This demand, it turned out, was more elastic in the long run than it had appeared to be.

Because the character of immediate response differs from long-run adjustment, it is useful to define, at least loosely, two time periods, the long run and the short run. Two assumptions define the **short run**: (1) a fixed scale, or a fixed factor, of production, and (2) no entry to or exit from the industry. First, the short run is defined as that period during which existing firms have some *fixed factor of production*, that is, during which some factor locks them into their current scale of operations. Second, new firms *cannot enter* an industry, and existing firms *cannot exit* in the short run. Firms may curtail operations, but they are still locked into some costs, even though they may be in the process of going out of business.

Just which factor or factors of production are hard to change in the short run differs from industry to industry. For a manufacturing firm, the actual physical plant is the easiest to see. A factory is built with a given production rate in mind. While that rate can be increased, output cannot increase beyond a certain limit. For a private physician, the limit may be her own capacity to see patients. The day has only so many hours, and her endurance has a limit. In the long run, she may invite others to join her practice and expand, but for now, in the short run, she is the firm, and her capacity is the firm's capacity.

In the **long run**, there are *no fixed factors of production*. Firms can plan for any output level they find desirable. They can double or triple output, for example. In addition, new firms can *start up operations*, and existing firms can *go out of business*.

Short run   *The period of time for which two conditions hold; the firm is operating under a fixed scale (fixed factor) of production and firms can neither enter nor exit an industry.*

Long run   *That period of time for which there are no fixed factors of production. Firms can increase or decrease scale of operation and new firms can enter and existing firms can exit the industry.*

No hard-and-fast rule specifies how long the short run is. The point is simply that there are two basic kinds of decisions: those that govern the day-to-day operations of the firm and those that involve longer-term planning. Sometimes major decisions can be implemented in weeks; often, however, it takes years.

The Basis of Decisions: Market Prices and Technology

As we said earlier, the three fundamental decisions of firms are made in order to maximize profits. Since profits equal total revenues minus total costs, each firm needs to know how much it costs to produce its product and how much its product can be sold for.

To know how much it costs to produce a good or service, I need to know something about the production techniques that are available and about the prices of the inputs required. To estimate how much it will cost me to operate a gas station, I need to know what equipment I need, how many workers, what kind of a building, where to locate the plant, and so forth. I also need to know the going wage rates for mechanics and unskilled laborers, the cost of gas pumps, hydraulic lifts, and Coke machines, interest rates, rents per square foot on high-traffic corners, and the wholesale price of gasoline. And, of course, I need to know how much I can sell gasoline and repair services for.

In the language of economics, I need to know three things:

1.   The price of output
2.   The techniques of production that are available
3.   The prices of inputs

Output price determines potential revenues. The techniques available tell me how much of each input I need, and input prices tell me how much they will cost. The last two, then, determine costs.

The rest of this discussion and the whole next chapter focus on *costs* of production. We begin at the heart of the firm, with the process of production itself. Faced with a set of input prices, firms must decide on the best, or optimal, method of production. The optimal method is the one that minimizes cost. With cost determined and the market price of output known, a firm will make a final judgment about the quantity of its product to produce and the quantity of each input to demand.

PRODUCTION AND PRODUCTION TECHNOLOGY

Production   The process through which firms combine and transform inputs into outputs.

Production is the process of combining and transforming inputs and making them into outputs. The process takes many forms. General Motors uses land, buildings, different kinds of labor, steel, rubber, and many other ingredients to produce automobiles. The San Francisco Symphony Orchestra uses land, a building, highly skilled labor, musical instruments (capital), and so on to produce performances.

Production technology   The relationship between inputs and outputs.

It is **production technology** that relates inputs to outputs. To produce any given service or good, it takes specific quantities of inputs. Just as a loaf of bread requires certain amounts of water, flour, and yeast, some kneading, and patting, as well as an oven, gas, or electricity, so a trip from downtown New York to Newark, New Jersey, can be produced with a taxicab, 45 minutes of a driver's labor, some volume of gasoline, and so forth.

Most outputs can be produced in more than one way—that is, by using a number of different techniques. You can tear down an old building and clear a lot to create a park in several ways, for example. Five hundred men and women with small hammers could descend upon it and carry the pieces away by hand; that would be a *labor-intensive* technology. The same park could be produced by two people with a wrecking crane, a steam shovel, a backhoe, and a dump truck; that would be a *capital-intensive* technology. Similarly, different inputs can be combined to transport people from New York to New Jersey. A PATH train that carries many people simultaneously under the Hudson River requires a large amount of capital relative to labor. Cab rides to Newark require much more labor relative to capital.

An insurance company needs office space to produce its product, but office space can be assembled in a variety of ways. In suburban locations, office parks are often spacious, with trees and grass and buildings of two or three stories. In central cities, offices are stacked on top of one another in glass towers. To be in the insurance business, you need capital in the form of a building and land, but the two can be combined in several ways. In central cities, only a small amount of land is combined with a great deal of capital to produce insurance services. In suburban office parks, the same services are produced with more land and less capital.

In choosing the most appropriate technology, firms presumably choose the one that minimizes the cost of production. For a firm in an economy with a plentiful supply of inexpensive labor but not much capital, that choice will no doubt involve labor-intensive techniques. Firms in an economy with high wages and high labor costs, however, have an incentive to "substitute" away from labor and to use more capital-intensive, or *labor-saving*, techniques. Suburban office parks use more land and have more open space in part because land there is plentiful and less expensive than land in the middle of a big city. Spreading out is cheaper than building a tower.

Production Functions

Production function   A mathematical expression of a relationship between quantities of inputs and outputs.

When the relationship between inputs and outputs, that is, the technology of production, is expressed numerically or mathematically, it is called a **production function**. Table 7.1 and Figure 7.3 illustrate a simple production function for a small sandwich shop. Most of the sandwiches are grilled, and the shop owns only one grill, which can easily accommodate only two people. One person working alone can produce only 10 sandwiches per hour. He has to answer the phone, wait on customers, keep the tables clean, and so on. The second worker can stay at the grill full time and not worry about

TABLE 7.1
Production Function

Labor units (employees)	Total product (sandwiches per hour)	Marginal product ($\Delta TP/\Delta L$)	Average product (TP/L)
0	0	—	—
1	10	10	10.0
2	25	15	12.5
3	35	10	11.7
4	40	5	10.0
5	42	2	8.4
6	42	0	7.0

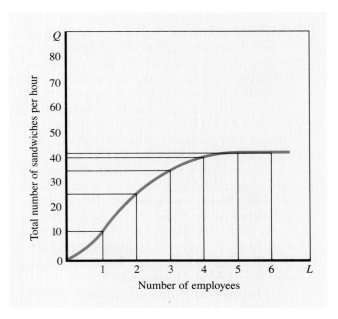

FIGURE 7.3
Production Function for
Sandwiches

A production function is a mathematical representation of the quantitative relationship between inputs and output. Here we see total product, sandwiches, graphed as a function of labor inputs.

anything except making sandwiches. Thus she can produce 15 sandwiches per hour. When a third person tries to use the grill, there is crowding, but, with careful use of space, more sandwiches can be produced. The third worker adds 10 sandwiches per hour.[1]

When the fourth and fifth workers are added, they can move to the grill while the others are putting on the pickles and onions, wrapping, and so on, but then the first three must wait to get back to the grill. Worker four adds a net of five sandwiches per hour to the total, and worker five adds just two. Hiring a sixth worker adds no output at all: the current maximum capacity of the shop is 42 sandwiches per hour.

Marginal product The additional output that can be produced by adding one more unit of a specific input ceteris paribus.

Marginal Product and the Law of Diminishing Returns   **Marginal product** is the additional output that can be produced by hiring an additional unit of input, holding all other inputs constant. Thus from Table 7.1 you can see that the marginal product of the first unit of labor is 10 sandwiches; the marginal product of the second is 15, the third, 10, and so forth. Notice that the marginal product of the sixth worker is 0. Figure 7.4 graphs the marginal product curve. Geometrically, it presents a graph of the slope of the production function.[2]

Law of diminishing returns The observation that when additional units of a variable input are added to fixed inputs after a certain point, the additional product of a unit of the added variable input declines.

The **law of diminishing returns** states that after a certain point, *when additional units of a variable input are added to fixed inputs* (in this case the building and grill), *the marginal product of the variable input declines.* The British economist David Ricardo first formulated the law of diminishing returns based on his observations of agriculture in nineteenth century England. With a given area of land, he noted that successive "doses" of labor and capital yielded smaller and smaller increases in crop output. This is true in agriculture because either less fertile land must be farmed or the same land must be farmed more intensively. In manufacturing diminishing returns set in when limited plant capacity becomes overburdened.

[1] Be sure to note that the added output from hiring a third worker is less because of the capital constraint, *not* because the third worker is somehow less efficient or hard working. We assume that all workers are of equal quality.
[2] Because slope is the change in Y divided by the change in X, the slope of a production function is the change in total product (measured on the Y axis) divided by the change in labor inputs. The slope is thus the additional output *per additional unit* of labor, or the marginal product of labor.

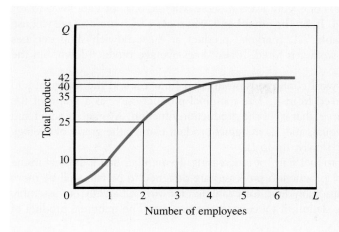
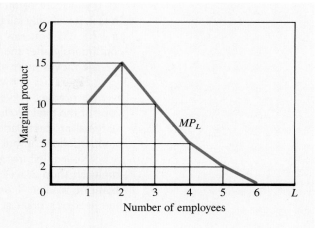

FIGURE 7.4
Derivation of Marginal Product from a Production Function

The marginal product of labor is the additional output that one additional unit of labor produces. The marginal product of the second unit of labor is 15 units of output; the marginal product of the fourth unit of labor is 5 units of output. Diminishing returns implies that the marginal product curve slopes downward.

Diminishing returns set in at our sandwich shop when worker three is added. The marginal product of the second worker is actually higher than the first. The first worker takes care of the phone and the tables, and that frees up the second worker to concentrate on sandwich making. But from that point on, the grill gets crowded.

Diminishing returns characterize many productive activities. Consider, for example, an independent accountant who works primarily for private citizens preparing their tax returns. As he adds more and more clients, he must work later and later into the evening. At some point, the additional hours spent yield little or no product. Here the "fixed" factor of production is the worker himself for whom there is a limited number of available hours. Similarly, adding the hundredth floor onto a building is more difficult than adding the twentieth; the fixed input, land, ultimately becomes a binding constraint.

Diminishing returns, or diminishing marginal product, begin to show up when more and more units of a variable input are added to a fixed input, such as scale of plant. In defining the short run, you recall, we assumed that some fixed factor of production constrains the firm. The fact is that *diminishing returns always apply in the short run*, and in the short run every firm will face diminishing returns. This means that every firm finds it progressively more difficult to increase its output as it approaches capacity production.

Marginal Product versus Average Product   **Average product** is the average amount produced by each unit of a variable factor. At the sandwich shop with one grill, that variable factor is labor. In Table 7.1, you saw that the first two workers together produce 25 sandwiches per hour, so their average product is 12.5. The third worker adds only 10 sandwiches per hour to the total. These 10 sandwiches are the *marginal* product of labor. (Recall that marginal product is the product of only the *last* unit of labor.) The *average product* of the first three units of labor, however, is 11.7, the average of 10, 15, and 10.

Average product "follows" marginal product, but it does not change as quickly. If marginal product is above average, the average rises; if marginal product is below average, the average falls. Suppose, for example, that you have had six exams and your average is

86. If you score 75 on the next one, your average score will *fall*, but not all the way to 75. In fact, it will only fall to 84.4. If, on the other hand, you score a 95, your average will rise to 87.3. As you saw in Table 7.1, marginal product at the sandwich shop declines continuously after the third worker is hired. It also drags average product down, but the average moves more slowly.

Figure 7.5 shows a typical continuous-production function and the marginal and average product curves derived from it. The marginal product curve is a graph of the slope of the total product curve, that is, of the production function. Average product and marginal product start out equal, and, as marginal product climbs, the graph of average product follows it, but more slowly, up to L_1.

Notice that marginal product starts out increasing. Remember that it did that in the sandwich shop as well. Most production processes are designed to be run well by more than one worker. Take an assembly line, for example. To work efficiently, an assembly line needs a worker at every station; it's a cooperative process. The marginal product of

FIGURE 7.5

Typical Continuous Production Function

Marginal and average product curves can be derived from total product curves. The marginal product of labor is defined as $\Delta Q / \Delta L$; thus, it is the *slope* of the total product curve. Average product follows marginal product; it rises when marginal product is above it and falls when marginal product is below it.

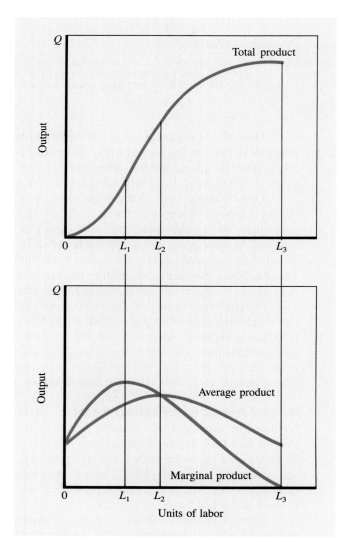

the first workers is low or zero. Only upon reaching the number of workers that the plant was designed for does marginal product peak out.

At L_1, marginal product turns around and begins to fall. Just as the third sandwich maker began to crowd the grill, every plant has a finite capacity, and efforts to increase production will always run into the limits of that capacity. At L_2, marginal product has fallen back to the average product, which has been increasing. Between L_2 and L_3, marginal product falls below average, and thus average product begins to follow it *down*. Average product is thus at its maximum at point L_2, where it is equal to marginal product.

At L_3, the total product curve is flat—that is, it has a zero slope. At this point, more labor yields no more output, and marginal product at that point is zero—the assembly line has no more positions, the grill is jammed, and the doctor is so tired that she can't see another patient. (If you have trouble understanding the relationships among the three curves in Figure 7.5, go back over the calculations in Table 7.1 and review the section on graphing in Chapter 2.)

Two Variable Factors of Production   So far we have considered production functions with only one variable factor of production. But inputs work together in production. In general additional capital increases the productivity of labor. Capital—buildings, machines, and so on—is of no use without people to operate it, so capital and labor are *complementary* inputs.

To see this, consider again the sandwich shop. If the demand for sandwiches began to exceed the capacity of the shop to produce them, one option would be to expand capacity. This would mean opening up more space and purchasing more capital in the form of a new grill.

A second grill would essentially double the productive capacity of the shop. Table 7.2 shows what a new grill would do to the marginal product of labor in the shop. With only one grill, the first worker produces 10 sandwiches per hour and the second produces 15. With the third worker, diminishing returns set in. The third can crank out only 10 sandwiches and the fourth only five per hour. But with two grills, diminishing returns don't set in until there are two workers at *each* grill. The third and fourth workers produce 15 sandwiches each per hour. Remember, number one is handling the phone and the tables, so numbers two, three, and four can go full speed on the grills.

The fifth worker is now the one that begins to crowd. The fifth worker is the third sandwich maker on the first grill. She can produce only 10. The sixth worker is the third worker on the second grill, and he can also produce 10 sandwiches an hour. It is not until

TABLE 7.2
Marginal Product of Labor in Sandwich Production with Two Grills

	ONE GRILL		TWO GRILLS	
	Total Product	Marginal Product	Total Product	Marginal Product
0	0	0	0	0
1	10	10	10	10
2	25	15	25	15
3	35	10	40	15
4	40	5	55	15
5	42	2	65	10
6	42	0	75	10
7	42	0	80	5

Robotics

The ultimate substitution of capital for labor is robotics. Fifteen years ago robots were confined to the world of science fiction. Today, robots are everywhere in industry. *The Statistical Abstract of the United States* actually has data on the number of robots produced in the United States to do tasks such as welding, soldering, machine-tool loading and unloading, assembly of components, painting, gluing, sealing, and so forth. The Japanese have used robots extensively in automobile production for years. In 1986, 60 U.S. companies reported over $300 million in sales of robots, accessories, and components.

Whenever robots are introduced, it is, of course, a threat to employees. The following article from the *New York Times* appeared in December, 1987:

> Starting in February the NBC "Nightly News" anchor, Tom Brokaw, will have three fewer people in his audience—the camera operators.
>
> NBC will start using robot cameras on "Nightly News," and within a couple of months also on "Sunrise" and "Before Hours," the

network's early morning business program, as well as on specials and election reports. The studio work in all those programs primarily involves head shots.

A director in the control booth will send his instructions to the camera by way of a computer instead of by relaying them to a camera operator.

"It's all based on a philosophy that we're trying to put our creative people as close to the end product as we possibly can, and where there are people translating somebody's instructions from a person to a device, the more we can reduce the number of translators the better off we are," the NBC vice president for editorial production services, Tom Wolzien, said yesterday.

Mr. Wolzien said the robot cameras would eventually eliminate the equivalent of four employees on "Nightly News." NBC said no one would be dismissed because of the robot cameras. The network has been scaling back its personnel by not replacing people who quit or retire.

Robot cameras could eventually save the company close to $1 million a year, Mr. Wolzien said.*

*From the Associated Press, *New York Times*, Dec. 22, 1987. Reprinted by permission.

we have hired seven workers that marginal product drops to five. We have enhanced the productivity of labor by adding capital to the production process.

Figure 7.6 shows graphically how the increase in capital enhances the productivity of labor and shifts the marginal product curve out to the right. This simple relationship lies at the heart of worries about "productivity" at the national and international levels. Building new, modern plants and equipment enhances a nation's productivity. Since the 1950s for example, Japan has accumulated capital—built plant and equipment—faster than any other country in the world. The result is very high quantity of output per worker on average.

FIGURE 7.6

Shift of a Marginal Product of Labor Curve Resulting from an Increase in Capital

When more capital is added in the form of a new grill, the productivity of labor is enhanced. The added capital shifts the marginal product of labor curve to the right.

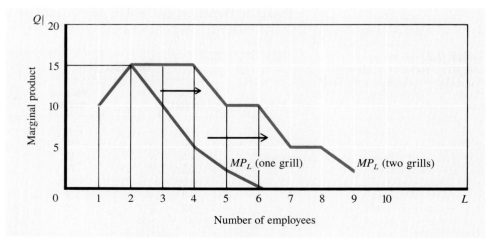

More Complex Production Functions

Many empirical studies have used data on actual quantities of inputs and outputs to estimate the shapes of real production functions. These econometric studies use data to construct formal mathematical relationships between input and output quantities. In order to do these estimates, economists generally use a mathematical relationship that embodies both diminishing returns to single inputs and the complementarity that exists between inputs.

The most commonly used relationship was first investigated in the 1920s by Paul H. Douglas, a University of Chicago economist and later a U.S. Senator, and C.W. Cobb, a mathematician. A very simple **Cobb-Douglas production function** is

$$Q = \sqrt{K \cdot L}.$$

It says that the quantity of output is equal to the square root of the number of units of capital times the number of units of labor. If a firm using this technology hired four workers and used nine units of capital, it would be able to produce six units of output in a given time period: $4 \times 9 = 36$, and the square root of 36 is 6. If the firm doubled the amount of labor and capital, to eight workers and 18 units of capital, output would also double to 12 units: $8 \times 18 = 144$, and the square root of 144 is 12.

Table 7.3 presents some numbers derived from the Cobb-Douglas production function. First, notice that several combinations of inputs can be used to produce each level of output. Six units of output can be produced with four units of labor and nine units of capital or with six units of each, and so forth. Table 7.4 shows that when units of labor are added to 12 units of capital, each successive unit produces a smaller amount of additional product; it exhibits diminishing returns to labor when capital is held constant.

TABLE 7.3

Combinations of Inputs Which Can Be Used to Produce 6 Units of Output ($Q = \sqrt{K \cdot L}$.)

Q	K	L
6	36	1
6	18	2
6	12	3
6	6	6
6	3	12
6	2	18
6	1	36

TABLE 7.4

Diminishing Marginal Product of Labor ($Q = \sqrt{K \cdot L}$)

K	L	Total Product (Q)	Marginal Product ($\Delta Q / \Delta L$)
12	0	0	—
12	1	3.46	3.46
12	2	4.90	1.44
12	3	6.00	1.10
12	4	6.93	.93
12	5	7.75	.82
12	6	8.49	.74
12	7	9.17	.68

This particular function does not correspond to any actual business. It is presented to illustrate the kind of mathematical expression that does embody the properties that real technologies seem to exhibit. The Cobb-Douglas functions that are estimated from real data are slightly more complicated mathematically, but they are identical in character to this simple one.

CHOICE OF TECHNOLOGY AND COST OF PRODUCTION: A LOOK AHEAD

The assumption that firms strive to maximize profits implies that they also strive to *minimize costs of production*. Firms have a number of production techniques to choose among, and it follows that they will pick the technique that produces output at the least cost. The choice they make depends on the current market prices of inputs, or factors of production.

Consider the three techniques presented in Table 7.5, where cost of production is calculated under two alternative sets of factor prices. Where labor and capital each cost $1.00 per unit, the firm chooses technique B, at $14.00 per unit. However, if capital costs were to rise to $2.00 per unit, the firm would choose technique C, substituting labor for capital in response to the change in factor price. In other words, it would use a more labor-intensive technique because that would be its least costly option.

In thinking about Table 7.5, think about some of the examples presented at the beginning of the chapter. In economies where labor is plentiful and inexpensive, firms use technologies that are labor intensive because those are the lowest-cost techniques available. In developing countries, agricultural goods are produced with a lot of labor and a limited amount of machinery and equipment—machinery can be obtained, but it is expensive relative to the inexpensive labor. In the United States, agriculture has become increasingly capital intensive. The amount of farm equipment per farm worker has increased dramatically. Rising wages have made labor more expensive relative to capital.

In central cities, where land is scarce and expensive, office buildings and apartment buildings rise to great heights. In the suburbs, we build single-family homes, and even apartment complexes are low-rise garden apartments or town houses. Business properties are spread out and landscaped. Why? Because inputs can be substituted one for another, and input prices are different in the central city and in the suburbs. Where land is expensive, capital will be substituted for land. That is why we have skyscrapers.

The cost of producing any product depends on the quantities of inputs needed to produce it and the prices of those inputs. So far we have discussed the technical relationships between inputs and outputs. In doing so, we have actually been describing part of the analysis and decision making that lies behind cost curves. As we shall see in the next chapter, each point on a cost curve represents the lowest possible cost at which that level of output can be produced.

TABLE 7.5
Choice of Technique to Minimize Cost

Technique	Input requirements per unit of output K	L	Cost per unit of output $P_L = \$1, P_K = \$1$	$P_L = \$1, P_K = \$2$
A	10	5	$15	$25
B	7	7	$14	$21
C	4	12	$16	$20

SUMMARY

1. Firms come in different sizes and internal organizations, but they all take *inputs* and transform them into *outputs*.
2. In perfect competition, no single firm has any control over prices. This follows from two assumptions: (1) that perfectly competitive industries are composed of many firms, each small relative to the size of the industry and (2) that each firm in a perfectly competitive industry produces exactly the same, or homogeneous, products.
3. It follows then, that the demand curve facing a competitive firm is perfectly elastic. If a single firm raises its price above the market price, it will sell nothing. Because it can sell all it produces at the market price, a firm has no incentive to reduce price below the market price.
4. Firms in a competitive industry must make three choices: (1) how much output to supply, (2) how to produce that output, and (3) how much of each input to demand.
5. From this point on, we assume that all firms behave so as to maximize profits.
6. Profit equals total revenue minus total cost. Economic cost includes (1) a normal return, or profit, to the owners and (2) the opportunity cost, rather than the money cost, of each factor of production.
7. A "normal rate of return" to capital is included as a cost because tying up resources in the capital stock of a firm has an opportunity cost. If you start a business or buy a share of stock in a corporation, you do so because you expect a profit. That profit is not real profit unless it exceeds some normal rate of return that you could get at a bank or by buying a safe bond.
8. Economic profits are thus profits over and above a normal rate of return. A firm earning zero economic profits is a firm earning just exactly a normal rate of return. Since we include normal profits as a cost, a firm does not show economic profits unless it is earning above a normal return for its owners. A firm actually earning a profit as an accountant measures it is suffering a loss from the perspective of economics if the profit rate is below normal—that is, it is losing money relative to the return on generally available alternative investments.
9. Two assumptions define the short run: (1) a fixed scale or, more specifically, a fixed factor of production and (2) no entry to or exit from the industry. In the long run firms can choose any scale of operations they want, and new firms can enter and leave the industry.
10. To make decisions, firms need to know three things: (1) the market price of their output, (2) the techniques of production that are available, and (3) the price of inputs.
11. When the relationship between inputs and outputs, that is, the technology of production, is expressed numerically or mathematically, it is called a production function.
12. The marginal product of a variable input is the additional product that an added unit of that input will produce if all other inputs are held constant.
13. The law of diminishing returns states that when additional units of a variable input are added to fixed inputs, the marginal product of the variable input will decline.
14. Average product is the average amount produced by each unit of a variable factor. If marginal product is above average, the average rises; if marginal product is below average, the average falls.
15. Capital and labor are at the same time complementary and substitutable inputs. Capital enhances the productivity of labor, and it can also be substituted for labor.
16. The cost side of the profit equation depends on factor prices and techniques of production. The next chapter combines the two to develop cost curves.

REVIEW CONCEPTS

REVIEW QUESTIONS

1. The diagram below shows the various combinations of capital and labor that can be used to produce 100 units of output:

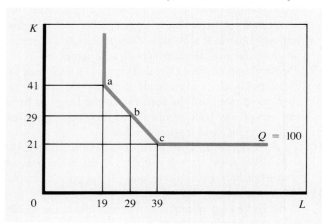

   a. Consider the techniques represented by points *a*, *b*, and *c*. If the price of labor and capital were $2.00 each and the firm decided to produce 100 units of output, which technique would the firm employ?
   b. If a payroll tax were imposed that pushed the price of labor to $3.00 but left the price of capital at $2.00, which technique would the firm choose?
   c. If a profits tax pushed the price of capital up to $3.00 but left the price of labor at $2.00, which technique would the firm choose then?

2. Assume that widgets can be produced using two different techniques, A and B. The following table provides data on the total input requirement of each at four different output levels:

	Q = 1		Q = 2		Q = 3		Q = 4	
	K	L	K	L	K	L	K	L
A	5	2	8	4	11	5	15	5
B	3	3	6	5	8	7	11	10

   a. If labor is $2.00 per unit and capital is $3.00 per unit, what is the minimum cost of producing one widget? Two widgets? Three widgets? Four widgets?
   b. Graph cost of production as a function of output. (Put output on the X axis and cost on the Y axis.)
   c. How much did it cost to go from an output of one to an output of two? To go from an output of two to three? From three to four?

3. Do you think demand (supply) is likely to be more elastic in the short run or in the long run? Why? What factors are likely to influence long-run supply elasticity? Long-run demand elasticity?

4. Suppose that it cost $500,000 to start an ice cream store (including all the equipment necessary to operate the business). Assume that annual revenues from operating the store would be $80,000 and that all costs (as an accountant would measure them) would be $50,000. The costs include rental of the store, labor, supplies, and full maintenance of the equipment. Full maintenance implies that if our owner went out of business she could sell the equipment for the full $500,000. Suppose finally that the ice cream business is risky, and that a rational capitalist would demand a 20-percent return on investment to enter.
   a. What is profit as an accountant would measure it if our capitalist bought the equipment with her own money?
   b. If you consider 20 percent a "normal return" to investment, how much economic profit would the enterprise earn? Explain your answer.

8

The Firm: Short-Run Costs and Competitive Output Decisions

COSTS: INPUT PRICES
  AND TECHNOLOGY OF PRODUCTION
  Fixed and Variable Costs:
    The Short Run
  Fixed Costs
  Variable Costs
  Total Costs
  Costs: Only Part of the
    Profit Equation
REVENUES: THE OUTPUT MARKET

Total Revenue (TR)
  and Marginal Revenue (MR)
Maximizing Profit:
  Comparing Costs and Revenues
The Marginal Cost Curve
  as the Supply Curve of a Competitive
  Firm in the Short Run
A QUICK LOOK AHEAD
SUMMARY

This chapter continues our examination of the decisions behind competitive supply and demand curves. You have seen that firms in perfectly competitive industries make three very specific decisions. (Figure 8.1 shows this as well.) Those decisions are

1. How much output to supply
2. How to produce that output, that is, what production technique to use
3. What quantity of each input to demand

We have assumed so far that firms are in business to earn profits and that they make choices in order to maximize those profits. The level of profits is the difference between revenues and costs. Because firms in perfectly competitive markets are price-takers in both input and output markets, much depends upon prices over which firms have no control. Like households, firms also face market constraints.

FIGURE 8.1
Decisions Facing Competitive Firms

DECISIONS:	Are Based On	INFORMATION:
1. The quantity of output to *supply*		1. The price of inputs*
2. How to produce that output (which technique to use)		2. Techniques of production available*
3. The quantity of each input to *demand*		3. The price of output
		*determines production costs

The focus in this chapter is on costs of production. To calculate costs, a firm must know two things: what inputs in what combinations it needs to produce its product and how much those inputs cost. As we begin to examine how technology and input prices determine costs, we focus first on input markets. By the end of the chapter, we return to the output market, with enough information to figure out how much of its product a firm is likely to supply at each possible price. In other words, we will have derived the supply curve of a competitive firm in the short run.

COSTS: INPUT PRICES AND TECHNOLOGY OF PRODUCTION

Fixed and Variable Costs: The Short Run

In this chapter, we discuss costs *in the short run only*. You have seen that the short run is that period during which two conditions hold: (1) existing firms face limits imposed by some factor of production that is "fixed" and (2) new firms cannot enter an industry and existing firms cannot exit, that is, they cannot go completely out of business. This notion of the short run, as distinct from the long run, has implications for costs.

All firms have costs that they must bear regardless of their output. Some costs, in fact, must be paid even if the firm stops producing anything, that is, even if output is zero. These are called **fixed costs**, and the important thing to remember about them is that firms can do nothing *in the short run* to avoid them or to change them. In the long run, of course, a firm has no fixed costs, because it can change its scale of operation or get out of the industry. Therefore, all long-run costs are *variable*.

Firms do have certain costs in the short run that depend on the level of output they have chosen, and these are called **variable costs**. Fixed costs and variable costs together make up **total costs**:

$$TC = TFC + TVC,$$

where TC denotes total costs, TFC denotes total fixed costs, and TVC denotes total variable costs.

Fixed cost   Any cost that a firm bears in the short run that does not depend on its level of output. These costs are incurred even if the firm is producing nothing. There are no fixed costs in the long run.

Variable cost   Any cost that a firm bears as a result of production and which depends on the level of production chosen.

Total costs   Fixed costs plus variable costs.

Fixed Cost

Total Fixed Cost (TFC)   Fixed costs taken all together are sometimes called *overhead*. If you operate any kind of plant facilities, you must heat the building to keep the pipes from freezing in the winter. You may have to keep the roof from leaking, pay a guard to protect the building from vandals, and make payments on a long-term lease, even if no production is taking place. Then there are insurance premiums, taxes, and city fees, and perhaps contract obligations to workers and administrative salaries to pay.

Fixed costs represent a larger portion of total costs for some firms than for others. Electric companies, for instance, maintain generating plants, thousands of miles of distribution wires, poles, transformers, and so forth. Usually, such a plant is financed by issuing bonds to the public—that is, by borrowing. The interest that must be paid on these bonds represents a very substantial part of the utilities' operating cost. It is a fixed cost in the short run, no matter how much, if any, electricity is being produced.

For the time being, we assume that capital and labor are the only inputs used by firms.[1] It is sometimes assumed that capital—plant, equipment, and inventory—is a fixed input in the short run and that labor is the only variable input. To be a bit more realistic, however, we will assume that capital has both a fixed *and* a variable component. After all, some capital can be purchased in the short run.

Consider a small consulting firm. The firm employs several economists, research assistants, secretaries, a receptionist, and an engineer. It rents space in an office building and has a five-year lease. The rent it pays on the office space can be thought of as a fixed cost in the short run. Certainly the monthly electric bill and heating bills are essentially fixed although the amounts may vary slightly. So are the salaries of the basic administrative staff. Payments on some capital equipment—a large copying machine, for instance, and the main word processing system—can also be thought of as fixed. Everything else depends on the number of consulting contracts the firm has.

The same firm, however, also has costs that vary with output. When there is a lot of work, the firm hires more employees at both the professional and research assistant level. The capital used by the consulting firm may also vary, even in the short run. Payments on the computer system it owns do not change, but it may rent additional computer time from a time sharing company when necessary. The firm can buy additional personal computers and word processing terminals quickly if need be. It must pay for the copy machine, but the machine costs more when it is running than when it is not. This consulting firm, like many businesses, including law firms, architects, and designers, actually breaks out fixed and variable costs when it bills clients, reporting first costs directly attributable to the case or the project and then adding a certain amount for "overhead."

Total fixed costs (**TFC**), then, are those costs that do not change with output, even if output is zero. Table 8.1 presents data on just the fixed costs of a hypothetical firm. Fixed costs are $1000 at all levels of output. The top diagram in Figure 8.2 shows total fixed costs as a function of output. Since *TFC* does not change with output, the graph is simply a straight horizontal line at $1000.

The important thing to remember here is that firms cannot control fixed costs in the short run. For this reason, these costs are sometimes called **sunk costs**.

Average Fixed Cost (AFC)   Average fixed cost (**AFC**) is total fixed cost divided by output. For example, if the uncomplicated firm in Figure 8.2 produced three units of output, average fixed costs would be $333 ($1000 divided by three). If the same firm produced five units of output, average fixed cost would be $200 ($1000 divided by five). *Average fixed cost falls as output rises*, because the same total is being spread over, or divided by, a larger number of units (see Table 8.1), a phenomenon sometimes called **spreading overhead**.

Graphs of average fixed cost, like that in the bottom diagram in Figure 8.2 which presents the average fixed cost data from Table 8.1, are downward-sloping curves. Notice that AFC approaches zero as the quantity of output gets large. For example, if output were 100,000 units, average fixed cost would equal only one cent per unit in our example. Of course, it never actually reaches zero.

TABLE 8.1

Short-Run Fixed Cost (Total and Average) of a Hypothetical Firm

Q	TFC	AFC
0	$1000	$ —
1	1000	1000
2	1000	500
3	1000	333
4	1000	250
5	1000	200

Sunk costs   *Another name for fixed costs (or total fixed costs) in the short run because firms have no choice but to pay them.*

Average fixed costs (AFC)   *Total fixed cost divided by the number of units of output; a per unit cost measure.*

Spreading overhead   *The process of dividing total fixed costs by more units of output. What happens is that average fixed cost declines as Q rises.*

---

[1]While this may seem unrealistic, virtually everything that we will say about firms using these two factors can easily be generalized to the case of firms that use many factors of production—different kinds of labor and land, for example.

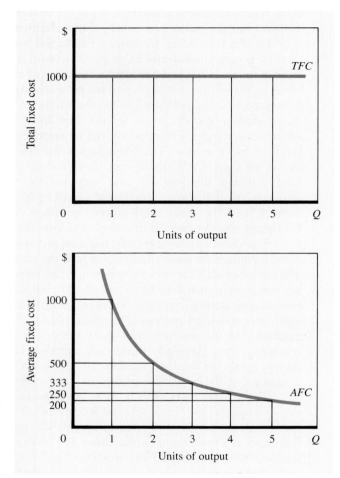

FIGURE 8.2
Short-Run Fixed Cost (Total and
Average) of a Hypothetical Firm

Average fixed cost is simply total fixed
cost divided by the quantity of output.
As output increases, average fixed
cost declines because we are dividing
a fixed number ($1000) by a bigger
and bigger quantity.

Variable Costs

Total Variable Cost (TVC)   Total variable costs (TVC) are those costs that depend
on, or vary with, output in the short run. To produce more output, a firm uses more
inputs. The cost of additional output depends directly on what additional inputs are
required and how much they cost.

As you saw in Chapter 7, input requirements are determined by technology. Firms
generally have a number of production techniques available to them, and the option they
choose is assumed to be the one that produces the desired level of output at the *least cost*.
To find out which technology does this best, each firm must compare the total variable
costs of producing that level of output using different production techniques.

This applies to small businesses as well as large manufacturing firms. Suppose that
you are a small farmer. A certain amount of work has to be done in order to plant and
harvest your 120 acres, and you can get it done in a number of ways. You might hire four
farm hands and divide up the tasks, or you might buy several pieces of complex farm
machinery (capital) and do the work single-handedly. Clearly, your final choice depends
on a number of things. What machinery is available? What does it do? Will it work on

small fields such as yours? How much will it cost to buy each piece of equipment? What wage will you have to pay farm hands? How many will you need to get the job done? If the machinery is expensive and the labor is cheap, you will probably choose the labor-intensive technology. If farm labor is expensive and the local farm equipment dealer is going out of business, you might get a good deal on some machinery and choose the capital-intensive method.

Having compared the costs of alternative production techniques, the firm may be influenced in its choice by the current *scale* of its operation. Remember, in the short run we are locked into a *fixed* scale of operations. A firm currently producing on a small scale may find that a labor-intensive technique is the least costly, whether or not labor is comparatively expensive; the same firm producing on a larger scale might find a capital-intensive technique less costly.

In general, then, the relationship between total variable costs and output, that is, the total variable cost curve, depends on (1) what techniques of production are available and (2) the prices of the inputs required by each technology. To see this in more detail, let us look at some production figures for "frumps."

Table 8.2 presents an analysis that might lie behind the total variable cost curve of a typical frump firm. In this case, there are two production techniques available, one somewhat more capital-intensive than the other. We also assume that the price of labor is $1.00 per unit and the price of capital is $2.00 per unit. (Because our firm shops in competitive input markets, it takes those prices as given, you recall.) For purposes of our frump example we are focusing on *variable* capital, that is, on capital that can be changed in the short run. In practice, some capital is fixed in the short run, capital such as buildings and large, specialized machines. In our example we will use K to denote variable capital. Remember, however, that the firm has other capital, capital that is fixed in the short run.

Analysis reveals that to produce one unit of output, the labor-intensive technique is least costly. Technique A requires four units of both capital and labor, which would cost a total of $12.00. Technique B requires six units of labor but only two units of capital for a total cost of only $10.00. Thus to produce one frump the firm would use technique B, and the total variable cost of producing one unit of output would be $10.00.

The relatively labor-intensive technique B is still the best method of production for two units of output. Using B, the firm can produce two frumps for $18.00. When we get to three frumps, however, technique A becomes the cheapest. The total variable cost of production is $24.00. The firm will use nine units of capital at $2.00 each and six units of labor at $1.00 each.

TABLE 8.2
Derivation of Total Variable Cost Schedule from Technology and Factor Prices

Produce	Using Technique	Units of input required (production function) K	L	Total Variable Cost Assuming $P_K=\$2\ P_L=\$1$
1 Unit of	A	4	4	$12.00
Output	B	2	6	$10.00
2 Units of	A	7	6	$20.00
Output	B	4	10	$18.00
3 Units of	A	9	6	$24.00
Output	B	6	14	$26.00

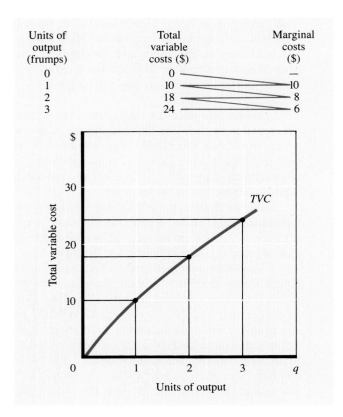

Units of output (frumps)	Total variable costs ($)	Marginal costs ($)
0	0	—
1	10	10
2	18	8
3	24	6

FIGURE 8.3
Total Variable Costs Schedule and Curve

In Table 8.2 total variable cost is derived from production requirements and input prices. When expressed in relation to total output, the result is a total variable cost schedule or curve.

Figure 8.3 summarizes the relationship between variable costs and output in this case. The important point to remember here that *the total variable cost curve embodies information about both factor, or intput, prices and technology*: it shows the cost of production using the best available technique at each output level, given current factor prices.

Marginal costs (MC)   An increase in total cost that results from producing one additional unit of output; a per unit cost measure.

Marginal Cost (*MC*)   The most important of all cost concepts is that of **marginal cost** (**MC**), the increase in total cost that results from the production of one more unit of output. Let us say, for example, that a firm is producing 1000 units of output and decides to raise output to 1001. This raises costs, and the increase, that is, the cost of the 1001st unit, is the marginal cost. Notice that focusing on the "margin" is one way of looking at variable costs: marginal costs reflect variable costs because they vary when output changes. Fixed costs do not change when output changes.

The table in Figure 8.3 shows how marginal cost is derived from total variable cost by simple subtraction. The cost of producing the first unit is $10.00. Raising production from one unit to two units increases total variable cost from $10.00 to $18.00; the difference is the *marginal cost* of the second unit, $8.00. Raising output from two to three units increases total variable cost from $18.00 to $24.00. The marginal cost of the third unit, therefore, is $6.00.

Table 8.3 shows that marginal cost is simply the cost of the additional inputs, or resources, needed to produce the marginal unit of output. You saw in Table 8.2 that the least expensive method of production for one frump and for two frumps was technique *B*. Here is what happens when the firm raises output from one unit to two units. To produce

TABLE 8.3

Derivation of Marginal Cost from Total Variable Cost, Technology, and Factor Prices

	Least-cost technology	Input requirements K	Input requirements L	Total variable cost
Unit 1	B	2	6	$10.00
Unit 2	B	4	10	$18.00
	Additional inputs needed	+2	+4	
	Price of inputs	× $2.00	× $1.00	
	Marginal costs (of unit 2)	$4.00	$4.00 ⟶	$8.00
Unit 2	B	4	10	$18.00
Unit 3	A	9	6	$24.00
	Additional inputs needed	+5	−4	
	Price of inputs	× $2.00	× $1.00	
	Marginal costs (of unit 3)	+$10.00	−$4.00 ⟶	$6.00

one unit of output, it uses two units of capital at $2.00 per unit and six units of labor at $1.00 per unit, for a total variable cost of $10.00. Technique *B* requires four units of capital (at $2.00 per unit) and 10 units of labor (at $1.00 per unit) to produce two units of output, for the total variable cost of $18.00. To produce the second unit, our frump producer needs to use two units of additional capital (at $2.00 each) and four units of additional labor (at $1.00 each), for a total additional cost of $8.00. Thus the marginal cost of the second unit is $8.00—the cost of the added resources needed to produce it.

Now what happens when total output goes up by one more unit? To produce three frumps, the firm switches to technique *A*, which requires nine units of capital (at $2.00 each), more than twice as much capital as it took to produce two frumps. Why spend so much more on variable capital? Because this expenditure means that the firm can cut down on the amount of labor it uses. Two frumps required 10 units of labor (at $1.00 each); three frumps require only six. Thus, although increasing output from two frumps to three requires the firm to spend an additional $10.00 on capital (five additional units at $2.00 each), it also means that it can cut back on labor, using four fewer units (at $1.00 each) and saving the firm $4.00. The marginal cost of the third unit is thus $6.00.

Clearly, however, an example that shows firms hiring less labor when output rises is not typical. Normally, when firms expand, they use more capital and hire more labor, as our firm does in moving from one unit of output to two. But the example is extreme to drive home two points: (1) that *costs* at any level of output depend on technology *and* factor prices and (2) that the technology appropriate at one level of production may not be appropriate at other levels of production.

While the easiest way to get at marginal cost is to look at total variable cost and just subtract (as in Figure 8.3), don't lose sight of the fact that when a firm increases its output level, it hires or demands more inputs. *Marginal cost* measures the *additional* cost of inputs required to produce each successive unit of output.

The Shape of the Marginal Cost Curve in the Short Run   The assumption of a *fixed factor of production* in the short run means that the firm is stuck at its current scale of operation. As a firm tries to increase its output, it will eventually find itself trapped by that scale. Thus our definition of the short run also implies that marginal cost eventually rises with output. The firm can hire more labor and use more materials—that is, it can add variable inputs—but diminishing returns eventually set in.

FIGURE 8.4
Declining Marginal Product
Implies that Marginal Cost Will
Eventually Rise with Output

In the short run, every firm is constrained by some fixed factor of production. Having a fixed input implies
diminishing returns (declining marginal product) and a limited capacity to
produce. As that limit is approached,
marginal costs rise.

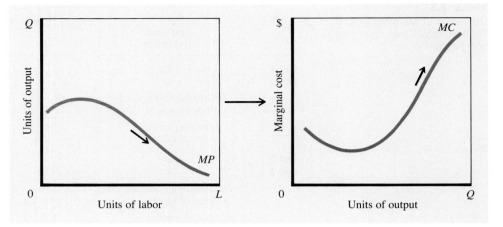

Now recall the sandwich shop, with one grill and too many workers trying to fix
sandwiches on it, from Chapter 7. With a fixed grill capacity, more laborers could make
more sandwiches, but the *marginal product* of each successive cook declined as more
people tried to use the grill. If each additional unit of labor adds less and less to total
output, it follows that each additional unit of output costs more to produce. Thus
diminishing returns, or decreasing marginal product, implies increasing marginal cost (see
Figure 8.4).

Recall too the accountant who makes a living helping people file their federal and
state tax returns. He has an office in his home and works alone. His fixed factor of
production is his own time: there are only so many hours in a day, and he has only so
much stamina. In the long run, he may decide to hire and train an associate, but in the
meantime (the short run) he has to decide how much to produce, and that decision is
constrained by his current scale of operations. The fact that he has no trained associate
and that each day contains only 24 hours constrains the number of clients that he can take
on. Because of this, the firm will see increased marginal costs. The biggest component of
the accountant's cost is time. When he works, he gives up leisure and other things that he
could do with his time. With more and more clients, he works later and later into the
night; as he does, he becomes less and less productive, his hours become more and more
valuable for sleep and relaxation—in other words, the marginal cost of doing each
successive tax return rises.

To reiterate, in the short run, every firm is constrained by some fixed input that
leads to diminishing returns to variable inputs and limits its capacity to produce. As a firm
approaches that capacity, it becomes increasingly costly to produce successively higher
levels of output. In other words, marginal costs ultimately increase with output.

Graphing Total Variable Costs and Marginal Costs   Figure 8.5 shows how the total
variable cost curve and the marginal cost curve of a typical firm might look. The numbers
for the first two units of output are those arrived at by the frump producer (see Figure
8.3). Notice first that the shape of the marginal cost curve is consistent with short-run
diminishing returns. At first it declines, but eventually the fixed factor of production
begins to constrain the firm, and marginal cost rises. Up to 29 units of output, each
successive unit of output costs slightly less than the one before. Beyond 29 units, however,
the cost of each successive unit is greater than the one before.

Clearly, more output costs more in total than less output, and therefore total
variable costs (TVC) always increase when output increases. Even though the cost of

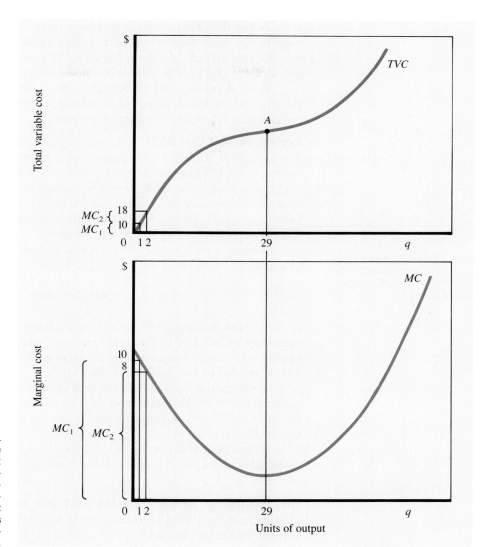

FIGURE 8.5

Total Variable Cost and Marginal
Cost for a Typical Firm

Total variable costs always increase
with output. Marginal cost is the cost
of each additional unit. Thus, the figure shows graphically how total variable cost changes with single unit increases in total output. When output
rises from one to two units, cost goes
from $10.00 to $18.00. Thus the marginal cost of the second unit is $8.00.

each additional unit changes, as long as this marginal cost is positive total variable cost rises
when output rises. Thus the *total* variable cost curve always has a positive slope.

The *slope* of the total variable cost curve, however, varies. The slope of the curve
reveals how quickly costs increase with output, and that is reflected in marginal cost. Look
carefully at the diagrams in Figure 8.5. The marginal cost of the first unit is $10.00.
Going from zero to one unit of output increases total variable cost by $10.00, from zero
to $10.00. The point on the total variable cost curve at two units is $18.00, but the
increase from one to two units, that is, the marginal cost of the second unit, is only $8.00.

Remember that the numerical value of the slope of a line is equal to the change in Y
divided by the change in X; the slope of a total variable cost curve is thus the change in
total variable cost divided by the change in output ($\Delta TVC/\Delta Q$). Since marginal cost is by
definition the change in total variable cost resulting from an increase in output of one unit
($\Delta Q = 1$), *marginal cost actually is the slope of the total variable cost curve*, or

$$\text{slope of } TVC = \Delta TVC/\Delta Q = \Delta TVC/1 = \Delta TVC = MC.$$

Notice that as marginal cost decreases, up to 29 units of output the slope of the total variable cost curve flattens out—that is, total variable cost increases, but at a *decreasing rate*. Beyond 29 units of output, marginal cost increases and the total variable cost curve gets steeper; total variable costs continue to increase, but at an *increasing rate*.

Point A on the total variable cost curve, the point at which a decreasing slope becomes an increasing slope, or at which marginal cost stops declining and begins increasing, is referred to as an *inflection point*.

Average Variable Cost (AVC)   A more complete picture of the costs of a hypothetical firm appears in Table 8.4. The second column shows total variable costs—derived, we assume, from information on input prices and technology. The third column derives marginal cost simply by subtraction. For example, raising output from three units to four units increases variable costs from $24.00 to $32.00, making the marginal cost of the fourth unit $8.00. The marginal cost of the fifth unit is $10.00, the difference between $32.00 for four units and $42.00 for five units.

Average variable cost (AVC)
Total variable cost divided by the number of units of output; a per unit cost measure.

Average variable cost (**AVC**) is total variable cost divided by the number of units of output:

$$AVC = TVC/Q.$$

In Table 8.4, the AVC in the fourth column is simply the numbers in the second column (*TVC*) divided by the numbers in the first column (*Q*). For example, if the total variable cost of producing five units of output is $42.00, then the average variable cost is $42.00 divided by five units, or $8.40.

Look again at Table 8.4. Since total variable cost rose from $18.00 to $24.00, the marginal cost of the third unit is $6.00. The average variable cost of the first three, if the first costs $10.00, the second costs $8.00, and the third costs $6.00, is $8.00, or $24.00 divided by three.

The important distinction to remember here is that *marginal* cost is the cost of *one single additional unit*. *Average* cost is the average per unit cost *of all the units* being produced.

The Relationship Between Average Cost and Marginal Cost   Average cost and marginal cost are related in a very specific way. When marginal cost is *below* average, average cost declines toward it. Think again of test scores. If you have an average score of 85 on three exams, and you then receive a 75, your average will fall. In Table 8.4, the *average* variable cost of producing two units is $9.00. The *marginal* cost of the third is $6.00, and thus the average falls to $8.00.

TABLE 8.4
Short-Run Costs of a
Hypothetical Firm

(1) Q	(2) TVC	(3) MC	(4) AVC	(5) TFC	(6) TC	(7) AFC	(8) ATC
0	$ 0	$—	$—	$1000	$1000	$ —	$ —
1	10	10	10	1000	1010	1000	1010
2	18	8	9	1000	1018	500	509
3	24	6	8	1000	1024	333	341
4	32	8	8	1000	1032	250	258
5	42	10	8.4	1000	1042	200	208.4
—	—	—	—	—	—	—	—
—	—	—	—	—	—	—	—
—	—	—	—	—	—	—	—
500	8000	20	16	1000	9000	2	18

Similarly, when marginal cost is *above* average, average cost increases toward it. If you had received a 95 on your last test instead of a 75, your average would have risen. In Table 8.4 the average cost of four units is $8.00. The fifth unit costs $10.00, and the average rises to $8.40. *Average cost, then, always moves in the direction of marginal cost.*

Graphing Total, Average, and Marginal Costs   All of this can be illustrated graphically. Figure 8.6 duplicates the diagrams in Figure 8.5 but with the addition of average variable cost. Average cost *follows* marginal cost, but it lags behind because it is the average of all previous units.

The marginal cost of the first unit is the same as the average variable cost of producing just that unit, so marginal cost and average variable cost start together at point D on the diagram. (If this is not clear, go back to Table 8.4 and see why for *one unit* AVC=MC=$10.00.) Average variable costs from there follow marginal cost down to point C. Marginal cost begins to rise at 29 units, but average cost does not begin to rise until marginal cost crosses it and *rises above it.* In this case, that occurs at 48 units, point C. It is always true that *marginal cost intersects average variable cost at the lowest, or minimum, point of AVC.*

Another example using test scores should help you to see this. Consider the following sequence of test scores: 95, 85, 92, 88. The average of these four is 90. Now suppose you get an 80. Obviously that drags down your average. In fact, after five tests

FIGURE 8.6
More Short-Run Costs

The relationship between marginal cost and average cost is important. When marginal cost is *below* average cost, average cost is declining. When marginal cost is *above* average cost, average cost is increasing. It follows that rising marginal cost will cut average variable cost at its minimum point.

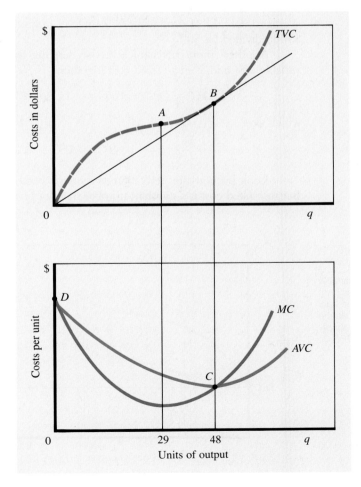

your average is down to 88. Now suppose you get an 85. That's up from 80, but it's still *below* your average. As a result your average continues to fall (from 88 to 87.5), even though your marginal test score rose. But if instead of an 85 you get an 89, just one point over your average, you've turned your average around, and, in fact, it is rising.

Total Costs

We are finally ready to complete the cost picture with the addition of fixed costs to variable costs. **Total cost (TC)** is simply the sum of total fixed and total variable costs. That is,

$$\text{total cost} = \text{total fixed cost} + \text{total variable cost}.$$

This is shown in Figure 8.7, where the same vertical distance (equal to *FC*) is simply added to *TVC* at every level of output. In Table 8.4 the sixth column adds the fixed cost of $1000 to total variable cost.

Average Total Cost (ATC)   Average total cost **(ATC)** is total cost divided by the number of units of output, or *TC/Q*. Column 8 in Table 8.4 shows the result of dividing the numbers in column 6 by the numbers in column 1. For example, at five units of output, *total* cost is $1042; *average* total cost is $1042 divided by five, or $208.40. The average total cost of producing 500 units of output, however, is only $18.00—that is, $9000 divided by 500.

Another, more revealing, way of deriving average total cost is to add average variable cost and average fixed cost together:

$$TC = TFC + TVC \qquad TC/Q = TFC/Q + TVC/Q,$$

which says

$$ATC = AFC + AVC.$$

Look back at the derivation of average fixed cost in Table 8.1 and Figure 8.2. Because fixed cost is a constant number that does not change with output, *average fixed*

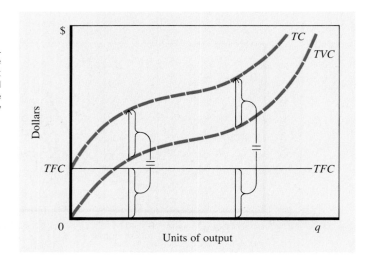

FIGURE 8.7
Total Cost Equals Fixed Cost Plus Variable Cost

Adding total fixed cost to total variable cost means adding the same amount at every level of output. Thus the total cost curve has the same shape as the total variable cost curve; it is simply higher by an amount equal to TFC.

cost, or *TFC/Q*, is simply that constant divided by an ever-increasing number of units of output. This means that as output increases, average fixed cost declines steadily. If the output level is very high, average fixed cost is very small. The data used in Figure 8.2, where the *AFC* of two units of output is $500.00, and in Table 8.4, where the *AFC* drops to $200.00 at five units, show this quite clearly. If the firm goes on to produce 500 units of output, *AFC* declines to only $2.00 (see column 7 in Table 8.4).

We can now derive average total cost a second way. In Table 8.4, the figure in column 8 was derived simply by dividing total cost by the quantity of output. That figure is also equal to the sum of *AFC* and *AVC*, that is, the sum of columns 4 and 7. This second derivation makes it clear that as output increases, average cost and average variable cost get closer and closer together. Because average fixed cost gets smaller and smaller, we have a smaller and smaller number to add to *AVC* in order to get *ATC*.

Figure 8.8 graphs average total cost. The bottom part of the figure graphs the average fixed cost from Figure 8.2. The top part shows the declining average fixed cost added to average variable cost at each level of output. Again, because *AFC* gets smaller and smaller, *ATC* gets closer and closer to *AVC* as output increases.

FIGURE 8.8

Average Total Cost = Average Variable Cost + Average Fixed Cost

To get average total cost, we add average fixed and average variable costs. Since average fixed cost falls with output, an ever-declining amount is added vertically to *AVC*. Thus *AVC* and *ATC* get closer together as output increases.

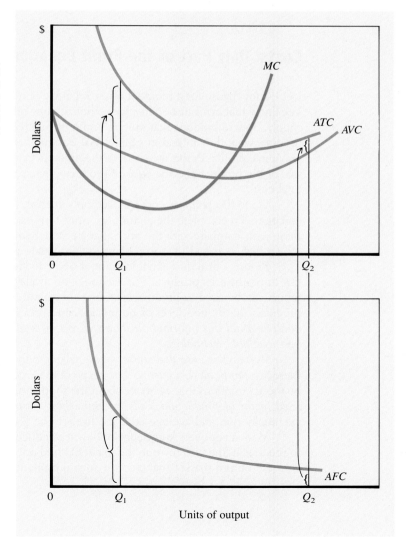

The Relationship Between Average Total Cost and Marginal Cost   The relationship between average *total* cost and marginal cost is exactly the same as the relationship between average *variable* cost and marginal cost. That is, average total cost follows marginal cost, but because it is an average over all units of output, it lags behind. It lags behind even more now; not only is it being averaged with the variable cost of all previous units produced, we have tossed in fixed costs in as well. The added fixed cost, in a sense, increases the "load" that is being dragged around by marginal cost.

The first unit of output in the example in Table 8.4 costs $1010 to produce—$1000 fixed cost plus $10.00 variable cost. Since fixed costs are now covered, the second unit costs in total $8.00. The total cost of two units is $1018; average total cost of the two is ($1010 + $8.00)/2, which is $509.00. The third unit cost in total is only $6.00. The total cost of three units is thus $1024, or $1018 + $6.00, and the average total cost of three units is ($1010 + $8.00 + $6.00)/3, which is $341.00.

As you saw with the test scores, the marginal cost is what drives the changes in average total cost. If marginal cost is *below* average total cost, average total cost will *decline* towards it; if marginal cost is *above* average total cost, average total cost will *increase*. As a result, marginal cost intersects average *total* cost at its *minimum* point, just as it did with average *variable* cost.

Costs: Only Part of the Profit Equation

Let us now pause for a moment to see what we know so far about the behavior of firms. We know that firms make three basic choices: how much product or output to produce or supply, how to produce that output, and how much of each input to demand in order to produce what they intend to supply. We assume that these choices are made in order to maximize profits. Profits are equal to the difference between what a firm takes in from the sale of the product and the costs of producing what it sells: profit = total revenue minus total cost.

Up to this point, we have looked only at costs, and costs are only a part of the profit equation. To complete the picture, we must turn back to the output market and see how these costs compare with the price that a product commands when a firm sells it. Before we do that, however, it is important to consolidate what we have said about costs.

Before a firm does anything else, it needs to know the different methods that it can use to produce its product. The technologies available determine what combinations of inputs can be used to produce each level of output. Firms choose that technique which produces the desired level of output at least cost. *The cost curves that result from the analysis of all this information show the cost of producing each level of output using the best available technology.*

Remember here that so far we are talking only about short-run costs and therefore these are *short-run cost curves*. The shape of these curves is determined in large measure by the assumptions that we make about the short run, especially the assumption that *some fixed factor of production leads to diminishing returns*. This being true, marginal costs eventually rise, and average costs are likely to be U-shaped.

With a complete knowledge of how to produce a product and how much it will cost to produce it, the firm turns to the market to find out what it can sell its product for, and it is to the output market that we now turn our attention.

REVENUES: THE OUTPUT MARKET

In order to calculate profits, firms must combine their cost analyses with information on potential revenues from sales. After all, if a firm can't sell its product for more than it costs to produce it, it won't be in business long. On the other hand, if the market gives the firm a price that is significantly greater than the cost it incurs to produce a unit of its product, that may give the firm an incentive to expand output. Large profits might also attract new competitors to the market.

A competitive industry has many firms that are small relative to the size of the market. We are talking about wheat farmers in Kansas, not about IBM. In this environment, such firms have no control over the market price of their products. Product price is determined by the interaction of many suppliers and many demanders.

Figure 8.9 shows a typical firm in a competitive industry. Price is determined in the market at P^*. The firm can certainly charge any price that it wants for its product, but if it charges above P^*, the quantity demanded at that price falls to zero, and the firm won't sell anything. After all, many other firms are producing exactly the same product. The firm could also sell its product for less than P^*, but there is no reason to do so. If the firm can sell all it wants to sell at the going market price of P^*, and we assume that it can, it would not be sensible to sell it for less.

All this implies that in the short run a competitive firm faces a demand curve that is simply a horizontal line at the market equilibrium price, in this case P^*. In Figure 8.9, that curve is labeled d. We say that such firms face a perfectly elastic demand.

Total Revenue (TR) and Marginal Revenue (MR)

Total revenue (TR)   The product of price per unit and the quantity of output the firm decides to produce (P × Q).

Profit is the difference between total revenue and total cost. **Total revenue** is the total amount that a firm takes in from the sale of its product. A perfectly competitive firm sells each unit of product for the same price, regardless of the output level it has chosen.

FIGURE 8.9
Demand Facing a Typical Firm in a Competitive Market

Because in competition we assume that firms are very small relative to the market, they have no control over price. A firm can sell all it wants at the market price but would sell nothing if it charged a higher price. Thus the demand curve facing a competitive firm is simply a horizontal line at P^*.

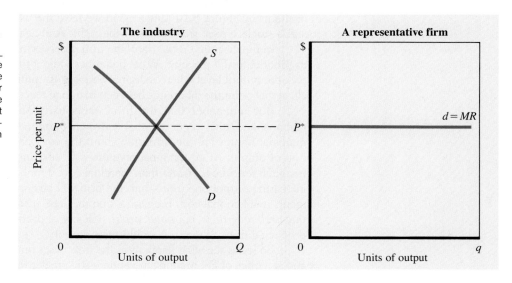

Therefore, *total revenue* (TR) is the simple product of price times the quantity of output that the firm decides to produce:

$$\text{total revenue} = \text{price} \times \text{quantity}$$
$$TR = P \times Q.$$

Because price is assumed to be fixed in a competitive industry, total revenue depends only on the amount of output the firm decides to sell. Remember, our firm is so small relative to the industry that changes in its output do not affect the market price.

Marginal revenue is the added revenue that a firm takes in when it increases output by one additional unit. If a firm producing 10,521 units of output per month increases that output to 10,522 units per month, it will take in an additional amount of revenue each month. The revenue associated with the 10,522nd unit is simply the amount that the firm sells that one unit for. Thus, for a competitive firm, **marginal revenue (MR)** is simply equal to the current market price of each additional unit sold.

In Figure 8.9, the market price is P^*. Raising output from 1000 to 1001 will increase revenue by P^*. A firm's marginal revenue curve is a curve that shows how much revenue the firm will gain by raising output by one unit at every level of output. For a competitive firm, its marginal revenue curve and its demand curve are identical. The horizontal line in Figure 8.9 can be thought of as both the demand curve facing the firm and its marginal revenue curve.

Marginal revenue product (MRP) *The additional revenue gained by producing and selling one more unit of output. In competition, $P \times MR$.*

Maximizing Profit: Comparing Costs and Revenues

The logic in the next few paragraphs conveys one of the most important concepts in all of economics. As we pursue this point, remember that we are working under two assumptions: (1) that the industry is perfectly competitive and (2) that firms choose the level of output that yields the maximum total profit.

The Profit-Maximizing Level of Output: An Example   Now look carefully at the diagrams in Figure 8.10. Once again we have the whole market, or industry, on the left and a single typical small firm on the right. And again the current market price is P^*.

In the diagram on the right, the firm observes market price and knows that it can sell its product for P^* per unit. What quantity should it produce? It might seem reasonable to pick the output level where marginal cost is at its minimum point, in this case, at q_1. After all, at that point the difference between marginal revenue and marginal cost is the greatest.

But remember that the firm wants to maximize the difference between total revenue and total cost, not that between *marginal revenue* and *marginal cost*. The marginal figures tell the firm only about the costs and revenues associated with a single unit of output. At q_1, marginal revenue is P^* and marginal cost is MC_1. In other words, marginal revenue is *greater* than marginal cost. Think carefully about what that means. By increasing output one more unit, the firm will take in more in additional revenue than it incurs in additional cost. Increasing output, then, means that total profits will rise because *the next unit adds marginal profit*. Clearly a profit-maximizing firm would not stop producing at q_1. Instead, it would raise output.

So let us see what happens as the firm raises output to, say, q_2 in the diagram. At q_2, and at a price of P^*, marginal revenue is still greater than marginal cost. Just as before, this means that the firm can earn higher profits by raising output even further. As *long as*

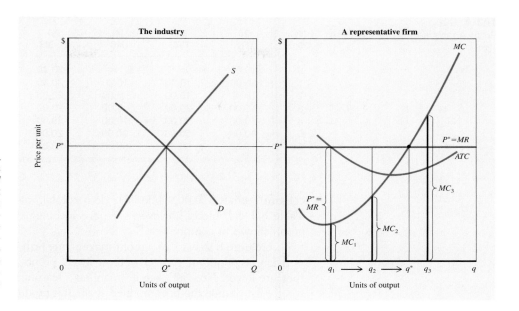

FIGURE 8.10
The Profit-Maximizing Level of
Output for a Competitive Firm

If price is above marginal cost, as it is
at q_1 and q_2, profits can be *increased*
by raising output; each additional unit
increases revenues by more than it
costs to produce the additional output. Beyond q^*, however, added output will reduce profits. At q_3, an additional unit of output costs more to
produce than it will bring in revenue
when sold on the market. Profit-
maximizing output is thus q^* where
$P^*=MC$.

marginal revenue is greater than marginal cost, even though the difference may be getting smaller, added output means added profit—that is, the revenue gained by raising output one unit exceeds the cost incurred by doing so.

This logic takes us up to q^*. At an output of q^*, marginal cost, because of diminishing returns, has increased to the point where it is equal to output price ($P^*=MR=MC$). If the firm produced *more* than q^* units, marginal cost would in fact rise *above* marginal revenue, and profits would fall. At q_3 units of output, marginal revenue is still P^*, but marginal cost has risen above P^* to MC_3. It does not pay the firm to increase output if marginal cost is greater than marginal revenue, because any additional output adds more to total cost than it adds to total revenue. In other words, it *reduces* profits.

The inevitable conclusion, then, is that *a profit-maximizing competitive firm will produce up to the point where the price of its output is just equal to short-run marginal cost,*[2] or

$$P = MC.$$

The Profit-Maximizing Level of Output: A Numerical Example   Table 8.5 presents some data for another hypothetical firm. Let's assume that the market has set a $20.00 unit price for the firm's product. Total revenue is the simple product of $P \times Q$ (the numbers in

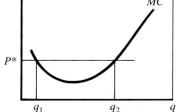

[2]To be very precise, it is possible that price is equal to marginal cost at two points, one where marginal cost is declining and another where marginal cost is increasing. Profit is maximized where marginal cost crosses price on its way *up* (q_2). The marginal costs of the first few units of production are high, because at such a low level of output the firm is not using its plant very efficiently. It would never make sense to produce at these low levels. In fact, to stop at the first point where $P=MC$ (q_1) would be to *minimize* profits. Can you figure out why?

TABLE 8.5
Profit Analysis for a Simple Firm

(1) Q	(2) TFC	(3) TVC	(4) MC	(5) P=MR	(6) TR	(7) TC	(8) Profit
0	$10.00	$0	$ —	$20.00	$0	$10.00	$−10.00
1	10.00	10.00	10.00	20.00	20.00	20.00	0
2	10.00	15.00	5.00	20.00	40.00	25.00	15.00
3	10.00	20.00	5.00	20.00	60.00	30.00	30.00
4	10.00	30.00	10.00	20.00	80.00	40.00	40.00
5	10.00	50.00	20.00	20.00	100.00	60.00	40.00
6	10.00	80.00	30.00	20.00	120.00	90.00	30.00

column 1 times $20.00). The table derives total, marginal, and average costs, exactly as Table 8.4 did. Here, however, we have included revenues, and we can calculate the profit, shown in column 8.

Column 8 shows that a profit-maximizing firm would choose to produce either four or five units of output. At each of those levels, profits are $40.00; at all other output levels, they are lower. Now let's see if "marginal" reasoning gets us to the same conclusion.

First, should the firm produce at all? If it produces nothing, it suffers losses equal to $10.00. If it increases output to one unit, marginal revenue is $20.00 (remember that it sells each unit for $20.00), and marginal cost is $10.00. Thus it gains $10.00, just enough to cover fixed costs and break even. But that is better than a $10.00 loss.

Should the firm increase output to two units? The marginal revenue from the second unit is again $20.00, and the marginal cost is only $5.00. Thus by producing the second unit it increases its profits by $15.00. The third unit adds the same amount to profits. Again marginal revenue is $20.00 and marginal cost is $5.00, an increase in profit of $15.00, for a total of $30.00.

The fourth unit offers still more profit. Price is above marginal cost, which means that producing that unit will increase profits. Price, or marginal revenue, is $20.00, and marginal cost is just $10.00. Thus the fourth unit adds $10.00 to profit. At unit number five, however, diminishing returns push marginal cost up until it is just equal to price. The marginal revenue from producing the fifth unit, therefore, is just equal to the marginal cost incurred, and nothing is either added to or subtracted from profits.

At unit number six, marginal cost rises above price, and added production reduces profits. The marginal cost of the sixth unit is $30.00, but producing and selling it will bring in only $20.00, a reduction in total profit of $10.00. Clearly the firm will not produce the sixth unit.

The profit-maximizing level of output is thus four or five units. The firm produces up to the point that price and marginal cost are equal.

The Marginal Cost Curve as the Supply Curve of a Competitive Firm in the Short Run

Consider how the typical firm described in Figure 8.10 would behave in response to an increase in price. On the left in Figure 8.11, demand shifts, driving price from P_0 to P_1 and finally to P_2. When price is P_0, a profit-maximizing firm will choose output level q_0. To produce any less, or to raise output above that level, would lead to a lower level of profit. At P_1 the same firm would increase output to q_1, but it would stop there. At P_1, the firm would supply q_1 units of output to the market. Similarly at P_2, the firm would raise output to q_2 units of output.

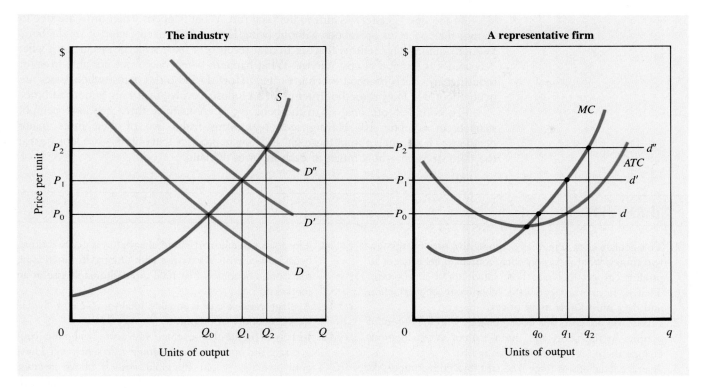

FIGURE 8.11
Marginal Cost Is the Supply Curve of a Competitive Firm

At any market price* the marginal cost curve shows the output level that maximizes profit. Thus the marginal cost curve of a competitive firm is the firm's short-run supply curve.
*This is true except when price is so low that it pays a firm to shut down—a point that will be discussed in Chapter 9.

The right half of the diagram shows a curve that relates price and quantity supplied. At any market price, the marginal cost curve shows the output level that maximizes profit. That statement also describes a supply curve, and therefore *the marginal cost curve of a competitive firm is the firm's short-run supply curve.*

There is, of course, some price level below which the firm will shut down its operations and simply bear losses equal to fixed costs even if price is above marginal cost. This important point is part of the subject of the next chapter.

A QUICK LOOK AHEAD

At the beginning of this chapter we set out to combine information on technology, factor prices, and output prices to derive the supply curve of a competitive firm. That has now been done.

The *marginal cost curve*, which you saw how to derive in Table 8.4, carries information about both *input prices* and *technology*. The firm looks to output markets for information on potential revenues, and the current market price defines the firm's marginal revenue curve. The point where price, or marginal revenue, is just equal to marginal cost is the profit-maximizing level of output. Thus, the marginal cost curve *is* the firm's supply curve in the short run.

In the next chapter we turn to the long run. What happens when firms are free to choose their scale of operations without being limited by a fixed factor of production? Without diminishing returns that set in as a result of a fixed scale of production, what determines the shape of cost curves? What happens when new firms are able to enter industries in which profits are being earned? How do industries adjust when losses are being incurred? How does the structure of an industry evolve over long periods of time?

To complete our analysis of the behavior of competitive firms, we look at input markets in Chapter 10. Having seen how firms make two of their three major decisions—how much output to supply and how to produce that output—we look next at the third decision—how much of each input to demand.

SUMMARY

1. To calculate costs, a perfectly competitive firm must know two things: what inputs in what combinations it needs to produce its product and how much those inputs cost. That is, firms must know the technology of production and they must know input prices.

2. Fixed costs are costs that do not change with the output of a firm. In the short run, firms cannot avoid them or change them, even if production is zero.

3. Average fixed cost is total fixed cost divided by output. As output rises, average fixed cost declines steadily: you are dividing a fixed number by a larger and larger quantity of output.

4. Variable costs are those that depend on the level of output chosen. Fixed costs plus variable costs equal total costs.

5. Numerous combinations of inputs can be used to produce each level of output. Total variable cost is the cost of the combination of inputs that produces each level of output at minimum cost.

6. Marginal cost is the increase in total cost that results from the production of one more unit of output. If a firm is producing 1000 units, the cost of increasing output to 1001 is marginal cost (MC).

7. Marginal cost measures the cost of the additional inputs required to produce each successive unit of output.

8. In the short run, there is a fixed factor of production, or a fixed scale of plant. As a firm increases output, it will eventually find itself trapped by that scale. Because of the fixed scale, marginal cost eventually rises with output.

9. Marginal cost is the slope of the total variable cost curve.

10. The total variable cost curve always has a positive slope, because total costs always rise with output. But increasing marginal cost means that total costs ultimately rise at an increasing rate.

11. Average variable cost is equal to total variable cost divided by the quantity of output.

12. Just as a higher-than-average test score will raise your average and a lower-than-average test score will lower your average, when marginal cost is above average variable cost, average variable cost is *increasing*, and when marginal cost is below average variable cost, average variable cost is *declining*.

13. Marginal cost intersects average variable cost at its minimum point.

14. Average total cost is equal to total cost divided by Q. It is also equal to the sum of average variable cost and average fixed cost.

15. Total revenue is simply price times the quantity of output that a firm decides to produce and sell. Marginal revenue is the additional revenue that a firm takes in when it increases output by one unit.

16. For a competitive firm, marginal revenue is simply equal to the current market price of its product.

17. A profit-maximizing firm in a perfectly competitive industry will produce up to the point that the price of its output is just equal to short-run marginal cost: $P = MC$. Except at very low prices, the marginal cost curve of a competitive firm is the firm's short-run supply curve.

REVIEW CONCEPTS

fixed costs   182
variable costs   182
total costs   182

total fixed costs   183
sunk costs   183
average fixed cost (AFC)   183

REVIEW QUESTIONS

1. A firm's cost curves are given by the following table:

Q	TC	FC	VC	AVC	ATC	MC
0	$100.00	$100.00				
1	130.00	100.00				
2	150.00	100.00				
3	160.00	100.00				
4	172.00	100.00				
5	185.00	100.00				
6	210.00	100.00				
7	240.00	100.00				
8	280.00	100.00				
9	330.00	100.00				
10	390.00	100.00				

   a. Copy and complete the table.
   b. Graph ATC, AVC and MC on the same graph. What is the relationship between the MC curve and ATC? Between MC and AVC?
   c. Suppose the market price is $30.00; how much will the firm produce in the short run? How much are the profits? Show them on the graph.
   d. Suppose the market price is $50.00; how much will the firm produce in the short run? How much are the profits? Show them on the graph.
   e. Suppose market price were $10.00; how much would the firm produce in the short run? How much would the profits be? Show them on the graph.

2. The total cost curve for producing a record is given below. Draw the total fixed cost curve, the average fixed cost curve, the AVC curve, the ATC curve, and the MC curve.

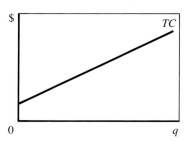

3. A 1973 Berkeley graduate inherited her mother's printing company. The capital stock of the firm consists of three machines of various vintages, all in excellent condition:

	Cost of printing and binding per book	Maximum total capacity per month
Machine 1	$1.00	100 books
Machine 2	$2.00	200 books
Machine 3	$3.00	500 books

   a. Assume that "cost of printing and binding per book" includes *all* labor and materials, including the owner's own wages. Assume further that Mom signed a long-term contract (50 years) with a service company to keep the machines in good repair for a fixed fee of $100.00 per month.
   (1) Derive the marginal cost curve of the firm.
   (2) Derive the total cost curve of the firm.
   b. If she could sell all the books she wanted at $3.00 each, how many per month would the printing company owner produce? What would her total revenues be? Total costs? Total profits?

4. "If marginal cost is rising, average cost must also be rising." Do you agree or disagree? Explain.

5. The following curve is a production function for a firm that uses just one variable factor of production, labor. It shows total output, or product, for every level of inputs:

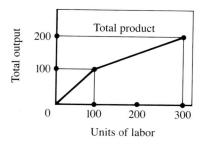

   a. Derive and graph the marginal product curve.
   b. If the wage rate is $4.00, derive and graph the marginal cost curve for the firm.
   c. If output sells for $6.00, what is the profit-maximizing level of output? How much labor will the firm hire?

9 The Firm: Costs and Competitive Supply in the Long Run

The last two chapters have presented a theory of how a profit-maximizing competitive firm behaves in the short run. We laid out the three fundamental decisions that all firms must make: (1) how much output to produce or supply, (2) how to produce that output, and (3) how much of each input to demand.

Firms use information on input prices, output prices, and technology in order to make the decisions that will lead to the most profit. Since profits are the difference between revenues and costs, *firms must know how much their products will sell for and how much production will cost, using the most efficient technology*.

In Chapter 8 we saw in detail how cost curves can be derived from production functions and input prices. Once a firm has a clear picture of its short-run costs, the price at which it sells its output determines the quantity of output that will maximize profit. Specifically, we argued that a profit-maximizing competitive firm will supply output up to the point that price equals marginal cost. As a result, the marginal cost curve of such a firm is the same thing as its supply curve.

In this chapter, we turn from the *short run* to the *long run*. The condition in which firms find themselves in the short run (Are they making profits? Are they incurring losses?) determines what is likely to happen in the long run. Remember that output (supply) decisions in the long run are less constrained than they are in the short run. First of all, the firm has *no fixed factor of production* that confines its production to a given scale of plant. Second, firms are free to *enter* industries in order to seek profits and to *leave* industries in order to avoid losses.

Moving to the long run has important implications for the shape of cost curves. As we saw, in the short run the assumption of a fixed factor of production, or scale of plant, eventually causes marginal cost to increase along with output. This assumption does not hold in the long run, however. With no fixed scale, the shape of cost curves becomes more complex and less easy to generalize about. The shape of long-run cost curves has important implications for how an industry's structure is likely to evolve over time. Later in the chapter we will discuss long-run costs in detail.

We begin our discussion of the long run by looking at firms in three short-run circumstances: (1) firms earning economic profits, (2) firms suffering economic losses but continuing to operate to reduce or minimize those losses, and (3) firms that find it in their interest to shut down and bear losses just equal to fixed costs.

In general, industries in which firms are earning economic profits are likely to expand: firms already in the industry will find an incentive to enlarge their existing scales of plant, and new firms are likely to join the competition. Industries in which firms are suffering losses are likely to contract: some firms will cut their losses and get out of the business, and others may reduce their scale.

SHORT-RUN CONDITIONS AND LONG-RUN DIRECTIONS

Before we begin our examination of firm behavior, let us review the concept of profit that we are using here. A normal rate of profit is *included* in costs as we measure them in economics. Thus when we say that a firm is earning profits, we mean that it is earning a profit over and above a normal rate of return to capital. The phrase "normal rate of return" means that the profit rate is just sufficient to keep current investors interested in the industry. Thus when we speak of profits, we really mean "extranormal" profits. Sometimes, for emphasis, these are called *economic profits*.

When we use "profit" in this sense, we are simply taking into account the opportunity cost of capital. By investing in one firm, the owners or lenders are forgoing what they could earn by investing somewhere else. That is why the normal rate of return must be at least equal to the interest rate on "safe" investments—government bonds, for example. Only when investors earn profits *above* this level are they earning a real profit. And only when they are earning real profits are new investors likely to be attracted to the industry.

When we say that a firm is suffering *losses*, we mean that it is earning a profit rate for its investors that is *below* normal. Such a firm may be suffering losses as an accountant would measure them or simply be earning at a very low, that is, below normal, profit rate. Investors in a firm are not going to be happy if they earn a return of only two percent when they can get seven percent in a simple bank money market account. By the same token, a firm that is *breaking even*, or earning zero economic profits, is one that is earning exactly a normal profit rate. New investors are not attracted, but current ones are not running away either.

With this in mind, then, we can say that for any firm at any moment, one of three conditions holds: (1) the firm is making a profit, (2) the firm is suffering losses, or (3) the firm is just breaking even.

Profit-Making Firms

A Numerical Example: The Blue Velvet Car Wash   When a firm earns revenues in excess of cost, including a normal profit rate, it is earning economic profits. Let us take as an example the Blue Velvet Car Wash. Suppose that investors have put up $500,000 to construct a building and purchase all the equipment required. Let's also suppose that investors expect to earn a minimum return of 10 percent on their investment. If the money to set up the business were borrowed from the bank, the car wash owners would pay a 10-percent interest rate. In either case, we cannot say that the firm is earning an economic profit until it has paid its investors, or the bank, 10 percent of $500,000, or $50,000 every year. Thus, that $50,000 is part of costs.

The car wash is open 50 weeks per year, and it can handle up to 800 cars per week. Now, whether it is open and operating or not, it has certain *fixed* costs. Those costs include $1000 per week to investors—that is, the $50,000 per year that represents normal return on investment or the interest paid to the bank—and $1000 per week in other fixed costs—a basic maintenance contract on the equipment, a long-term lease on the location, and so forth.

When the car wash is operating, there are also *variable* costs. Workers must be paid, and materials such as soap and wax must be purchased. The wage bill, let's say, is $1000 per week, and materials, electricity, and so forth run $600 if the car wash is run at full capacity. If the car wash is not in operation, *there are no variable costs.* Table 9.1 summarizes the costs of the Blue Velvet Car Wash.

This car wash business is competitive—there are many car washes of equal quality in the area, and they offer their service at $5.00. If Blue Velvet washes 800 cars each week, it takes in revenues of $4000 from operating. Is this enough to make an economic profit?

The answer is yes. Revenues of $4000 are sufficient to cover both fixed costs of $2000 and variable costs of $1600, leaving an economic profit of $400.00 per week (see Table 9.2, case 2.) Shutting down would mean suffering losses equal to fixed costs of $2000, and so it is clearly in the firm's interest to continue operating.

TABLE 9.1
Blue Velvet:
Weekly Costs of a Car Wash

Total fixed costs	
1. Normal Return (Profit) to Investors	$1000
2. Other Fixed Costs (maintenance contract, heat, etc.)	1000
Total fixed costs	**$2000**
Total variable costs (800 washes)	
1. Labor	$1000
2. Materials	600
Total variable costs	**$1600**
Total costs	**$3600**

TABLE 9.2
Decision to Shut Down Depends
on Variable Costs and Revenues

Fixed Costs		$ 2000
Case 1 Shut Down		
Revenues	$0	
Variable costs	0	
Profit on operations	$0	
Profit/loss		$ −2000
Case 2 P=$5		
Revenues ($5.00×800)	$4000	
Variable Costs	1600	
Profit on Operations	$2400	
Profit/loss		$ 400
Case 3 P=$3		
Revenues ($3.00×800)	$2400	
Variable costs	1600	
Profit on operations	$ 800	
Profit/loss		$ −1200
Case 4 P=$1.50		
Revenues ($1.50×800)	$1200	
Variable costs	1600	
Profit on operations	$ −400	
Profit/loss		$ −2400

A Profit-Making Firm Presented Graphically   Figure 9.1 graphs the performance of a firm that is earning economic profits. As before, in the left-hand diagram we have the industry, or the market, and in the right-hand diagram we have a representative firm. At present, the market is clearing at a price of P^*. Thus we assume that the firm can sell all it wants at P^*, but that it is constrained by its capacity; its marginal cost curve rises in the short run because of the assumption of fixed scale. You already know that a profit-maximizing firm produces up to the point that P^* equals marginal cost. As long as price exceeds marginal cost, firms can push up profits by increasing short-run output. The firm in the diagram, then, will produce, or supply, q^* units of output.

Both revenues and costs are shown graphically. *Total revenue* (TR) is simply the product of price and quantity ($P^* \times q^*$). On the diagram, total revenue is equal to the area of the rectangle P^*Aq^*0 (the area of a rectangle is equal to its length times its width).

At output q^*, *average total cost* is C; numerically, it is equal to the length of line segment q^*B, which is the same as $0C$. Since average total cost was derived by *dividing* total cost by q, we can get back to total cost by *multiplying* average total cost by q. That is,

$$ATC = TC/q \text{ and } TC = ATC \times q.$$

Total cost, then, is the area of rectangle $0CBq^*$. *Total economic profit* is simply the difference between total revenue (TR) and total cost (TC), and this is the area P^*ABC, which is shaded in the diagram.

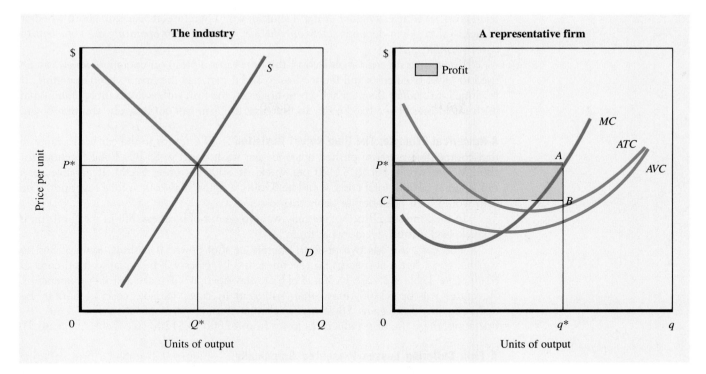

FIGURE 9.1

Firm Earning Economic (Excess) Profits in the Short Run

A profit-maximizing firm will produce up to the point where $P^*=MC$. At q^* total revenues are equal to P^*Aq^*0. Total costs are equal to ATC at q^* times q^* or CBq^*0. Thus profits ($TR-TC$) are equal to P^*ABC.

A firm that is earning economic profits in the short run and expects to continue to do so has an incentive to expand in the long run. Those profits also give new firms an incentive to enter the market and compete for them. These adjustments change the appearance of this graph quite significantly, as you will soon see.

Firms Suffering Losses

Shut-down point   *The lowest point on the average variable cost curve. When price falls below AVC, total revenue is insufficient to cover variable costs and the firm will shut down and bear losses equal to fixed costs.*

You might think that all firms suffering losses would shut down. In fact, such firms fall into two categories: (1) those that find it advantageous to shut down operations immediately and bear losses equal to fixed costs and (2) those that continue to operate in the short run in order to reduce their losses. The most important thing to remember is that firms are stuck in the industry in the short run. The firm can shut down, but it cannot get rid of its fixed costs by going out of business. We assume that fixed costs must be paid in the short run no matter what the firm does.

Whether a firm suffering losses decides to produce or not to produce in the short run depends on the advantages and disadvantages of continuing production. If it shuts down, it earns no revenues and has no variable costs to bear. If, on the other hand, it continues to produce, it both earns revenues and incurs variable costs. A firm must bear fixed costs, of course, *whether or not* it shuts down. Therefore, its decision about whether or not to shut down depends *solely on whether revenues from operating are sufficient to cover variable costs.*

If revenues *exceed* variable costs, the firm earns a profit on operation which can be used to offset fixed costs and reduce losses, and it may pay the firm to keep operating. If revenues are *smaller* than variable costs, however, the firm suffers losses on operation that push total losses above fixed costs. In this case, the firm can cut losses by shutting down.

A Numerical Example: The Blue Velvet Revisited   To return to the car wash, suppose that competitive pressure pushed the price per wash down to $3.00. Total revenues for Blue Velvet would fall to $2400 per week, or 800 cars times $3.00. If variable costs remained at $1600, total costs would be $3600, a figure higher than total revenues. The firm would then be suffering economic losses.

In the long run, Blue Velvet may want to go out of business, but in the short run it is stuck, and it must decide what to do.

The car wash has two options: operate or shut down. If it shuts down, it has no variable costs, but it also earns no revenues, and its losses will be equal to fixed costs of $2000 (see Table 9.2, case 1). If it decides to stay open, it will make a profit on operation. Revenues will be $2400, more than sufficient to cover variable costs of $1600. By operating, the firm gains $800 per week that it can use to offset its fixed costs. By operating, then, the firm reduces its losses from $2000 to $1200 (see Table 9.2, case 3).

A Firm Suffering Losses Presented Graphically   Figure 9.2 graphs a firm suffering economic losses. The market price is P^*. If the firm decides to operate, it will do best by producing up to the point where price is equal to marginal cost, in this case, at an output of q^* units.

Once again, total revenue (TR) is simply the product of price and quantity ($P^* \times q^*$), or the area of rectangle P^*Aq^*0. Average total cost is C, and it is equal to the length of q^*B and $0C$. Total cost is the product of average total cost and q^* ($ATC \times q^*$), and on the graph it is equal to the area of rectangle CBq^*0. Total cost is greater than total revenue, and the firm is suffering economic losses, shown on the graph by the area of rectangle $CBAP^*$.

Profits from operation, that is, the difference between total revenue and total *variable* cost, can also be identified. On the graph, total revenue is the area P^*Aq^*0. *Average* variable cost at q^* is D, or the length of q^*E. *Total* variable cost is the product of average variable cost and q^* and is therefore equal to the area of rectangle DEq^*0. Profit on operation is thus the rectangle P^*AED.

Remember that average total cost is equal to average fixed cost plus average variable cost. That means that at every level of output average fixed cost is the difference between average total and average variable cost:

$$TC = TFC + TVC \qquad TC/q = TFC/q + TVC/q,$$

which says

$$ATC = AFC + AVC \text{ or } AFC = ATC - AVC.$$

In Figure 9.2, therefore, average fixed cost is equal to the length of BE (the difference between ATC and AVC at q^*). Since total fixed cost is simply average fixed cost times q^*, total fixed cost is equal to the area $CBED$. Thus if the firm had shut down, its losses would be equal to $CBED$, the entire shaded rectangle. By operating, the firm

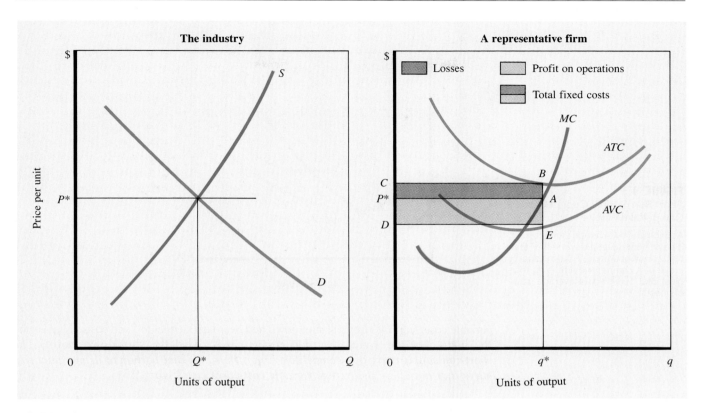

FIGURE 9.2

Firm Suffering Economic Losses but Showing a Profit on Operation in the Short Run

When price is sufficient to cover average variable costs, firms suffering short-run losses will continue to operate rather than shut down. Total revenues or P^*Aq^*0 cover variable costs DEq^*0 leaving a profit on operation of P^*AED to cover part of fixed costs and reduce losses.

earned a profit on operation equal to area P^*AED, covering some fixed costs and reducing losses to $CBAP^*$.

If we think only in averages, it seems logical that a firm in this position will continue to operate. Price is the average revenue per unit. As long as that is sufficient to cover average variable costs, the firm stands to gain by operating rather than shutting down.

Firms that Will Shut Down in the Short Run   When revenues are insufficient to cover even variable costs, firms suffering losses find it advantageous to shut down, even in the short run.

Suppose, for example, that competition and the availability of sophisticated new machinery pushed the price of a car wash all the way down to $1.50. Washing 800 cars per week would then yield revenues of only $1200 (see Table 9.2, case 4). With variable costs at $1600, operating would mean losing an additional $400 *over and above* fixed costs of $2000. This means that total losses would amount to $2400. Clearly, a profit-maximizing/loss-minimizing car wash would reduce its losses from $2400 to $2000 by shutting down, even in the short run.

As you have seen, in the short run competitive firms will produce up to the point where price and marginal cost are equal *unless price falls below average variable cost*. When price is below average variable cost, total revenue is insufficient to cover even

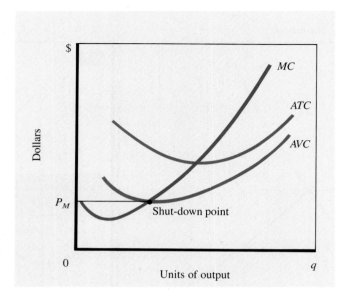

FIGURE 9.3
Short Run Supply Curve of a
Competitive Firm

At prices below average variable cost,
it pays a firm to shut down rather than
to continue operating. Thus the supply
curve of a competitive firm is its marginal cost curve *above* average variable cost.

variable costs, and the firm will shut down and bear losses equal to fixed costs. That is why
the bottom of the average variable cost curve is called the **shut-down point.** *The
short-run supply curve of a competitive firm is thus only that portion of its marginal cost
curve that lies above its average variable cost curve* (see Figure 9.3).

The Industry Supply Curve in the Short Run and the Long Run

Industry supply curve (in the
short run)   *The sum of marginal*
cost curves (above AVC) *of all*
firms in an industry.

Supply in a competitive industry is simply the sum of all the products supplied by all the
individual firms in the industry. It follows, then, that the short-run **industry supply curve**
is the horizontal sum of the marginal cost curves (above AVC) of all the firms in the
industry.

Figure 9.4 shows the supply curve for an industry with just three firms. At a price of
P_1, firm 1 produces 100 units, the output where $P=MC$. Firm 2 produces 200 units, and
firm 3 produces 150 units. The total amount supplied on the market at P_1 is thus 450
(100+200+150). Similarly, at a price of P_2, firm 1 produces 90 units, firm 2 produces
180 units, and firm 3 produces 120 units. At P_2, the industry thus supplies 390 units
(90+180+120).

Two things can cause the industry supply curve to move. First, in the short run if
something—say an increase in the price of some input—moves the marginal cost curves
of all the firms together, the entire industry supply curve also moves. For example, when
the cost of producing components of home computers decreased, the marginal cost
curves of all computer manufacturers shifted downward. Such a shift amounted to the
same thing as an outward shift in their supply curves.

Second, in the long run an increase or decrease in the number of firms, and
therefore in the number of individual firms' supply curves, shifts the total industry supply
curve. If new firms enter the industry, the industry supply curve moves to the right; if
firms exit the industry, the industry supply curve moves to the left.

We return to shifts in industry supply curves and discuss them further when we take
up long-run adjustments later in this chapter.

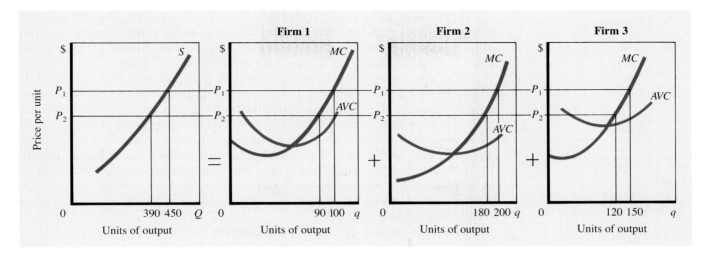

FIGURE 9.4
The Industry Supply Curve in the Short Run Is the Horizontal Sum of the Marginal Cost
Curves of all the Firms in an Industry

Assuming there are only three firms in the industry, the industry supply curve is simply the total supplied
by the three firms at each price. For example, at P_1, firm 1 supplies 100 units, firm 2 supplies 200 units,
and firm 3 supplies 150 units, for a total of 450.

Profits, Losses, and the Long Run: A Review

Table 9.3 summarizes the different circumstances that firms may face as they plan for the
long run. Profit-making firms will produce up to where price and marginal cost are equal
in the short run. Since "profits" means "economic profits," there is an incentive for firms
to expand and for new firms to enter in the long run.

Firms suffering losses will produce if, and only if, revenues are sufficient to cover
variable costs. If a firm can earn a profit on operations, it can reduce the losses it would
suffer if it shut down. Such firms, like profitable firms, will also produce up to where $P =
MC$. If firms suffering losses cannot cover variable costs by operating, they will shut down
and bear losses equal to fixed costs. Whether or not a firm decides to shut down in the
short run, if it is suffering losses, it has an incentive to contract in the long run. The simple
fact is that when profits are less than opportunity costs, existing firms will either scale back
or get out of the industry altogether.

TABLE 9.3
Profits, Losses, and Firms'
Decisions in the Long and Short
Run

Short-run condition	Short-run decision:	Long-run decision:
Profits	$P=MC$: operate	Expand: new firms enter
Losses 1. With profit on operations	$P=MC$: operate	Contract: firms exit
Losses 2. With loss on operations	Shut down: losses=fixed costs	Contract: firms exit

In the short run, a firm's decision about how much to produce depends upon the market price of its product and the shapes of its cost curves. Remember that the short-run cost curves show costs that are determined by the *current* scale of plant. In the long run, however, firms have to choose among many *potential* scales of plant.

The long-run decisions of individual firms will depend on what their costs are likely to be at different scales of operation. Just as firms have to analyze different technologies to arrive at a structure of costs in the short run, they must also compare their costs at different scales of plant in order to arrive at long-run costs. Perhaps a larger scale of operations will reduce production costs and provide an even greater incentive for a profit-making firm to expand. Perhaps large firms will run into bureaucratic problems that constrain growth. The analysis of long-run possibilities is even more complex than the short-run analysis, because more things are variable—scale of plant is not fixed, for example, and there are no fixed costs. In theory, firms may choose *any* scale of operation, and so they must analyze many possible options.

Now let us turn to the shape of cost curves in the long run.

LONG-RUN COSTS: ECONOMIES AND DISECONOMIES OF SCALE

As you know by now, the shapes of *short-run* cost curves follow directly from the assumption of a fixed factor of production. As output increases beyond a certain point, the fixed factor, which we usually think of as fixed scale of plant, causes *diminishing returns* to other factors and thus increasing marginal costs. In the long run, however, there is no fixed factor of production. Firms can choose any scale of production: they can double or triple output or go completely out of business. Thus we have no assumption from which to deduce the shapes of long-run cost curves.

The shape of a firm's long-run average cost curve depends on how costs vary with scale of operations. For some firms, increased scale, or size, reduces costs; for others, increased scale might lead to inefficiency and waste. When an increase in a firm's scale of production leads to *lower average costs*, we say there are **increasing returns to scale**, or **economies of scale**. When average costs *do not change* with the scale of production, we call this **constant returns to scale**. Finally, when an increase in a firm's scale of production leads to *higher average costs*, we talk about **decreasing returns to scale**, or **diseconomies of scale**.

Increasing returns to scale, or economies of scale When an increase in scale of production leads to lower average costs per unit produced.

Constant returns to scale When an increase in scale of production has no effect on average costs per unit produced.

Increasing Returns to Scale (Economies of Scale)

Technically, the phrase *increasing returns to scale* refers to the relationship between inputs and outputs. When a production function exhibits increasing returns, it means that a given percentage increase in the production of output requires a smaller percentage increase in the inputs. For example, if a firm were to double output, it would need less than twice as much of each input to produce that output. Stated the other way around, if a firm doubled or tripled inputs, it would more than double or triple output.

When firms can count on fixed input prices, increasing returns to scale also means that as output rises, average cost of production falls. The term "economies of scale" refers directly to this reduction in cost per unit of output that follows from larger-scale production.

The Nature of Economies of Scale   Most of the economies of scale that immediately come to mind are technological in nature. Automobile production would obviously be more costly per unit if a firm were to produce 100 cars per year by hand. Henry Ford introduced standardized production techniques early in this century that increased output volume, reduced costs per car, and made the automobile available to almost everyone.

Some economies, however, do not result from technology but from *sheer size*. Very large companies, for instance, can buy in volume at discounted prices. Large firms may also produce some of their own inputs at considerable savings. And they can certainly save in transport costs when items can be shipped in bulk.

A Numerical Example: Economies of Scale in Egg Production   Nowhere are economies of scale more visible than in agriculture. In a small town in rural Ohio, farmers have been producing eggs for local markets for many years. A few years ago a major agribusiness moved into town and set up a huge egg-producing operation.

The new firm, Chicken Little Egg Farms, Inc., is completely mechanized. Complex machines feed the chickens, collect the eggs, and box them. Large refrigerated trucks transport the eggs all over the state daily. The company has a contract with a major soup company to sell the chickens after they are no longer useful for egg production. In the same town, some small farmers still own small flocks of less than 200 chickens and drive their own eggs to markets around the county. They collect the eggs, feed the chickens, and clean the coops by hand.

Table 9.4 presents some hypothetical cost data for Homer Jones's small operation and for Chicken Little Inc. Jones has his operation working well. He has several hundred chickens and spends about 15 hours per week feeding, collecting, delivering, and so forth. In the rest of his time he raises soybeans. We can value Jones's time at $8.00 per hour, because that is the wage he could earn working at a local manufacturing plant that has job openings. When we add up all Jones's costs, including a rough estimate of the land and capital costs attributable to egg production, we arrive at $177.00 per week. Total production on the Jones farm runs about 200 dozen, or 2400, eggs per week, which means that his average cost comes out to $.073 per egg.

TABLE 9.4
Weekly Costs Showing Economies of Scale in Egg Production

Jones Farm	Total weekly costs
15 hours of labor (implicit value $8)	$120
Feed, other variable costs	25
Transport costs	15
Land and capital costs attributable	17
	$177
Total output	2400 eggs
Average cost	$.073 per egg

Chicken Little Egg Farms Inc.	Total weekly costs
Labor	$5,128
Feed, other variable costs	4,115
Transport	2,431
Capital and land	19,230
	$30,904
Total output	1,600,000 eggs
Average cost	$.019 per egg

The costs of Chicken Little Inc. are much higher in total; indeed, weekly costs run over $30,000. A much higher percentage of costs are capital costs: the firm uses lots of sophisticated machinery that cost millions to put in place. Total output is 1.6 million eggs per week, and the product is shipped all over the Midwest. The comparatively huge scale of plant has driven average production costs all the way down to $.019 per egg.

While these numbers are hypothetical, you can see why small farmers in the United States are finding it difficult to compete with large scale agribusiness concerns that can realize significant economies of scale.

Economies of Scale Presented Graphically   Figure 9.5 shows short-run and long-run average cost curves for a firm that realizes economies of scale up to about 100,000 units of production and roughly constant returns to scale after that. The diagram shows three potential scales of operation, each with its own set of short-run cost curves.

Once the firm chooses a scale on which to produce, it becomes locked into one set of cost curves in the short run. If the firm were to settle on scale 1, it would not realize the major cost advantages of producing on a larger scale. By roughly doubling its scale of operations from 50,000 to 100,000 units (scale 2), the firm reduces average costs per unit significantly.

Constant Returns to Scale

Technically, the term *constant returns* means that the quantitative relationship between input and output stays constant, or the same. That is, if a firm doubles inputs, it doubles output; if it triples inputs, it triples output; and so forth. Furthermore, if input prices are fixed, constant returns implies that average cost of production does not change with scale. In other words, the long-run average cost curve remains flat.

The firm in Figure 9.5 exhibits roughly constant returns to scale between scale 2 and scale 3. That is, average cost of production is about the same in each. If the firm exhibited constant returns at higher levels, the long-run average cost curve (*LRAC*)

FIGURE 9.5

A Firm Exhibiting Economies of Scale

The long-run average cost curve of a firm shows the different scales on which the firm can choose to operate in the long run. Each scale of operation defines a different "short run." Here we see a firm exhibiting economies of scale; moving from scale 1 to scale 3 reduces average cost.

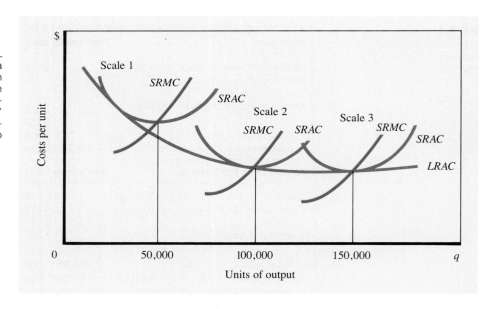

would continue as a flat straight line. We could draw some additional short-run curves showing larger scales out to the right.

Economists have studied cost data extensively over the years in order to estimate the extent to which economies of scale exist. Evidence suggests that in most industries firms don't have to be gigantic to realize whatever cost savings from scale economies are available. For example, automobile production is accomplished in thousands of separate assembly operations, each with its own economies of scale. Once it was thought that beer would one day be produced most cost-effectively in a small number of huge breweries; now the industry is completely decentralized, with each brand operating many smaller production plants all over the country.

One simple theoretical argument supports the empirical result that most industries seem to exhibit constant returns to scale after some level of output. Competition always pushes firms to adopt the least-cost technology and scale. If cost advantages result with larger-scale operations, those firms that shift to that scale will drive the smaller, less efficient firms out of business. A firm that wants to grow once it has reached its "optimal" size can do so by simply building another identical plant. It seems logical that most firms face constant returns to scale *as long as* they can replicate their existing plants. Thus when you look at developed industries, you can expect to see firms of different sizes operating with similar costs. These firms produce using roughly the same, or optimal, scale of plant, but larger firms simply have more plants.

Decreasing Returns to Scale (Diseconomies of Scale)

Decreasing returns to scale, or diseconomies of scale When an increase in scale of production leads to higher average cost per unit produced.

When average cost increases with scale of production, a firm has what are called decreasing returns to scale, or diseconomies of scale. The most often cited example of a diseconomy of scale is bureaucratic inefficiency. As size increases beyond a certain point, operations tend to become more difficult to manage. You can easily imagine what happens when a firm grows top-heavy with managers who have accumulated seniority and high salaries. It is clear that the coordination function is more complex for larger firms than for smaller ones, and the chances that it will break down may be greater.

A large firm is also more likely than a small firm to find itself facing organized labor. Unions can demand higher wages and more benefits, go on strike, force firms to incur legal expenses, and take other actions that increase production costs. (This does not mean that unions are bad, simply that their activities often increase costs. A more detailed discussion of unions and labor appears in Chapter 19.)

Figure 9.6 describes a firm that exhibits both economies of scale and diseconomies of scale. Average costs decrease with scale of plant up to q^* and increase with scale after that. A long-run average cost curve that looks like this also looks very much like the short-run average cost curves we have examined in the last two chapters. But *do not confuse the two*. All *short-run* average costs curves are U-shaped, because we assume a fixed scale of plant that constrains production and drives marginal cost upward after a point of diminishing returns. In the *long run*, we make no such assumption; rather, we assume that scale of plant can be changed.

The shape of a given firm's *long-run* average cost curve depends on how costs react to changes in scale. Some firms do see economies of scale, and their long-run average cost curves slope downward. Most firms seem to have flat long-run average cost curves. Still others encounter diseconomies, and their long-run average costs slope upwards. Thus the same firm can face diminishing returns, a *short-run* concept, and still have a *long-run* cost curve that exhibits economies of scale.

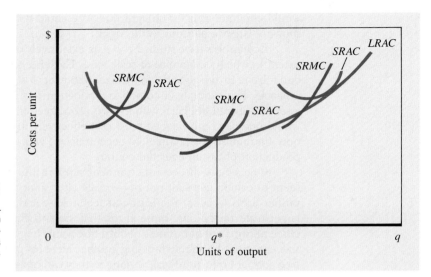

FIGURE 9.6

A Firm Exhibiting Economies and Diseconomies of Scale

For this firm, economies of scale push costs down to q*. Beyond q*, it experiences diseconomies of scale. q* is the level of production at lowest average cost, using optimal scale.

External Economies and Diseconomies of Scale

External economies and diseconomies of scale   If industry growth results in a decrease *of long-run average costs, that means there are external economies of scale; if industry growth results in an* increase of *long-run average costs, that means there are* external diseconomies of scale.

Sometimes average costs increase or decrease with the size of the *industry*, in addition to responding to changes in the size of the firm itself. When long-run average costs *decrease* as a result of industry growth, we say that there are **external economies of scale**. When average costs *increase* as a result of industry growth, we say that there are **external diseconomies of scale**.

Consider, for example, the growth of the "high-tech" manufacturing industry in the United States. The 1970s saw a revolution of sorts concentrated around Boston, Massachusetts, and in the "Silicon Valley," which lies in the peninsula south of San Francisco. So many new firms began to produce highly technical computer products that a new industry was born. Firms such as The Digital Equipment Company, Prime, Wang Laboratories, Apple, Hewlett-Packard, and many others experienced very rapid rates of growth.

Before the high-tech boom, the Massachusetts economy had been stagnant. The unemployment rate was the highest among the industrialized states. Many textile mills and shoe factories had gone out of business or moved their operations to the South or out of the United States altogether. As the new technology firms began to expand in the mid 1970s, they found a labor force that needed to be trained. In the infancy of the industry, the expanding firms bore virtually all the training costs themselves. As the industry grew and flourished, however, people began to acquire the necessary technical skills on their own in order to compete for the jobs. Private schools grew up all around Boston and San Jose, in the Silicon Valley, to train people for jobs in the high-tech field.

Once these training costs were shifted from the firms to the employees, or to the government through scholarship aid, average cost of production in the industry fell. Notice that this decline in costs, which resulted from an *external economy of scale*, was due to growth of the *industry*—it had nothing to do with cost advantages that any *individual* firm might have secured by producing on a larger scale.

Now let us consider construction, an industry made up of thousands of individual small firms. Recent decades have seen several construction booms, and during a boom the industry expands. One of the biggest expansions came between 1975 and 1979. Expansion, of course, puts pressure on the price of lumber and lumber products.

Empirical Cost Functions in the Brewing Industry

The shape of the long-run average cost function determines the optimal firm size. You have seen that firms that face cost curves that decline with firm size have an incentive to grow. Optimal firm size, in turn, determines the structure of the industry in the long run. If large-scale operations have significant cost advantages over small operations, one would expect to see a smaller number of large firms in an industry.

Over the years, economists have studied the cost structure of virtually every major industry using data gathered from individual firms. An excellent recent example is Victor Tremblay's work on the brewing industry, "Scale Economies, Technological Change, and Firm-Cost Asymmetries in the U.S. Brewing Industry," published in the *Quarterly Review of Economics and Business,* Summer, 1987.

Tremblay begins with a general discussion of the industry's structure since 1950. From 1950 to 1983 the number of independent U.S. brewing companies decreased from 369 to 33, and the average size of firms in the industry grew dramatically. One possible reason for such a change is that economies of scale may have risen over the years making survival possible for fewer and fewer firms.

To test this hypothesis, Tremblay puts together a data set that contains observations on three national producers (Anheuser-Busch, Pabst, and Schlitz) and 19 regional producers from 1950 to 1978. From these data, he estimates short-run average cost functions for six different time periods and estimates economies of scale by comparing them. From the results he concludes that significant scale economies do indeed exist in the brewing industry, and that they have increased markedly over the period of the study.

The results tell an interesting story of the development of an industry:

> Survival in brewing required that each firm build additional capacity and sell enough beer to take advantage of the rising scale economies. This competitive drive for greater production put

downward pressure on beer prices and forced firms who were unable to exploit all economies of scale out of business. Thus, over 300 firms exited the industry, and concentration rose rapidly during this period.

Many factors may have caused economies of scale in brewing to increase during this time. At the plant level, faster packaging equipment and greater plant automation caused scale economies to rise. For example, modern canning lines fill 2,000 12-ounce cans per minute, whereas a typical high speed canning line operated at a rate of just 300 cans per minute in 1952. In order to keep canning lines operating efficiently, it is estimated that a brewer would have to increase plant production from 0.3 to 2.2 million barrels from 1952 to 1986.

Numerous innovations made large automated brewhouses less and less expensive to build and operate. For 1973, Keithahn [21, p. 48] found that plant construction costs per barrel of productive capacity declined by more than 35 percent for a plant with a 5.0 million barrel capacity compared to a 1.0 million barrel plant. Furthermore, greater automation reduced labor expenses by reducing the number of workers needed to produce a given level of output. This is evident from the fact that the total number of production workers in brewing declined from a high of 64,800 in 1953 to just 29,500 in 1983, a period when annual production increased from 88.2 to 195.1 million barrels.

Multiplant scale economies, which developed in the late 1940s and early 1950s, were also an important determinant of optimal firm size in brewing. During this period, innovations in water treatment made it less costly to hold water (and therefore beer) quality constant across the country. This enabled brewers to decentralize their production operations while maintaining product homogeneity among different production facilities across the country. There were no multiplant producers in 1945, but most of the major brewers operated more than one plant by 1956. Decentralization enabled firms to cut shipping costs to distant customers and make use of national advertising campaigns.*

*Victor Tremblay, "Scale Economies, Technological Change, and Firm-Cost Asymmetries in the U.S. Brewing Industry," *Quarterly Review of Economics and Business,* Summer 1987.

Increases in construction activity cause the demand for lumber products to rise, and that causes the cost of construction to shift upward for all construction firms.

Table 9.5 shows one indicator of construction activity: new housing units started. In 1976 and 1977, the industry grew at a very rapid pace. In 1978 over 2 million new units were started in a single year. This growth was accompanied by a very rapid run-up in lumber prices as demand for lumber products ballooned. From 1975 to 1979, the price of lumber products increased over 83 percent, while prices in general increased only about 35 percent.

In the construction industry, a change in the scale of any individual firm's operations has no impact on the price of lumber, because no one firm has any control over the price. The increase in costs in the late 1970s resulted from expansion of the *industry.* In other words, it was an *external* diseconomy of scale.

TABLE 9.5
Construction Activity and the
Price of Lumber Products,
1975–1979

Year	New housing units started (millions)	Percentage increase	Percentage change in the price of lumber products	Percentage change in consumer prices
1975	1.16	—	− 6.8	+ 9.1
1976	1.54	+32.8	+20.7	+ 5.8
1977	1.99	+29.2	+18.9	+ 6.5
1978	2.02	+ 1.5	+16.2	+ 7.7
1979	1.74	−13.9	+ 9.9	+11.3

Source: U.S. Bureau of the Census, *Construction Reports*, series C20; U.S. Bureau of Labor Statistics, *Producer Price Indexes,* annual.

This concept of external economies and diseconomies is critical to our next discussion of long-run industry adjustments. As industries grow in response to profits or contract in response to losses, their costs of production can change.

LONG-RUN ADJUSTMENTS IN COMPETITIVE INDUSTRIES

We began this chapter with an outline of the different short-run positions in which firms may find themselves. Firms can be operating at a profit or suffering economic losses; they can be shut down or producing. When firms are earning economic profits (profits above normal) or are suffering economic losses (profits below normal, or negative) the industry is not at an equilibrium, and firms will change what they are doing. What is likely to happen depends in part on the behavior of costs in the long run. That is why we spent a good deal of time discussing the notion of economies and diseconomies of scale.

Now we can put the two ideas together and discuss the actual long-run adjustments that are likely to take place in response to short-run profits and losses.

The Expansion of Firms and Industries in Response to Short-Run Profits

We begin the analysis of long-run adjustments with an industry in which firms are earning economic profits. We assume that all firms in the industry are producing with the same technology of production, and that each firm has a long-run average cost curve that is U shaped. This implies that there are some economies of scale to be realized in the industry, and that all firms ultimately begin to run into diseconomies at some scale of operation.

Figure 9.7 shows a representative firm initially producing at scale 1. Market price is P_1, and firms are enjoying economic profits. Without the long-run cost curve drawn in, the diagram is the same as the one in Figure 9.1. Total revenue ($P_1 \times q_1$) exceeds total cost ($SRAC$ at $q_1 \times q_1$), and profit per period is equal to the shaded rectangle.

At this point, notice that our representative firm has not realized all the economies of scale available to it. By expanding to scale 2, it will reduce average costs significantly, and unless price drops it will increase profits. Thus as long as firms are enjoying profits, and economies of scale exist, firms will expand. We assume that the firm in Figure 9.7 shifts to scale 2.

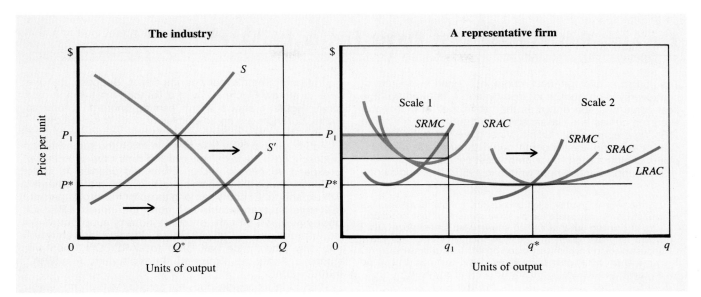

FIGURE 9.7

Firms Expand in the Long Run when Increasing Returns to Scale Are Available

When there are economies of scale to be realized, firms have an incentive to expand to realize them. Thus firms will be pushed by competition to produce at their optimal scales. Price will be driven to the bottom of the *LRAC* curve.

At the same time, the existence of economic profits will attract new entrants. New firms have an incentive to enter, and we assume that they do. Both the entrance of new firms and the expansion of existing firms have the same effect on the left-hand diagram. Both cause the short-run supply curve to shift to the right. Because the short-run industry supply curve is the sum of all the marginal cost curves of all the firms in the industry, it will shift to the right. First, since all firms in the industry are expanding to a larger scale, their individual short-run marginal cost curves shift to the right. Second, with new entries, there are more firms and thus more marginal cost curves to add up.

As capital flows into the industry, the supply curve in the left-hand diagram shifts to the right and price falls. The question is, where will the process stop? Firms will continue to expand as long as there are economies of scale to realize, and new firms will continue to enter as long as economic profits are being earned. Final equilibrium is achieved only when price falls to P^* and firms have exhausted all the economies of scale available in the industry.

Look carefully at the final equilibrium in Figure 9.7. Each firm will choose the scale of plant that produces its product at minimum long-run average cost. That is, competition drives firms to adopt not just the most efficient technology in the *short* run, but also the most efficient scale of operation in the *long* run. In the long-run, equilibrium price (P^*) is equal to long-run average cost, short-run marginal cost, and short-run average cost. Economic profits are driven to zero:

$$P^* = SRMC = SRAC = LRAC,$$

where $SRMC$ denotes short-run marginal cost, $SRAC$ denotes short-run average cost, and $LRAC$ denotes long-run average cost.

The Long-Run Average Cost Curve: Flat or U-Shaped?

The long-run average cost curve has been a source of controversy in economics for many years. A long-run average cost curve was first drawn as the "envelope" of a series of short run curves in a classic article written by Jacob Viner in 1931.[*] In preparing that article, Viner gave his draftsman the task of drawing the long run curve through the minimum points of all the short run average cost curves.

In a supplementary note written in 1950, Viner comments:

> . . . the error in Chart IV is left uncorrected so that future teachers and students may share the pleasure of many of their predecessors of pointing out that if I had known what an envelope was, I would not have given my excellent draftsman the technically impossible and economically inappropriate task of drawing an AC curve which would pass through the lowest cost points of all the ac curves yet not rise above any ac curve at any point.[†]

While this is an interesting part of the lore of economics, a more recent debate concentrates on the economic content of this controversy. In the November-December 1986 issue of *Challenge*, Professor Herbert Simon of Carnegie-Mellon University puts it bluntly:

> I think the textbooks are a scandal. . . . the most widely used textbooks use the old long-run and short-run cost curves to illustrate the theory of the firm. . . . [the U-shaped long-run cost curve] postulated that in the long run the size of the firm would increase to a scale associated with the minimum cost on the long-run curve. It was supposed to predict something about the size distribution of firms in the industry. It doesn't do that and there are other problems. Most serious is the fact that most empirical studies show the firm's cost curves not to be U-shaped, but in fact to slope down to the right and then level off, without a clearly defined minimum point.[‡]

Professor Simon's point is important. Suppose that we were to redraw Figure 9.7 with a flat long-run average cost curve. Figure 1 shows a firm earning short-run economic profits, but there are no economies of scale to be realized.

Despite the lack of economies of scale, expansion of such an industry would likely take place in much the same way as we described in the text. First, existing firms have an incentive to expand. At current prices, a firm that doubles its scale would earn twice the economic profits even if cost did not fall with expansion. Of course as long as economic profits persist, new firms have an incentive to enter the industry. Both of these events will shift the short-run industry supply curve to the right, and price will fall. As before, expansion and entry will stop only when price has fallen to LARC. Only then will economic profits be eliminated. At equilibrium, $P = SRMC = SRAC = LRAC$.

This model, of course, does not predict the final firm size or the structure of the industry. When the long run AC curve is U-shaped, firms stop expanding at the minimum point since further expansion means higher costs; thus, optimal firm size is determined technologically. If the LRAC curve, however, is flat, small firms and large firms have identical average costs.

If this is true, and it seems to be in many industries, the structure of the industry in the long run will depend on whether existing firms expand faster than new firms enter. If new firms enter quickly in response to profit opportunities, the industry will end up with large numbers of small firms. If, on the other hand, existing firms expand more rapidly than new firms enter, the industry may end up with only a few very large firms. Thus, there is an element of randomness in the way industries expand. In fact, most industries contain some large firms and some small firms, which is exactly what Simon's flat LRAC model predicts.

Figure 1
Long-Run Expansion in An Industry with Constant Returns to Scale

If price remained at P_1, the hypothetical firm producing at scale I would double its profits by expanding to scale II. With economic profits, existing firms have an incentive to expand and new firms have an incentive to enter. As they do, the supply curve shifts to S_2 driving price down to P_2, but nothing determines the final size of a firm.

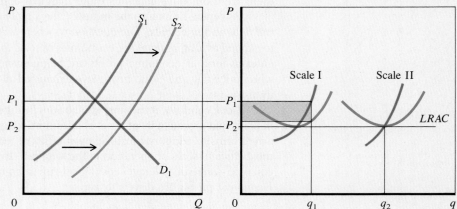

[*]Jacob Viner, "Cost Curves and Supply Curves," *Zeitschrift fur Nationalokonomie*, vol. III (I-1931), pp. 23–46.

[†]George J. Stigler and Kenneth E. Boulding, ed., *AEA Readings in Price Theory*, vol. VI Chicago; Richard D. Irwin, 1952. p. 227.

[‡]Interview with Herbert A. Simon, "The Failure of Armchair Economics," *Challenge*, November/December 1986, pp. 23–24.

The Contraction of Industries Suffering Short-Run Losses

Firms that suffer short-run losses have an incentive to leave the industry in the long run, but in the short run they cannot. As we have seen, some firms incurring losses will choose to shut down and bear losses equal to fixed costs. Others will continue to produce in the short run in an effort to minimize their losses.

Figure 9.8 depicts a firm that will continue to produce q_O units of output in the short run, despite its losses. With losses, however, the long-run picture will change. Firms in this position have an incentive to get out of the industry, and as they exit the short-run supply curve of the industry shifts to the left. As it shifts, the equilibrium price rises.

Once again the question is, How long will this adjustment process continue? As long as there are losses, firms will shut down and leave the industry. As this happens, price rises. The gradual price rise, however, reduces losses for firms remaining in the industry until those losses are ultimately eliminated. In the diagram, this occurs when price rises to P^*. At that point, remaining firms will maximize profits by producing q^* units of output. Price is just sufficient to cover average costs, and economic profits and losses are zero.

The final long-run competitive equilibrium is the same when we start with losses as it is when we start with profits:

$$P = SRMC = SRAC = LRAC,$$

and economic profits are zero.

FIGURE 9.8

Long-Run Contraction and Exit in an Industry with Constant Returns to Scale

When firms in an industry suffer losses, there is an incentive for them to exit; disinvestment will result as capital seeks a higher return in other sectors. As firms exit, the supply curve shifts to S', driving price up to P^*. As price rises, losses are gradually eliminated.

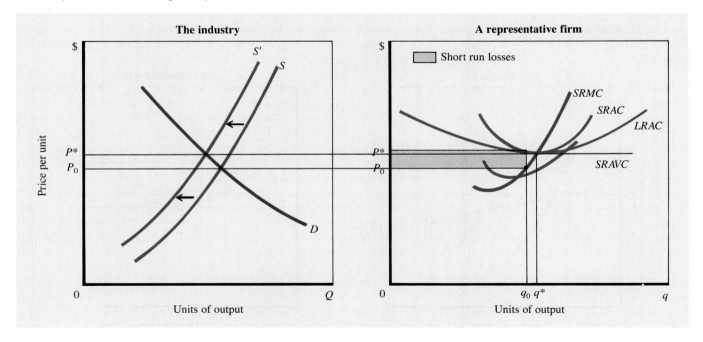

The Long-Run Industry Supply Curve

You have already seen that in some industries costs react to changes in the size of the industry itself rather than to changes in an individual firm's scale of production. Let us reconsider, now, an industry that exhibits *external economies* of scale, that is, as the industry grows, average costs decrease. Such industries, an example of which appears in Figure 9.9, are called **decreasing-cost industries**.

Decreasing-cost industry   An industry that shows external economies of scale—that is, its average costs decrease as the industry grows. The long-run supply curve for such an industry has a negative slope.

Assume that the industry is in long-run equilibrium at price P_1. Then, over time, demand increases, shifting the demand curve from D_1 to D_2, driving price up to P_2. That, of course, creates economic profits. In response, existing firms expand, and new firms enter, shifting the supply curve out to the right, S_1 to S_2.

As the industry expands, external economies of scale come into play, and the increased size of the industry creates cost savings for all firms. Thus the average cost curve facing each firm in the industry shifts *downward*. As a result, profits are not eliminated until the shift in supply drives price down below its original point, all the way to the bottom of the *new* average cost curve.

Presumably, further expansion would lead to even greater savings. The dark line in Figure 9.9, which traces out price and total output over time as the industry expands, is called the **long-run industry supply curve (LRIS)**. If the industry enjoys external economies of scale, its long-run supply curve will slope down.

In Figure 9.10, we derive the long-run industry supply curve for an industry that faces *external diseconomies* of scale. (These were suffered in the construction industry, for example, when increasing activity drove up lumber prices.) Once again, as demand expands, price is driven up to P_2. In response to the resulting higher profits, firms enter,

FIGURE 9.9
A Decreasing Cost Industry: External Economies of Scale

In a decreasing cost industry, average cost declines as the industry expands. As demand expands to D_2, price rises to P_2. As new firms enter and existing firms expand, supply shifts to S_2, driving price down. If costs decline as a result of the expansion to $LRAC_2$, the final price will be below P_1 at P_3. The long-run industry supply curve *(LRIS)* slopes downward.

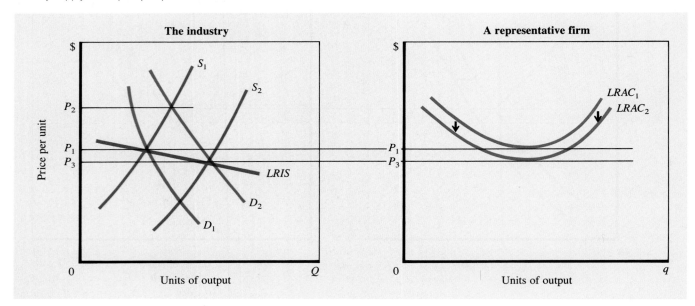

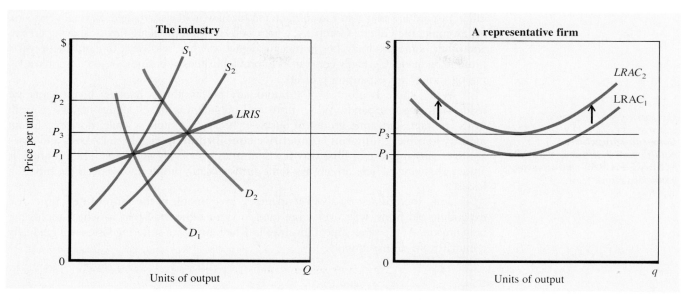

FIGURE 9.10

An Increasing Cost Industry: External Diseconomies of Scale

In an increasing-cost industry, average cost increases as the industry expands. As demand shifts to D_2, price rises to P_2. As new firms enter and existing firms expand output, supply shifts to S_2, driving price down. If long-run average costs rise as a result to $LRAC_2$, the final price will be P_3—above P_1. The long-run industry supply curve (*LRIS*) slopes up.

Increasing-cost industry   *An industry that shows external diseconomies of scale—that is, its average costs increase as the industry grows. The long-run supply curve for such an industry slopes up.*

Constant-cost industry   *An industry that shows no economies or diseconomies of scale as the industry grows. Such industries have flat, or horizontal, long-run supply curves.*

shifting the short-run supply schedule to the right and driving price down. But this time, as the industry expands, the long-run average cost curve shifts up to $LRAC_2$ owing to external diseconomies of scale. Now, price has to fall back only to P_3, not all the way to P_1, to eliminate economic profits. Such an industry, whose long-run industry supply curve thus slopes up to the right, is called an **increasing-cost industry**.

It should not surprise you to know that industries in which there are no external economies or diseconomies of scale have flat, or horizontal, long-run industry supply curves, and are called **constant-cost industries**.

The Long-Run Adjustment Mechanism in Practice

This discussion of entry and exit and expansion and contraction has been vague on purpose because the actual process is extremely complex, and it varies from industry to industry. The general idea of capital flowing in response to profit opportunities, however, is critical. In Chapter 1 we talked about the notion of efficient markets. The logic of efficient markets is that as profit opportunities develop they are quickly eliminated. To illustrate that point, we described driving up to a toll booth on a freeway and suggested that shorter-than-average lines are quickly eliminated as cars shift into them. So too profits in competitive industries are eliminated as new competing firms move into open slots, or perceived opportunities, in the industry.

In practice, the **entry and exit** of firms in response to profit opportunities usually involves the financial capital market. In capital markets, people are looking day in and day out for profits. When firms in an industry do well, capital is indeed likely to flow into that industry. Entrepreneurs actually start new firms. In addition, firms producing entirely different products may join the competition for new markets far afield. Several years ago, for example, the Gillette Company, a firm well known for making razors, shaving cream, and other home products, began making digital watches because it thought there was a profit to be made. Certainly companies in profitable lines of business have no trouble at all raising money for expansion projects.

Long-run competitive equilibrium When P = SRMC = SRAC = LRAC *and economic profits are zero.*

When there is promise of extraordinary profits, things happen: investments are made and output expands. When firms end up suffering losses, things happen as well: firms contract, and some go out of business. It can take quite a while, however, for an industry to achieve **long-run competitive equilibrium**. In fact, because costs and tastes are in a constant state of flux, very few industries ever really get there. The economy is always changing. There are always some firms making profits and some firms suffering losses.

This, then, is a story about tendencies. Investment, in the form of new firms and expanding old firms, will, over time, tend to favor those industries in which profits are being made. At the same time, industries in which firms are suffering losses will gradually contract from disinvestment.

BEGINNING TO CLOSE THE CIRCLE

You have now seen what lies behind the demand curves and supply curves in competitive *output* markets. The next two chapters take up competitive *input* markets and complete the picture.

Perhaps you can already begin to see how market systems answer the basic questions that we defined at the outset of this discussion. We said that every society has some mechanism for answering three fundamental questions: *What* will be produced? *How* will it be produced? and *For whom* will it be produced?

In the last four chapters, we have been building a model of a simple market system under the assumption of perfect competition. Let us expand on just one more example in order to review the response of a competitive system to a change in consumer preferences.

Over the past decade, Americans have developed a taste for wine in general and for California wines and "wine-coolers" in particular. We know that household demand is constrained by income, wealth, and prices, and that income is, at least in part, determined by the choices that households make. Within those constraints, however, households choose, and, increasingly, they choose—or demand—wine. The demand curve for wine has shifted to the right, causing excess demand followed by an increase in price.

With higher prices, wine producers find themselves earning economic profits. *This increase in price and consequent rise in profits is the basic signal that leads to a reallocation of society's resources.* In the short run, wine producers are constrained by their current scales of operation. California has only a limited number of vineyards and only a limited amount of vat capacity; for example.

In the long run, however, you would expect to see resources flow in to compete for those nice economic profits, and you do. New firms enter the wine-producing business. New vines are planted and new vats and production equipment are purchased and put in place. Vineyard owners move into new states—Rhode Island, Texas, and Maryland —and established growers also increase production. Overall, more wine is produced to meet the new consumer demand. At the same time, firms are being pushed to operate using the most efficient technology available.

What starts as a shift in preferences ends up as a shift in resources. Land is reallocated, labor moves into wine production, and all this is accomplished without any central planning or direction.

To complete the picture now, we turn in Chapter 10 to competitive input markets.

SUMMARY

1. For any firm at any moment, one of three conditions holds: (1) the firm is earning economic profits, (2) the firm is suffering losses, or (3) the firm is just breaking even—that is, earning a normal rate of return.

2. A firm earning economic profits in the short run, if it expects to continue to do so, has an incentive to expand in the long run. Profits also provide an incentive for new firms to enter the industry.

3. In the short run, firms suffering losses are stuck in the industry. They can shut down operations ($Q=O$), but they must still bear fixed costs. In the long run, of course, firms suffering losses can liquidate and exit the industry.

4. Some firms suffering losses will operate and by doing so reduce their losses. Operating earns revenues, as well as incurring variable costs. If revenues exceed variable costs, the profit from operating can be used to pay some fixed costs and thus reduce losses.

5. Some firms suffering losses will decide to shut down in the short run. This decision results when revenues are insufficient to cover even variable costs. This occurs when the price of output falls below average variable costs.

6. The minimum point on the average variable cost curve, that is, the point where marginal cost and average variable cost intersect, is called the shut-down point. At all prices above it, the *MC* curve shows the profit-maximizing level of output. At all prices below it, optimal short-run output is zero.

7. The short-run supply curve of a firm in a perfectly competitive industry is the portion of its marginal cost curve that lies above average variable costs.

8. Two things can cause the industry supply curve to move: (1) in the short run, anything that causes marginal costs to change across the industry, such as an increase in the market wage, and (2) in the long run, entry or exit of firms.

9. When a firm exhibits economies of scale (increasing returns to scale) it means that producing on a larger scale saves on inputs. If a firm doubles inputs, it will *more* than double output, and long-run average costs decrease with output.

10. When a firm exhibits diseconomies of scale (decreasing returns to scale) a doubling of inputs will *not* double output. Average costs *increase* with output.

11. When short-run profits exist in an industry, firms will enter and existing firms will expand. That shifts the industry supply curve to the right. When this happens, price falls and ultimately profits are eliminated.

12. When short-run losses are suffered in an industry, some firms exit and some firms may reduce scale. That shifts the industry supply curve to the left, raising price and eliminating losses.

13. Long-run competitive equilibrium is reached when $P=SRMC=SRAC=LRAC$ and economic profits are zero.

14. A decreasing-cost industry is one in which costs fall as the industry expands. It exhibits external economies of scale, and the long-run industry supply curve slopes downward.

15. An increasing-cost industry is one in which costs rise as the industry expands. It exhibits external diseconomies of scale, and the long-run industry supply curve slopes upward.

REVIEW CONCEPTS

REVIEW QUESTIONS

1. Explain how it is possible that a firm with a production function that exhibits increasing returns to scale can run into diminishing returns at the same time.

2. Suppose that firms in industry X had production functions that exhibited increasing returns to scale up to 150,000 units of output, but decreasing returns to scale above that level. Sketch a typical firm's long-run average cost function. If each firm started on a small, inefficient scale, but earned economic profits, at what scale would they ultimately settle?

3. Suppose that there were only two sectors of the economy, one of which used a great deal of energy. In addition, suppose that the government, in its desire to achieve independence from foreign sources, placed a large tax on energy use. Describe in detail the long-run adjustments you would expect to see following such a tax.

4. Consider an industry that exhibits external diseconomies of scale in the long run. Suppose that over the next ten years demand for its product increases rapidly. Describe in detail the adjustments likely to follow. Where would market price ultimately settle? Use diagrams in your answer.

5. The following two long-run production functions show the relationship between inputs and outputs:

$$(1)\ Q = 3K + 2L.$$
$$(2)\ Q = \sqrt{K\,L}.$$

a. Show that both exhibit constant returns to scale.

b. If the price of capital is $5.00 and the price of labor is $4.00, show that the average cost curve is flat.

c. If in the short run capital is fixed, do these two production functions exhibit diminishing returns? Show using a numerical example.

6. For each of the following, say whether you agree or disagree and explain why in a sentence or two:

a. A firm will never sell its product for less than it costs to produce it.

b. If the short-run marginal cost curve is U-shaped, the long-run average cost curve is likely to be U-shaped as well.

c. Input prices are assumed to be fixed in deriving the long-run supply curve for a competitive industry.

10 The Firm: Demand in Competitive Input Markets

As you have seen, business firms in perfectly competitive industries must make three fundamental decisions: (1) how much to produce and supply in output markets; (2) how to produce that output, that is, which technology to use; and (3) how much of each input to demand. So far, our discussion of firm behavior has focused on the first two questions. In Chapters 7–9, we developed a model to explain how profit-maximizing firms choose among alternative technologies and decide how much to supply in output markets. In essence, we went behind the short- and long-run industry supply curves.

Throughout our discussion of firm behavior, however, we have focused on *output* markets. We now turn to the behavior of firms in competitive *input* markets (highlighted in Figure 10.1), going behind input demand curves in much the same way that we went behind output supply curves in the previous two chapters. One lesson here is that when we look behind input demand curves, we discover the exact same set of decisions, seen from a different point of view. In a very real sense, we have already talked about everything covered in this chapter. It is the *perspective* that is new.

The next chapter discusses the capital and land markets in some detail. This chapter is about input markets in general, but we concentrate on the labor market, because the relationship between households and firms is direct; firms pay workers a wage directly in exchange for their labor. The capital market is institutionally more complex than the labor market, but in fact it is very similar. In order to buy a capital asset—a machine, for instance—a firm must use funds that it obtains from households. In exchange, firms pay profits, or interest, to those households. In a sense, households supply this capital, just as they supply labor, but this is the subject of Chapter 11.

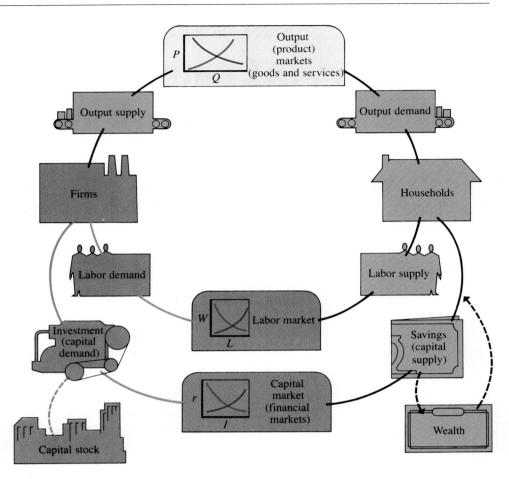

FIGURE 10.1
Firm and Household Decisions

Firms and households interact in both input and output markets. This chapter highlights firm choices in input markets.

THE FIRM IN INPUT MARKETS

Demand for Inputs: A *Derived Demand*   A firm cannot make a profit unless there is a demand for its product: households must be willing to pay for its output. The quantity of output that a firm produces in both the long run and the short run thus depends on the value that the market places on what that firm produces. Therefore, because it really depends on the demand for outputs, *the demand for inputs is a* **derived demand**. The key point you should take away from this chapter is that the value of any input—land, labor, or capital—depends on how society values the things (output) that the input produces. The price of any factor of production (input) depends on its productivity in competitive markets.

Prices in competitive input markets, of course, depend on demand by firms, supply by households, and how the two interact. In the labor market, for example, households must decide whether to work and how much to work. In Chapter 6 we saw that the opportunity cost of working for a wage is either leisure or the use value derived from nonpaid labor—working in the garden, for instance, or rearing children. Firms will demand workers as long as the value of what those workers produce exceeds what they must be paid. Households will supply labor as long as the wage exceeds the value of leisure or the value that they derive from nonpaid work.

An examination of the links between input and output markets reveals a great deal about the nature of the allocative process. In addition, because the distribution of income depends to a large extent on the wages, profits, and rents paid to the various factors of production, understanding how these markets work helps us to understand the distribution of output better and, ultimately, to answer the basic question of who gets what and why.

Complementary and substituteable inputs   *Factors of production are used together to enhance each other and can also be used in place of each other.*

Inputs: Complementary and Substitutable   Another major theme running through this chapter is that inputs are simultaneously **complementary** and **substitutable**. Two inputs used together may enhance, or complement, each other. A new machine that raises the productivity of labor may not be any good without someone to run it. Machines can also be substituted for labor, or less often perhaps, labor can be substituted for machines.

All this means that a firm's input demands are tightly linked one to another. An increase or decrease in wages naturally causes the demand for labor to change, but it may also have an effect on the demand for capital or land. If we are to understand the demand for inputs, therefore, these interconnections must be sorted out.

A Firm Using Only One Variable Factor of Production: Labor

Diminishing returns   *When successive units of a variable factor are added to a production process with a fixed factor of production, the marginal product of the variable factor falls.*

Marginal product   *The additional output produced with the addition of one additional unit of input ceteris paribus.*

Diminishing Returns Revisited   Recall that we defined the *short run* as that period during which some fixed factor of production limits a firm's capacity to expand. Under these conditions, the firm that decides to increase output will eventually encounter **diminishing returns**. To state this more formally, a fixed scale of plant means that the marginal product *of variable inputs declines*. Recall also that **marginal product** of labor is the additional output that is produced if a firm hires one additional unit of labor. For example, if a firm pays for 400 hours of labor per week—10 workers working 40 hours—and asks one worker to stay an extra hour, the product of the 401st hour is the *marginal product of labor* for that firm.

In Chapter 7, we talked at some length about declining marginal product at a sandwich shop. The first two columns of Table 10.1 reproduce some of the production data from that shop. You may remember that the shop has only one grill, at which only two or three people can work comfortably. In this example, the grill is the fixed factor of production in the short run and labor is the variable factor. The first worker can produce 10 sandwiches per hour, and the second can produce 15. The second worker can produce

TABLE 10.1

Marginal Revenue Product per Hour of Labor in Sandwich Production (One Grill)

Total labor units (employees)	Total product (sandwiches per hour)	Marginal product (sandwiches per hour)	Price (value added per sandwich)*	Marginal revenue product (per hour)
0	0	—	—	—
1	10	10	$.50	$5.00
2	25	15	.50	7.50
3	35	10	.50	5.00
4	40	5	.50	2.50
5	42	2	.50	1.00
6	42	0	.50	0

*The "price" is essentially profit per sandwich; see discussion in text.

more because the first is also busy answering the phone and taking care of customers, as well as making sandwiches. From there on, however, marginal product declines; the third worker adds only 10 sandwiches per hour, because the grill gets crowded. The fourth worker can squeeze in quickly while the others are serving or wrapping, but adds only five additional sandwiches each hour, and so forth.[1]

In this case, the capacity of the grill ultimately limits output. In order to see how the firm might make a rational choice about how many workers to hire, however, we need to know more about the value of that product and the cost of labor.

Marginal revenue product (MRP)   *The additional revenue earned by the use of one additional unit of input, ceteris paribus.*

Marginal Revenue Product   The **marginal revenue product (MRP)** of a variable input is the additional revenue a firm earns by employing one additional unit of that input, *ceteris paribus*. If labor is the variable factor, for example, hiring an additional unit will presumably lead to added output, called the *marginal product of labor*. The sale of that added output will yield some revenues. Marginal revenue product is the revenue that is produced by selling the good or service that the marginal unit of labor produces. For a competitive firm, marginal revenue product is the value of a factor's marginal product.

Using labor as our variable factor, we can state this proposition more formally by saying that if MP_L is the marginal product of labor and P_X is the price of output, then the marginal revenue product of labor is

$$MRP_L = MP_L \times P_X.$$

Figure 10.2 shows how a marginal revenue product curve can be derived from a marginal product curve. In the lower diagram, the 1000th unit of labor adds ten units of output. If each unit sells for $5.00, marginal revenue product is $50.00. The 1300th unit of labor adds five units of output, which sell for a total of $25.00. As long as the sales price per unit of output is a constant, the marginal revenue product curve has exactly the same shape as the marginal product curve except that the scale on the Y axis is in dollars, not in units of output.

When calculating marginal revenue product, we need to be very precise about just what product is being produced. A sandwich shop, to be sure, sells sandwiches, but it does not produce the bread, meat, cheese, mustard, and mayo that go into the sandwiches. What the shop is producing is "sandwich cooking and assembly services": the shop is "adding value" to the meat, bread, and other ingredients by preparing and putting it all together in ready-to-eat form. With this in mind, let's assume that each finished sandwich in our shop sells for $.50 over and above the costs of its ingredients. Thus, the price of the service the shop is selling is $.50 per visit, and the only variable cost of providing that service is that of the labor used to put the sandwiches together.

Table 10.1 calculates the marginal revenue product of each worker if the shop takes in $.50 per sandwich over and above the costs of its ingredients. The first worker produces 10 sandwiches per hour which, at $0.50 each, generates revenues of $5.00 per hour. The addition of a second worker yields $7.50 an hour in revenues. After that diminishing returns drive *MRP* down. The marginal revenue product of the third worker is $5.00 per hour; for the fourth worker, it is only $2.50, and so forth.

Marginal Revenue Product, Input Price, and Factor Demand   Demand for input depends on the marginal revenue product of an input and its unit cost, or price. The price of labor, for example, is the wage that is determined in the labor market. (Remember that

[1]As we said in Chapter 7, we assume that all workers are equally skilled and motivated. The third worker is no less hard working or skilled than the first two. Rather, the grill is getting crowded. To put this another way, *the capital constraint is binding.*

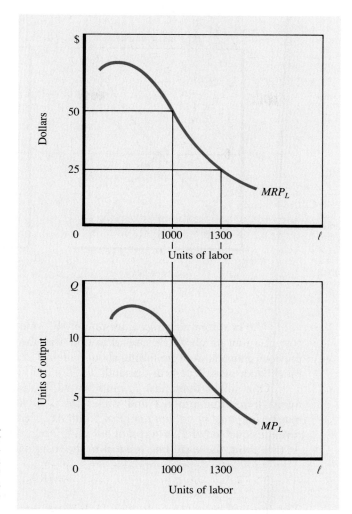

FIGURE 10.2

Deriving a Marginal Revenue Product Curve from Marginal Product Assuming $P_x = \$5$

The marginal revenue product of labor is the price of output times the marginal product of labor. In competition it is the market value of labor's marginal product. As long as output price is constant, the *MRP* curve has the same downward slope as the *MP* curve.

we are still dealing only with competitive firms that are price-takers in both output and input markets. Such firms can hire all the labor they want to hire as long as they pay the market wage.) We can think of the "hourly wage" at the sandwich shop, then, as the marginal cost of a unit of labor.

A profit-maximizing firm will add inputs—in the case of labor, it will hire workers—as long as the marginal revenue product of that input exceeds its price. Look again at the figures for the sandwich shop in Table 10.1 and then suppose that the going wage for sandwich makers is $4.00 per hour. A profit-maximizing firm would hire three workers. The first worker would yield $5.00 per hour in revenues and the second would yield $7.50, but they would cost only $4.00 each per hour. The third worker would bring in $5.00 per hour, but still cost only $4.00 in marginal wages. The marginal product of the fourth worker ($2.50), however, would not bring in enough revenue to pay his salary.

Figure 10.3 presents the same information graphically. The labor market appears on the left; on the right is a single firm that employs workers. This firm, incidentally, does not represent just the firms in a single industry. Because firms in many different industries demand labor, the firm in the graph represents any firm in any industry that uses labor.

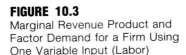

FIGURE 10.3

Marginal Revenue Product and Factor Demand for a Firm Using One Variable Input (Labor)

A competitive firm using only one variable factor of production will use that factor as long as its marginal revenue product exceeds its unit cost. The firm will hire labor as long as MRP_L is greater than the going wage, W^*. The hypothetical firm will demand l^* units of labor.

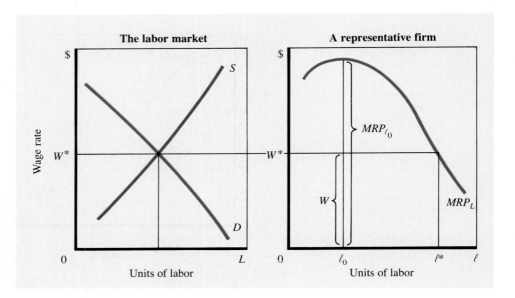

The firm faces a *market wage rate* of W^*, and we can think of this as the marginal cost of a unit of labor. (Be careful to note that the margin is now in units of *labor*; in previous chapters we were talking about marginal units of *output*.) Given W^*, then, how much labor would the firm demand?

One might think that l_o units would be hired, where the difference between marginal revenue product and wage rate is greatest. But the firm is interested in maximizing total profit, not marginal profit. At l_o, hiring one more unit of labor generates revenue equal to MRP_{l_o} at a cost of only W^*. Thus, the firm will continue to hire up to l^*. At that point, the wage rate is equal to the marginal revenue product of labor, or

$$W^* = MRP_L.$$

The firm will not produce beyond l^*, because the cost of hiring the *next* unit of labor, W^*, would be greater than the value of what that unit produces. (Recall that the fourth sandwich maker can produce only an extra $2.50 an hour in sandwiches, while his salary is $4.00 per hour.)

Thus for a firm that uses only one variable factor of production, the curve in the right hand diagram of Figure 10.3 tells us how much labor the firm will hire at each potential market wage rate. That description should sound familiar to you—it is, in fact, the description of a demand curve. Therefore we can now say that *when a firm uses only one variable factor of production, that factor's marginal revenue product curve is the firm's demand curve for that factor in the short run.*

A Familiar Logic: Marginal Revenue and Cost   In Chapter 8 we saw that the marginal cost curve of a competitive firm is the same as its supply curve. That is, at any output price, the marginal cost curve determines how much output a profit-maximizing firm will produce. We came to that conclusion by comparing the marginal revenue that a firm would earn by producing one more unit of output with the marginal cost of producing it.

There is absolutely no difference between the reasoning in Chapter 8 and this reasoning: the only difference is that what is being measured at the margin has changed.

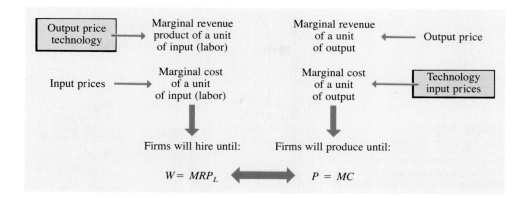

FIGURE 10.4
The Two Profit-Maximizing Conditions Are Simply Two Views of the Same Choice Process

There the firm was comparing the marginal revenues and costs of another unit of output. Here, the firm is comparing the marginal revenues and costs of employing another unit of input. To see this, look at Figure 10.4. (You may also find it helpful to compare Figure 10.3 with Figure 8.10.) If the only variable factor of production is labor, the condition $W = MRP_L$ is the same condition as $P = MC$. In other words, the two statements say exactly the same thing.[2]

In both cases, the firm is comparing the cost of production with potential revenues from the sale of product at the margin. In Chapter 8 the firm compared the price of output (P) directly with cost of production (MC) where cost was derived from information on factor prices and technology. (Go over the derivation of cost curves if this is unclear.) Here information on output price and technology is contained in the marginal revenue product curve, which is compared with information on input price to determine the optimal level of input to demand. This means that firms make *simultaneous* decisions about how much output to supply and how much of each input to demand. In effect, one decision *is* the other.

The assumption of one variable factor of production makes the trade-off facing firms easy to see. Figure 10.5 shows that in essence firms weigh the value of labor as reflected in the market wage against the value of the product of labor as reflected in output market prices. If society values a good more than it costs firms to hire the workers to produce that good, the good will be produced. In general the same logic also holds for more than one input. Firms weigh the value of outputs as reflected in output price against the value of inputs as reflected in marginal costs.

Deriving input demands: Some examples   For the small sandwich shop, calculating the marginal product of a variable input (in this case, labor) and marginal revenue product was easy. Although it may be more complex, the decision process is essentially the same for big corporations and for individuals.

When an airline hires more flight attendants, it increases the quality of its service in order to attract more passengers from other airlines and thus sell more of its product.

---

[2]This can also be shown algebraically as:

$$W = MRP_L = MP_L \cdot P_x = \frac{\Delta Q}{\Delta L} \cdot P_x \rightarrow P_x \frac{\Delta Q}{\Delta L} = W \rightarrow P_x = W \cdot \frac{\Delta L}{\Delta Q} = MC.$$

$\frac{\Delta Q}{\Delta L}$ = Output per unit input (*MP*) $\frac{\Delta L}{\Delta Q}$ = Input per unit output.

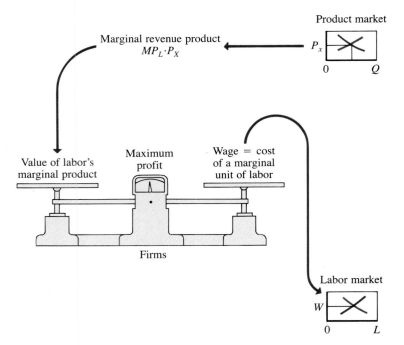

FIGURE 10.5

The Trade-Off Facing Firms

Firms weigh the cost of labor as reflected in wage rates against the value of labor's marginal product. If society values a good more than the cost of hiring workers to produce it, it will be produced.

Flight attendants cost the airline something, however; they must be paid a wage. In deciding how many to hire, then, the firm must figure out how much new revenue the added flight attendants are likely to generate relative to their wages.

As at the sandwich shop, diminishing returns clearly set in at a certain point. Once a sufficient number of attendants are on a plane, marginal additions add little to the quality of service, and their marginal product diminishes. Like the grill, the airplane has a fixed physical capacity, and the addition of a variable factor beyond a certain level might even give rise to negative marginal product. Too many attendants could bother the passengers and make it difficult to get to the restrooms.

In making your own decisions, you too compare marginal gains with input costs in the presence of diminishing returns. Suppose you grow vegetables in your yard. You do this for a number of reasons. First, you save money at the grocery store—vegetables are an output with a measurable pecuniary value. Second, you can plant what you like, and the vegetables taste better fresh from the garden. Third, you simply like to work in the garden—you get sun, exercise, fresh air, and a sense of being "with the earth."

Like the sandwich shop and the airline, you also face diminishing returns in your garden, however. You have only 625 square feet to work with, and with land as a fixed factor in the short run, your marginal product will certainly decline. You can work all day every day, but your limited space will produce only so many string beans. The first few hours you spend each week watering, fertilizing, and dealing with major weed and bug infestations probably have a high marginal product. But after five or six hours, there is little else you can do to increase yield. Diminishing returns also apply to your own satisfaction. The farmers' markets are now full of cheap fresh produce that tastes nearly as good as yours. And once you have been out in the garden for a few hours, the hot sun and hard work start to lose their charm and the earth under your fingernails gives way to the less gritty pleasure of watching a baseball game on TV.

Although your gardening does not involve money (unlike the sandwich shop and the airline which pay out wages), the labor you supply has a value that must be weighed, even if the cost of a unit of your labor is only the value you could derive by using that time doing something else, such as watching TV. And when the returns from gardening

234

diminish beyond a certain point, that's exactly what you do.

It is as true for the sandwich shop as for you that if the cost of labor rises, less of it is likely to be employed. If the competitive labor market pushed the daily wage to $6.00 per hour, the sandwich shop would hire only two workers instead of three. If you suddenly became very busy at school, your time would become more valuable and you would probably devote fewer hours to gardening.

A Firm Employing Two Variable Factors of Production

When a firm employs more than one variable factor of production, the analysis becomes more complicated, but the principles stay the same. We shall now consider a firm that employs variable capital (K) and labor (L), and thus faces factor prices P_K and P_L.[3] (Quickly recall here that *capital* refers to plant, equipment, and inventory used in production. We have assumed that some portion of the firm's capital stock is fixed in the short run, but that some of it is variable—for example, some machinery and equipment can be installed quickly.) Our analysis can be applied to any two factors of production, and it can easily be generalized to three or more. It can also be applied to the long run when all factors of production are variable.

You have seen that inputs are both *complementary* and *substitutable* at the same time. Land, labor, and capital are used *together* to produce outputs. The worker who uses a shovel digs a bigger hole than one with no shovel; add a steam shovel and that worker becomes really productive. When an expanding firm adds to its stock of capital, it raises the productivity of its labor, and vice versa. Thus each factor complements the other.

At the same time, of course, land, labor, and capital can also be substituted one for another. If labor becomes expensive, some labor-saving technology may take its place. In central cities where land is very expensive, capital is substituted for land—that is, floor space is stacked up on top of itself in tall buildings.

When we confined our analysis to firms employing just one variable factor of production, a change in the price of that factor affected only the demand for the factor itself. When more than one factor varies, we must consider the impact of a change in one factor price on the demand for *other* factors as well.

Substitution and Output Effects of a Change in Factor Price   Table 10.2 presents data on a hypothetical firm that employs variable capital and labor. Now suppose that the firm faces a choice between two available technologies of production, technique A, which is capital intensive, and technique B, which is labor intensive. When the market price of labor is $1.00 per unit and the market price of capital is $1.00, the labor-intensive method

TABLE 10.2

Response of a Firm to an Increasing Wage Rate

Technology	Input requirements per unit of output		Unit cost if $P_L = \$1.00$ $P_K = \$1.00$	Unit cost if $P_L = \$2.00$ $P_K = \$1.00$
	K	L		
A (capital intensive)	10	5	$15.00	$20.00
B (labor intensive)	3	10	$13.00	$23.00

[3] The price of labor, P_L, is the same as the wage rate W. We will, however, use the term "P_L" instead of W for the rest of the chapter to stress the symmetry between labor and capital.

Do Factor Returns Really Reflect Productivity?

This chapter presents a theory that suggests that competitive markets reward each factor of production in accordance with its productivity at the margin. Using labor as an example, the equilibrium wage rate will be equal to the value of labor's marginal product. How does this part of competitive market theory square with reality?

The proposition that rewards and productivity are tightly linked is clear in firms with only one employee. Consider, for example, a portrait photographer who works for herself. The Department of Labor reports:

> Photographers and camera operators held about 101,000 jobs in 1984. About half of all jobs are salaried positions. The rest are held by self-employed photographers who do individual projects for those wishing to use their services.

What rewards does our photographer earn? She takes photographs of people for a fee. Buyers pay her directly. When she produces a portrait of an individual, she is paid a fee that reflects the value of her "product." No one is coerced into using her services; the amount that a given client pays reflects his willingness to pay for the product.

Of course, the total fee paid to a photographer is in part a return to capital: she uses a camera and must have a dark room equipped with chemicals, paper and so forth. She also has acquired skills over the years, and those skills add to the value of her final product. The better the product, the more she can charge.

The following are descriptions of several labor markets published by the Department of Labor. As you read through them, think about the factors that determine the market wages paid to each profession. Can you see the links to the value of labor's product in each case?

Dentists

> Employment of dentists is expected to grow faster than the average for all occupations through the mid-1990's. Among the factors responsible for anticipated job growth are changes in

population size and structure, which are expected to boost demand for restorative dentistry. As the baby-boom generation matures, large numbers of middle-aged Americans will be candidates for more intensive dental care. Unlike younger people, who have benefited from advances in dental health, people born before the 1950's tend to have intricate dental work that will require complicated maintenance as they grow older.

Pilots

> Employment of pilots is expected to increase faster than the average for all occupations through the mid-1990's. While computerized flight engineering systems may reduce the demand for flight engineers, the expected growth in airline passenger and cargo traffic will create a need for more aircraft, more pilots, and more flight instructors. Businesses are expected to operate more planes and employ more pilots to fly passengers and cargo to the increased number of locations that the scheduled airlines do not service.

Photographers

> Demand for photographers will be stimulated as business and industry place greater importance upon visual aids in meetings, stockholders' reports, sales campaigns, and public relations work. Photography is becoming increasingly important in scientific and medical research, where opportunities are expected to be good for those with appropriate technical skills. Employment in photojournalism is expected to grow slowly.

Ministers

> The pressures of rising costs and inadequate financial support due to the anticipated slow growth in church membership are expected to result in only limited growth in the need for minsters through the mid-1990's. The number of persons being ordained has been increasing, and this trend is likely to continue. As a result, new graduates of theological schools are expected to face increasing competition in finding positions, and more experienced ministers will face competition in moving to larger congregations with greater responsibility. The supply-demand situation will vary among denominations and geographic regions.

All quotes from U.S. Department of Labor, *Occupational Outlook Handbook*, 1986–87.

of producing output is least costly. Each unit costs only $13.00 to produce using technique *B*, while the unit cost of production using technique *A* is $15.00. If the price of labor rises to $2.00, however, technique *B* is no longer least costly. The unit cost rises to $23.00 for labor-intensive technique *B*, but to only $20.00 for capital-intensive technique *A*.

Table 10.3 shows the impact of such an increase in the price of labor on both capital and labor demand when a firm produces 100 units of output. With each input factor costing $1.00 per unit, the firm chooses technique *B* and demands 300 units of capital

TABLE 10.3

The Substitution Effect of an Increase in Wages on a Firm Producing 100 Units of Output

| | To produce 100 units of output: | | |
	total capital demanded	total labor demanded	total variable cost
When P_L = $1.00, P_K = $1.00, firm uses technology B.	300	1000	$1300
When P_L = $2.00, P_K = $1.00, firm uses technology A.	1000	500	$2000

and 1000 units of labor. Total variable cost is $1300. An increase in the price of labor to $2.00 causes the firm to switch from technique B to technique A. In doing so it *substitutes capital for labor*. The amount of labor demanded drops from 1000 to 500 units; the amount of capital demanded increases from 300 to 1000 units.

The tendency of firms to substitute away from a factor whose price has risen and toward a factor whose price has fallen is called the **factor substitution effect**. The factor substitution effect is part of the reason that *input demand curves slope downward*. When an input, or factor of production, becomes less expensive, firms tend to substitute it for other factors and thus buy *more* of it. When a particular input becomes more expensive, however, firms tend to substitute other factors and buy *less* of it. When energy prices rose in the 1970s, for example, the big push toward conservation included new heating plants, insulation, and smaller cars. Firms, as well as private citizens, tried to substitute capital for energy wherever they could.

The firm described in Tables 10.2 and 10.3 continued to produce 100 units of output after the wage rate doubled. An *increase* in the price of a *production factor*, however, also means an increase in the *costs of production*, and cost curves shift upwards. When a firm faces higher costs, it is likely to produce less in the short run. If you stop and recall that the supply curve of a competitive firm is the same thing as its marginal cost curve, you can see that when the marginal cost curve shifts upward, quantity supplied declines, as shown in Figure 10.6. Now when a firm decides to cut output, its demand for all factors declines, including, of course, the factor whose price increased in the first place. This is called the **output effect** *of a factor price increase*.[4]

A *decrease* in the price of a factor of production, on the other hand, means lower costs of production, and cost curves shift downward. If their output price remains unchanged, firms will increase output, and that, in turn, means that demand for all factors of production will increase—the *output effect of a factor price decrease*.

The output effect also helps explain why input demand curves slope downward. Output effects and substitution effects almost always work in the same direction.[5] Consider, for example, a decline in the wage rate. Lower wages mean that a firm will substitute labor for capital and other inputs—that is, the factor substitution effect leads to an increase in demand for labor. Lower wages mean lower costs, and lower costs lead to more output. This increase in output, then, means that the firm will hire more of all

---

[4]It is certainly possible that a cut in output involving a major switch in the optimal technique of production will *increase* the demand for some input factor. When this happens, the factor in demand is called an inferior factor. But for purposes of our discussion, we will assume that increases in output *increase* the demand for all factors, and that decreases in production *decrease* the demand for all factors.

[5]In the rare case of an inferior factor, they work against each other. Can you figure out why?

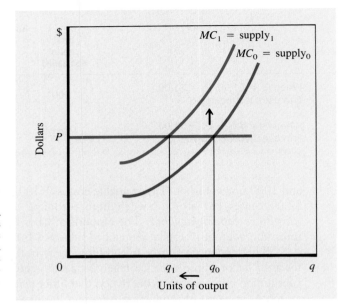

FIGURE 10.6

Decrease in Output From an Increase in Cost

When a factor price increases it raises the cost of production. Since a firm's marginal cost curve acts just like a supply curve, an increase in costs drives supply down. Firms will produce less and as a result they demand fewer inputs.

FIGURE 10.7

Summary of Output and Substitution Effects: Why Labor Demand Slopes Down

Input demand curves slope downward. That is, when a factor price declines, firms tend to use more of it and vice versa. The actual change in quantity demanded is the sum of two effects: the output effect and the factor substitution effect.

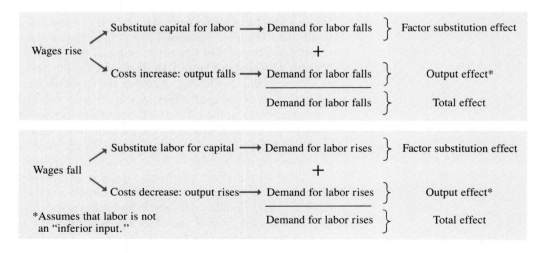

factors of production, including labor itself. That is the output effect. Notice that both effects lead to an increase in the demand for labor when the wage rate falls. Figure 10.7 summarizes these output and substitution effects.

Deriving an Input Demand Curve When Two Factors Are Variable   Deriving a firm's input demand curve is more complicated when two factors of production are variable than when just one factor varies. Let's go back to the sandwich shop again. Table 10.1 gave the marginal product and marginal revenue product schedules, assuming a fixed grill capacity. If the market wage for sandwich makers were $4.00 per hour, the shop would hire three workers. Each would generate more than $4.00 in revenues. Only if the market wage rate went below $2.50 per hour and labor were the only variable factor of production, would the firm increase the amount of labor demanded, from three to four units. (The marginal revenue product of the fourth worker, $2.50 per hour, would then exceed the new market wage.)

But now let's assume grill capacity is also variable. Suppose that a decline in wages reduces cost enough to warrant an expansion. The purchase of a second grill will raise the productivity of labor and shift the marginal revenue product curve out to the right. When we earlier discussed marginal revenue product as the additional revenue earned by hiring one additional unit of labor at the margin, ceteris paribus, we assumed that all other inputs—specifically, the grill capacity at the sandwich shop—remained constant. If we now change grill capacity, we get a new *MRP* schedule.

Let's consider the productivity of labor with two grills. Table 10.4 shows the marginal product and marginal revenue product of labor at a sandwich shop that has two grills. We know that two workers can fit comfortably at each of the grills. The first worker can produce 10 sandwiches per hour and the next three workers can each produce 15. When there was only one grill, the marginal product of the fifth worker was just two sandwiches, but with the new grill her productivity goes up to ten sandwiches, and she will now be the third worker on one of the grills.

Marginal revenue product also increases. The *MRP* of the second, third, and fourth workers is now $7.50 per hour each. The fifth adds revenues of $5.00 per hour instead of just $1.00, and on down the line. Figure 10.8 shows how the addition of new capital shifts the marginal revenue product curve of labor to the right. With the new grill in place, a wage rate of $4.00 per hour means that the shop can hire six workers instead of just three. The marginal revenue product of the sixth worker is $5.00 per hour, still above that worker's price of $4.00. The shop will draw the line at the seventh worker, whose *MRP* is only $2.50, however.

Figure 10.9 shows the typical response of a firm to a decline in the market wage. At the outset, the market is in equilibrium, with supply and demand equal at W_o, and the firm is operating with a capital stock K_1. At the initial wage, the firm will hire as long as the marginal revenue product of labor exceeds the wage rate. The profit-maximizing level of labor demand is l_o.

TABLE 10.4

Marginal Revenue Product per Hour of Labor in Sandwich Production (Two Grills)

Total labor units	Total product (sandwiches per hour)	Marginal product (sandwiches per hour)	Price (value added) per sandwich	Marginal revenue product ($per hour)
0	—	—	—	—
1	10	10	$.50	$5.00
2	25	15	.50	7.50
3	40	15	.50	7.50
4	55	15	.50	7.50
5	65	10	.50	5.00
6	75	10	.50	5.00
7	80	5	.50	2.50
8	85	5	.50	2.50
9	87	2	.50	1.00
10	89	2	.50	1.00
11	89	0	.50	0

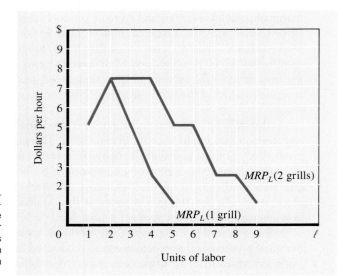

FIGURE 10.8
Effect of Increase in Capital on Labor Productivity in Sandwich Production

Expanding capacity by purchasing additional capital, a grill, increases the productivity of labor. The fifth worker added only $1.00 per hour to revenues with one grill. With two grills, the fifth worker brings in $5.00 per hour in revenue.

FIGURE 10.9
Factor Demand for a Firm Employing Two Variable Factors of Production (Capital and Labor)

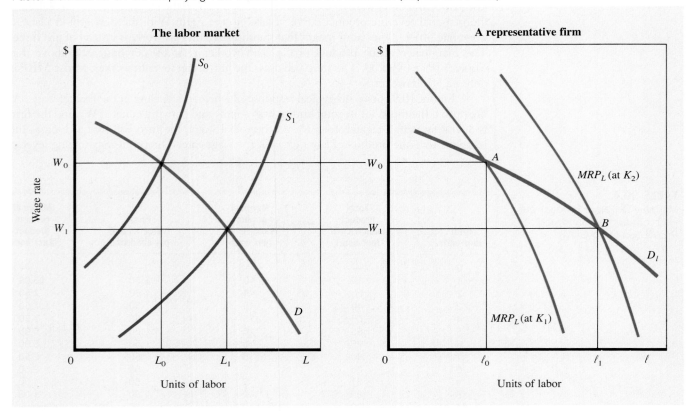

Given these conditions, let us now assume that a sudden influx of "guest workers" from a neighboring region drives down the wage rate in the labor market. The new lower wage, W_1, reduces the firm's costs, and in response, the firm increases output and decides to purchase more variable capital. Just as the new grill did for the sandwich shop, the new capital increases the productivity of labor and shifts the marginal revenue product curve out to the right.

The new marginal revenue product curve is labeled MRP_L/K_2 in Figure 10.9. With the new capital in place, the firm now hires labor up to l_1. At that point, the new wage is equal to the new MRP_L. The *demand-for-labor curve is the line connecting all points such as A and B.* Be sure to note that at every point along the demand curve $W=MRP$.

This section was meant to illuminate two important points. First, demand for any factor of production in a competitive industry depends upon its productivity and upon how its product is valued in the marketplace. Second, the productivity of any factor depends critically on the amount of other factors employed with it. The productivity of labor, for example, is enhanced when additional capital is used by a firm.

A critical factor in increasing a nation's output and living standard is capital. Whether it is an additional grill in a restaurant, tractors on farms, or steam shovels, capital raises the productivity of the laborers that use it and enhances a producer's ability to produce.

The Profit-Maximizing Condition for the Firm   Every firm has an incentive to use variable inputs as long as the revenue those inputs generate covers their costs at the margin. More formally, firms will employ an input up to the point that its price equals its marginal revenue product. This condition holds for *all* factors at *all* levels of output. Thus we can write

$$P_L = MRP_L,$$

$$P_K = MRP_K,$$

$$P_A = MRP_A,$$

where L is labor, K is capital and A is land (acres).

When all these conditions are met, the firm will be using the optimal, or least costly, combination of inputs. Also, if all these conditions hold at the same time, it is possible to rewrite them in a form that has an intuitive interpretation. Rewriting the first condition:

$$P_L = MRP_L.$$

$$P_L = MP_L \times P_X.$$

Thus

$$MP_L/P_L = 1/P_X.$$

Similarly we get that $1/P_X = MP_K/P_K$, and that $1/P_X = MP_A/P_A$. It therefore follows that

$$MP_L/P_L = MP_K/P_K = MP_A/P_A.$$

Your intuition tells you much the same thing that these equations do. All of this simply says that the marginal product of the last dollar spent on capital must be equal to the marginal product of the last dollar spent on labor, which must be equal to the marginal product of the last dollar spent on land, and so forth. If this were not so, the firm could produce more with less and reduce cost. Suppose, for example, that

$$MP_L/P_L > MP_K/P_K.$$

What happens is that by shifting dollars out of capital and into labor, the firm can produce more output. Hiring more labor drives down the marginal product of labor, and using less capital increases the marginal product of capital. This means that the ratios come back to equality as the firm shifts out of capital and into labor.

So far we have used very general terms to discuss the nature of input demand by firms in competitive markets where input prices and output prices are taken as given. The most important point is that demand for a factor depends on the value that the market places on its marginal product. The rest of the chapter explores the forces that determine the actual shapes and positions of demand curves.

THE SHAPES AND POSITIONS OF INPUT DEMAND CURVES

When we discussed supply and demand in Chapter 5, we spent a good deal of time talking about the factors that influence the responsiveness, or elasticity, of *output* demand curves. We have not talked about *input* demand curves in any detail, however, and we now need to say more about what lies behind them.

The Positions of Factor Demand Curves: Why Do They Shift?

Factor (input) demand curves are derived from information on technology, that is, production functions, and output price. Thus changes that occur in output markets and changes in technology can and do influence the demand for inputs. These shifts in demand are important because they directly affect the allocation of resources among alternative uses, as well as the level and distribution of income.

The Demand for Outputs   By now you know that firms will demand an input as long as its marginal revenue product exceeds its market price. Marginal revenue product, which in perfect competition is equal to a factor's marginal product times the price of output, is the value of the factor's marginal product:

$$MRP_L = MP_L \times P_X.$$

The value of a resource to a firm, then, depends directly on the value of the things that the firm produces. If product demand shifts out, product price will rise and marginal revenue product (factor demand) will shift to the right. If product demand declines, product price will fall and marginal revenue product (factor demand) will shift to the left. To see this, go back and raise the price of sandwiches from $.50 to $1.00 in the sandwich shop example examined in Table 10.1.

To the extent that any input is used intensively in the production of some product, changes in the demand for that product cause factor demand curves to shift and the prices of those inputs to change. In Chapter 9, we saw how increases in the demand for new construction affected lumber prices.

Land prices are another good example. Twenty-five years ago, the area in Manhattan along the west part of Central Park from about 80th Street north was a run-down neighborhood full of abandoned houses. The value of land there was virtually zero. Landlords walked away from properties or sold them at very low prices because the demand for housing in that area was very low. The only prospective tenants were poor, and land used for housing of the poor has a low marginal revenue product because the *output* sells, or in this case rents, for low prices.

Then things changed. Manhattan's economy boomed, and many more people wanted to live on the Upper West Side. The basic structures in that area were well built, and developers began to renovate them as early as the late 1960s. Now there is a huge demand for housing, and rents have hit record levels. Some single-room apartments, for example, go for as much as $1400 per month, and the price is going higher.

With the higher price of output, input prices have increased substantially. Small buildings on 80th Street and Central Park West sell for well over a million dollars, and the value of the land figures very importantly in these building prices. In essence, a shift in demand for an output, housing in the area, has pushed up the marginal revenue product of land from zero to very high levels.

The Demand for Other Inputs

THE LEVEL AND PRODUCTIVITY OF OTHER INPUTS   In our discussion we have kept coming back to the fact that factors of production complement each other, that is, they work together. Clearly the productivity of, and thus the demand for, any one factor of production depends upon the quality and quantity of the other factors with which it works. This was evident at the sandwich shop, where the simple addition of the second grill raised the productivity of labor and shifted the shop's demand curve up to the right.

The *effect of capital accumulation on real wages* is one of the most important themes in all of economics. In general, the production and use of capital enhances the productivity of labor, increases demand, and drives up wages.

Take transportation. In a poor country like Bangladesh, one person with an ox cart can move a small load over bad roads very slowly. The product of an additional worker with a cart is not great. By contrast, in the United States, the stock of capital used by workers in the transportation industry is enormous. A truck driver in the United States works with a substantial amount of capital. The typical 18-wheel tractor trailer, for example, is a piece of capital worth over a hundred thousand dollars. The roads themselves are capital, which was put in place by the government. The amount of material that a single driver can now move between distant points in a short time is staggering relative to what it was just 20 years ago. That increase in productivity has resulted directly from the addition of new capital to the industry, and it is reflected in the wages and incomes of truckers.

The infusion of capital into an industry raises the productivity of other inputs in that industry. However, it may also serve as a substitute for labor and thus cause the demand for labor to fall. Nowhere is this more evident than in agriculture, where the shift to modern capital-intensive methods of production has greatly enhanced the productivity of land but has substantially reduced the demand for labor. Table 10.5 shows the increases in productivity recorded for several agricultural outputs. As a result of productivity increases like these farm employment declined from just under 10 million in 1950 to 3.75 million in 1984.

TABLE 10.5
Increased Productivity and
Reduced Demand for Labor in
Agriculture, 1960–1982

Crop	1960–1974	1978–1982
Corn		
Yield per acre	62.2	105.2
Labor hours per 100 bushels	11	3
Wheat		
Yield per acre	25.2	34.0
Labor hours per 100 bushels	12	8
Potatoes		
Yield per acre	195	270
Labor hours per short ton	5	3
Milk		
Milk per cow	75	118
Labor hours per hundred weight of milk	1.2	.3

Source: Department of Agriculture, Economic Research Service, *Agricultural Statistics.*

THE PRICES OF OTHER INPUTS   When a firm has a choice among alternative technologies, the choice it makes will depend to some extent on relative input prices. You saw in Tables 10.2 and 10.3 that an increase in the price of labor substantially increased the demand for capital as the firm switched to a more capital-intensive production technique.

During the 1970s, the large increase in energy prices relative to prices of other factors of production had a number of effects on the demand for those other inputs. Insulation of new buildings, installation of more efficient heating plants, and similar efforts substantially raised the demand for capital as capital was substituted for energy in production. But it has also been argued that the energy crisis led to an increase in demand for labor. If capital and energy are complementary inputs, that is, if technologies that are capital intensive are also energy intensive, the argument goes, these higher energy prices tended to push firms toward more labor-intensive techniques.[6] A new highly automated technique, for example, might need fewer workers but it would also require a vast amount of electricity to operate. High electricity prices could lead a firm to reject the new techniques and stick with an old, more labor-intensive, one.

The Impact of Technological Change   Closely related to the impact of capital accumulation on factor demand is the potential impact of **technological change**, that is, the introduction of new methods of production or new products. A new technique of production is nearly always developed in order to reduce production costs. Usually new technologies introduce ways to produce outputs with fewer inputs by increasing the productivity of existing inputs or by raising marginal products. Because marginal revenue product is marginal product times the price of output, increases in productivity directly shift input demand curves.

Think for a moment about the dramatic impact of modern technology on the production of automobiles. Early in this century, the invention of assembly lines gave new meaning to the concept of mass production and raised the productivity of labor substantially. Today the word in automotive technology is robotics. Many of the tasks

[6]This argument was made in a series of papers by Professor Dale Jorgenson of Harvard University.

once performed along assembly lines by human workers are now handled by highly automated robots. These robots are clear substitutes for labor, but they also increase the productivity of those human beings remaining on the job. NBC News, in 1988, introduced robotic TV cameras, each of which was expected to reduce costs substantially.

New products born of technological advance also influence factor demands. The computer age has made many skills obsolete, but it has created a demand for many more. In 1965 people who could repair mechanical calculators were needed. Twenty years later, no one repaired cheap electronic calculators. If they ever broke, you simply threw them away and bought new ones. As for the descendant of the old calculator, in 1979 there were 279,000 personal computers manufactured in the United States; in 1983 the figure was 4.5 million.[7] An enormous industry that did not even exist ten years ago now employs thousands of people in thousands of companies producing software to make those machines work.

All in all, technological change can and does have a powerful influence on factor demands. As new products and new techniques of production are born, with them come demands for new inputs and new skills. As old techniques and old products become obsolete, so too do the labor skills and other inputs needed to produce them.

The Shapes of Factor Demand Curves: Elasticity of Demand in Input Markets

A demand schedule, or demand curve, expresses the relationship between the price of an output or input and the quantity demanded, *ceteris paribus*. The shape of the curve itself expresses the way demand reacts to changes in price while all the other influences on it are held constant.

You have just seen how variables *other than the price of the factor itself* influence demand. Changes in the use of other inputs, technological advances, and changes in output demands all cause factor demands to shift. Here we need to discuss the changes in quantity of a factor demanded that result from a change in its *own* price. In general, responsiveness, or elasticity, of input demand at the level of an individual firm depends on the magnitude of the substitution effects and output effects discussed above.

The Size of the Factor Substitution Effect   As you already know, when the price of a factor of production rises, firms tend to substitute other factors for it. Conversely, when the price of a factor of production falls, firms tend to substitute it for other factors. The size of such an effect depends upon how easy it is to substitute one factor for another.

Substitution among factors is more difficult in some industries than in others. Consider two factors, land and capital, as they are used in two different kinds of industries, manufacturing and the large sector collectively called "finance, insurance, and real estate." In manufacturing, goods must move from station to station, often along an assembly line. The most efficient plan for most manufacturing firms is to have all production work done on the same level. This is essential for a firm producing bulky products like automobiles, which it would be hard to move from level to level in a

---

[7]U.S. Department of Commerce, Bureau of the Census, *Statistical Abstract of the United States, 1985*, table 1394, p. 777.

high-rise building during production. Finance, insurance, and real estate firms, on the other hand, provide services to businesses and households. The work is done on video display terminals and, less frequently, on paper in office buildings. The only things that need to be regularly moved from floor to floor are people, and this is relatively easy to accomplish.

When a firm builds a high-rise office tower, it is substituting capital for land in production. Office firms, which can conveniently be housed in high-rise office buildings, use less land and more capital by stacking up capital floor by floor in a building. Manufacturing firms find it more difficult to substitute capital for land, and they tend to be housed in single-story, sprawling plant facilities.

This observation goes a long way toward explaining why urban areas look the way they do. In city centers, land is scarce and expensive. Land area increases with the square of the distance from the center, and thus the farther out one goes, the more land there is to develop and the lower the price of land. Office firms that find it easy to substitute capital for land tend to locate in skyscrapers near the centers of cities. Manufacturing firms that find it difficult to substitute capital for land have in recent years been locating farther and farther out from the city.

The demand for land in manufacturing, then, is *inelastic*, because it is not easy to substitute capital for it. The demand for land in finance, insurance, and real estate, however, is quite *elastic*, because substitution possibilities are great.

The Size of the Output Effect   When the price of an input rises, costs increase; when the price of an input falls, costs decrease. Increasing costs tend to reduce output, and thus they reduce factor demand across the board. Decreasing costs increase total factor demand. Given these propositions, the *size* of the output effect that results from a change in a factor price depends on two things: (1) the relative intensity with which that factor is used, and (2) the elasticity of demand in the output market.

The effect of intensity of factor use is easy to see. If my firm uses little labor, a rise in wages does not have a large impact on my costs. Firms in the North felt the rise in energy prices during the 1970s much more than firms in the South and Southwest because they used more energy to heat their plants.

To take just one more example, late in the 1970s, the price of silver increased dramatically from about $10.00 per ounce to about $50.00. Some claim that hoarding by a small number of speculators caused the run-up. But whatever the reason for this sharp increase, its impact, while modest on most firms, hit a few firms very hard. The hardest hit, perhaps, was the photography industry, which used silver very intensively in the production of film.

It is not as easy to understand why the elasticity of demand in *output* markets has anything to do with the size of the output effect, and thus the elasticity of demand, in factor markets. To shed some light on this, let us suppose that an increase in wages drives up costs for all firms in an industry by 25 percent. All of those firms then cut back on production, and the industry supply curve shifts left. As this shift occurs, the price of output rises. If output demand is inelastic, it will quickly push up the price of output, and firms will recover a large part of the cost increase in higher revenues. Thus the output effect is small—or, in other words, output does not change very much. If output demand is elastic, however, the rise in price leads consumers to choose substitute products, and production drops off more. Thus the output effect is large—in other words, output changes a great deal.

Figure 10.10 shows the impact of an increase in marginal cost on output for an industry with inelastic output demand and for an industry with elastic output demand.

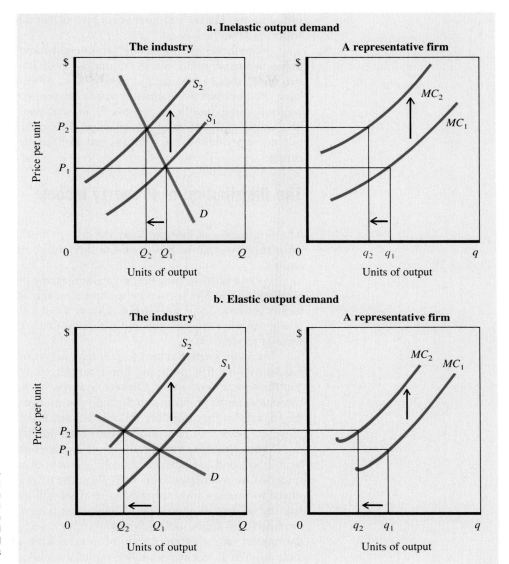

FIGURE 10.10

The Size of the Output Effect Depends on the Elasticity of Demand for Output

The industry supply curve is the sum of the marginal cost curves of all the firms in the industry. Thus an increase in marginal costs for all firms shifts the industry supply curve to the left and drives up the price of output. The final decrease in industry output depends on the elasticity of demand for output.

MARGINAL PRODUCTIVITY AND INCOME DISTRIBUTION

We have now in a sense come full circle. In Chapter 6 we began discussing household choice, arguing that choice in output markets depends on a household's willingness and ability to pay under the constraints of income and wealth. The final distribution of output among members of a society, we said, depends on the **distribution of income and wealth.**

The brief discussion here summarizes in part our analysis of perfectly competitive markets. Chapter 17 discusses the income distribution in the United States fully, including the market and nonmarket factors that affect distribution, poverty, and public policy options.

Households in our model of a competitive economy earn incomes by supplying factors of production to the market. Look back at Figure 10.1 and note again the two basic kinds of income: (1) income from property, or wealth, and (2) income from labor. Part of labor income is very much like property income. Some people earn higher wages because they have "invested" in acquiring marketable skills. Those skills can be thought of as a form of intangible property called *human capital*. The higher wages that come to those with skills are just like the returns on an investment in physical capital.

The Distribution of Property Income

The distribution of income from property, or wealth, depends on two things: (1) who owns property, that is, how wealth is distributed, and (2) the return to property in the market.

As to who owns property, we are here taking the distribution of wealth as given, as a result of history. The present generation of wealth holders came to have their wealth in a variety of ways. Some inherited it. Others saved it themselves. Some won a lottery. Still others may have started a successful business that grew and prospered (which is really the same as saving).

As to the market return to property, in our model, market return depends on the *productivity* of that property. For example, land earns a rent equal to its marginal contribution to production. Owners of firms, be they proprietors or shareholders in a corporation, earn profits that in the long run are equal to the marginal revenue product of the capital that they own directly or indirectly. If we think of acquired skills as intangible property, those skills also earn a return equal to their marginal revenue products.

Note especially that the theory of income distribution we are building here views land, labor, and capital symmetrically—it sees each as productive, and each as being rewarded in accordance with the value that it adds to what gets produced. Providing capital to workers, or simply adding workers, will increase output. You can dig a bigger hole by adding people or by adding more powerful shovels; you can produce more sandwiches by adding sandwich makers or by adding a new grill. Other theories of income distribution take a different view of income from property. For example, in Marxian theory, profit is not a reward for capital's usefulness in production but rather it is a wrongful appropriation of value that was actually created exclusively by labor. (This point of view is explained more fully in Chapter 17.)

Labor Income

The distribution of labor income depends in part on decisions made by households and in part on market wage rates. Households must decide whether to work for pay and how much to work. Clearly, there is not just one labor market; there are many. Each separate labor market has its own equilibrium wage, and different people end up earning different wage rates. How income gets distributed depends, for one thing, on the size of these wage differentials.

A COMPLETE VIEW OF THE ALLOCATIVE PROCESS

We now have a complete, but simplified, picture of household and firm decision making. Review Figure 10.1 one more time to see how both households and firms interact in two arenas, output markets and input markets. We have also examined some of the basic forces that determine the allocation of resources, the mix of output and the distribution of output in perfectly competitive markets.

In this competitive environment, profit-maximizing firms make three fundamental decisions: (1) how much to produce and supply in output markets, (2) how to produce products (which technology to use), and (3) how much of each input to demand. Chapters 7–9 looked at these three decisions as they apply in the output market. We derived the supply curve of a competitive firm in the short run and discussed output market adjustment in the long run. Deriving cost curves involved evaluating and choosing among alternative technologies. Finally, you saw how a firm's decision about how much product to supply in output markets implicitly determines input demands.

To show the connection between output and input markets, this chapter took this same set of decisions and examined their applications to input markets. Figure 10.11 shows just how close the connection between output and input decisions really is. Diagram A presents information on technology and input prices embodied in the marginal cost curve. Here firms hire up to the point where output price, that is, marginal revenue, is equal to marginal cost: $P_X^* = MC$. In the middle and bottom diagrams, output price and technological information are embodied in marginal revenue product curves. Here firms hire up to the point where each factor's marginal revenue product is equal to its price: $P_K^* = MRP_K$, and $P_L^* = MRP_L$.

The key is that k^* and l^* must be fully consistent with q^*. That is, using the best available (or least costly) technology, k^* units of capital and l^* units of labor will produce q^* units of output. The choice of q^* as the amount of output to *supply* implies that the firm must *demand* l^* units of labor and k^* units of capital.

Looking at output and input markets together also helps to shed light on why firms and households choose what they do. Let us start with firms and then move on to households. Firms are in business to make a profit, and they must sell their output for more than it costs them to produce it. Output price reflects what households are willing to pay for consumer goods. *A firm will hire an input only if it can be used to produce a product that someone is willing to pay for.* (In this connection, review Figure 10.5.) Furthermore, a firm will hire an input, or factor of production, as long as the value of what it produces—its marginal revenue product—exceeds the price the firm has to pay for that factor.

Factor prices are determined by the interaction of supply and demand in input markets. A factor supply curve shows the prices required to attract the factor from its alternative use. The alternative to supplying labor, for example, is either leisure or unpaid work. The alternative to supplying financial resources for capital formation is consuming today.

Thus firms weigh the values of products against the values of resources. With their goal of maximizing profits, firms weigh what households reveal they are willing to pay in output markets against the wages that households require in order to supply resources. The firm provides the technology for transforming the resources into useful form.

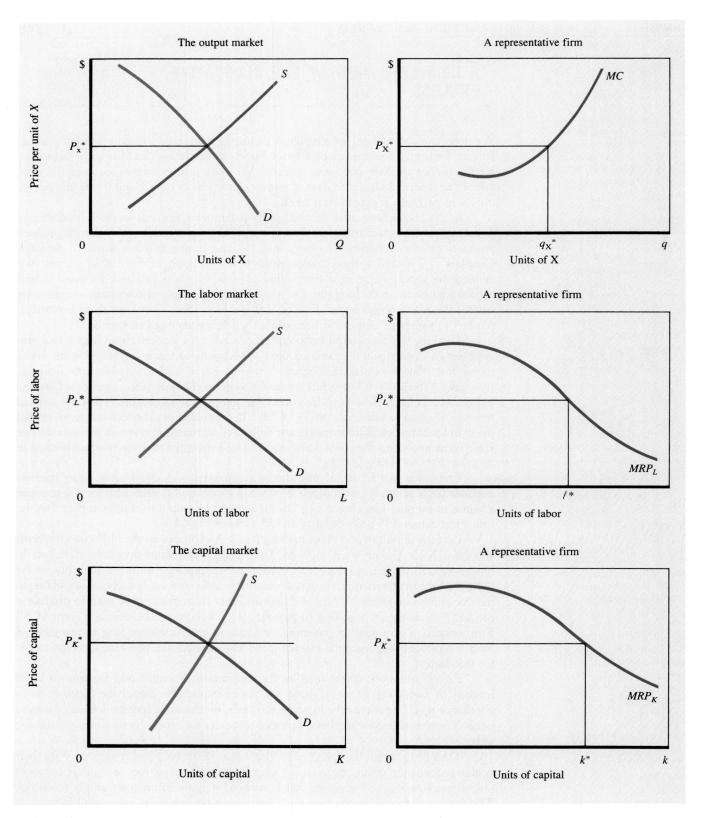

FIGURE 10.11
Short-Run Decisions of a Competitive Firm

Households too weigh the values of products supplied to the market against the values of the resources at their disposal. A household can consume leisure or it can work and use the income derived from it to buy goods. (Figure 6.7 projects this point graphically.)

The next chapter takes up the complexity of what we have here been loosely calling the "capital market." There we discuss the relationship between the market for physical capital and financial capital markets and look at some of the ways that firms actually make investment decisions. Once we examine the nature of overall competitive equilibrium in Chapter 12, we can finally begin the process of relaxing some of the assumptions that have restricted the scope of our inquiry so far.

SUMMARY

1. When you look behind input demand curves, you discover the exact same set of decisions that lie behind output supply curves but from a different point of view.

2. Demand for inputs depends on demand for the outputs that they produce; input demand is thus a *derived demand*.

3. Inputs are at the same time complementary and substitutable. For example, capital raises the productivity of labor, and thus it complements labor; at the same time, capital may be substituted for labor.

4. The marginal revenue product of a variable input is the additional revenue a firm will earn by employing one additional unit of the input, ceteris paribus. MRP is equal to the input's marginal product times the price of output.

5. Demand for an input depends on the marginal revenue product of the input. Firms will buy an input (or hire labor) up to the point where marginal revenue product of the input equals the price of the input. For a firm employing only one variable factor of production, the MRP curve *is* the firm's demand curve for that factor.

6. For a firm employing one variable factor of production, labor, the condition $W = MRP_L$ is exactly the same as the condition $P = MC$.

7. When a firm employs two variable factors of production, a change in factor price has both a factor substitution effect and an output effect.

8. A wage increase may lead a firm to substitute capital for labor, and thus the demand for labor will decline. This is the factor substitution effect of the wage increase.

9. A wage increase increases cost, and higher cost may lead to lower output and less demand for all inputs, including labor. This is the output effect of the wage increase.

10. The position of a firm's demand curve for a factor of production depends on the demand for the firm's product, the level and productivity of other inputs used, the prices of other inputs, and the state of technology.

11. The shape (elasticity) of a firm's factor demand curve depends on the size of output and substitution effects that in turn depend on the ease of substitutability among inputs, the elasticity of demand for outputs, and the relative intensity with which that factor is used.

12. The distribution of output in a competitive economy depends on the distribution of income. There are two basic kinds of income: income from property, or wealth, and income from labor. Property income depends on profits, interest, and rents earned in capital and land markets. Labor income depends on wages earned in labor markets.

13. Because the price of a factor at equilibrium in competitive markets is equal to its marginal revenue product, the distribution of income depends in part on the relative productivity of factors.

REVIEW CONCEPTS

REVIEW QUESTIONS

1. Assume that a firm which produces twits can produce them with one of three processes, used alone or in combination. The following table indicates the amounts of capital and labor required by each of the three processes to produce one twit.

	Units of labor	Units of capital
Process 1	4	1
Process 2	2	2
Process 3	1	3

   a. Assuming that capital costs $3.00 per unit and labor costs $1.00, which process will be employed?
   b. Plot the three points on the firm's TVC curve corresponding to $q=10$, $q=30$, and $q=50$.
   c. At each of the three output levels, how much K and L will be demanded?
   d. Repeat parts a–c, assuming the price of capital is $3.00 and the price of labor has risen to $4.00.

2. Assume that shoes are produced with one variable factor of production, labor. Using the following production function, estimate the amount of labor that a competitive firm would hire, assuming that labor is available for $35.00 per day and that shoes sell for $10.00 per pair.

Units of labor (days)	Total output
1	5
2	9
3	12
4	14
5	15

3. Suppose that the government raised the payroll tax imposed on employees from 7.13% to 15 percent. Describe potential impacts on the demand for labor. Be sure to discuss output and substitution effects in your answer.
   Now suppose that the government raised the payroll tax imposed on employers from 7.13% to 15 percent. What would happen? How would the results differ from the same change for employees?
4. The demand for land is a derived demand. Think of a popular location near where you are attending school. What determines the demand for land in that area? What are the outputs that are sold by businesses located there? Discuss the relationship between land prices and the prices of those products.
5. In a perfectly competitive economy, the distribution of income depends on productivity. Some people argue that rewarding factors in accordance with their productivity is both fair and efficient.
   But if there were no redistribution, those with no "productivity" would have no income. Can you think of groups unable (through no fault of their own) to earn wages in the labor market? (*Hint:* you might start with children under five.) Suppose you were appointed philosopher of the king's court to recommend what should be done to care for these people. Who, if anyone, should be responsible for them?
6. Many states provide firms with an "investment tax credit" that effectively reduces the price of capital facing companies in the state. In theory, these credits are designed to stimulate new investment and thus create jobs. Critics have argued that if there were strong factor substitution effects, these subsidies could actually *reduce* employment in the state. Explain their arguments.

11 Capital Markets and Land Markets: Profit, Interest, and Rent

Firms and industries expand and contract in response to economic profits and losses. When firms expand, they put into place physical capital in the form of new plant and equipment, and they hire variable inputs. So far, we have said, rather loosely, that firms demand these inputs—land, labor, and capital—and that households supply them.

Transactions between households and firms in the labor and land markets are fairly direct and easy to understand. Households offer their labor directly to firms in exchange for wages; land owners lease or sell their land directly to firms in exchange for rent or an agreed-upon price. In the capital market, transactions between households and firms are less direct. Firms purchase, or in some way demand, capital assets, but not directly from households. Households do, however, ultimately supply the financial resources necessary for firms to procure capital assets. The mechanism by which this takes place involves a complex set of institutions—the stock market, banks, venture capital funds, brokerage houses, and so forth—collectively called the *financial capital market*.

In this chapter, we begin to analyze the basic functions of the capital market. First, we must review the basic concepts of capital, investment, and depreciation. After we describe interest, profits, and the motive to invest, we look in detail at the mechanics of individual investment decisions. Finally, we return to the land market, the nature of rent, and the land allocation process. Before we start, look back at Figure 10.1.

CAPITAL, INVESTMENT, AND DEPRECIATION

Capital

Capital Anything that is produced by the economic system which is used subsequently as an input in the production of future goods and services.

Physical, or tangible, capital Material things used as inputs in the production of future goods and services, such as buildings, machinery, and inventories.

One of the most important concepts in all of economics is the concept of **capital**. *Capital goods are those goods produced by the economic system itself that are used as inputs to produce other goods and services in the future.* Capital goods thus yield valuable productive services over time.

Tangible Capital When we think of capital, we generally think of the physical capital employed by business firms. The major categories of **physical**, or **tangible, capital** are (1) nonresidential structures (office buildings, power plants, factories, shopping centers, warehouses, and docks, for example), (2) durable equipment (machines, trucks, sandwich grills, automobiles, and so on), (3) residential structures, and (4) inventories of inputs and outputs that firms have in stock.

Most firms need tangible capital, along with labor and land, to produce their products. A restaurant's capital requirements include a kitchen, ovens and grills, tables and chairs, silverware, dishes, light fixtures, and carpeting. Those items must be purchased up front and maintained in order for the restaurant to function. A manufacturing firm must have a plant, specialized machinery, trucks, and inventories of parts. A winery needs oak casks, vats, piping, temperature-control equipment, and cooking and bottling machinery. In addition to its shelves and display cases, the capital stock of a retail drugstore is largely made up of inventories. Drugstores do not produce the aspirin, vitamins, and toothbrushes that they sell. Those things are bought from manufacturers and put on display. The product actually produced and sold by a drugstore is *convenience*. Like any other product, convenience is produced with labor and capital in the form of a store with lots of products, or inventory, displayed on the sales floor and kept in storerooms.

An apartment building is also capital. Produced by the economic system, it yields valuable services over time, and it is used as an input to produce housing services, which are rented out.

Intangible capital Invisible, nonmaterial things that contribute to the output of future goods and services, such as reputation and good will.

Human capital A form of intangible capital that includes the skills and other knowledge that workers have or acquire through education and training and which yields valuable services to a firm over time.

Intangible Capital Not all capital is physical. Some intangible forms of capital satisfy every part of our definition. When a business firm invests in advertising to establish a brand name, it is producing **intangible capital**, called "**goodwill**." That goodwill is produced, and it yields valuable services to the firm over time.

When a firm establishes a training program for employees, it is investing in the skills of its workers. One can think of such an investment as the production of an intangible form of capital called **human capital**. It is produced with labor (instructors) and capital (classrooms, computers, projectors, and books). Human capital in the form of new or augmented skills is an input—it will yield valuable productive services for the firm in the future.

When research produces valuable results—a new process of production that reduces costs or a new formula that creates a new product—the new technology itself can be thought of as capital. Furthermore, even ideas can be patented and the rights to them can be sold.

Who Produces Capital? Households and governments, as well as firms, produce capital. *Households* produce and use both tangible and intangible capital. If you build a vacation home for yourself, for example, you will use that capital over time to produce a flow of valuable services. Whoever is paying for your college education is investing in

Social capital or infrastructure A form of tangible capital, produced largely by governments but in some cases also by private firms, that renders services that contribute to the public good. Roads, highways, bridges, water and sewer systems, public utilities, transportation systems, telecommunications networks, and so forth are a few examples.

intangible capital. Knowledge and skills are human capital that should, if you succeed as expected, yield valuable services for a long time.

One of the major functions of *government* is to produce **social capital** called **infrastructure**. The most common form of social capital is public works such as highways, roads, bridges, and sewer and water systems. They are certainly produced, and most of them yield productive services over time. Nearly all firms use roads and highways to transport their inputs and outputs. Fire stations, police stations, city halls, courthouses, police cars, and telecommunications systems are all forms of social capital that are used as inputs to produce the things that governments produce: public safety, social order, fire protection, and so forth.

The Time Dimension   The most important dimension of capital is that it exists through *time*. Labor services are used at the time they are provided. Households consume nondurable goods and services as purchased. But capital exists now and into the future, and *its value is only as great as the value of the services it will render over time*. In a very real sense, capital is the physical embodiment of those future services.[1]

Measuring Capital   Labor is measured in hours, and land is measured in square feet or acres. But because capital comes in so many forms, it is virtually impossible to measure directly in physical terms. The indirect measure generally used is *present market value*. The measure of a firm's **capital stock** is the current market value of its plant, equipment, inventories, and intangible assets. Although this allows business managers, accountants, and economists to add buildings, barges, and bulldozers, it is not a physical measure of capital.[2]

Capital is measured as a *stock value*. That is, like the volume of water in a tub, it is measured at a point in time. Stop the clock and measure. The capital stock of the XYZ Corporation on July 31 is $3,453,231. Or at the beginning of 1987, the gross nonresidential fixed capital stock (buildings and equipment) of all private industries, including farms, in the United States was $7 trillion, including $3.6 trillion in structures and $3.4 trillion in equipment.[3]

Although it is measured in terms of money, or value, *it is very important to think of the actual capital stock itself*. That is, when we speak of capital, we refer not to money or financial assets such as bonds or stocks, but to the physical plant, equipment, and inventory of the firm.

Investment and Depreciation

Investment The creation of capital. While capital is measured at a given point in time—a stock—investment is measured over a period of time—a flow. The flow of investment enhances the stock of capital.

Stocks of capital are affected over time by two flows: investment and depreciation. When a firm produces or puts in place new capital—a new piece of equipment, for example—it has invested in something. **Investment** is a *flow* that increases the stock of capital. It has a *time dimension*, and thus we speak of investment per period (by the month, quarter, or year).

[1]Conceptually, consumer durable goods, such as automobiles, washing machines, and so forth, are capital. They are produced, they yield services over time, and households use them as inputs to produce services such as transportation and clean laundry.

[2]It is important to distinguish between concept and practice in the measurement of capital. Business firms keep records in accordance with what are called "generally accepted accounting principles." These principles include formal rules for calculating and reporting the values of capital assets.

Take "goodwill," for example. Because it is difficult to value precisely, accepted principles do not allow firms to include it in their financial statements as an asset. In concept, however, goodwill is indeed capital. As we pursue our discussion here, therefore, we will not be bound by generally accepted accounting principles.

[3]U.S. Department of Commerce, *Survey of Current Business*, (January 1986).

TABLE 11.1
Investment in the U.S. Economy, 1987

	Billions of current dollars	As a percentage of total investment	As a percentage of GNP
Nonresidential structures	134.1	18.7	3.0
Durable equipment	308.0	43.0	6.9
Inventories	45.7	6.4	1.0
Residential structures	228.5	31.9	5.1
Total gross private investment	716.3	100.0	16.0
Depreciation	−479.4	− 66.9	−10.7
Net investment (gross investment minus depreciation)	236.9	33.1	5.3

Source: U.S. Department of Commerce.

Before we proceed any further with this discussion, you should be careful to remember that the term "investing" is not used here to describe the act of buying a share of stock or a bond. Although we commonly use the term that way ("I invested in some Union Carbide stock" or "he invested in treasury bonds"), and despite the fact that real investments are often made with the proceeds of a stock sale, the term *investment* when correctly used refers only to the *creation of capital*.

Table 11.1 presents data on investment in the United States economy in 1987. Nearly half of the total was new durable equipment. Almost all the rest was investment in structures, split evenly between residential—apartment buildings, condominiums, houses, and so forth—and nonresidential—factories, shopping malls, and so forth. A very small percentage of total investment in 1987 went into inventories, that is, the stocks of inputs and outputs that business firms maintain to insure that production flows smoothly and that outputs are available to meet demand.

Depreciation   The decline in the economic value of an asset that occurs over time.

Depreciation is the decline in economic value of an asset over time. If you have ever owned a car you are aware that its resale value falls over time. Suppose you bought a new Pontiac in 1987 for $10,500 and you decide to sell it two years and 25,000 miles later. Checking the newspaper and talking to several dealers, you find out that, given its condition and the mileage, you can expect to get $7100 for it. It has depreciated $3400.

Depreciation is also a flow—that is, it too has a time dimension. To pursue the comparison with the amount of water in a tub, investment is like the amount of water that flows from the tap into the tub per hour; depreciation is like the amount running down the drain when the stopper is not quite tight, or the amount that evaporates each hour.

A capital asset can depreciate because it physically wears out or because it becomes obsolete. Take, for example, a computer control system in a factory. If a new, technologically superior, system is developed that does the same job for half the price, the old system may be replaced even if it still functions well. The Pontiac depreciated because of wear and tear *and* because new models were available.

FINANCING CAPITAL INVESTMENT: FINANCIAL MARKETS

While governments make some capital investment decisions and households make others, most decisions to produce new capital goods, that is, to invest, are made by firms. A firm cannot invest, however, unless it has the funds to do so. The funds that firms use to buy capital goods come, directly or indirectly, from households. When a household decides not to consume a portion of its income, it saves, and various financial institutions facilitate the transfer of those savings to firms that use them for capital investment.

Let us take a simple example in order to see how the system works. Suppose that some firm wants to purchase a machine costing $1000, and some household decides at the same time that it wants to save $1000 from its income. Figure 11.1 shows one way that the household's decision to save might connect with the firm's decision to invest.

Interest *The fee paid by a borrower to a lender over time.*

Either directly or through a financial intermediary, the household agrees to loan the money to the firm, and in exchange the firm contracts to pay the household **interest** at some agreed-upon rate each period. The firm gives the household a bond, which is nothing more than a piece of paper that promises to repay the loan at some specific time in the future. The bond also specifies the flow of interest to be paid in the meantime.

The new saving enhances the household's stock of wealth. The household's net wealth has increased by the $1000, which it holds in the form of a bond.[4] The bond is an asset to the household because it represents the firm's promise to repay the $1000 at some future date with interest. Meanwhile the firm takes the proceeds and buys a new $1000 machine, which it adds to its stock of capital. Presumably this investment will generate added **profits** that will facilitate the payment of interest to the household. Such projects are undertaken as long as the profits likely to be realized are sufficient to cover the interest payments to the household.

Financial capital markets *A set of institutions that together channel household saving into productive capital investment projects by firms.*

The **financial capital market** is a set of institutions that channels household saving into productive investment projects. The flow of new saving each period (per month, per year) can thus be thought of as the supply of capital. Firms look at the alternative projects available, make judgments about their desirability, and decide whether to go ahead. Seen in this way, their investment can be thought of as the demand for new capital.

FIGURE 11.1
$1000 in Saving becomes $1000 of Investment

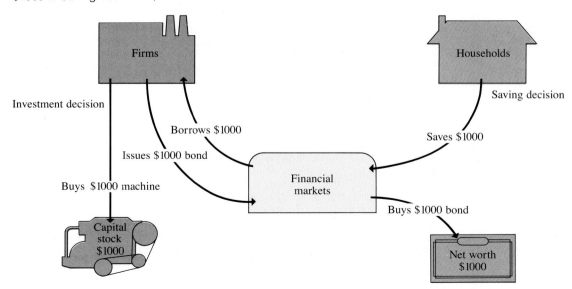

[4]Note that it is the *act of saving* that increases the household's net worth, not the act of buying the bond. Buying the bond simply transforms one financial asset—money—into another—a bond. The household could simply have held onto the money.

The Crash of 1987

On October 19, 1987—Bloody Monday—the stock market suffered its worst single day loss in history. The Dow Jones industrial average fell 508 points, wiping out some $500 billion in wealth in just a few hours. It was one of the most dramatic days in Wall Street's history. What is the stock market? Why did it crash in October?

The stock market is a market in which shares of stock in corporations are bought and sold. When a person or an institution buys a share of stock in a company the person or institution becomes part owner of the company. For example, if I own 1000 shares of the Xerox corporation, I own about 1/110,000 of the company since there are about 110 million shares outstanding. As a share holder, I am entitled to a share of the profits of the company. In the first quarter of 1988, Xerox made a profit of $152 million, which amounts to $1.37 per share. That means my share of the profits comes to $1370.

As we described in the text of this·chapter, sometimes companies pay these profits directly to shareholders as dividends and sometimes profits are retained inside corporations to finance investment projects. When a company retains earnings and invests, it grows, and presumably each outstanding share is worth more. Thus, shareholders receive their share of profits in an indirect way—the market value of their shares increases. Increases in the market value of shares are called "capital gains." Prior to the Tax Reform Act of 1986, capital gains received special tax treatment; capital gains were taxed at lower rates than dividend income. The purpose was to encourage firms to retain earnings and invest.

When a firm initially issues shares of stock, it does so for several possible reasons. Sometimes it is a new corporation that needs to raise money to build plant and equipment. Sometimes it is a proprietorship that has grown and prospered and wants to "go public"; in this case the proceeds of the stock sale go to the proprietor who is, in essence, selling his company to the public. Sometimes it is an established company that issues new shares of stock to finance major investment projects.

Once a share of stock has been issued, it may be sold and resold hundreds of times, but none of the proceeds of those subsequent sales go to the firm that issued the stock. Each day hundreds of millions of shares are sold and bought. For every share that changes hands there is a buyer and a seller.

Some buyers and sellers are big institutions. Some colleges, for example, have endowment funds contributed over the years primarily by alumni. Harvard has the largest endowment of any university in the United States, totaling over $4 billion in 1988. The College Equities Retirement Fund (CREF) holds the retirement funds of college teachers and administrators. In 1988, CREF owned over $25 billion worth of stock. But private citizens, the so-called "small investors," also buy and sell stocks.

When a person or an institution decides to buy or sell some shares, orders are sent electronically to one of several markets or exchanges. The largest single exchange is the New York Stock Exchange, which lists thousands of companies. On an average day well over 100 million shares will change hands on the New York Stock Exchange.

The price of a share of stock depends on what buyers are willing to pay and what sellers are willing to accept. It is like any other market; prices are determined by the forces of supply and demand. If, at a given price, there are more shares of a particular stock being offered than demanders are willing to buy, the price will fall. Similarly, if buyers want to buy more shares on a given day than sellers are offering, the price will rise. In fact, stock prices rise and fall hour by hour and minute by minute—data on transactions are recorded and sent out over the wire to brokers who watch the "tape" all day long.

The most common index of stock prices is the Dow Jones industrial average. It is the simple sum of the current selling price of shares in thirty different industrial companies. In August 1987 the Dow stood at over 2700; in October it fell as low as 1738. The average share lost over one-third of its value.

Many people think that a falling stock market means that companies are losing out. Remember, once a share of stock is issued, the subsequent exchanges do not involve the company at all. If I buy Digital stock at $150 a share and sell at $100, I lose *$50* a share—Digital loses nothing.

What then causes stock prices to rise or fall as much as they do? Because the direct reward for owning stock is a share of company profit, current and potential shareholders are influenced by expectations of future profits. If the general economic climate seems favorable and conducive to growth of profits, stock prices are expected to rise. When the economy encounters trouble, expectations may dim, pushing stock prices down. For five years before the crash, the stock market rose steadily. This was due in part to favorable expectations and healthy corporate profits; it was also due in part to an influx of foreign buyers, particularly the Japanese.

There are many theories for why the crash occurred. One thing we know is that many people and institutions decided to sell stocks all at once. When that happens, prices can fall rapidly until enough buyers are found to clear the market. Some large sellers had computer programs that automatically sold shares when prices fell by a predetermined amount, and that accelerated the decline. Some claim the decline was triggered by bad economic signs warning of future economic problems; during the preceding summer, there were signs of inflation and higher interest rates.

Whatever the cause of the decline, expectations seemed to improve. By April 1988, the Dow was back over 2100.

The Stock Market, Venture Capital, and Other Exotica

When a firm issues a fixed-interest-rate bond, it borrows money and pays interest at an agreed-upon rate to the person or institution that buys the bond. Many other mechanisms, four of which are illustrated below (and see Figure 11.2), also serve the same exact purpose, that is, the channeling of household savings into investment projects.

CASE A   As I look around my home town, I see several ice cream stores doing very well, but I think that I can make better ice cream than they do. To go into the business, I need to buy ice cream making equipment, tables, chairs, freezers, and signs, and to lease a store. Because I put up my house as collateral, I am not a big risk, and the bank grants the loan at a fairly reasonable interest rate. Banks have money to lend like this only because households deposit their savings there.

CASE B   A scientist at a leading university develops an inexpensive method of producing a very important family of virus-fighting drugs, using microorganisms created through gene splicing. This is a new process and a new business, and no one really knows whether it will work out and be profitable. The business could very well fail within 12 months, but if it makes it, the potential for profit is huge.

Our scientist goes to a venture capital fund for financing. Such funds take household savings and put them into high-risk ventures in exchange for a share of the profits if the new businesses make it. By investing in many different projects, the funds reduce the risk of losing money. Once again, household funds make it possible for firms to undertake investments. If a venture succeeds, those owning shares in the venture capital fund receive substantial profits.

CASE C   General Motors Corporation decides that it wants to build a new assembly plant in Tennessee, and it discovers that it has enough to pay for the new facility out of this year's profits. The new investment is thus funded out of internal funds, or *retained earnings*.

FIGURE 11.2
Financial Markets Link Household Saving and Investment by Firms

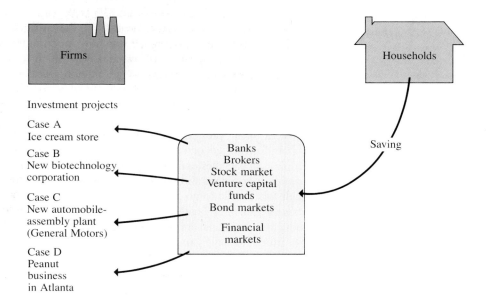

Firms

Households

Investment projects

Case A
Ice cream store

Case B
New biotechnology corporation

Case C
New automobile-assembly plant (General Motors)

Case D
Peanut business in Atlanta

Banks
Brokers
Stock market
Venture capital funds
Bond markets

Financial markets

Saving

The result is exactly the same as if the firm had gone to households via some financial intermediary and borrowed the money to pay for the plant. General Motors is owned by its shareholders. When it earns a profit, the profit really belongs to those shareholders. If GM uses its profits to buy new capital, this is done only with the shareholders' implicit consent. When a firm takes its own profit and uses it to buy capital assets, instead of paying it out to its shareholders, the total value of the firm goes up, as does the value of the shares held by stockholders. As in the other examples, GM's capital stock ends up higher, and so does the net worth of households.

When a household owns a share of stock that appreciates, or increases in value, the appreciation is income, and unless the household sells the stock and consumes the gain, it is part of saving. In essence, when a firm retains earnings for investment purposes, it is actually *saving on behalf of its shareholders*.

CASE D   A former high-ranking government official decides to start a new peanut processing business in Atlanta, and he further decides to raise the funds needed by issuing shares of stock. Households buy the shares, paying, again, with income that they decide not to consume, and in exchange they are entitled to a share of the profits of the firm.

The shares of stock become part of the net worth of households. The proceeds from stock sales are used to buy plant equipment and inventory. Savings flow into investment, and the firm's capital stock goes up by the same amount as household net worth.

The Process of Capital Accumulation and Allocation

You can see from these examples that various, and sometimes complex, connections between households and firms facilitate the movement of saving into productive investment. All of these, however, accomplish the same thing.

Think again about Colleen and Bill who found themselves on a deserted island in Chapter 2. They had to make choices about how to allocate available resources, including their time. One important choice was how much energy to devote to producing goods and services for present enjoyment and how much to devote to investment that would bring future enjoyment. By spending long hours working on a house or a boat that might take a year to build, for example, Colleen and Bill are saving and investing. First, they are using resources that could be used to produce more immediate rewards—they could gather more food or simply lie in the sun and relax. Second, they are applying those resources to the production of *capital*.

Industrialized or agrarian, small or large, traditional and simple or modern and complex, all societies exist through time and must allocate resources over time. In simple societies, investment and saving decisions are made by the same people: Colleen and Bill decide whether to forgo present pleasures (consumption) and whether to produce capital goods (a house, a boat). In modern industrial societies, investment decisions (capital production decisions) are made primarily by firms. Households, on the other hand, decide how much to save, and in the long run saving limits or contrains the amount of investment that firms can undertake. The capital market exists in between to direct saving into profitable investment projects.

Profit and Interest

Before we look any further into the decision to invest, we need to reflect for a moment on the nature of interest and profit. *Interest and profit are the income flows that are paid to owners of capital.* Sometimes this payment is *direct*, and sometimes it is *indirect*.

If I am a sole proprietor, I reap the rewards of investment decisions that I make personally. If I am a shareholder, the specific investment decisions are made by others, but I own a part of the firm and I am entitled to my share of its profits. These profits may be paid directly to me as dividends, or they may be retained by the firm, in which case the value of my shares increases. If I buy a bond or make a deposit to an interest-bearing bank account, my saving is still channeled into investment, and I reap at least some of the reward in the form of interest. Regardless of the mechanism we choose, all of us expect our ownership to yield some sort of positive income flow.

Interest and profit may function as *incentives to postpone gratification*. When you save, you pass up the chance to buy things that you want right now. Rather than spending and consuming something today, you decide to spend and consume something in the future, using what you hope will be increased funds. One view of interest and profit, therefore, holds that they are the rewards for postponing consumption.

Interest and profit also serve as *rewards for innovation and risk taking*. Someone who takes a new idea or a new product and turns it into a successful business is called an **entrepreneur**. The entrepreneur's goal is to reap rewards in the form of profits from the new enterprise.

Not all new businesses make it, of course. When someone starts a business, he or she takes a risk. If the product doesn't sell, or if the new company is badly managed, the investors can lose. In 1981, a recession year, 16,794 businesses failed in the United States.[5]

When a new firm does make it, however, the rewards can be enormous. Successful entrepreneurs have accumulated huge fortunes. Ray Kroc, founder of McDonald's, made billions. Every year *Fortune Magazine* publishes the names of the richest people in America, and virtually every major fortune listed there is traceable to the founding of some business enterprise that "made it big." In recent years, the big winners have been high-tech companies, such as Apple Computer and Wang Laboratories, whose founders, Steve Jobs and An Wang, have indeed amassed enormous personal wealth.

When a successful entrepreneur takes an idea and turns it into a profitable product or service, the return is more than just compensation for postponing consumption. It is a reward for innovation and risk taking,[6] and many argue that this is the essence of our free enterprise system. Clearly the potential of big financial rewards motivates innovation, and innovation is good for society. Ideas lead to new products and new ways of producing things. Innovation is at the core of economic growth and progress. More efficient production techniques mean that we can use the resources saved to produce new things.

Critics of the free enterprise system claim that such large rewards are not justified and that accumulations of great wealth and power are not good for society. Proponents,

---

[5]U.S. Department of Commerce, Bureau of the Census, *Statistical Abstract of the United States, 1982, 1983*, table 889, p. 533.

[6]Interest is often defined as the return to "postponement," and profit is defined as the return to risk and entrepreneurship. In practice high fixed interest rates are often set on high-risk loans. In recent years many risky ventures and "buy outs" have been financed with so-called "junk bonds" that pay the buyer an interest rate substantially above the risk-free rate of interest offered by insured banks or the federal government.

on the other hand, argue that large rewards are necessary because the social benefits of innovation are very high, and reducing the potential for large personal gains could substantially reduce beneficial risk taking.

THE DECISION TO INVEST: DEMAND FOR CAPITAL

In Chapter 9 we talked about incentives for investment by business firms in very general terms. There you saw that if firms in an industry earn *economic profits*, that is, profits over and above a normal rate of return, or if *economies of scale* that lower average costs are possible, then existing firms have an incentive to expand. You also saw that economic profits in an industry stimulate the entry of new firms into those markets. The expansion of existing firms and the creation of new firms both involve investment in new capital.

Even when there are no economic profits in an industry, however, firms must still do some investing. First, equipment wears out and must be replaced if the firm is to stay in business. Second, firms are constantly changing. A new technology may become available, sales patterns may shift, or the firm may expand or contract its product line, for example. With this background, then, we now focus on the investment decision process within an individual firm. (As you proceed, you will see that this discussion elaborates on our analysis of factor demand in the last chapter, as well as on the mechanics of the capital market that we have just reviewed.)

Forecasting the Future

The Expected Benefits of Investments   We have already said that the most important dimension of capital is that of time. In other words, capital produces useful services over *some period of time*. In building an office tower, a developer makes an investment that will be around for decades. In deciding where to build a branch plant, a manufacturing firm commits a large amount of resources to purchase capital that will be in place for a long time.

It is important to remember, though, that capital goods do not begin to yield benefits until they are actually being used. Often the decision to build a building or purchase a piece of equipment must be made years before the actual project is completed. While the acquisition of a small business computer may take only days, the planning process for downtown development projects in big American cities has been known to take decades.

Thus the investment decision of necessity involves looking into the future, or *forecasting*. Decision makers must have expectations about what is going to happen in the future. A new plant will be worth a lot—that is, it will produce much profit—if the market for a firm's product grows and the price of that product remains high. The same plant will be worth little if the economy slides into a recession or consumers grow tired of the firm's product. An office tower may turn out to be a wonderful investment if all the space gets rented at market rents that are as high as, or higher than, current rents, but it may be a poor investment if many new office buildings go up at the same time, flooding the office space market, pushing up the vacancy rate, and driving down rents. The first requirement, then, is that the potential investor evaluate the *expected flow of future productive services* that an investment project will yield.

Remember that households, business firms, and governments all undertake investments. A household must evaluate the future services that a new roof or a new car will yield. A firm must evaluate the flow of future revenues that a new plant will generate. Governments must estimate how much benefit society will derive from a new bridge or a war memorial.

An official of the General Electric Corporation in 1981 described the difficulty involved in such evaluations. GE subscribes to a number of different economic forecasting services. Those services provided the firm with 10-year predictions of new housing construction that ranged from a low of 400,000 new units per year to a high of 4 million units per year. Because General Electric sells millions of household appliances to contractors building new houses, condominiums, and apartments, the forecast was critical. If the high number turned out to be correct, the company would spend literally billions of dollars on new plant and equipment to prepare for the extra demand. If new construction reached only the low number, GE would begin closing several of its larger plants and disinvesting. In fact, GE took a middle road. It assumed that housing production would be between 1.5 and 2 million units, and that turned out to be correct.

General Electric is not an exception. All firms must rely on forecasts to make sensible investment and production decisions, but of course forecasting is an inexact science because so much depends on random events that cannot be foreseen.

The Expected Costs of Investments   The benefits of any investment project flow from it in the form of future profits. Those profits must be forecast. But costs must also be evaluated. We assume that firms have access to financial markets, both as borrowers and as lenders. If a firm borrows, it must *pay* interest over time; if it lends, it will *earn* interest. If the firm borrows to finance a project, the interest on the loan is part of the cost of the project.

But even if a project is financed with the firm's own funds, rather than by borrowing, there is still a cost. A thousand dollars put into a capital investment project will generate an expected flow of future profit; the same $1000 put into the financial market (in essence, loaned to another firm) will yield a flow of interest payments. Unless the project is expected to yield more than the market interest rate will yield, it will not be undertaken.

The availability of interest means that there is an *opportunity cost* associated with every investment project. Thus the evaluation process involves not only estimating future benefits, but comparing them with the possible alternative uses of the funds required to undertake the project. At a minimum, those funds could earn interest in financial markets. The cost of an investment project may thus be direct or indirect.

A DIGRESSION ON INTEREST RATES   Because we refer repeatedly to "the interest rate" in the pages that follow, a few words of clarification are in order. It is something of a fiction to speak of *the* interest rate; in fact, there are many interest rates. *Interest* is the fee that a borrower pays to a lender for the use of her or his money. The *interest rate* on a given loan depends on the length of the loan, the perceived risk of the loan, and the expectations of the lender about future interest rates. The greater the risk, the higher the interest rate that the lender demands. When the City of New York was near bankruptcy in the mid 1970s, it was nearly forced to borrow money at an interest rate of 40 *percent per year*. Loaning money to the City of New York was indeed risky at that time.

Interest rates on long-term loans tend to move along with interest rates on short-term loans—sometimes higher, sometimes lower—but they also reflect expectations about future rates. Between 1982 and 1987, interest rates fell. But nobody believed they would stay low forever. In 1987 the interest rate on short-term loans was significantly below the interest rate on long-term loans, because people wanted to be compensated more for agreeing to tie up their money for many years. At the same time, borrowers are willing to pay somewhat more for a long-term loan because they can "lock in" a rate and not have to worry about rates rising. Back in 1981, when short-term interest rates were nearly 20 percent, however, few believed that they would stay that high. Thus the rate on long-term loans was comparatively lower because borrowers were unwilling to agree to those very high rates for a long period of time when they expected that short-term rates would fall.

Real interest rate *The interest rate minus the rate of inflation.*

There is also a distinction between the rate of interest and the "real rate of interest" on a loan. The **real rate of interest** is the interest rate minus the rate of inflation. If A loans B $100.00 for one year at an interest rate of 10 percent, B will pay back $110.00. But if the price of goods and services has increased 10 percent due to inflation, A has in fact earned no "real" interest at all; he would get back the exact same "real" value that he loaned out. He has not been compensated for making the loan, because what he gets back will buy no more than what he loaned. If the loan had been made at 12 percent and prices had risen 10 percent, A would have received real interest amounting to two percent. As you can see, the true cost of an investment depends on the real rate of interest.

The Nuts and Bolts of Investment Decisions   Once expectations have been formed, firms must quantify them—that is, they must assign some dollars-and-cents values to them. One way is to calculate an **expected rate of return** on the investment project. For example, if a new computer that costs $400,000 is likely to save $100,000 per year in data-processing costs for a long time to come, the expected rate of return on that investment is 25 percent per year. If the same machine saved the firm only $40,000 per year, the expected rate of return would be 10 percent.

Table 11.2 presents a menu of investment choices and expected rates of return that face a hypothetical firm. Expected rates of return are based on forecasts of future profits attributable to the investments. Any change in expectations would change all the numbers in the right-hand column of the table.

Figure 11.3 graphs the total amount of investment in thousands of dollars that the firm would undertake at various interest rates. If interest rates were 24 percent, it would fund only Project A, the new computer—it can borrow at 24 percent and invest in a computer that is expected to yield 25 percent. Stated another way, faced with the choice of earning a return of 24 percent in the market or a 25 percent return by buying the computer, the computer wins. At 24 percent, then, total investment is $400,000. (At such a high interest rate, of course, only very profitable projects would be funded if we were talking about the real world and not the hypothetical world of the table and figure.)

TABLE 11.2
Potential Investment Projects and Expected Rates of Return for a Hypothetical Firm, Based on Future Profits Attributable to the Investment

Project	Total investment amount (dollars)	Expected rate of return (percentage)
A. New main frame computer	400,000	25
B. New branch plant	2,600,000	20
C. Sales office in another state	1,500,000	15
D. Word-processing system	100,000	12
E. Ten new delivery trucks	400,000	10
F. Advertising campaign	1,000,000	7
G. Employee cafeteria	100,000	5

FIGURE 11.3

Total Investment as a Function of the Market Interest Rate

The demand for capital depends on interest rates. When interest rates are low, firms are more likely to invest in new plant and equipment than when interest rates are high. This is because interest rates determine the direct cost (interest on a loan) or the opportunity cost (alternative investment) of each project.

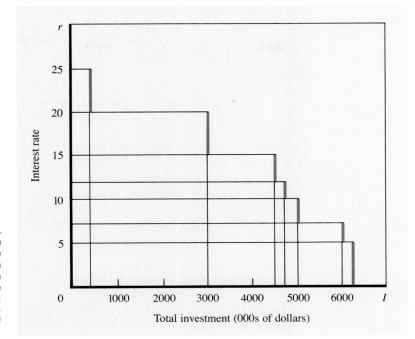

FIGURE 11.4

Investment Demand or Marginal Efficiency of Investment

The aggregate investment function shows the demand for capital in the economy as a function of interest rates. As is true for individual firms, lower interest rates are likely to stimulate investment in the economy as a whole.

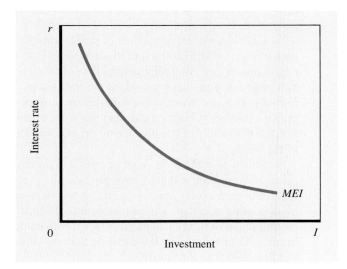

If interest rates were 18 percent, the firm would fund projects A and B, and its total investment would rise to $3 million. Again, if the firm could borrow at 18 percent, the flow of additional profits from the new plant and the new computer would more than cover the costs of borrowing, but none of the other projects would be justified. At an interest rate of 14 percent, it would undertake the first three projects at a total cost of $4.5 million. Only if interest rates fell below 5 percent would it fund all seven investment projects.

The investment schedule in Table 11.2 and its graphic depiction in Figure 11.3 describe the firm's demand for capital, expressed as a function of the market interest rate. The horizontal sum of all the individual firms' investment schedules describes the demand for capital in the economy as a whole (see Figure 11.4). Keynes called this curve

Marginal efficiency of investment *A curve that shows the total amount of investment that would be undertaken in an economy in a given period of time at every possible interest rate.*

the **marginal efficiency of investment** (**MEI**) schedule. In a sense, it is a ranking of all the investment opportunities in the economy in order of expected yield. *Only those investment projects in the economy that are expected to yield a rate of return higher than the market interest rate will be funded.* At lower market interest rates, more investment projects are undertaken.

The most important thing to remember about the marginal efficiency of investment, or *MEI,* curve is that its shape and position depend critically on the *expectations* of those making the investment decisions. Many influences affect those expectations, and thus they are usually volatile and given to frequent change. Clearly, upswings and downswings, or booms and recessions, in the economy as a whole influence them. As Keynes said, expectations and investment depend on the "animal spirits of entrepreneurs." So while lower interest rates tend to *stimulate* investment, and higher interest rates tend to *slow* it, other hard-to-measure and hard-to-predict factors that play upon "animal spirits" also affect the level of investment spending. These might include, for example, policy changes, election results, international affairs, inflation, or changes in currency exchange rates.

Discounting and Present Value

As we have seen, the firm's basic problem is to evaluate streams of value, or income, that will materialize only in the future. We have just argued that one way to decide whether or not to undertake an investment project is to calculate its expected rate of return and then compare that with the interest rate available in financial markets. This section describes an alternative, nearly equivalent, method of analysis.

Consider the expected flow of profits from the investment shown in Table 11.3. If such a project cost $1200 to put in place, would the firm undertake it? At first glance, you might answer yes. After all, the total flow of profit is $1600. But this flow of profit comes only after five years have passed, so the firm has to wait for it. The same $1200 could be loaned out or put into a money market account now. There it would earn interest, and perhaps produce a higher yield than if it were invested in the project. You can easily see that the desirability of the investment project will depend on what interest rate is available in the market.

One way of thinking about interest is to say that it *allows us to buy and sell claims to future dollars.* Future dollars have prices in the present. That is, a contract for one dollar to be delivered in one year, two years, or ten years can be purchased today. How? Simply by depositing a certain amount in an interest-bearing certificate or account. Using the present prices of future dollars gives us a way to compare values that will be realized in the future with present costs. If we can do that, we can evaluate investment projects that will yield benefits into the future.

It is not difficult to figure the "price" today of one dollar to be delivered in one year. You must pay an amount (X) such that when you get X back in one year with interest you will have one dollar. If r is the interest rate available in the market, r times X, or rX, is the amount of interest that X will earn for you in one year. Thus at the end of a year you will have $X+rX$, or $X(1+r)$, and you want this to be equal to one dollar. Solving for X algebraically:

$$\$1 = X(1+r) \qquad X = \$1/(1+r).$$

We say that X is the **present value**, or **present discounted value**, (these mean the same thing) of one dollar one year from now. Actually, X is the current market price of

TABLE 11.3
Expected Profits from an Investment Project

End of . . .	$
Year 1	100.00
Year 2	100.00
Year 3	400.00
Year 4	500.00
Year 5	500.00
All later years	0

Present discounted value *The present discounted value of R dollars to be paid t years in the future is the amount you need to put aside today, at current interest rates, to insure that you end up with R dollars t years from now. It is the current market value of a contract to deliver R dollars in t years.*

one dollar to be delivered in one year. In other words, it is the amount you have to put aside now if you want to end up with one dollar a year from now.

Now let's go more than one year into the future and consider more than a single dollar. For example, What is the present value of a claim on $100.00 in two years? Notice that the investment project described in Table 11.3 will yield $100.00 profit in year two, as well as $400.00 in year three, and so forth.

Using the same logic, let X be the present value, or current market price, of $100.00 payable in two years. Thus, X plus the interest it would earn compounded for two years is equal to $100.00. After one year, you would have $X + rX$, or $X(1+r)$. After two years, you would have this amount plus another year's interest on the whole amount:

$$X(1+r) + r[X(1+r)] \text{ or } X(1+r)(1+r) \text{ which is } X(1+r)^2.$$

Again solving algebraically for X:

$$\$100.00 = X(1+r)^2 \qquad X = \$100.00/(1+r)^2.$$

If the market interest rate were 10 percent, or .10, then the present value of $100.00 in two years would be

$$X = \$100.00/(1.1)^2 = \$82.65.$$

If you put $82.65 in a certificate earning 10 percent per year, you would earn $8.26 in interest after one year, giving you $90.91. Interest in the second year would be $9.09, leaving you with exactly $100.00 at the end of two years.

In general, the present value, or present discounted value, of R dollars t years from now is

$$PDV = \frac{R}{(1+r)^t}.$$

Table 11.4 calculates the present value of the income stream in Table 11.3 at an interest rate of 10 percent. The total present value turns out to be $1126. This tells the firm that it can simply go to the financial market today and buy a contract for $100.00 one year from now, and another for $100.00 two years from now, still another for $400.00 three years from now, and so forth, all for the low price of $1126. To put this another way, it could loan out or deposit $1126 in an account paying a 10 percent interest rate, withdraw $100.00 next year, withdraw $100.00 in the following year, take another $400.00 at the end of three years, and so forth. When it takes its last $500.00 at the end of the fifth year, the account will be empty—the balance in the account will be exactly zero.

TABLE 11.4

Calculation of Total Present Value of a Hypothetical Investment Project (assuming $r = 10$ percent)

End of . . .	$	Divided by	=	Present Value ($)
Year 1	100.00	(1.1)		90.91
Year 2	100.00	$(1.1)^2$		82.65
Year 3	400.00	$(1.1)^3$		300.53
Year 4	500.00	$(1.1)^4$		341.51
Year 5	500.00	$(1.1)^5$		310.46
Total present value:				1126.06

Thus, *at current market interest rates*, it has exactly duplicated the income stream that the investment project would have yielded for a total present price of $1126. Why then would it pay out $1200 to undertake this investment? The answer, of course, is that it would not.

We can restate the point this way: If the present value of the income stream associated with an investment is *less* than the full cost of the investment project, it should *not* be undertaken.

It is important to remember here that we are discussing the *demand for capital*. Business firms must evaluate potential investments in order to decide whether they are worth undertaking. That involves predicting the flow of potential future profits arising from each project and comparing those future profits with the return available in financial markets at current interest rates. The present-value method allows firms to calculate how much it would *cost today* to purchase or contract for the exact same flow of earnings in financial markets.

Lower Interest Rates, Higher Present Values   Suppose that interest rates fall from 10 percent to five percent. With a lower interest rate, the firm will have to *pay more* to purchase the same number of future dollars. Take for example the present value of $100.00 in two years. You saw that if the firm puts aside $82.65 at 10 percent interest, it will have exactly $100.00 in two years; at a 10-percent interest rate, the present discounted value, or current market price, of $100.00 in two years is $82.65. But $82.65 put aside at a five-percent interest rate would generate only $4.13 in interest in the first year and $4.34 in the second year, for a total balance of $91.12 after two years. In order to get $100.00, the firm needs to put aside *more* than $82.65. Solving for X as we did before,

$$X = \$100.00/(1+r)^2 = \$100.00/(1.05)^2 = \$90.70.$$

Thus you can see that at five percent interest, the present value of $100.00 in two years has risen by $8.05.

Table 11.5 recalculates the present value of the full stream at the lower interest rate; it shows that the total present value has risen to $1334.59. The investment project will yield the same stream of earnings for a present price of only $1200, and thus it is now a better deal than the financial markets when the market interest rate falls to five percent. Under these conditions, a profit-maximizing firm will make the investment.

Here is the basic rule: if the present value of an expected stream of earnings from an investment exceeds the cost of the investment necessary to undertake it, then the investment should be undertaken. But if the present value of an expected stream of earnings falls short of the cost, then the financial market can generate the *same stream* for *less money*, and the investment should not be undertaken. When the interest rate or the rate of return offered by the market exceeds the rate of return on a project, the investment is not justified *at current interest rates*.

TABLE 11.5

Calculation of Total Present Value for a Hypothetical Investment Project (assuming $r = 5$ percent)

End of . . .	$	Divided by	=	Present Value ($)
Year 1	100.00	(1.05)		95.24
Year 2	100.00	$(1.05)^2$		90.70
Year 3	400.00	$(1.05)^3$		345.54
Year 4	500.00	$(1.05)^4$		411.35
Year 5	500.00	$(1.05)^5$		391.76
Total present value:				1334.59

Rate of Return versus Present-Value Calculations   In the menu of possible investment projects that you saw in Table 11.2, the right-hand column listed an *expected rate of return* for each project.

To arrive at the rate of return on a project, a firm first needs to estimate the same stream of earnings that is used to arrive at present value. Then it needs to know what interest rate would be necessary to generate the exact same stream of earnings if the capital cost of the project were simply put into the financial market rather than into the project. For the project we have been analyzing, the question is, If the firm puts $1200 (the cost of the investment) into an interest-bearing bond or account instead of purchasing the machine, what interest rate would that $1200 have to draw to allow us to take out $100.00 after one year, another $100.00 after two years, $400.00 after three years, and so forth? In other words, What market interest rate would make the firm *just indifferent* between the investment in the project and loaning the money out in the market?

To get those returns at an interest rate of 10 percent, it had to deposit only $1126.06. Had it deposited $1200 at that rate, the firm would have been able to realize more earnings from interest. This means that the rate of return for the project is *less* than 10 percent. But the rate of return is *greater* than five percent. As you recall, to get the same stream at five percent, the firm had to deposit $1334.59.

In fact, the expected rate of return on this project is 8.09%. If the firm deposits $1200 in an account yielding 8.09%, it can withdraw exactly the stream of earnings in Table 11.3 and have nothing left over after it withdraws the last $500.00 at the end of the fifth year. If the market rate of interest were 8.09%, therefore, it wouldn't matter whether the firm made the investment or put $1200 into the market.[7]

Now we have two ways to evaluate a given project. One way is to compare, as we did in Table 11.3, the market interest rate with the rate of return on the investment. For that hypothetical project, the implicit rate of return was 8.09%. When the market yields only five percent interest, returns on the project beat those available in the market, and the project is undertaken. When the market rate of interest is 10 percent, however, the market wins, and the project is not undertaken.

The other way is to calculate the present discounted value of the project at the market rate of interest. If the present discounted value of the expected stream of earnings is *less* than the cost of the project, the market will generate the same stream of earnings for a lesser amount. Thus the market is a better deal, and the project is not undertaken. This was the case when we used a market rate of 10 percent. With the interest rate at five percent, however, the present value of the project was higher than $1200, and the project was undertaken.

These two methods of evaluating an investment project are, for all practical purposes, equivalent. Whether you use present-value calculations or compare expected rates of return on the project against those in the market, lower market interest rates make investments look more attractive, and higher market interest rates make investments look less attractive.

---

[7]It would be a good idea to work through the calculations and prove this to yourself. To calculate the implicit rate of return on a project, you solve for the interest rate that equates project cost to the present value of the profit stream from the project. For our project

$$\$1200 = \$100/(1+r) + \$100/(1+r)^2 + \$400/(1+r)^3 + \$500/(1+r)^4 + \$500/(1+r)^5.$$

This is an equation with a single unknown. The solution, which can be obtained analytically or by simple trial and error, is $r = .0809$, or 8.09%.

Asset Values, Present Values, and Future Income Streams

We have said often enough that the value of a capital investment is only as great as the value of the services it will produce over time. To put this more formally, we can now say that the *market price of an asset is generally driven to the present discounted value of the stream of earnings that the asset is expected to produce over time for the owner.* Two examples should show clearly enough how the market does this.

A Bond   Consider a **bond**, which generally represents a fixed guaranteed stream of earnings to be paid at specified times in the future. An eight-percent, 10-year $1000 bond, for example, entitles the owner to $80.00 per year for 10 years and the $1000 back at the end of 10 years, no matter what happens to the market interest rate.

The company or government that issues that bond does so because it wants to borrow the money for 10 years. It has no obligation whatsoever to pay the money back before the 10 years are up. There is, however, a market for previously issued bonds; they have a value at present because whoever owns them is entitled to a stream of future earnings. A bond represents a claim to future dollars, and the market value, or price, of a bond derives directly from that stream of future dollars.

Suppose that you bought such a bond at eight percent a year ago and now want to sell it. But now, a year after you bought it, the interest rate on *new* 10-year bonds is 12 percent. How much would a *rational* person be willing to pay for your bond? She would certainly *not* pay $1000, because now spending $1000 would buy her title to $120.00 per year with $1000 back, and that is significantly more than $80.00 per year. Table 11.6 shows that she could, with interest rates at 12 percent, buy the *exact same income stream* for $786.87. That is the *present discounted value* of the stream to which your bond entitles the bearer. If she pays you more than that for it, she is, in fact, accepting a yield of *less* than 12 percent. If you offered it to her for less than $786.87, she would be getting a yield of *more* than 12 percent.

Rental Property   While it is easy to see that the value of a financial asset such as a bond depends on the stream of income that it generates over time, the same is true of *all other assets* as well. Businesses are often bought and sold, and when they are, the parties to the sale must estimate the present value of the expected future profits of the business.

Take, for example, a large house in San Francisco. Assume that the house is in excellent physical condition, that it is located near San Francisco State College, and that it has ten rooms that can be rented out to students for $300.00 each per month. Full

Bond   *An I.O.U. A promise to pay some specific amount at some specific time in the future. Usually bonds specify a flow of payments to the owner that is determined by a specific annual interest rate applied to a specified face value. A 10 year 8% $1000 bond, for example, is a promise to pay the holder $1000 in 10 years and $80 each year in the interim.*

TABLE 11.6
Present Value of an 8 Percent $1000 Bond when Interest Rates Rise to 12 Percent

End of year	$	Divided by	=	Present Value ($)
1	80	(1.12)		71.43
2	80	$(1.12)^2$		63.78
3	80	$(1.12)^3$		56.94
4	80	$(1.12)^4$		50.84
5	80	$(1.12)^5$		45.39
6	80	$(1.12)^6$		40.53
7	80	$(1.12)^7$		36.19
8	80	$(1.12)^8$		32.31
9	1080	$(1.12)^9$		389.46
Total present value:				786.87

occupancy of such a house would generate $3000 per month, or $36,000 per year, in revenues to the owner. Now assume further that insurance, maintenance, repair, and property taxes cost a total of $6000 per year. The maintenance and repair are sufficient to maintain the value of the property indefinitely. How much would you be willing to pay to purchase the house if these flows were likely to continue unchanged for a long period of time?

Under these assumptions, the house is just like a bond. The owner would receive a net profit of $30,000 each year. If interest rates were 10 percent, and if there were no risks associated with the house, a rational buyer would pay about $300,000. That is because $30,000 is 10 percent of $300,000. A continuous flow of $30,000 is a 10-percent rate of return on a $300,000 asset.[8] To pay more would mean that the buyer was accepting a return lower than 10 percent; to pay less would mean a return of more than 10 percent. In fact, the present discounted value of $30,000 for a long period of time at an interest rate of 10 percent is $300,000.

LAND AND LAND MARKETS

The **land market** is yet another input market that is closely related to, but different in important ways from, the capital market. Land, of course, is not a produced input, as capital is. There is only a certain amount of land—it is in fixed supply, and it is owned by someone. The only real questions about land are how much it is worth and what use it will be put to.

Because land in general and each parcel in particular is fixed in supply, we say that its price is **demand determined** (see Figure 11.5). The return to any factor of production in fixed supply is called a **pure rent**. Any given site has a number of different

Demand determined   *When a good is in fixed supply, its price is determined exclusively by what firms or households are willing to pay for it. When a good is in fixed supply we say that its price is demand determined.*

Pure rent   *The return to any factor of production that is in fixed supply.*

FIGURE 11.5
The Rent on Land Is Demand Determined

Because land in general (and each parcel in particular) is in fixed supply, its price is demand determined. Graphically, a fixed supply is represented by a vertical, perfectly inelastic, supply curve. Rent, R_0, depends exclusively on demand—what people are willing to pay.

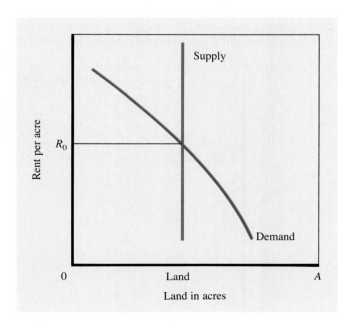

[8]This assumes that the value of the house remains at $300,000, just as the final value of the bond remained at $1000. If buyers anticipate increases in house values, however, the increase can be thought of as added future yield, or income. That would raise the present value of the house, because buyers should be willing to pay to receive those future gains. We also are ignoring the role of taxes. Real estate investment returns depend critically on the tax code.

alternative uses, and so, as with any other factor in a market setting, it will presumably go to the potential user who is willing to pay the most for it. The value of land to a potential user may derive from the *characteristics* of the land itself or from its *location*. For example, it may be very fertile and thus of great value in agriculture; it may be at a conjunction of waterways and thus of value for commerce; or it may be at an accessible and aesthetically pleasing location and thus of great value as a residential site.

Land use patterns clearly change over time as economies grow and develop. Urbanization, population growth, and rising productivity in agriculture inevitably lead to a shift of land out of agriculture and into industrial and residential use. The process of land allocation in the absence of regulation is no different from the process of labor or capital allocation, except that its supply is perfectly inelastic. Any potential user will bid for it as long as the bid is below the marginal revenue product of the land.

David Ricardo's Explanation of Rent

In the early nineteenth century, David Ricardo wrote about rent as the return to a factor in strictly limited supply. Ricardo explained the notion with a story. Suppose that a country has within its borders land of several qualities. At the beginning of the story, food for the entire population can be grown on the highest-quality land. As population grows and the demand for food increases, however, people stake claims to lower-quality land and begin to farm it. When they do, of course, they discover that it is not as productive as the land of higher quality.

Figure 11.6 shows that the high-quality land produces 100 bushels of corn per acre per year. Low-quality land with a similar "dose" of capital and labor can produce only 80 bushels of corn per acre per year.

The owners of high-quality land can now earn an income simply by owning it. Suppose, for example, that the owner of high-quality land says to a farmer thinking of staking a claim to a few free acres of low-quality land, "You are welcome to go use that lousy land, but if you want, you can use my land for the paltry sum of 19 bushels of corn

FIGURE 11.6
Ricardo's Explanation of Rent

On the highest quality of land, a "dose" of capital and labor can produce 100 bushels of corn. On the next best land, a similar dose can produce only 80 bushels. Even if the low quality land is free and open, owners of the high quality land will be able to extract a *rent* because of its added productivity.

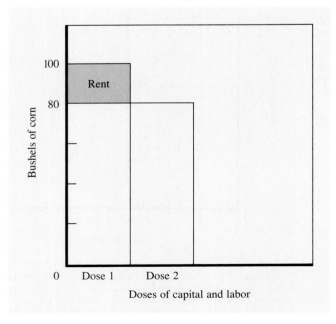

per year per acre." Clearly the farmer rents the better land. By doing so, he ends up with 81 bushels per acre instead of 80, and the landlord now earns a *pure rent*, the return to the strictly limited high-quality land.

The Allocation of Land Among Competing Uses

As a simple example of how a competitive market allocates land among alternative uses, consider two potential uses for a plot of land. Use A requires a $100,000 capital investment and will yield a profit of $20,000 per year after maintenance, depreciation, and taxes but *before rent is paid*. Use B requires a $150,000 capital investment and will yield a $50,000 flow of annual profits under the same conditions.

If we assume that the *interest rate*—that is, the normal rate of return to investment in the sectors of the economy in which the businesses are involved—is 10 percent, then we can calculate the maximum bid that the land owner should be able to extract from each potential user. This logic is really the same as that behind the events in Ricardo's story.

In use A, $10,000 of the $20,000 annual profit is required as the compensation for capital. That is, 10 percent, or $10,000 on an investment of $100,000 is by definition just sufficient to interest investors in this sector. Alternatively, the capital might be purchased with the proceeds from a loan. In that case, the simple interest on the loan would be $10,000. If the location is what enables the owner who proposes use A to earn the full $20,000, the landowner should be able to demand up to $10,000 per month for access to the location.

In use B, capital must receive $15,000—that is, 10 percent of $150,000—but profits are $50,000. That leaves $35,000 for land. Thus land use B will generate significantly more rent, and presumably the developer proposing that use will end up with the land.

Another way to look at the same problem is to ask, if interest rates are 10 percent, how much would an investor be willing to pay in total (land *and* capital) to receive a flow of $20,000 in profits, which she would receive in use A? Since $20,000 is 10 percent of $200,000, an investor should be willing to pay up to $200,000. Any amount under that means that the investor will earn more than 10 percent.

Because the capital costs $100,000, the full value of the plot of land in use A is $100,000—$200,000 total minus $100,000 for capital. Notice that $100,000 is exactly equal to what a land buyer would be forced to pay to earn a rental stream of $10,000 per year. Stated another way, $100,000 is the *present discounted value* of the $10,000 annual stream of rent. For use B the gross yield is $50,000 per year, and we therefore arrive at a total value of $500,000 when the interest rate is 10 percent. The amount required for the capital is $150,000, so land can claim a total of $350,000. Once again, this is the *present value* of the $35,000 rental stream that flows from use B, and it will clearly be the highest bid.

Land Rent and the Value of Output Produced on Land

We have seen that rent depends on what the potential users of land are willing to pay for it. Presumably, land will end up being used by whoever is willing to pay the most for it. But what determines willingness to pay? Let us now connect our discussion here with the discussion of factor markets in general from Chapter 10.

As our example of two potential users bidding for a plot of land shows, the bids depend on the potential for profit. That is, if the land were free, use A would generate a profit of $10,000 per year and use B would generate a profit of $35,000 per year. But these profits do not just materialize. They presumably come from producing and selling an output that is valuable to households. Land in a popular downtown location is expensive because of what can be produced on it. A restaurant located next to a popular theatre can charge a premium price because it has a relatively captive clientele. Clearly, it still has to produce a quality product, but the location provides a substantial opportunity to make a profit.

This is exactly the essence of what we said in the last chapter about factor demand in general. Recall that a profit-maximizing firm will employ a factor of production *as long as its marginal revenue product exceeds its market price*. *Marginal revenue product,* we said, is the additional revenue earned by using one more unit of a factor—it is the marginal physical product of the *input* times the price of *output*. For example, for labor

$$MRP_L = MP_L \times P_X,$$

where P_X is the price of output being produced.

In Chapter 10, you saw that a profit-maximizing firm will hire labor as long as the revenue earned from selling labor's product is sufficient to cover the cost of hiring labor—the wage rate, W. The same thing is true for land. A firm will pay for and use land as long as the revenue earned from selling the product produced on it is sufficient to cover its price. The profitability of the restaurant located next to the theatre results from the fact that the meals produced there command a price in the marketplace. Similarly, just as the demand curve for labor reflects the value of labor's product as determined in output markets, so does the demand for land depend on the value of land's product in output markets.

Thus the allocation of a given location or a given plot of land between competing uses depends on the trade-off between competing products that can be produced on the same plot. Agricultural land becomes developed when its value in producing housing or manufactured goods or providing space for a shopping center exceeds its value in producing crops.

One final word about land: because land cannot be physically moved, the value of any one parcel depends to a large extent upon the uses to which adjoining parcels are put. A factory belching acrid smoke will probably reduce the value of adjoining land, while a new highway which increases accessibility may enhance it.

As you can see, the demand for capital and land depend on their productivity. Each in its own way contributes to the value of final products, and so the market value of these final products determines the *allocation* of land and capital, as well as the final *values* of land and capital. To close, we return briefly to capital markets.

CAPITAL FORMATION: PUTTING OUTPUT AND INPUT MARKETS TOGETHER

One of the central ideas in economics is the concept of capital. Capital is produced by the economic system itself; it generates services over time; and it is used as an input in the production of goods and services.

The enormous productivity of modern industrial societies is due in part to the tremendous amount of capital that they put into place or have accumulated over the years. It may surprise you to know that the *average* worker in the United States works with over $50,000 worth of capital. There is no question that the "economic miracle" of modern Japan resulted first and foremost from the very high rates of investment that began after World War II and have continued for 40 years.

The bulk of this chapter has been describing the institutions and processes that determine the amount and character of capital produced in a market economy. Existing firms in search of increased profits, potential new entrants, and entrepreneurs with new ideas are all continuously evaluating potential investment projects. At the same time, households are saving. Each year households save some portion of their disposable incomes. That new saving becomes part of their net worth, and they want to earn a return on it. Each year at least a good portion of the new saving finds its way into the hands of firms who use it to buy new capital goods.

Between households and firms is the *financial capital market*. Millions of people participate in financial markets every day. There are literally thousands of money managers, pension funds, mutual funds, college portfolios, brokerage houses, options traders, and banks whose very existence have as their purpose earning the highest possible rate of return on people's saving.

Everyone wants the best possible yield, and most people are willing to pay to find it. Money managers are continuously scanning the financial horizons for profitable investments. What businesses are doing well? What businesses are doing poorly? Is there an opportunity to fill a hole in the market by backing this entrepreneur or that one? Should we loan money to an expanding firm? All of the analysis done by financial managers seeking to earn a high yield for clients, by managers of firms seeking to earn high profits for their stockholders, and by entrepreneurs seeking profits from innovation channels capital into its most productive uses. Within single firms, the evaluation of individual investment projects by its nature involves *forecasting* and valuing *streams of potential income* that will be earned only in future years.

In planned economies, decisions about capital investment are made centrally as a part of a plan. Those who advocate the market system argue that investment decisions are best made by specialists who know a great deal about the product and market involved, and who are risking their own money or the money of their clients.

We have now completed our discussion of competitive input and output markets. We have looked at household and firm choices in output markets, labor markets, capital markets, and land markets.

We next return to our starting point in Chapters 4 and 5 and reflect on the nature of the allocative process that we have described. How does it function when we put it all together? Is the result good or bad? Can we improve on it? All this is the subject of Chapter 12.

SUMMARY

1. Capital goods are those goods produced by the economic system itself that are used as inputs to produce other goods and services in the future. Capital goods yield valuable productive services over time.

2. Usually we think of physical, or tangible, capital. Human capital (skills, training, health, and so on) and goodwill are examples of intangible capital.

3. Firms, households, and governments all produce and use capital.

4. The most common measure of a firm's capital stock is the

current market value of its plant, equipment, inventories and intangible assets. However, in thinking about capital it is best to think of the actual capital stock.

5. The term "investment" correctly refers to the creation of capital, not to the purchase of a share of stock or a bond.

6. Depreciation is the decline in the economic value of an asset over time.

7. The funds that firms use to buy capital come, directly or indirectly, from households. Financial capital markets work to channel household savings into investment projects.

8. Profit and interest are the income flows that are paid to the owners of capital. They reward households for postponing consumption and for risk taking and entrepreneurship.

9. Investment decisions of necessity involve forecasting. Investors must evaluate the expected flow of future productive services that an investment project will yield.

10. The availability of interest to lenders means that there is an opportunity cost associated with every investment project. This must be weighed against the stream of earnings that a project is expected to yield.

11. Interest is the fee that a borrower pays to a lender for the use of her or his money. The interest rate on a given loan depends on the length of the loan, the perceived risk of the loan, and the interest rate that the lender demands. The real rate of interest is the interest rate minus the rate of inflation.

12. The aggregate investment function, or the marginal efficiency of investment schedule, shows the demand for capital in the economy as a function of the market interest rate. Lower interest rates should stimulate investment.

13. An individual project can be evaluated by calculating the present discounted value of the future profits expected to flow from the project and comparing it with up-front project costs. A second method is to calculate the rate of return implicit in the project and compare it with the market interest rate.

14. The present value of some amount to be received or realized in the future is the amount you would have to put aside today at current interest rates to end up with that amount in the future. It is nothing more than the present market value of those future dollars.

15. The market value of an asset is normally driven to the present value of the stream of earnings that the asset will yield to its owner.

16. Because land in general, and each parcel in particular, is fixed in supply, we say that its value is demand determined.

17. The return to any factor in fixed supply is called a pure rent.

18. Financial capital markets channel capital into its most productive uses, just as land markets channel land into its most productive uses.

REVIEW CONCEPTS

capital   254
physical, or tangible, capital   254
intangible capital   254
goodwill   254
human capital   254
social capital   255
infrastructure   255
capital stock   255
investment   255
depreciation   256
interest   257

profits   257
financial capital market   257
entrepreneur   261
real rate of interest   264
expected rate of return   264
marginal efficiency of investment   266
present (discounted) value   266
bond   270
land market   271
demand determined   271
pure rent   271

REVIEW QUESTIONS

1. Give at least three examples of how savings can be channeled into productive investment.

2. Explain what we mean when we say that "households supply capital and firms demand capital."

3. Assume that a household decides to have a house built that costs $100,000. This year the household has an income of $40,000, of which $25,000 is spent on current consumption and the rest is used as a down payment on the house. The additional $85,000 is borrowed from an aged relative who earns no income and currently lives off her wealth. Assume that she sells some shares of stock to acquire the cash for the loan. A third party who earned $200,000 last year bought the stock from the aged relative for $85,000 and spent $115,000 on current consumption.

    For each of the four parties, calculate
    a. The amount of saving during the period
    b. The quantity of investment during the period
    c. Any change in net worth
    d. Any change in capital stock

4. Calculate the present value of the income streams A-E at an 8 percent interest rate and again at a 10 percent rate:

End of year	A	B	C	D	E
1	$ 80	$ 80	$100	$100	$500
2	80	80	100	100	300
3	80	80	1100	100	400
4	80	80	0	100	300
5	1080	80	0	100	0
6	0	80	0	1100	0
7	0	1080	0	0	0

5. If investment E in Question 4 were a machine that cost $1235, would you, as a member of the board, vote to purchase it if the market interest rate were eight percent? What if the interest rate were 10 percent?

6. The owner of a piece of land has determined that it has two potential uses: (1) For $150,000, he could build an apartment building that would contain 10 apartments, each of which would rent for $200.00 *per month*. It would cost a total of $4000 *annually* to maintain and operate. (2) For $130,000, he could build a small office building that would contain 10 offices, each of which would rent for $150.00 *per month*. It would cost $3000 *per month* to maintain and operate the offices.

    Assume that the interest rate is 10 percent, and calculate how much the land is worth. Explain your answer.

7. Describe the capital stock of your college or university. How would you go about measuring its value?

    Has your school made any major investments in recent years? If so, describe them.

12 General Equilibrium, the Efficiency of Competition, and Sources of Market Failure

The last six chapters have built a model of a simple competitive economy. Our discussion has revolved around the two fundamental decision-making units, *households* and *firms*, that interact in two basic market arenas, *input markets* and *output markets*. (Look again at the circular flow diagram, shown in Figure 12.1.)

Households make constrained choices in both input and output markets. We began in Chapter 5 with an individual household demand curve for a single good or service. Then in Chapter 6 we went behind the demand curve and saw how income, wealth, and prices define the budget constraints within which households exercise their tastes and preferences. We soon discovered, however, that we could not look at household decisions in output markets without thinking about decisions in input markets at the same time. Household income, for example, depends on choices made in input markets: whether to work, how much to work, what skills to acquire, and so forth. Capital income (income from ownership) depends in part on the amount that households decide to save out of each year's income. Input market choices are constrained as well by factors such as current wage rates, the availability of jobs, and interest rates.

A *firm* exists when someone or some group decides to produce a product or service for the market. Profit-making firms, to which we have confined our discussion, earn those

279

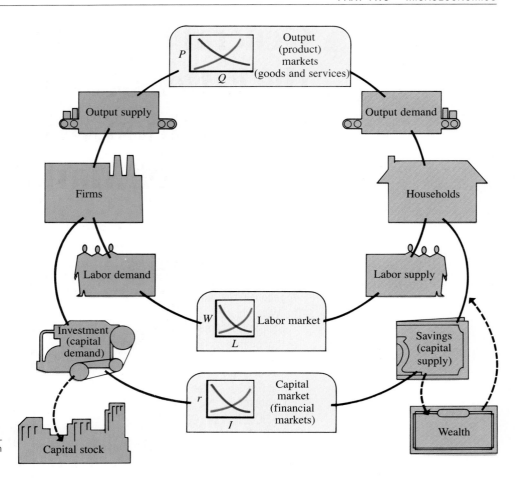

FIGURE 12.1
Firm and Household Decisions

Firms and households interact in both input and output markets.

profits by selling products and services for more than it costs to produce them. With firms, as with households, we saw that output markets and input markets could not be analyzed separately. Firms make three specific decisions, and they must make them simultaneously: (1) how much output to supply, (2) how to produce that output, that is, which technology to use, and (3) how much of each input to demand.

In Chapters 7–9, we explored these three decisions from the viewpoint of output markets. We saw that the marginal cost curve above average variable cost is the supply curve of a competitive firm in the short run. Implicit in the marginal cost curve itself is a choice of technology and a set of input demands. In Chapters 10 and 11, we looked at these same decisions from the viewpoint of input markets.

Output and input markets are connected because firms and households make simultaneous choices in both arenas. There are other connections among markets as well. Firms buy in both capital and labor markets, for example, and they can substitute capital for labor and vice versa. A change in the price of one factor can easily change the demand for other factors. Buying more *capital*, for instance, clearly changes the marginal revenue product of *labor* and shifts the labor demand curve. Households also shop in many output markets at the same time. A change in the price of a single good or service usually affects household demand for other goods and services, as when a price decrease makes one good more attractive than other close substitutes. The same change also makes households better off when they find that the same amount of income will buy more. Such additional "real income" can be spent on any one, or all, of the other goods and services that the household buys.

The point here is that markets cannot be considered separately as if they operated independently. While it is important to understand the decisions of *individual* firms and households and the functioning of *individual* markets, we now need to "add it all up," to look at the operation of the system as a whole.

You have seen the concept of equilibrium being applied to markets and to individual decision-making units. In individual markets, supply and demand determine an equilibrium price. Firms are in short-run equilibrium when price and marginal cost are equal. In the long run, however, equilibrium in a competitive market is achieved only when economic profits are eliminated. Households are in equilibrium when they have equated the marginal utility per dollar spent on each good to the marginal utility per dollar spent on every *other* good. This process of examining the equilibrium conditions in individual markets and for individual households and firms separately is called **partial equilibrium** analysis.

General equilibrium *The condition in which equilibrium prevails simultaneously in all markets in an economy.*

A **general equilibrium** exists when all markets in an economy are in simultaneous equilibrium. When an event disturbs the equilibrium in one market, it may disturb many other markets as well. The ultimate impact of the event depends upon how all markets adjust to it. Thus partial equilibrium analysis, which looks at adjustments in one market in isolation, may be misleading.

Thinking in terms of a general equilibrium leads to some important questions. Is it even possible for all agents and all markets to be in equilibrium simultaneously? Are the equilibrium conditions that we have discussed separately compatible with one another? Why is an event that disturbs an equilibrium in one market likely to disturb many others simultaneously?

In talking about general equilibrium, the first concept we explore in this chapter, we continue our exercise in *positive economics*—that is, we seek to understand how systems operate *without making value judgments* about outcomes. Later in the chapter, we turn from positive economics to normative economics as we begin to evaluate the results of how the system functions. Are its outcomes good or bad? Can we make them better?

Efficiency *The condition in which the economy is producing what people want at least possible cost.*

In judging the outcomes of any economic system, as you recall, it is essential first to establish specific criteria to judge by. In this chapter, we use two such criteria, *efficiency* and *equity*. First we demonstrate that *if all the assumptions we have made hold*, then the resulting allocation of resources is **efficient**—that is, the system produces what people want and does so at least cost. More formally, we can say that any change that is made to improve the welfare of one person or group makes some other person or group worse off. When we begin to *relax some of our assumptions*, however, it becomes apparent that free markets may *not* be efficient. Several sources of market failure, or inefficiency, naturally occur within an unregulated market system. Finally, we turn to the potential role of government in correcting market failure and achieving fairness in distribution.

GENERAL EQUILIBRIUM ANALYSIS

Three cases should illustrate some of the insights that we can gain when we move from partial to general equilibrium analysis. Let us first consider the impact on the economy of a major technological advance, next, of a shift in consumer preferences, and finally, of the imposition of a tax on one sector of an economy. As you read, remember that we are looking for the connections between markets, and particularly between input and output markets.

General Equilibrium Effects—Links Between Output and Input Markets

One of the important points made in this chapter is that markets are interconnected. When one market adjusts to changes in supply or demand conditions, other markets are affected as well. Nowhere is this connection more clear then in the construction industry. In 1981 and 1982 interest rates in financial capital markets increased dramatically. The prime rate, the lowest interest rate banks charge their best customers, rose above 20 percent. High interest rates discourage investment as we saw in Chapter 11. As a result, the demand for houses, apartments, factories, and shopping centers declined dramatically, and the construction industry sank into a recession. The following article reprinted from the newsletter of the Federal Reserve Bank of San Francisco traces the rest of the story. These events disturbed equilibria in many output and input markets.

> In the last few years, the lumber industry of the Pacific Northwest has suffered from its worst slump since World War II. Lumber mills have been forced to close or to curtail operations in response to the downturn in the demand for timber products. As of January 1, for example, 82 out of 197 mills in Oregon were closed. In fact, softwood lumber production in the Pacific Northwest has dropped nearly 35 percent from its peak level in 1978. Although there are

now signs that the lumber industry is reviving, the recovery remains jeopardized by a variety of special demand and supply problems.

DEMAND PROBLEMS

The forest products industry depends on the housing industry for almost half of the demand for its products. Thus, when high interest rates and the recession precipitated a 40-percent decline in housing starts between 1979 and 1981, the effect was transmitted directly to the forest products industry. A strong dollar further depressed sales by weakening the competitive position of U.S. producers in world export markets.

The downturn in demand affected the economies of the Pacific Northwest dramatically because of their dependence on a thriving forest products industry. Over one-fourth of total manufacturing employment in Washington and Oregon (which together produce over half of the nation's softwood lumber), for example, is in the forest products industry. Cutbacks in mill production caused massive job layoffs, raising unemployment rates in some timber processing areas of the two states to nearly 30 percent, and contributing to state unemployment rates that are above national levels.

Source: "Northwest Timber Dilemma," From the Federal Reserve Bank of San Francisco Newsletter, February 18, 1983. Reprinted by permission.

The Electronic Calculator: A Technological Advance

Graduate students working in quantitative fields of study in the late 1960s, and even as late as the early 1970s, recall rooms in academic buildings filled with noisy mechanical calculators. A single calculator weighed about 40 pounds and was able to add, subtract, multiply, and divide. These machines couldn't remember anything, and they took 20 to 25 seconds to do one multiplication problem.

Major corporations had rooms full of accountants with such calculators on their desks, and the sound when thirty or forty of them were running at once was deafening. During the 1950s and 1960s, most firms had these calculators, but most people did not have them in their homes, because a single machine cost several hundred dollars. A few homes had "adding machines," but hardly anyone had a calculator. Some high schools had calculators for accounting classes, but most school children in the United States had never seen one.

In the 1960s, Wang Laboratories developed an electronic calculator. Bigger than a modern personal computer, it had several keyboards that attached to a single main processor. It could add, subtract, multiply, and divide, but it also had a memory. Its main virtue was speed and quiet: it did calculations instantaneously without any noise. The Wang machine sold for around $1500.

The outset of the 1970s saw rapid developments in the industry. First, calculators shrank in size. The Bomar Corporation made one of the earliest hand calculators—the Bomar Brain. Again, these early versions could do nothing more than add, subtract, multiply, and divide, they had no memories, and they still sold for several hundred dollars. Then, in the early 1970s, a number of technological breakthroughs made it possible to mass produce very small electronic circuits (micro chips). That, in turn, made these machines very inexpensive to produce, and it is here that we begin our general equilibrium story. Costs if the industry shifted downward dramatically. As costs fell, profits increased. With economic profits, new firms rapidly entered the market, Instead of one or two firms producing state-of-the-art machines, dozens of firms began cranking them out by the thousands. As that happened, the industry supply curve shifted out to the right, driving down prices toward the new lower costs.

As the price of electronic calculators fell, the market for the old mechanical calculators died a quiet death. With no more demand for their product, producers found themselves suffering losses and got out of the business. As the price of electronic calculators kept falling, thousands of people who had never had a calculator began to buy them. By 1973 calculators were available at discount appliance stores for $60.00 to $70.00, and by 1975, over 18 million were produced annually, at an average price of $62.00. Gross sales were over a billion dollars per year. The average price fell to under $30.00 by the mid 1980s, and you can now buy a basic calculator for less than $5.00, or get one free with a magazine subscription. Nearly 30 million of them are produced each year.[1]

Thus the rapid decline in cost led to a rapid expansion of supply and a decline in price. The lower prices increased the quantity demanded until most American homes have at least one calculator, and thousands of people walk around with calculators in their pockets.

So far, this is a *partial equilibrium story*, however. These events, of course, had effects on many other markets; in other words, they disturbed the *general equilibrium*. When mechanical calculators became obsolete, many people who had over the years developed the skills required to produce and repair those complex machines found themselves unemployed. At the same time, demand for workers in the production, distribution, and sales of electronic calculators boomed. New skills were required, and the expansion of the industry led to an increase in demand for the kinds of labor needed. The new technology thus caused a reallocation of labor across the labor market.

Capital too was reallocated. New firms invested in the plant and equipment needed to produce electronic calculators. Old capital owned by the firms that previously made mechanical calculators became obsolete and depreciated, and it ended up on the scrapheap. The mechanical calculators themselves, part of the capital stocks of accounting firms, banks, and so forth, were scrapped as they became obsolete and were replaced by the cheaper and more efficient new models.

When a new billion-dollar industry appears from nowhere, it earns billions of dollars in revenues that might have been spent on other things. Even though the effects of this success on any one other industry were probably small, general equilibrium analysis tells us that in the absence of the new industry and the demand for its product, households would demand other goods and services, and other industries would be producing more. In this case, society has benefited a great deal. Everyone can now buy a very useful, and to many of us indispensable, product cheaply. It has raised the productivity of certain kinds of labor and reduced costs in many industries.

The point here is that a significant—if not sweeping—technological change in a single industry had effects on many markets. Households faced a different structure of prices and adjusted their consumption of many products. Labor reacted to new skill requirements and was reallocated across markets. Capital was likewise reallocated.

[1]U.S. Department of Commerce, Bureau of the Census, *Statistical Abstract of the United States, 1983/1984*, table 1434, p. 797. Compiled from reports of associations and manufacturers.

The Wine Industry: A Shift in Consumer Preferences

For a more formal view of the general equilibrium effects of a change in one market on other markets consider an economy with just two sectors, X and Y. For purposes of the discussion, let us say that the rapidly growing wine business in the United States is industry X and everything else is industry Y. (Of course the sequence of adjustments would be the same for any expanding sector of the economy.)

During the 1970s, American consumer preferences in alcoholic beverages clearly changed in favor of wine. Table 12.1 provides some data. Domestic wine production increased by 74 percent between 1965 and 1980. In addition, in 1980 we imported more than nine times as much wine as we had in 1965. Overall demand increased 86.6%. Part of this increase was simply due to increased population, part was probably due to a change in the age distribution of the population, and some was due to a simple change in preferences. Per capita consumption of wine rose 53 percent.

Figure 12.2 shows the initial equilibrium in sectors X and Y. We assume that both are initially in long-run competitive equilibrium. Total output in sector X is Q_X^0, the product is selling for a price of P_X^0, and firms produce up to where P_X^0 is equal to marginal cost—q_X^0. At that point, price is just equal to average cost, and economic profits are zero. The same condition holds initially in sector Y. The market is in zero profit equilibrium at a price of P_Y^0.

Now assume that a change in consumer preferences, or in the age distribution of the population, or in something else shifts the demand for X out to the right from D_X^0 to D_X^1. That shift drives price up to P_X^1. At the same time, since the demand for Y must decline, the demand curve for Y shifts back to the left from D_Y^0 to D_Y^1.

With the shift in demand for X, price rises to P_X^1 and profit-maximizing firms immediately increase output to q_X^1. But now there are economic profits in X, profits over and above a normal rate of return. With the downward shift of demand in Y, price falls to P_Y^1. Firms cut back to q_Y^1, and the lower price causes firms producing Y to suffer economic losses.

In the short run, adjustment is simple. Firms in both industries are constrained by their current scales of plant. Firms can neither enter nor exit their respective industries. Each firm in X raises output somewhat, from q_X^0 to q_X^1. Firms in Y cut back from q_Y^0 to q_Y^1.

In response to the existence of economic profit in sector X, the capital market begins to take notice. In Chapter 9 we said that existing firms have an incentive to expand

TABLE 12.1
Production and Consumption of Wine in the United States, 1965–1980

Year	U.S. production (millions of gallons)	Imports (millions of gallons)	Total (millions of gallons)	Consumption per capita (gallons)
1965	565	10	575	1.32
1970	713	22	735	1.52
1975	782	40	822	1.96
1980	983	91	1073	2.02
Percent Change, 1965–1980	+74.0	+810	+86.6	+53.0

Source: U.S. Department of Commerce, Bureau of the Census, *Statistical Abstract of the United States, 1985*, table 1364, p. 765.

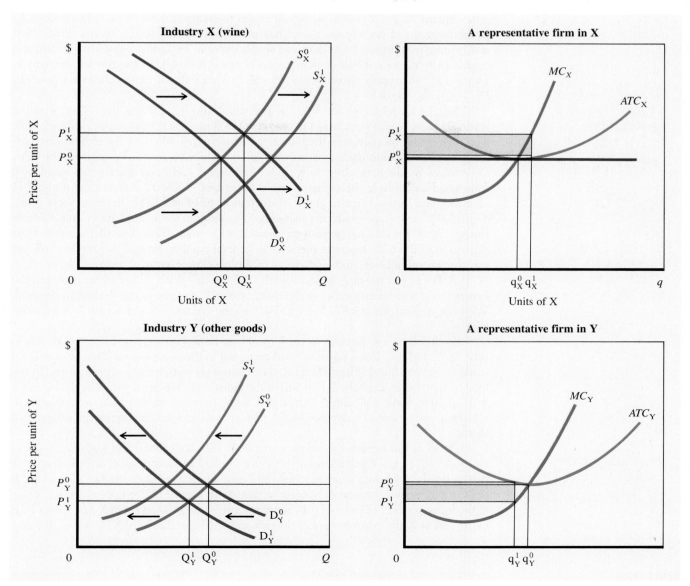

FIGURE 12.2

Adjustment in an Industry with Two Sectors

Initially demand for X shifts from D_x^0 to D_x^1. This shift pushes the price of X up to P^1, creating economic profits. Demand for Y shifts from D_y^0 to D_y^1 pushing the price of Y down to P_y^1, and creating economic losses. Firms have an incentive to leave sector Y and firms have an incentive to enter sector X. Leaving shifts supply in Y to S_y^1, raising price and eliminating losses. Entry and expansion shift supply in X to S_x^1 reducing price and eliminating profits.

in, and new firms are likely to enter, an industry in which there are economic profits to be earned. In Chapter 11, we discussed the mechanics of capital allocation in more detail. Firms in an industry that is turning economic profits find their expectations rising and undertake investment projects that look attractive. Financial analysts also see the economic profits as a signal of future healthy growth, and entrepreneurs may get interested in the industry.

Adding all this together, we would expect to see investment begin to favor sector X. In the language of economics, capital begins to flow into this sector. As new firms enter and existing firms expand, the short-run supply curve in the industry shifts to the right and continues to do so until all economic profits are eliminated. In the top left diagram in Figure 12.2, the supply curve moves from S_X^0 to S_X^1, a shift that drives price back down to P_X^0.

But let us return to the story of the wine industry. During the 1970s, demand gradually picked up. Prices began to rise, profits followed, and wine makers did very well. The high profits brought with them investment and expansion. Dozens of new vineyards set out vines in California, and a number of companies began mass production of wine.

Wine production is relatively "land intensive," and good wine is produced only from good land where the climate is right for grapes. Table 12.2 shows the number of vineyards and total acreage in grape production in 1974 and 1982. Between those years, over 10,000 new grape producers started up operations in the United States. In California alone, 150,000 additional acres were planted with vines. Thus one of the other ways expansion in the wine business affected the general equilibrium was that the land market was thrown off balance, and land prices in the good wine-growing regions increased.

Returning to the diagrams in Figure 12.2, we saw there that as sector X reaped the benefits of a shift of consumer preferences, sector Y experienced a decline in demand. With the decline, the price of Y fell to P_Y^1, creating economic losses shown in the shaded area.

In the short run, firms in sector Y must bear those losses. Some firms may decide to shut down and take losses equal to fixed costs, but in the short run we have assumed that while firms can shut down production, they cannot go completely out of business. In the long run, however, capital will flow out of the industry. Some firms will leave the business, and no new firms will enter. Firms that hang on may restrict their investments to replacing equipment as it depreciates. Certainly financial markets will not smile on such a sector.

As all of this occurs, the supply curve in Y shifts back to the left, pushing up prices and reducing losses. Capital continues to exit until all economic losses are eliminated. A new general equilibrium is not reached until equilibrium is reestablished in all markets. If costs of production remain unchanged, as they do in Figure 12.2, this equilibrium occurs at the initial product prices, but with more resources and production in X and less in Y. If expansion in X drives up the prices of resources used specifically in X, however, the cost

TABLE 12.2
Land in Grape Production in the United States and in California Alone, 1974 and 1982

	Number of vineyards	Number of acres
United States		
1974	14,208	712,804
1982	24,982	874,996
Percent change	+75.8	+22.8
California		
1974	8,333	607,011
1982	10,481	756,720
Percent change	+25.8	+24.7

Source: U.S. Department of Commerce, Bureau of the Census, Census of Agriculture (1974 and 1982), 1, part 51.

curves in X shift upward and the final, post-expansion, zero-profit equilibrium occurs at a higher price. In Chapter 9 we referred to such an industry as an *increasing-cost industry*. This is exactly what happened in the case of premier California wines.

The Importance of General Equilibrium Analysis for Policy Making: A Tax Example

Because most changes in an economy affect more than one sector, looking at just one sector of the economy using partial equilibrium analysis can be misleading. Whenever the government considers policy changes, then, it must consider their effects on general equilibrium.

Take the question of who ultimately "pays" a tax, for example. A corporation income tax is a tax on the "net income," or profit, of corporations. It does not apply to other forms of business organization (proprietorships and partnerships). As of 1988, the federal corporate tax was levied on most firms at 34 percent. (During President Reagan's two terms in office, corporate taxes took a roller coaster ride. The Economic Recovery Tax Act of 1981 sharply cut corporate taxes in the United States. But the Tax Reform Act of 1986 increased them by over $100 billion.)

For years there has been a debate about whether we should have a separate tax on corporations. If revenues must be raised, one of the things we need to know, in order to decide whether one tax is better than another, is who pays them. Certainly the corporate income tax is paid *initially* by the owners of corporations—it is levied on profits, and thus it reduces the profits that owners earn. But that is far from the end of the story. Markets and prices adjust to the presence of a tax, and its "burden" may be shifted to others, who are not directly responsible for writing the check to the Internal Revenue Service.

The corporate tax might, for example, be passed on to consumers of corporate products in the form of higher prices. It might be passed backward to workers in the form of lower wages, and so forth. To disentangle all of these effects requires *general equilibrium analysis*.

Most analyses of the corporate tax assume that there are two sectors in the economy, the corporate and noncorporate sectors (remember the sectors X and Y that we examined in connection with the wine industry). If we assume that the two sectors are in equilibrium before the tax is levied, profit rates in both sectors will be equal. Now the new tax reduces the after-tax profit rate in the corporate sector, and economic losses, or profits below normal, are the immediate result.

The differential in after-tax profits created by the tax will then cause investment and capital formation to favor the noncorporate sector. That sector will expand, and supply will shift to the right, driving down prices and reducing profits. Thus part of the burden of the corporate tax gets shifted to owners of capital in the noncorporate sector, and their profits fall. As you saw in the case of the wine industry, capital will continue to flow toward the more profitable sector until *after-tax profit rates* are equal in the two sectors.

Labor markets may also be affected. If the expanding noncorporate sector demands more labor than the contracting corporate sector, wages could actually rise. And as the corporate sector contracts, the prices of corporate products may rise relative to noncorporate products.

Because the general equilibrium effects are complex, economists strongly disagree about where the ultimate burden of the corporate income tax lies. Most believe that both the price and the wage effects of the tax are small, but that the burden is at least in part shifted outside of the corporate sector to the owners of capital in general, reducing after-tax profits in both the corporate and noncorporate sectors.

Formal Proof of a General Competitive Equilibrium

Economic theorists have struggled with the question of whether a set of prices that equates supply and demand in all markets simultaneously can actually exist when there are literally thousands and thousands of markets. If it were not possible, that could mean continuous cycles of expansion, contraction, and instability.

The nineteenth century French economist Leon Walras struggled with the problem, but he could never provide a formal proof. Using advanced mathematical tools, economists Kenneth Arrow and Gerard Debreu and mathematicians John von Neumann and Abraham Wald have now shown the existence of at least one set of prices that *will* clear all markets in a large system simultaneously.

THE EFFICIENCY OF COMPETITIVE EQUILIBRIUM

Chapters 3 through 11 in effect built a complete model of a simple, perfectly competitive system. Recall that in Chapters 4 and 5 we made a number of important assumptions. We assumed that both output markets and input markets are competitive—that is, that no individual household or firm is large enough relative to the market to have any control over price. In other words, firms and households are price-takers.

We further assumed that households have perfect information on product quality and on all prices available, and that firms have perfect knowledge of technologies and input prices. Beyond this, we said that decision makers in a competitive system always consider all the costs and benefits of their decisions, that there are no "external" costs.

We are about to argue now that *if all these assumptions hold*, the economy will produce an efficient allocation of resources. Later, as we relax these assumptions one by one, you will discover that the result is no longer efficient, and that a number of sources of market failure occur naturally.

The Idea of Allocative Efficiency

In Chapter 1 we introduced several specific criteria used by economists to judge the performance of economic systems and to evaluate alternative economic policies. These criteria are (1) *efficiency*, (2) *equity*, (3) *growth*, and (4) *stability*. In Chapter 1 you also learned a brief definition of the efficiency criterion, that is, *an efficient economy is one that produces the things that people want and does so at least cost*. The idea is that the economic system exists to serve the wants and needs of the people in a society, and if resources can be reallocated to somehow make the people "better off," they should be. We want to use the resources at our disposal to produce maximum well-being; the trick is to define "maximum well-being."

For many years, social philosophers wrestled with a problem of "aggregation." When we say "maximum well-being" we mean "maximum" *for society*. Societies are made up of many people, however, and the problem has always been how to add up satisfaction, or well-being, for *all* members of society. What has emerged is the now

Pareto efficiency, or optimality   *A condition in which no change is possible that will make some member of society better off without making some other member of society worse off.*

widely accepted concept of *allocative efficiency*, first developed by the Italian economist Vilfredo Pareto in the nineteenth century. This very precise definition of efficiency is often referred to as **"Pareto efficiency"** or **"Pareto optimality."**

Specifically, a change is said to be *efficient* if it *at least potentially* makes some members of society better off without making other members of society worse off. An efficient, or *Pareto optimal*, system is one in which no such changes are possible. An example of a change that makes some people better off and nobody worse off is a simple voluntary exchange. I have apples; you have nuts. I like nuts; you like apples. We trade. We both gain, and no one loses.

In order for such a definition to have any real meaning, of course, we have to be precise about two things: (1) what do we mean by "better off" and (2) what about changes that make some people better off and others worse off?

First of all, people *themselves* must decide what "better off" and "worse off" mean. I am the only one who knows whether I'm better off after a change, but sometimes my behavior "reveals" whether I am. If you and I exchange one item for another because I like what you have and you like what I have, we both "reveal" that we are better off after the exchange, because we agreed to it voluntarily. On a somewhat larger scale, if everyone in the neighborhood wants to have a park and they all contribute to a fund to build one, they have changed the allocation of resources, and they are clearly all better off for it.

But nearly every change that one can imagine making in an economic system leaves some people better off and some people worse off. If, because of a change, some gain and some lose, and it can be demonstrated that the value of the gains exceeds the value of the losses, then the change is said to be *potentially efficient*. In theory, if we could arrange costless transfers of income, those who gain could fully compensate those who lose, and something would be left over. In practice, however, the distinction between a *potential* and an *actual* efficient change is often ignored, and all such changes are simply called *efficient*.

A Change Justified on the Basis of Allocative Efficiency

Several years ago, in an effort to reduce state spending, the budget of the Massachusetts Registry of Motor Vehicles was cut substantially. This meant, among other things, a sharp reduction in the number of clerks in each office. Almost immediately Massachusetts residents found themselves waiting in line for hours when they had to register their automobiles or get their drivers' licenses.

Clearly, drivers and car owners began paying a price—standing in line, which uses time and energy that could otherwise be used more productively. Now before we can make sensible efficiency judgments, we must be able to *measure*, or at least *approximate*, the value of gains and losses. To approximate the losses to car owners and drivers, we might ask *how much they would be willing to pay to avoid standing in those long lines*.

In one office, estimates showed that 500 people stood in line every day for about one hour each. If each person were willing to pay just $2.00 to avoid the line, the damage imposed would be $1000 per day. If the registry were open 250 days per year, the reduction in labor force at that office alone created a cost, conservatively estimated, of $250,000 per year.

Estimates also showed that taxpayers in Massachusetts saved about $80,000 by having fewer clerks at that office. If the clerks were reinstated, there would be some gains and some losses. Car owners and drivers would gain, and taxpayers would lose. But since we can show that the value of the gains would substantially exceed the value of the losses, it can be argued that reinstating the clerks would be an *efficient change*. Note that the only *net* losers would be those taxpayers who don't own a car and don't get driver's licenses.[2]

The Efficiency of Competition

In order to demonstrate that the competitive mechanism leads to an efficient allocation of resources, we need to show that no changes are possible that will make some people better off without making others worse off. In order to do that, we need to demonstrate three things: (1) that resources are allocated among firms efficiently, (2) that final products are distributed among households so that transferring them between households won't improve well-being, and (3) that the system is producing the things that people want.

The intuitive discussion that follows does not prove that a perfectly competitive economy is efficient. It does, however, follow the basic logic of a formal proof that is highly mathematical.

Efficient Allocation of Resources Among Firms

The simple definition of efficiency holds that firms must produce their products using the best available—that is, lowest cost—technology. Clearly if more output could be produced with the same inputs, it would be possible to make some people better off without making others worse off.

The competitive model we have been using rests on several assumptions that assure us that resources in such a system would indeed be efficiently allocated among firms. Most important of these is the assumption that individual firms maximize profits. In order to maximize profit, a firm must minimize the cost of producing its chosen level of output. With a full knowledge of existing technologies, firms will choose the one that produces the output it wants at least cost.

There is more to it than that, however. Inputs must be allocated *across* firms in the best possible way. If we found it possible, for example, to take capital from firm A and swap it for labor from firm B and produce more product in both firms, then the original allocation was inefficient. Back in Chapter 2 we gave an example. Farmers in Ohio and Kansas both produce wheat and corn. The climate and soil in most of Kansas is best suited to wheat production; the climate and soil in Ohio is best suited to corn production. Clearly Kansas should produce most of the wheat and Ohio should produce most of the corn. A law that forced Kansas land into corn production and Ohio land into wheat production would result in less of both, and that would be inefficient. But if markets are free and open, Kansas farmers will naturally find a higher return by planting wheat, and Ohio farmers will find a higher return in corn. The free market, then, should lead to an efficient allocation of resources among firms.

The same argument can be made more general. Misallocation of resources among firms is unlikely as long as *every single firm* faces the same set of prices and trade-offs in input markets. Recall from Chapter 10 that firms will hire each factor of production as long as its marginal revenue product exceeds its market price. As long as all firms have access to the *same* factor markets and the *same* factor prices, a marginal unit of a factor will produce the *same* value in each firm. Certainly firms will use different technologies

---

[2]But, you might ask, aren't there other gainers and losers? What about the clerks themselves? What is normally assumed in analyses like this one is that the citizens who pay lower taxes now spend that money on other things. The producers of those other things need to expand to meet the new demand, and they hire more labor. Thus a contraction of 100 jobs in the public sector will open up 100 jobs in the private sector. If the economy is fully employed, the transfer of labor to the private sector is assumed to create no net gains or losses to the workers themselves.

and factor combinations, but at the margin, no single profit-maximizing firm can get more value out of a factor than that factor's current market price. If it could, it would—or should—have hired more of that factor in the first place.

Thus the assumptions that factor markets are competitive and open, that all firms pay the same prices for inputs, and that all firms maximize profits lead to the conclusion that the allocation of resources among firms is efficient.

Efficient Distribution of Outputs Among Households   Even if the system is producing the right things, and they are produced efficiently, they still have to get to the right people. The Boggses shouldn't end up with the things that the Mattinglys like, and the Mattinglys shouldn't end up with the things that the Boggses like. Just as open, competitive factor markets ensure that firms don't end up with the wrong inputs, open, competitive output markets ensure that households don't end up with the wrong goods and services.

Within the constraints imposed by income and wealth, households are free to choose among all the goods and services available in output markets. A household will buy a good as long as it generates utility, or subjective value, greater than its market price. Utility value is revealed in market behavior—you don't go out and get something unless you are "willing to pay" *at least* the market price.

Figure 12.3 shows a market demand curve for a good, X. Everyone who values X at more than P^* per unit buys it and gets a "surplus." Those who subjectively value it at less than P^* do not buy it. Thus an additional unit of X will never yield more value than P^* as long as everyone faces the same set of prices, that is, as long as there is no price discrimination.[3]

FIGURE 12.3
Demand Curves Reveal
Household "Willingness to Pay"

A demand curve illustrates conceptually how the market forces households to reveal their preferences. You do not get a product unless you pay for it. Those "willing to pay" as much as or more than the going price, P^*, buy it; those who are not, do not.

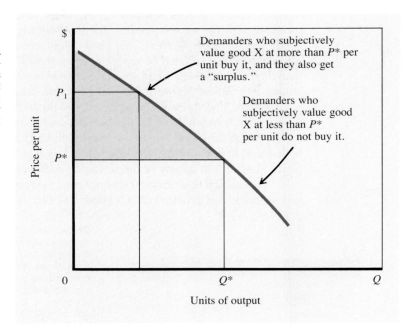

[3]Remember that the value you place on any one good depends on what you must give up to have it. The trade-offs available to you depend on your budget constraint. The trade-offs that are desirable depend on your preferences. If you buy a cassette deck costing $100.00 for your dorm room, you may be giving up a trip home. If I buy it, I may be giving up two new tires for my car. But we've both revealed that the cassette deck is worth to us at least as much as all the other things that $100.00 could buy. As long as we are free to choose among all the things that $100.00 can buy, we will not end up with the wrong things. It's not possible to find a trade that will make us both better off.

We all know that people have different tastes and preferences, and that they will buy very different things in very different combinations. But as long as everyone shops freely in the same markets, no redistribution of final outputs among people will make them better off. It is just this simple: if you and I buy in the same markets and pay the same prices, and I buy what I want and you buy what you want, neither of us can possibly end up with the wrong combination of things. *But free and open markets are essential to this result.*

Producing What People Want: The Efficient Mix of Output   It does no good to produce things efficiently or to distribute them efficiently if the system produces the wrong things. Will competitive markets produce the things that people want?

If the system is producing the wrong mix of output, we should be able to show that producing more of one good and less of another will make people better off. In order to show that perfectly competitive markets are efficient, we must demonstrate that no such changes in the final mix of output are possible.

The condition that ensures that the right things are produced is $P = MC$. That is, in the long run and in the short run, a firm will produce where the price of its output is equal to the marginal cost of production. The logic goes like this: when a firm weighs price and marginal cost, it weighs the value of its product to society *at the margin* against the value of the things that could otherwise be produced with the same resources. If some product is worth more to people than what otherwise could be produced with the same resources, then competition ensures that that product will be produced instead of those other things. Figure 12.4 summarizes this logic graphically.

But this is true *only if price is a good measure of the worth of a good to society and if* marginal cost *is a good measure of the value of the things that might otherwise be produced with the same resources*. We have already made the argument that price *is* a good measure of the worth of a marginal unit of a good or service to society. Anyone who subjectively values a good or service at more than P^* buys it; anyone who values it less than P^* does not buy it. Thus, when a *marginal* unit of product is produced, the person or household that ends up with it is that person or household that values it just at P^*.

To see that this is so, imagine supply expanding by one unit. Price will drop an infinitesimal amount to clear the market, and someone—some person or household which, before the supply expansion, was indifferent between buying and not buying—will be induced to buy just that one unit. All of this is to say that P^* is a good measure of the actual "benefit" to society of producing an additional unit of product X.

To establish that marginal cost is a good measure of the societal cost, or opportunity cost, of additional production of a good, let's turn back to input markets. Resources are

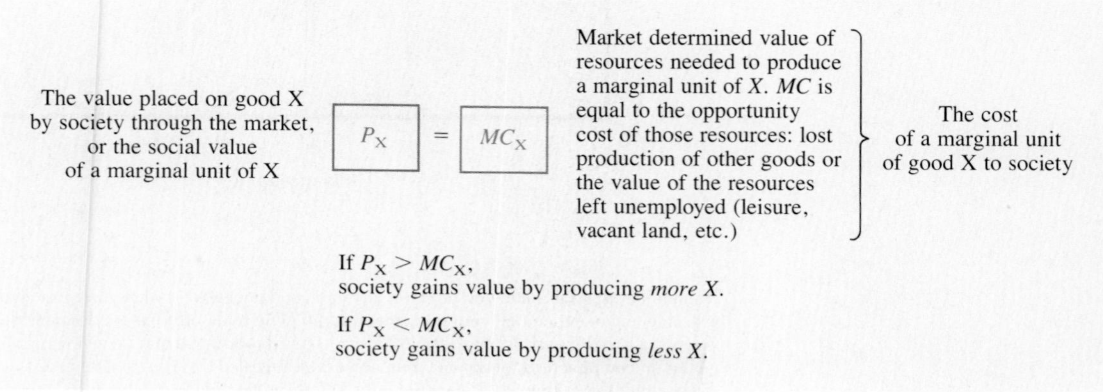

The value placed on good X by society through the market, or the social value of a marginal unit of X

$$P_X = MC_X$$

Market determined value of resources needed to produce a marginal unit of X. *MC* is equal to the opportunity cost of those resources: lost production of other goods or the value of the resources left unemployed (leisure, vacant land, etc.)

The cost of a marginal unit of good X to society

If $P_X > MC_X$, society gains value by producing *more* X.

If $P_X < MC_X$, society gains value by producing *less* X.

FIGURE 12.4
The Key Condition: Price Equals Marginal Cost
Society will produce the efficient mix of output if all firms equate price and marginal cost.

required to produce an added unit of output. Those resources come from one of two sources: either they were previously *unused*, or *unemployed*, or they were used, or employed, *but in the production of some other good or service.*

Consider labor as an example of a factor that would otherwise have been employed producing something else. Recall that workers are paid a wage just equal to marginal revenue product, which in competitive markets is the value of the marginal product of labor ($W = MRP_L = P_X \cdot MP_L$). Thus if a certain amount of *labor* is drawn out of the production of good Y, what is lost to society is an amount of *product* Y equal in value to the value of the labor withdrawn.

At equilibrium, with many firms each buying labor up to the point where $W=MRP_L$, if a unit of labor is attracted from one firm to another, it is because the *product* of that unit of labor is valued more highly there. If all resources are valued in competitive markets, the marginal cost of a unit of output is just equal to the value of the goods that otherwise would have been produced with the same inputs.

Again using labor as the example, consider what happens with resources that would otherwise have been *unemployed*. If each firm equates the market clearing wage to the value of labor's marginal product, and a person *chooses* not to be in the labor force, that person reveals that either leisure or the value of nonpaid labor is worth more to him or her than the value that society places on his or her potential product in the market. It is therefore efficient *not* to work. (This, by the way, does not hold when markets do not clear, as in the case of *involuntary unemployment.*)

Thus if you are voluntarily unemployed, or out of the labor force, and you get attracted into a job producing goods or services for the market, you are giving up leisure that is less valuable to you than the wage you are paid. Those who value leisure more highly will not take a job; those who place an even lower value on leisure are already working.

Marginal cost, then, is a good measure of what society *gives up* by using resources to produce more of a good or service. Staying with the example of labor, if the resources needed to produce something come from the production of something else, MC measures the value of the *product* given up; if those resources were previously unused, MC measures the value of *leisure* that is given up.

The reasoning then, is that because competitive firms will produce as long as the price of their product is greater than the marginal cost of production, they will produce as long as a gain for society is possible. That is, if society values good X more than it values good Y or what otherwise would be produced with the same resources, then more X will indeed be produced. The market guarantees that the right things are produced, and therefore competitive markets yield an efficient mix of output.[4]

Note that by this same reasoning, however, if the price of some good ends up above the marginal cost of production at equilibrium, additional production will provide benefits in excess of the real costs to society. This means that the good is being underproduced and that the outcome is *inefficient*. Figure 12.4 also covers this point.

Figure 12.5 shows how a simple market system leads individual households and firms to make efficient choices in input and output markets. For simplicity, the figure assumes only one factor of production, labor. Households weigh the market wage against the value of leisure and time spent in unpaid household production. But the wage is a measure of labor's potential product, because firms weigh labor cost (wages) against the

[4]It is important to understand that firms do not act consciously to balance social costs and benefits. The assumption is, in fact, that firms are self-interested, private profit-maximizers. It just works out that in perfectly competitive markets, when firms are weighing private benefits against private costs, they are actually, perhaps without knowing it, weighing the benefits and costs to society as well.

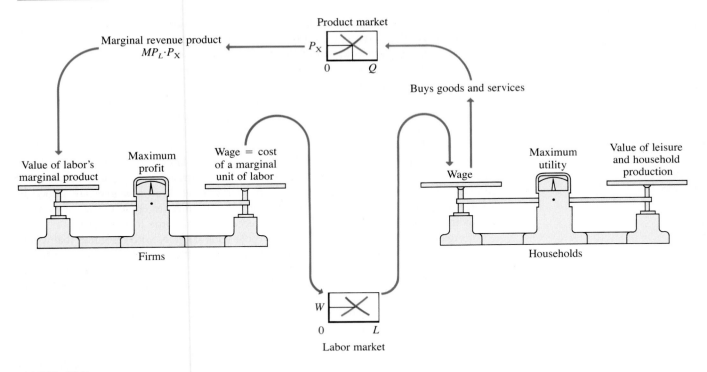

FIGURE 12.5
Efficiency Follows from a Weighing of Values by both Households and Firms

For simplicity assume that there is just one variable factor of production, labor. Households are presumed to weigh the value of market produced goods against the value of leisure and household production. To buy products, households must earn income from wages. But, since firms weigh the cost of labor, as reflected in wages, against the value of labor's product, households are actually weighing the value of leisure and home production against the value of what they would produce ($W=MP_L \cdot P_x$) if they entered the labor force. The result is an efficient balance in both product and input markets.

value of the product produced and hire up to the point that $W=MRP_L$. Households use wages to buy market-produced goods. Thus households implicitly weigh the value of market-produced goods against the value of leisure and household production.

When a *firm's* scale is balanced, it is earning maximum profit; when a *household's* scale is balanced, it is maximizing utility. No changes can then improve social welfare.

"Perfect Competition" versus Real Markets

So far, we have built a model of a *perfectly competitive market system* that produces an efficient allocation of resources, an efficient mix of output, and an efficient distribution of output. But the perfectly competitive model is built on a set of assumptions, all of which must hold for the result to have meaning. We have assumed that all firms and households are price-takers in input and output markets, that firms and households have perfect information, that no external effects exist, that all firms maximize profits, and so forth.

But these assumptions do not always hold in real-world markets. When they do not, the conclusion that free, unregulated markets will produce an efficient outcome breaks down. The remainder of this chapter discusses some inefficiencies that occur naturally in markets and some of the strengths, as well as the weaknesses, of the market mechanism. We also discuss the usefulness of the competitive model for understanding the economy.

THE ECONOMICS OF MARKET FAILURE

Market failure   What happens when some malfunction in the market mechanism results in a misallocation or unproductive use of resources, that is, in inefficiency.

In suggesting some of the problems encountered in real markets and some of their possible solutions, the rest of this chapter previews the next major section of this book. Here we briefly outline four major sources of **market failure**: (1) *imperfect market structure*, or noncompetitive behavior, (2) the existence of *"public goods,"* (3) the presence of *"external costs and benefits,"* and (4) *imperfect information*. Each of these phenomena results from the failure of one of the assumptions basic to the perfectly competitive model, and each is discussed in more detail in later chapters. Each also points to a potential role for government in the economy. The desirability and extent of actual government involvement in the economy is, as you are no doubt already aware, a hotly debated subject.

Imperfect Markets

Imperfectly competitive industry   An industry in which single firms can raise the price of their products without losing all demand for those products.

Up until now we have operated on the assumption that the number of buyers and sellers in each market is large. When each buyer and each seller is only one of a great many in the market, no single one of them can independently influence price. Thus all economic decision makers are by virtue of their relatively small size forced to take input prices and output prices as given. When this assumption of perfect competition is relaxed, and we examine the behavior of firms that have a degree of control over price and potential competition, the result is **imperfect competition** and an *inefficient allocation of resources*.

A Kansas wheat farmer is probably a "price-taker," but IBM, Xerox, and AT&T most certainly are not. Many firms in many industries do have some control over price. The degree of control that is possible depends on the character of competition in the industry itself.

Pure monopoly   An industry made up of only one firm that produces a product for which there are no close substitutes and in which significant barriers exist to prevent new firms from entering the industry.

An industry with just a single firm producing a product for which there are no close substitutes is called a **monopoly**. While a monopoly has no other firms to compete with, it is still constrained by market demand. To be successful, the firm still has to produce something that people want. Essentially, a monopoly must choose both price and quantity of output simultaneously because the amount that it will be able to sell depends on the price it sets. If the price is too high, it will sell nothing. Presumably a monopolist sets price in order to maximize profit. That price is generally significantly above average costs, and such a firm usually earns economic profits.

In competition, economic profits will attract the entry of new firms hungry for the business. A rational monopolist without government restraint does everything possible to block any such entry in order to preserve economic profits in the long run. As a result, society loses the benefits of more product and lower prices. A number of **barriers to entry** can be raised. Sometimes a monopoly is actually licensed by government, and entry into its market is prohibited by law. Taiwan has only one beer company; most areas in the United States have only one local telephone company. Sometimes the cost of starting up is extraordinarily high and the established firm is well known. Ownership of a natural resource can be the source of monopoly power as well. If I buy up all the coal mines in the United States and I persuade Congress to restrict imports, no one can enter the coal industry and compete with me.

Between monopoly and perfect competition are a number of other imperfectly competitive market structures. *Oligopolistic industries* are made up of a small number of firms, each with a degree of price-setting power. *Monopolistically competitive industries* are made up of a large number of firms that acquire price-setting power by differentiating their products or by establishing a brand name. Only General Mills can produce Wheaties, for example, and only Miles Laboratories can produce Alka-Seltzer. What all imperfectly competitive industries have in common is that *output is lower*—the product is underproduced—and *price is higher* than it would be under perfect competition. The condition $P=MC$ no longer holds, and the system no longer produces the most efficient product mix.

In the United States, many forms of noncompetitive behavior are illegal. The Sherman Act of 1890 makes "combinations or conspiracies in restraint of trade" illegal. A firm that attempts to monopolize an industry or conspires with other firms to reduce competition risks serious penalties. The Clayton Act of 1914 strengthened the Sherman Act and made a few more things explicitly illegal, such as buying the stock of competitive firms, interlocking boards of directors, and price discrimination. The most famous recent antitrust case ended in 1982 with the breakup of the American Telephone and Telegraph Company. The case was originally filed in 1974 by the Justice Department, charging that AT&T had used its power to freeze out competition in the long-distance and equipment markets. Again, this sort of behavior prevents society from enjoying the benefits of free competition and thus the right mix of output and prices that reflect true cost.

This, however, provides just a glimpse of imperfect competition. All of this is discussed in much more detail in chapters 13, 14, and 15.

Public Goods

A second major source of market failure is that private producers simply do not find it in their best interest to produce everything that members of society want. More specifically there is a whole class of goods, called **public goods,** or **social goods,** that will be underproduced or not produced at all in a completely unregulated market economy.[5]

Public goods *Goods or services that bestow collective benefits on members of society; they are, in a sense, collectively consumed. Generally, since benefits are collective, one cannot be excluded from enjoying them once they are produced. The classic example is national defense.*

Public goods are goods or services that bestow collective benefits on society; they are, in a sense, collectively consumed. The classic example is national defense, but there are countless others—police protection, preservation of wilderness lands, and public health, to name a few. Some public goods, such as national defense, benefit the whole nation. Others, such as clean air, may be limited to smaller areas—the air may be clean in a Kansas town but dirty in a Southern California city.

The difficulty with a public good is that in general everyone gets to consume it, whether they pay for it or not. Once the good is produced, no one can be excluded from enjoying its benefits. Producers of **private goods,** like hamburgers, can make a profit because they don't hand over the product until you pay for it. (Chapters 4–11 of this book have been about the production of *private* goods, products produced by firms for sale to individual households.)

If the provision of public goods were simply left to private, profit-seeking producers with no power to force payment, a dilemma would be encountered. Suppose I value some

---

[5]While they are normally referred to as public *goods*, many of the things we are talking about are *services*.

public good, X; if there were a functioning market for it, I would be willing to pay for it. Now suppose that I am asked to contribute voluntarily to the production of X. Should I contribute? Perhaps I should on moral grounds, but not on the basis of pure self-interest. There is absolutely no contingency associated with paying. First, since I can't be excluded for nonpayment, I get the good whether I pay or not. Second, my contribution, no matter how large it seems *to me*, is so small that it will not affect the level of output.

Thus private provision of public goods fails. A completely laissez-faire market system will not produce everything that all members of a society might want. Citizens must band together to ensure that desired public goods are produced, and this is generally accomplished through government provision financed with taxes. The purpose of government provision is to correct for a naturally occurring failure of the market to produce everything that consumers want. (Public goods are the subject of Chapter 16.)

Externalities

Externality *A cost or benefit resulting from some activity or transaction that is imposed or bestowed upon parties external to the activity or transaction. Sometimes called spillovers or third-party effects. Often externalities are in the form of public goods, falling collectively on many people.*

A third major flaw in the market is the existence of external costs and benefits. By **externality** we mean some cost or benefit imposed or bestowed on an individual or group that is outside, or external to, the transaction—in other words, something that affects a third party. In an urban society, external effects are pervasive, more the rule than the exception. The classic example is pollution, but there are thousands of others, such as airport noise, traffic accidents, loud radios, congestion, and painting your house a color that the neighbors think is ugly—or unhistorical.

Not all externalities are negative. Housing investment, for example, may yield benefits for neighbors. Operating a farm near a city provides residents in the area with nice views, fresher air, and a less congested environment.

Externalities are a problem only if decision makers do not take them into account. The logic of efficiency presented in the previous section of this chapter required that firms weigh social benefits against social costs. If a firm in a competitive environment produced a good, it was because the value of a good to society exceeded the social cost of producing it—that is the logic of $P=MC$. If social costs or benefits are overlooked or left out of the calculations, the decisigns that result are likely to be wrong, or inefficient.

The market itself has no automatic mechanism that provides decision makers with an incentive to consider external effects. Society, however, through government, established over the years a number of different institutions for dealing with externalities. Tort law, for example, is a body of legal rules that deal with third-party effects. Under certain circumstances, those who impose costs are held strictly liable for them; in other circumstances, liability is only assessed if the cost resulted from "negligent" behavior. Tort law deals with small problems as well as larger ones. If a neighbor sprays her lawn with a powerful chemical and kills off your prize shrub, you can take her to court and force her to pay for it. If an oil tanker springs a leak and thousands of gallons of black oil are washed ashore, fouling the beaches, the owners of beach front property can take the shipping company to court and force payment for damages.

The effects of externalities can be enormous. The case that received the most attention during the early 1980s was the problem of acid rain. Many factories and power plants in the Midwest burn coal and emit waste products containing sulphur compounds. In the atmosphere, these compounds mix with water and produce sulfuric acid that is carried north and east by the prevailing winds.

This means that for some years the rain in Canada and in the northeastern United States has had a high acid content. The potential damage from acid rain over a long

External Effects and Efficiency

The analysis presented in this chapter indicates that a competitive market structure will lead to an efficient allocation of resources when decision makers weigh the costs and benefits of their decisions. Unfortunately, decision makers do not always have a natural incentive to do so. The following article describes the inefficiency that can result.

EXTERNAL EFFECTS CAN DISTORT RESOURCE USE

Even with such a simple resource as residential land, we often find that a system of individual ownership needs public regulation because of "external effects." One person's use of a natural resource can inflict damage on other people who have no way of securing compensation, and who may not even know that they are being damaged. We would like to insure that each resource is allocated to that use in which its net social value is highest. But if the full costs of some use of a resource do not fall upon the private owner or public decision-maker, but upon someone else, then the resource is unlikely to find its way into its socially best use. We could not allow pig farmers to bid freely for residential land, for example. (There is a symmetrical case where use of a resource confers external benefits that cannot be captured by the owner or decision-maker.)

We are used to these consequences of "external effects." I mean that we are accustomed to them as citizens, and we understand them as economists. But economists realize, as citizens sometimes do not, that the implications of external effects must be traced further. They have secondary effects on the system of resource allocation. If electric power is "too cheap" to the customer, because he is not charged with its full social cost, then other things will happen. Other commodities that are produced with the help of large amounts of electric power will also be cheap, and they will be overproduced. Other industries will be tempted to adopt techniques of production that use more electric power than they would if the price of electric power were higher. The rest of the society will find itself subsidizing those people—if they are an identifiable group—who consume a lot of electricity or a lot of goods made with a lot of electricity.

Similarly, if society is in fact subsidizing the private automobile —by not charging it for all the damage it does—then the location patterns of suburbs and of industry will be affected. A change in the private costs of automobile travel will have effects on house rents, residential choices, and eventually on the location of industry. If the use of DDT and other toxic chlorinated hydrocarbons were prohibited, or merely made more expensive, one would naturally expect certain changes in food prices and availability. But there might also be corresponding effects on the regional distribution of income and population, and these in turn might have further consequences difficult to calculate.

Source: From 'Robert Solow, "The Economists' Approach to Pollution and its Control," *Science*, August 1971.

period of time is very high. There is evidence now that it may be killing fish in lakes and rivers, defoliating forests, causing serious damage to buildings, and so forth. The Canadian Prime Minister has been to Washington on several occasions looking for a response from the U.S. government. Estimates of potential damage from acid rain run into billions and billions of dollars.

Another recent example of an externality with potentially horrifying damages is toxic waste dumping. For years, companies piled chemical wastes indiscriminately into dump sites near water supplies and residential areas. In some locations, those wastes seeped into the ground and contaminated the drinking water. In the Love Canal case in New York State, an entire community was forced to move and abandon its homes. Had those potential costs been considered at the time the dumping took place, the chemicals would not have been disposed of in this fashion and enormous damages would have been avoided.

Economists have for years suggested that a carefully designed set of taxes and subsidies could help to "internalize" these external effects. For example, if a paper mill was polluting the air and waterways, and it was taxed in proportion to the damage actually caused by that pollution, it would consider those costs in its decisions.

Sometimes, interaction among and between parties can lead to the proper consideration of externality without government involvement. If someone plays her radio loudly on the fourth floor of your dormitory, that person imposes an externality. The residents, however, can get together and negotiate a set of mutually acceptable rules. In a now-famous article published in 1960, Ronald Coase pointed out that where small numbers of people are involved, the parties can indeed get together and bargain or negotiate, a process that will lead to full consideration of external costs and benefits.[6]

Calculating damages from externalities in dollar terms is a difficult task, but often it is unavoidable. Judges in liability cases are forced to make judgments of this sort all the time. Public policies to deal with problems like acid rain will hurt one sector at the expense of another. If the costs of acid rain are as large as some suggest, for example, imposing them on industrial firms in the Midwest will make it very difficult for many of them to survive. Installing air "scrubbers" to take out the troublesome particulates is so costly that some firms simply cannot do it. If a large plant is forced out of business, people will be unemployed. If a power plant must install every possible measure to reduce pollution, electric bills will rise sharply. Unless absolute rights are involved, gains and losses must be *weighed*. There are no easy answers.

For our purposes here, the point is that the market does not always force consideration of all the costs and benefits of decisions. Yet for an economy to achieve an efficient allocation of resources, all of them must be weighed. We will discuss externalities in more detail in Chapter 16.

Imperfect Information

A fourth major source of market failure is **imperfect information** on the part of buyers and sellers. The conclusion that markets work efficiently rests heavily on the assumption that consumers and producers have full knowledge of product characteristics, available prices, and so forth. The absence of full information can, of course, lead to transactions that are ultimately disadvantageous.

Some products are so complex that consumers find it difficult to judge the potential benefits and costs of purchase. Certainly demanders in the market for medical care do not fully understand what they buy. Buyers of life insurance have a very difficult time sorting out exactly what the terms of the more complex policies are and what the true "price" of the product is. Consumers of almost any service that requires expertise, such as plumbing or TV repair, have a hard time evaluating what is needed, much less how well it is done.

Some forms of misinformation can be corrected with simple rules such as "truth-in-advertising" regulations. In some cases, the government provides information to citizens; there are job banks and consumer information services. In some industries, such as medical care, there is no clear-cut solution to the problem of noninformation or misinformation.

Is the Market Mechanism Good or Bad?

Where does all of this leave us? Is the market system good or bad? Should the government be involved in the economy, or should it leave the allocation of resources to the free market? So far, our information is mixed and incomplete. To the extent that the perfectly competitive model reflects the way markets really operate, there seem to be some clear advantages to the system. On the other hand, when we relax the assumptions and expand the model to include noncompetitive behavior, public goods, externalities, and the possibility of imperfect information, we see at least a potential role for government.

[6]Ronald Coase, "The Problem of Social Cost," *Journal of Law and Economics*, (1960).

The market system does seem to provide most participants with the incentive to weigh costs and benefits in an efficient way. Firms can make profits only if there is a demand for their products. If there are no externalities, or if such costs or benefits are properly internalized, firms *will* weigh social benefits and costs in their production decisions. And the profit motive should provide competitive firms with an incentive to minimize cost and to produce their products using the most efficient technologies. Likewise, competitive input markets should provide households with the incentive to weigh the value of their time against the social value of what they can produce in the labor force.

But markets are far from perfect. Market failure occurs for a number of reasons that might be at least partially influenced by government involvement in the economy.

The answer to the opening question is at this point incomplete for yet another reason. Thus far we have discussed only the criterion of efficiency, and economic systems and economic policies must be judged by many other criteria, not the least of which is *equity*, or *fairness*. Indeed, some contend that the outcome of any free market is unfair, because some get very rich and others cannot get by.

The chapters that follow explore many of these issues in more depth. In Chapter 13, we begin with a discussion of output and pricing decisions in monopoly markets.

PERFECT COMPETITION AS A STARTING POINT

In this chapter we have wrapped up the model of perfect competition described in detail in the last eight chapters. In discussing the idea of "general equilibrium," we saw how the markets described separately in earlier chapters are all interrelated and how adjustments in any one of them can cause subsequent adjustments in many or all of the others. In order to understand the way any economic system functions and to think properly about public policy issues, it is essential to consider these interconnections. Partial equilibrium analysis can lead to wrong answers.

We also turned for the first time to *normative economics*. We began by defining again the concept of *efficiency*. Next, we took an intuitive look at the efficiency of the perfectly competitive system. Under all the assumptions of perfect competition, the result is efficient. No changes could be made in the allocation of resources among firms, in the mix of output or in the distribution of output among members of society, that would even potentially make some better off without making some worse off.

But these assumptions simply do not hold in the real world. When we relax them in order to describe the world more accurately, we see some of the problems that the unconstrained market does not solve for itself.

SUMMARY

1. Chapters 6-11 built a model of a perfectly competitive market economy in which firms and households interact in output markets and input markets.

2. Both firms and households make simultaneous choices in both input and output markets. For example, input prices determine output costs and affect output supply decisions of firms; wages in the labor market affect labor supply decisions, income, and ultimately how much output households can and do purchase.

3. A *general equilibrium* exists when all markets in an economy are in simultaneous equilibrium.

4. When an event disturbs the equilibrium in one market, it may disturb many other markets as well. Partial equilibrium analysis can be misleading, because it looks only at adjustments in one market in isolation. But an increase in the preference for wine may affect the market for beer, for grapes, for land in California, for farm workers, and so forth. The imposition of a tax on corporate profits may

affect the earnings of shareholders, the wages of workers, and the prices of products, among many other things.

5. An efficient economy is one that produces the goods and services that people want, and does so at least cost. Specifically, a change is said to be efficient if it at least potentially makes some members of society better off without making others worse off. An efficient, or Pareto optimal, system is one in which no such changes are possible.

6. If a change makes some people better off and some people worse off, but it can be shown that the value of the gains exceeds the value of the losses, the change is said to be potentially efficient.

7. If all the assumptions of perfect competition held, the result would be an efficient, or Pareto optimal, allocation of resources.

8. To prove the last statement, it is necessary to show that resources are allocated efficiently among firms, that final products are distributed efficiently among households, and that the system is producing what people want.

9. When the assumptions of perfect competition do *not* hold, the conclusion that free, unregulated markets will produce an efficient allocation of resources breaks down.

10. Monopolists have an incentive to block the entry of competitors to protect economic profits. If they are successful, consumers are deprived of the lower prices and additional product that competition would bring. Clearly these results are inefficient.

11. Public, or social, goods bestow collective benefits on members of society. Because benefits are collective, people in most cases cannot be excluded from enjoying them for nonpayment, as they can be with private goods. Thus private firms do not find it profitable to produce public goods, and this results in inefficiency.

12. Externalties are costs or benefits that are imposed or bestowed on an individual or group that is outside, or external to, the transaction—in other words, something that affects a third party. If such social costs or benefits are over looked or left out of the calculations, the decisions of households or firms are likely to be wrong, or inefficient.

13. Market efficiency depends on the assumption that buyers have perfect information on product quality and price and that firms have perfect information on input quality and price. Clearly, misinformation can lead to bad choices and inefficiency.

REVIEW CONCEPTS

partial equilibrium   281
general equilibrium   281
efficiency   281
pareto efficiency, or optimality   289
market failure   295
imperfect competition   295

monopoly   295
barriers to entry   295
public goods, or social goods   296
private goods   296
externality   297
imperfect information   299

REVIEW QUESTIONS

1. Consider the market for personal computers that began booming during the late 1970s. In what ways did that boom affect the labor market? What new skills were demanded? How were those skills produced? Suppose John just bought a PC for $3000. If PC's didn't exist, how might John have spent the same $3000? What happens to employment in the sectors where those things are produced?

2. A major source of chicken feed in the United States is anchovies, small fish that can be scooped up out of the ocean at low cost. Every seven years, the anchovies disappear to spawn, and producers must turn to grain, which is more expensive, to feed their chickens. What is likely to happen to the cost of chicken? What are substitutes for chicken? How are those markets affected? Name some complements to chicken. How are those markets affected? How might the allocation of farm land be changed as a result?

3. Suppose two passengers both end up with a reservation for the last seat on a train from San Francisco to Los Angeles. Two alternatives are proposed:
   a. Toss a coin.
   b. Sell the ticket to the highest bidder.
      Compare the two from the standpoint of efficiency and equity.

4. Assume that there are two sectors in an economy: housing (H) and other goods (X). Assume that housing services are produced with capital alone and no labor. Describe the adjustments that would take place if a tax was levied on profits in the housing sector. Who would end up bearing the burden of such a tax? In your answer, talk about the adjustment that you would expect in capital, labor, and output markets.

5. In Chapter 9 we argued that when a firm employs just one variable factor of production, the condition $W = MRP$ and the

condition $P=MC$ are "the same condition"—that is, these two equations say the same thing. Explain why the condition $P=MC$ ensures that the system will produce the right mix of output. Using similar logic, use the condition $W=MRP$ to explain why household decisions about whether to work or to consume leisure are efficient if markets are competitive.

6. If the private market doesn't produce public goods in efficient quantities, how might society go about ensuring adequate production? How would the public goods be paid for? What problems are there with your method of provision? How do you find out what public goods people want? Is that easy or difficult? Why?

7. Explain carefully how a tax can correct for an external cost. Next, explain how a subsidy can correct for an external benefit.

13 Imperfect Competition: Monopoly Markets

Since Chapter 6, we have devoted most of our attention to building a model of an economy made up of *perfectly competitive markets*. In order to do this, we had to make some fairly restrictive assumptions, and in Chapter 12 we began to see what happens when we relax one or another of them.

A number of very important assumptions underlie the logic of perfect competition. One is that a large number of firms and households are interacting in each market. Another is that firms in a given market produce undifferentiated, or homogeneous, products. Taken together, these two conditions limit the choices that firms find open to them. With many firms in each market, no single firm has any control over market prices. Single firms may decide how much to produce and how to produce it, but the market determines output price. We also assumed that new firms are free to enter industries and to compete for profits. This assumption led us to conclude that opportunities for economic profit are eliminated in the long run as competition drives price to a level equal to the average cost of production.

In the next three chapters, we relax these basic assumptions as we explore the important implications, both positive and normative, that follow. As we said we would in Chapter 12, here we look closely at the behavior of firms that *do* control the character of what they produce and that *do* have some control over the prices of their products. We also look at the behavior of firms in industries with few firms and with barriers to the entry of new firms.

IMPERFECT COMPETITION AND MARKET POWER

Imperfectly competitive industry An industry in which single firms exercise some degree of market power. A firm exercises market power when it is able to raise the price of its product without losing all of its demand.

A market, or industry, in which individual firms have some control over price is **imperfectly competitive**. Under imperfect competition, all successful firms have one thing in common: they exercise **market power**, that is, the ability to raise price without losing all demand for their product.

Imperfect competition does not mean that there is *no* competition, of course. In fact, in some imperfectly competitive markets, competition takes place in even *more* arenas than it does when there is perfect competition. Firms can differentiate their products, improve quality, market aggressively, cut prices, and so forth.

Getting and Keeping Market Power

In order for a firm to exercise control over the price of its product, it must be able to *limit competition*. If your firm produces sweatbands, and if other firms can enter freely into the sweatband industry and produce exactly the same sweatbands that you produce, the result will be just what we have spent the last seven chapters describing: the price of sweatbands will be driven down to their average cost, and economic profits will be eliminated.

If your firm can prevent other firms from producing exactly the same sweatbands, however, or if it can prevent other firms from entering the market, then it has a chance of preserving its economic profits. At one extreme is a *pure monopoly*. A monopoly is an industry with a *single firm*, in which the entry of new firms is blocked. There are a number of ways that a single firm monopolizing the industry may be able to set barriers in the way of firms that wish to begin producing competitive products.

But a firm need not be a monopolist to exercise market power. An *oligopoly* is an industry in which there are a small number of firms, each large enough to have an impact on market price. To preserve their market power in the long run, of course, oligopolists too must erect barriers to entry. When new firms producing the exact same product can enter the market freely, no one has market power.

Even when an industry has a large number of firms, individual firms may still be able to acquire market power. Establishing a brand name, getting a reputation for producing high-quality products, or acquiring a patent have the effect of creating a somewhat separate market for the products of a single firm. Even though there are many close substitutes, only Procter & Gamble can produce Ivory Soap. In a sense, P&G monopolizes the market for Ivory Soap—entry to this market is legally blocked by their copyright on the brand name. Firms that differentiate their products in industries that have many producers and free entry are called *monopolistic competitors* (review Table 3.1).

Industry Boundaries

We can say that a monopoly is an industry with just one firm, and an oligopoly is an industry with just a few competitors, but where do we set the boundary of an industry? For example, while it is true that Procter & Gamble is the only firm that can produce Ivory Soap, there are many other brands of soap. The ease with which consumers can substitute for a product limits the extent to which a monopolist can exercise market power. By the same token, the more broadly a market is defined, the more difficult it becomes to find substitutes.

Consider hamburger, for example. A single firm that produces Brand X hamburger faces stiff competition from other hamburger sellers, even though it is the only producer of Brand X. It has no market power, because near-perfect substitutes are available. If a firm were the *only* producer of hamburger, however, or better yet, the only producer of beef, it would have more market control, because fewer, or no, alternatives would be available. When fewer substitutes exist, a monopolist has more power to raise price, because demand is less elastic, as Figure 13.1 shows. A monopolist that produced *all food* would exercise enormous market power because there are no substitutes at all for food as a category.

Pure monopoly   An industry with a single firm that produces a product for which there are no close substitutes and in which significant barriers prevent other firms from entering to compete away profits.

To be meaningful, therefore, our definition of a monopolistic industry must be more precise. A **pure monopoly**, then, is an industry with a single firm that produces a product for which there are no close substitutes and in which there are significant barriers to entry.

Barriers to Entry

Barriers to entry   Those factors that prevent new firms from entering an industry in which economic profits are being earned.

Firms that already have market power can preserve it either by preventing other firms from producing an exact duplicate of their product or by preventing firms from entering the industry. A number of potential **barriers to entry** can be raised.

Legal Barriers: Government Franchises   Many firms are monopolies by virtue of government directive. Local telephone-operating companies, for example, are granted exclusive licenses by states to provide "local exchange service." No other firms are permitted to offer telephone service within specific local areas. State governments also grant electric companies the sole right to supply power within given areas. The usual

FIGURE 13.1

The Boundary of a Market and Elasticity

In a sense, we can define an industry as broadly or narrowly as we like. The more broadly we define it, however, the fewer substitutes there are, and the less elastic demand is likely to be. A monopoly is an industry with one firm that produces a product for which there are *no close substitutes*. The producer of Brand X hamburger cannot properly be called a monopolist.

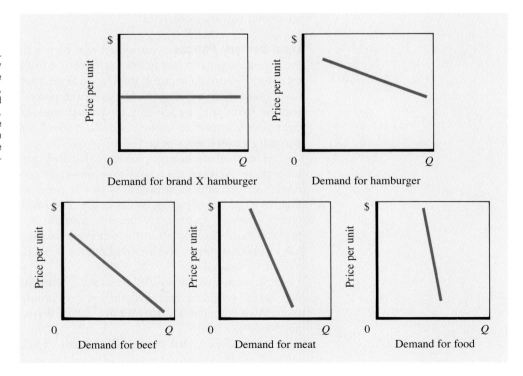

reasoning offered to defend granting this kind of monopoly power by **government franchise** is that it is more efficient for a single firm to produce the particular product—usually a service—than it is for many firms to duplicate it. If very large economies of scale are possible, it makes no sense to have many small firms each producing the same thing at much higher unit costs. These so-called "natural monopolies" are discussed more formally at the end of this chapter.

Usually governments regulate monopolies to which they have granted exclusive licenses. Public utility commissions in each state watch over electric companies and locally operating telephone companies. One of their responsibilities, for example, is to regulate the prices charged by these utilities to insure that they don't abuse their monopoly power.

Large economies of scale are not the only reason that governments grant monopoly licenses. A monopoly is easier to control than a competitive industry. Iowa, Maine, New Hampshire, Ohio, and some other states, for example, permit liquor to be sold only through state-controlled and -managed liquor stores. Many states have state-run lotteries; competition exists, but it is illegal. When large economies of scale do not exist in an industry, the logic for having government-run monopolies is less solid. One possibility is that the state wants to prevent private parties from encouraging, and profiting from, sin. Another is that government monopolies are a convenient source of revenues; how can anyone criticize the state-licensed, implicit taxation of drinking and gambling!

Fairness, or equity, is another frequently offered justification for the operation of a government-regulated monopoly. Technological progress in the telecommunications industry has reduced the advantages that come from size, but states are clearly not ready to open local exchange service to competition. The reason is that states want to insure that everyone has access to a telephone at affordable rates. In most states, private households are provided with telephone service at a price below the cost of producing it, and local telephone companies earn the bulk of their profits from business users, who are charged a price above cost. Obviously, then, deregulating local service would mean higher telephone bills for households.

Legal Barriers: Patents Another legal barrier that prevents entry into an industry is the invention **patent** that grants exclusive use of the patented product or process to the inventor. Patents are issued in the United States under authority of Article I, Section 8, of the Constitution, which gives Congress the power to "promote the progress of science and the useful arts, by securing for limited times to authors and inventors the exclusive right to their respective writings and discoveries." Patent protection in the United States is currently granted for a period of 17 years.

The thinking behind patents is that they provide an incentive for invention and innovation. New products and new processes come from research and development undertaken by individual inventors and by firms. Research requires resources and time that have opportunity costs. Without the protection that a patent provides, the results of research would immediately become available to the general public, and very little research would be done. On the other side of the coin, however, patents do serve as a barrier to competition, and they do keep the benefits of research from flowing through the market to consumers.

Suppose that the industry producing blank video tape cassettes is competitive, and that the full economic cost (including normal profit) of producing video cassettes is $5.00 each. With competition, market price will be driven to average cost, and consumers will pay $5.00 per tape.

Now suppose that the BASF company develops a new type of tape material that makes it possible to produce tapes of equal quality for $3.00. With no patent protection, every company in the industry will quickly analyze the material and begin producing tapes at a cost of $3.00. Soon competition will drive the price of tapes to $3.00, and consumers will enjoy the full benefits of the new technology. But that would take away BASF's incentive to do research on new materials.

If, instead, BASF can protect its new material with a patent, it can produce tapes for $3.00, charge a price closer to $5.00, and make significant economic profits.[1] Those profits reward the development of the new material, but they also keep the benefits from consumers.

The expiration of patents after 17 years really represents a compromise: on the one hand, it is important to stimulate invention and innovation; on the other hand, invention and innovation do society no good unless their benefits eventually flow to the public.

Sometimes the conflict between patents as an incentive to innovation and patents as a barrier to competition is difficult to resolve. In the early 1960s, General Motors developed through research a number of innovations that substantially improved the quality of the intercity busses that they produced. One, for example, was a superior-quality, transversely mounted engine. GM secured patents on these developments, of course, and proceeded to produce better busses.

Before too long, General Motors had gobbled up over 85 percent of the intercity bus market and found itself in trouble with the Justice Department. The courts held that GM was indeed in violation of the antitrust laws; the patents were a barrier to entry that permitted GM to monopolize the intercity bus market. As a result, the courts issued a "consent decree," forcing GM to give up its patents and to make available to the competition any new advances for several years into the future. Needless to say, not much research was done to improve the quality of intercity busses while that decree was in effect.

Economies of Scale and Capital Cost Advantages   Some products can be produced efficiently only in big, expensive production facilities. For example, the Federal Trade Commission has estimated that an oil refinery large enough to achieve maximum-scale economies in the production of gasoline would cost more than $500 million dollars. No matter how high her animal spirits are running, a small entrepreneur is not going to jump into the refining business in search of economic profit. The need to raise an initial investment of half a billion dollars certainly limits the pool of potential entrants, and this is particularly true when the business is risky to boot.

Sometimes there are large economies of scale that are not production related. Breakfast cereal can be produced efficiently on a very small scale, for example; large-scale production does not reduce costs. But the breakfast cereal market is dominated by heavily advertised brand names. To compete successfully, a new firm would have to mount an advertising campaign costing millions of dollars, an enormous investment in the intangible capital called goodwill. Once again, the large front-end capital requirement in the presence of risk is certainly likely to deter would-be entrants.

The actual significance of large economies of scale as a deterrent to firms wishing to enter a new market is the subject of much debate. The capital market in the United States has grown and developed to the point that very large sums of money can be obtained if the investors see a good chance to reap economic profits. Certainly, scale economies are not as powerful a barrier to entering an industry as legal restrictions and patents.

---

[1]Another alternative is licensing. Suppose BASF licenses the use of its material for $1.00 per tape produced. If firms use the material, costs will fall to $4.00 ($3.00 per tape plus the license fee). The price of tapes will fall to $4.00, and BASF will get a royalty of $1.00 for every tape produced using the new material. Here the inventor splits the benefits with consumers. Some analysts have proposed adding *mandatory* licensing to the current patent system.

Ownership of a Scarce Factor of Production   You can't enter the diamond-producing business unless you own a diamond mine. There are not many diamond mines in the world, and most are already owned by a single firm, the DeBeers Company of South Africa. Once upon a time, the Aluminum Company of America (now Alcoa) owned or controlled virtually 100 percent of the bauxite deposits in the world, and until the 1940s Alcoa monopolized the production and distribution of aluminum. Obviously if the production of a product requires a particular input, and one firm owns all of it, that firm will control the industry; the fact of ownership alone serves as a barrier to entry.

Price as a Fourth Decision Variable

A firm has market power when it has some control over the price of its product—that is, it can raise its price without losing all demand. The exercise of market power requires that the firm be able to limit competition in some way. Either it erects barriers to the entry of new firms or it prevents other firms from producing the exact same product. Regardless of the source of this power, output price is no longer taken as given by the firm. Now price is a decision variable, and firms with market power must decide not only: (1) how much to produce, (2) how to produce it, and (3) how much to demand in each input market, but also (4) *what price to charge*.

This does not mean that having "market power" gives a firm the ability to charge any price it likes, however. A market demand curve still *constrains* the behavior even of a pure monopolist. To sell its product successfully, a firm must, of course, produce something that people want and sell it at a price they are willing to pay.

As we explore the behavior of firms with market power in this chapter we concentrate on pure monopolies. Chapter 14 takes up the more common industry structures of oligopoly and monopolistic competition. In Chapter 15, we look at the history of antitrust rules, regulations, and laws in the United States.

PRICE AND OUTPUT IN PURE MONOPOLY MARKETS

A *pure monopoly market* is one in which a single firm produces a product for which there are no close substitutes. For purposes of building a model of monopoly behavior, we make two basic assumptions: (1) that entry to the market is strictly blocked, and (2) that firms behave so as to maximize profits.

Initially we assume that our pure monopolist buys in competitive input markets. Even though the firm is the only one producing for its product market, it is only one among many firms buying factors of production in input markets. The local telephone company, for example, must hire labor like any other firm, and to attract workers it must pay the market wage; to buy fiber-optic cable, it must pay the going price. In these input markets, therefore, our firm is a price-taker—that is, input prices are exogenous.

On the *cost* side of the profit equation, then, a pure monopolist differs not one bit from a perfect competitor. Both choose the technology that minimizes the cost of production. The cost curve of each represents the minimum cost of producing each level of output.

The difference arises on the *revenue* side of the ledger. A competitive firm faces a fixed, market-determined price, and we assume that it can sell all that it wants to sell at that price; it is constrained only by its current capacity in the short run. The demand curve

FIGURE 13.2
The Demand Curve Facing a
Competitive Firm Is Perfectly
Elastic

Competitive firms are price takers;
they are small relative to the size of
the market and thus cannot influence
market price. The implication, as we
saw in Chapter 8, is that the demand
curve facing a competitive firm is perfectly elastic. If the firm raises its price,
it sells nothing. There is no reason to
lower its price if it can sell all it wants
at P^*.

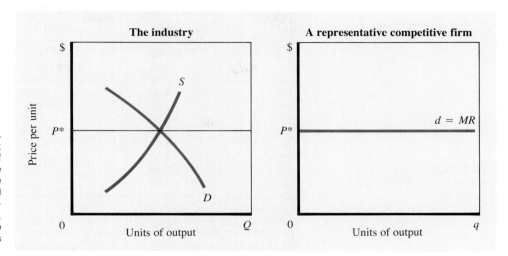

Marginal revenue   The
additional revenue that a firm
would earn by raising its level of
output by one unit.

facing a competitive firm is simply a horizontal line (see Figure 13.2). Raising its price
means losing all demand, because perfect substitutes are available. On the other hand, it
has no incentive to charge a lower price either.

Because a competitive firm can charge only one price, regardless of the output level
chosen, its **marginal revenue**—that is, the additional revenue that a firm earns by raising
output one unit—is simply the price of the output, or P^*. Remember that marginal
revenue is important because a profit-maximizing firm will increase output as long as
marginal revenue exceeds marginal cost.

The Market Demand Curve Facing Monopolists

With only one firm in a monopoly market, there is no distinction between the firm and
the industry—the firm *is* the industry. The market demand curve *is* the firm's demand
curve, and the quantity supplied *is* what the firm decides to produce.

We shall start by discussing a monopoly that *cannot price discriminate*. That is, it
sells its product to all demanders at the same price. (*Price discrimination* means selling to
different consumers or groups of consumers at different prices.)

Let us also say that the monopoly faces a *known demand curve*—that is, the firm
has enough information to predict how households will react to different prices. Many
firms use sophisticated statistical methods to estimate the actual *elasticity of demand* for
their products. Other firms may use less formal methods, including trial and error,
sometimes called "price searching." All firms with market power must have some sense of
how consumers are likely to receive their products at various prices, however. Knowing
the demand curve it faces, the firm must simultaneously choose both the quantity of
output to supply and the price of its output. Once the firm chooses a price, the market
determines how much will be sold. To put this another way, the firm chooses the single
point where it wants to be on the market demand curve.

Marginal Revenue and Market Demand   Just like a competitor, a profit-maximizing
monopolist will continue to produce output as long as marginal revenue is greater than
marginal cost. When a firm faces a downward-sloping demand curve, however, the nature
of marginal revenue changes. An increase in output involves not just producing more and
selling it, but also *reducing its price in order to sell it*.

QUANTITY	PRICE	TOTAL REVENUE	MARGINAL REVENUE
0	$11.00	$ 0	$ –
1	10.00	10.00	10.00
2	9.00	18.00	8.00
3	8.00	24.00	6.00
4	7.00	28.00	4.00
5	6.00	30.00	2.00
6	5.00	30.00	0.00
7	4.00	28.00	−2.00
8	3.00	24.00	−4.00
9	2.00	18.00	−6.00
10	1.00	10.00	−8.00

TABLE 13.1
Marginal Revenue Facing a
Monopolist

Consider the hypothetical demand schedule in Table 13.1, also graphed in Figure 13.3. The third column gives figures for the total revenue that the firm would take in at each potential level of output. If the firm produced one unit, it could sell it for $10.00, and total revenue would be $10.00. If it decided to produce two units, it could sell them for $9.00 each, and total revenue would be $18.00. As the fourth column shows, *marginal revenue* from the second unit would thus be $8.00 ($18.00 minus $10.00). Notice that the marginal revenue from increasing output from one unit to two units is *less* than the price of the second unit.

FIGURE 13.3
Marginal Revenue Facing a
Monopolist

At every level of output, marginal revenue for a monopolist is below price. That is because (1) we assume the monopolist must sell all its product at a single price (no price discrimination) and (2) to raise output and sell it, the firm must *lower* the price it charges. Selling the additional output will raise revenue, but this increase is offset somewhat by the lower price charged for all units sold. Therefore the increase in revenue from increasing output by one (the marginal revenue) is less than price.

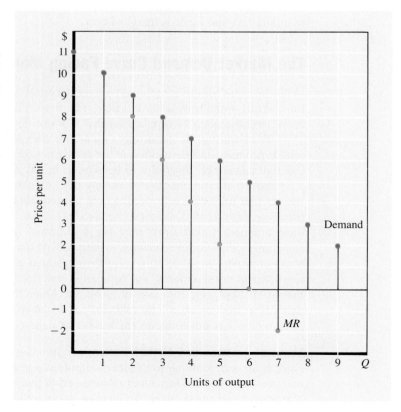

Now look what happens when the firm considers setting production at four units rather than three, again increasing output by a single marginal unit. It is true that the fourth unit would sell for $7.00, but because the firm can't price discriminate, it must sell *all four* for $7.00. Had it chosen to produce only three, they would have sold for $8.00 each. Thus, offsetting the revenue *gain* of $7.00 is a revenue *loss* of $3.00, that is, $1.00 for each of the three units that would have sold at the higher price. Marginal revenue is thus $7.00 minus $3.00, or $4.00, which is considerably below price. Remember, a perfectly competitive firm does *not* have to charge a lower price to sell more; thus $P=MR$ in competition.

Marginal revenue can also be derived simply by looking at the change in total revenue. At three units of output, total revenue is $24.00; at four units of output, total revenue is $28.00. Marginal revenue is the difference, or $4.00.

Moving from six units of output to seven units of output actually *reduces* total revenue for the firm; that is to say marginal revenue is *negative*. While it is true that the seventh unit will sell for a positive price, $4.00, in order to sell it the firm must sell *all seven* units for $4.00. If output had been restricted to six units, each would have sold for $5.00. Thus, offsetting the revenue gain of $4.00 is a revenue loss of $6.00, that is, $1.00 for each of the six units that the firm would have sold at the higher price. Thus *increasing* output by one unit actually *decreases* revenue by $2.00. Figure 13.3 graphs the marginal revenue schedule derived in Table 13.1. Notice that at every level of output except one unit, marginal revenue is *below* price. Marginal revenue turns from positive to negative after six units of output; in the diagram, the marginal revenue curve drops below the quantity axis at six units. When the demand curve is a straight line, the marginal revenue curve bisects the quantity axis between the origin (where P_X and Q_X are both 0) and where the demand curve hits the quantity axis.

Notice that the *marginal revenue curve shows the change in total revenue that results as the firm moves along the segment of the demand curve that lies directly above it.*

Marginal Revenue and Elasticity   Whether an increase in output increases revenue or decreases revenue depends on the elasticity of demand. Since total revenue is the product of price and quantity ($P \times Q$), the impact of an increase in quantity depends on *how great a price decrease* accompanies it. Recall that price elasticity of demand is the ratio of the percentage change in quantity to the percentage change in price as the firm moves between two points along a demand curve.

If demand is *elastic*, the percentage increase in quantity will be bigger than the percentage decrease in price. Total revenue will thus *increase* if output is raised, and marginal revenue will be *positive*:

$$\%\Delta Q > \%\Delta P \qquad \downarrow P \cdot Q \uparrow \; = TR \uparrow$$

On the other hand, if demand is *inelastic*, the percentage increase in quantity will be smaller than the percentage decrease in price. Total revenue will thus *fall* if output is increased, and marginal revenue will be *negative*:

$$\%\Delta P > \%\Delta Q \qquad \downarrow P \cdot Q \uparrow \; = TR \downarrow .$$

If demand has *unitary elasticity*, that is, elasticity equal to -1, any increase in quantity will be exactly offset by a decrease in price. Total revenue thus will not change, and marginal revenue will be zero.

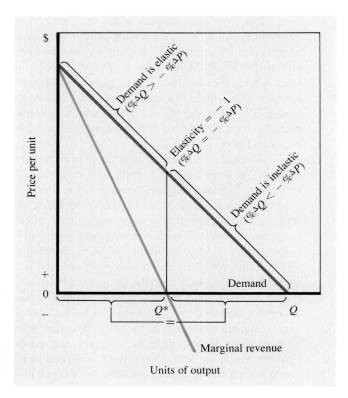

FIGURE 13.4

Marginal Revenue and Elasticity

As you learned in Chapter 5, elasticity changes as you move along a straight-line demand curve. Marginal revenue depends on elasticity of demand. When demand is elastic, increasing output increases revenue (*MR* is positive); when demand is inelastic, increasing output reduces revenue (*MR* is negative).

Figure 13.4 graphs the relationship between marginal revenue and elasticity. Along the upper portion of a straight-line demand curve, demand is elastic, and that portion of the marginal revenue curve that corresponds to it is positive. At the midpoint of a straight-line demand curve, elasticity is unitary, and marginal revenue is zero. Along the lower portion, demand is inelastic, and that portion of the marginal revenue curve that corresponds to it is negative and falls below the quantity axis. (If you need to review elasticity and the fact that it changes along a straight-line demand curve, see Chapter 5.)

The Choice of a Profit-Maximizing Price and Output   The purpose of spending so much time in defining and explaining marginal revenue is that it is an important factor in choosing the profit maximizing price and quantity for a monopolist. Figure 13.5 superimposes a demand curve and the marginal revenue curve derived from it over a set of cost curves. A monopolistic firm must now go through the same basic decision process that a competitive firm goes through. Any profit-maximizing firm will raise its production target as long as the added revenue from the increase outweighs the added cost. To put this in more specific terms, it is profitable to raise output *as long as marginal revenue is greater than marginal cost.* Any positive difference between marginal revenue and marginal cost can be thought of as *marginal profit.*

The optimal price/output combination for the monopolist in Figure 13.5 is Q_m and P_m. At any output below Q_m, marginal revenue is greater than marginal cost. Above Q_m, increasing output would reduce profits, because marginal cost exceeds marginal revenue. Thus, *the profit-maximizing level of output for a monopolist is the one at which marginal*

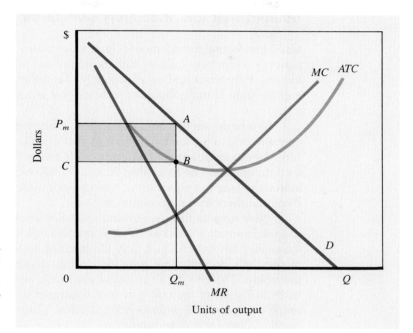

FIGURE 13.5
Price and Output Choice for a
Profit-Maximizing Monopolist

A profit-maximizing monopolist will
raise output as long as marginal revenue exceeds marginal cost. Maximum
profit is achieved at an output of Q_m
and a price of P_m. To the right of Q_m,
MC is greater than marginal revenue;
increasing output would *reduce* profit.

revenue equals marginal cost: $MR = MC$. Because marginal revenue for a monopoly lies
below the demand curve, the final price chosen by the monopolist is above marginal cost,
where $P_m > MC$.

At Q_m, price will be fixed at P_m, and total revenue will be $P_m \times Q_m$, or the area of
rectangle P_mAQ_m0. Total cost is the product of average total cost and Q_m, or the area of
rectangle CBQ_m0. Total profit is the difference between total revenue and total cost, or
the area of P_mABC.

Among competitive firms, the presence of economic profits provides an incentive
for new firms to enter, shifting supply to the right, driving down price and eliminating
profits. Remember, however, that for monopolies we assumed that barriers to entry have
been erected and that profits are protected.

The Absence of a Supply Curve in Monopoly   In perfect competition, the supply curve
of a firm in the short run is the same as the marginal cost curve of the firm (above average
variable costs). As the price of the good it produces changes, the firm simply moves up or
down its marginal cost curve in choosing how much output to produce. As you can see,
however, Figure 13.5 contains nothing that we can point to and call a supply curve. The
amount of output that a monopolist produces depends on its marginal cost curve *and* on
the shape of the demand curve that it faces. In other words, the amount of output that a
monopolist supplies is not independent of the shape of the demand curve, and so a
monopoly firm has no supply curve that is independent of the demand curve for its
product.

In perfect competition, we can draw a firm's supply curve without knowing
anything more than the firm's marginal cost curve. As we have seen, the situation for a
monopolist is more complicated. A monopolist sets both price and quantity, and the
amount of output that it supplies depends on *both* its marginal cost curve and the demand
curve that it faces.

Competition and Monopoly Compared

One way to understand monopoly is to compare equilibrium output and price in a perfectly competitive industry with the output and price that would be chosen if the same industry were organized as a monopoly. To make this comparison meaningful, let us exclude from consideration any technological advantage that a single large firm might enjoy.

We begin, then, with a competitive industry made up of a large number of firms operating with a production technology that exhibits constant returns to scale in the long run. (As you recall, *constant returns to scale* means that average cost is the same whether the firm operates one large plant or many small ones.) Figure 13.6 shows a competitive industry at long-run equilibrium, a condition in which price is equal to long-run average costs, and there are no economic profits.

Now suppose that the government nationalizes the industry and turns over control to a single private monopolist. The monopolist now owns one firm with many plants, but technology has not changed, only the locus of decision-making power. To analyze the monopolist's decisions, we must derive the consolidated cost curves now facing the monopoly. The new firm's marginal cost curve and average cost curve are simply the horizontal sums of the cost curves of what used to be those of the old firms and now simply represent the monopoly's individual plants. Figure 13.7 shows average and marginal costs for a three-plant firm.

If the new monopoly decides to produce 9000 units of output, it could do so at an average cost of $12.00. Two thousand would be produced in plant 1 at an average cost of

FIGURE 13.6
A Competitive Industry in Long-Run Equilibrium

In a competitive industry in the long run, price will be driven to long-run average cost. The market supply curve is the sum of all the short-run marginal cost curves of the firms in the industry. Here we assume that firms are using a technology that exhibits constant returns to scale: *LRAC* is flat. Big firms enjoy no cost advantage.

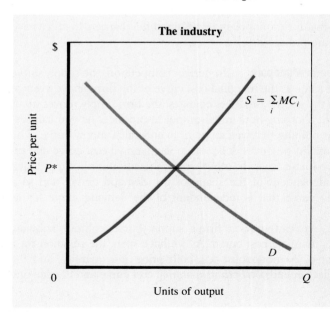
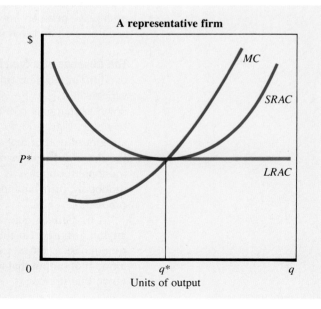

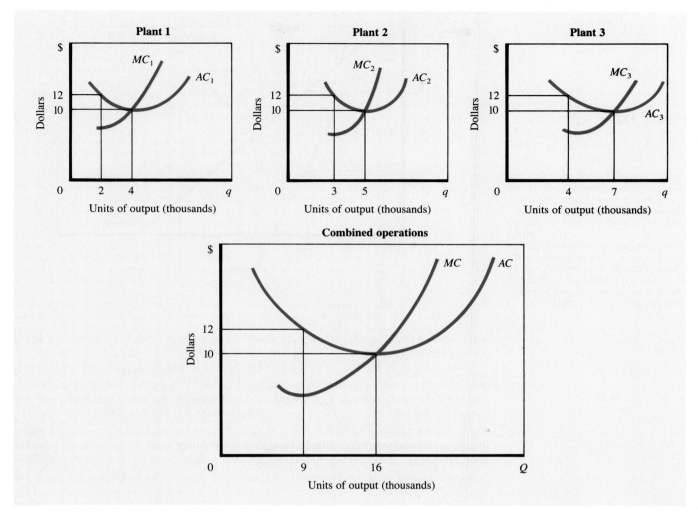

FIGURE 13.7

Cost Curves for a Consolidated Multiplant Firm

The cost curves of a single consolidated multi-plant firm are simply the horizontal sum of the cost curves of the individual plants. This is easy to see in the case where there are just three plants.

$12.00; 3000 would be produced in plant 2 at an average cost of $12.00; 4000 would be produced in plant 3 at an average cost of $12.00. The average cost of producing 16,000 units in the three plants of the consolidated firm would be $10.00. The marginal cost of the sixteen thousandth unit is $10.00 when 4000 units are being produced in plant 1, 5000 in plant 2, and 7000 in plant 3.

The important conclusion is that if the marginal cost curve of the consolidated firm is the horizontal sum of the marginal cost curves of the individual plants, then the marginal cost curve of the monopoly firm is *exactly the same* as the supply curve in the industry when it was competitively organized.

Figure 13.8 superimposes the cost curves of the consolidated monopoly industry on the diagram of the competitive industry in Figure 13.6. Since the marginal cost curve of the monopoly firm is the *same* as the former supply curve, it intersects the demand curve

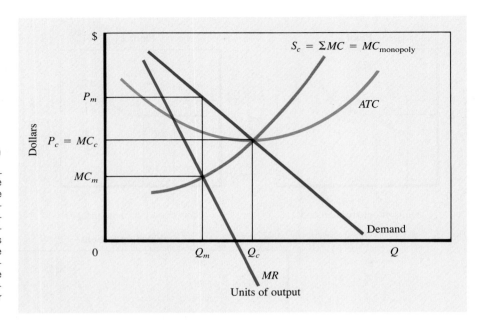

FIGURE 13.8

Comparison of Monopoly and Competitive Outcomes for a Firm with Constant Returns to Scale

In the newly organized monopoly, the marginal cost curve is exactly the same as the supply curve that represented the behavior of the independent firms when the industry was organized competitively. This enables us to compare the monopoly outcome with the competitive outcome. Quantity produced by the monopoly will be less than the competitive level of output, the monopoly price will be higher than the price under competition.

at P^*, labeled P_c in Figure 13.8, a point which also appears at the bottom of the new firm's average total cost curve.

No longer at the mercy of the market, however, the monopolist can choose any price/quantity combination along the demand curve. The output level that maximizes profits to the monopolist is Q_m, where marginal revenue intersects marginal cost, and output will be priced at P_m. To increase output beyond Q_m or to charge a price below P_m would reduce profit. The final result is that, relative to a competitively organized industry, a monopolist *restricts output, charges higher prices,* and *earns economic profits.* And remember, all we did was to transfer decision-making from the individual small firms to a consolidated owner. The new firm gains nothing at all technologically from being big.

Collusion and Monopoly Compared

Collusion   The act of joining with other producers in an effort to limit competition and increase joint profits.

Suppose now that an industry was not nationalized and no monopoly thus created. Instead, the individual firm owners simply got together and jointly maximized profits, a behavior called **collusion**. In this case, the outcome would be just the *same.* Firms certainly have an incentive to collude. When they act independently, they compete away whatever profits they can find. But, as we saw, when price was increased to P_m across the industry, the monopolistic firm earned economic profits.

Despite the fact that collusion is illegal, it has gone on in some industries. In one of the most significant cases, a number of executives of well-known electrical equipment manufacturers were successfully prosecuted in the early 1960s for meeting secretly to fix prices and divide up markets. In January 1987, a judge moved to end a pricing agreement between milk producers in New York City that had existed since the 1930s. The wholesale price of milk dropped *between* \$.30 and \$.71 per gallon in one week!

THE SOCIAL COSTS OF MONOPOLY

So far you have seen that a monopoly produces less output and charges a higher price than a competitively organized industry, if we assume that no large economies of scale exist for the monopoly. You are probably thinking at this point that producing less and charging more to earn economic profits is likely to be bad for consumers, and you are right.

Inefficiency and Consumer Loss

In Chapter 12, we argued that the condition that price equals marginal cost ($P = MC$) is central to the conclusion that markets produce what people want. This argument rests on two propositions: (1) that price provides a good approximation of the social value of a unit of output, and (2) that marginal cost, in the absence of externalities (costs or benefits to external parties not weighed by firms), provides a good approximation of the social opportunity cost of the product. In pure monopoly, price ends up above marginal cost. When this happens the firm is underproducing from society's point of view—that is, society would be better off if the firm produced more and charged a lower price. Monopoly, therefore, leads to an inefficient mix of output.

A slightly simplified version of the monopoly diagram appears in Figure 13.9. It shows how we might make a rough estimate of the size of the loss to social welfare that is due to monopoly. For clarity here, we ignore the short-run cost curves and assume constant returns to scale in the long run. Under competitive conditions, firms would produce output up to Q_c, and price would ultimately settle at P_c, equal to long-run average cost. A monopoly firm in the same industry would produce Q_m and charge a price of P_m.

FIGURE 13.9

Welfare Loss from Monopoly

A demand curve shows the amounts that people are willing to pay at each potential level of output. Thus the demand curve can be used to approximate the benefits to the consumer of raising output above Q_m. MC reflects the marginal cost of the resources needed. The triangle ABC roughly measures the net social gain of moving from Q_m to Q_c (or the loss due to monopoly).

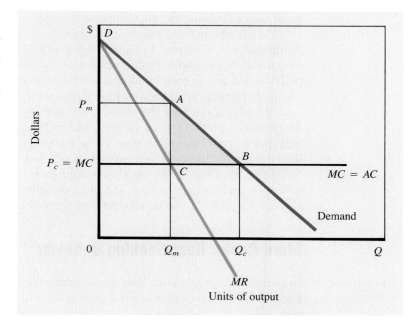

Now consider the gains and losses associated with increasing price from P_c to P_m and cutting output from Q_c to Q_m. You might guess that the winner will be the monopolist and the loser will be the consumer, but let us see how it works out.

Initially, at P_c there are no economic profits. Consumers are being charged a price of P_c, but many are actually willing to pay more than that. For example, a substantial number of people would pay P_m. Those people willing to pay more than P_c are receiving what we earlier called a *consumer surplus*. The demand curve shows approximately how much households are willing to pay at each level of output, and thus the area of triangle DBP_c gives us a rough measure of the "consumer surplus" being enjoyed by households when the price is P_c. Consumers willing to pay just P_m get a surplus equal to the length AC. Those who place the highest value on this good—that is, those who are willing to pay the most—get a surplus equal to DP_c.

Now along comes the government, which nationalizes the industry and turns it over to a monopolist who goes right ahead and cuts output to Q_m and raises price to P_m. The big winner is the monopolist, who ends up earning economic profits equal to the area P_mACP_c—that is, total revenue ($P_m \times Q_m = P_mAQ_m0$) minus total cost ($P_c \times CQ_m = P_cCQ_m0$).

The big losers are the consumers. Their "surplus" now shrinks from the area of triangle DBP_c to the area of triangle DAP_m. Part of that loss is covered by the monopolist's gain, *but not all of it*. The loss to consumers exceeds the gain to the monopoly by the area of triangle ABC. Thus, triangle ABC roughly measures the *net* loss in social welfare associated with monopoly power in this industry. If we could push price back down to the competitive level and increase output up to Q_c, however, consumers would gain more than the monopolist would lose, and the gain in social welfare would approximate the area of ABC.

In a classic article in the *American Economic Review* in 1954, Arnold Harberger showed that these losses, or **welfare costs of monopoly**, can actually be measured if data are available on elasticity of demand. In essence the Harberger method involves nothing more than calculating the areas of these triangles from data on real demand curves.[2]

In this example, the presence of a monopoly also causes an important change in the distribution of real income. In Figure 13.9, area P_mACP_c is economic profit flowing to the monopolist. If price were pushed down to P_c by competition or regulation, those excess profits would pass to consumers in lower prices. Society may value this resource transfer on equity grounds in addition to the efficiency gain.

Finally, there may be social costs that do not show up on these diagrams. Monopolies, protected from competition by barriers to entry, do not face the same pressures to cut costs and to innovate as competitive firms do. A competitive firm that does not use the most efficient technology will find itself being driven out of business by firms that do. One of the significant arguments against tariffs and quotas to protect industries such as automobiles and steel from foreign competition is that protection removes the incentive to be efficient and competitive.

More Costs: Rent-Seeking Behavior

Rent seeking   *Actions taken by firms or households to preserve extranormal profits. For example, a monopolist might lobby the government for an exclusive license that would prevent competition.*

In recent years, economists have found another serious worry. While triangle ABC in Figure 13.9 indeed represents a real net loss to society, part of rectangle P_mACP_c may also end up lost. To understand this, we need to think about the incentives facing *potential* monopolists.

[2]See Arnold Harberger, "Monopoly and Resource Allocation," *American Economic Review*, Vol. XLIV No. 2 (May 1954), pp. 77–87.

Competition and Milk Prices

Prior to January 1987, five dairies controlled the entire milk supply to New York City except for Staten Island. Entry into the city's milk market was blocked by the New York State Department of Agriculture and Markets, from which a potential entrant had to obtain a license to compete.

Not surprisingly, New Yorkers paid more for their milk than did others in adjacent areas. The first real evidence came in December 1985, when a New Jersey dairy, Farmland, was licensed to sell milk on Staten Island. Almost immediately, the price of milk there dropped more than 40 cents per gallon.

Late in 1986, New York Agriculture Commissioner Joseph Gerace denied Farmland a license to distribute milk in the rest of New York City, saying that a license would bring "destructive competition." On December 13, 1986, the *New York Times* carried an editorial strongly critical of Governor Cuomo for not firing Gerace and pointing out that Cuomo had received over $58,000 in campaign contributions from the dairy cartel. Recall the discussion in the text of "rent seeking behavior."

On January 3, 1987, Gerace resigned under pressure from the governor, and 6 days later, Farmland won in the courts what it could not win from the regulatory commission: permis-

sion to compete. On January 9, Federal District Court Judge Leonard Wexler ruled that the denial of license to Farmland amounted to economic protectionism and was unconstitutional. The following day, Governor Cuomo agreed that the State would not appeal and that it would pay all of Farmland's court costs and attorney fees. It was the end of a cartel that had dominated the New York City milk market for over 50 years.

On January 16, the *New York Times* carried a headline reading "Milk Prices Plunge in New York City in a Burst of Competition:"

> Milk prices dropped between 30 and 71 cents a gallon in New York City supermarkets this week in the face of new competition from a New Jersey dairy. A&P, Grand Union, D'Agostino, Red Apple and Sloan's were all charging $1.99 a gallon for whole milk yesterday —a sharp drop from last week when the first shipment of milk from Farmland Dairies of Wallington, N.J. reached grocery shelves in Manhattan, Brooklyn, the Bronx and Queens. Previously, Farmland's sales had been limited to Staten Island. . . .

> Asked why Farmland's prices were lower than those of its New York competitors, its president, Marc Goldman, said, 'It's not that we are so much cheaper, but that they have been overcharging.'

New York Times, January 17, 1987, pg. 30.

The area of rectangle P_mACP_c is the difference between total revenue and economic cost. It is profit over and above a normal return to capital. If entry were free and competition were open, those profits would be competed to zero. Clearly, owners of businesses earning economic profits have an incentive to prevent this from happening. In fact, the diagram shows exactly how much they would be willing to pay to prevent it from happening. A rational owner of such a firm would be willing to pay anything less than the entire rectangle. Any portion of it left over after expenses is better than zero, which would be the case if free competition eliminated it all.

There are many things that a potential monopolist can do to protect his or her position. One obvious approach is to hire lobbyists to push the government for restrictions on competition. A classic example of this behavior can be seen in organizations of taxicab drivers in New York and other large cities. In order to operate a cab legally in New York City, you need a license. The number of licenses is tightly controlled by the city. If entry into the business were open, competition would hold down cab fares to the cost of operating cabs. But cab drivers have become a powerful lobbying force and have muscled the city to restrict the number of licenses issued. That holds up fares and preserves monopoly profits.

There are countless other examples. The steel industry and the automobile industry spend large sums lobbying Congress for tariff protection. It is claimed that the establishment of the now-defunct Civil Aeronautics Board in 1937 to control competition in the airline industry, and extensive regulation of trucking by the FTC prior to deregulation in the 1970s, both came about in part through industry efforts to restrict competition and preserve profits.

This kind of behavior is called **rent seeking**. Recall from Chapter 11 that *rent* is the return to a factor of production in strictly limited supply. When economic profits appear in a competitive industry, they represent a return to a factor of production in limited supply in the short run. The short run is defined as a period in which some factor of production is fixed or limited. In the long run, resources are attracted to profit opportunities. Rent-seeking behavior consists of actions that firms and households take to preserve extranormal profits.

This line of reasoning has two important implications. First, rent-seeking behavior itself consumes resources. Lobbying and building barriers to entry are not costless activities. Periodically faced with the prospect that the City of New York will issue new taxi licenses, cab owners and drivers are so well organized that they could bring the city to a standstill with a strike or even a limited job action. Second, rent-seeking behavior presents us with a somewhat different view of government involvement in the economy. Both of these points deserve some elaboration.

In the story that we told in Figure 13.9, we saw the area of rectangle P_mACP_c as a transfer from consumers to monopolists. That is, consumers received less consumer surplus, and monopolists got excess profits. But if those profits are in part consumed by the expenses of rent-seeking behavior, they are lost entirely. That is, the resources consumed produce nothing of social value. All they do is help to preserve the present distribution of income. Thus the true net social cost is the sum of triangle ABC *and that portion of rectangle P_mACP_c* that ends up paying for the rent-seeking behavior itself—lobbyists' wages, expenses of the regulatory bureaucracy, and so forth.

The possibility of rent-seeking behavior also leads us to another view of government. So far we have considered the role government might play in helping to achieve an efficient allocation of resources in the face of market failure, in this case, the failures due to imperfect market structure. In Chapter 15 we survey the measures government might take to insure that resources are efficiently allocated when monopoly power actually arises. The idea of rent-seeking behavior introduces the important new notion of *government failure*. In this view of the world, the government becomes the tool of the rent seeker, and the allocation of resources is made even less efficient than before.

This view is at the center of what is called **public choice theory**. The key idea is that governments are made up of people, just as business firms are. These people —politicians and bureaucrats—can be expected to act in their own self-interest, just as owners of firms are expected to. Analyzing government behavior from this perspective yields a number of important conclusions, and we return to the **economics of public choice** in Chapter 16.[3]

Public choice theory   An approach to economic theory which proceeds on the assumption that the elected and nonelected public officials who set economic policies and regulate the players act in their own self interest (just as firms do).

POTENTIAL REMEDIES FOR MONOPOLY

Chapter 15 deals with regulation, antitrust law, and public policy toward concentrated industries in which firms have market power. At this point, however, we should look briefly at the two main approaches that federal and state governments, regulatory agencies, and the courts have taken to deal with undesirable market power: *restructuring the industry* and *regulation*.

[3]The term "rent-seeking" behavior was coined by Ann Krueger in an important article published in 1974. Much of the theory dates to earlier work by Gordon Tullock. See Ann O. Krueger, "The Political Economy of the Rent-Seeking Society," *American Economic Review*, 64, (1974) 291–303, and J. Buchanan, R. Tollison, and G. Tullock (eds.), *Toward a Theory of the Rent-Seeking Society* (College Station, Texas: Texas A and M University Press, 1980).

Restructuring an Industry

If an industry is restructured to make it more competitive and firms are then forced to compete, the argument goes, price will be bid down and output should rise back to the efficient level. Industries have been restructured by the courts in a number of ways. One is to remove barriers that prevent competitors from entering the industry and to arrange conditions that give new entries a better chance of making it. This was the approach taken by the court in the dismemberment, at least in part, of AT&T.

Prior to 1982, the American Telephone and Telegraph Company, also known as the Bell System, was very close to being a national monopoly in the provision of telecommunications services. It was by far the biggest long-distance carrier, it operated the vast majority of the local exchange services, produced most of the telecommunications equipment, and controlled various other aspects of the business. In a suit brought against AT&T, the Justice Department claimed that the company used its monopoly of local exchange service to block the entry of competing long-distance carriers. Ultimately, all parties to the case reached an agreement that was approved by the court.

Part of the final solution agreed to by AT&T in 1982 was that it would sell off its local exchange operating companies, and that other long-distance carriers would have access to the local networks on the same terms as AT&T. The local operating companies, now no longer owned by AT&T, retained their state-granted monopoly powers to provide local service. The whole point of the restructuring was to allow more firms to compete for long-distance service.

The AT&T case certainly led to a major restructuring of the industry and the breakup of a large firm into smaller separate firms, but the smaller companies retained their monopoly powers. Provision of local exchange service by companies such as New York Telephone, Pacific Bell, and so forth, is not competitive, and it was not intended to be. The goal was to remove a barrier and to allow new competitors to enter the *long-distance* market.

The intercity bus case discussed earlier is another example of a remedy involving removal of barriers to entry in order to permit more competition. In that case, the courts took General Motors' patents and gave them to the competition.

On a number of occasions, the courts have actually carved up monopoly firms into pieces that ended up directly competing with one another. Two examples are the Standard Oil Company and the American Tobacco Company, both of which were broken up into smaller competing companies by court order in 1911.

Regulation of an Industry

Price ceiling   A maximum price per unit above which producers of a good or service may not legally charge; usually imposed by government regulation.

Monopolies may also be regulated. Consider how a monopoly might react to the government's imposition of a price ceiling. The efficient price of any good is the price that is equal to the marginal cost of producing the good ($P=MC$). Figure 13.10 reproduces the diagram shown in Figure 13.5. Now suppose that some regulatory body imposes a **price ceiling**, or maximum price, at P_R. No regulation of quantity is imposed; the ruling simply says that the firm cannot charge more than P_R for its product.

Such a rule changes the nature of marginal revenue. Prior to the imposition of the ceiling, the unregulated monopolist could choose any price/quantity combination it wanted along the demand curve, and it chose to produce Q_m and to charge P_m in order to maximize profits. It didn't supply more than Q_m because that was the level at which marginal cost rose above marginal revenue; producing more would have reduced profits.

FIGURE 13.10

Imposition of a Price Ceiling
Changes Marginal Revenue and
the Profit-Maximizing Output
Level

Imposing a price ceiling at P_R changes
the nature of marginal revenue. Once
the ceiling is in place, the revenue
gained from raising output one unit
(MR) is exactly equal to P_R, the amount
the unit would be sold for. But this is
only true up to Q^*. Beyond Q^* the firm
is still constrained by market demand,
and marginal revenue drops to the old
curve.

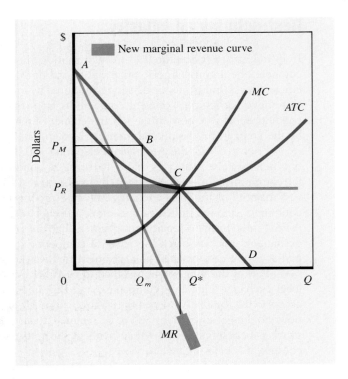

(Remember that at Q_m, if the firm wants to increase output, it must lower price below P_m.
Remember, too, that a monopolist cannot price discriminate, so the lower price that it
must charge for *all* output offsets the gain from selling more output. Such is the nature of
marginal revenue for a monopolist.)

How does a ceiling change all this? To start with, for any quantity between zero and
Q^*, the firm can charge no more than P_R. Now the demand curve between A and C no
longer means anything. If it wants to sell Q_m units, the firm will charge P_R; if it wants to
sell Q^* units, it will charge P_R. *Raising output by one unit at any quantity between zero
and Q^* will increase revenues by just P_R.* Thus, as in competition, marginal revenue is
simply equal to the ceiling price at any level of output up to Q^*.

To the right of Q^*, however, the old demand curve becomes relevant again. If the
firm decides to produce more than Q^* units of output, it will have to charge a price below
P_R. (This is not a violation, of course, because P_R is a *ceiling*, or *upper limit*.) Remember
that the marginal revenue curve in monopoly is derived from changes along the demand
curve that lies *directly above it*. Thus, to the right of Q^*—that is, below point C on the
demand curve—the old marginal revenue curve comes into play. With the price ceiling,
marginal revenue is simply P_R up to Q^*, at which point it falls to the old MR curve that
drops off the graph below the quantity axis.

Just as it did before, the firm will produce as long as marginal revenue is above
marginal cost, now up to Q^* rather than Q_m. Because marginal revenue is now P_R, MR
will not fall below marginal cost until point C, or at Q^* units of output. The mere
imposition of the price ceiling without any other regulatory action simply leads the
profit-maximizing monopolist to produce at the efficient level of output.[4]

---

[4]We would not want to leave the impression that choosing the optimal price was a trivial task for a regulator. On the
contrary, because competition is absent, there is no market in which to look for P_R. It must be estimated from cost
data. As we shall see, price regulation is inevitable for natural monopolies, but as anyone who has ever served on a
public utility commission will tell you, it is hard to do.

Note that this result does not coincide with what common sense predicts. A regulatory agency says to a firm, "You must charge a *lower* price." While firms in a competitive industry would *reduce* quantity supplied, a monopolistic firm responds by producing *more*.

Some exceptions to this result do exist, even when industries are not competitive. Price ceilings placed on the oil industry during the 1970s reduced output when some producers decided to keep their oil in the ground in anticipation of future price increases or of deregulation. Nonetheless, the general proposition that imposing a price ceiling on an otherwise unregulated monopoly will actually increase output remains valid.

So far we have restricted our discussion to situations in which a single large firm in an industry has no technological advantage over many smaller ones. We now turn to situations in which large firms use production technologies that involve very large economies of scale.

NATURAL MONOPOLY

In comparing monopoly and competition, we assumed that the efficient scale of operation was small. When the efficient scale of operation is small, there is no technological reason to have big firms instead of small firms. In some industries, however, there are technological economies of scale so large that it makes sense to have just one firm. Examples are rare, but public utilities—the electric company, for example, or the local telephone company—are among them. A firm that has such a structure is called a **natural monopoly**.

Natural monopoly   An industry which realizes such large economies of scale in producing its product that single-firm production of that good or service is most efficient. An industry with a continuously declining average cost curve.

Although Figure 13.11 presents an exaggerated picture, it does serve to illustrate the point. One large-scale plant (scale 2) can produce 500,000 units of output at an average cost of $1.00. If the industry were restructured into five firms, each producing on a smaller scale (scale 1), the industry could produce the same amount, but average cost

FIGURE 13.11
A Natural Monopoly

A natural monopoly is a firm where efficient scale is very large. Here average cost declines until a single firm is producing nearly the entire amount demanded in the market. With one firm producing 500,000 units, average cost is $1.00. With five firms each producing 100,000 units, average cost is $5.00.

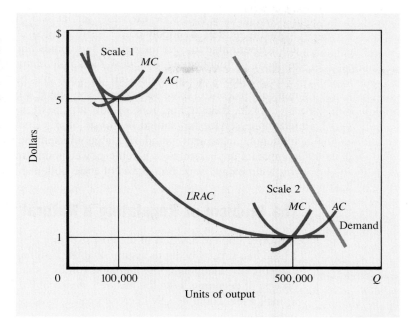

would be five times as high. Consumers see a considerable gain when these potential economies of scale are realized.

The critical point here is that *these economies must be realized at a scale that is close to total demand in the market*. Notice in Figure 13.11 that the long-run average cost curve is still declining when it hits the market demand curve. If at a price of $1.00 market demand was 5 *million* units of output, there would be no reason to have only one firm in the industry. Ten firms could each produce 500,000 units, and each could reap the full benefits of the available economies of scale.

The Problem of Identifying a Natural Monopoly

Empirical studies suggest that very few true natural monopolies exist. The most often-cited example has always been the local telephone system. Would it make any sense to have two or more telephone cables running down each street? Providing local exchange service requires an enormous initial investment in switching equipment, wires, trenches, poles, and the like. Thus fixed costs are very high, while marginal costs are very low. This means that average costs will continuously decline, which defines a natural monopoly.

Lately, however, even this conventional wisdom has come under fire as modern technology opens up new ways of doing business in this industry. For example, more and more telephone traffic is being transmitted through the air by microwave. Microwave transmitters can now be installed at relatively low cost, and no poles or connected wires are needed. As a result, we have "smart buildings" that can bypass the local telephone company. Small firms are also stringing newly developed fiber-optic cable from location to location at relatively low cost. During the early 1980s, a company called The Teleport ran cable up the center of Manhattan, into the other boroughs of New York, across to New Jersey, and all the way to Princeton. The cable connects customers to a set of microwave antennae that communicates with over 1000 orbiting satellites. All of this was done at very low cost.

Many analysts have concluded that monopoly power can no longer justifiably be granted to local telephone exchange services on the basis of large economies of scale. Nonetheless, that monopoly power is still granted, and small start-up "bypass" operations are not permitted to offer their customers connections to other local users. The argument in favor of maintaining the local monopoly status is now that states want to assure universal access to the system at low cost, and public utility commissions, with their mandate to control basic service, can see that this happens.

Even though the bulk of the argument for maintaining monopolies in local telephone service has shifted from one of efficiency to one of equity, the basic natural monopoly argument based on large efficient scale still seems valid where power companies are concerned. Electric power is still transmitted only over wires, and given this technology, huge economies of scale undeniably exist.

The Problem of Regulating a Natural Monopoly

A more complete diagram of the cost structure of a natural monopoly appears in Figure 13.12. For simplicity, let us assume that the firm has very large initial fixed costs and very low constant marginal costs. Demand is fully exhausted while average cost is still in the process of declining. Like the business shown in Figure 13.11, operating this business on a small scale would be silly because production costs would rapidly rise if firm size were reduced.

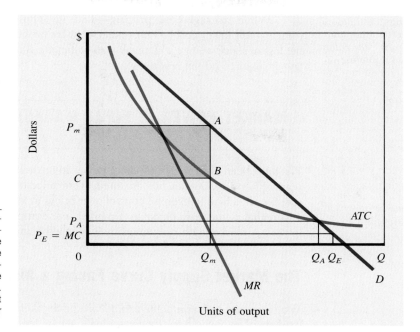

FIGURE 13.12

A Natural Monopoly

An unregulated monopolist would produce only up to the point where *marginal cost* and *marginal revenue* were equal—Q_m. If price were set at the efficient level, P_E, the firm would always suffer losses, because that price is insufficient to cover average costs. A compromise is for regulators to set price at P_A, just sufficient to cover costs including a normal profit rate.

If an exclusive government license were issued to a single firm, which was then allowed to choose price and quantity freely, the firm would price at P_m, produce Q_m units of output, and earn economic profits of P_mABC. Such a firm, unregulated, would turn around and take all the benefits from the economies of scale away from consumers. All of this is simply to say that acknowledging a single firm as a natural monopoly and allowing it to operate under the protection of a government franchise essentially requires that the government become involved in its regulation.

In talking about potential remedies, we said that the "efficient" regulation would be to place a price ceiling on the firm where price equals marginal cost. Unfortunately, that does not work in the case of a natural monopoly. When average cost is declining, marginal cost must be below it. If a price ceiling were placed at $P = MC$ (P_E in Figure 13.12), the ceiling would be below average cost and the firm would suffer losses. A simple ceiling at marginal cost would be "efficient" in the short run, but it would drive the firm out of business in the long run.

Two other solutions to this regulatory dilemma are possible. The efficient solution would be to enforce the price ceiling at marginal cost and to subsidize the monopoly to keep it in business. This requires the use of tax dollars, however, and therefore it is rarely used.[5]

By far the most common regulatory approach is to control price in a way that allows the owners of the public utility to earn a "fair rate of return." The state regulator's "fair rate of return" sounds very much like the economist's "normal rate of return," and, in fact, the language of some state regulations sounds suspiciously as if it came from an elementary economics textbook. Because a normal return to capital is included in economic costs, a price that allowed a firm to earn a normal return (which we assume is the same as the regulator's "fair return") would be a price just sufficient to cover average total costs (ATC). In Figure 13.12, a price ceiling set at P_A would leave the firm with zero profits and earning just a normal rate of return.

[5]If the tax itself imposes no excess burden by distorting decisions, you can show that the gains to consumers from the lower "efficient" utility price exceed the cost to taxpayers. This makes the result potentially efficient.

Average-cost pricing *Setting price to cover average cost per unit including a "fair return"; the policy most often applied in regulating monopoly pricing.*

While **average-cost pricing**—that is, setting price to cover costs and a fair return—will lower cost to consumers, transfer profits from monopolists, and reduce the net loss of social welfare, the result is *not* efficient. It is a compromise whose chief virtue is that it requires no tax revenues.

MARKET POWER IN INPUT MARKETS: MONOPSONY

Monopsony *A market in which there is only one buyer for a good or service.*

We have been talking about market power in terms of output, or product, markets to this point. Even monopolies, we assumed, were price-takers in input markets. But it is also possible for a firm to exercise control over prices in input markets. Consider, for example, a firm that is the *only buyer* in a market, *the* company that hires labor in a "company town." A market with only one buyer is called a **monopsony**.[6]

The Market Supply Curve Facing a Monopsonist

We have said that competitive firms are price-takers in input markets as well as output markets. The wage rate, for example, is set by the interaction that results when many firms demand labor and many households supply it. An individual firm takes an externally determined wage rate as a given. We have also said that a competitive buyer of an input will demand the input as long as the marginal revenue product of the input exceeds its price. The marginal revenue product of labor, for example, is the added revenue that the firm earns by hiring one additional unit of labor. The unit of labor produces some product—its marginal product—which, when sold, brings in revenues. The firm compares the "marginal gains" from hiring each unit of labor, that is, what the product of that unit sells for, against the "marginal cost" of that unit, that is, the wage rate. (If this sounds unfamiliar, you might want to review Chapter 10.)

When a firm hires labor competitively, it hires all the labor it needs at the current market wage. But now suppose that the firm is the *only* buyer of laborers with some particular skill. This means that instead of being able to hire all it wants at the equilibrium wage, it faces the market supply curve. The wage rate thus becomes a *decision variable*. If the market supply curve slopes upward, and the monopsony firm wants more labor, it must offer a *higher wage*. Now the marginal cost of an additional unit of labor is no longer just equal to the wage rate. This leads us to the concept of **marginal factor cost (MFC)**, that is, the additional cost of using one additional unit of a factor of production at the margin.

Marginal factor cost (MFC) *The additional cost of adding one more unit of a given factor of production, such as labor.*

Using the supply schedule in Table 13.2, suppose that the firm wants to increase its use of labor from three units to four. The fourth unit of labor will work for a wage of $8.00 per hour, but our firm cannot price discriminate, and it must pay *all* workers the higher wage. When it employed three workers, it had to pay them each only $6.00 per hour; now those three will each earn an additional $2.00 per hour. The total cost of going from three to four units of labor, therefore, is the $8.00 that goes to the fourth worker, and $2.00 to each of the other three. The *marginal factor cost* is thus $14.00. In other words,

[6]The terms "monopoly" and "monopsony" both derive from Greek root words. In both cases *mon(o)* means "sole" or "single." "Monopoly" adds a form of the Greek verb *polein*, "to sell." "Monopsony" adds a form of the Greek verb "opsonein," to buy food.

Units of labor supplied	Wage	Total factor cost (TFC)	Marginal factor cost (MFC)
0	$ 0	$ —	$ —
1	2.00	2.00	2.00
2	4.00	8.00	6.00
3	6.00	18.00	10.00
4	8.00	32.00	14.00
5	10.00	50.00	18.00
6	12.00	72.00	22.00
7	14.00	98.00	26.00

TABLE 13.2
Deriving Marginal Resource Cost for a Monopsonist

increasing the use of labor by one unit will cost the firm $14.00. The marginal factor cost is higher than the wage rate at *every level* of labor demand, because the higher wage needed to attract any additional labor supply goes to all workers, not just to the marginal worker.

Figure 13.13 shows a typical marginal factor cost schedule that is above the labor supply schedule facing a monopsonist in a labor market. It is superimposed on the firm's marginal revenue product schedule. Using our now-familiar marginal logic, *a profit-maximizing firm hires labor as long as its marginal revenue product exceeds its marginal factor cost.*

The monopsonist in Figure 13.13 would hire labor up to L_m and thus set a wage equal to W_m. In competition, the wage would be W_c, where supply and demand (marginal revenue product) are equal. Thus, much like a monopolist who curtails production and

FIGURE 13.13
A Monopsonist Will Hold Wages Below Marginal Revenue Product and Hire Less Labor than a Competitor

For a monopsonist the marginal cost of hiring one additional unit of labor is higher than the wage rate, because the firm must increase the wage of all workers to attract the new worker into the labor force. The monopsonist will hire only up to L_m and pay a wage W_m.

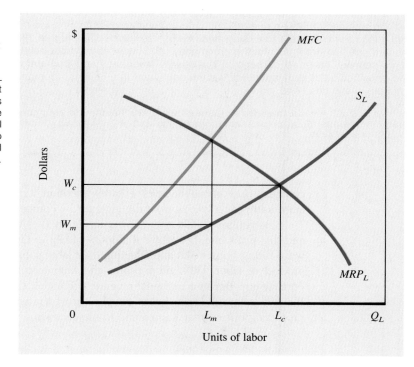

Monopsony Power and the Nursing Profession

There is substantial evidence that the supply of nurses in the United States is declining at precisely the same time that the demand for nurses is increasing. In a competitive labor market, the result would be a rapid rise in nurses' wages to attract people into the profession and to clear the market.

But something seems to be preventing nurses' salaries from rising enough to eliminate the shortage. A registered nurse earns a median annual salary of $21,000 according to 1984 statistics from the Occupational Outlook Handbook. For their pay, nurses work under stressful conditions in hospitals and clinics, often on evening or nighttime shifts. Doctors may treat them poorly, and patients may abuse them.

It is no surprise, then, that people have begun turning away from this job, choosing instead to pursue more lucrative positions as doctors or to work outside the medical profession. To meet expected demand, the nation's 1.4 million registered nurses will have to increase their ranks 44% to 2 million by the year 2000. The number of licensed practical nurses will have to grow 37% from 631,000 to 869,000. These increases are not likely. A study by UCLA's Cooperative Institutional Research Program (CIRP) showed a 50% decline between 1974 and 1986 in the proportion of college freshman women who planned to pursue a nursing career.

According to the CIRP, these college women's career preferences have shifted from the traditionally female fields of teaching, social work, and nursing to business, law, medicine—apart from nursing—and engineering. In 1986, for the first time, the number of women among the nation's freshmen in four-year colleges who aspired to be physicians surpassed the number of women who aspired to be nurses.

Some who have become nurses are also turning away from traditional health care roles in order to make more money. Some registered nurses get master's degrees in business administration and enter the fields of hospital administration, marketing, and human resources. And many are finding it worth the effort: nurses with MBAs command salaries of $50,000–$80,000 a year.

However, the demand for nurses in various health care areas has increased even as the number of people entering the profession drops. Demand began to rise in 1983, when the federal government introduced a "prospective payment" system for Medicare patients. Under this program, hospitals had to assign patients one of 486 diagnoses. Medicare then paid the hospital a fixed amount for that particular diagnosis, whether the patient required minor medical care or a lengthy hospital stay. Faced with this fixed payment, hospitals began cutting costs by admitting patients later and discharging them quicker. Many discharged patients required intensive services such as intravenous feeding and respirator support. As a result, the use of home care and community clinics rose, increasing the need for nurses.

Total demand for health care has increased as rising income and the growing availability of health care insurance have made paying for medical help easier. Also, the elderly population has grown, with the number of people 85 and over increasing six times as fast as the rest of the population. These people require nursing home care, and nursing homes are a major employer of registered nurses.

Why do salaries for nurses remain low if there is an increased demand for their services? One possible explanation may be that the health care industry behaves somewhat like a monopsonist. For example, many argue that hospitals in a given area often agree to set a fixed pay scale for nurses. To attract more nurses with higher wages would mean substantially higher costs since the wages of all nurses would have to be raised. (See Figure 13.13.)

Most economists believe that such arrangements are hard to enforce and that eventually wages will be driven upward until the quantity demanded and the quantity supplied are once again equal.

Sources: "Who wants to be a nurse?" *American Demographics*, January 1988; "Critical Condition: Supply of Nurses Wearing Thin," *The Margin*, October 1987; *Occupational Outlook Handbook*; "Nurse-MBAs Find a Growing Demand," "Nursing's Need is People Power,"; *Chicago Tribune*, March 6, 1988

charges a price *above* the level set by competition, a monopsonist cuts back on demand for labor and pays a wage *below* the level set by competition.

As you saw in Chapter 12, the condition $W = MRP$ insures that households supply, and that firms hire, the efficient amount of labor. This condition implies that the market wage facing households and affecting their labor supply behavior reflects the value of the product of labor. With monopsony, the wage rate is held considerably below MRP at equilibrium. Because marginal revenue product is the value of labor's product, keeping the offered wage lower keeps people out of the work force who would otherwise be producing output that has a value to society. Thus, monopsony is inefficient.

Remedies for Monopsony

The remedies for monopsony are similar to the remedies for monopoly. On the regulatory side, imposition of a minimum wage at W_c in Figure 13.13 would *increase* employment. The reasoning behind this is very similar to the reasoning that led us to conclude that a price ceiling imposed on a monopolist would actually increase production. Again, this runs counter to expectations, because a minimum wage in a competitive labor market decreases employment.

Just as colluding firms can unite to behave as a monopoly, so colluding firms can unite to behave as a monopsony. They have a real incentive to get together and offer a low wage. If the market power of a monopsonist results from collusion on the part of buyers, it can be stopped by the courts. In most cases, restructuring the industry is not an option, however. In recent years, baseball players have been complaining that team owners have made a deal to limit offers to free agent players. Several players actually charged the teams with collusion and price fixing, and in 1987 the courts agreed.

A MOST IMPERFECT MARKET

A firm has *market power* when it exercises control over the price of its output or the prices of the inputs that it uses. The extreme case of a firm with market power is the pure monopolist. In pure monopoly, a single firm produces a product for which there are no close substitutes and from which all new competitors are barred.

Our focus in this chapter on the relatively rare case of pure monopoly has served a number of purposes. First, the model does indeed describe a number of industries quite well. Second, the monopoly case clearly illustrates the observation that imperfect competition leads to an inefficient allocation of resources. Finally, the analysis of pure monopoly offers a number of important insights that will help in studying the more commonly encountered models of monopolistic competition and oligopoly discussed in Chapter 14.

SUMMARY

1. Three important assumptions underlie much of the logic of pure competition: (1) that a large number of firms and households are interacting in each market; (2) that firms in a given market produce undifferentiated, or homogeneous, products; and (3) that new firms are free to enter industries and to compete for profits.

2. The first two assumptions imply that firms have no control over input prices or output prices.

3. A market in which individual firms have some control over price is imperfectly competitive; such firms exercise market power.

4. A pure monopoly is an industry with a single firm that produces a product for which there are no close substitutes, and in which there are significant barriers to entry.

5. There are many potential barriers to entry; they include legal barriers (government franchises and licenses), patents, economies of scale, and ownership of scarce factors of production.

6. Market power means that firms must make four decisions each period instead of just three: (1) how much to produce, (2) how to produce it, (3) how much to demand in each input market, and (4) what price to charge.

7. Market power does not imply that a monopolist can charge any price it wants. Monopolies are still constrained by market demand. They can only sell what people will buy and can only sell at a price that people are willing to pay.

8. Marginal revenue, to a monopolist, is not equal to product price, as it is in competition. Rather, marginal revenue is lower than price because to raise output one unit *and to be able to sell* that one unit, the firm must lower the price it charges to all buyers.

9. A profit-maximizing monopolist will produce up to the point that marginal revenue is equal to marginal cost ($MR = MC$).

10. When demand is elastic, marginal revenue is positive—to sell more output, firms must lower price, but not by much. When demand is inelastic, marginal revenue is negative—to sell more output, firms must lower price substantially.

11. Since MR lies below the demand curve, the monopolist will charge a price above marginal cost.

12. Monopolies have no identifiable supply curves. Each firm simply chooses a point on the market demand curve —that is, it chooses a price and quantity to produce.

13. If a single owner were to take over a competitive industry and run it as a monopoly, it would increase price and reduce output. Owners would earn economic profits, and consumers would lose the benefits of low competitive prices.

14. When firms price above marginal cost, the result is inefficient. The decrease in consumer surplus is larger than the monopolist's profit, thus causing a loss in social welfare.

15. Actions that firms may take to preserve excess economic profits, such as lobbying the government to restrict competition, are called rent seeking. Rent-seeking behavior consumes resources and adds to social cost, further reducing social welfare.

16. The two main approaches to the problem of monopoly are restructuring the industry and regulation.

17. When a firm exhibits large economies of scale so that average costs continuously decline with output, it may be efficient to have only one firm in an industry. Such an industry is called a natural monopoly.

18. When there is only a single buyer in an input market, the firm is a monopsony. The problem of firms that exercise market power in input markets is similar to the problems of monopoly.

REVIEW CONCEPTS

imperfect competition   304
market power   304
pure monopoly   305
barriers to entry   305
government franchise   306
patent   306
marginal revenue   309
collusion   316

welfare cost of monopoly   318
rent seeking   319
public choice theory, the economics of public choice   320
price ceiling   321
natural monopoly   323
average-cost pricing   326
monopsony   326
marginal factor cost (MFC)   326

REVIEW QUESTIONS

1. "Market power implies that firms can charge any price they wish for their product." Do you agree? Explain.

2. Explain why the marginal revenue curve facing a competitive firm differs from the marginal revenue curve facing a monopolist.

3. Assume that the potato chip industry in the Northwest in 1986 was competitively structured and in long-run competitive equilibrium; firms were earning a normal rate of return. In 1987 two smart lawyers quietly bought up *all* the firms and began operations as a monopoly called "Wonks." In order to operate efficiently, Wonks hired a management consulting firm, which estimated long-run costs and demand. These results are presented in the following figure:

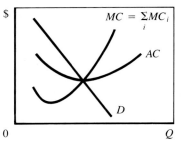

($\sum_i MC_i$ = the horizontal sum of the marginal cost curves of the individual branches/firms)

a. Indicate 1986 output and price on the diagram.
b. Assuming that the monopolist is a profit-maximizer, indicate total revenue, total cost, and total profit after the consolidation.
c. Assuming that about 25 percent of the potatoes grown in Idaho are used for potato chips in the Northwest, what would you expect to happen to the price of Idaho potatoes in the short run after the consolidation?
d. Suppose that after three years of successful operation, the annual accounting statement looked like the following:

Price per bag: $.50
Total sales (bags): 4,000,000
Cost of potatoes: $1,000,000
Total additional cost: $500,000*
*Includes labor, maintenance, depreciation, etc.

Noticing Wonks's success, in 1990 General Foods begins to research the prospects for a possible takeover. Its research indicates

1. Wonks has a strong brand name and several patents that serve as effective barriers to entry.
2. Demand and costs are likely to remain unchanged for many years to come.

How much would General Foods be willing to pay for 100 percent of Wonks's stock if a normal rate of return in the business is 10 percent?
e. The following year an old buddy from law school files a complaint with the antitrust division of the Justice Department claiming that Wonks has monopolized the potato chip industry. Justice concurs and prepares a civil suit. Suppose you work in the White House and the President asks you to prepare a brief memo (two or three paragraphs) outlining the issues. In your response, be sure to include

1. the economic justification for action
2. a proposal to achieve an efficient market outcome

4. Consider the following monopoly:

Fixed costs = $1000
Marginal cost = $1.00 (and is constant)

a. Draw the total cost schedule.
b. Draw the average total cost curve and the marginal cost curve on the same graph.
c. Assume that all households have the same demand schedule, given by the following relationship:

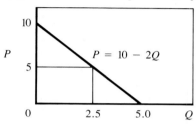

If there are 400 households in the economy, draw the aggregate (market) demand curve and the marginal revenue schedule facing the monopolist.
d. What is the monopolist's profit-maximizing output? What is the monopolist's price?
e. What is the "efficient price," assuming no externalities?
f. Suppose that the government "imposed" the efficient price by passing a law giving the President authority to set a ceiling on price at the efficient level. What is the long-run output of the monopoly?
g. Can you suggest an alternative approach for achieving an efficient outcome?

14 Imperfect Competition: Monopolistic Competition and Oligopoly

---

MONOPOLISTIC COMPETITION
  The Structure of Monopolistic Competition
  Product Differentiation, Advertising,
    and Social Welfare
  The Behavior of Firms
    under Monopolistic Competition (Conduct)
  Economic Efficiency
    and Resource Allocation (Performance)

OLIGOPOLY
  The Structure of Oligopoly
  The Behavior of Firms
    under Oligopoly (Conduct)
  The Performance of Firms in an Oligopoly
SUMMARY

We have now examined two "pure" market structures. At one extreme is *perfect competition*, a market structure in which many firms, each small relative to the size of the market, produce undifferentiated products and have no market power at all. Each competitive firm takes price as given and faces a perfectly elastic demand for its product. At the other extreme is *pure monopoly*, a market structure in which only one firm, with the power to set price and protected by barriers to entry, dominates an industry. Its market power would be complete if it did not face the discipline of the market demand curve. Even a monopoly, however, must produce a product that people want and are willing to pay for.

Most industries in the United States fall somewhere in between these two extremes. In this chapter, we focus on two types of industry in which firms exercise some market power but at the same time face competition. The first, *monopolistic competition*, differs from perfect competition only in that firms can differentiate their products. Entry to a given industry is free, and each industry is made up of many firms.

The second, *oligopoly*, is an extremely broad category that covers many different kinds of firm behavior and industry structure. An oligopoly is an industry with a small number of competitors. Each firm in an oligopoly is large enough to have some control over market price, but beyond that the character of competition varies greatly from industry to industry. An oligopoly may have two firms or fifty, and those firms may produce differentiated or undifferentiated products.

Before we go on, it is useful to outline the approach that we will take to studying and analyzing industries. In Chapter 1 we described several special fields of concentration within economics, one of which was *industrial organization*. Over the years, industrial organization economists have developed a standard approach to the study of industries that is presented schematically in Figure 14.1.[1]

---

[1] This approach dates to the work of Edward S. Mason at Harvard in the 1930s, and it has been extended by numerous scholars since.

333

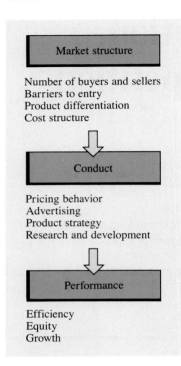

FIGURE 14.1
A Model of Industrial
Organization Analysis

Monopolistic competition   The most common form of industry (market) structure in the United States, characterized by a large number of firms, no one of which can influence market price by virtue of size alone. Some degree of market power is achieved by firms producing differentiated products. New firms can enter and established firms can exit such an industry with ease.

Most analyses start with a description of the **structure of an industry.** How many firms are there? What portion of the industry's total sales is accounted for by the top four firms in the industry? By the top eight? Are there barriers to entry? If so, how do they operate? Do firms produce homogeneous or differentiated products? Are there economies of scale? The answers to these and similar questions define an industry's structure.

From structure, analysts turn to the **behavior,** or **conduct,** of firms in the industry. How are prices set? Does a dominant firm in effect set price for other, smaller, firms? Do firms advertise? If so, what portion of total cost is advertising expense? How much research do the firms do? How often are new product lines introduced?

Sometimes formal models help to predict how firms are likely to behave. For example, if an industry is competitively structured and no serious barriers to entry are in place, high profits should attract new firms. Where firms have market power, they can be expected to hold back on production and charge a price above marginal cost. The real purpose of analyzing an industry, however, is to determine the impact of its structure and conduct on the allocation of resources. Do its behavior and structure lead to inefficiency? Does the industry enhance or retard economic growth? What impact does it have on the distribution of income? These are all aspects of the **performance** of the industry.

MONOPOLISTIC COMPETITION

The Structure of Monopolistic Competition

A **monopolistically competitive industry** has the following structural characteristics: (1) *a large number of firms;* (2) *no barriers to entry;* and (3) *product differentiation.*

While pure monopoly and perfect competition are rare, monopolistic competition is a very common form of organization in the United States. Take, for example, the restaurant business. The San Francisco Yellow Pages devote 26 pages to a listing of over 1500 different restaurants in the area. Each one of them produces a slightly different product and makes an attempt to distinguish itself in the minds of consumers. Entry to the market is certainly not blocked. One location near Union Square saw five different restaurants start up and go out of business in five years. Although many restaurants fail, small firms can nonetheless compete and survive, because there are no large economies of scale.

The structural feature that distinguishes monopolistic competition from monopoly and oligopoly (we treat oligopoly fully later in this chapter) is that firms cannot influence market price *by virtue of their size.* No one restaurant is big enough to affect the *market* price of a prime rib dinner, for example, even though all restaurants can certainly control their *own* prices. Rather, firms gain control over price in monopolistic competition by *differentiating their products.* You make it in the restaurant business by producing a product that people want that others are not producing and/or by establishing a reputation for good food and good service. By producing a unique product or establishing a particular reputation, a firm becomes, in a sense, a "monopolist"—that is, no one else can produce the *exact same* good.

The structural feature that distinguishes monopolistic competition from pure monopoly is that *good substitutes are available.* With 1500 restaurants in the San Francisco area, there are dozens of reasonably good Italian, Chinese, and French restaurants. Thus if I open an Italian restaurant, there is plenty of competition—lots of good, but not perfect, substitutes. Carving out a market niche is difficult, and the failure rate is high. Some parts of the city have many restaurants that are very similar; there the situation resembles perfect competition.

San Francisco's Chinatown probably has fifty small Chinese restaurants, with over a dozen packed on a single street. The menus are nearly identical, and they all charge virtually the same prices. At the other end of the spectrum are those restaurants, with very well-established names and prices far above the cost of production, that are always booked. That, of course, is the goal of every restaurateur who ever put a stockpot on the range to simmer.

Table 14.1 presents some data on eight national manufacturing industries that have the structural characteristics of monopolistic competition.[2] Each of these industries includes hundreds of individual firms, some of which are larger than others, but all of which are small relative to the industry. In book publishing, for example, the top four firms account for only 17 percent of total shipments. The top 20 firms account for 56 percent of the market, while the market's remaining 44 percent is split among nearly 2000 separate firms.

To review *monopolistic competition*, then, firms in this industry structure are small relative to the total market, new firms can enter the industry in pursuit of profit, and relatively good substitutes for the firms' products are available. Firms in monopolistically competitive industries try to achieve a degree of market power by differentiating their

TABLE 14.1
Percentage of Value of Shipments Accounted for by the Largest Firms in Selected Industries, 1982

SIC#	Industry Designation	Four largest firms	Eight largest firms	Twenty largest firms	Number of firms
3792	Traveler trailers and campers	36	48	63	446
2834	Pharmaceutical preparations	26	42	69	584
2515	Mattresses and bedsprings	23	31	43	786
2599	Furniture and fixtures	19	28	42	819
2321	Men's and boys' dress shirts	19	29	48	535
2731	Book publishing	17	30	56	2007
3564	Blowers and fans	14	24	43	450
3079	Misc. plastic products	7	10	17	10,152

Source: U.S. Department of Commerce, Bureau of the Census, 1982 Census of Manufactures, *Concentration Ratios in Manufacturing*, Subject Series MC82-S-7.

[2]The data are tabulated and reported by Standard Industrial Classification, or SIC, codes. This classification system for industries has been developed over a period of years and is administered by the Department of Commerce. The system operates in such a way that industry definitions become progressively narrower, and thus industry descriptions become more specific, with successive additions of digits. There are 20 *major groups* (SIC 20: food and kindred products), 150 *groups* (SIC 201: meat products), 450 *industries* (SIC 2011: meat-packing plants), 1500 *product classes* (SIC 20112: bacon), and 13,000 *products* that add two more digits to make up a seven-digit code. (The *Standard Industrial Classification Manual*, (1987), from the U.S. Government Printing Office in Washington, D.C., describes the system).

The Census Bureau compiles its numbers from data collected in the Census of Manufactures, done every five years. The data from the 1987 census will not be released for a few years.

products—by producing something new, different, or better, or by creating a unique identity in the minds of consumers. Before we go on to discuss the behavior of such firms, a few words about advertising and product differentiation are in order.

Product Differentiation, Advertising, and Social Welfare

Product differentiation   One strategy that firms use to achieve market power. Accomplished by producing truly different products and by creating differentiated product images by means of advertising.

Monopolistically competitive firms achieve whatever degree of market power they command through **product differentiation**. In order to be chosen over competitors, products must have distinct positive identities in the minds of consumers, and this differentiation is often accomplished through *advertising*.

Monopolistic Competition and Product Differentiation

The analysis of perfect competition in Chapters 6 through 12 assumed that firms produce homogeneous, or undifferentiated, products. The analysis in this chapter, however, illustrates that firms have an incentive to differentiate their products in the minds of consumers. A firm that produces a "better" product or establishes itself a reputation for quality can charge a higher price and earn more profits, at least in the short run. In perfect competition, when a firm charges a price above that of its competitors, it sells nothing. Product differentiation is a source of limited "market power."

Some people believe that advertising and product differentiation are wasteful. They argue that valuable resources are used to create minute and meaningless differences in consumers' minds. Others argue that product innovation and marketing are at the heart of what's good about our system —product competition gives us new and better products and plenty of variety. Read the following article, and judge for yourself.

Ronald Bownds quit his oil company job three years ago and came home to this pretty hill-country town to bottle the spring water that bubbles up on the family ranch.

Mr. Bownds had modest plans for his Hill Country Spring Water of Texas Inc. at first. He hauled spring water two miles to an old meatpacking plant at the ranch and, with a friend, poured it into plastic jugs.

Mr. Bownds isn't thinking small anymore. This summer, he built a 35,000-square-foot automated bottling plant where he now has 80 employees. His sales will double to $2 million this year from customers in nine states, including New York and Connecticut. "I'm fixing to make Utopia the No. 1 brand" of sparkling spring water in the country, declares the 34-year-old cowboy.

Mr. Bownds is one of many water entrepreneurs riding the crest of the swelling bottled water business. Consumers, worrying about polluted tap water and avoiding calories and chemicals in soft drinks, are lapping up bottled waters at a quickening pace. With sales rising about 15% in each of the past five years to about $1 billion this year, water is the second-fastest-growing segment of the beverage industry, after wine coolers. Per capita consumption in the U.S. grew from 1.5 gallons in 1976 to 5.2 gallons in 1985.

With the exception of the French import Perrier, water has typically come from small-business men, like Mr. Bownds in scenic rural places like Utopia, who tap ancient springs or artesian wells and vie for slivers of regional markets. Most of them bottle "still" or noncarbonated water for home delivery and retail stores. Others, including Mr. Bownds, are tapping into the lucrative upscale market for mineral and carbonated waters.

But it is Mr. Bownds's dream to beat the Goliaths to win over consumers. The secret to gaining customers, he figures, is to find good distributors who keep his product stocked on grocery shelves and wrangle for aisle displays. And the faster he signs up the best distributors, the sooner he wins consumers.

COUNTRY CHARM

So, like the fictitious Frank Bartles of wine-cooler fame, he puts his country charm to work. He invites top beer and soda distributors to Utopia and woos them from the high perch of his dirty-white Chevy Suburban. Dressed in a cowboy shirt and boots, with his wide belly spilling over a hand-tooled Western belt, he drives them over the ranch, past red Hereford cattle, to the shady spring.

The sales pitch seems to work. Gulf Coast distributor Lawrence Del Papa of Houston sold nothing but Budweiser products before he took the tour with Mr. Bownds. He carries Utopia water now. "That hill country has a magic to it," he says.

Mr. Bownds has a long shot. Major corporations with big advertising and marketing budgets will win the national game, predicts Mr. Carpenter of Anheuser-Busch. "The pressure on retail shelf space gives the advantage to producers with a total program rather than just a regional brand," he says.

Source: Marj Charlier, "Bottled Water Business Swelling Quickly," reprinted by permission of the *Wall Street Journal,* ©Dow Jones & Co. Inc., 1987. All rights reserved.

TABLE 14.2
Total Advertising Expenditures in 1985 by Medium

	Dollars (millions)
Newspapers	25,170
Magazines	5,155
Television	20,770
Radio	6,490
Direct mail	15,500
Other	21,665
Total	94,750

Source: McCann Erickson Inc. Reported in U.S. Bureau of the Census, *Statistical Abstract of the United States, 1987*, table 925, p. 538.

In 1985 firms spent over $94 billion dollars on advertising (see Table 14.2). You couldn't possibly go through life, and probably not through a day, without hearing that "Coke is it," or that you can "reach out and touch someone" through AT&T. Advertising reaches us through every medium of communication. Driving down most major highways we see billboards. It is actually possible to rate television shows by how much the water pressure in a community drops when competing shows are interrupted by commercials. Table 14.3 shows national network television advertising expenditures by major industrial category. The food products industry leads the pack with expenditures of over $1.5 billion on television alone in 1985. In the fall of 1986, it cost $338,000 for 30 seconds of commercial advertising time during breaks of "The Bill Cosby Show."

The effects of product differentiation in general and advertising in particular on the allocation of resources has been hotly debated for years. Advocates claim that these forces are what gives the market system its vitality and power; critics argue that they cause waste and inefficiency. Before we proceed to the formal models of monopolistic competition and oligopoly, the major points of this debate are well worth reviewing.

The Case for Product Differentiation and Advertising   The most important advantage to open product competition is that it provides us with the *variety* inherent in a steady stream of new products, while ensuring that the quality of these products remains high. We have said before that one of the most important characteristics of a modern economy is the tremendous variety of tastes and preferences that it can satisfy. A walk through several neighborhoods of a big city, or even a hour in a modern department store or mall, should be enough to convince you that one thing we can say for certain about human wants is that they are infinite in their variety.

Free and open competition with differentiated products is the only way to satisfy all of us. Think of the variety of music we listen to—bluegrass, heavy metal, folk, classical. Business firms engage in constant market research. What do consumers want? What colors? What cuts? What sizes? The only firms that succeed are the ones that answer these questions correctly and thereby satisfy an existing demand that was not being satisfied by the market.

In recent years, quite a few of us have taken up the sport of running. The market has responded in a very big way. Now there are numerous running magazines; hundreds

TABLE 14.3
Expenditures for Network Advertising in 1985

	Dollars (millions)
Food and food products	$1,502
Toiletries and toilet goods	955
Automobiles	848
Proprietary medicines	700
Beer and wine	428
Soft drinks and confectionary	388
Laundry soap, cleansers, polishes	397
All industries	8,313

Source: Television Bureau of Advertising, Inc. (New York). Reported in U.S. Department of Commerce, Bureau of the Census, *Statistical Abstract of the United States, 1987*, table 928, p. 539.

of orthotic shoes designed specifically for runners with particular running styles; running suits of every imaginable color, cloth, and style; weights for the hands, ankles, and shoe laces; tiny radios to slip into your sweatbands; and so forth. Even physicians have differentiated their products: sports medicine clinics have diets for runners, therapies for runners, and doctors specializing in shin splints or Morton's toe. There is even a running shoe with a small computer built into the heel to monitor a runner's time, distance, and calories expended.

The products that satisfy a real demand survive, but the market has no mercy for products that no one wants. They sit on store shelves, are sold at heavy discount prices or not at all, and eventually disappear. Firms making products that don't sell go out of business, the victims of economic Darwinism in which only the products that can thrive in a competitive environment survive. Without open competition, if we had running suits at all, they might all be gray.

A significant portion of economic growth involves product innovation. Just think of the things that we have and use today that didn't exist ten or fifteen years ago. The standard of living rises when the technology of production improves—that is, when we learn to produce more with fewer resources. Developing and using better techniques of production involves innovation. But the standard of living also rises when we have *product innovation*, when new and better products come on the market.

Variety is also important to us psychologically. The astonishing range of products available exists not just because your tastes differ from mine. Human beings get bored easily. We grow tired of things, and diminishing marginal utility sets in. I don't go just to French restaurants; it's nice to eat Greek or Chinese food once in a while too. To satisfy many people with different preferences that change over time, the market must be free to respond with new products.

People who visit planned economies always comment on the lack of variety. The classic story is one of driving from West Berlin into East Berlin; color and variety seem to vanish. Visitors to China since the economic reforms of the mid-1980s claim that the biggest visible sign of change is the increase in the selection of products available to the population.

Proponents of product differentiation also say that it leads to *efficiency* and *higher quality*. If my product is of higher quality than that of my competition, my product will sell more and my firm will do better. If I can produce something of high quality cheaper, that is, more efficiently, than my competition can, I will force them to do likewise, or force them out of business.

Creating a *brand name* through advertising also helps to insure quality. Firms that have spent millions to establish a brand name or a reputation for quality have something of value to protect. Soviet planners discovered many years ago that requiring producers to imprint their individual "production marks" on products improved quality.[3]

In order for product differentiation to work, of course, consumers must know about product quality and availability. In perfect competition, where all products are alike, we assume that consumers have perfect information; without it, the market fails to produce an efficient allocation of resources. *Complete information* is even more important when we allow for product differentiation. How do consumers get this information? The answer is, at least in part, through advertising. The basic function of advertising, according to its proponents, is to assist consumers in making informed, rational choices.

Supporters of product differentiation and advertising also claim that these tech-

---

[3]See Marshall I. Goldman, "Product Differentiation and Advertising: Some Lessons from the Soviet Experience," *Journal of Political Economy* (August 1960).

niques promote competition. New products can compete with old established brands only if they can get their messages through to consumers, and when consumers are informed about a wide variety of potential substitutes, they can more effectively resist the power of monopolies.

To sum up, the advocates of free and open competition, with its differentiated products and advertising, believe that this is what gives the market system its vitality and power. It is the only way to begin to satisfy the enormous range of tastes and preferences in a modern economy, they say. Product differentiation also helps insure high quality and efficient production, and advertising provides consumers with the valuable information on product availability, quality, and price that is needed for efficient choice in the marketplace.

The Case Against Product Differentiation and Advertising   To all this the critics cry, "Baloney!" To this way of thinking, product differentiation and advertising waste society's scarce resources. Enormous sums of money are spent to create minute, meaningless differences among products, which often exist only in our minds.

Drugs, both prescription and nonprescription, are a prime example. Companies spend millions and millions of dollars to "hype" brand name drugs that contain *exactly* the same compounds as those available under their generic names. The antibiotics erythromycin and erythrocin have the same ingredients. Yet the former is half again as expensive. Aspirin is aspirin, yet we pay twice the price for an advertised brand, because the manufacturer has convinced us that there is a tangible—or intangible—difference.

Do we really need fifty different kinds of soap, the price of each of which is inflated substantially by the cost of advertising? For a firm producing a differentiated product, advertising is part of the everyday cost of doing business; its price is built into the average cost curve and thus into the price of the product in the short run and the long run. Consumers pay for it.

In a way, advertising and product differentiation turn the system completely around. We have been talking about an economic system designed to meet the needs and satisfy the desires of members of society, that is, as a means to an end, which is the social good. Advertising is intended to *change* people's preferences and to *create* wants that otherwise would not have existed. From the advertiser's viewpoint, people exist to satisfy the needs of the economy, that is, the *goal* of the economic system has been lost sight of, and instead, the *means* has become the end.[4]

Critics also argue that the information content of advertising is minimal at best and deliberately deceptive at worst. It is meant to change our minds, to persuade us, and to create brand "images." Take a look and see how much *real* information there is in the next ten advertisements you see on television. To the extent that no information is conveyed, critics argue, advertising creates no real value, and thus a substantial portion of the $90 billion worth of resources that we devote to advertising is wasted.

Competitive advertising can also easily turn into unproductive warfare. Suppose there are five firms in an industry and one begins to advertise heavily. In order to survive, the others respond in kind—if one firm drops out of the race, it will certainly lose out. Advertising of this sort may not increase demand for the *product* or improve profitability for the *industry* at all. Instead, it is all too often what is called a "zero sum game," a game that, on balance, no one wins.

---

[4]This point was well made by John Kenneth Galbraith in *The Affluent Society* (Boston: Houghton Mifflin, 1958).

Advertising may reduce competition by creating a barrier to the entry of new firms. One famous case study taught at the Harvard Business School calculates the cost of entering the breakfast cereal market. In order to be successful, a potential entrant would have to start with millions of dollars in an extensive advertising campaign to establish a brand name recognized by consumers. Entry to the breakfast cereal game is not completely blocked, but such requirements make it much more difficult.

Finally, some argue that advertising by its very nature imposes a cost on society. We are continuously being bombarded by bothersome jingles and obtrusive images. Driving home from work, we pass 50 billboards and listen to 15 minutes of news and 20 minutes of advertising on the radio. When we get home, we open and throw away 10 pieces of unsolicited junk mail, glance at a magazine containing 50 pages of writing and 75 pages of advertisements, and perhaps watch a television show that is interrupted every three-and-a-half minutes for a "message."

The bottom line, critics argue, is waste and inefficiency. Enormous sums are spent to create minute, meaningless, and possibly nonexistent, differences among products. Advertising raises the cost of products and frequently contains very little information. Often, it is merely an annoyance. Product differentiation and advertising have turned the system upside down: people exist to satisfy the needs of the economy and not vice versa. Advertising can lead to unproductive warfare and may serve as a barrier to entry, thus reducing real competition.

Is There a Right Answer?   One of the things that you will see over and over as you study economics, and many other subjects too, is that a lot of questions have no right answers. There are strong arguments on both sides of this one, and even the empirical evidence leads to conflicting conclusions. Some studies show that advertising leads to concentration and excess profits; others, that advertising improves the functioning of the market.[5]

The Behavior of Firms Under Monopolistic Competition (Conduct)

When we first defined this market structure we said that monopolistically competitive industries are made up of a large number of firms, each small relative to the size of the total market. Thus no one firm can affect market price *by virtue of its size alone*. Firms do differentiate their products, however, and by doing so, they gain some control over price.

Product Differentiation and Demand Elasticity   Purely competitive firms face a perfectly elastic demand for their product: all firms produce exactly the same product, and if any one firm tried to raise price, buyers would simply go elsewhere and the firm would sell nothing. When a firm can distinguish its product from all others in the minds of consumers, as we assume it can under monopolistic competition, it probably can raise price without losing all demand. Figure 14.2 shows how product differentiation might make demand somewhat less elastic for a hypothetical firm.

---

[5]The most widely quoted study showing that advertising restricts competition is William S. Comoner and Thomas A. Wilson, *Advertising and Market Power* (Cambridge, Mass.: Harvard University Press, 1974). As one example of the opposing argument, see John M. Scheidell, *Advertising, Prices, and Consumer Reaction: A Dynamic Analysis* (Washington, D.C.: American Enterprise Institute, 1978).

FIGURE 14.2

Product Differentiation Reduces the Elasticity of Demand Facing a Firm

While the demand curve faced by a monopolistic competitor is likely to be *less* elastic than the demand curve faced by a perfectly competitive firm, it is likely to be *more* elastic than the demand curve faced by a monopolist because *close* substitutes for the products of a monopolistic competitor are available.

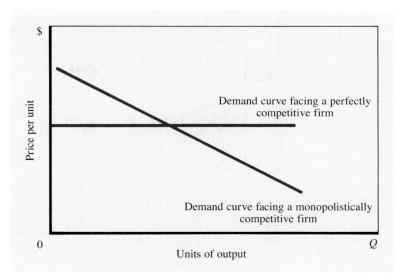

A monopoly, we said, is an industry with a single firm that produces a good for which there are no close substitutes. A monopolistically competitive firm is like a monopoly in that it is the only producer of its unique product—remember, there is only one Ivory Soap. But unlike in a monopoly market, the product of a monopolistically competitive firm has *many close substitutes* competing for the consumer's favor. While the demand curve faced by a monopolistic competitor is likely to be *less* elastic than the demand curve faced by a perfectly competitive firm, it is likely to be *more* elastic than the demand curve faced by a monopoly.

Price/Output Determination in the Short Run   Under conditions of monopolistic competition, a profit-maximizing firm behaves very much like a monopolist in the short run. First, marginal revenue is not equal to price, because the firm has some control over output price. As with monopoly, in order to increase output and sell it, a firm must lower price. The marginal revenue curve thus lies *below* the demand curve, falling below the quantity axis midway between the origin and the intercept of the demand curve, as you can see in Figure 14.3. (If necessary, review Chapter 13 to get a grip on this idea.)

The firm then chooses that combination of output and price that maximizes profit. In order to maximize profit, the firm will produce as long as the marginal revenue from increasing output and selling it exceeds the marginal cost of producing it. In Figure 14.3a, the profit-maximizing output is q_o. To sell q_o units of product, the firm must charge P_o. Total revenue is $P_o \times q_o$, or the area of P_oAq_oO. Total cost is equal to average total cost times q_o, or CBq_oO. Thus, total profit is equal to the difference, or area P_oABC.

Nothing guarantees that a firm in a monopolistically competitive industry will earn economic profits in the short run. Figure 14.3b shows what happens when a firm with the same cost curves faces a weaker market demand. Even though the firm does have some control over price, market demand is insufficient to make the firm profitable.

As in pure competition, such a firm *minimizes its losses* by producing up to the point where marginal revenue is equal to marginal cost. Of course, as in competition, the price that it charges must be sufficient to cover variable costs or else the firm will shut down and suffer losses equal to total fixed costs, rather than increasing losses by producing more. In other words, the firm must make a profit on operation. In Figure 14.3b, the

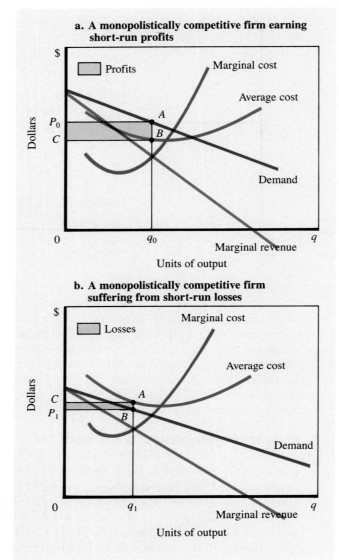

a. A monopolistically competitive firm earning short-run profits

Profits

Marginal cost

Average cost

A

P_0

B

C

Demand

Dollars

0 q_0 Marginal revenue q

Units of output

b. A monopolistically competitive firm suffering from short-run losses

Losses

Marginal cost

Average cost

C A

P_1 B

Demand

Dollars

0 q_1 Marginal revenue q

Units of output

FIGURE 14.3

Monopolistic Competition in the Short Run

a. In the short run, the diagram of a typical monopolistically competitive firm is identical to the diagram of a monopolist. But with free entry, the equilibrium will change in the long run. b. Here average variable costs are kept out of the diagram; we assume that price, P_1, is sufficient to cover variable costs.

loss-minimizing level of output is q_1. Total revenue is $P_1 \times q_1$, or P_1Bq_10. Total cost, or CAq_10, is greater than revenue, and the firm suffers a loss equal to $CABP_1$.

Price/Output Determination in the Long Run   In analyzing monopolistic competition, our key assumption is that entry and exit are, in the long run, free. Firms can enter an industry when there are profits to be made, and firms suffering losses may fold up and go out of business. But entry into an industry of this sort is somewhat different from what it is in pure competition, because products are differentiated. A firm that enters a monopolistically competitive industry is producing a close substitute for the good in question, *but not the same good.*

Let us begin with a firm earning economic profits in the short run. Its economic profits provide an incentive for new firms to enter. As they come into the industry, the

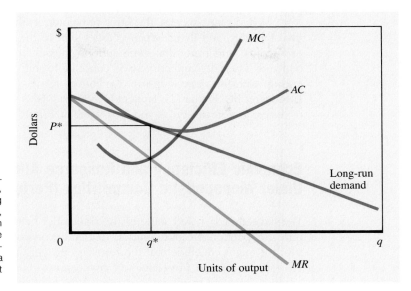

FIGURE 14.4
Monopolistically Competitive
Firm at Long-Run Equilibrium

As new firms enter, seeking profits,
the demand curves of profit-making
existing firms begin to shift to the left,
pushing marginal revenue with them
as consumers switch to the new close
substitutes. This continues until profits are eliminated. That occurs for a
firm when its demand curve is just
tangent to its average cost curve.

new firms compete by offering close substitutes, and this drives down the demand for the
product of the firm that was previously earning economic profits. If several restaurants
seem to be doing very well in a particular location, for example, others may start up and
attract business from them.

New firms will continue to enter the market until excess profits are eliminated. As
this happens, the demand curve facing each old firm in Figure 14.3a begins to shift to the
left, pushing the marginal revenue curve along with it. This shift continues until profits
are eliminated. This occurs when the demand curve slips down to the average total cost
curve, at which point the demand curve and the average total cost curve are tangent.
(That is, they just touch and have the same slope). Figure 14.4 shows a monopolistically
competitive industry in long-run equilibrium. At q^* and P^*, price and average total cost
are equal, and there are no economic profits or losses.

If you look carefully at this tangency, which in Figure 14.4 is at output level q^*, it is
clear that it occurs at the profit-maximizing level of output. Move a bit to the left and
average cost is higher than price; move a bit to the right and average cost is higher than
price. It is also interesting that at q^* not only is the demand curve tangent to the ATC
curve, but marginal revenue and marginal cost are equal.[6]

Even if a firm starts with losses in the industry, it will arrive at the same equilibrium.
(Look back at Figure 14.3b, which shows a firm suffering losses). Suppose that too many
restaurants opened up in a given small area, for example. Near Philadelphia, along a strip
of highway called City Line, there are a dozen or so "quick dinner" restaurants crowded
into a very small area. Most diners go to one or two of the popular spots, while business is
slow at the others. It thus seems likely that there will be a "shake-out" sometime in the
near future—that is, one or more firms suffering losses will decide to drop out of the
business.

[6]Remember the relationship between "marginal" and "average." Essentially the margin is what makes the average
move. If my marginal test score is 70 and my average is 90, my average will fall. For a firm, *price* is average
revenue, and it is being pulled downward by marginal revenue. By the same token, at q^* it is marginal cost that is
dragging average cost downward. At q^*, marginal cost and marginal revenue are equal, and average cost and
average revenue are equal, and the effect of the margin on the average should be the same for cost and revenue. In
other words, average cost and average revenue should be declining *at the same rate* at q^*, and this means that they
are tangent.

When that happens, the firms remaining in the industry get a larger share of the total business, and their demand curves shift to the right. Prosperous firms grow more prosperous, and firms that were suffering losses find them reduced by the additional demand. Their demand curves will continue to shift until losses are eliminated. Thus we end up with the same long-run equilibrium as we did when we started out with a firm earning profits. Demand is tangent to average total cost, and there are no economic profits or losses, as you can see if you look again at Figure 14.4.

Economic Efficiency and Resource Allocation Under Monopolistic Competition (Performance)

We have already noted some of the similarities between monopolistic competition and pure competition. Because entry is free and economic profits are eliminated in the long run, we might conclude that the result is efficient. There are two problems, however.

First, once a firm achieves any degree of market power by differentiating its product, its profit-maximizing strategy is to hold down production and charge a price above marginal cost, as you can see from Figures 14.3 and 14.4. Remember from Chapter 12 that price is the value that society places on a good, and marginal cost is the value that society places on the resources needed to produce it. Thus by holding production down and price above marginal cost, monopolistically competitive firms prevent the efficient use of resources. More product could be produced at a resource cost below the value that consumers place on the product.

Second, notice in Figure 14.4 that the final equilibrium is necessarily to the left of the low point on the average total cost curve. In a monopolistically competitive industry, a typical firm will therefore not realize all the economies of scale available. In pure competition, as you recall, firms were pushed to the bottom of their long-run average cost curves.

In the real world, let us say that a number of firms enter an industry and build plants based on initially profitable positions. But as more and more firms compete for those profits, individual firms find themselves with smaller and smaller market shares, and they end up eventually with "excess capacity." The firm in Figure 14.4 is not fully utilizing its existing capacity because competition drove its demand curve to the left. Thus in monopolistic competition we end up with many firms, each producing a slightly different product at a scale that is less than optimal. Would it not seem better to have a smaller number of firms, each producing on a slightly larger scale?

These costs, however, need to be balanced against the potential gains that can accrue from aggressive competition among products. If, as we said earlier, product differentiation leads to the introduction of new products, improvements in old products, and greater variety, then a rather important gain in economic welfare counteracts, and perhaps outweighs, the loss of efficiency from pricing above marginal cost or not fully realizing all economies of scale.

Most industries that comfortably fit the model of monopolistic competition are very competitive. Price competition coexists with product competition, and firms do not earn outrageous profits. Nor do they violate any of the antitrust laws that we discuss in detail in the next chapter.

Such firms have not been a subject of great concern among economic policy makers. Their behavior appears to be sufficiently controlled by competitive forces, and no serious attempt has been made to regulate or control them.

OLIGOPOLY

The Structure of Oligopoly

Oligopoly   A form of industry (market) structure characterized by a few firms that are each large enough to influence market price by virtue of size. Products may be homogeneous or differentiated. The behavior of any one firm in an oligopoly very much depends on the behavior of others.

An **oligopoly** is a market dominated by a few firms that, by virtue of their individual sizes, are large enough to influence the market price. Oligopolies come in a great variety of different structures. In some oligopoly markets, products are differentiated—the classic example is the automobile industry. In others, products are nearly homogeneous—in primary copper production, for example, only eight firms produce all the basic metal. Some oligopolies have a very small number of firms, each large enough to influence price. Only four firms are in primary lead production, for example. Others have many firms, and only a few control market price—four firms control 90 percent of the market for electric lamps, but 128 firms compete in the industry.

Table 14.4 contains some data on nine industries that are relatively concentrated. While the largest firms account for most of the output in each, some seem to support a large number of smaller firms. When an industry has a relatively small number of firms that dominate the market we call it a "concentrated industry." Oligopolies are *concentrated industries.*

TABLE 14.4
Percentage of Value of Shipments Accounted for by the Largest Firms in High-Concentration Industries, 1982

SIC Number	Industry Designation	Four largest firms	Eight largest firms	Number of firms
3332	Primary lead	NA	100	5
3711	Motor vehicles	92	97	284
2067	Chewing gum	95	NA	9
3996	Hard surface floor covering	99	99	12
3641	Electric lamps	91	96	113
2043	Cereal breakfast foods	89	98	32
3331	Primary copper	NA	100	7
3635	Vacuum cleaners	80	96	29
2296	Tire cord and fabric	81	99	12

Source: U.S. Department of Commerce, Bureau of the Census, 1982 Census of Manufactures, *Concentration Ratios in Manufacturing*, Subject Series MC-82-S-7. NA = Not available.

What makes oligopoly so difficult to analyze precisely is the complex interdependence that usually exists among and between firms in these industries. The behavior of any one firm depends on what reactions it expects of all the other firms in the industry. Because individual firms make so many decisions—how much output to produce, what price to charge, how much advertising to do, whether and when to introduce new product lines, and so forth—industrial strategies can be, and usually are, very complicated and difficult to generalize about.

The Behavior of Firms under Oligopoly (Conduct)

Many different kinds of market structure qualify as oligopolies. As a result, a number of different models of oligopoly have been developed. A complete survey would exceed our

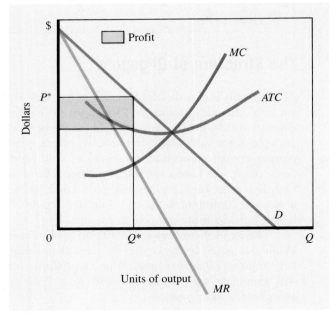

FIGURE 14.5
Market Equilibrium for a
Colluding Oligopoly is Just Like
a Monopoly

If all firms in a competitive industry
jointly profit-maximize, the result is
just as it would be under a pure monopoly. The cartel would face market
demand and produce only up to the
point where marginal revenue and
marginal cost are equal.

purposes, but what follows provides a good sample of alternative approaches to the
behavior, or conduct, of oligopolistic firms. As you will see, all kinds of oligopoly have one
thing in common: the behavior of any given firm depends on the behavior of the other
firms in the industry.

The Collusion model   In Chapter 13, we examined what happens in a purely
competitive industry when it falls under the control of a single profit-maximizing firm. In
that analysis, we presupposed no technological or cost advantages to having one firm
rather than many. There you saw that when many competing firms act independently,
they produce more, charge a lower price, and earn less profit than if they acted as a single
unit. If they get together and agree to cut production and increase price—that is, if firms
can agree *not* to price compete—they will have a bigger total-profit pie to carve up.
When a group of profit-maximizing oligopolists collude on price and output, the result is
exactly the same as it would be if a monopolist controlled the entire industry, as you can
see in Figure 14.5.

Cartel   A group of firms that get together and make joint price and output decisions.

A group of firms that get together and make price and output decisions jointly is
called a **cartel**. Perhaps the most familiar example of a cartel today is the Organization of
Petroleum Exporting Countries (OPEC). As early as 1970, OPEC began to cut
production, and its decisions in this matter led to a rise in the price of crude oil on world
markets during 1973 and 1974 of over 400 percent in less than a year.

Price fixing is not controlled internationally, but it is illegal in the United States
under the antitrust laws. Nonetheless, the incentive to fix prices can be irresistible, and
industries are caught doing it from time to time. One very famous case in the 1950s
involved explicit agreements among a number of electrical equipment manufacturers. In
that instance, 12 people from five companies met secretly on a number of occasions and
agreed to set prices and split up contracts and profits. The scheme involved rotating
among the firms the winning bids on alternate contracts in accordance with the phases of
the moon. Ultimately the scheme was exposed, and the participants were tried, convicted,
and sent to jail.

For a cartel to work, a number of conditions must be present. First, demand for the

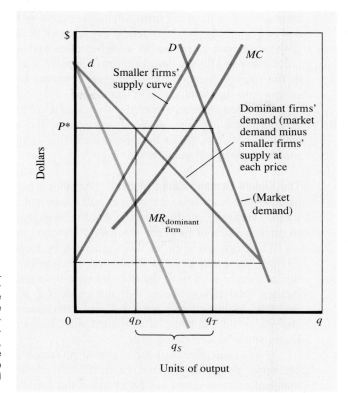

FIGURE 14.6

Price Leadership with a Single Dominant Firm

The demand curve facing the dominant firm is derived by subtracting the amount supplied at the average price by the smaller firms from market demand. For example, at P* market demand is q_T, smaller firms supply q_S, leaving q_D for the dominant firm. The dominant firm then sets Q and P to maximize profit, subject its demand curve.

Collusion and tacit collusion   *Collusion occurs when price- and quantity-fixing agreements among producers are explicit. Tacit collusion occurs when such agreements are implicit.*

Price leadership   *The result when one firm that dominates an oligopoly sets prices and all the smaller firms in the industry follow its pricing policy.*

cartel's product must be inelastic. If a lot of substitutes are readily available, the cartel's price increases may be self-defeating as buyers simply switch to the substitutes. Second, the members of the cartel must play by the rules. If a cartel is holding up prices by restricting output, there is a big incentive for members to cheat by increasing output, even a little bit. Breaking ranks can mean very large profits.

Both of these problems have plagued the OPEC cartel in recent years. First, demand turned out to be much more elastic in the long run than it was in the short run. The United States and most other consuming nations now import far less oil than they did in the mid 1970s. Second, individual members, finding their revenues eroded by lower world prices, have cheated on the agreement by increasing production. The problem of member discipline has been exacerbated because many more non-OPEC nations now produce oil than were producing it in 1973.

Collusion occurs when price-fixing agreements are explicit. When firms end up fixing price without a specific agreement, it is called **tacit collusion**. A small number of firms with market power may fall into the practice of setting similar prices or following the lead of one firm without ever meeting or setting down formal agreements.

The Price-Leadership Model   A similar, but not identical, result may ensue when one firm dominates an industry and all the smaller firms decide to follow the leader's pricing policy—hence the descriptive term **price leadership**. If the dominant firm knows that the smaller firms will follow its lead, it will derive its own demand curve by simply subtracting from total market demand the amount of demand that the smaller firms will satisfy.

Figure 14.6 diagrams price leadership behavior when a single firm dominates an industry. The dominant firm begins by deriving its own demand curve under the assumption that the small firms will follow its pricing lead. The shapes of its demand curve and marginal revenue curve reflect the behavior of both consumers and competing firms. If the dominant firm charges a higher price and smaller firms follow suit, two things reduce demand for the dominant firm's product. First, of course, consumers buy less of it in the market. Second, the competing firms are likely to supply more output, further cutting into the dominant firm's sales.

The demand curve labeled with a small d in Figure 14.6 embodies both the reaction of consumers and the assumed reaction of the smaller firms. The dominant firm maximizes its own profit by setting price P^*, supplying quantity q_D, and allowing the smaller firms to sell quantity q_s.

Kinked demand curve model *A model in which the demand curve facing each individual firm has a "kink" in it. The kink follows from the assumption that competitive firms will follow suit if a single firm cuts price but will not follow suit if a single firm raises price.*

The Kinked Demand Curve Model   Another common model of oligopolistic behavior assumes that firms believe that rivals will follow suit if they *cut* prices but not if they *raise* them. In other words, they assume that the elasticity of demand in response to an increase in price is different from the elasticity of demand in response to a price cut.

You can see some of these reactions by examining the demand curve in Figure 14.7. If the initial price is P^*, a firm considering raising price would face an elastic demand curve if its rivals did not also raise their prices. That is, in response to the price increase undertaken above, demand would fall off quickly. The reaction to a price decrease would not be as great, because rivals would decrease price too. The firm under analysis would lose some of its market share by increasing price, but it would not get a bigger share by decreasing price.

Now remember that the marginal revenue curve reflects the changes in demand occurring along the demand curve *directly above it*. (Review the derivation of the marginal revenue curve in Chapter 13 if this is not fresh in your mind.) That being the case, MR_1 reflects the changes in P and q along demand curve segment d_1. MR_2 reflects changes in P and q along demand curve segment d_2.

As always, profit-maximizing firms will produce as long as marginal revenue is greater than marginal cost. If, as in Figure 14.7, the marginal cost curve passes through q^* at any point between A and B, the optimal price is P^* and optimal output is q^*. To the left of q^*, marginal revenue is greater than marginal cost; to maximize profits, then, the firm should increase output. To the right of q^*, marginal cost is greater than marginal revenue; in this case the firm should not increase output, because producing above q^* will reduce profits.

Notice that this model predicts that in oligopolistic industries price is likely to be more stable than costs. In Figure 14.7, the marginal cost curve can shift up or down by a substantial amount before it becomes advantageous to change price at all. A number of attempts have been made to test whether oligopolistic prices are indeed more stable than costs. While the results do not support the hypothesis of stable prices, the evidence is far from conclusive.[7]

The **kinked demand curve model** has been criticized on a number of grounds. First, it fails to explain why the price is at P^* to begin with. Second, the assumption that competing firms will follow price cuts but not price increases is overly simple; real-world oligopolistic pricing strategies are much more complex.

Strategic Reaction: The Cournot Model   Perhaps the oldest model of oligopoly behavior was put forward by Augustin Cournot almost a hundred and fifty years ago. The

---

[7]See for example Julian Simon, "A Further Test of the Kinky Oligopoly Demand Curve," *American Economic Review* (December 1969), and George Stigler, "The Kinky Oligopoly Demand Curve and Rigid Prices," *Journal of Political Economy*, 55 (1947).

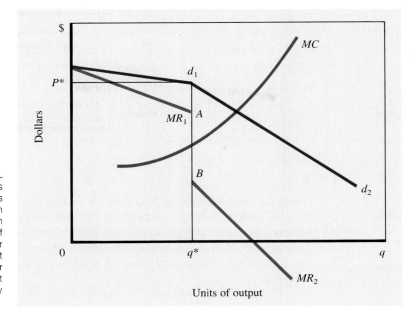

FIGURE 14.7
A Kinked Demand Curve
Oligopoly Model

The kinked demand model assumes that competing firms follow price cuts but not price increases. Thus if a firm increased its price, the competition would not, and demand would fall off quickly. But if a firm cuts price, other firms would as well, and the price cut would not gain as much demand for that firm as it would if they did not follow. Above d_1 demand is relatively elastic. Below d_1 elasticity falls.

The Cournot model   *A model of a two-firm industry (duopoly) in which each firm fails to properly anticipate the reaction of its competitor to its own output and pricing decisions.*

Cournot model is based on three assumptions: (1) that there are just two firms in an industry—this is called a *duopoly*; (2) that each firm takes the output of the other as given; and (3) that both firms maximize profits.

The story begins with a new firm producing nothing and the existing firm producing everything—that is, the existing firm simply takes the market demand curve as its own, acting like a monopolist. When the new firm starts operating, it assumes that the existing firm will continue to produce the same level of output and charge the same price as before. The market demand of the new firm, then, is simply market demand less the amount that the existing firm is currently selling. In essence, the new firm assumes that its demand curve is everything on the market demand curve below the price charged by the older firm.

When the new firm starts operation, the existing firm discovers that its demand has eroded. Now it assumes that the output of the new firm will remain constant, subtracts it from market demand, and produces a new, lower level of output. But that throws the ball back to the new firm, which now finds that the competition is producing less.

These adjustments get smaller and smaller, with the new firm raising output in small steps and the initial firm lowering output in small steps until the two firms split the market and charge the same price.

While the Cournot model illustrates the interdependence of decisions in oligopoly, its assumption about strategic reactions are quite naïve. The two firms in the model react only after the fact and never come to anticipate the moves of the competition.

Strategic Reaction Anticipated: Game Theory   The firms in Cournot's model do not anticipate the moves of the competition. Yet in choosing among strategies in an oligopolistic market, real-world firms can and do try to guess what the opposition will do in response to any move they might make.

In 1944 John von Neumann and Oskar Morgenstern published a path-breaking work in which they analyzed a set of problems, or *games*, in which two or more people or

FIGURE 14.8
Payoff Matrix for Advertising Game

		B'S STRATEGY: Don't Advertise	B'S STRATEGY: Advertise
A'S STRATEGY	Don't advertise	A's profit = \$50,000 B's profit = \$50,000	A's profit = \$25,000 B's loss = \$75,000
A'S STRATEGY	Advertise	A's profit = \$75,000 B's loss = \$25,000	A's profit = \$10,000 B's profit = \$10,000

organizations pursue their own interests and no one of them can dictate the outcome.[8]

Game theory *Analyzes oligopolistic behavior as a complex series of strategic moves and reactive countermoves among rival firms. In game theory firms are assumed to anticipate rival reactions.*

Game theory goes something like this: as in all conflict situations, and thus all games, there are decision makers, or players, rules of the game, and payoffs, or prizes. Players choose strategies without knowing with certainty what strategy the opposition will use, but some information may be available to the players that indicates how their opposition may be "leaning."

Figure 14.8 illustrates what is called a "payoff matrix" for a very simple game. Two firms, A and B, each must decide whether to mount an expensive advertising campaign. If neither firm decides to advertise, each will earn a profit of \$50,000. But if one firm advertises and the second does not, the firm that does will increase its profit by 50 percent, to \$75,000, while driving the competition into the loss column. If both firms decide to advertise, they will each earn \$10,000. They may generate a bit more demand by advertising, but that is completely wiped out by the expense of the advertising itself.

If they could collude (and we assumed they cannot), the optimal strategy would be to agree not to advertise. That solution maximizes the joint profits to both firms. If neither firm advertises, joint profits are \$100,000. If both firms advertise, joint profits are only \$20,000. If only one of the firms advertises, joint profits are \$50,000.

The strategy that firm A will actually choose depends on the information available concerning B's likely strategy and on A's preferences for risk. In analyzing games, it is often assumed that players will adopt strategies that minimize the damage that the opposition can do. In other words, they first assume that the competition will choose the strategy that will cause them the most damage. For example, if A advertises, the *worst* thing that can happen is that it will earn \$10,000. If A does not advertise, the worst thing that can happen is that it will lose \$25,000. To minimize the potential damage, A would choose to advertise. If both followed the same strategy of minimizing potential damage, both would advertise and end up with \$10,000 profits.

If the players don't assume the worst, but we allow them to switch strategies, the results are the same. Let A choose a strategy. *Once A has chosen, it* always *pays B to advertise*. If A advertises, B suffers a \$25,000 loss by not advertising but earns \$10,000 by advertising. If A does *not* advertise, it still pays B to advertise. By advertising when A does not, B earns profits of \$75,000 rather than the \$50,000 it would earn by not advertising. Similarly, *once B has chosen, it* always *pays A to advertise*.[9]

When game theory first appeared in the late 1940s, it seemed that it would in time

[8]See J. von Neumann and O. Morgenstern, *Theory of Games and Economic Behavior* (Princeton, N.J.: Princeton University Press, 1944).

[9]The lower right corner of the payoff matrix, \$10,000 profit to each firm, is a stable outcome called a *Nash equilibrium*. A Nash equilibrium has the property that given firm 1's strategy, firm 2 can do no better, and given firm 2's strategy, firm 1 can do no better.

be able to explain the behavior of oligopoly firms in great detail. However, when we move from two potential strategies to three or four, and particularly when we move to more than two players, the number of potential outcomes and the properties of the strategy pairings become enormously complex, and it becomes very difficult to predict which strategy, or which combination of strategies, a firm might choose in any given circumstance.

In the end, game theory leaves us with a greater understanding of the *problem* of oligopoly but with an incomplete and somewhat inconclusive set of propositions about the *likely behavior* of oligopolistic firms. Some very interesting conclusions emerge about a fairly small number of specific game circumstances, but game theory doesn't provide much help with an industry of five firms, each simultaneously choosing product, pricing, output, and advertising strategies.

About all we are left with is the certainty of *interdependence*—the strategy that a firm chooses is likely to depend on that firm's perceptions of the responses of competing firms.

Contestable Markets   Before we turn to the performance of oligopolies, we should note one relatively new theory of behavior that has limited applications but some important implications for understanding imperfectly competitive market behavior.

Perfectly contestable market   A market in which entry and exit are costless. If capital were fully mobile, a firm could enter a market, compete for profits, and leave without incurring start-up or shut-down costs.

A market is defined as **perfectly contestable** if entry to it *and* exit from it are costless. That is, a firm can move into a market in search of excess profits, but if it fails, it loses nothing. In order to do this, a firm must have capital that is both mobile and easily transferable from one market to another.

Take, for example, a small airline that can move its capital stock from one market to another with little cost. Provincetown Boston Airlines (PBA) runs routes between Boston, Martha's Vineyard, Nantucket, and Cape Cod during the summer months. During the winter, the same planes are taken to Florida, where they fly up and down that state's west coast between Naples, Fort Meyers, Tampa, and other cities. Or, when a new industrial complex is built at a fairly remote site, a number of trucking companies may offer their services. Their capital stock, too, is mobile, and if a competing firm does not do well, it can move its trucks somewhere else at no great cost.

Because entry is cheap, participants in a contestable market are continuously faced with competition or the threat of competition. Even if there are only a few firms competing, the openness of the market forces them to produce efficiently or be driven out. This threat of potential competition remains high simply because new firms face very little risk in going after a new market. If things don't work out in a crowded market, they don't lose their investment. They can simply transfer their capital to a different place or different use.

In contestable markets, even large firms end up behaving like perfectly competitive firms. Prices are pushed to long-run average cost by competition, and economic profits do not persist.

As you can see, oligopoly is a market structure that is consistent with a variety of behaviors, or conducts. All that is necessary is that firms are large enough to have some control over price; oligopolies are concentrated industries. At one extreme is the cartel, in which the few firms get together and jointly maximize profits—in essence acting as a monopolist. At the other extreme, the firms within the oligopoly vigorously compete for small contestable markets by moving capital quickly in response to observed economic profits. In between the two are a number of alternative models, all of which stress interdependence of firms.

The Performance of Firms in an Oligopoly

As with other market structures, the final question to ask about oligopoly is How well does it perform? Are oligopolistic industries good or bad? Should they be regulated or changed? Are they efficient, or do they lead to an inefficient use of resources? With the exception of the contestable-markets model, all the models of oligopoly we have looked at lead to the conclusion that concentration in a market leads to pricing above marginal cost with output below the efficient level. When price is above marginal cost at equilibrium, consumers are paying more for the good than it costs to produce it in terms of products forgone in other industries. To increase output would be to create value that exceeds the social cost of the good, but firms have an incentive not to do so.

Entry barriers in many oligopolistic industries also prevent new capital and other resources from responding to profit signals. Under competitive conditions or in contestable markets, excess profits would attract new firms and thus increase production. This problem is most severe when entry barriers exist and firms explicitly or tacitly collude. The results are essentially identical to the results of a monopoly: firms jointly profit-maximize by fixing prices at a high level and splitting up the profits among themselves.

Product differentiation under oligopoly also presents us with the same dilemma that we encountered in monopolistic competition. On the one hand, vigorous product competition among oligopolistic competitors produces variety and leads to innovation in response to the wide variety of consumer tastes and preferences. It can be argued that vigorous product competition is efficient. On the other hand, product differentiation may lead to waste and inefficiency. Product differentiation accomplished through advertising may have nothing to do with product quality, and advertising itself may have little or no information content. If it serves as an entry barrier that blocks competition, product differentiation can cause the market allocation mechanism to fail.

To sum up, oligopolistic, or concentrated, industries are likely to be inefficient for several reasons. First, profit-maximizing oligopolists are likely to produce where product price is above marginal cost. When price is above marginal cost, there is underproduction from society's point of view: in other words, society could get more for less, but it doesn't. Second, strategic behavior can lead to outcomes that are not in society's best interest. Specifically, strategically competitive firms can force themselves into deadlocks that waste scarce resources. Finally, to the extent that oligopolies differentiate their products and advertise, there is the promise of new and exciting products. At the same time, however, there remains a real danger of waste.

Industrial Concentration and Technological Change   One of the major sources of economic growth and progress throughout history has been technological advance. Innovation, both in methods of production and in the creation of new and better products, is one of the engines of economic progress. Much innovation starts with research and development efforts undertaken by firms in search of profit.

Several economists, most notably Joseph Schumpeter and John Kenneth Galbraith, argued in works now considered classics that industrial concentration actually increases the rate of technological advance. As Schumpeter put it in 1942:

> As soon as we . . . inquire into the individual items in which progress was most conspicuous, the trail leads not to the doors of those firms that work under conditions of comparatively free competition but precisely to the doors of the large concerns . . . and

a shocking suspicion dawns upon us that big business may have had more to do with creating that standard of life than keeping it down.[10]

The Schumpeterian hypothesis caused the economics profession to pause and take stock. The conventional wisdom had always been that concentration and barriers to entry insulated firms from competition and led to sluggish performance and slow growth.

The evidence as to where innovation comes from is mixed. Certainly, most small businesses do not engage in research and development, and most large firms do. When taken as a percentage of sales, firms in industries with high concentration ratios spend more on research and development than firms in industries with low concentration ratios.

Oligopolistic companies such as IBM and AT&T have done incredible amounts of research. AT&T's Bell Laboratories probably did more important primary research than any other organization in the country over the last several decades. It has been estimated that Bell Labs did 10 percent of *all* the basic industrial research in the United States during the 1970s. IBM, which set the industry standard in personal computers, has certainly introduced as much new technology to the computer industry as any other firm.

On the other hand, the "high-tech revolution" grew out of many tiny start-up operations. Companies such as the Digital Equipment Corporation, Wang Laboratories, Apple Computers, and many others barely existed only a few years ago. The new biotechnology firms that are just beginning to work miracles with genetic engineering are still tiny operations that started with research done by individual scientists in university laboratories.

Here again, as with the debate about product differentiation and advertising, significant ambiguity remains. Indeed, there may be no right answer. Technological change seems to come in fits and starts, sometimes from small firms and sometimes from large ones.

Industrial Concentration and Government   Certainly there is much in the behavior of large, concentrated industries to guard against. Barriers to entry, large size, and product differentiation all lead to market power and potentially to inefficiency. Barriers to entry and collusive behavior stop the market from working toward an efficient allocation of resources.

For several reasons, however, economists no longer attack industry concentration with quite the same fervor that they once did. First, the theory of contestable markets shows that even firms in highly concentrated industries can be pushed to produce efficiently in certain market circumstances. Second, the benefits of product differentiation and product competition are real, at least in part. After all, a constant stream of new products and new variations of old products does come to the market almost daily. Third, the effects of concentration on the rate of research and development spending are, at worst, mixed. It is certainly true that large firms do a substantial amount of the total research in the United States. Fourth and finally, in many industries, substantial economies of scale simply preclude a completely competitive structure.

In addition to the debate about the desirability of industrial concentration, there is a never-ending debate about the historical role of government in regulating markets and what the proper role of government should be. One view is that high levels of concentration lead to inefficiency and that it is proper for government to act in an effort to improve the allocation of resources—to help the market work more efficiently. This logic

---

[10]J.A. Schumpeter, *Capitalism, Socialism and Democracy* (New York: Harper, 1942) and J.K. Galbraith, *American Capitalism* (Boston: Houghton Mifflin, 1952).

has been used to justify the antitrust laws and other regulations aimed at noncompetitive behavior.

Another view is that the clearest examples of effective barriers to entry are ones actually created by government. This view holds that government regulation in past years has been anticompetitive and has made the allocation of resources worse than it would have been with no government involvement. Recall from our discussion in Chapter 13 that those who earn economic profits have an incentive to spend resources to protect themselves and their profits from competitors. This *rent-seeking* behavior may include using the power of government.

In the next chapter, we look carefully at the role of government and the potential role of government in imperfectly competitive markets.

SUMMARY

1. Most analyses of industries start with a discussion of market structure. How many firms are there? What portion of the industry's total sales is accounted for by the top four firms? By the top eight firms? Do firms produce homogeneous, or differentiated, products? Are there economies of scale?

2. Next, analyses turn to conduct. How do firms behave? How are prices set? Is there a dominant firm that smaller firms follow? Do firms advertise?

3. The ultimate purpose of most industry analyses is to determine the effect of structure and conduct on performance. Is the industry efficient? Does it enhance or retard economic growth?

4. A monopolistically competitive industry has the following characteristics: (1) a large number of firms, (2) no barriers to entry, and (3) product differentiation.

5. An example of monopolistic competition is the restaurant business (leaving out the big national chains).

6. Some argue that product differentiation and advertising give the market system its vitality and power. Others argue that they are wasteful and inefficient.

7. By differentiating their products, firms hope to be able to raise price without losing all demand, as would be the case if all firms produced identical or homogeneous products. The demand curve facing a monopolistic competitor is less than perfectly elastic.

8. When firms enter a monopolistically competitive industry, they introduce close substitutes for the goods being produced. This attracts demand away from the firms already in the industry. Demand faced by each firm shifts left, and profits are ultimately eliminated.

9. Monopolistically competitive firms end up pricing above marginal cost. This is inefficient, just as it was in the case of monopoly. This model also predicts that firms will find themselves producing below full capacity; they will end up with wasted excess plant capacity.

10. An oligopoly is a market dominated by a few firms that, by virtue of their individual sizes, have the power to influence market price.

11. The behavior of a single oligopolistic firm depends on what reactions it expects of all the other firms in the industry. Industrial strategies can be, and usually are, very complicated and difficult to generalize about.

12. When firms collude, either explicitly or tacitly, they jointly maximize profits by charging an agreed-upon price or by setting output limits and splitting profits. The result is exactly the same as it would be if only one firm were in the industry.

13. The price-leadership model gives a similar but not identical result. In this organization, the leader sets a price and allows competing firms to supply all they want.

14. A firm faces a kinked demand curve if competitors follow price cuts but fail to respond to price increases.

15. Game theory analyzes the behavior of participants as if their behavior were a series of strategic plays. It helps us understand the problem of oligopoly but leaves us with an incomplete and inconclusive set of propositions about the likely behavior of individual firms.

16. A market is defined as perfectly contestable if entry and exit are free. That is, a firm can move into a market in search of excess profits, but if it fails, it loses nothing. Firms in such industries must have mobile capital.

17. The behavior of oligopolistic firms is likely to lead to an inefficient allocation of resources.

REVIEW CONCEPTS

industry structure   334

firm behavior, or conduct   334

industry performance   334

monopolistic competition   334

product differentiation   336

oligopoly   345

cartel   346

collusion   347

tacit collusion   347

price leadership   347

kinked demand curve model   348

the Cournot model   349

game theory   350

perfectly contestable markets   351

REVIEW QUESTIONS

1. Which of the following industries is likely to be monopolistically competitive? Why?
   a. Specialty ice cream stores
   b. Retail pharmacies
   c. Steel production
   d. Lumber products

2. Suppose that a new specialty ice cream store opens in your hometown. Soon people are lining up outside the place every day for hours. The store sells ice cream cones for $2.00, and they cost $.50 to produce. Describe the likely response of the market over time. Be specific. What type of industry are we dealing with?

3. Which of the following markets are likely to be contestable? Explain your answers.
   a. Shipbuilding
   b. Trucking
   c. House-cleaning services
   d. Wine production

4. The matrix below shows payoffs based on the strategies chosen by two firms. If they collude and hold prices at $10.00, each will earn profits of $5 million. If A cheats on the agreement, lowering his price, but B does not, A will get 75 percent of the business and earn profits of $8 million and B will lose $2 million. Similarly, if B cheats and A does not, B will earn $8 million and A will lose $2 million. If both cut prices, they will end up with $2 million each in profits.

   Which strategy minimizes the maximum potential loss for A? For B? If you were A, which strategy would you choose? Why? If A cheats, what will B do? If B cheats, what will A do? What is the most likely outcome of such a game? Explain.

5. Write a position paper on industrial concentration for the new President. Is this a problem in the United States? What are the advantages and disadvantages of strong actions against concentrated industries?

| | | B'S STRATEGY | |
		Stand by agreement	Cheat
A'S STRATEGY	**Stand by agreement**	A's profit: $5 million B's profit: $5 million	A's profit: −$2 million B's profit: $8 million
	Cheat	A's profit: $8 million B's profit: −$2 million	A's profit: $2 million B's profit: $2 million

15 Imperfect Markets and Public Policy: Antitrust and Regulation

If all the assumptions of perfect competition hold, the allocation of resources is efficient—the system produces the goods and services that people want, and it does so at least cost. No reshuffling of resources or output can improve the welfare of some without reducing the welfare of others. That was the message of Chapter 12.

As we began to relax some of those assumptions, however, we found several naturally occurring sources of "market failure." Chapters 13 and 14 dealt with the first of these, *imperfect markets*. Firms that are able to achieve some degree of control over the price of their products are likely to end up charging more and producing less than what is socially optimal. Thus far we have looked carefully at three different market structures that are apt to be inefficient: *monopoly*, *monopolistic competition*, and *oligopoly*.

When unregulated markets fail to produce efficiently, governments can and do act to improve the allocation of resources. Some of their actions, of course, lead to a *less* efficient allocation of resources as well. This chapter discusses in some detail the history and theory of government involvement in imperfectly competitive markets.

Historically, governments have assumed two basic and seemingly contradictory roles with respect to imperfectly competitive industries: (1) they *promote* competition and restrict market power primarily through antitrust laws and other Congressional acts and (2) they *restrict* competition by regulating industries.

FEDERAL ANTITRUST LAWS

Post-Civil-War America

The period immediately following the Civil War was one of rapid growth and change in the United States. As migrants headed to the open spaces, population swelled in the West as well as in the East. Railroads were built between all major cities, and in May of 1869 a golden spike driven at Promontory Point, Utah, completed the transcontinental line linking the East with California. Between 1864 and 1874, what was already a substantial rail network doubled in size. At the same time, factories sprang up to accommodate new methods of production that were constantly being introduced. Between 1870 and 1913, the economy grew at its fastest rate in U.S. history.

Before the Civil War, most firms had been small and their markets local. The high cost of transportation limited access to large market areas, and production technologies were efficient only on a small scale. But the railroads opened up the nation, and firms began to compete for national markets. Many of the new technologies exhibited economies of scale; real advantages to size in some industries soon became apparent.

Communications technology also changed dramatically during the same period. In 1877 an inventor offered to sell Western Union, for $100,000, a patent on a new method of sending information over wires. Alexander Graham Bell's asking price was just too high for Western Union, and it turned down the offer. Within ten years, telephone lines operated by Bell companies crisscrossed the country, linking city after city.[1]

As all of these forces drew the United States together, the character of the economy changed. Small firms selling to local markets were replaced by large firms selling to regional and national markets. With size came power, and with power came hunger for more power. Competition was fierce and often warlike.

The successful exercise of power meant driving out competition and controlling markets, and for many businesses these became explicit goals. Thousands of small firms, often under coercion, were gobbled up by big ones. Cartels fixed prices and controlled output. Price cutting to drive competitors out of business was common. Large firms got secret rebates from railroads. In this climate, the *trust* flourished. Shareholders of independent firms agreed to give up control of their stock in exchange for trust certificates that entitled them to a share of the common profits. A group of trustees then operated the combined firm as a monopoly, controlling output and setting price.

Before long, however, people saw that something was wrong with the system that had emerged. Small independent farmers facing large powerful railroads, monopsonistic buyers, and declining agricultural prices, began to organize. Formed in 1867, the National Grange became a strong pressure group on behalf of farmers against the power of big business. At the same time, life for the laboring classes in the cities and in factory towns was grim. Child labor, long hours, meager wages, and crowded housing in slums were reminiscent of conditions in England during the Industrial Revolution that began a century earlier.

"Big business" was held responsible, and its image was probably best captured in cartoons of grotesquely fat men with big cigars and diamond stickpins crushing workers and farmers underfoot. Perhaps the best known and most vilified of these "robber barons" was Jay Gould, who made a fortune manipulating railroad stocks and trying to monopolize the railroad business. In 1881 Gould controlled more railroad mileage than

[1]See Gerald Brock, *The Telecommunications Industry* (Cambridge, Mass.: Harvard University Press, 1980).

The Industrialists

Andrew Carnegie built a steel empire. Jay Gould monopolized the railroad business and manipulated its stock. Cornelius Vanderbilt improved steamship travel and technology.

These three men were nineteenth-century industrialists whose business wheelings and dealings earned them substantial fortunes and the title "robber barons." They and the other men like them—for example, J. P. Morgan and John D. Rockefeller,—controlled America's mills, banks, and railroads. Because of their immense power and wealth, these men were portrayed as greedy and vicious individuals who made their fortunes at the expense of the masses. Some robber barons deserved the title. Others, however, were simply good businessmen who worked hard and seized opportunity.

Cornelius Vanderbilt was one such smart businessman. In 1817, a New Jersey capitalist hired Vanderbilt to challenge Robert Fulton's monopoly on New York's waterways. Fulton was the only authorized carrier of steamboat passengers in the state. Defying the New York authorities, Vanderbilt ferried passengers between Elizabeth, NJ, and New York City at reduced fares. He was so successful that he drove Fulton's business to bankruptcy and extended steamboat transportation throughout the Northeast. Vanderbilt stayed ahead of the competition by taking advantage of technical innovations that lowered his costs. For example, he switched to a new type of boiler and used less expensive coal for fuel instead of costly wood. More important, he took risks. On the New York to Albany route he carried passengers without charge, depending on their purchases of food along the way to cover his costs. Vanderbilt did so well on this route that his competitors, to stay afloat, had to buy him out, paying him $100,000 outright plus $5,000 per year for ten years just to stay away.

Andrew Carnegie, another so-called robber baron, founded the largest and most profitable steel empire in the world. He forged his fortune by manufacturing new products and opening up new markets as necessary.

For twenty years, Carnegie's steel mills made rails. The great railroad systems were being built across the country, and the new routes required Carnegie's product. Eventually railroad expansion slowed, and the market for rails began to dry up. A steel manufacturer was going to have to look elsewhere for his bread and butter. Carnegie foresaw that growing urban centers would need steel beams for the multistoried structures made possible by the invention of the elevator. He ordered his plants to begin manufacturing structural beams used in constructing the increasingly popular skyscrapers.

Although Carnegie had been somewhat contemptuous of world trade, he realized that he needed to tap foreign markets to keep his steel empire growing. Carnegie Steel Co. hired a full-time sales manager to search out the European market. Sales agents were also appointed for China and Australia. Carnegie was never totally reconciled to foreign business ("Bad days for us when we have to take foreign trade," he once said), but he felt pride in his company's growing business abroad. Even when foreign trade became less profitable, Carnegie continued to deal with those markets, saying, "We need to sell a limited amount of product to foreign markets even though prices are low just so as to keep up connections there."

At home, Carnegie had two business concerns. He wanted to keep costs below those of his competitors in order to maintain the lowest price, and he wanted to gain total control over every aspect of steel production. The company had been focusing on only one operation, converting raw materials into steel. Carnegie decided to expand manufacturing under his roof to include the entire production cycle, from processing the raw materials to fashioning the final product. To make the company self-sufficient, Carnegie also gained part ownership or leases in 34 working mines. By achieving this vertical structure and gaining control over his raw material sources, Carnegie turned his highly successful business into an industrial empire.

The names of Rockefeller, Carnegie, Vanderbilt, and others are known today primarily because of the many charitable foundations, libraries, and museums that they founded. In fact, John D. Rockefeller gave away more wealth to charity —approximately $550 million—than any American before him had even possessed.

SOURCES: "The Rise of Big Business in America," *The World & I*, March 1988; Thomas B. Brewer, ed., *The Robber Barons*, New York: Holt, Rinehart and Winston, *1973.* Joseph Frazier Wall, *Andrew Carnegie*, New York: Oxford University Press.

Interstate Commerce Commission (ICC)   A federal regulatory group created by Congress in 1887 to oversee and correct abuses of the railroad industry.

any other individual or group. While recent research shows that Gould may not have been as evil as most history books portray him, there is no question that he wielded enormous power.

While public sentiment increasingly favored reform, faith in the market and in private enterprise also remained strong. In response to public pressure, Congress began to formulate **antitrust** legislation. In 1887, it created the **Interstate Commerce Commis-**

Sherman Act   *Passed by Congress in 1890, the Act declares every contract or conspiracy to restrain trade among states or nations illegal and declares any attempt at monopoly, successful or not, a misdemeanor. Interpretation of what specific behaviors were illegal fell to the courts.*

sion to regulate the railroads; in 1890 it passed the **Sherman Act**, which declared monopoly and trade restraints illegal. To control monopoly power in general, however, the Sherman Act turned not to regulation and public enterprise, but to *competition* and *the market*.

Landmark Antitrust Legislation

The Sherman Act of 1890   The real substance of the Sherman Act is contained in two short sections:

> *Section 1.* Every contract, combination in the form of trust or otherwise, or conspiracy, in restraint of trade or commerce among the several States, or with foreign nations, is hereby declared to be illegal. . . .

> *Section 2.* Every person who shall monopolize, or attempt to monopolize, or combine or conspire with any other person or persons, to monopolize any part of the trade or commerce among the several States, or with foreign nations, shall be deemed guilty of a misdemeanor, and, on conviction thereof, shall be punished by fine not exceeding five thousand dollars, or by imprisonment not exceeding one year, or by both said punishments, in the discretion of the court.

The biggest problem with the Sherman Act lay in its interpretation. The language of the statute seems to declare monopolistic *structure*, as well as certain kinds of *conduct* or behavior, to be illegal, but it was unclear what *specific* acts were to be considered "restraints of trade." Competition itself can act as a restraint, for example.

When a statute is unclear, it usually falls to the courts to provide clarification. Unfortunately, the courts only added to the confusion in the early years. In 1911 two major antitrust cases made it to the Supreme Court. The two companies, Standard Oil and American Tobacco, seemed to epitomize the textbook definition of monopoly, and both appeared to exhibit the structure *and* the conduct that was outlawed. Standard Oil controlled about 91 percent of the refining industry, and although the exact figure is still disputed, the American Tobacco Trust probably controlled between 75 and 90 percent of the market for all tobacco products except cigars. Both had used tough tactics to swallow up competition or to drive it out. Not surprisingly, the Supreme Court found each firm guilty of violating both sections 1 and 2 of the Sherman Act, and ordered their dissolution.[2]

Rule of reason   *The criterion introduced by the Supreme Court in 1911 and used to determine whether a particular action was illegal ("unreasonable") or legal ("reasonable") within the terms of the Sherman Act.*

The court's opinion made it clear, however, that the law did not outlaw *every* action that seemed to restrain trade, but only those that were *unreasonable*. In enunciating this **"rule of reason,"** the court also seemed to say that structure alone was not a criterion for unreasonableness. Thus it was possible that a near-monopoly did not violate the Sherman Act as long as it had won its market using "reasonable" tactics.

Subsequent court cases confirmed that only if a firm had exhibited unreasonable *conduct* could it be convicted of violating the Sherman Act. Between 1911 and 1920, cases were brought against Eastman Kodak, International Harvester, United Shoe Machinery, and United States Steel, the first three of which controlled overwhelming shares of their respective markets and the fourth of which controlled 60 percent of the country's capacity to produce steel. But all four cases were dismissed on the grounds that no evidence of "unreasonable conduct" had been brought.

[2]U.S. v. Standard Oil Co. of New Jersey, 221 U.S.1 (1911); U.S. v. American Tobacco Co., 221 U.S. 106 (1911).

The enunciation of the rule of reason did little to clarify the language of the Sherman Act, and just what explicit acts the courts would deem unreasonable remained a mystery. The original supporters of the act were upset by the lack of enforcement; business simply wanted to know the rules of the game. In response, Congress went back to the drawing board in 1914 and passed the *Clayton Act* and the *Federal Trade Commission Act.*

The Clayton Act and the Federal Trade Commission, 1914

Designed both to strengthen the Sherman Act and to clarify the "rule of reason," the **Clayton Act** of 1914 outlawed a number of very specific practices. First, it made *tying contracts* illegal. Such a contract binds a customer to buy one product in order to obtain another. Second, it *limited mergers* that would "substantially lessen competition or tend to create a monopoly." Third, it banned *price discrimination*, that is, charging different customers different prices for reasons other than changes in cost or the matching of competitors' prices.

The **Federal Trade Commission (FTC)** was given broad powers to investigate "the organization, business conduct, practices, and management" of companies that engage in interstate commerce. At the same time, the act establishing the Commission added another vaguely worded prohibition to the books: "Unfair methods of competition in commerce are hereby declared unlawful." The determination of what constituted "unfair" behavior was left up to the commission. The FTC was also given the power to issue "cease and desist orders" where it found behavior in violation of the law.

The legislation of 1914, however, retained the focus on *conduct*, and thus the "rule of reason" remained central to all antitrust action in the courts.

From Conduct to Structure: The Alcoa Case, 1945

In a series of cases after 1911, the court reaffirmed that simply *being* a monopoly did not constitute a violation of the antitrust laws. Even though United States Steel grew large enough to dominate the market for iron and steel, for example, it did not coerce its remaining rivals or conspire to fix prices, and thus it did not engage in unreasonable *conduct*. As the court said, "The law does not make *mere size* [italics added] an offense or the existence of unexerted power an offense." In short, it was not illegal to be a benevolent monopoly.

This was the basic position of the courts until 1945, when the "rule of reason" was challenged in the landmark **Alcoa case**.[3] In that case, the United States charged the Aluminum Company of American (Alcoa) with violating Section 2 of the Sherman Act by monopolizing the market for newly refined aluminum, an argument essentially based on the fact that Alcoa controlled 90 percent of the raw aluminum market.

The court did not hold that any specific *behavior*, or conduct, by which Alcoa achieved its monopoly position was in itself illegal. It said, in fact, that Alcoa had used "normal, prudent, but not predatory business practices. . . . These included building capacity well ahead of demand." Rather it was the *structure* of the market itself that led Judge Learned Hand to rule in favor of the United States and order the dissolution of Alcoa.

> No monopolist monopolizes unconscious of what he is doing. So here "Alcoa" meant to keep, and did keep, that complete and exclusive hold upon the ingot market with which it started. That was to "monopolize" that market, however innocently it otherwise proceeded.

[3]U.S. v. Aluminum Co. of America, 148 F. 2nd 416 (1945).

Clayton Act   *Passed by Congress in 1914, it clarified the "rule of reason" and outlawed specific monopoly behaviors such as tying contracts, unlimited mergers, and price discrimination.*

Federal Trade Commission (FTC)   *A federal regulatory group created by Congress in 1914 to investigate the structure and behavior of firms engaging in interstate commerce, to determine what was unlawful "unfair" behavior, and to issue "cease-and-desist" orders to those found breaking the law.*

One other case is worth a brief note here, because it extended the Sherman Act as it was interpreted in the Alcoa case to cover an oligopoly that was acting like a monopolist. In 1946 the United States brought suit against the three largest domestic cigarette producers. The decision found no specific evidence of collusion, but the court did find that the firms had acted *as if* they were taking account of each other's behavior in setting prices. The case, in essence, extended the law to include *tacit collusion* as well as explicit conspiracy.[4]

Other Legislation   Other pieces of legislation designed to deal with specific problem areas followed in the wake of the Clayton Act. In 1921 the **Willis-Graham Act** formally exempted telephone mergers from antitrust review. (Later in the chapter we discuss the telecommunications industry in some detail.) The telephone industry was one of the very few industries that the government essentially declared a **natural monopoly** and decided to regulate rather than dissolve.

The **Wheeler-Lea Act** of 1938 extended the language of the Federal Trade Commission Act to include *"deceptive"* as well as *"unfair"* methods of competition. This empowered the FTC to deal with false and deceptive advertising and the sale of harmful products.

The **Celler-Kefauver Act** of 1950 extended the government's authority to ban mergers. The original legislation could only block *horizontal mergers* in which firms producing the same product joined together. The Celler-Kefauver Act extended the government's power to block *vertical mergers*, in which firms at various stages in a production process combined—movie-making companies, movie-distribution companies, and theatre chains, for example—as well as conglomerate mergers in which firms producing unrelated products combined. In all cases, however, the fact that the merger would substantially lessen competition had to be established.

The same act closed an important loophole in the Clayton Act. Earlier legislation had prevented one firm from acquiring the *stock* of another company if such a purchase would lessen competition, but firms got around the legislation by buying the *physical assets* (plant and equipment) of a competing firm. This strategy was explicitly banned in 1950 under Celler-Kefauver.

Further Regulation of Mergers

The Clayton Act of 1914 had given government the authority to limit mergers that might "substantially lessen competition in an industry." The Celler-Kefauver Act of 1950 enabled the Justice Department to monitor and enforce these provisions effectively.

In 1968 the Justice Department issued its first guidelines designed to reduce uncertainty about the mergers that it would find acceptable. The 1968 guidelines were very strict. For example, if the largest four firms controlled 75 percent or more of a market, an acquiring firm with a 15-percent market share would be challenged if it wanted to acquire a firm that controlled as little as an additional 1 percent of the market.

In 1982 the Antitrust Division, in keeping with President Reagan's "hands off" attitude toward big business, issued a new set of far more lenient guidelines. Revised in 1984, they remain in place today. The 1982/1984 standards are based on a measure of market structure called the **Herfindahl-Hirshman Index (HHI)**. To calculate the HHI,

Herfindahl-Hirshman index   A *mathematical calculation using existing firm market share figures that is currently used by the Antitrust Division of the Justice Department to determine whether a proposed merger is in the public interest.*

---

[4]See William H. Nicholls, "The Tobacco Case of 1946" *American Economic Review* (May 1949), p. 296. Also American Tobacco Co. et. al. vs. U.S., 328 U.S. 781 (1946). In the American Tobacco case fines totaling $255,000 were levied against the tobacco companies and their executives, but no structural remedies were applied. There is little evidence that their behavior changed after the fines were paid.

TABLE 15.1
Calculation of a Simple Herfindahl-Hirshman Index for Four Hypothetical Industries, each with only Four Firms

	Firm 1	Firm 2	Firm 3	Firm 4	Herfindahl-Hirshman Index
Industry A	50	50	—	—	$50^2 + 50^2 = 5000$
Industry B	80	10	10	—	$80^2 + 10^2 + 10^2 = 6600$
Industry C	25	25	25	25	$25^2 + 25^2 + 25^2 + 25^2 = 2500$
Industry D	40	20	20	20	$40^2 + 20^2 + 20^2 + 20^2 = 2800$

you take the market share of each firm expressed as a percentage, square these figures, and add. For example, in an industry in which two firms each control 50 percent of the market, the index is

$$50^2 + 50^2 = 2500 + 2500 = 5000.$$

For an industry in which four firms each control 25 percent of the market, the index is

$$25^2 + 25^2 + 25^2 + 25^2 = 625 + 625 + 625 + 625 = 2500.$$

Table 15.1 shows calculations for several hypothetical industries.

If the Herfindahl-Hirshman index is less than 1000, the industry is considered unconcentrated, and any proposed merger will go unchallenged by the Justice Department. If the index is between 1000 and 1800, the department will challenge any merger that would increase the index by over 100 points. Herfindahl indexes above 1800 mean that the industry is considered concentrated already, and the department will challenge any merger that pushes the index up more than 50 points (Table 15.2).

In 1982 two breweries, Pabst and Heileman, proposed a merger. At the time, the Herfindahl index in the beer industry was about 1772. Before the merger, each firm had about 7.5% of the market. After a merger, then, the new firm would have a combined share of 15 percent, and that would raise the index by 112.5:

$$(15^2) - (7.5^2 + 7.5^2) = 225 - 112.50 = 112.50.$$

Because the merger increased the index by more than 100 points, it was challenged by the Justice Department.

TABLE 15.2
Department of Justice Merger Guidelines (revised 1984)

Herfindahl-Hirshman Index	Action
Less than 1000 (unconcentrated)	No challenge
1000–1800 (moderate concentration)	Challenge if index is raised more than 100 points by the merger
1800 and over (concentrated)	Challenge if index is raised more than 50 points by the merger

Note: See Phillip Areeda, *Antitrust Analysis*, 3rd ed., 1986 supplement (Boston: Little, Brown, 1986), p. 185.

In 1984 the same two companies reapplied to the Justice Department for permission to merge. This time Pabst agreed to sell four of its brands—accounting for over one third of its total production—and one brewery to a third party. The sale was sufficient to bring the merger within the guidelines, and the Antitrust Division dropped its objections. As of 1988, however, the merger had not been consummated.

ENFORCEMENT, SANCTIONS, AND REMEDIES

In Chapters 13 and 14, we discussed the basic economic logic behind government concern with monopoly and market power. In the last section, we briefly sketched the development of the antitrust laws. We now turn to the equally important area of enforcement.

The Antitrust Division and the FTC

Two different administrative bodies have the responsibility for initiating actions on behalf of the United States government against individuals or companies thought to be in violation of the antitrust laws, the *Antitrust Division of the Justice Department* and the *Federal Trade Commission*.

The 1914 legislation that established the FTC gave it broad powers to forbid "unfair and deceptive" conduct. The FTC has five members appointed by the President and confirmed by the Senate for terms of seven years. A large staff of lawyers and economists investigate and "prosecute" offenders. The FTC can issue *"cease-and-desist" orders* to offenders, but such orders carry neither criminal or civil penalties for past damages nor monetary fines. Thus the FTC exists to prevent *further* unlawful action, and in practice most FTC proceedings end in formal agreements rather than cease-and-desist orders.

The FTC has also established a set of *Trade Regulation rules* that makes clear what practices it deems unfair and subject to action. One such "rule," for example, states that a service station that fails to display octane ratings clearly on gas pumps is guilty of an "unfair or deceptive act or practice." These rules simplify the process of adjudication by making the standards of conduct clear.

The FTC acts to prevent future acts of unfair or deceptive conduct. It also, along with the **Antitrust Division** of the Department of Justice, initiates actions against those who actually violate the law. The power to impose penalties and remedies formally rests with the courts, but the Antitrust Division decides which cases to prosecute. All cases involving criminal complaints against individuals or companies originate in the Antitrust Division, but it is fairly small. Its resources are limited, and the vigor with which it pursues antitrust violators changes with the views of the President and the attorney general.

Antitrust Division (of the Justice Department)   One of two federal agencies empowered to act against those in violation of antitrust laws. It initiates action against those who violate antitrust laws and decides which civil cases to prosecute and against whom to bring criminal charges.

Private Actions

Antitrust cases may also brought to the courts by private citizens. Since 1914 private persons have been empowered to bring suits as long as they can clearly demonstrate a significant injury or threat of injury. The original suit against AT&T that ended in the divestiture in 1982 was brought by a private company, MCI. In 1987 major league baseball players who were free agents found that team owners seemed reluctant to bid against each other for the top players. Several actually brought private action against what they saw as a "conspiracy in restraint of trade," and the courts ruled in their favor. A final settlement, however, had not been reached by 1988.

Sanctions and Remedies

The courts are empowered to impose a number of remedies if they find that the law has been violated. Certain civil and criminal penalties can be exacted for past wrongs, and other measures can prevent future wrongs. Specifically, the courts can "(1) forbid the continuation of illegal acts, (2) force the defendant to dispose of the fruits of his or her wrong, and (3) restore competitive conditions."

> In fashioning effective relief, the courts have considerable discretion in their choice of remedy. Antitrust decrees have, for example, ordered defendants to dispose of subsidiary companies; to create a company with appropriate assets and personnel to compete effectively with defendant; to make patents, trademarks and trade secrets or know-how available to competitors at reasonable royalties or even without any royalties; to provide goods and services to all who wish to buy; to revise the terms on which defendant buys or sells; and to cancel, shorten or modify outstanding agreements with competitors, suppliers or customers.[5]

Consent decrees Formal agreements on remedies drawn before, during, or after litigation among all parties to an antitrust case.

Consent Decrees   Between 75 and 80 percent of all government-initiated civil suits are settled with the signing of what is called a *consent decree*. **Consent decrees** are formal agreements between the prosecuting government and the defendants that must be approved by the courts. Such decrees can be signed before, during, or even after a trial takes place. Because antitrust cases are long and expensive to litigate, both parties obviously benefit if settlement comes early in the process.

Consent decrees have encompassed a wide variety of agreements. A company may agree to give up a patent that is serving as a barrier to effective competition, for example, or it may agree to be broken up into separate competing companies, as in the AT&T case described below.

Criminal Actions   In 1955 and again in 1974, the sanctions for violating the Sherman Act were changed. The original act held that violations were misdemeanors, and made no distinction between individuals and corporations. Today the penalties are more pointed and considerably more severe:

> Every person who shall make any contract or engage in any combination or conspiracy hereby declared to be illegal shall be deemed guilty of a *felony*, and on conviction thereof, shall be punished by a fine not exceeding *one million dollars* if a corporation, or, if any other person, *one hundred thousand dollars* or by imprisonment not exceeding three years, or by both said punishments, in the discretion of the court.[6]

The practice of the Antitrust Division has been to limit criminal proceedings to only the most outrageous violations, where intent to violate is clear. In 1961 seven prominent

[5]Phillip Areeda, *Antitrust Analysis: Problems, Text and Cases*, 3rd. ed. (Boston: Little, Brown, 1986), p. 61.
[6]26 Stat. 209 (1890), as amended 15 U.S.C.A. 1–7 (1980). Changes to the statute are italicized in the text.

executives of major U.S. corporations that produced electrical equipment were found guilty of flagrantly violating well-established laws. They had secretly met and agreed to fix prices. All seven received 30-day jail sentences.

Treble Damages   Any person or private company that sustains injury or financial loss because of an antitrust violation can recover damages from the guilty party over and above any fines levied. The award made by the court must be three times the actual damages:

> any person injured in his business or property by reason of anything forbidden in the antitrust laws . . . shall recover threefold the damages by him sustained, and the cost of suit, including a reasonable attorney's fee.[7]

This, of course, provides a powerful incentive for private parties to have recourse to the antitrust laws.

The Effectiveness of Antitrust Enforcement

Should the antitrust division be more aggressive? Administration and enforcement of the law is costly, and there are clearly diminishing returns. Furthermore, laws and penalties neither can nor do stop all undesirable behavior. Just what level of enforcement activity we ought to settle for is a highly controversial subject. Critics of business who favor more enforcement argue that the Antitrust Division does not have the resources to enforce the law.[8] Others argue that while some level of enforcement activity is useful, the Antitrust Division is *overly* aggressive and should be scaled back.

The breakup of AT&T in 1982 brought the debate to the public arena. Some people believe that the AT&T case was a disaster, that it tore apart the greatest telephone company in the world and left consumers worse off than before. In fact, local telephone rates have risen substantially since 1982. Others argue, quite to the contrary, that the outcome of the case has been an enormous success, and that we are just beginning to see the fruits of intense competition in the form of new and better products and services. They point out that the rise in local rates is due to the gradual elimination of an inefficient subsidy to local rate payers that regulators had, over the years, unwisely built into long-distance rates. They also point out that long-distance rates have fallen sharply.

The issues raised by this debate require some further discussion. In the next section, we review the economic logic behind the antitrust laws before turning to the substance of recent criticism leveled at enforcement practices.

ARGUMENTS FOR AND AGAINST ANTITRUST ENFORCEMENT

The Case for Antitrust Enforcement

In a sense, the first part of this book, and particularly Chapters 13 and 14, have already made the case for having and enforcing antitrust laws. As you have seen, competition has

---

[7]See Areeda, *Antitrust*.

[8]For fiscal years 1985–1987, the budget of the Antitrust Division was about $45 million per year. Staffing has remained unchanged at 649 full-time employees during this period. (See *Budget of the United States*, Fiscal Year 1987, section I-06.)

some real potential benefits. It drives firms to produce at least cost and provides an incentive for them to introduce new, efficient production techniques and new products. When anticompetitive behavior or monopoly power threatens to rob society of the benefits of open competition, therefore, public policy should step in to prevent it.

The antitrust laws do more than just condemn monopoly; they also restrict certain specific kinds of conduct, whether the industry is monopolistic or not. Most of the specific acts and practices outlawed by the various antitrust laws can result in serious social costs and waste of society's scarce resources. Thus it is fairly easy to build an economic case for having and enforcing prohibitions against unfair and deceptive practices, price fixing, collusion, and price discrimination.

Unfair or Deceptive Practices

For a market to work, the first requirement is that consumers have valid *information on product availability, quality, and product price*. The variety and complexity of modern life forces the average consumer to consider many products that cannot be fully understood or personally evaluated. Medical care, financial services, insurance, drugs, food products, consumer electronics, and products in other areas too numerous to mention are so complicated and specialized that the consumer may well be misinformed about them, if not deliberately deceived. In such cases, it may be reasonable for the government to act on behalf of consumers to prevent "unfair and deceptive acts or practices."

Price fixing and collusion

Firms can use **price fixing** and **collusion** to protect themselves from competition. Both practices allow firms that would otherwise compete to act together as a monopoly and reap monopoly profits. Competitive markets drive product prices close to the cost of production, and in the long run firms will earn only normal profits. Were a monopolist to gain control of the same industry, it would clearly be in his or her interest to cut output, raise price, and do everything possible to prevent competition. When this happens, consumers lose. They pay more for the same product, and less of it is produced. (In Chapter 13 you saw how the size of the net loss to society from the monopolization of an industry is calculated.)

Price discrimination What happens when a firm charges different buyers different prices for the same product. Such strategies are illegal if they drive out competition.

Price Discrimination

Under the Clayton Act, **price discrimination** that tends to lessen competition is illegal. For example, suppose that several companies buy rolled steel to make filing cabinets. The largest producer, by virtue of size and bargaining power, may be able to extract a very low price from the steel producers, a price not justified by cost savings due to large volume. The bargaining power thus gives the large producer an arbitrary advantage over its smaller competitors. This can lead to monopoly power in the longer run.

Not all price discrimination is illegal. It goes on all around us. Airlines, druggists, movie theatres, public transit systems, telephone companies, and so forth charge different prices for children, senior citizens, students, military personnel, and other identifiable groups. Professional journals charge individuals and institutions (libraries) very different subscription fees. Rental car companies offer discounts to members of AAA, frequent fliers, employees of certain businesses, and weekend renters.

Despite its common occurrence, there is an economic argument against any form of price discrimination. Suppose that two groups, A and B, pay two different prices, P_A and P_B, for the same good. Assume that P_A is higher than P_B. There will be some members of group A who will be willing to pay more than P_B but not as much as P_A. These people will not buy the product. If trading among the groups was permitted, the higher price would be meaningless, because those in group B would simply buy at P_B and sell to members of group A at a slight markup. If a member of group B makes a markup sale to a member of group A who would *not* have bought the good at price P_A, both are clearly better off.

Thus for price discrimination to work the firm must be able to prevent the groups being discriminated against from trading with each other. But if voluntary trading has to be prevented, that is prima facie evidence of *inefficiency*.

For a variety of reasons, then, price discrimination implies that goods are being distributed inefficiently and that firms are producing less than they would under competitive conditions.[9]

Highly Concentrated Industries   Antitrust action against firms in highly concentrated industries on the basis of *industry structure alone* is a different case and a more difficult one to make. In theory, a monopoly can be just as efficient as a competitive industry if it does not exercise its power and if it continues to minimize costs and to innovate *as if it had rivals*. Those who favor antitrust action on the basis of structure alone argue, however, that such behavior is extremely unlikely.

Between 1911 and 1945, the courts and the Antitrust Division were stuck with the "rule of reason." It often required months of testimony to demonstrate "unreasonable conduct," and even then it was difficult to do. In the Alcoa decision, Judge Learned Hand essentially said "enough is enough." When a firm controls 90 percent of a clearly defined market, we have an illegal monopoly, and there is no such thing as a benevolent monopoly, he decided.

The Antitrust Laws as a Deterrent   Because we can only speculate about what would have happened without them, we cannot say in fact whether the antitrust laws have worked or not. Some actual decisions have clearly produced the desired results. The Standard Oil decision, for example, gave us several regional oil companies that came to compete vigorously in the refining business. And clear evidence indicates that the bringing of price-fixing complaints lowers prices.

But you cannot measure the success of the speed limit laws by looking only at the behavior of those who get speeding tickets; you must also look at how fast most people drive. Proponents of antitrust enforcement argue that the real gains of such a policy lie in the cases that never make it to court, because antitrust laws and rules serve as a significant *deterrent*. Without them, they argue, the temptation to fix prices, collude, engage in deceptive advertising, and so forth would be irresistible. If there were no prohibitions against it, can anyone doubt that firms would merge, dominate markets, and exploit monopoly power? As you saw in chapters 13 and 14, the profit incentive for firms to do so is extremely compelling.

In Chapter 13 we also introduced the theory of *rent-seeking* behavior. Firms earning monopoly profits should be willing to pay to prevent competition from eroding those profits. Presumably that means that there is an incentive for firms to lobby for protection from the antitrust laws. In 1945 Congress passed the McCarran-Ferguson Act, which effectively exempts the insurance industry from prosecution under the antitrust laws. While regulated in some states, insurance companies in most states are able to fix

[9]The conclusion that price-discriminating monopolists under-produce does not hold for a firm that can "perfectly discriminate." Such a firm can charge a different price for *every unit* of output, that is, it can charge the same buyer different prices for the same product. In theory, a "perfect" price-discriminating monopolist would charge each person successively lower prices, driving every buyer down on his or her demand curve to a price equal to the marginal cost of production. Thus, *at the margin*, every buyer faces the same price, and the monopolist can extract *all* the consumer surplus from each consumer. In practice, however, the best that a firm can do is to segment the market into many groups.

prices, carve up markets, and engage in tying contracts. In 1988 a number of members of Congress, with the backing of the Reagan administration, called for the repeal of the act. Their efforts were met with a well-organized and powerful lobbying campaign funded by the industry itself.

The Case Against Antitrust Enforcement

In recent years, antitrust laws have come under increasing criticism. While few complain about the laws that make certain kinds of *conduct* illegal, concern is gathering about remedies aimed at concentrated industries that seem to be performing fairly well. Several themes recur in this recent criticism.

Regulations as the Penalty for Success   Critics of regulation contend that the Antitrust Division and the FTC are not concerned with inefficient firms that have not done well; rather, they are interested only in the firms that, in a sense, have done *too well*. In other words, if a company produces a "better mouse trap" and comes to dominate an industry, the government nails it for being a monopoly.

One example was discussed in Chapter 13. In the early 1960s, extensive research led the General Motors Corporation to come up with a number of important improvements in the design of intracity busses. One, for example, was a very efficient transversely mounted engine. Those improvements were patented, and as a result, GM came to dominate the market for intracity busses completely.

After a long legal battle, the court issued a consent decree forcing GM to give up its patents to the competition. In addition, any further design improvements that GM made through research and development would likewise have to be made available to its competitors. The result was that GM stopped developing new and better busses, and travelers ended up with worse busses than they might have had.

Many people made the same argument about the breakup of AT&T in 1982. We had a well-managed and enormously successful private company—the best telephone company in the world. No one argued that AT&T had done anything wrong or unethical. Rather, the argument was that competition might lead to an even better result—new products, better service, and lower rates. But, the critics cried, the key word was *"might."* And, they added, resorting to familiar and compelling logic, "If it ain't broke, don't fix it!"

The Need for Big, Strong Companies to Face Foreign Competition   For most of our history, the United States did not have to worry much about foreign competition. Today everyone knows the names Toyota, Sony, Mitsubishi, Yamaha, and many others. Giant corporations in the Far East and Europe are flooding American markets with sophisticated products and masterful marketing techniques.

It is said that the old theory of competitive markets doesn't work when our industries face competition from foreign companies whose governments aid and abet their activities. The Japanese government, for example, does everything in its power to help its giant firms penetrate foreign markets and to grow, while the United States government forces American megafirms to defend themselves in court against antitrust judgments.

It may also be that if cooperation among firms—a major joint research effort, for example—were allowed, or even encouraged, it might help industries fight foreign competition. But firms in concentrated industries are unlikely to participate in joint ventures for fear of antitrust action.

Negative Effects on Research, Development, and Growth   The Schumpeterian hypothesis, outlined in Chapter 14, lays the foundation for the argument that large firms can devote significant resources to research and development activities, while lower levels of industrial concentration lead to less R&D. But, as you have seen, the evidence is mixed. Larger firms are indeed more likely to have research staffs than smaller firms, but when you count the number of patents procured or look at the number of important developments, they do not seem to show any systematic correlation with firm size.[10]

> After the Alcoa case in 1945, Kaiser, Reynolds, and several other new firms entered the aluminum industry: A study examined technical progress [before and after the Alcoa case] and concluded that the reduction in seller concentration was responsible at least in part for increased progressiveness. . . . the existence of several producers has led to competitive marketing, increasing the pressures to develop new alloys and new uses for aluminum, including many consumer products such as foil. Reduced concentration seems to have provided a significant competitive stimulus to innovation.[11]

Conflicting evidence comes from the telecommunications industry. AT&T maintained an enormous research facility called Bell Laboratories. Founded in 1925, at its peak it had 17 research centers in nine states and employed thousands of scientists and engineers. We can safely say that no single research program was responsible for more important breakthroughs, including the transistor, the solar battery, the laser, and many more. Yet research and new product development are proceeding at an amazing rate in the new companies that were broken off from AT&T in 1982 and in those that are springing up around it.

Efficient Capital Flows and Relatively Contestable Markets   Another argument against more vigorous antitrust enforcement is that barriers to entry are not as formidable as they once were. Capital markets have become more efficient; investors are always looking for profitable ventures and are now able to mobilize the huge sums necessary to enter almost any industry if there are economic profits to be earned. The efficiency of capital markets serves to make more and more markets contestable. Either entry or just the threat of new entry makes market power less of a problem.

Distrust of Government   Even if it can be shown that antitrust enforcement is a good idea in theory, many people simply distrust putting power in the hands of government. They feel that government intervention creates more problems than it solves. For example, bureaucracy is slow and wasteful, and people in the industry clearly know more about what they do than those government employees charged with regulating or prosecuting it.

The next section of this chapter takes up regulation. Another approach to monopoly power is to let the monopoly firm continue to exist as a monopoly but to regulate its price. The logic for regulation rather than antitrust enforcement usually rests on the perception that the firm is a natural monopoly—that large economies of scale justify having just one firm in the industry. Criticisms of government regulation resemble the criticisms of

---

[10]See Richard Caves, *American Industry: Structure, Conduct, Performance.* 6th ed., (Englewood Cliffs, N.J.: Prentice-Hall, 1987), p. 76.

[11]See Caves, *American Industry*, p. 77.

government prohibition we have rehearsed here. Critics charge that true natural monopolies are extremely rare and that when governments regulate an industry, they generally restrict competition and often protect monopoly profits for no good reason. Recall the discussion of "rent-seeking" behavior in Chapter 13.

Antitrust Laws and Enforcement on Balance

One of the lessons you will take from this course (and from your whole education) is that complicated questions have no simple answers. There are strong arguments for government involvement in the economy to restrain behavior. Unchecked monopoly power, collusion, price fixing, and so forth can be enormously expensive to a society. It is also easy to show that competition provides incentives for efficient production, innovation, and a healthy economy.

It is equally clear, unfortunately, that enforcement of the antitrust laws has imposed some costs on society. Successful companies have paid a price for their success. Some, such as GM, were forced to give back markets that they won through vigorous competition. Antitrust activities may also have played a part in reducing our ability to compete for international markets.

The role of policy makers is to understand the arguments, weigh the evidence, and proceed in one direction or the other. While policy decisions must be made without knowledge of the outcome, enlightened uncertainty is better than ignorance.

REGULATION AND NATURAL MONOPOLY

At the beginning of this chapter we said that the government plays two basic roles that seem contradictory: (1) it *promotes* competition and restricts market power, primarily through antitrust laws and other acts of Congress and (2) it *restricts* competition by regulating and simultaneously protecting certain industries. So far, we have looked exclusively at the former. Now we turn to government activities that end up protecting monopoly power.

The government, of course, regulates many areas in the economy that have nothing whatsoever to do with market structure. Some of these areas, environmental protection, for example, are discussed in later chapters. This section, however, deals only with regulation of those sectors that have come to be called "*natural monopolies*."

The Logic of Regulation

In Chapter 13 you saw how the market fails when market power is unrestrained. Firms that can control price and bar the entry of new firms find it advantageous to overprice and underproduce relative to what is best for society. A number of solutions to this problem are possible, at least in theory. One solution is to restructure the industry into a more competitive one. A second is to impose some sort of price regulation—a price ceiling at marginal cost, for example.

The antitrust laws that we have just examined rest on the proposition that competition, not regulation, is the best way to achieve efficiency in an economy. Although the courts exercise great discretion, everything they do, from requiring firms to give up patents to breaking firms up into smaller competing units, aims at stimulating competition.

But it has always been understood that not all markets can be, or should be, competitively structured. Most important among these exceptions are firms or industries that can take advantage of very large economies of scale—the *natural monopolies* alluded to earlier in this chapter and described in Chapter 13. In the extreme case, it may be true that all economies of scale available to a natural monopoly are not exhausted, even when all the product demanded in the market is being produced in a single plant.

Figure 15.1 reproduces a diagram from Chapter 13. Notice that average total cost is still declining when the demand curve hits the quantity axis. To break such a firm into smaller pieces, each producing some fraction of total demand, would mean that each of the small firms would have to produce at a much higher average cost.

Most natural monopolies have very high fixed costs and low marginal costs. Take, for example, the local electric company. Building a generation plant and putting up poles and wires is costly, but once they are in place, the cost of generating and distributing one additional kilowatt of electricity is low. Large-scale initial investments are required, but once the plant is built, marginal costs are quite low. Part of the thinking behind the protection of such industries is that having more than one firm undertake the very large initial investment is a waste of resources.

One solution to the natural monopoly problem is to let it exist as a monopoly, but to regulate the price of its product and its rate of return. If the natural monopoly in Figure 15.1 went unregulated, it would charge price P^*, far above marginal costs. But a simple

FIGURE 15.1
A Natural Monopoly

A natural monopoly exists when a firm exhibits very large economies of scale. Here long-run average costs facing the firm continue to decline with output even when a single firm is producing all the output demanded in the market. With no regulation, the firm would produce at Q^* and price at P^*. Regulating price to be equal to marginal cost results in losses. Setting price at P_A means that average cost is covered and that investors earn a normal rate of return.

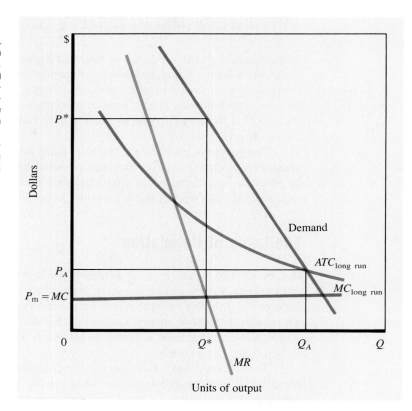

price ceiling imposed at MC would not work, because marginal cost is *below* average cost, and the firm could not make even a normal profit.

Theory suggests three options for regulation: (1) set the *efficient price* ($P=MC$) and provide a *subsidy* out of general revenues; (2) set price equal to *average cost* (P_A), which allows firms to charge a price that covers all costs, including a normal return on invested capital; or (3) impose a *two-part tariff,* with a basic service charge as a lump sum and a price for usage equal to marginal cost. Both of the last two options require that some regulatory commission set the firm's rate of return.

Some industries have been explicitly protected from antitrust laws since their beginnings. The Interstate Commerce Commission was actually set up expressly to regulate the railroads three years before passage of the Sherman Act. It made no sense to have two railroads laying separate tracks between two cities. As a natural monopoly, the railroad was a textbook case. Its big costs came in securing rights of way, laying tracks, and building engines and rolling stock. Initially, the railroads held unregulated monopoly power. It was the unrestrained exercise of that power against farmers, who had to rely on the railroads to ship their product, that aroused the anger which became organized as the antitrust movement.

The Bell Telephone Company also behaved like a textbook monopoly until some of its patents expired in 1894. After 1894 increasing competition in the telecommunications industry actually led Bell to argue *for* regulation. Worried about both antitrust actions and the emergence of new competition, Bell argued that it was a natural monopoly. It made as little sense, it said, to have two or more sets of telephone lines down the same road as to run two railroad lines down the same right of way.

In response, many states set up public utility commissions in the early years of this century. Pro-regulation sentiment reached its peak in 1907, when seven states established new regulatory bodies. Mergers between firms in the telecommunications market were finally exempted from antitrust review by the Willis-Graham Act of 1921, and by that time telephone companies were strictly regulated in all states.

The Decline of Regulation

During the last part of the 1970s and the early 1980s the feeling grew that the government was regulating industries that were not really natural monopolies. In some cases, the reasons for regulation had eroded with technological advances in the industries; in other cases, the industries were not natural monopolies to begin with. As a result, there has been a movement toward deregulation, and the mandates of various regulatory agencies are gradually changing.

The *Federal Energy Regulatory Commission* regulates the price of natural gas that travels through interstate pipelines. It may also fix the wholesale rates for electricity transmitted interstate. In 1978 Congress began gradually deregulating the price of natural gas over a ten-year period.

The *Federal Communications Commission* regulates interstate telephone and telegraph rates and services. Regulation of local operating companies remains with state-run public utility commissions. Clearly an industry in transition, telecommunications is likely to see much less regulation in the future.

Technological change has made it possible—and even necessary—for long-distance telephone service to become competitive. This was signaled when a new company, MCI, filed a private action against AT&T, arguing that it used its monopoly in local service areas and in the manufacture of equipment to monopolize the long-distance market. In 1982 AT&T reached a settlement in which it agreed to separate its long-distance service and equipment manufacturing business from its local operating companies. Although the FCC still regulates AT&T's long-distance rates in part to give the new companies a chance in the face of AT&T's "100-year head start," it is clear that the FCC sees this residual regulation of the long-distance market as transitional and that ultimately long-distance rates will be competitively set.

Even local public utility commissions have recently moved toward deregulation. In nearly every state, PUCs still regulate the price of local service and the rate of return of the local operating companies, but increasing competition from many sources has become a real challenge. Firms are setting up private networks that bypass the system altogether. "Telecommunications-enhanced real estate," or "smart buildings," are wired with private systems or microwave transmitters that bypass the local exchange network. So far, those competitive services are not permitted to provide local exchange service, but they are making the life of the regulator difficult, and the local telephone companies are asking for the ability to get out and compete with them.

Thus the rationale for continued regulation of the telecommunications industry seems to be changing. Advancing technology has weakened the natural monopoly argument, but state and local governments want to insure that all citizens continue to have access to low-cost basic telephone service. The argument is that there are social gains to having everyone on the network. PUC regulation still maintains subsidies that keep down the cost of basic local exchange service. This is done by allowing the local operating companies to charge long-distance carriers an access charge. Open competition would see the end of this subsidy, and it would mean higher rates for basic service. Many states in the mid 1980s have been experimenting with gradual deregulation of telecommunications firms, but only time will tell how far such changes will go.

The authority of the oldest regulatory agency granted nationwide powers, the *Interstate Commerce Commission*, expanded for a time to include interstate trucking as well as the railroads. Its control over truckers' services and rates is essentially gone now, and only those railroads that exhibit "market dominance" remain under its direct control. The trucking industry never had the characteristics of a natural monopoly in the first place, but its regulation continued into the 1970s largely for political reasons. Trucking deregulation began in 1978, and by 1983 competition had pushed the real price of truckload shipments down by 25 percent.[12]

The airlines were once tightly regulated by the *Civil Aeronautics Board*, which controlled routes and fares for all interstate carriers. Now the CAB is out of business, and deregulation is complete. A great deal of evidence shows that competition has reduced air fares considerably since deregulation began in the mid-1970s. While airline deregulation has certainly reduced fares, the final impact of free-for-all competition is yet to be known. By 1987 there was seeming chaos. Texas Air bought Eastern, Continental, and People Express; US Air bought Piedmont. TWA was having serious union problems trying to cut costs. Some fear that the new "bottom line" competitive pressures may lead the industry to cut services and compromise on safety.

Perhaps the only remaining pure natural monopoly is the electric power industry. The various *state public utility commissions* still exercise control over rates and service, and the basic logic remains valid. It makes sense to have only one firm producing and selling power in any given area, and for these companies deregulation is essentially out of the question.

---

[12]Thomas G. Moore, "Rail and Truck Reform—The Record So Far," *Regulation*, VII (November/December 1983), pp. 33–41.

The Problems of Regulation

The theory of natural monopoly sounds fairly simple. Regulatory commissions are charged with setting prices that allow regulated monopolies to earn a normal rate of return. A number of problems are inherent in regulation, however, and these will probably always perplex the regulator to some degree.

Commanding the Necessary Data   Regulation requires analyzing a great deal of information. The first problem is calculating the base—presumably some measure of the "value" of the firm's capital investment—on which a fair return should be allowed. Debate over the value of the utility's property can go on and on. Should the commission use purchase price adjusted for increases in prices? Replacement cost? Some estimate of market value?

The commission must also analyze costs. Should all costs be allowed? Which costs are reasonable? Public utility commissions have developed methods for analyzing all the information necessary, but it is a difficult process, subject to differences of opinion and to error.

Then, too, the political process that attends rate regulation is time-consuming and cumbersome. Public utility commissions are impaneled to act in the "public interest." Whenever decisions such as rate setting are made, the public must be consulted. These consultations take the form of public hearings and open sessions. And of course the final decisions made by PUCs can be reviewed in the courts. Interested parties have not been shy about filing suits after an unfavorable or unpopular decision. When a firm makes a pricing mistake, it can act quickly to change its price. When a utility commission makes a mistake, however, correcting it may take over a year.

Averch-Johnson effect   *The observed tendency for regulated monopolies to build more capital than they need. This usually occurs when allowed rates of return are set by a regulatory agency at some percent of fixed capital stocks.*

Lack of Incentives to Be Efficient   Because the return to a regulated natural monopoly is set by a commission, it may not use efficient production techniques. For example, if a regulatory commission fixes the return by setting a *rate* expressed as a percent of the utility's assets, the *dollar amount* of profit depends only on the total value of those assets. Thus firms may actually have an incentive to overinvest in capital if the allowed return exceeds the cost of capital. This tendency is called the **Averch-Johnson effect**, after the scholars who noted the proclivity of regulated firms to build more capital capacity than they need.[13]

In general, then, we can say that when regulated firms are guaranteed a standard rate of return, they have no incentive to keep costs at a minimum. When profits are not linked to some measure of performance, there is no reason to perform well and no severe penalty for weak performance.

Excessive Nonprice Competition   Regulated monopolies do not have a problem with nonprice competition, because they don't *have* competition. In regulated industries where several firms compete directly with each other while being required to charge the *same price*, however, product differentiation can become excessive.

The marketing zeal of the airlines in the early 1970s is the example most often cited. During that time, airlines offered frequent flights, designer-painted planes, a choice of five menus, free carpet slippers, and all kinds of other little frills that are hard to imagine now, in an effort to increase ticket sales. As a result of deregulation, today competition drives airlines to produce the service that people want, at least cost and thus at a more reasonable price.

[13]Harvey Averch and Leland Johnson, "Behavior of the Firm under Regulatory Constraint," *American Economic Review*, LII (December 1962), pp. 1052–1069, and Richard Caves, *American Industry*, p. 107.

Is There Too Much Regulation?

Those who contend that regulation has been excessive make two basic arguments. First, few real natural monopolies actually exist, and thus there is rarely a reason for government regulation on the basis of market structure. Second, many, if not most, instances of government regulation have succeeded in reducing competition in industries where competition might be beneficial.

It is important to understand that this chapter is not about *all* government regulation. In later chapters, we take up other kinds of government involvement, including environmental protection, occupational health and safety, and food and drug regulation. Here we are talking simply about government regulation of firms that are allowed to operate essentially as monopolies on the grounds that economies of scale make antitrust enforcement impractical. Critics argue that even the classic natural monopoly —the electric power company—may no longer fit the definition very well. While large economies of scale may still exist in power *distribution*, power *generation* can be done on a relatively small scale, at scattered sites, and sold. Small plants can efficiently produce power and feed it into the "grid." It is possible technologically, they say, for the industry to be quite competitive.

Those who contend that the government has actually stifled potentially beneficial competition argue that most examples of real barriers to entry are barriers actually *created* by governments. We have already talked about regulation in the taxicab, trucking, and airlines industries. A box in Chapter 13 discusses government protection of New York milk producers. Certainly none of these industries could possibly be called a natural monopoly, and yet all are, or were, highly regulated.

Most of these examples are consistent with the theory of rent-seeking behavior discussed in Chapter 13. Recall that basic argument. If a firm finds that it is possible to earn economic profits and to protect them by preventing competition, it will expend resources to do so; that may include lobbying for regulatory protection. AT&T figured out in 1905 that regulation was a better fate than all-out competition, so it actually sought out regulation. Similarly, the trucking industry favored continued regulation, as did most of the airlines, when deregulation of each of those industries was first proposed.

Be careful not to confuse the criticism of regulation with the criticism of antitrust enforcement, however. While both call for less government, the logic behind the two agreements is quite different. Antitrust enforcement is undertaken to *promote* competition. In a way, it is the opposite of market regulation, which nearly always serves to *restrict* competition.

IMPERFECT STRUCTURE: THE ROLE OF GOVERNMENT AND PUBLIC POLICY

This chapter has introduced you to the world of economic public policy. What is the proper role of government in industries that are not structured competitively? Three possible approaches are open to government: (1) do nothing; (2) attempt to make the industry more competitive through the application of the antitrust laws or other regulations that restrict anticompetitive conduct; or (3) preserve the monopoly structure, but regulate it.

None of these is a perfect solution. Doing nothing inevitably results in significant social losses. Industries with market power rob consumers of value and misallocate society's scarce resources. The antitrust laws have strengths and weaknesses, but most economists feel that they deter behavior that might otherwise cost society too much.

Regulation, however, presents another set of problems altogether. Where very large economies of scale make it logical to preserve monopoly structure in an industry, regulation is the only reasonable course of action. Even though few true natural monopolies exist, governments have a long history of regulating industries and restricting potentially beneficial competition.

SUMMARY

1. When unregulated markets fail to produce efficient results, there may be things that governments can do to improve the allocation of resources.

2. Governments have assumed two basic roles: (1) to *promote* competition and restrict market power, primarily through antitrust laws and other Congressional acts, and (2) to *restrict* competition by regulating industries.

3. Congress created the Interstate Commerce Commission in 1887 to regulate the railroads and in 1890 passed the Sherman Act that declared monopoly and trade restraints illegal.

4. In 1914 Congress passed the Clayton Act designed to strengthen the Sherman Act and to clarify exactly what specific forms of conduct were "unreasonable" restraints of trade. In the same year, the Federal Trade Commission was established and given broad powers to investigate and regulate unfair methods of competition.

5. Subsequent legislation extended the government's power to limit mergers that might substantially lessen competition in an industry. Currently the Justice Department operates within specific guidelines, known as the Herfindahl-Hirshman index, based on the measure of market structure.

6. Responsibility for the enforcement of the antitrust laws rests primarily with the Antitrust Division of the Justice Department and the Federal Trade Commission. Antitrust complaints may also be brought to the courts by private citizens.

7. The courts are empowered to impose a number of remedies if they find that the law has been violated. These include civil and criminal penalties for past wrongs, as well as decrees that specifically forbid future illegal acts.

8. Between 75 and 80 percent of all government-initiated suits are settled with the signing of consent decrees. Consent decrees have included a wide variety of agreements ranging from eliminating a barrier to entry, such as a patent, to the breakup of major corporations.

9. The case for government concern with the structure and conduct of industries has been well established; unchecked monopoly power, collusion, price fixing, and so forth can be enormously expensive to society. But in recent years, voices have been raised in opposition to vigorous antitrust enforcement. The basic arguments are that it penalizes success, that we need strong companies to face foreign competition, that it may reduce basic research and development, and that most markets are reasonably contestable.

10. Proponents of antitrust enforcement point out that the real gains are in the cases that never make it to court because the antitrust rules and laws serve as a significant deterrent. Without them the temptation to fix prices, collude, engage in deceptive advertising, and so forth would be irresistible.

11. When an industry demonstrates very large economies of scale, it may be efficient to have only one large firm in that industry. Such a firm is called a natural monopoly. If a single-firm industry is protected on the grounds that it is a natural monopoly, it must be regulated to prevent exploitation of its monopoly power.

12. In past years, the government has been involved in regulating industries that are not natural monopolies. In the last decade, a number of these industries have been totally or partially deregulated. They include trucking, airlines and telecommunications.

13. The proper role of government in the world of business is hard to define. Doing nothing about noncompetitive industries inevitably results in significant social losses. The antitrust laws have strengths and weaknesses, but most economists feel they deter behavior that might otherwise cost society too much. Where very large economies of scale make it logical to preserve monopoly structure in an industry, regulation is the only reasonable course of action.

REVIEW CONCEPTS

REVIEW QUESTIONS

1. What was the "rule of reason" enunciated by the courts in 1911? What problems did the court encounter in implementing the rule of reason? In what ways did the Clayton Act help to clarify its meaning?
2. With the Alcoa case, the position of the courts changed dramatically. What important principle was changed by Judge Hand's opinion in the Alcoa case? List the advantages and disadvantages of the structural approach to antitrust enforcement introduced by the Alcoa decision.
3. Suppose the widget industry were made up of five firms each controlling 10 percent of the market, and 10 firms each controlling 5 percent of the market. If two firms that each control 10 percent of the market in this industry proposed merging, would the merger be challenged by the Justice Department under the 1982/1984 guidelines? Explain your answer.
4. Suppose the widget industry were made up of two firms each with a market share of 20 percent, three firms each with a market share of 10 percent, and six firms each with a market share of five percent. If two of the firms each controlling 10 percent of the market proposed a merger, how would the Justice Department react? Explain your answer.
5. What federal agency is charged with the responsibility of regulating unfair and deceptive competition? Give several examples of trade practices you have personally encountered

that you think are unfair.
6. Explain, using graphs, why restructuring a monopoly into a number of competing firms is likely to lead to a more efficient allocation of resources.
7. Explain why the restructuring alternative fails as a remedy in the case of a natural monopoly. Illustrate your answer with a graph. What alternatives are there to restructuring in the case of a natural monopoly?
8. The Clayton Act makes price discrimination illegal. Define price discrimination. How might price discrimination lead to a lessening of competition in an industry? Can you give another, more general, reason for public concern about price discrimination?
9. What are the arguments in favor of continued regulation of local operating companies in the telecommunications industry? What are the arguments in favor of complete deregulation of that industry?
10. One of the objectives of the AT&T breakup was to bring lower prices to consumers through competition. Long-distance rates have indeed fallen since 1983, but the price of local service has gone up. Does this mean that restructuring and deregulation have failed? Explain.
11. Write an essay on the government's current approach to concentrated industries. Do we need more government involvement or less? Defend your position.

16 Government in the Economy: Externalities, Public Goods, and Public Choice

In Chapters 5 through 12, we built a complete model of a perfectly competitive economy under a set of fairly restrictive assumptions. When we finished, we had demonstrated that the resulting allocation of resources was efficient. In other words, a competitive system produces what people want, and it does so at least cost. We can prove this formally by showing that no change in the allocation of resources, in the mix of output, or in the distribution of output will improve the well-being of some people without reducing the well-being of others.

At the end of Chapter 12, we began to relax some of the assumptions on which the competitive model depends. We introduced the idea of **market failure**, and in Chapters 13 and 14 we talked about three kinds of imperfect markets: *monopoly*, *oligopoly*, and *monopolistic competition*. Chapter 15 discussed some of the ways government has responded to the inefficiencies of imperfect markets and to the development of market power through antitrust action and regulation. We also discussed some of the problems that crop up when government gets involved in regulating the economy.

As we continue our examination of market failure, we look first at the problem of externalities. Often when we engage in transactions or make economic decisions, second or third parties suffer consequences that decision makers have no incentive to consider. For example, for many years manufacturing firms and power plants had no reason to worry about what impact the smoke from their operations might have on the quality of the air we breathe. Now we know that air pollution harms people, and it has become one of the most often-cited example of an externality. When the *costs* of externalities are left out, we may engage in activities or produce products that are not "worth it." When we fail to consider *social benefits*, we may fail to do things or produce things that are indeed "worth it." The result is an inefficient allocation of resources.

Market failure   *What happens when some malfunction in the market mechanism results in a misallocation or unproductive use of resources, that is, in inefficiency.*

The idea of an externality is one of the most powerful in all of economics. Consider all the things that you do or might be tempted to do in a day. A substantial percentage of those actions has some impact on others. One of the functions of social rules, customs, and laws in a civilized society is to induce the members of that society to consider the social consequences of their actions and adjust their behavior accordingly.

Later in the chapter, we consider another naturally occurring market failure that involves a class of products called *public goods*, or *social goods*, that private firms find it unprofitable to produce even if members of society want them. Public goods yield *collective* benefits, and in most societies, it is governments that either produce them or arrange for their provision. The process of choosing what social goods to produce, that is, the problem of social choice, is by nature very different from the process of private choice.

While the existence of public goods and the presence of externalities are examples of market failure, it does not follow that government involvement will necessarily improve matters, of course. Just as markets can fail, so too can governments. In fact, when we look carefully at the incentives facing government decision makers, we find some reasons for government failure.

In the perfectly competitive model, efficiency was achieved because each decision maker had an incentive to weigh all the costs and benefits of his or her actions. By the end of this chapter, you will see that although the market does not always provide private decision makers with the incentive to weigh the full costs and benefits of their decisions properly, neither does the organization and operation of the public sector—the government—provide public-sector decision makers—politicians and bureaucrats—with incentives to weigh the full costs and benefits of *their* decisions.

The material that follows may seem theoretical, but no debate in economics has more practical importance than the age-old argument over the "proper" role of government in the economy. Differences on this issue lie at the heart of the tensions between alternative economic systems—capitalism, socialism, and communism.

Problems of externalities are also pervasive and far-reaching. There are very few private transactions that do not have spillover effects. The costs of actual damage to the environment, for example, as well as the costs of protecting the environment, are enormous, and they are paid by every citizen. The potential cost of cleaning hazardous-waste dump sites in the United States, to name only an isolated example, has been put in the tens of billions of dollars.

EXTERNALITIES

Externality A cost or benefit resulting from some activity or transaction that is imposed or bestowed upon parties external to the activity or transaction. Sometimes called spillovers or third party effects.

An **externality** is said to exist when the actions or decisions of one person or group impose a cost or bestow a benefit on some second or third parties. Sometimes externalities are referred to as *spillovers* or *neighborhood effects*. Inefficient decisions result when decision makers fail to consider social costs and benefits.

The presence of externalities is a significant phenomenon in modern life. Examples are everywhere: air, water, land, sight and sound pollution, traffic congestion, automobile accidents, abandoned housing, nuclear accidents, and cigarette smoking in enclosed public places are only a few of them. A whole body of law called tort law is designed in large measure to deal with externalities. We pay billions for insurance to protect us from liability claims that might result from harm we impose on others.

As societies become more and more urbanized, externalities become more and more important. The reason is clear: when we live closer together, our actions are more likely to have effects on others.

The Logic of Marginal-Cost Pricing with Externalities

As you have seen, profit-maximizing competitive firms will produce output up to the point that price is equal to marginal cost ($P=MC$). Let us pause for a moment here to review why this condition is essential to the proposition that competitive markets produce what people want—that is, an efficient mix of output.

When a firm weighs price and marginal cost and no externalities exist, it is in fact weighing the full benefits to society of additional production against the full costs to society of that production. Those who benefit from the production of a product are the people or households who end up consuming it. The price of a product (P_X) is a good measure of what an additional unit of that product is "worth," since those who value it more highly than P_X already buy it. People who value it less than P_X are not buying it. If marginal cost captures all costs—that is, all costs *to society*—of producing a marginal unit of a good, then producing as long as P_X is greater than MC is efficient. Up to that point, each unit of production yields benefits in excess of cost.

Consider a firm in the business of producing laundry detergent. As long as the price per unit that consumers pay for that detergent in the market exceeds the cost of the resources needed to produce one marginal unit of it, the firm will continue to produce. Producing up to that point is *efficient*, because for every unit of detergent produced, consumers derive benefits that exceed the cost of the resources needed to produce it. Producing more than that amount is *inefficient*, because marginal cost will rise *above* the unit price of the detergent. For every unit produced beyond that level, society uses up resources that have a value in excess of the benefits that consumers place on detergent. Figure 16.1a shows such a firm and such an industry.

But suppose that the production of the firm's product imposes external costs on society as well. If it does not factor those additional costs into its decisions, the firm is likely to overproduce. In Figure 16.1b, a certain measure of external costs is added to the firm's marginal cost curve. We see them in the diagram, but the firm is ignoring them. The curve labeled *MSC*, which stands for **marginal social cost** (**MSC**), is the simple sum of the marginal costs of producing the product plus the correctly measured damage costs imposed in the process of production.

Marginal social cost (MSC)   The total cost to society of producing an additional unit of a good or service. MSC is equal to the sum of marginal resource costs and marginal damage costs.

If we assume for the moment that the firm does not have to pay for these damage costs, it will produce exactly the same level of output (q^*) as before, and price (P^*) will continue to reflect only the costs that the firm actually pays to produce its product. The firms in this industry will continue to produce, and consumers will continue to consume their product, but the market price takes into account only part of the full cost of producing the good. At equilibrium (q^*), marginal social costs are considerably greater than price. Recall that price is a measure of the full value to consumers of a unit of the product at the margin.

Let us say that our soap plant freely dumps its untreated toxic waste products into a river. The waste imposes a number of specific costs on people who live downstream: it kills the fish in the river, it makes the river ugly to look at and rotten to smell, and it destroys the river for recreational use. There may also be real health hazards, depending on what chemicals the firm is dumping. Obviously the plant's product also provides certain benefits. Its soap is valuable to consumers, and they are willing and able to pay for it. The firm employs people and capital, and its revenues are sufficient to cover all costs. The issue is, however, how the *net benefits* produced by the plant compare with the value of the damage that it does. You don't need a sophisticated economic model to know that *someone* should consider those costs.

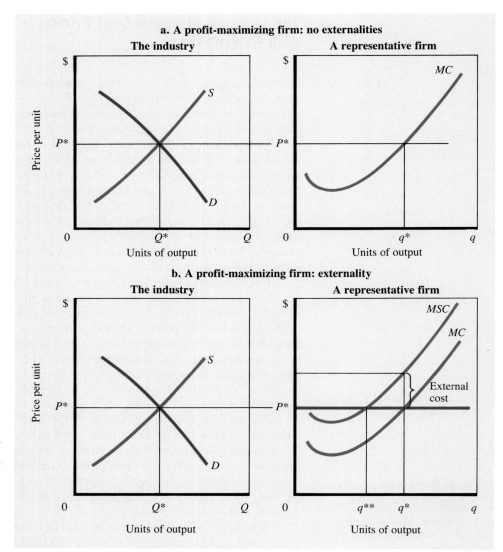

FIGURE 16.1

Profit Maximizing Firms Will Produce up to the Point that Price Equals Marginal Cost (*P=MC*)

If we assume that the current price reflects what consumers are willing to pay for a product at the margin, firms that produce external costs without weighing them in their decisions are likely to produce too much. Every unit of output produced above *q*** in Figure b costs society more than the benefits it provides to consumers.

The case of acid rain, discussed briefly earlier, is a very complex, but very good, example of an externality and of the issues and conflicts involved in dealing with externalities. Manufacturing firms and power plants in the Midwest burn coal with a high sulphur content. When the smoke from those plants mixes with moisture in the atmosphere, the result is a dilute acid that is blown by the prevailing winds north to Canada and east to New York and New England, where it falls to earth in the rain. The subject of a major conflict between the U.S. and Canadian governments and between industry and environmental groups, this acid rain is imposing potentially enormous costs where it falls. Estimates of damage from fish kills, building deterioration, and deforestation range well up into the billions of dollars.

Decision makers at the manufacturing firms and public utilities using high-sulphur coal should weigh these costs, but the issue is not all one-sided. Burning cheap coal and not worrying about the acid rain that may be falling on someone else means jobs and cheap power for residents of the Midwest, and both of these benefits weigh heavily on the minds of Midwestern governors. Without question, forcing a cleanup would hurt the industries involved. Jobs might be lost, but if the costs of the acid rain were correctly measured and the plants in the Midwest were forced to pay, then the result would be a *net* increase in benefits. If the cheap electricity and other products produced in the Midwest are *worth* the full costs, plants would *not* shut down; consumers would simply pay higher prices. If those goods are *not* worth the full cost, they should not be produced, at least in current quantities or using current production methods.

The case of acid rain highlights the fact that efficiency analysis ignores the *distribution* of gains and losses. That is, for efficiency we need only demonstrate that the total value of the gains exceeds the total value of the losses. If Midwestern producers and the consumers of their products were forced to pay an amount equal to the damages they cause, the gains from reduced damage in the East would exceed costs in the Midwest. The beneficiaries of forcing Midwestern firms to consider these costs would be the households and firms in the East.

Perhaps one of the most significant cases of an externality that affected people in many parts of the world was the 1986 explosion and fire in a nuclear power plant at Chernobyl, a small city near Kiev in the Soviet Union. Within a few hours after the fire began, radioactive particles were detected in the air in Scandinavia. Food products contaminated by the fallout had to be destroyed all over Europe. Within a week of the disaster, radioactivity was detected across the United States. The long-term health consequences of the Chernobyl explosion are, of course, still unknown.

Private Choices and External Effects

To understand externalities, let us start with a simple two-person example. Harry lives in a dormitory at a big public college in the Southwest, where he is a first year student. When he graduated from high school, his family gave him a terrific stereo system. Unfortunately, when Harry's dorm was built, the university's capital budget was tight, and the walls are made of quarter-inch sheetrock over three-inch aluminum studs. You can hear people sleeping four rooms away. Harry likes bluegrass music of the particularly "twangy" kind. Because of a hearing loss after an accident on the Fourth of July some years ago, he often does not notice the volume at which he plays his music.

Jake, who lives next door, isn't much of a music lover, but when he does listen, he listens to Brahms concerti and occasionally to Mozart. Needless to say, Harry's music bothers him.

Let's assume for a moment that there are no further external costs or benefits to anyone other than the two of them. Figure 16.2 diagrams the decision process that they face. The downward-sloping curve labeled *MB* represents the value of the marginal benefits that Harry derives from listening to his music. Now of course Harry doesn't sit down to draw this curve, any more than anyone else (other than an economics student) sits down to draw actual demand curves. Curves like this are simply abstract representations of the way people behave. But if you think carefully about it, such a curve must exist in Harry's case (and in everyone else's). To ask how much an hour of listening to music is worth to you is to ask how much you would be willing to pay to have it. Start at $0.01 and raise the "price" slowly in your mind. Presumably, you must stop at some point; where you stop depends on your taste for music and your income.

You can think, then, about the benefits that Harry derives from listening to bluegrass as some maximum amount of money between $0.01 and $50.00 that he would

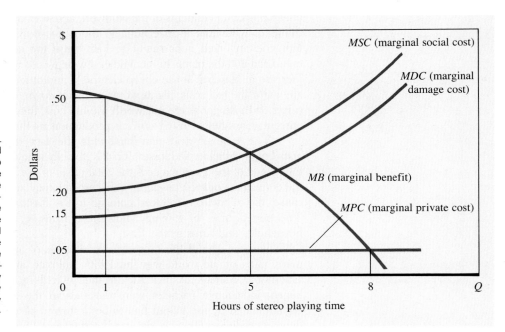

FIGURE 16.2
Externalities in a College Dormitory

The marginal benefits to Harry exceed the marginal costs he must bear to play his stereo at stereo playing time of up to eight hours. But when the stereo is playing, a cost is being imposed on Jake. When we add the costs borne by Harry to the damage costs imposed on Jake we get the full cost of the stereo to society—made up of Harry and Jake. To play the stereo more than five hours is inefficient because the benefits to Harry are less than the social cost for every hour above five. If Harry considers only his private costs, he will play the stereo for too long a time.

Marginal damage cost (mdc)   *The additional harm done by increasing the level of an externality producing activity by one unit. If producing product x pollutes the water in a river, MDC is the additional cost imposed on residents by the added pollution that results from increasing output by one unit of x per period.*

be willing to pay to listen for an hour. For the first hour, let us say, the figure for *MB* is $0.50. We assume diminishing marginal utility, of course. The more hours Harry listens, the lower the benefits from each successive hour. In the diagram, the *MB* curve falls below $.05 per hour after eight hours of playing time.

We call the costs that Harry must pay per hour in order to listen to music *marginal private costs*, labeled *MPC* in Figure 16.2. These include wear and tear on the records, the needle, electricity, and so forth. In the diagram, these costs are constant at $0.05 per hour.

Then there is Jake. Although Harry's music doesn't poison Jake, give him lung cancer, or even cause him to lose money, it damages him nonetheless. Jake is harmed, and, as in the case of Harry's benefits, it is possible, at least conceptually, to measure that harm in terms of the amount that he would be willing to pay to avoid it. The *damage*, or *cost*, imposed on Jake is represented by the **marginal damage cost** (**MDC**) curve in Figure 16.2. Assuming that Jake would be willing to pay some amount of money to avoid the music, it is also reasonable to assume that the amount increases with each successive hour.

In the simple two-person society of Jake and Harry, it's easy to add up social benefits and costs. Consider first what would happen if Harry simply ignored Jake.[1] If Harry decides to play the stereo, Jake will be damaged. As long as Harry gains more in personal benefits from an additional hour than he incurs in costs, the stereo will stay on. He will play it for eight hours. It is clear that this result is inefficient; for every hour of play beyond five, the cost borne by society, in this case, a society made up of Harry and Jake, exceeds the benefits to Harry.

It is generally true, then, that when economic decisions ignore external costs,

[1] It may actually be easier for someone to ignore the social costs imposed by their actions when those costs fall on large numbers of people that they do not know personally. For the moment, however, we simply assume that Harry takes no account of Jake.

Industrial Waste

Trees and shrubs withered away. Fish in the river died, and the population of muskrat and ringneck pheasant began dwindling. People began suffering nervous disorders, headaches and epilepsylike seizures. Some lost their hair, and others developed cancer.

The villain? Industrial pollution. The Hooker Chemical Company had been dumping its toxic wastes in Love Canal in upstate New York since the 1930s. The company, which manufactures pesticides and other chemical products, had used the canal as a dumping ground for some 20,000 tons of waste residues. By the time Hooker's practice came to light in the 1970s, the entire Love Canal area, including adjoining houses and a school, had been permeated with dangerous industrial wastes, and the local population had begun suffering severe health consequences.

Hazardous wastes are defined by the Environmental Protection Agency as those that may cause or significantly contribute to serious illness or death or that, if improperly managed, pose a strong threat to human health or the environment. These wastes are the results of our highly technological society. They are generated through production of fuel, plastic, rubber, medicine, and a host of other products that Americans use daily. According to the EPA, the characteristics of hazardous wastes are ignitability (they burn easily), corrosivity (they may eat through other materials), reactivity (they can generate dangerous gases or explode), and toxicity (they may release harmful fumes and gases).

The danger inherent in industrial wastes often comes to light when the materials are not disposed of properly. An EPA study of 17 industries conducted in the 1970s showed that approximately 90 percent of the waste they generated was not safely disposed of. The least expensive, environmentally sound method for getting rid of this waste is a secure landfill, but few of these exist. The cheapest disposal method—and the one most often used—is to have the waste carted off by truckers who dump it illegally in fields and open lots.

Waste stored out in the open—legally or illegally—has resulted in some near disasters. In Lowell, Massachusetts, a private corporation set up to process waste materials from local industries went bankrupt. It left behind approximately 20,000 barrels containing 1 million gallons of toxic wastes. The barrels, many of which were rusted and leaking, were stored near a stream that flowed into the Concord River, and from there, into the Merrimack River, from which local inhabitants got their drinking water. Another 250,000 to 300,000 gallons of toxic wastes were left in leaking storage tanks a few hundred yards from the town of Lowell itself.

Who foots the bill for cleanup? In Lowell, the state had to spend $1.5 million to clean up the site. More often than not, the question of who pays for disposal is answered in court. In 1987, Westinghouse Electric Corp. filed suit against more than 140 insurance companies it had used since 1948 to try and force them to pay cleanup and liability costs at 90 of its toxic waste sites. The bill for this operation is expected to total hundreds of millions of dollars.

Cleaning up all the country's industrial waste sites is going to be an extraordinarily expensive task. In 1987, the EPA placed 951 waste sites on its national priority list—meaning that the sites required urgent attention. However, the government estimates that the list of priority sites could climb to as many as 10,000, which would require expenditures of $100 billion—$400 for every U.S. resident. The government has started in on this mammoth job. Congress enacted legislation in 1986 that established an $8.5 billion, 5-year program called the Superfund to begin the cleanup process. Congress has also passed legislation establishing a national program to protect human health and the environment from improper handling of waste and to encourage conservation of natural resources.

Industry has joined government in tackling the toxic waste problem. The Minnesota Mining and Manufacturing Company (3M) began its "Pollution Prevention Pays" program in 1975 and has saved itself nearly $300 million by cutting its waste in half. Perhaps other companies will rally around 3M's slogan and also begin working to prevent industrial waste pollution.

Sources: Sandra Postel, "Defusing the Toxics Threat: Controlling Pesticides and Industrial Waste," *Worldwatch Paper*; September 1987. "The Toxic Waste Battle is Boiling Over," *Business Week*, August 3, 1987; "Mobilizing New Protection for Natural Resources," *Environment Magazine*, May 1987; Michael Brown, *Laying Waste*, New York: Washington Square Press, 1981.

whether those costs are borne by one person or by society as a whole, the decisions are likely to be inefficient. A number of mechanisms are available to provide decision makers with incentives to weigh the external costs and benefits of their decisions, to *internalize* them, as we say. In some cases, externalities are internalized without government involvement through bargaining and negotiation; in other cases, private bargains fail, and the only alternative may be government action of some kind.

We will return shortly to Harry and Jake to see how they deal with their problem. First, however, we need to discuss the general problem of correcting for externalities.

Alternative Approaches to the Problem of Externalities

Four basic approaches have been taken to the problem of externalities: (1) government-imposed taxes and subsidies, (2) private bargaining and negotiation, (3) legal rules and procedures such as injunctive relief and liability rules, and (4) direct government regulation. While each approach is best suited for a different set of circumstances, all three provide decision makers with an incentive to weigh the external effects of their decisions.

Taxes and Subsidies   Traditionally, economists have advocated the use of marginal taxes and subsidies as a direct way of forcing firms to consider external costs or benefits. When a firm imposes an external social cost, a tax should be imposed equal to the damages of each successive unit of output produced by the firm. In other words, the tax should be *exactly equal to* marginal damage costs.

Figure 16.3 uses the diagram that appears as Figure 16.1, but this time the damage costs are actually paid by the firm in the form of a tax. The firm now faces a marginal *cost* curve that is the same as the marginal *social* cost curve. Remember that the industry supply curve is the sum of the marginal cost curves of the individual firms. This means that the industry supply curve shifts back to the left, driving up price.

Because a profit-maximizing firm equates price with marginal cost, the new price to consumers now covers both the resource costs of producing the product and the damage costs. The consumer-decision process is now once again efficient at the margin, because social benefit as reflected in market price is equal to the full marginal cost of the product.

MEASURING DAMAGES   The biggest problem with this approach is that the damages must be estimated in money terms. For the soap plant polluting the nearby river to be properly taxed, the government must evaluate the damages done to residents downstream

FIGURE 16.3

Tax Imposed on a Firm Equal to Marginal Damage Cost

If a tax is imposed on a firm exactly equal to marginal damage costs, the firm will weigh the tax, and thus the damage costs, in its decisions. At the new equilibrium price, P_1, consumers will be paying an amount sufficient to cover full resource costs as well as the cost of damage imposed. q_1 is the efficient level of output.

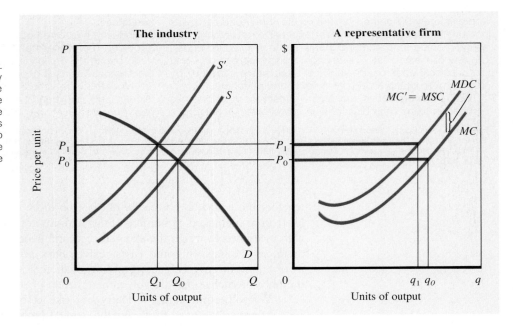

in money terms. This is a difficult but not an impossible task. When legal remedies are pursued, judges are forced to make such estimates all the time as they decide on compensation to be paid. Surveys of "willingness to pay," studies of property values in affected versus nonaffected areas, and sometimes the market value of recreational activities can provide basic data.

The monetary value of damages to health and loss of life is, naturally, much more difficult to estimate, and any measurement of such losses is certainly controversial. But even here, policy makers frequently make judgments that implicitly set values on life and health. Tens of thousands of deaths and millions of serious injuries result from traffic accidents in the United States every year, yet Americans are unwilling to give up driving or to reduce the speed limit to 40 miles per hour—the cost would be too high. Indeed, in 1987 the Congress, in response to public demand, passed legislation to allow states to increase the speed limit to 65 miles per hour on rural parts of interstate highways. If most Americans are willing to increase the risk of death in exchange for shorter driving times, clearly the value we place on life has its limits.

The value of health also has its limits. We do not allocate *all* our national wealth to the provision of health care. We spend billions on recreation, for example, while many health-care facilities are pushed for resources.

Life and health are certainly valuable, but those values, while high, are not infinite. Any agency, whether private or public, that engages in activities that are potentially damaging to life or health must carefully consider the consequences of its actions. It is better to estimate those costs systematically rather than arbitrarily.

It is important to note that taxing externality-producing activities *may not eliminate damages*. Taxes on these activities are not designed to eliminate externalities; they are simply meant to force decision makers to consider the full costs of their decisions. Even if we assume that a tax correctly measures *all* the damage done, the decision maker may find it advantageous to go right on causing the damage. For example, the soap manufacturers may find it most profitable simply to pay the tax and go on polluting the river in lieu of cleaning up. That is, it may find that it can continue to pollute because the revenues from selling its product are sufficient to cover the cost of resources used *and to fully compensate the damaged parties*. In such a case, producing the product in spite of the pollution is "worth it" to society. It would be inefficient for the firm to stop polluting. Only if damage costs were very high would it make sense to stop. Thus you can see the importance of proper measurement of damage costs.

Some pollution is thus efficient. If consumers are willing to pay a price for a product that covers both the resource costs of producing it *and* an amount sufficient to compensate the damaged parties fully, then the level of production is efficient. To produce less would be inefficient. The imposition of the tax makes the polluter choose the efficient level of output and the best technology of production.

REDUCING DAMAGES TO AN EFFICIENT LEVEL   Taxes do provide an incentive to use the most efficient technology for dealing with the damage. If the tax reflects true damages, and if it is reduced when damages are reduced, firms may choose to avoid or reduce the tax by using a different technology that causes less damage. Suppose that our soap manufacturer, for example, is taxed $10,000 per month for polluting the river. If the soap plant can ship its waste to a disposal site elsewhere at a cost of $7000 per month and thereby avoid the tax, it will certainly do so. If a plant belching sulfides into the air can install "smoke scrubbers" that eliminate emissions for less than the tax imposed for polluting the air, it too will do so.

THE INCENTIVE TO TAKE CARE AND TO AVOID HARM   But now suppose that the damaged parties could do something to avoid the damages. If full compensation is paid to the damaged parties, *they may have no incentive to avoid them*. People who are fully compensated for damages have no reason to exert effort or spend money to avoid the harm.

Take, for example, a laundry located next to the exhaust fans from the kitchen of a Chinese restaurant. Suppose damages run to $1000 per month because the laundry must use special air filters to operate its dryers lest the clothes smell of Szechuan spices. The laundry looks around and finds a perfectly good alternative location away from the restaurant that rents for only $500.00 per month above its current rent. Absent any compensation, the laundry will move and the total damage will be $500.00 per month. But if the restaurant compensates it for damages of $1000 a month, why should it move? Under these conditions, a move is unlikely, even though it would be efficient.

Thus payment of compensation in an externality case can encourage the victim to make an inefficient decision. On the other hand, if imposing the cost on the victim is seen as unjust, compensation may be justified on the basis of equity. This case is an example in which the criteria of efficiency and equity can lead to conflicting policies.

SUBSIDIZING EXTERNAL BENEFITS   Sometimes activities or decisions generate external benefits instead of costs. Real estate investment provides a clear example. When I fix up my house, I am the primary beneficiary, but those in my neighborhood also gain. Not only does my place look nicer, the street becomes more stable, and that is a social benefit. Investors who revitalize a downtown area—an old theatre district in a big city, for example—provide benefits to many people, both in the city and in surrounding areas.

Activities that provide such external social benefits may be subsidized at the margin to give decision makers an incentive to consider them. Just as ignoring social costs can lead to inefficient decisions, so too can ignoring social benefits. Government subsidies for housing and other development, either directly through specific expenditure programs or indirectly through tax exemptions and abatements, have been justified on such grounds.

Bargaining and Negotiation   In a notable article written in 1960, Ronald Coase pointed out that the government need not be involved in every case of externality.[2] In the case of Harry, the stereo nut, and his victim Jake, for example, taxes and subsidies would be irrelevant. Coase argues that private bargains and negotiations are likely to lead to an efficient solution in many social damage cases without any government involvement at all. This argument is referred to as the **Coase theorem**.

Coase theorem   *The proposition that if bargains were reached costlessly, then externalities would not result in an inefficient allocation of resources. Through bargaining and negotiations, private parties can and will arrive at the efficient solution when externalities are present without government involvement.*

In order for Coase's solution to work, three things must be true. First, the basic rights at issue must be clearly understood. Either Harry has the right to play his stereo or Jake has the right to silence. These rights will probably be spelled out in dorm rules. When basic rights are truly at issue, of course, the courts decide what they are and which takes precedence. Second, there must be no impediments to bargaining. Parties must be willing and able to discuss the issues openly and without cost. Third, only a few people can be involved. Serious problems develop when one of the parties to a bargain is a large group of people who are only voluntarily associated.

For the sake of the story, let us say that all three of these conditions hold for Harry and Jake. The dorm rules establish basic rights in this case by specifying that during certain hours of the day, Harry has an absolute right to play his stereo as loudly as he pleases. Returning to Figure 16.2 again, suppose that under the rules Harry is free to

[2]See Ronald Coase, "The Problem of Social Cost," *Journal of Law and Economics* (1960).

choose any number of hours between zero and eight.

Because Harry is under no legal constraint to pay any attention to Jake, you might be tempted to think that he will ignore Jake and play his stereo for eight hours. Recall that up to eight hours, the marginal benefits to Harry exceed the marginal costs that he must pay. Jake is, however, willing to offer Harry a bribe to have Harry play his stereo less than eight hours. For the first hour of play, the marginal damage to Jake is $0.15, and so Jake would be willing to pay Harry $0.15 in the first hour to have Harry cease playing. The opportunity cost to Harry of playing the first hour is thus $0.15 plus the (constant) marginal private cost of $0.05, or $0.20. Since the marginal gain to Harry in the first hour is $0.50, Harry would not accept the bribe. Likewise, for hours two through five the marginal benefit to Harry exceeds the bribe that Jake would be willing to pay plus the marginal private cost.

After five hours, however, Jake is willing to pay $0.25 per hour to have Harry cease playing, which means that the opportunity cost to Harry is $0.30, and the marginal benefit to Harry of another hour of playing has fallen to $0.25. Harry will thus accept the bribe not to play the sixth hour. Similarly, a bribe of $0.25 per hour is sufficient to have Harry not play the seventh and eighth hours, and Jake would be willing to pay such a bribe. Five hours is thus the efficient amount of playing time. More hours or fewer hours reduces net total benefits to Harry and Jake.

Coase also points out that bargaining will get the contending parties to the right solution regardless of where rights are initially assigned. For example, suppose that the dorm rules state that Jake has the right to silence. This being the case, he can go to the head residents and have them enforce the rule. Now when Harry plays the stereo and Jake asks him to turn it off, Harry must comply.

But Harry now has the same option that Jake had before. He can offer compensation that it is clearly in Jake's interest to accept. Since Harry gets far more than $0.15 in net benefit from the first hour, he will certainly be willing to pay enough to fully compensate Jake in order to keep the stereo on. If Jake takes the compensation and Harry plays the stereo, Jake has, in effect, sold to Harry his right to have silence. As before, bargaining between the two parties will lead to five hours of stereo playing. At exactly five hours, Jake will stop taking compensation and tell Harry to turn the stereo off. (Look again at Figure 16.2 and convince yourself that this is true.)

Note that in both cases the offer of compensation might be made in some form other than cash. Jake may offer Harry goodwill, a favor or two, or the use of his Harley Davidson for an hour.

Coase's critics are quick to point out that the conditions required for bargaining to produce the efficient result are not always present. The biggest problem with Coase's system is also a common problem. Very often one party to a bargain is a large group of people, and our reasoning may be subject to a *fallacy of composition.*

Suppose that a power company in Pittsburgh is polluting the air, and the damaged parties are the 100,000 people who live near the plant. For the sake of argument, let's assume that the plant has the right to pollute. The Coase theorem predicts that the people who are damaged by the smoke will get together and offer a bribe (just as Jake offered a bribe to Harry). If the bribe is sufficient to induce the power plant to stop polluting or reduce the pollutants with scrubbers, then it will take the bribe and cut down on the pollution. If it is not, the pollution will continue, but the firm would be weighing all the costs (just as Harry did when he continued to play the stereo) and the result would be efficient.

But, *not everyone will participate.* First, each contribution is so small relative to the whole that no one contribution makes much of a difference. Thus making a contribution seems unimportant. Second, everyone gets to breathe the cleaner air, whether he or she contributed to the bribe or not. Human nature, therefore, dictates that many people will not participate, because they don't have to, and the private bargain breaks down—the bribe that the group comes up with will be less than the full damages unless everyone participates. (These two problems—the "drop-in-the-bucket" and the "free-rider"—are discussed more fully later in this chapter.) Thus when the number of damaged parties is large, government taxes or regulation may be the only avenue to a remedy.

Injunction *A court order forbidding the continuation of behavior that leads to damages.*

Liability rules *Legally enforced requirements that those who do damage must compensate those who can establish the fact of and the degree of damage.*

Legal Rules and Procedures For bargaining to result in an efficient outcome, the initial assignment of rights has to be clear to both parties. When rights are established by law, more often than not some mechanism to protect those rights is also built into law. In some cases where a nuisance exists, for example, there may be injunctive remedies. In such cases, the victim can go to court and ask for an **injunction** forbidding the nuisance from continuing. When the dorm rules specifically gave Jake the right to have silence, his getting the head resident to speak to Harry was something like getting an injunction.

Injunctive remedies are irrelevant, however, when the damage has already been done. Consider accidents, for example. If your leg has already been broken as the result of an automobile accident, enjoining the driver of the other car from drinking and driving won't work—it's already too late. In these cases, rights must be protected by **liability rules**, that is, rules that require A to compensate B for damages imposed. In theory such rules are designed to do exactly the same thing that taxing a polluter is designed to do: provide decision makers with an incentive to weigh all the consequences, actual and potential, of their decisions. Just as taxes do not stop all pollution, liability rules do not stop all accidents.

The threat of liability, however, does induce people to take more care than they might otherwise take. Product liability is a good case in point. If a person is damaged in some way because a product is defective, the producing company is in most cases held strictly liable for the damages, even if the company took reasonable care in producing the product. Thus producers have a powerful incentive to be careful. If consumers know they will be generously compensated for any damages, however, they may not have as powerful an incentive to be careful when using the product.

Direct Regulation of Externalities Taxes and subsidies and legal rules are designed to induce firms and households to weigh the social costs and benefits of their actions. The size of the external cost/benefit that ends up actually being imposed depends on the reaction of households and firms to the incentives that the taxes, subsidies, and rules provide.

For obvious reasons, many externalities are too important to be regulated indirectly. Dumping cancer-causing chemicals into the ground near a public water supply is simply illegal, and those who do it can be prosecuted and sent to jail.

The Environmental Protection Agency was established by act of Congress in 1970. In addition, every state has a division or department charged with regulating activities likely to harm the environment. Since the 1960s, Congress has passed a number of pieces of legislation that set specific standards for permissible discharges into the air and water. Direct regulation of externalities is not only imposed when damages are severe; most airports in the United States have landing patterns and hours that are regulated by local governments to minimize aggravating noise.

Another example of an externality that can be controlled both directly and indirectly is traffic congestion. When people decide to drive to work in the morning they add to congestion, imposing an external cost on other drivers. In Los Angeles, access to freeways in some places is limited by signals to keep traffic flowing. Many urban mass transit systems are subsidized or priced below cost in an effort to attract people out of their cars and off the roads. If a million-dollar subsidy to a mass transit system reduces congestion and saves commuters two million dollars worth of time and aggravation, the result is efficient.

In fact, many criminal penalties and sanctions for violating environmental regulations are like taxes imposed on polluters. Not all violations and crimes are stopped, but violators and criminals face "costs." For the outcome to be efficient, the penalties they expect to pay should reflect the damage their actions impose on society.

The Ubiquitous Problem of Externalities

The problem of externalities is everywhere. Once Colleen joins Bill on the desert island we have externalities. In large technological societies, there are millions of them. The Chernobyl nuclear power plant disaster in the Soviet Union showed again just how far-reaching external effects can be.

The problem of externalities has no single best solution. In this country we use all the solutions available, and then some. Private bargains are sufficient to ensure an efficient allocation of resources in a great many cases. They fail in many others. The law sets forth rules dealing with many specific kinds of externalities—traffic accidents, for example. Regulatory agencies such as the Environmental Protection Agency (EPA) also impose rules on households and firms—"effluent charges," for example, that force polluters to consider the costs of their wastes.

The critical point is that when externalities are ignored, bad decisions and an inefficient allocation of resources are likely to result.

SOCIAL, OR PUBLIC, GOODS

Another source of market failure lies in the existence of **public goods**, often called **social**, or **collective, goods**. These kinds of goods represent a market failure because they have characteristics that make it difficult for the private sector to produce them profitably. In an unregulated market economy with no government to see that they are produced, public goods would at best be produced in insufficient quantity and at worst not produced at all.

Nonrival in consumption A characteristic of public goods: one person's enjoyment of the benefits of a public good does not detract from another's enjoyment of them.

Nonexcludable Another characteristic of most public goods: their benefits fall on all members of a group or a society and no one can be excluded from enjoying those benefits once the good is produced.

Characteristics of Public Goods

Public goods are defined by two closely related characteristics: they are **nonrival in consumption** and/or their benefits are **nonexcludable**, that is, it is difficult or impossible to exclude anyone from enjoying their benefits, once produced.

A good is called *nonrival* in consumption when A's consumption of it does not interfere with B's consumption of it. This means that the benefits of the goods are *collective*—they accrue to everyone. National defense, for instance, benefits us all. The fact that I am protected in no way detracts from the fact that you are protected, and indeed every citizen is protected just as much as every other citizen. If the air is cleaned up, my breathing that air does not interfere with your breathing it, nor (under ordinary circumstances) is it used up as more people breathe it. Private goods, on the other hand, are *rival* in consumption—if I eat a hamburger, you cannot eat it too.

Some goods can sometimes generate collective benefits and still be rival in consumption. This happens when there is crowding. A park or a pool, for example, can accommodate many people at the same time, generating collective benefits for everyone. But when too many people crowd in on a hot summer day, they begin to interfere with each other's enjoyment. Beyond a certain level of use, then, the park or the pool becomes rival in consumption.

Most public goods also have the property that once the good is produced, people *cannot be excluded* for any reason from enjoying its benefits. Once a national defense system is established, it protects everyone. When the police department sets up a successful crime-prevention program, everyone in town is less likely to be the victim of a crime.

For a private profit-making firm to produce a good and make a profit, it must be able to *withhold* that good from those who do not pay. If a private firm cannot exclude people from enjoying the benefits of its product, it has a real problem. McDonald's can make money selling fish sandwiches only because you don't get the fish sandwich unless you pay for it first. If payment were voluntary, it's not clear how long McDonald's would be in business.

Let us consider a clever entrepreneur who decides to offer better police protection to the city of Metropolis. Very careful, and we will assume correct, market research reveals that the citizens of Metropolis do indeed want high-quality protection, and they are willing to pay for it. Clearly, not everyone is willing to pay the same amount; some can afford more, others can afford less, and people have different preferences and different feelings about risk. Our entrepreneur nevertheless hires a sales force and begins to sell his service. Soon, however, he encounters a problem. Because his is a private company, payment is strictly voluntary, and he can't force anyone to pay. Payment for a hamburger is voluntary too, but a hamburger can be withheld for nonpayment. The good that our new firm is selling, however, is by nature a public good.

As a potential consumer of a public good, I face a dilemma. I want more police protection, and, let's say, I'm even willing to pay $50.00 a month for it. But nothing is contingent upon my payment. First, if the good is produced, the crime rate falls and all residents benefit; I get that benefit whether or not I pay for it. In other words, I get a free ride, and that is why this dilemma is called the **free-rider problem**. Second, my payment is very small relative to the amount that must be collected to provide the service. Thus the amount of police protection actually produced will not be significantly affected by the amount that I contribute, or whether I contribute at all. This is appropriately called the **drop-in-the-bucket problem**.

The conclusion is self-evident. A consumer acting in his or her own self-interest has no incentive to contribute voluntarily to the production of public goods. To be fair, some will feel a moral responsibility or social pressure to contribute, and those people indeed may do so. But the economic incentive is missing, and most people do not find room in their budgets for lots of voluntary payments.

Sometimes public, or government, provision is called for even if exclusion is possible. An oft-cited example is the "empty bridge." If a very large bridge spans a river, many cars and trucks can cross on it simultaneously. Its benefits are thus collective, and as long as there is no crowding, they are nonrival. Except perhaps for some very minor

Free-rider problem   A *problem intrinsic to public goods: because people can enjoy the benefits of public goods whether or not they pay for them, everyone is disinclined to pay for them. Consumption is not contingent upon payment.*

Drop-in-the-bucket problem   *Another problem intrinsic to public goods: the service is usually so costly that the level of its provision does not depend on whether or not any single person pays or not.*

depreciation, the marginal cost of providing "crossing services" is zero. It is easy to exclude people from crossing a bridge—you simply erect a barrier at each end. But because the marginal costs of using the bridge are nearly zero, excluding people from crossing is inefficient. Crossing the bridge presumably generates a benefit to anyone who chooses to do so, and it costs society virtually nothing.

An Aside: Income Distribution as a Public Good   In the next chapter, we add the issues of justice and equity to the matters of economic efficiency that we are considering here. There we argue that the government may wish to change the distribution of income that results from the operation of the unregulated market on the grounds that the distribution is not fair. Before we get to that, however, you should note that some economists have argued for redistribution of income on grounds that it generates benefits that are public.

For example, let us say that many members of American society want to eliminate hunger in the United States. Suppose that you yourself are willing to give $200.00 per year in exchange for the knowledge that people are not going to bed hungry. Many private charities in the United State use the money they raise to feed the poor. If you want to contribute to this activity, you can certainly do so privately, through charity. So why do we need government involvement?

We have seen that activities which generate public benefits—say, national defense—may be underproduced privately. If redistribution of income produces public benefits, might it not also lead to underproduction? And if so, how might that be so?

First, the elimination of hunger (the goal we set in our example) generates collective psychological benefits; simply knowing that people are not starving helps us sleep better. Second, however, eliminating hunger may reduce disease, and this in turn has a number of clearly beneficial effects. People who are fit and strong are more likely to stay in school and to get and keep jobs. This reduces welfare claims and contributes positively to the economy. If people are less likely to get sick, insurance premiums for everyone will go down. People who work are less likely to use drugs heavily. Robberies may decline, because fewer people are desperate for money. This means that all of us are less likely to be victims of crime, both now and in the future, and so on.

These are goals that members of society may very well want to achieve. But just as there is no economic incentive to contribute voluntarily to national defense, so there is no economic incentive to contribute to private causes. If hunger is eliminated, you benefit whether you contributed or not—the free-rider problem again. At the same time, poverty is a huge problem, and your contribution cannot possibly have any influence on the amount of hunger nationally—the drop-in-the-bucket-problem again.

Thus the goals of income redistribution may be more like national defense than like a hamburger. If we accept the idea that redistributing income generates a public good, private endeavors may fail to do what we want them to do, and government involvement may be called for.

Public Goods So Far   In sum, there are two types of public good: (1) those that are nonrival and nonexcludable (national defense) and (2) those that are nonrival but from which it is possible to exclude people (the empty bridge). Where exclusion is not possible, private provision of public goods fails. Where consumption is really nonrival, marginal cost of provision is zero and efficiency calls for free access even though exclusion is possible. Private provision of such goods at a price is possible but inefficient.

Public Provision of Public Goods

All societies, past and present, have had to face the problem of providing public goods. When members of society get together and form a government in the first place, they do so to provide themselves with goods and services that will not be provided if they act separately. Like any other good or service, a body of laws (or system of justice) is produced with labor, capital, and other inputs. Law and the courts yield social benefits, and they must be set up and administered by some sort of collective, cooperative effort. There are hundreds of other examples of pure public goods; among them national defense, police and fire protection, public health, weather forecasting, and the list goes on.

Notice that we have specified **public provision**, not **public production**. Often the government decides what service it wants to provide, but it contracts with the private sector to produce the good. Much of the materiel for national defense is produced by private defense contractors. Highways, government offices, data processing services, and so forth are usually produced by private firms.

One of the immediate problems of public provision, of course, is that it leads to *public dissatisfaction*. Government is easy to be angry at. Part, but certainly not all, of the reason for this lies in the nature of the goods that it provides. Firms that produce or sell private goods post a price—we can choose any quantity that we want, or we can walk away without any. It makes no sense to get mad at a shoe store, because no one can force you to shop there.

You cannot shop for collectively beneficial public goods, however. When it comes to national defense, for example, the government must choose one and only one kind and quantity of (collective) output to produce. Because none of us can choose how much should be spent or on what, we are all dissatisfied. Even if the government does its job with reasonable efficiency, at any given time about half of us think that we have too much national defense and about half of us think that we have too little.

Optimal Provision of Public Goods

In a famous article first published in the early 1950s, Paul Samuelson, of MIT, demonstrated that there existed an *optimal*, or *most efficient*, level of output for every public good.[3] The discussion of the Samuelson solution that follows leads us straight in to the thorny problem of how societies, as opposed to individuals, make choices.

The Samuelson Theory　　As you recall, an efficient economy is one that produces what people want. Private producers, whether competitors or monopolists, are constrained by the market demand for their products. If they can't sell their products for more than it costs to produce them, they are out of business. But, since private goods permit exclusion, firms can withhold their products until households pay. This contingency of delivery upon payment forces households to *reveal* something about their preferences. No one is forced to buy or not to buy, but if you want a product, you have to pay for it. Buying a

---

[3]Paul A. Samuelson, "Diagrammatic Exposition of a Theory of Public Expenditure," *Review of Economics and Statistics*, XXXVII (1955).

Privatization

Public *provision* and public *production* of services are not the same thing. Often, the government provides a service, but the actual production is done in the private sector. Even pure public goods are often, at least in part, produced by private firms under contract to the government. The best example is national defense. While the Congress appropriates the money and pays the bill, rocket boosters for the space program and for weapons systems are produced by private companies like Morton Thiokol, Inc.

This combination of public provision and private production of services began as early as the Revolutionary War. When the Continental Congress wanted British ships captured or sunk, they would hire "privateers"—private shippers—to do the job. The Congress knew that these commercial entrepreneurs were faster and better than government forces.

In recent years, the town of Elkgrove, Illinois, cut escalating municipal budget costs by using private fire fighters. In Auburn, Alabama, a private company built, owns, and operates the waste-water treatment plant that cleans the city's sewage. This arrangement should save the city's residents $25 million over 25 years.

In recent years, there has been increasing pressure to shift functions out of the public sector and into the private sector. This privatization can take two forms. First, the government can contract with corporations and other nongovernment agencies to provide services the government wants to continue to provide but not produce. Second, the government may want to get out of the business completely on the grounds that provision is best left to the private sector.

In Japan, privatization of the national railways is expected to curtail heavy losses. In China, privatizing agriculture has resulted in an explosion of food supply and a dramatic improvement in the rural standard of living. In Africa, the Marxist governments of such countries as Angola, Benin, and Congo are planning to sell money-losing state companies. Many other countries, including Britain and France, have chosen to sell stock in their state-owned bank, energy, and telecommunications firms to "privatize" them to make them more financially viable. In fact, a leading bank estimates that at least 55 major state enterprises worldwide have been privatized since 1980 at a total sales price of $48 billion and that another 2,000 concerns, worth approximately $130 billion,

will be sold by 1990.

Those who approve private production note that competitive profit-making firms have an incentive to be efficient and to produce high-quality products. Firms that perform poorly will lose contracts. However, advocates of privatization also want the government to leave *provision* of some services to the private sector. They advocate that the government should get out of certain businesses altogether. Why should the government produce steel, provide rail service, or produce beer as it does in some countries? If private producers are turned loose in a competitive environment they will better respond to the needs of consumers, and price competition will lead to lower prices.

The biggest push for privatization focuses on those government agencies considered the most inefficient. The President's Commission on Privatization recommended that private companies take over the U.S. Post Office's role of delivering advertising and rural mail—the first steps toward eventual removal of the government from all of the country's postal operations. The commission also suggested privatization of prisons, air traffic control operations, public housing, and other areas that might be improved through competition in the private sector.

Those opposed to privatization argue that the government actually does quite a creditable job. They note that more than 90 percent of social security checks arrive on time and in the proper amount. And 75 percent of people receiving government services say that they are satisfied with their treatment.

In a sense, this chapter provides a counterargument to complete privatization. If a good is a public good by nature, the private sector will not produce it, at least in adequate amounts, without government involvement.

Second, private producers do not always have an incentive to consider the full costs and benefits of producing their product. Where externalities exist, government involvement may be called for.

Third, public provision often takes place in the name of redistribution. For example, the Housing Act of 1946 declared that the government had a responsibility to ensure that every American had a decent place to live. It is clear that if the government left provision of housing completely to the private sector, many more people would be homeless.

Sources: "In defense of bureaucracy," *State Government News*, July 1986; "Report Sees Government Role in Privatizing," *City & State*, February 1, 1988; "Panel Ask Private Firm Mail Delivery," *Chicago Sun-Times*, March 18, 1988; "Privately Run Prisons, Air Traffic Control Proposed," *Chicago Sun-Times*, March 1988; "The Global Appeal of Privatization," *The World & I*, January 1988.

product at a posted price reveals that it is "worth" at least that amount to you and to everyone who buys it.

Market demand for a private good is simply the *sum of the* quantities that each household decides to buy. The diagrams in Figure 16.4 review the derivation of a market demand curve. Here, assume that society consists of two people, A and B. At a price of

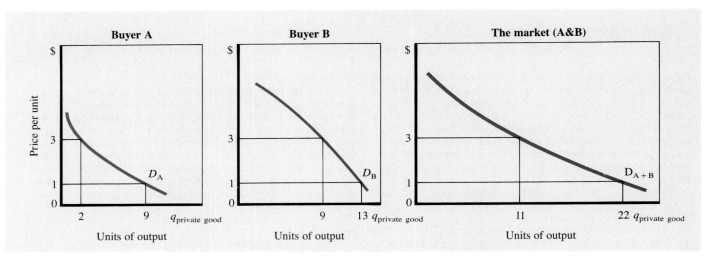

FIGURE 16.4

With Private Goods, Consumers Decide what Quantity to Buy; Market Demand Is the Sum
of Those Quantities at Each Price

At a price of $3.00, A buys two units and B buys nine for a total of 11. At a price of $1.00, A buys nine units
and B buys 13, for a total of 22. We all buy the quantity of each private good that we want. Market
demand is the horizontal sum of all individual demand curves.

$1.00, A demands nine units of the private good and B demands 13. Market demand at a
price of $1.00 is 22 units. If price were to rise to $3.00, A's demand would drop back to
two units and B's would drop back to nine units; market demand at a price of $3.00 is 11
units. The point is that the price mechanism forces people to reveal what they want, and it
forces firms to produce only what people are willing to pay for, *but it works this way only
because exclusion is possible.*

People's preferences and demands for public goods are conceptually no different.
To demonstrate that an efficient level of production exists, Samuelson assumes that we
know people's preferences. Figure 16.5 has demand curves for A and B. If there were a
market and the public good were available at a price of $6.00, A would buy X_1 units. Or,
to put this another way, A is willing to pay $6.00 per unit to obtain X_1 units of the public
good. B, on the other hand, is willing to pay only $3.00 per unit to obtain X_1 units of the
public good.

Remember, however, that public goods are nonrival, that is, benefits accrue
simultaneously to everyone. One, and only one, quantity can be produced, and that is the
amount that everyone gets. If X_1 units are produced, A gets X_1 and B gets X_1. If X_2 units
are produced, A gets X_2 and B gets X_2.

To arrive at market demand for public goods, then, we do not sum quantitites;
rather, *we add up the amounts that individual households are willing to pay for each
potential level of output.* In Figure 16.5, for example, A is willing to pay $6.00 per unit
for X_1 units and B is willing to pay $3.00 per unit for X_1 units. Thus if a society consists
only of A and B, society is willing to pay $9.00 per unit for X_1 units of public good X. For
X_2 units of output, society is willing to pay a total of $4.00 per unit.

For private goods, market demand is the horizontal sum of individual demand
curves—we add the different *quantities* that households consume. For public goods,

market demand is the vertical sum of individual demand curves—we add the different *amounts* that households are willing to pay to obtain each level of output.

Samuelson argues that once we know how much society is willing to pay for a public good, we need only compare that with the cost of its production. Figure 16.6 reproduces A's and B's demand curves and the total demand curve for the public good. As

FIGURE 16.5

With Public Goods, There Is Only *One* Level of Output, Consumers Are Willing to Pay Different Amounts for Each Level

A is willing to pay $6 per unit for X_1 units of public good. B is willing to pay only $3.00 per unit. Society—in this case A & B—is willing to pay a total of $9.00 per unit for the good. Since only one level of output can be chosen for a public good, we must add A's contribution to B's; that means adding demand curves vertically.

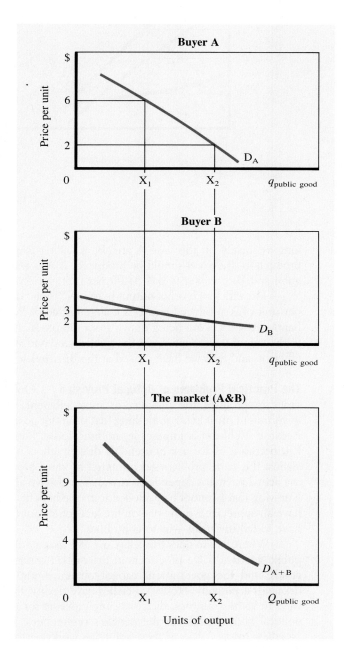

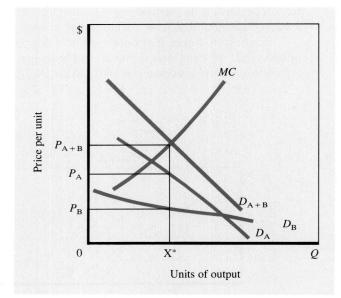

FIGURE 16.6
Optimal Production of a Public
Good

Optimal production of a public good
means producing as long as society's
total willingness to pay per unit (D_{A+B})
is greater than the marginal cost of
producing the good.

long as society, in this case A and B, is willing to pay more than the marginal cost of
production, the good should be produced. If A is willing to pay $5.00 per unit of public
good and B is willing to pay $3.00 per unit, society is willing to pay $8.00.

The efficient level of output here is X^* units. If at that level A is charged a fee of P_A
per unit of X produced and B is charged a fee of P_B per unit of X, everyone should be
happy. Resources are being drawn from the production of other goods and services only
to the extent that people want the public good and are willing to pay for it. Everything is
efficient, and thus we have arrived at the **optimal level of provision for public goods**.

The Practical Problems of Optimal Provision   One big problem remains, however. In
order to produce the optimal, or most efficient, amount of each public good, the
government must know something that it cannot possibly know—everyone's preferences.
Because exclusion is impossible, nothing forces households to reveal their preferences.
Furthermore, if we ask households directly about their willingness to pay, we run up
against the same problem encountered by our "protection-services" salesman above. If
my actual payment depends on my answer, I have an incentive to hide my true feelings.
Knowing that I cannot be excluded from the benefits and that my payment is likely not to
have an appreciable influence on the level of output finally produced, what incentive do I
have to tell the truth—or to contribute?

Where, then, does this leave us? We *assume* that members of society want certain
public goods. Private producers in the market cannot make a profit by producing these
goods, and the government cannot obtain enough information to measure society's
demands accurately. No two societies have dealt with this dilemma in precisely the same
way. In some countries, dictators simply decide for the people. In others, representative
political bodies speak for the people's preferences. In still others, people vote directly.
Needless to say, none of these solutions works perfectly.

THE PROBLEM OF SOCIAL CHOICE

Social choice   The problem of deciding what societies want. The process of somehow aggregating or adding up individual preferences to make a choice for the whole.

One view of government, or the public sector, holds that it exists to provide things that "society wants." A society is a collection of individuals, and each individual has a unique set of preferences. Defining "what society wants," therefore, becomes a problem of **social choice**—of somehow adding up, or aggregating, individual preferences.

It is also important to understand, however, that government is made up of individuals—politicians and government workers—whose *own* objectives in part determine what government does. To understand government, then, we must understand the incentives facing politicians and public servants, as well as the difficulties of aggregating the preferences of the members of a society.

Voting and the Rule of the Majority

Democratic societies use the ballot to arrive at aggregate preferences and to make the social decisions that follow from them. If all votes could be unanimous, it would certainly guarantee efficient decisions; after all, anyone likely to be made worse off by a decision would surely vote against it. Unfortunately, unanimity is difficult to achieve with three people, and virtually impossible to achieve among hundreds of millions of people, because each person has different preferences.

Impossibility theorem   A proposition demonstrated by Kenneth Arrow which shows that no system of aggregating individual preferences into social decisions will always yield consistent, non-arbitrary results.

The most common social decision-making mechanism is, of course, majority rule. But it too has problems. In a well-known work published in 1951, Kenneth Arrow proved what has come to be called the **impossibility theorem**.[4] Arrow has shown that it is impossible to devise a voting scheme that respects individual preferences and gives consistent nonarbitrary results.

One example of a seemingly irrational result emerging from majority-rule voting that is often used to shed light on Arrow's work is the voting paradox. Suppose that, faced with a decision about the future of the institution, the president of a major university opted to let her three top administrators vote on the following options: should the university (1) increase the number of students and hire more faculty, (2) maintain the current size of the faculty and student body, or (3) cut back on faculty and reduce the student body? Figure 16.7 represents the preferences of the three administrators diagrammatically.

FIGURE 16.7
Preferences of Three Top University Officials

VP1 prefers *A* to *B* and *B* to *C*. VP2 prefers *B* to *C* and *C* to *A*. The Dean prefers *C* to *A* and *A* to *B*.

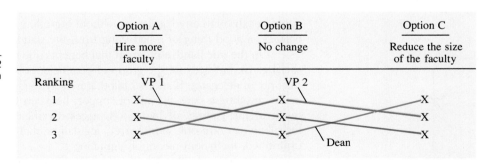

	Option A Hire more faculty	Option B No change	Option C Reduce the size of the faculty
Ranking	VP 1	VP 2	
1	X	X	X
2	X	X	X
3	X	X (Dean)	X

[4]Kenneth Arrow, *Social Choice and Individual Values* (New York: Wiley 1951).

TABLE 16.1
Results of Voting on University's
Plans

Vote	VP1	Votes of: VP2	Dean	Result*
A versus B	A	B	A	A wins: A>B
B versus C	B	B	C	B wins: B>C
C versus A	A	C	C	C wins: C>A

*A>B is read "A is preferred to B"

Voting paradox *A simple*
demonstration of how majority rule
voting can lead to seemingly
contradictory and inconsistent
results. A commonly cited
illustration of the kind of
inconsistency described in the
impossibility theorem.

The vice president for finance (VP1) wants growth. He prefers A to B and B to C. The vice president for development (VP2), however, has been heavily involved in fund raising, and she doesn't want to rock the boat. She prefers maintaining the current size of the institution, option B, to either of the others. If the status quo was out of the question, she would prefer option C. The dean believes in change; he wants to shake the place up, and he doesn't much care whether that means increase or decrease. He prefers C to A and A to B.

Table 16.1 gives the results of the vote. When the three vote on A versus B, they vote in favor of A, that is, to increase the size of the university rather than keeping it the same. VP1 and the dean outvote VP2. Voting on B and C produces a victory for option B; two of the three would rather hold the line than decrease the size of the institution. After two votes we have the result that A (increase) is preferred to B (no change) and that B (no change) is preferred to C (decrease).

The problem arises when we then have the three vote on A against C. Both VP2 and the dean vote for C, giving it the victory; C is actually preferred to A. But if A beats B, and B beats C, how can C beat A? The results are inconsistent.

The **voting paradox** illustrates several points. Most important is the fact that when preferences for public goods differ across individuals, any system for adding up, or aggregating, those preferences can lead to inconsistencies. In addition, it illustrates just how much influence the person who sets the agenda has. If a vote had been taken on A and C first, the first two votes might never have occurred. This is why rules committees in both houses of Congress have enormous power; they establish the rules under which, and the order in which, legislation will be considered.

Another worry about majority-rule voting is that it leads to **logrolling**. Logrolling occurs when representatives trade votes—D helps get a majority in favor of E's program, and in exchange E helps D get a majority on her program. It is not clear whether any bill could get through any legislature without logrolling. Neither is it clear whether it is, on balance, a good thing or a bad thing from the standpoint of efficiency.

On the one hand, a program that benefits one region might generate enormous net social gains, but because the group of beneficiaries is fairly small, it will not command a majority of delegates. If another bill that is likely to generate large benefits to another area is also awaiting a vote, a trade of support between the two sponsors of the bills should result in the passage of two good pieces of efficient legislation. On the other hand, logrolling can turn out "pork barrel" legislation, that is, coalitions may be formed around unjustified, inefficient pieces of legislation.

A number of other problems also follow from voting as a mechanism for public choice. For one thing, voters do not have much of an incentive to become well informed. When you go out to buy a car or, on a smaller scale, a CD player, you are the one who suffers the full consequences of a bad choice. Similarly, you are the beneficiary of the gains from a good choice. Not so in voting. One person's vote is not likely to determine whether a bad choice or a good choice is actually made. While many of us feel that we have a civic responsibility to vote, no one really believes that his or her vote will actually determine the outcome of an election. The time and effort it takes just to get to the polls is enough to deter many people—look at the low turnout in most elections. Getting informed involves even more costs, and it is not surprising that most people do not do it.

But beyond the fact that a single vote is not likely to be decisive is the fact that the costs and benefits of wise and unwise social choices are widely shared. If the congressman that I elect makes a bad mistake and wastes a billion dollars, I bear only a small fraction of that cost. It may be that the direct consequences of a vote are so widely shared and seem so remote that voters perceive them to be infinitely small or zero. Thus even though the sums involved are large in aggregate, individual voters find no incentive to become informed.

Yet another problem with voting is that choices are almost always limited to *bundles* of publicly provided goods, and we vote infrequently. Most of us vote for Republicans or Democrats. We vote for President only every four years. We elect senators for six-year terms. In private markets, we can look at each item separately and decide how much of each we want. We also can shop daily. In the public sector, however, we vote for a platform or a party that takes a particular position on a whole range of issues. In the public sector it is very difficult, or impossible, for voters to unbundle issues.

There is, of course, a reason why bundling occurs in the sphere of public choice. It is difficult enough to convince people to go to the polls once a year. If we voted separately on every appropriation bill, we would spend our lives at the polls. This is in fact one reason for representative democracy. We elect officials who we hope will become informed and represent our interests and preferences.

Government Officials as Utility Maximizers

Recent work in economics has focused not just on the government as an extension of individual preferences but also on government officials as people with their own agendas and objectives. To understand the way government functions, we need to look less at the preferences of individual members of society and more at the incentive structures that exist around public officials.

One group of officials that we seem to worry about constantly are the people who run government agencies—the Social Security Administration, the Department of Housing and Urban Development, and state registries of motor vehicles, for example. What incentive do they have to produce a good product and to be efficient, and might such incentives be lacking?

In the private sector, where firms compete for profits, only efficient firms producing goods that consumers will buy survive. If a firm is inefficient, that is, if it is producing at a higher-than-necessary cost, the market will drive it out of business. Not necessarily so in the public sector. If your bureau is producing a necessary service, or one mandated by law, you do not need to worry about customers. No matter how bad the service is at the registry of motor vehicles, everyone with a car must buy its product. If we are to have a social security system, people will always submit forms, and somebody has to process them.

Whether the internal structure of production is efficient depends on how the incentives facing workers and agency heads are structured. If the budget allocation of an agency is based on the last period's spending alone, for example, agency heads have a clear incentive to spend more money, however inefficiently. This obvious point is not lost on government officials, who have tried out many ways of rewarding agency heads and employees for cost-saving suggestions.

But critics point out that these efforts to reward productivity and punish inefficiency are rarely successful. It is difficult to punish, let alone dismiss, a government employee. Elected officials are subject to recall, but it usually takes gross negligence to raise the anger of voters high enough for such a measure. And elected officials are rarely associated with problems of bureaucratic mismanagement, which they all decry on a daily basis.

Critics of "the bureaucracy" argue that no set of internal incentives can ever match the discipline of the market, and they point to studies of private versus public garbage collection, airline operations, fire protection, mail service, and so forth which suggest significantly lower costs in the private sector. One of the major themes of the Reagan administration was "privatization." According to this argument, if the private sector can possibly provide a service, it is likely to do so more efficiently, and the public sector should get out. (See box on p. 395.)

One of the worries about wholesale privatization is its potential consequences for distribution. Late in his administration, for example, President Reagan suggested that the federal government sell the entire stock of public housing to the private sector. But would the private sector continue to provide housing to poor people? The worry is that it would not, because it is not profitable to do so.

Like voters, public officials suffer from a lack of incentive to become fully informed and to make tough choices. Consider, for example, an elected official. If the real objective of an elected official is to get reelected, then her real incentive must be to provide visible goods for her constituency while hiding the costs or spreading them thin. In short, self-interest may easily lead to poor decisions and public irresponsibility.

Rent Seeking Revisited

Another problem with public choice is that special interests can and do spend resources to influence the legislative process. Although if, as we said before, voters individually have little incentive to become well informed and to participate fully in the legislative process, favor-seeking special interests certainly do. We saw in Chapter 13 that a monopolist should be willing to pay a substantial amount to prevent competition from eroding its economic profits. Many—if not all—industries lobby for favorable treatment, softer regulation, or antitrust exemption. We called this behavior *rent seeking*.

In fact, rent seeking extends far beyond those industries that lobby for government help in preserving monopoly powers. Any group that benefits from a government policy has an incentive to use its resources to lobby for that policy. Farmers lobby hard for farm subsidies, oil producers lobby hard for oil import taxes, the American Association of Retired Persons lobbies hard against cuts in social security, and so forth.

In the absence of well-informed and active voters, special-interest groups assume an important and perhaps a critical role. Some have argued that favorable legislation is, in effect, for sale in the marketplace. Those willing and able to pay the most are more successful in accomplishing their agendas than those with less.

Government Failure

The point of all this is simple. Theory may well suggest that unregulated markets fail to produce an efficient allocation of resources. But this should not lead you to the conclusion that government involvement necessarily leads to efficiency. There are good reasons to believe that government attempts to produce the right goods and services in the right quantities efficiently may also fail.

GOVERNMENT OR THE MARKET?

Whether or not markets are competitive, if left free to operate without any regulation or constraint they are likely to fail to produce an efficient allocation of resources. For one thing, external costs and benefits are omnipresent, and when decision makers are not required to consider them or add them into their calculations, the consequences can be extremely serious. For another, the private sector will simply not produce public, or social, goods adequately. Because such goods are nonrival in consumption and because the benefits that flow from them are nonexcludable, the private sector cannot produce them profitably, and so it produces them in insufficient quantities or does not produce them at all.

In theory, both problems have optimal solutions. To solve the problem of externalities, government can impose a tax equal to the external marginal costs caused by the offending activity. It can also subsidize beneficial activities. As an alternative, it may establish liability rules and/or injunctive remedies in the law to help internalize external costs, or it can directly regulate the activity that generates the externality. To solve the problem of the correct production level for public goods, Samuelson demonstrated that adding up the total willingness to pay at every potential level of public-good output and comparing those to cost of production will result in a level of production that is potentially efficient.

There is no question that government must be involved in both the provision of public goods and the control of externalities. No society has ever existed in which citizens did not get together to protect themselves from the abuses of an unrestrained market and to provide for themselves certain goods and services that the market did not provide. The question is not *whether* we need government involvement. The question is *how much* government involvement there should be, and what kind.

Critics of government involvement correctly point out that the existence of an "optimal" level of public-goods production does not guarantee that governments will achieve it. In fact, it is easy to show that governments will generally fail to achieve the most efficient level. Nor is there any reason to believe that governments are capable of achieving the "correct" amount of control over externalities. Markets do indeed fail to produce an efficient allocation of resources, but governments also "fail" for a number of reasons.

1. Measurement of social damages and benefits is difficult and imprecise. For example, estimates of the costs of acid rain range from practically nothing to incalculably high sums.

2. There is no precise mechanism through which citizens' preferences for public goods can be correctly known. All voting systems lead to inconsistent results. Samuelson's

optimal solution works only if each individual pays in accordance with his or her own preferences. Since that is impossible, we all must be taxed to pay for the mix of public goods that the imperfect voting mechanism happens to grant us.

3. Government agencies are not subject to the discipline of the market, and therefore we have little reason to expect that they will be efficient producers. The amount of waste, corruption, and inefficiency in government is a hotly debated issue. While government is not subjected to the discipline of the market, it must, however, submit to the discipline of the press, tight budgets, and the opinion of the voters.

4. Once in power, both elected and appointed officials have needs and preferences of their own, and it is naive to expect them to act selflessly for the good of society (even if they know what would be best). Bureaucrats in the Department of Defense, for example, have a clear incentive to increase the size of their budgets, and elected officials rely heavily on those same bureaucrats for information.

Just as critics of government involvement concede that the market fails to achieve an efficient result, defenders of government must acknowledge government's failures. To their critics they simply respond that we get *closer* to an efficient allocation of resources by trying to control externalities and by doing *our best* to produce the public goods that people want with the imperfect tools we have than we would by leaving everything to the market.

We should worry about inefficiency and corruption. We should try to be as precise as possible about the measurement of social costs. We should look continuously for new and better ways of getting at the citizens' preferences. But we cannot stop doing what needs to be done on the grounds that we cannot do it perfectly.

SUMMARY

1. This chapter continues our discussion of market failure. In Chapters 13–15 we examined the problem of noncompetitive market structures. Here we turn to externalities and public goods.

2. Often when we engage in transactions or make economic decisions, second or third parties suffer consequences that decision makers have no incentive to consider. These are called externalities.

3. A classic example of an external cost is pollution.

4. When external costs are left out of economic decisions, we may engage in activities or produce products that are not "worth it." When external benefits are not considered we may fail to do things that are indeed "worth it." The result is an inefficient allocation of resources.

5. The idea of an externality is one of the most powerful in all of economics. A substantial percentage of all the things you do in a day has some impact on others. One of the functions of social rules, customs, and laws in a civilized society is to induce the members of that society to consider the social consequences of their actions and adjust their behavior accordingly.

6. Government has used a number of alternative mechanisms to control externalities: (1) taxes and subsidies, (2) legal remedies such as injunctions and liability rules, and (3) direct regulation.

7. When the number of parties is small, bargaining and negotiation can take care of externalities without government involvement.

8. Another failure of the free market is that certain goods and services that people want will not be produced in adequate amounts. Public goods have characteristics that make it difficult or impossible for the private sector to produce them profitably.

9. Public goods are nonrival in consumption; their benefits fall collectively on members of society or on groups of members. It is generally impossible to exclude people from enjoying the benefits of public goods for not paying. An obvious example of a public good is national defense.

10. One of the immediate problems of public provision is that it leads to public dissatisfaction. We can choose any quantity of private goods that we went, or we can walk away without any. When it comes to public goods such as national defense, however, the government must choose one and only one kind and quantity of (collective) output to produce. Even if the government does its job with reasonable efficiency, at any given time about half of us think that we have too much national defense and about half think we have too little.

11. Theoretically, there exists an optimal level of provision for each public good. To discover it, however, we would need to know the preferences of each individual citizen.

12. Because there is no way to know everyone's preferences about public goods, we are forced to rely on imperfect social choice mechanisms, such as majority rule.

13. The theory that suggests that free markets do not achieve an efficient allocation of resources should not lead one to conclude that government involvement necessarily leads to efficiency. Demonstrably, governments also fail.

14. Defenders of government involvement in the economy acknowledge its failures but believe that we get closer to an efficient allocation of resources with government than we would without it. By trying to control externalities and by doing the best we can with imperfect tools to provide the public goods that society wants, we do better than we would if we left everything to the market. We cannot stop doing what needs to be done on the grounds that we cannot do it perfectly.

REVIEW CONCEPTS

market failure   379
externality   380
marginal social cost (MSC)   381
marginal damage cost (MDC)   384
Coase Theorem   388
injunction   390
liability rule   390
public goods (social, or collective goods)   391
nonrival in consumption   391
nonexcludable benefits   391

free-rider problem   392
drop-in-the-bucket problem   392
public provision of public goods   394
public production of public goods   394
optimal level and provision for public goods   398
social choice   399
impossibility theorem   399
voting paradox   400
logrolling   400

REVIEW QUESTIONS

1. If government imposes on the firms in a polluting industry penalties (taxes) that exceed the actual value of the damages done by the pollution, the result is an inefficient and unfair imposition of costs on those firms and on the consumers of their products. Discuss. Using the diagrams in Figure 16.3, show how consumers end up bearing the burden.

2. Suppose that a city decides to sponsor a free concert series in a public park surrounded by high-rise apartment buildings. The city's economist endorses the concerts on the grounds that they will provide a number of external public benefits.
   a. Explain his logic. Would you support such a series? Could it have been done by the private sector?
   b. The people who reside in the buildings surrounding the park object on the grounds that an external cost is being imposed on them. How would you go about resolving the conflict? What information would you need?

3. A steel plant built in the heart of a nice residential district would impose a rather severe externality on its neighbors. How does your city or town deal with such problems? Explain the logic.

4. It has been argued that the following are examples of "mixed goods." They are essentially private but partly public. For each one, describe the private and public parts and discuss briefly why the government should or should not be involved in their provision.
   Elementary and secondary
      education
   Higher education
   Medical care
   Air traffic control

5. A paper factory dumps polluting chemicals into the Snake River. Thousands of citizens live along the river (Hint: a large number), and they bring suit claiming damages. You are asked by the judge to testify at the trial as an impartial expert. The court is considering four possible solutions, and you are asked to

comment on the potential efficiency and equity of each. Your testimony should be brief.

a. Deny the merits of the case and simply affirm the polluter's right to dump. The parties will achieve the optimal solution without government.

b. Find for the plaintiff. The polluters will be held liable for damages and must fully compensate citizens for all past and future damages imposed.

c. Order an immediate end to the dumping. No damages awarded.

d. Refer the matter to the Environmental Protection Agency. It will impose a tax on the factory equal to the marginal damage costs. Proceeds will not be paid to the damaged parties.

6. One of the arguments for government redistribution of income is based on the idea that the income distribution itself can be thought of as a public good. As we will see in the next chapter, distributional arguments are generally made on the grounds of equity or economic justice. This, however, is an efficiency argument. How can redistribution be justified on efficiency grounds?

7. Government involvement in general scientific research has been justified on the grounds that advances in knowledge are public goods—once produced, information can be shared at virtually no cost. A new production technology in an industry could be made available to all firms, reducing costs of production, driving down price and benefiting the public. The patent system, however, allows private producers of "new knowledge" to *exclude* others from enjoying the benefits. Inventors would have no incentive to produce new knowledge without the possibility of profiting from their inventions. If only one company keeps the knowledge, it produces at lower cost, but can use the exclusion to acquire monopoly power and hold price up. On balance, is the patent system a good or a bad thing? Is government involvement in scientific research a good idea? Discuss.

17

Income Distribution and Poverty

Equity *Fairness. Often, people refer to a distribution of income that is more equal across households as more equitable, or fair. As the text points out, equity is a much more complex concept than that.*

What role should government play in the economy? The last few chapters have focused on actions the government might be called upon to take to improve the *efficiency* of markets. But even if we achieved markets that were perfectly efficient, would the result be fair? We now turn to the question of **equity**, or *fairness*.

The first 12 chapters of this book attempted to identify the basic market forces that determine *what* gets produced, *how* it gets produced and *who* gets it. Somehow, the goods and services produced in every society get distributed among its citizens. Some of those citizens end up with palatial mansions in Palm Beach, weekend ski trips to Gstaad, and Maseratis; others end up without enough to eat, in back-country shacks. This chapter focuses on distribution. Why do some people get more than others? What are the sources of inequality? Should the government change the distribution that the market generates?

Ideally we should talk not about the distribution of *things* but about the distribution of *well-being*. In the nineteenth century, philosophers used the concept of *utility* as a measure of well-being. As they saw it, people make choices among goods and services on the basis of the utility that they yield, and people act so as to *maximize utility*. If someone prefers a night at the symphony to a rock concert, it is because that person expects to get more utility from the symphony performance. If we extended that thinking, we might argue that if household A gets more total utility than household B, A is better off than B.

Utility, of course, is not observable or measurable. But thinking about it as if it were can help one understand some of the ideas that underlie debates about distribution. Suppose, for example, that society consisted of only two people, "I" and "J." Next suppose that the line *PP'* in Figure 17.1 represents all the combinations of I's utility and

FIGURE 17.1
Utility Possibility Frontier

If society were made up of just two people, I and J, and all of the assumptions of perfect competition held, the market system would lead to some point along *PP'*. Every point along *PP'* is Pareto optimal, or efficient; it is impossible to make I better off without making J worse off, and vice versa. But which among all points is best? Is *B* better than *C*?

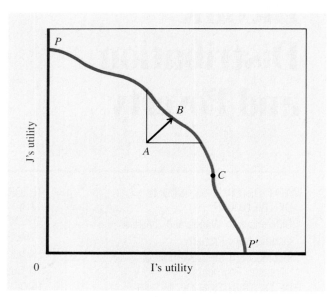

Utility possibility frontier   A graphical representation of a two person world that shows all points at which A's utility can only be increased if B's utility is decreased. That is, it represents all Pareto efficient points at which A can be made better off only by making B worse off.

J's utility that are possible, given the resources and technology available in their society. (Note that this is a step beyond the ppf discussed in Chapter 2, which had outputs on the X and Y axes).

Any point inside *PP'*, or the **utility possibilities frontier**, is *inefficient*, because both I and J could be better off. A is such a point. *B* is one of many possible points along *PP'* that society should prefer to A, because both members are better off at *B* than they are at A.

While point *B* is clearly preferable to point A from everyone's point of view, how does point *B* compare with point *C*? Both *B* and *C* are efficient; I cannot be made better off without making J worse off, and vice versa. Indeed, all the points along *PP'* are efficient, but they may not be equally desirable. If all the assumptions of competitive market theory held, the market system would lead to one of the points along *PP'*. The actual point reached would depend upon I's and J's initial endowments of wealth, skills, and so forth.

But the market solution leaves some people out. The rewards of a market system are linked to productivity, and some people in every society are simply not capable of being very productive. All societies make some provision for the very poor. Most often, public expenditures on behalf of the poor are financed with taxes collected from the rest of society. Society thus makes a judgment that those of us who are better off should give up some of our rewards so that those at the bottom can have more than the market system would allocate to them. In a democratic state, such *redistribution* is presumably undertaken because a majority of the members of that society think that it is fair, or just.

Early economists drew analogies between social choices among alternative outcomes and consumer choices among alternative outcomes. A *consumer* chooses on the basis of his own unique *utility function*, or measure of his own well-being; a *society*, they said, chooses on the basis of a *social welfare function* that embodies the society's ethics.

Such theoretical discussions of fairness and equity focus on the distribution and redistribution of utility. But because utility is neither observable nor measurable, most discussions of actual policy deal with the distribution of income or the distribution of wealth as indirect measures of well-being. It is important throughout that you remember that income and wealth are indeed *imperfect* measures of well-being. Someone with a profound love of the outdoors may choose to work in a national park for a low wage rather than to work for a consulting firm in a big city for a high wage. The choice reveals that she is *better off*, even though her measured income is lower. To see this another way, think about five people with $1.00 each put into a room together. Now suppose that one has a magnificent voice, and four give up their dollars to hear her sing. The exchange leads to inequality of measured wealth—the singer has $5.00, and no one else has any, but all are better off than they were before.

While income and wealth are imperfect measures, they have no observable substitutes and therefore they are the measures we use throughout the chapter. First, we review the factors that determine the distribution of income in a market setting. Second, we look at the data on income distribution, wealth distribution, and poverty in the United States. Third, we talk briefly about some theories of economic justice. Finally, we describe a number of current redistributional programs, including public assistance, or welfare, food stamps, Medicaid, and public housing.

WHAT DETERMINES INCOME DISTRIBUTION?

Why do some people and some families have more income than others? Before we turn to data on the actual distribution of income, let us review what we already know about the sources of inequality. Households derive their incomes from three basic sources: (1) from wages or salaries received in exchange for labor; (2) from property, that is, capital, land, and so forth; and (3) from government. The amount of income received from each of these sources varies widely from household to household (see Figure 17.2).

FIGURE 17.2
Sources of Inequality

Households derive their incomes from three basic sources: (1) from wages and salaries in exchange for their labor; (2) from property, that is, capital, land, and so forth; and (3) from the government in the form of transfer payments such as welfare.
Source: Statistical Abstract of the U.S., 1987 Table 733 p. 438.

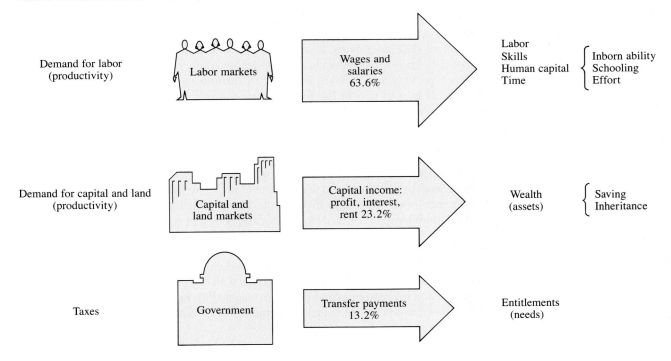

Differences in Wages and Salaries

About 64 percent of personal income in the United States in 1987 was received as wages and salaries. Hundreds of different wage rates are paid to employees for their labor in thousands of different labor markets. As you saw in Chapter 9, competitive market theory predicts that all factors of production are paid a return equal to their marginal revenue products, that is, the market value of what they produce at the margin. There are a number of reasons one type of labor might be more productive than another.

Required Skills and Working Conditions   Clearly, some people are simply born with attributes that translate into valuable skills. Kareem Abdul Jabbar and Robert Parish are great basketball players, in part because they happen to be over seven feet tall. They didn't decide to go out and invest in height; they were born with the right genes. Some people have perfect pitch and beautiful voices, while others are tone deaf. Some people have quick mathematical minds, while others cannot subtract two from two.

Where a particular skill is in strictly limited supply, everything depends upon the demand for it. Men's professional basketball is extremely popular, and the top NBA players make millions of dollars per year. There are some great women basketball players, too, but women's professional basketball has not become popular, and with little demand, their skills go comparatively unrewarded. In tennis, however, people want to see women play, and women therefore earn prize money similar to the money earned by men.

Some people with very rare skills can make enormous salaries in a free market economy. Whitney Houston has a powerful and lovely voice that millions of people are willing to pay to hear in person, and on tapes, CD's, records, and videos. Before Pablo Picasso died, he could sell small sketches for vast sums of money. Were they worth it? They were *worth* exactly what the highest bidder was willing to pay.

Every year over 45 million Americans go to professional baseball games, and millions more watch on television. People who watch are willing to pay to see the skills of the players and to see their teams win. The best players can demand huge salaries, sometimes millions of dollars per year. Once again, their skills are worth as much as people and companies are willing to pay to see them exhibited.

Not all skills are inborn. Some people have invested in training and schooling to improve their knowledge and skills, and therein lies another source of inequality in wages. When we go to school, we are investing in **human capital** that we expect to yield dividends, at least in part in the form of higher wages later on. Human capital is also produced through on-the-job training. People learn their jobs and acquire "firm-specific" skills as long as they are on the job. Thus in most occupations there is a reward for experience. Often the pay scale reflects numbers of years on the job, and those with more experience earn higher wages than those in similar jobs with less experience.

Some jobs are more desirable than others. Entry-level positions in "glamour" industries such as publishing and television tend to be low-paying. On the other hand, less desirable jobs often pay wages that include **compensating differentials**. Of two jobs requiring roughly equal levels of experience and skills that compete for the same workers, the job with the worse working conditions usually has to pay a slightly higher wage to attract workers away from the job with the better working conditions.

Compensating differentials are required when the job is clearly very dangerous. Those who take great risks are usually rewarded with high wages. High-beam workers on skyscrapers and bridges command premium wages. Fire fighters in cities that have many old, run-down buildings are usually paid more than those in relatively tranquil rural or suburban areas.

Human capital   The stock of knowledge, skills, and talents that people possess; it can be inherited or acquired through education or training.

Compensating differentials   Differences in wages that result from differences in working conditions. Risky jobs usually pay higher wages; highly desirable jobs usually pay lower wages.

The Controversy Over Comparable Worth

On average, women earn significantly less than men. In 1988, the median weekly earnings of women were 69.3 percent of men's earnings. Since women holding full time jobs work fewer hours than men, women's average hourly earnings are a slightly larger fraction of men's—77 percent in 1988. In addition, the degree of occupational segregation between men and women in the United States is striking. For example, in 1986, women accounted for 94.3 percent of registered nurses, 98.3 percent of kindergarten and preschool teachers, 99.0 percent of secretaries, and 65.0 percent of social workers. A study of 393 companies in California found that only 10 percent of established job categories had both men and women assigned to them.*

There are two views about why such a difference exists. One view holds that most of the difference can be attributed to choices women make about what jobs to take, how many hours to work, and when to enter and leave the labor force. The argument here is that labor markets are efficient, and that wages come to reflect productivity. Women earn lower wages because they have chosen to enter occupations that require little training and have low productivity, or because they avoid dangerous occupations and seek those that allow free movement into and out of the labor force.

This view further argues that the gap between women's and men's wages will close when women obtain the same amount of training as men, when they enter the same professions, and when they remain on the job without taking time off to raise families.

A second view holds that women's choices are not free and that wage differentials cannot be explained by differences in productivity. This second view maintains that women are channeled into certain occupations by custom, tradition, and discrimination and that wages in those occupations are kept artificially low. It is argued that jobs requiring similar skills, contributing similar amounts to employer earnings, and having similar working conditions are likely to be paid low wages when they are traditionally filled by women.

Those who espouse this second view argue that the wage gap can be closed in a number of ways. First, employers could be persuaded or forced to accept women in previously all male jobs. Second, wages across occupations of "comparable worth" could be equalized.

Under this approach, expert panels would evaluate the intellectual and physical demands of jobs within a particular company or controlled by a single employer (such as a state or local government). The panel would assign points to each job based on its working conditions, responsibility, and other characteristics, and would weigh each of these factors. The result would be a composite score, or index, that, it is claimed, would measure the "worth" of each job. People holding jobs of comparable worth as measured by these scores would receive equal pay.[†]

In 1963, Congress passed the Equal Pay Act, which prohibited unequal pay for *equal* work. The current move is to require equal pay for *comparable* work. A large number of states including California, Iowa, Minnesota, Montana, Oregon, and Washington have passed comparable worth laws for state employees. In the mid–1970s Australia adopted such a plan nationwide. As a result, base pay for women rose from 65 percent of men's to 94 percent between 1970 and 1980.

Critics of the comparable-worth approach argue that such laws will end up hurting women. Raising wages above their equilibrium levels, it is argued, will cause employers to hire fewer women. Those who end up with jobs will earn higher wages, but some will be left out. There is mixed evidence of this score from the Australian experience. One study found that pay equalization slowed the growth of women's employment by one-third and increased women's unemployment by 0.5 percentage points. Other studies found virtually no effect.

Critics also claim that the job evaluation process is hopelessly complex. They argue that the only reliable indicator of a job's worth is the wage rate that an employer must pay to fill it.

Source: Henry Aaron and Cameran Lougy, *The Comparable Worth Controversy*, Washington, DC: The Brookings Institution, 1986.

*William T. Bielby and James N. Baron, "A Woman's Place Is with Other Women: Sex Segregation within Organizations," in Barbara F. Reskin Ed., *Sex Segregation in the Workplace: Trends, Explanations, Remedies* (Washington, D.C.: National Academy Press, 1984). P. 35. Other data in the first paragraph from US. Dept of Labor, B.L.S, *Employment and Earnings* April, 1988.

† Aaron and Lougy, *The Comparable Worth Controversy*, p. 2

More than One Household Income   Another source of wage inequality among households is the fact that many households have more than one earner in the labor force. Second, and even third, incomes are becoming more the rule than the exception for American families. In 1960 about 37 percent of women over the age of 16 were in the labor force. By 1978 the figure had increased to over 50 percent, and it continued to climb slowly but steadily to a 1988 level of 56 percent.

Comparing two-earner and one-earner households highlights another problem with money income as a measure of well-being. Consider, for example, a family of four with both parents working, and an identical family with only one wage earner. The two-earner family will have a significantly higher money income, but the comparison ignores the value of what the non-wage-earning spouse produces. When one member of a family stays home, that person normally provides services that would otherwise have to be purchased. The children are cared for, the house is maintained, food may be grown in the garden. When both parents work, there are expenses for day care, housecleaning, yard work, home repairs, and so forth.

If one member stays home voluntarily, that family has revealed that it values the home-produced services more than the income it would otherwise earn. It is "better off" than if two members were working even though it has a lower money income. Again, this means we must exercise caution when discussing the fairness of the distribution of money income.

Unemployment   Before turning to property income, it is important to mention another major cause of inequality in the United States that is the subject of much discussion in macroeconomics: **unemployment**.

People earn wages only when they have jobs. In recent years, the United States has been through two severe recessions. In 1975 the unemployment rate was over 9 percent, and over 8 million people were unable to find work; in 1982 the unemployment rate approached 11 percent, and over 12 million were jobless.

Unemployment hurts primarily those who get laid off, and thus its costs are narrowly distributed. For some workers, the costs of unemployment are lowered by unemployment compensation benefits paid out of a fund accumulated with receipts from a tax on payrolls.

Income from Property

Property income   *Income from the ownership of real property and financial holdings. It takes the form of profits, interest, dividends, and rents.*

Another important source of income inequality is that some people have **property income** while many others do not. Some people own a great deal of wealth, and some have no assets at all. Overall, about 23 percent of personal income in the United States comes from ownership of property. The amount of property income that a household earns depends upon (1) *how much* property it owns and (2) *what kinds* of assets it owns.

Households come to own assets through saving and through inheritance. Many of the big fortunes owned by people today were inherited from previous generations. The Rockefellers, the Kennedys, and the Fords, to name a very few, still have large holdings of property originally accumulated by previous generations. Thousands of families receive smaller inheritances each year from their parents. Under 1988 tax laws, nearly $700,000 can pass free of estate taxes. Most families receive little through inheritance, however, and most of their wealth or property comes from saving.

The income that flows to households from property depends on how it is held. Bonds, savings accounts, certificates of deposit, and money market accounts earn interest and are relatively safe—their yield is known with some certainty. Common stocks may pay more in dividends and yield capital gains for their owners, but they involve more risk.

The biggest fortunes in the United States today were accumulated by people who started companies that succeeded and then "made it really big." Among such recent success stories are Kenneth Olsen, founder of Digital Equipment Corporation, and An Wang of Wang Laboratories, both men supposedly worth over a billion dollars. Others who have made millions by selling their companies in recent years include Mitchell Kapor of Lotus Development and Stephen Jobs of Apple Computer. These people are entrepreneurs; they and those who back them take risks and, if they are lucky as well as good at what they do, they end up producing something that many people buy.

Another important component of wealth today is real estate. For most people, the biggest asset they will ever own is their home, and equity accumulated in owner-occupied houses is a major source of inequality. A house earns a return just like any other asset, a return that comes in the form of "housing services"—the owner lives in it rent free. In addition to these returns, houses can also appreciate, or increase in value. People who bought houses in California before 1976 and held onto them into the 1980s made a small fortune just living in their homes. The same thing happened in New York and Boston after 1983 when home prices in those two cities exploded upwards. If you had bought a $40,000 dollar house in a New York suburb in 1976, when mortgage rates were 8.5%, and put 20 percent down, you would have a monthly house payment of around $250. In 1987 your house would probably be worth over $200,000. To buy the same house in 1987 would require a down payment of $40,000 and a monthly payment of nearly $1500.

In recent years, then, the housing market has become an important source of inequality. Needless to say, a person who got into a hot housing market before a big run-up is considerably better off than a person who did not. If we could correctly measure his total income it would include a substantial return on that initial investment.

Income from the Government: Transfer Payments

Transfer payments   *Payments by government to people who do not supply goods or services in exchange.*

So far we have discussed sources of inequality in income received in the form of wages and salaries and from property. About 13 percent of personal income comes from governments in the form of "**transfer payments**." Transfer payments are payments made by government to people who do not supply goods or services in exchange. Most transfer payments, such as aid to families with dependent children (AFDC) and unemployment compensation, are made to those with low incomes, precisely because they have low incomes. As a result, transfer payments reduce the amount of inequality in the distribution of income.

Not all transfer income goes to the poor, however. The biggest single transfer program at the federal level is social security. Nearly everyone who is employed in the United States pays a social security tax out of wages. The tax for employed persons in 1988 and 1989 was set at 7.51% of earned income to be paid by the employee and 7.51% to be paid by the employer. Disabled workers, retired workers, or their survivors receive monthly benefit checks paid by the Social Security Administration out of those tax receipts. The size of the monthly payment depends on a complicated formula that includes the recipient's preretirement earnings and the number of years he or she worked and paid the tax.

Except for social security, however, transfer programs are by and large designed to provide income to those in need. They are part of the response of governments at several levels to inequality and poverty. Later in the chapter we examine the basic logic of redistribution and a number of specific programs in more detail.

THE DISTRIBUTION OF INCOME: HOW UNEQUAL IS IT?

Despite the many problems with using income as a measure of well-being, it is useful to know something about how income is actually distributed. Before we examine these data, however, we should once again pin down precisely what the data represent.

Economic income   *The amount of money a household can spend during a given time period without increasing or decreasing its net assets. Wages, salaries, dividends, interest income, cash and noncash transfer payments, rents, and so forth are sources of economic income.*

Economic income is defined as the amount that an individual or an individual family can spend during a particular period without reducing or increasing net assets. This means that anything that enhances your ability to spend is part of your economic income—wages, salaries, dividends, interest received, proprietors' income, transfer payments, rents, and so forth. In addition, if you own an asset, such as a share of stock, and it increases in value, that gain is part of your income, whether you sell the asset to "realize" the gain or not.

Recent Data on Income Distribution in the United States

Table 17.1 presents some calculations done by the Brookings Institution for 1985 estimating the distribution of several income components and of total income for family units. (The term "family" refers both to individuals living alone—one-person families—and to households with more than one person living together, who are related by blood, marriage, or adoption.) The measure of income used is very broad, including both taxable and nontaxable items, as well as estimates of capital gains.

The data are presented by "quintiles"—that is, the total number of families are first ranked by income and then split into five groups of equal size. In 1985 the top quintile earned 47.7% of total income, while the bottom quintile earned just 4.2%. The top one percent (which is part of the top quintile) earned nearly three times as much as the bottom 20 percent.

Wage and salary income, that is, labor income, was more evenly distributed than total income. The top one percent earned only 2.7%, and the middle groups earned a larger share. The combined middle three quintiles, or 60 percent of the total, received 58.7% of wages and salaries, compared with 48.1% of all income.

Not surprisingly, income from property is much more unevenly distributed than wages and salaries. Property income comes from owning things—land earns rent, stocks earn dividends and appreciate in value, bonds and deposit accounts earn interest, owners of small businesses earn profits, and so forth. In this category, the top 20 percent earns nearly 70 percent of property income, and the top one percent earns 27.4%.

TABLE 17.1
Distribution of Total Income and Components, 1985 (percentages)

Households	Total income	Wages and salaries	Property income	Transfer income
Bottom fifth	4.2	6.1	1.5	27.7
Second fifth	10.0	12.9	4.7	26.1
Third fifth	15.8	19.8	9.1	18.7
Fourth fifth	22.3	26.0	15.2	13.5
Top fifth	47.7	35.2	69.5	13.9
Top 1 percent	11.9	2.7	27.4	1.2

Source: Brookings Merge File.

Transfer payments include social security benefits, unemployment compensation, and welfare payments, as well as an estimate of nonmonetary transfers—food stamps, for example, and Medicaid and Medicare program benefits—from the government to households. Transfers flow to families at the bottom, but not only to them. Social security benefits, for example, which account for about half of all transfer payments, flow to everyone who participated in the system for the requisite number of years and who has reached the required age, regardless of income. Nonetheless, transfers represent a much more important income component at the bottom of the distribution than at the top. Although not shown in Table 17.1, transfers account for about 98 percent of the income of the bottom 10 percent of families, but only about 3 percent among the top 10 percent of families.

Changes in the Distribution of Income

Money income The measure of income used by the Census Bureau. Because it excludes noncash transfer payments, capital gains income, and a few other items, it is significantly less inclusive than "economic income."

Table 17.2 presents the distribution of money income among families rather than total economic income, at a number of points in time. **Money income**, the measure used by the Census Bureau in its surveys and publications, is slightly less complete than the income measure used in the Brookings calculations in Table 17.1. It does not include noncash transfer benefits, for example, nor does it include capital gains.

As you can see, income distribution in the United States has remained remarkably stable over a long period of time. Between the end of World War II and the late 1970s, there was a slight move toward equality, that is, the share of income going to both the top five percent and the top 20 percent declined, while the share going to the bottom increased slightly. Between 1979 and 1986, however, the trend was reversed, with the top two fifths gaining share and the bottom three fifths losing some.

The Lorenz Curve and the Gini Coefficient

Lorenz curve A widely used graph of the distribution of income, with cumulative "percent of families" plotted along the horizontal axis and cumulative "percent of income" plotted along the vertical axis.

The distribution of income can be graphed in several ways. The most widely used graph is the **Lorenz curve**, shown in Figure 17.3. Along the horizontal axis is the percentage of families, and along the vertical axis is the cumulative percentage of income. The curve shown here represents the year 1986, using data from the accompanying table.

During that year, the bottom 20 percent of families earned only 4.6% of total money income. The bottom 40 percent earned 15.4%, (4.6% plus 10.8%) and so forth. If income were distributed equally—if the bottom 20 percent earned 20 percent of the

TABLE 17.2
Distribution of Money Income of Families by Quintiles, 1947–1986 (percentages)

	1947	1960	1972	1979	1984	1986
Lowest fifth	5.0	4.8	5.4	5.3	4.7	4.6
Second fifth	11.8	12.2	11.9	11.6	11.0	10.8
Third fifth	17.0	17.8	17.5	17.5	17.0	16.8
Fourth fifth	23.1	24.0	23.9	24.1	24.4	24.0
Top fifth	43.0	41.3	41.4	41.6	42.9	43.7
Top 5 percent	17.2	15.9	15.9	15.9	16.0	17.0

Source: Statistical Abstract of the United States, various editions.

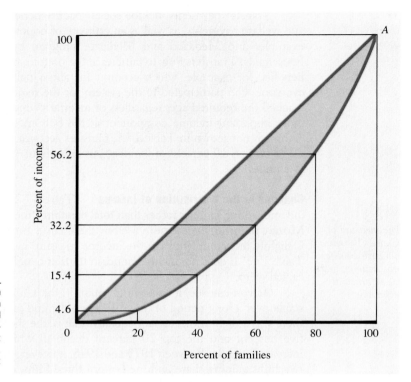

The Lorenz curve is the most common
way of presenting income distribution
graphically. The larger the shaded
area, the more unequal the distribution. If distribution were equal, so that
everyone received the same amount,
the Lorenz curve would be coincident
with the diagonal line OA.

*Gini coefficient   A commonly
used measure of inequality of
income derived from a Lorenz
curve. It can range from zero to a
maximum of one.*

income, the bottom 40 percent earned 40 percent of the income, and so forth—the
Lorenz curve would show this by following the 45-degree line between zero and 100
percent. More unequal distributions produce Lorenz curves that are farther from the
45-degree line.

The **Gini coefficient** is a commonly used measure of the degree of inequality in a
distribution. It is the ratio of the shaded area in Figure 17.3 to the total triangular area
below and to the right of the diagonal line OA. If income is equally distributed, the two
lines coincide, and the Gini coefficient is zero. The Lorenz curves for distributions with
more inequality are farther down to the right, their shaded areas are larger, and their Gini
coefficients are higher. The maximum Gini coefficient, of course, is one. As the Lorenz
curves down to the right, the shaded arc becomes a larger portion of the total triangular
area below OA. If one person earned all the income (with no one else receiving anthing),
the shaded area and the triangle would be the same, and the ratio would be equal to
one.

**Differences for Black Families and White Families and for People Not Living with a
Family**   So far we have been looking at income distribution among *all families* lumped
together. Looking just at families without differentiating them in any way hides some
important distinctions. First, the income distribution differs significantly between black
families and white families. Second, many people do not belong to a family—they may
live alone, or they may be part of a group of unrelated people living together. In 1984 the
Census Bureau estimated that in total 62.7 million families lived in the United States, and
of this number 6.8 million had a black "householder." About 30 million persons were
classified by the bureau as "unrelated individuals" in the same year.

Table 17.3 presents data on the distribution of money income for families by race
and for single-person households. The differences between the groupings are dramatic.

TABLE 17.3

Distribution of Money Income of
Families and Unrelated
Individuals, 1984 (percentages)

	All families	Black families	White families	One-person households
0–5,000	4.8	13.5	3.7	17.7
5–10,000	8.5	17.1	7.5	25.5
10–15,000	10.2	14.3	9.7	15.9
15–20,000	10.5	13.1	10.3	12.3
20–25,000	10.3	9.0	10.4	9.0
25–35,000	18.6	14.3	19.2	11.3
35–50,000	18.8	11.8	19.7	5.3
50,000 +	18.3	7.0	19.6	3.0
Total	100.0	100.0	100.0	100.0

Source: Statistical Abstract of the United States, 1987, tables 724 and 731.

Nearly 14 percent of black families, but only 3.7% of white families, have annual incomes below $5000. At the upper end, almost 40 percent of white families, but only about 19 percent of black families, have incomes above $35,000.

The category of single-person households includes quite a mixture of people, including the elderly living alone, college students, and single people in apartments. While it is hard to generalize about such a mixed bag, the income distribution of this group differs from that of families in very notable ways. Over 43 percent have incomes below $10,000, and 17.7% have incomes below $5000. Only three percent have incomes over $50,000, compared with 18.3% of all families.

The difference between families and single-person households is in part due to the fact that families very often contain more than one earner. Of 63.6 million families in 1985, 50.9 million had a husband and wife present. Of those 50.9 million families, 27.5 million, or 54 percent of the total, had both a husband and a wife working at least part of the time.[1]

Poverty

Most of the government's concern with the income distribution has focused on those in **poverty**. "Poverty" is a very complicated word to define, however. In simplest terms, it means people with very low incomes. The dictionary defines it simply as "lack of money or material possessions." But how low does your income have to be before you are classified as poor?

Philosophers and social policy people have long debated the meaning of "poverty." One school of thought argues that poverty should be measured by figuring how much it costs to buy the "basic necessities of life." For many years, the Bureau of Labor Statistics published "family budget" data designed to track the cost of specific "bundles" of food, clothing, and shelter that were supposed to represent the minimum standard of living.

Critics argue that defining bundles of "necessities" is a hopeless task. While it might be possible to define a "minimally adequate" diet, what is a "minimum" housing unit? Is a car a necessity? What about medical care? What if the church "requires" a significant donation? Low-income families end up actually using what income they have in an enormous variety of ways.

Some also argue that poverty is culturally defined and therefore a *relative* concept, not an *absolute* one. Poverty in Bangladesh, for example, is very different from poverty in

[1]*Statistical Abstract of the United States*, 1987, table 734.

The Homeless

In recent years, the number of homeless people in the United States has risen sharply. In a recent book, Jonathan Kozol recounts his stay at a shelter for the homeless in New York City's old Martinique Hotel:

The Martinique is not the worst of the hotels for homeless families in New York. Because its tenants have refrigerators—a refrigerator is a precious item for the mother of a newborn—some residents consider it to be one of the better shelters in the city. In visiting the Martinique, one tries to keep this point in mind, but at first it is not easy to imagine something worse. Three members of the New York City Council visited the building in July of 1986, and they were clearly shaken by their experience. "People passing by the hotel have no sense of the tragic dimensions of life inside," a report prepared by the Council's Select Committee on the Homeless said. "Upon entering the hotel, one is greeted by a rush of noise, made in large part by the many small children living there. These children share accommodations with a considerable cockroach and rodent population. The nearly 400 families housed at the Martinique are assisted by just seven HRA [Human Resources Administration] caseworkers, whose efforts to keep in contract with each family—at least once each month—often amount to no more than a note slipped under a door."

The City Council report offers this additional information about the people sheltered at the Martinique: the average family consists of a mother and three children. Thirty-four per cent of the families became homeless after eviction by a landlord, forty-seven per cent after being doubled up with other families or otherwise living in overcrowded conditions, nineteen per cent after living in substandard housing. Fifty per cent of the heads of households reported that they had once held full-time jobs. Seventy per cent had, since coming to the Martinique, visited at least five places to rent that they could not afford or from which they had been turned away by landlords who did not want children or welfare recipients. . . .

During the two years that I visited the Martinique, I found it to be the saddest place I had ever been in—partly, no doubt, because of the realization that some twelve hundred children were living there. What is life like for the children in this building? For many, the question may be answered briefly, as their lives will be extremely short. The infant-mortality rate in New York's welfare hotels from 1982 to mid-1984 was twenty-five per thousand—more than twice the national rate, and higher even than the rate in New York's housing projects. At the time of my first visit, in December of 1985, there was one nurse present—in daytime hours only—to meet the health needs of all the people in the building. The children who live at the hotel dwell in rooms devoid of light and fresh air. Play is a part of education, but these children do not have much opportunity for play. Their room doors open onto a narrow corridor; their windows look out on a courtyard strewn with glass, or on the street, or on the wall of an adjacent wing of the hotel. . . .

From any point of view, the most chilling fact is that families with small children have become the fastest-growing sector of the homeless. Today, there are twenty-eight thousand homeless people in emergency shelters in New York City. (Forty thousand more are believed by Robert Hayes to be living in abandoned buildings, public places, or the streets.) Of those twenty-eight thousand, ten thousand are single; eighteen thousand are parents and children, making up about five thousand families. The average homeless family includes one parent and two or three children. The number of homeless children in the shelters comes to over twelve thousand. The average age of these homeless children is six, the average age of the mothers twenty-seven. The number of homeless children that are not living in shelters is not known, but informal surveys indicate that there are many. In one abandoned building on the lower East Side, which I visited on a recent evening when the temperature went down below fifteen degrees, there were six children, the youngest of whom was two years old, trying to sleep beneath a blanket on the floor.

Reprinted from *Rachael and Her Children*. Copyright ©1988, Jonathan Kozol. Used by permission of Crown Publishers, Inc.

---

the United States. Even within the United States, urban poverty is very different from rural poverty. If poverty were a relative concept, it might change significantly as a society accumulates wealth and achieves higher living standards.

Although it is difficult to define precisely, the word "poverty" is one that we all understand intuitively to some degree. It conveys images of run-down, overcrowded, rat-infested housing, homeless people, untreated illness, and so forth. But it is also a word that we have been forced to define formally for purposes of keeping statistics and administering public programs.

Poverty line   *The officially established income level that distinguishes the poor from the non-poor. It is set at three times the cost of the Department of Agriculture's minimum food budget.*

The Official Poverty Line   Since the early 1960s, the government has observed an officially established poverty line. Based on the fact that poor families tend to spend about one third of their incomes on food, the **official poverty line** has been drawn at a figure that is simply three times the cost of the Department of Agriculture's minimum food budget.

Each year the Department of Agriculture sets out a nutritionally sound *minimum* food bundle. For example, a *week's* food for a woman between 20 and 34 years includes four eggs, one pound four ounces of meat, fish, or poultry, three pounds of potatoes, 12 ounces of dark green or yellow vegetables, three pounds of other vegetables, and eight ounces of fat or oil, as well as a few treats. In 1985, the department estimated that for a family of four people, such a bundle would cost about $70.00 per week. Multiply that times 52 weeks for a total of $3640 per year, triple that, and you have a poverty line for a family of four set at $10,920.

Poverty in the United States Since 1960   In 1962 Michael Harrington published *The Other America: Poverty in the United States*, a book that many credit with waking the American people up to the problem and stimulating the government to declare a "war on poverty" in 1964. In 1960 official figures had put the number of the poor in the United States at just under 40 million, or 22 percent of the total population. In his book, Harrington argued that that number had reached over 50 million.

As Table 17.4 shows, by the late 1960s the number of those living below the official poverty line declined to about 25 million, where it stayed for over a decade. Between 1978 and 1983, however, the number of poor jumped nearly 45 percent, from 24.5 million to 35.3 million, the highest number since 1964. As a percentage of the total population, the poor accounted for between 11 and 12.6% of the population throughout the 1970s. That figure increased sharply to 15.2% between 1979 and 1983. It has fallen back somewhat since 1983.

While the official 1985 figures put the poverty number at 14 percent of the population, some groups in society experience more poverty than others. Table 17.5 shows the official poverty count for 1964 and 1985 by demographic group. One of the problems with the official count is that because it considers only money income as defined by the census, it is somewhat inflated. Many federal programs designed to help people out of poverty include noncash benefits such as food stamps, public housing, and so forth, which, if added to income, would reduce the number of those officially designated as below the poverty line. The right-hand column in Table 17.5 shows how many would be classified as poor if we took into account noncash benefits received.

The poverty rate is nearly three times as high among blacks as among whites. Even after noncash benefits are counted, nearly one in five blacks lives in poverty. In addition, approximately the same proportion of Hispanics as blacks had incomes below the poverty line after in-kind transfers in 1985.

TABLE 17.4

Number and Percentage of Persons in Poverty, 1960–1985

	Millions	Percentage
1960	39.9	22.2
1966	28.5	14.7
1969	24.1	12.1
1970	25.4	12.6
1971	25.6	12.5
1972	24.5	11.9
1973	23.0	11.1
1974	23.4	11.2
1975	25.9	12.3
1976	25.0	11.8
1977	24.7	11.6
1978	24.5	11.4
1979	26.1	11.7
1980	29.3	13.0
1981	31.8	14.0
1982	34.4	15.0
1983	35.3	15.2
1984	33.7	14.4
1985	33.1	14.0

Source: Statistical Abstract of the United States, 1987, table 745.

TABLE 17.5

Percentage of Persons in Poverty by Demographic Group, 1964–1985

	Official measure 1964	Official measure 1985	Adjusted for in-kind transfers at market value, 1985*
All	19.0	14.0	9.3
White	14.9	11.4	7.8
Black	49.6	31.3	19.4
Hispanic	NA	29.0	19.1
Female householder— no husband present	45.9	33.5	NA
Elderly (65+)	28.5	12.6	3.2
Children under 18	20.7	22.1	15.5

Source: Statistical Abstract of the United States, 1986.
*Includes food, housing, and medical benefits.

The group with the highest incidence of poverty in 1985 was women living in households with no husband present. In 1964, 45.9% of such women lived in poverty. By 1984 the figure was still over one third. During the 1980s there has been increasing concern with the "feminization of poverty."

Poverty rates among the elderly have been reduced considerably since 1964, dropping from 28.5% to 12.6% in 1985. And with noncash benefits, especially health benefits, added in, the rate has fallen to 3.2%, the lowest rate in any single category. Certainly social security, supplemental security income, and Medicare have played a role in reducing poverty among the elderly.

The only category for which poverty rates have actually increased since 1964 is that of children. In 1964 20.7% of all children under 18 lived in poverty; in 1985, the figure had risen to 22.1%. Even after noncash transfers, the rate remains at 15.5%.

The Distribution of Wealth

As you probably recall, the distribution of property income is much more unequal than the distribution of income from labor. Because property income flows from ownership, it follows that the distribution of wealth is also quite unequal.

Data on the distribution of wealth are not as readily available as data on the distribution of income. In 1983, however, the government conducted a very detailed survey of the holdings that make up wealth, and some of the results are presented in Table 17.6. The top 10 percent of families ranked by income control more than half of all financial assets. The top two percent of income earners hold 50 percent of the stock held by households.

The term "property" in the table refers essentially to real estate, a substantial part of which exists in the form of owner-occupied housing. For many families, their home is the most important asset they own. The big run-up in the value of houses across the nation, especially in California and the large cities in the East during the 1970s and early 1980s, has exacerbated an already important source of inequality in the United States. Those who had houses or bought into the housing market early made large gains and will find housing relatively inexpensive from now on. Even with the drop in mortgage rates in the mid 1980s, however, new home buyers face enormous housing costs in some areas.

Critics of free-market systems point to the extreme inequality in the distribution of wealth as a major problem. As you will see later, in socialist and communist systems the government owns most of the capital stock. Most businesses are state businesses, and if

TABLE 17.6
Percent of Assets Held by Families Ranked by Income, 1983

	Top 2 percent	Top 10 percent
*Total Financial Assets**	30	51
Stocks	50	72
Bonds	39	70
Nontaxable bonds	71	86
Business assets	33	78
Property	20	50

*Checking, savings, certificates of deposit, IRA's, Keough, stocks, bonds, and so on.

Source: Survey of Consumer Finances, 1983.

there are profits, they go to the government to be used for the people. It is certainly true that if property income were left out of the calculations, the distribution of income and wealth in the United States would be much more equal.

But as you saw in Chapters 5 through 12, our culture holds profit to be the signal that directs private capital investment to its highest and best use. If private interest and profit did not exist, all investment would have to be centrally directed. Indeed, in centrally planned socialist states, the government does decide how all resources are to be allocated and which sectors will be developed and which will not.

Many see a trade-off here. Without property income, resources are more equally distributed. One major question that must be answered, however, is How much efficiency is lost to achieve more equality? (We explore answers to this question in Chapter 40.) What happens to incentives when the possibility of "making it" is lost? Can central planning work as effectively as the private market in allocating capital and in bringing new techniques and new products to market? While some people see a more equal distribution of rewards as desirable, others do not. The debate between these alternative views is aired in the next section.

THEORIES OF JUSTICE: THE ARGUMENTS FOR AND AGAINST REDISTRIBUTION

Debates about the role of government in correcting for inequity in the distribution of income revolve around two kinds of issues, philosophical ones and practical ones. *Philosophical* issues are those dealing with the "ideal." What *should* the distribution of income look like *if* we could give it any shape we desired. What is "fair"? What is "just"? *Practical* issues, on the other hand, deal with what is, and what is not, possible. Suppose we wanted to eliminate poverty altogether. How much would it cost, and what would we sacrifice to do it? When we take wealth or income away from higher-income people to give it to lower-income people do we destroy some incentives? What are the effects of this kind of redistribution?

Clearly, policy makers must deal with both kinds of issues, but it seems logical to deal first with the philosophical ones. If you do not know where you want to go, you cannot talk very well about how to get there or how much it costs to get there. You may find that you do not want to go anywhere at all. Many respected economists and philosophers do, in fact, argue quite ably that the government should *not* redistribute income.

In the discussion that follows, it is important to define the *community of reference*. We are all citizens of many communities. We live on blocks, in neighborhoods, and in towns. With one exception, American towns and cities are located within states. Most people are citizens of some established nation state, and we are all citizens of the world. In varying degrees, we all see ourselves as belonging to, or being members of, such groups.

The closer the group of reference, the stronger the sense of responsibility to the group most people feel. Many people would support a fund to aid the poor in their own town, but on a national or international level, they feel less of an obligation. Great debates on just such redistributional issues echo through the halls of Congress. Many feel, for example, that we have a stronger national obligation to feed the hungry in the United States than to feed those in Asia, Africa, or Latin America.

Discussions and debates about redistribution are often unclear about the community of reference. Most, however, refer to the policies of individual nations.

The Basic Argument Against Redistribution

Those who argue against government redistribution believe that, left to operate on its own, the market is fair. This argument rests on the proposition that "one is entitled to the fruits of one's efforts."[2] Remember that if market theory is correct, rewards paid in markets are linked to productivity. In other words, labor and capital are paid in accordance with the value of what they produce.

This view also holds that property income, that is, income from land or capital, is no less justified than labor income. All factors of production have marginal products. Capital owners receive profits or interest because the capital that they own is productive. (Recall from Chapter 7 that a production function shows the relationship between inputs and output. Output can be increased by adding labor or by adding capital or land.)

The argument against redistribution also rests on the principles behind "freedom of contract" and the protection of property rights. When I enter into an agreement either to sell my labor or to commit my capital to use, I do so freely, and in return I contract to receive payment, which becomes my "property." When a government taxes me and gives my income to someone else, that action violates these two basic rights.

The more common arguments against redistribution are not philosophical. Rather, they point to more practical problems. First, it is said that taxation and transfer programs interfere with the basic incentives that the market provides. Taxing higher-income people reduces their incentive to work, save, and invest. Taxing the "winners" of the economic game also discourages risk taking. Furthermore, providing transfers to those at the bottom reduces *their* incentive to work as well. All of this leads to a reduction in total output that is the "cost" of redistribution.

Another practical argument against redistribution is that it does not work. Some critics point to the recent rise in the poverty rate as an indication that antipoverty programs simply drain money without really helping the poor out of poverty. Whether they could help people break out of poverty or not, there is always the charge of bureaucratic inefficiency in administration. Social programs must be administered by people who must be paid. The Department of Health and Human Services employs over 120,000 people to run the social security system, process Medicaid claims, and so forth. Some degree of waste and inefficiency attends in any sizable bureaucracy.

Arguments in Favor of Redistribution

The argument most often used in favor of redistribution is that a society as wealthy as ours has a moral obligation to provide all its members with the basic necessities of life. The constitution does, after all, carry a guarantee of the "right to life. . . ." In declaring "war on poverty" in 1964, Lyndon Johnson put it this way:

> There will always be some Americans who are better off than others. But it need not follow that the "poor are always with us". . . . It is high time to redouble and to concentrate our efforts to eliminate poverty. . . . We know what must be done and this nation of abundance can surely afford to do it.[3]

[2]Powerful support for this notion of "entitlement" can be found in the works of the seventeenth century English philosophers Thomas Hobbes and John Locke.
[3]*Economic Report of the President* (1964).

Many people, often through no fault of their own, find themselves left out. Some are born with mental or physical problems that severely limit their ability to "produce." Then, of course, there are children. Even if some parents can be held accountable for their low incomes, do we want to punish children for sins of their parents and perpetuate the cycle of poverty? The elderly, without redistribution of income, would have to rely exclusively on savings to survive once they retire, and many conditions that have nothing to do with frugality can lead to inadequate savings. Should the victims of living too long or of bad luck be doomed to inevitable poverty? Illness is perhaps the best example: the accumulated fortunes of only a very few can withstand the drain of extraordinary hospital and doctors' bills and, ultimately, the cost of nursing home care.

Proponents of redistribution refute "practical" arguments against it by pointing, for example, to empirical studies that show little negative effect on the incentives of those who benefit from transfer programs. For many of those people—children, the elderly, the mentally ill—incentives are irrelevant, they say, and providing a basic income to most of the unemployed does not discourage them from working when they have the opportunity.[4]

The basic theoretical argument in favor of redistribution is that justice requires that the basics of life be provided to all members of society. But philosophers have made the case for redistribution more formally. We now turn briefly to several more formal arguments.

Utilitarian Justice   The essence of the utilitarian argument in favor of redistribution is that "a dollar in the hand of a rich person is worth less than a dollar in the hand of a poor person." The rich spend their marginal dollars on luxury goods—it is very easy to spend over $100.00 per person for a meal in a good restaurant in New York or Los Angeles. The poor spend their marginal dollars on necessities—food, clothing, and medical care. If the "marginal utility" of income declines as income rises, the value of a dollar's worth of luxury goods is worth less than a dollar's worth of necessity. Thus redistributing from the rich to the poor increases *total* utility. To put this notion of **utilitarian justice** in everyday language, the rich sacrifice a little and the poor gain a lot.

Each of the various utilitarian philosophers including, most notably, the Englishmen Jeremy Bentham and John Stuart Mill, who wrote in the late eighteenth and nineteenth centuries, took a slightly different approach to the argument. Some positions were quite formal. If, for example, the marginal utility of income declines with income and everyone has identical "utility functions,"[5] then as long as anyone has more income than anyone else, a utility gain will result from transferring income from those with more to those with less. If A has more income than B and **diminishing marginal utility of income** sets in, taking from A and giving to B will increase total utility, because A values those marginal dollars less than B does.

The purely utilitarian position has its problems, of course. People have very different tastes and preferences. Who is to say that you value a dollar more or less than I do? Utility is unobservable and unmeasurable, and thus comparisons cannot be made across individuals. Nonetheless, many people find the basic logic of the utilitarians quite

Utilitarian justice   The idea that a dollar in the hand of a rich person buys "less" than a dollar in the hand of a poor person. If the marginal utility of income declines with income, transferring income from the rich to the poor will increase total utility.

[4]For a discussion of the empirical evidence on the effects of transfer programs and taxation on incentives, see Chapter 19.
[5]A "utility function" is a way of expressing the relationship between goods or income and satisfaction or utility. $U = F(X_1, X_2, X_3. \ldots X_n)$ says that utility "is a function of" the goods, X_1 through X_n, that are consumed. To say that everyone has the same utility function means that everyone places the same subjective value on those goods.

persuasive. When you weigh luxuries against necessities in your own mind, you consult your own "utility function." And, as you know from your own experience, necessities are indeed by definition worth more than luxuries.

Social Contract Theory—Rawlsian Justice   The work of Harvard philosopher John Rawls has generated a great deal of recent discussion, both within the discipline of economics and between economists and philosophers.[6] In the tradition of the nineteenth century social contract theorists, Rawls argues that, as members of society, we have a contract with one another. In the theoretical world that Rawls imagines, the original **social contract** is drawn up, and all parties agree to it without knowledge of who they are or who they will be in society. This condition is called the "**original position**," or the "state of nature." With no vested interests to protect, members of society are able to make disinterested choices.

As we approach the contract, everyone has a chance to end up very rich or homeless, black or white. On the assumption that we are all "risk averse," Rawls believes that people will attach great importance to the position of the least fortunate members of society because anyone could end up there. **Rawlsian justice**, then, is argued from the assumption of risk aversion. Rawls concludes that any contract emerging from the original position would call for an income distribution that would "maximize the well-being of the worst-off member of society."

Any society bound by such a contract would allow for inequality, but only if that inequality had the effect of improving the lot of the very poor. If inequality provided an incentive for people to work hard and innovate, for example, as long as some of the fruits went to those at the bottom, those inequalities should be tolerated.

The Work of Karl Marx   **Marxian theory** and Marxian economics cannot be ignored in a world in which two dominant powers base their systems at least to some extent on Karl Marx's work. We talk at more length about Marx and Marxian theory in Chapter 40, but we should examine briefly some of the implications of his work here.

Marx did not write very much about socialism or communism. His major work, *Das Kapital*, was a three-volume analysis and critique of the capitalist system that he saw at work in the world around him. We know what Marx thought was wrong with capitalism, but he was not very clear about what would replace it. In one essay, written late in his life, he put forward the oft-quoted line "from each according to his ability, to each according to his needs,"[7] but he was not specific about the applications of such a principle.

Marx's view of capital income, however, does have important implications for income distribution. In the preceding chapters, we have been discussing profit as a return to a productive factor; in other words, capital, like labor, is productive and has a marginal product. By contrast, Marx attributes *all value to labor* and *none to capital*. According to Marx's **labor theory of value**, the value of any commodity depends only on the amount of labor needed to produce it. The owners of capital are able to extract profit, or "surplus value" because labor creates more value in a day than it is paid for. Like any other good, labor power is worth only what it takes to "produce" it. Translated into simple language, this means that under capitalism labor is paid a subsistence wage.

Marx sees profit as an illegitimate expropriation by capitalists of the fruits of labor's efforts. We might infer, then, that to a Marxian, what is wrong with the distribution of

Labor theory of value *Stated most simply, the theory that commodity values depend only on the amount of labor required to produce those commodities.*

[6]See John Rawls, *A Theory of Justice*, (Cambridge, Mass.: Harvard University Press, 1972).
[7]Karl Marx, "Critique of the Gotha Program" (May 1875), in Robert Tucker, ed., *The Marx-Engels Reader* (New York, W. W. Norton), p. 388.

income in the United States is its property income component. Without capital income, the distribution of income would be much more equal. (To see what difference this would make, look back at Table 17.1.)

Income Distribution as a Public Good   Those who argue that the unfettered market produces a just income distribution certainly do not forbid private charity. Voluntary redistribution does not involve any violation of property rights by the state.

In Chapter 16, however, you saw that there may be a problem with private charity. Suppose that people really do want to end hunger, for example. As they write out their checks to charity, they bump into the classic "public-goods" problem. First, there are "free riders." If starvation is eliminated, the benefits, even the merely psychological benefits, flow to everyone, whether or not they contributed. Second, any contribution is a "drop in the bucket." One individual contribution is so small that it can have no real effect.

With private charity, as with national defense, nothing depends upon whether I pay or not—there is no contingency. Thus private charity may fail for the same reason that the private sector is likely to fail to produce national defense. People will find it in their interest *not* to contribute. Thus we turn to government to provide things that we want that will not be provided adequately if we act separately—in this case, help for the poor.

A Question of Great Importance

The role of government in changing the distribution of income from that which follows from the operation of the market is a hotly debated and very important issue. The debate involves not only what government programs are appropriate to fight poverty but the character of the tax system as well. Unfortunately the quality of the public debate on the subject is low. Usually it consists of a series of claims and counterclaims about what social programs do to incentives, rather than a serious inquiry into what our distributional goal should be.

In the next section, we talk about the tools of redistributional policy in the United States. As we do this, you will have a chance to assess for yourself some of the evidence about their effects.

PROGRAMS AND POLICIES FOR REDISTRIBUTION

Redistribution always involves two parties or groups: those who end up with less and those who end up with more. Because redistributional programs are paid for out of tax dollars, it is important to know who the donors are—that is, who pays the taxes.

Taxes

The centerpiece of the U.S. tax system is the individual income tax, authorized by the Sixteenth Amendment to the Constitution passed in 1913. The income tax is "progressive." This means that those with higher incomes pay a higher percentage of their incomes in taxes. Even though the tax has many exemptions, deductions, and so forth that allow some taxpayers to reduce their tax burdens, all studies of the income tax show that its burden as a percentage of income rises as income rises.

With the passage of the Tax Reform Act of 1986, the Congress initiated a major change in the income tax. The purpose of the reforms was to simplify the tax and make it easier for people to comply with and harder to avoid. In addition, the act also significantly reduced the number of tax brackets and the overall progressivity of the rates. It also substantially reduced the tax burdens of those at the very bottom by increasing the amount of income one can earn before paying any tax at all.

The individual income tax is only one tax among many, however. What is important is the *overall* burden of taxation, including all federal, state, and local taxes. Unfortunately, it will be well into the 1990s before the full impact of the Tax Reform Act finds its way into the available statistics, but a large number of studies using pre-1987 data have estimated the overall tax burden by income class. The conclusion that emerges from nearly all of them, under a variety of assumptions about the actual incidence of all individual taxes, is that the overall burden is roughly proportional. In other words, everyone pays about the same percentage of their incomes in taxes. It is unlikely that the Tax Reform Act will change this conclusion in a major way.

Table 17.7 presents an estimate of "effective" tax rates paid by families that have been ranked by income in 1985. While some progressivity is visible, it is very slight. The bottom 10 percent of the income earners pay about 22 percent of their total incomes in tax. The top 10 percent pay 25.3%. Table 17.8 shows the impact of taxes on the cumulative distribution of income in 1980. After taxes have been paid, as you can see, the distribution of income is virtually unchanged. We can conclude from this that the tax side of the equation produces very little change in the distribution of income.

Expenditure Programs

Some programs designed to redistribute income or to aid the poor provide cash income to recipients. Others provide benefits in the form of health care, subsidized housing, or food stamps. Still others provide training or help workers find jobs. Table 17.9 gives 1987 expenditure levels for a number of the largest programs.

TABLE 17.7
Effective Rates of Federal, State, and Local Taxes, 1985 (taxes as a percentage of total income)

Population deciles	Percentage of total income
Bottom tenth	21.9
Second	21.3
Third	21.4
Fourth	22.5
Fifth	23.1
Sixth	23.5
Seventh	23.7
Eighth	24.6
Ninth	25.1
Top tenth	25.3

Source: Joseph Pechman, *Who Paid the Taxes 1966–1985?* (Brookings Institution, 1985).

TABLE 17.8
Cumulative Distribution of Family Income Before and After Taxes, 1980

Population deciles	Cumulative percentage of total income before paying taxes	Cumulative percentage of total income after paying taxes
Bottom tenth	1.3	1.4
Second	4.1	4.3
Third	8.3	8.7
Fourth	13.8	14.4
Fifth	20.8	21.5
Sixth	29.2	30.0
Seventh	39.1	40.1
Eighth	51.1	52.0
Ninth	66.2	66.9
Top tenth	100.0	100.0

Source: Joseph Pechman, *Taxes?*

TABLE 17.9
Government Social Welfare
Expenditures, 1987

	Billions of Dollars
Social insurance program	
Total	333
Old Age, Survivors, and Disability (OASDI)	208
Health insurance (Medicare)	80
Unemployment compensation	19
Workers compensation	26
Other Programs	
Total	108
Public assistance (AFDC and general assistance)	20
Medicaid	49
Supplemental security income	14
Food stamps	14
Veterans pensions	4
Housing	7
Overall Total	441

Source: Alecia Munnell, "The Current Status of Our Social Welfare System,"
New England Economic Review, (July/August 1987), 4. Updated.

Social security system The
federal system of social insurance
programs. It includes three separate
programs that are financed through
separate trust funds: an old age and
survivors insurance program, a
disability insurance program, and a
health insurance program for the
elderly.

Social Security   By far the largest income redistribution program in the United States, which is more or less incorrectly called a transfer program, is social security. The **social security system** is really three programs that are financed through separate trust funds. The *old age and survivors insurance program* (OASI) pays cash benefits to retired workers, their survivors, and their dependents, and it is the largest of the three. The *disability insurance program* (DI) pays cash benefits to disabled workers and their dependents. The third program, *health insurance (HI),* or *Medicare,* provides medical benefits to workers covered by OASDI and the railroad retirement program. Whatever the merits or demerits of the system, social security has been largely credited with reducing poverty among the elderly.

The social security program was established during the Great Depression because many of the elderly found that they were unable to support themselves after much of their savings had been wiped out by the stock market crash and subsequent bank failures. The system's primary purpose is to prevent the elderly from falling into poverty. In that it has succeeded.

Most workers in the United States have no choice but to participate in the system. For many years, federal employees, along with employees belonging to certain state and municipal retirement systems, were not required to participate, but federal employees are now being brought into the system. Today well over 90 percent of all workers in the United States contribute, with various degrees of enthusiasm.

Participants and their employers are required to pay a *payroll tax (FICA).* The tax in 1987 was 7.15% paid by employers and 7.15% paid by employees on wages up to $43,800 (1988–1989 rate = 7.51%). Self-employed people assume the entire FICA burden themselves.

If you participate in the system for 10 years, you are entitled to benefits. Benefits are paid monthly to you after you retire or, if you die, to your survivors. A complicated formula based on your average salary while you were paying into the system determines your benefit level. Those who earned more get a higher level of benefits. But there are maximum and minimum monthly benefits. By and large, low-salaried workers get out of the system more than they put in during their working lives. High-salaried workers usually get out of the system considerably less than they put in.

The social security system is self-financing, but it is different from a "funded" retirement system. In a "funded" system, deposits (either by the employer, the employee, or both) are made to an account in the employee's name. Those funds are invested and earn interest or dividends which accumulate until retirement, when they are withdrawn. Funded retirement plans operate very much like a savings plan that you might set up independently except that you cannot get at the contents until your retirement.

In the social security system, the actual tax receipts from today's workers are used to pay benefits to retired and disabled workers and their dependents today. Currently the system is collecting more than it is paying out, and the excess is accumulating in the trust funds. This is necessary to keep the system solvent, because after the year 2010 there will be a large increase in the number of retirees and a relative decline in the number of workers, owing to fertility patterns after World War II—the so-called "baby boom."

Public assistance, or "welfare" Government transfer programs that provide cash benefits to (1) families with dependent children whose incomes and assets fall below a very low line and (2) the very poor regardless of whether or not they have children.

Public Assistance   Next to social security, the biggest cash transfer program is **public assistance**, more commonly called *welfare*. Aimed specifically at the poor, welfare falls into two major categories.

By far the largest is *aid to families with dependent children (AFDC)*. Benefit levels for AFDC are set by the states, and they vary widely. In 1987 the maximum monthly payment to a single-parent family with two children was $118.00 per month in Alabama and $749.00 per month in Alaska; the overall median payment in the United States was $354.00. To participate, a family must have very low income and virtually no assets. In 1986 there were 11 million recipients in the United States, of which 7.3 million were children. Those adults who find jobs and enter the labor force lose benefits quickly as their incomes rise. This loss of benefits acts as a tax on beneficiaries, and some argue that it discourages welfare recipients from seeking jobs.

A second category of welfare payments is *general assistance*, which goes to the very poor regardless of family circumstances. In 1986 there were about 1.7 million recipients.

Supplemental Security Income   The *supplemental security income program (SSI)* is a federal program that was set up under the Social Security Administration in 1974. The program is financed out of general revenues—that is, there is no trust fund, nor are there any earmarked taxes.

SSI is designed to take care of the elderly who end up very poor with no, or very low, social security entitlement. There are over four million recipients, about half of whom also receive some social security benefits. As with welfare, qualified recipients must have very low incomes and virtually no assets.

Unemployment compensation A state government transfer program that pays cash benefits for a certain period of time to laid-off workers who have worked for a specified period of time for a covered employer.

Unemployment Compensation   In 1987 governments paid out over $15 billion in benefits to workers who were unemployed. The money to finance this benefit comes from taxes paid by employers into funds based in part on their own experience with laying off workers. Companies who hire and fire frequently pay a higher tax rate, while companies with relatively stable employment levels pay a lower tax rate. Both tax and benefit levels are determined by the states, within certain federal guidelines.

Workers who qualify for **unemployment compensation** begin to receive benefit checks soon after they are laid off, and those checks continue for a period of time that is specified by the state. Most unemployment benefits continue for 20 weeks, and the average unemployed worker receives about 36 percent of his or her normal wages in benefits. Not all workers are covered. To qualify for benefits, an unemployed person must have worked recently for a covered employer for a specified length of time for a given amount of wages. Recipients must also demonstrate willingness and ability to seek and accept suitable employment. Although nine of 10 employed persons are covered by unemployment insurance paid for by employers, only one third of the unemployed received benefits in 1986.

Unemployment benefits are not aimed at the poor alone, although many of the unemployed are poor. Unemployment benefits are paid regardless of a person's income from other sources and regardless of assets.

Medicare and Medicaid

In-kind government transfer programs that provide health and hospitalization benefits, Medicare to the aged and their survivors and to certain of the disabled, regardless of income, and Medicaid to people with low incomes.

Medicaid and Medicare   The largest in-kind transfer programs in the United States are Medicare and Medicaid. The **Medicaid** program provides health and hospitalization benefits to people with low incomes. Although administered by the states, about 56 percent of the cost is borne by the federal government. In 1986 about 23 million people received benefits; in that year, total payments were $44.7 billion and rising. Of all Medicaid recipients, 60 percent are technically below the poverty line and half are AFDC recipients.

Medicare, run by the Social Security Administration, is a health insurance program for the aged and certain disabled persons. Most U.S. citizens over 65 receive hospital insurance coverage regardless of income. In addition, they may elect to enroll in a supplementary medical insurance program under Medicare by paying a premium. If you are hospitalized, Medicare pays some, but not all, of your expenses. When the hospital stay is longer than 60 days, for example, patients are responsible for $130.00 per day.

In 1987, 28.4 million aged and three million disabled were covered, and approximately 6.5 million aged and 0.7 million disabled actually received reimbursed services.[8]

Food stamps   *Vouchers issued to low-income families and individuals by the government that can be used to purchase food.*

Food Stamps   This program, financed and run by the federal government, gives families and single individuals with low incomes the right to buy **food stamps**, or vouchers, that they can use to buy food at reduced prices at grocery stores. The program has been quite susceptible to abuse, and, for this and other reasons, the Reagan administration began to attack the program beginning in 1981.

In 1985 there were 19.2 million participants, down from 22 million in 1980. The total cost of the program in 1985 was $10.7 billion.

Housing Programs   Over the years, the federal government and state governments have administered many different housing programs designed to improve the quality of housing for low-income people. The biggest is the Public Housing program, which is financed by the federal government but administered by local public housing authorities. Public housing tenants pay rents equal to no more than 25 percent of their incomes. In many cases, that means that they pay zero. Among other programs, the largest is one called "Section 8" that provides housing assistance payments to tenants and slightly above-market rent guarantees to participating landlords.

In 1983, of the 29.2 million rental housing units in the United States, 2.2 million were in public housing projects and another 1.2 million received a government rent subsidy. Overall in that year, 11.6% of all rental units received a subsidy.[9]

In recent years, federal funding of housing programs has been sharply reduced. Budget authority for fiscal year 1986 was $9.5 billion, for 1987 it was $7.4 billion, and for 1988 it was $3.9 billion.[10]

---

[8]All statistics in this section are from U.S. House of Representatives Committee on Ways and Means, "Background Material and Data on Programs within the Jurisdiction of the Committee on Ways and Means" (March 1987).
[9]U.S. Department of Commerce/U.S. Department of Housing and Urban Development, *Current Housing Reports*, H-150-83 (Oct. 1984).
[10]*Budget of the United States*. Fiscal year 1988.

Do Poverty Programs Reduce Poverty?

Recall from Table 17.4 that the number of persons officially classified as poor dropped sharply during the 1960s and early 1970s. Between 1978 and 1983 however, the number increased nearly 40 percent. This increase is at the center of a great debate over the effectiveness of antipoverty programs.

One view holds that economic growth is the best way to cure poverty. Poverty programs are expensive and must be paid for with tax revenues. The high rates of taxation required to support these programs, their critics say, have eroded the incentive to work, save, and invest, thus slowing the rate of growth. In addition, the rise in poverty is cited as evidence that antipoverty programs do not work.

The opposite view is that poverty would be much deeper and more widespread without the programs. The increase in poverty has been the result not of *increasing* programs but in part because the "real" level of transfer payments has actually *fallen* significantly. In addition, the 1970s and 1980s witnessed two deep recessions, with substantial unemployment and major demographic changes. And there was a sharp increase in the number of households headed by women.

Despite the anti-big-government rhetoric of the Reagan years, most of what the government did to change the distribution of income before 1981 it still does today. The volume of redistribution is less, but most major programs have remained largely intact. Many still argue that what we do is far too little: poverty rates are rising, as are the numbers of homeless. But others continue to insist that government redistribution is taking its toll on incentives.

SUMMARY

1. Even if markets were perfectly efficient, the result might not be fair. Even in relatively free market economies, governments redistribute income and wealth, usually in the name of fairness, or equity.

2. Ideally, we should concern ourselves with the distribution of well-being, but because utility is neither observable nor measurable, most policy discussions deal with the distributions of income and wealth as imperfect substitutes for the concept of well-being.

3. Households derive their incomes from three basic sources: (1) from wages or salaries received in exchange for labor (about 64 percent); (2) from property such as capital and land (about 23 percent); and (3) from government (about 13 percent).

4. Differences in wage and salary incomes across households result from differences in the characteristics of workers (skills, training, education, experience, and so on) and from differences in jobs (dangerous, exciting, glamorous, difficult, and so forth). Household income also varies with the number of household members in the labor force, and it can decline sharply if members become unemployed.

5. The amount of property income that a household earns depends on the amount and kinds of property it owns. Property income is unevenly distributed. In the United States the top 20 percent of income earners earn about 70 percent of the property income.

6. Transfer income from governments flows substantially, but not exclusively, to lower-income households. Transfers account for 98 percent of the income for the bottom 10 percent of income earners but only 2.6% among the top 10 percent.

7. The top 20 percent of all income earners received 47.7% of the total income in the United States in 1985, while the bottom 20 percent earned just 4.2%. Income distribution in the United States has remained remarkably stable over a long period of time.

8. The Lorenz curve is a commonly used graphic device for describing the distribution of income. The Gini coefficient is an index of inequality that ranges from zero for perfect equality to one for total inequality.

9. The official poverty line in the U.S. is fixed at three times the cost of the Department of Agriculture's minimum food budget. In 1985 the poverty line for a family of four was $10,920.

10. Between 1960 and 1970, the number of people officially classified as poor fell from 40 million to 25 million. That

number did not change much between 1970 and 1978. Between 1978 and 1983, the number increased by nearly 45 percent to 35.3 million. Since 1983 the number has dropped slightly.

11. The basic philosophical argument against government redistribution rests on the proposition that one is entitled to the fruits of one's efforts. It also rests on the principles of freedom of contract and protection of property rights. More common arguments focus on the effects of redistribution on incentives to work, save, and invest.

12. The basic philosophical argument in favor of redistribution is that a society as rich as ours has a moral obligation to provide all its members with the basic necessities of life. More formal arguments can be found in the works of the utilitarians, Marx, Rawls, and others.

13. In the United States, redistribution is accomplished through mildly progressive taxation and through a number of government transfer programs. The largest of these are social security, public assistance, unemployment compensation, Medicare and Medicaid, food stamps, and various housing subsidy programs, including public housing.

14. The increase in poverty during the early 1980s is at the center of a great debate over the effectiveness of antipoverty programs. One view is that the best way to cure poverty is with economic growth. Poverty programs are expensive and must be paid for with tax revenues. The high rates of taxation required to support these programs have eroded the incentive to work, save, and invest, slowing the rate of growth. In addition, the rise in poverty is cited as evidence that antipoverty programs do not work. The opposite view is that without the programs, poverty would be much worse.

REVIEW CONCEPTS

equity   407
utility possibilities frontier   408
human capital   410
compensating differentials   410
unemployment   412
property income   412
transfer payments   413
economic income   414
money income   415
Lorenz curve   415
Gini coefficient   416
poverty   417
official poverty line   418

utilitarian justice   423
diminishing marginal utility of income   423
social contract   424
original position   424
Rawlsian justice   424
Marxian theory   424
labor theory of value   424
social security system   427
public assistance   428
unemployment compensation   428
Medicaid and Medicare   429
food stamps   429

REVIEW QUESTIONS

1. New Ph.D.'s in economics entering the job market find that academic jobs, jobs teaching at colleges and universities, pay about 30 percent less than nonacademic jobs such as working at a bank or a consulting firm. Those who take academic jobs are clearly worse off than those who take nonacademic jobs. Do you agree? Explain your answer.

2. Define economic income. What forms of real economic income have you earned this year that you do not have to report to the Internal Revenue Service?

3. Using the following data for 1981, plot two Lorenz curves on the same graph:

	Black	White
Lowest fifth	5.4	4.1
Second fifth	11.7	9.4
Third fifth	17.5	16.0
Fourth fifth	24.2	25.7
Highest fifth	41.2	44.8

Which has the highest Gini coefficient? How do you interpret the result?

4. How is the official poverty line in the United States established? How does it change from year to year? Suggest two alternative ways of measuring poverty.
5. Should welfare benefits be higher in California than they are in Mississippi? Defend your answer.
6. Poverty among the elderly has been sharply reduced in the last quarter century. How has this been accomplished?

7. Write a memo to your senator urging either an increase or a decrease in federal spending on public housing. Defend your position carefully, using both philosophical and practical arguments.
8. The tax system has had a larger impact on the distribution of income than government transfer programs. Do you agree or disagree? Explain.

18 Public Finance: The Economics of Taxation

A first course in economics has a number of goals. One of them is to introduce a body of theory about how economies work. The first seventeen chapters of this book contain what amounts to the core of microeconomic theory. We began with perfect markets. In Chapters 4 through 12, we built a model of a perfectly competitive market system, with no public sector, in which households and firms made self-interested choices. The result was efficient. The system seemed to produce what people wanted at least cost.

But to construct that model, we made a number of restrictive assumptions, and as we began to relax them in Chapters 13 through 17, we discovered some problems. We saw, for example, that imperfect market structures—monopoly, oligopoly, and so forth—can lead to underproduction and overpricing. Goods that bestow public or social benefits may not be produced by private, profit-seeking firms. External costs and benefits can lead to inefficient consumption and production decisions if these externalities are not taken into account by decision makers. In addition, the distribution of income and wealth may not be fair.

The previous five chapters have focused on the potential role that government might play in the economy to correct for these market failures. In theory, governments can do some things to improve the allocation of resources. Examples include production of public goods, antitrust enforcement and regulation of monopoly, rules and regulations to control externalities, and redistribution of income. Unfortunately, just as unregulated markets sometimes fail, so too do governments. Thus a constant tension between market allocation and government involvement runs through our whole discussion so far.

Another purpose of a first course in economics is to survey the discipline. In Chapter 1 we briefly described a number of the major subfields of economics. This chapter is the first of several that expand on those brief descriptions. Somewhat arbitrarily, we look first at public finance, labor economics, and urban economics. Later in the book, we take up international trade, development, and comparative systems.

The previous five chapters have dealt with the potential role of government in the economy, and it is an easy step from there to the field of *public finance*, with which we begin our survey of applied economics. No matter what functions we end up assigning to government, in order to do anything at all government must first raise revenues. The primary vehicle that the government uses to finance itself is, of course, *taxation*.

Before we can analyze the impact of taxes on the allocation of resources and the distribution of income, we need to introduce some basic principles of taxation. We must also review the arguments among those who would tax *income*, those who would tax *consumption*, and those who would distribute the tax burden according to *wealth*.

Here, too, we explore the important topic of *tax incidence*. Because households and firms change their behavior in response to taxes, the tax burdens are often shifted from those who are initially responsible for them to others through higher prices, lower wages, or reduced profits. The ultimate impact of taxes on the distribution of income depends on the extent to which these shifts take place.

Taxes can also impose excess burdens on society. When taxes cause households and firms to make choices that they would not otherwise make, the *cost*, or *burden*, of the tax to society may exceed the amount of revenue collected. Finally, the appendix to this chapter explores the tax reforms of 1986 and the tax system that emerged.[1]

THE ECONOMICS OF TAXATION

The most important thing to remember about taxes is that *ultimately they are paid by people, or by households*. Taxes may be imposed on transactions, institutions, property, meals, and all kinds of other things, but in the final analysis, they are paid by individuals or households.

Take the corporate tax, for example. The federal government imposes a tax on the net income, or profits, of corporations. Often you hear politicians and/or citizens' groups arguing for taxes on business because "business can afford to pay taxes and families cannot." People who use this rhetoric, however, assume that somehow taxes levied on business are paid by businesses and that is all there is to it. In fact, owners of corporations, that is, stockholders, and others who earn income from capital bear at least part of the corporate tax burden in lower after-tax profits. Consumers may pay part of the corporate tax in the form of higher prices for products. Finally, workers in some industries probably pay part of the corporate tax in the lower wages they earn because of its presence.

Types of Taxes

Before we begin our analysis of the tax system in the United States, we need to get some terms straight. There are many different kinds of taxes, and tax analysts use a very specific language to describe them. Every tax has two parts: a *base* and a *rate structure*. The **tax base** is the measure or value upon which the tax is levied. In this country, we levy taxes

Tax base *The measure or value upon which a tax is levied. Examples include income, sales, and home value.*

[1]Before we proceed, you may want to review the discussion of the public sector in Chapter 3. There we describe the basic sources of revenue for federal, state, and local governments, as well as the things those revenues are spent on.

Tax rate   *The percentage of a tax base that must be paid in taxes—15 percent of income, for example.*

on a variety of different bases including income, sales, property, and corporate profits. The **rate structure** determines the portion of the base that must be paid in taxes. A tax rate of 25 percent on income, for example, means that I pay a tax equal to 25 percent of my income.

Taxes on Stocks versus Taxes on Flows

Tax bases may be either stock measures or flow measures. The local property tax is a tax on the value of residential, commercial, or industrial property. A homeowner, for instance, is taxed on the current assessed value of his or her home. Current value is a *stock variable*—that is, it is measured or estimated at a point in time.

Other taxes are levied on *flows*. Income is a flow. Most people are paid on a monthly basis, and they have taxes taken out every month. Retail sales take place continuously, and a retail sales tax takes a portion of that flow. Figure 18.1 diagrams in simple form the important continuous payment flows between households and firms and the points at which the government levies six different taxes.

Proportional, Progressive, and Regressive Taxes

All taxes are ultimately paid out of income. If the burden of a tax is a *constant* proportion of income for all households, we call it a **proportional** tax. A comprehensive tax, with no deductions or exclusions, on all forms of income at 20 percent for all families, would be a proportional tax, for example.

Proportional tax   *A tax whose burden is the same proportion of income for all households.*

A tax that exacts a *higher* proportion of income from higher-income households than it does from lower-income households is a **progressive** tax. The U.S. Individual Income Tax is a progressive tax, because its rate structure increases with income. Under the current law, for example, a family with an income of $30,000 would pay a tax of roughly 15 percent, while a family with an income of $60,000 would pay a tax of about 22 percent.

Progressive tax   *A tax whose burden, expressed as a percentage of income, increases as income increases.*

A tax that exacts a *lower* proportion of income from higher-income families than it does from lower-income families is a **regressive** tax. The retail sales tax is a good example of a regressive tax, as well as of an indirect one. Suppose the retail sales tax in your state is five percent. You might assume that it is a proportional tax because everyone pays five

Regressive tax   *A tax whose burden, expressed as a percentage of income, falls as income increases.*

FIGURE 18.1
Taxes on Economic "Flows"

Most taxes are levied on measureable economic flows. For example, a profits, or net income, tax is levied on the annual profits earned by corporations.

Key (counterclockwise)
1   Personal income tax
2   Consumption tax (personal)
3   Retail sales tax
4   Payroll tax
5   Profits (net income) tax
6   Wage tax

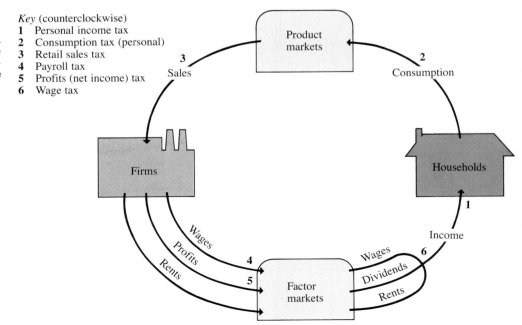

TABLE 18.1
The Burden of a Hypothetical
Five Percent Sales Tax Imposed
on Three Households with
Different Incomes

Because higher-income households
save a larger portion of their income
than lower-income households, a
seemingly proportional sales tax is actually *regressive*.

Household Income	Saving rate (in percent)	Saving	Consumption	5-percent tax	Tax as a percentage of income
A $10,000	20	$ 2,000	$ 8,000	$ 400	4.0
B 20,000	40	8,000	12,000	600	3.0
C 50,000	50	25,000	25,000	1250	2.5

percent. But not everyone spends the same fraction of their income on taxable goods and services. In fact, higher-income households save a larger fraction of their incomes. Thus, even though they spend more money on more expensive things and may pay more taxes in *dollars* than lower-income families, they end up paying a smaller *proportion of their income* in sales tax.

Table 18.1 shows how this works for three sample families. The lowest-income family saves 20 percent of its $10,000 income, leaving $8000 for consumption. With a five-percent sales tax, the household pays $400.00, or four percent of total income, in tax. The $50,000 family saves 50 percent of its income, or $25,000, leaving $25,000 for consumption. With the five-percent sales tax, the household pays $1250, only 2.5% of its total income.

Figure 18.2 gives an estimate of the actual burden of individual income taxes —federal, state, and local—and of state and local sales taxes in 1985. As you can quickly see, income taxes are progressive, and sales taxes are regressive.

Marginal versus Average Rates   When discussing a specific tax or taxes in general, it is often useful to distinguish between average tax rates and marginal tax rates. Your *average tax rate* is the total amount of tax you pay divided by your total income. For example, if you earned a total income of $15,000 and paid income taxes of $1500, your average income tax rate would be 10 percent. If you paid $3000 in taxes, your average tax rate would be 20 percent.

FIGURE 18.2
Income, Sales and Excise Taxes
as a Percent of Total Income in
1985.

The individual income tax is progressive; sales and excise taxes are regressive.
Source: Joseph Pechman, *Who Paid
the Taxes, 1966–85?* (Brookings,
1985).

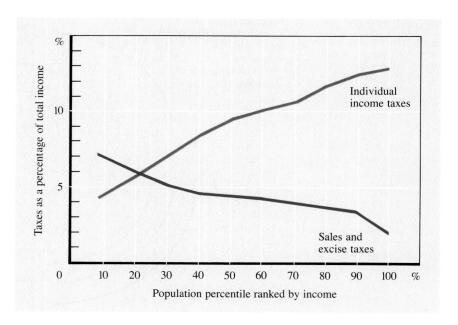

Your *marginal tax rate* is the tax rate that you pay on any additional income that you earn. That is, if you take a part-time job and earn an extra $1000 dollars and as a result pay an additional $280.00 in tax, your marginal tax rate is 28 percent.

Marginal and average tax rates are usually different. The U.S. individual income tax provides an excellent illustration of how and why marginal tax rates can diverge. If you have ever paid income taxes, you know that you must file a form called a tax return with the Internal Revenue Service each year before April 15. On the form you first figure out the total tax that you are responsible for paying for the year that ended in December. Next you see how much was withheld from your income and sent to the IRS by your employer. If too much was withheld, you get a refund. If not enough was withheld, you have to write a check to the government.

In figuring out the total amount of tax that you are responsible for paying, you first add up all your income. Then you are allowed to subtract a number of things from it. Among the things that virtually all taxpayers can subtract are the *personal exemption* and the *standard deduction*. After everything is subtracted, you are left with *taxable income*. Taxable income is then subject to a set of marginal rates that rise with income. Table 18.2 presents the marginal individual income tax rates for 1988.

Suppose that you were a single taxpayer who earned a total of $25,000 in 1988. To calculate your tax, you would first subtract a personal exemption of $1950 and a standard deduction of $3000. That leaves a taxable income of $20,050. The first $17,850 is taxable at a rate of 15 percent. That means a tax of $2677.50. Everything over $17,850 is taxable at a rate of 28 percent. For you, that means that $2200 ($20,050 − $17,850) is taxed at 28 percent, for an additional tax of $616.00. Your total tax is thus $616.00 + $2677.50 or $3293.50.

You can now see the difference between average and marginal rates. Your average tax rate is $3293.50 as a percent of $25,000, or 13.2%. But any additional income that you might have earned would have been taxed at 28 percent, because it would have been income over and above $17,850. These calculations are summarized in Table 18.3.

TABLE 18.2
Individual Income Tax Rates, 1988

Married couples filing jointly		Single taxpayers	
Taxable Income	**Tax Rate**	**Taxable Income**	**Tax Rate**
$0–$29,750	15%	$0–$17,850	15%
Over $29,750	28%	Over $17,850	28%

Source: Internal Revenue Service.

TABLE 18.3
Tax Calculations for a Single Taxpayer Who Earned $25,000 in 1988

Total income	$25,000
− Personal exemption	− 1,950
− Standard Deduction	− 3,000
= Taxable income	$20,050
Tax on first $17,850 @ 15% (17,850 × .15)	$2677.50
Amount subject to tax at 28%	
$20,050 − $17,850 = $2200	
Tax on $2200 @ 28% ($2200 × .28)	616.00
Total tax	$3293.50
Average tax rate = $3293.50/$25,000	13.2%
Marginal tax rate	28.0%

From the standpoint of analyzing behavior, it is *marginal* tax rates that matter the most. Decisions about how much to work, for example, depend on how much of the added income you get to take home. Similarly, a firm's decision about how much to invest will depend in part on the additional, or *marginal*, profits that the investment project would yield after tax.

Who Should Pay Taxes?

Benefits-received principle A *theory of fairness, dating back to Adam Smith and before, which holds that taxpayers should contribute to government (in the form of taxes) in proportion to the benefits that they receive from government spending.*

One of the criteria that we defined in Chapter 1 for evaluating the economy was *fairness*, or *equity*. Everyone agrees that tax burdens should be distributed fairly, that all of us should pay our "fair share" of taxes, but there is endless debate about what constitutes a fair tax system.

One theory of fairness is called the **benefits-received principle**. Dating back to Adam Smith and earlier writers, the benefits-received principle holds that taxpayers should contribute to government according to the benefits that they derive from public expenditures. This principle ties the tax side of the fiscal equation to the expenditure side. For example, the owners and users of cars pay gasoline and automotive excise taxes, which are paid into the Federal Highway Trust Fund that is used to build and maintain the federal highway system. The beneficiaries of public highways are thus taxed in rough proportion to their use of those highways.

The difficulty with the benefits principle is that the bulk of public expenditures are for public goods—national defense, for example. The benefits of public goods fall collectively on members of society, and there is no way to determine what values individual taxpayers place on them.

Ability-to-pay principle A *basis for taxation which stipulates that citizens should bear tax burdens in line with their ability to pay taxes.*

A different principle, and one that has dominated the formulation of tax policy in the United States, is the **ability-to-pay principle**. This principle holds that taxpayers should bear tax burdens in line with their ability to pay. Here the tax side of the fiscal equation is viewed quite apart from the expenditure side. This, of course, avoids the problem of attributing the benefits of public expenditures to specific taxpayers or groups of taxpayers.

Horizontal and Vertical Equity   If we accept the idea that ability to pay should be the basis for distributing tax burdens, two principles then follow. The principle of *horizontal equity* holds that those with equal ability to pay should bear equal tax burdens. The principle of *vertical equity* holds that those with greater ability to pay should pay more. While these notions have appeal, we must have answers to two interdependent questions before they can be meaningful. First, how is ability to pay measured? And second, if A has a greater ability to pay than B, *how much* more should A contribute?

Defining Ability to Pay, or What Is the "Best" Tax Base?

The three leading candidates for best tax base are *income*, *consumption*, and *wealth*. Before we debate the merits of each as a basis for taxation, however, let us review just what the terms mean.

Income, or, to be precise, *economic income*, is anything that enhances one's ability to command resources. The most often-used technical definition is the value of what one consumes plus any change in the value of what one owns:

$$\text{economic income} = \text{consumption} + \text{change in net worth}.$$

This broad definition includes many items that are not counted by the Internal Revenue Service and some items that the Census Bureau does not include in its definition of "money income." *Economic income* includes all money receipts, whether from employment, profits, or transfers from the government. It also includes the value of benefits not paid or received in money form, such as medical benefits, employer retirement contributions, paid country club memberships, and so forth. Increases or decreases in the value of stocks or bonds, whether or not they are "realized" through sale, are part of economic income. What difference really exists between someone who holds a share of stock that appreciates in value 10 percent and someone who earns 10 percent interest that is reinvested? For income tax purposes, capital gains count as income only when they are realized, but for purposes of defining economic income, *all increases in asset values count*, whether they are realized or not.

A few other items that we do not usually think of as income are included in a comprehensive definition of income. If I own my house outright and live in it rent free, income flows from my house just as interest flows from a bond or profit from a share of stock. By owning the house, I enjoy valuable benefits that I would otherwise have to pay rent for. I am my own landlord, and I am, in essence, earning my own rent. Other components of economic income include any gifts and bequests received and food grown at home.

The point is that in economic terms, *income is income, regardless of source and regardless of use*. For tax purposes, many income components are obviously hard to measure, and others are excluded for policy reasons. In fact, the definition of income used as a final tax base prior to the reforms of 1986 had become so riddled with holes that it was stretching a point to call it income.

Consumption is the total value of things that a household actually consumes during a period. It is equal to income minus saving, or

$$consumption = income - saving \text{ (change in net worth)}.$$

Wealth, or *net worth*, is simply the value of all the things that one owns, after one's liabilities are subtracted. If you were to sell off today everything of value that you own—stocks, bonds, houses, cars, other real assets, and so forth—at their current market prices and pay off everything that you owe—loans, mortgages, and so forth—you would end up with your "net worth." In other words,

$$net \ worth = assets - liabilities.$$

For years conventional wisdom among economists held that income was the best measure of ability to pay taxes. Many who feel that consumption is a better measure have recently challenged that assumption. The following arguments are not just arguments about fairness and ability to pay; they are really arguments about the best base for taxation.

Be careful to note as you proceed that the issue of the debate is which *base* is the best base, not which *tax* is the best tax. Not all consumption taxes, for example, are regressive sales taxes. It is perfectly possible to have a personal consumption tax with progressive rates by allowing people to deduct or exclude the value of what they save from income and applying a progressive rate schedule.

Consumption as the Best Tax Base   The view favoring consumption dates back at least to the seventeenth century English philosopher Thomas Hobbes, who argued that people should pay in accordance with "what they actually take out of the common pot, not what they leave in." The standard of living, so the argument goes, depends not on income but

The Tax Reform Act of 1986

The following article appeared on the front page of the *Wall Street Journal* on August 18, 1986, the day after the Congress finalized the bill which would be passed as the Tax Reform Act of 1986 and signed by the president later in the year. Virtually the entire issue of the *Journal* was devoted to the new tax laws.

WASHINGTON—The sweeping revision of the tax code agreed to by House and Senate tax writers over the weekend is virtually unprecedented in the 73-year history of the nation's income tax. It will touch the lives of all Americans.

The bill dramatically cuts tax rates and pays for this decline by eliminating or reducing a vast array of tax breaks. Tax shelters, which have proliferated in recent years, will be dealt a near-fatal blow. And corporations will find their opportunities to avoid taxes severely limited.

"I've been involved in trying to get tax reform for 25 years, and I never thought I'd live to see this," says Jerome Kurtz, a former commissioner of the Internal Revenue Service. "It's really spectacular."

The bill was completed by congressional tax conferees late Saturday evening, and both the Senate and House are expected to give final approval to the measure next month. President Reagan is expected to sign the measure into law soon thereafter.

POSSIBLE EFFECTS

The effects of the far-reaching legislation aren't easy to predict, but the plan clearly represents some fundamental changes in the direction of government policy. Among them:

—The bill marks a retreat from the use of the tax code for economic and social engineering. It cuts back many, though by no means all, of the tax credits and deductions now riddling the code. And it reduces the top tax rate so sharply that the remaining breaks lose much of their allure. "It's an abandonment, to some extent, of the mechanisms of fiscal policy,"

says Daniel Bell, a professor of social sciences at Harvard University.

—It reverses a 20-year slide in corporate tax revenues and reduces the tax code's traditional tilt toward smokestack industries. Many observers saw the 1981 tax law as the final blow to an effective corporate tax; its ample write-offs for capital-intensive companies enabled many of them to escape federal income taxes altogether. But the new bill will increase corporate taxes by about $120 billion over five years, roughly restoring the corporate tax to its levels in the 1970s. As long as budget deficits remain large, predicts John Palmer, a senior fellow at the Urban Institute in Washington, "corporations are not going to be let off from paying their fair share."

—It constitutes the most important antipoverty legislation in more than a decade. Rapid inflation and rising Social Security taxes have caused the tax burden of the poor to skyrocket during the past decade and a half; this measure will offset part of that increase. Six million impoverished people will be removed from the tax rolls. And for families of four below the poverty line, "this not only takes them off the tax rolls, it offsets half their Social Security payments," says Robert Greenstein, the director of the liberal Center on Budget and Policy Priorities.

MANY DECISIONS INVOLVED

In addition, the tax revisions will sharply alter the economics of many ordinary decisions. Some effects of these changes can be anticipated; others may take years to unfold.

"Nobody knows what the consequences will be," says Aaron Wildavsky, a professor of political science and public policy at the University of California at Berkeley. "All the models are based on the previous system of tax incentives. No one knowledgeable can tell you how this one will come out."

Source: Alan Murray, *The Wall Street Journal*, August 18, 1986; reprinted by permission of Dow Jones and Co., Inc, all rights reserved.

on what is *spent out of income*. If we want to redistribute well-being, therefore, the tax base should be consumption, because consumption is the best measure of well-being.

A second argument with a distinguished history dates back at least to work by Irving Fisher in the early part of the twentieth century. Fisher and many others have argued that a tax on income doubles taxes and discourages saving. A story told originally by Fisher, illustrates this theory quite nicely.[2]

Suppose that Alex builds a house for Frank. For this service, Alex is paid $10,000 and given an orchard containing 100 apple trees. Alex spends the $10,000 on consumption today, but he saves the orchard, and presumably he will consume or sell the

[2]Irving Fisher and Herbert Fisher, *Constructive Income Taxation: A Proposal for Reform* (New York: Harper, 1942), Chapter 8, p. 56.

fruit it bears every year in the future. Assume that at year's end the state levies a 10 percent tax on Alex's total income, which includes the $10,000 and the orchard. First, the government takes 10 percent of the $10,000, which is 10 percent of Alex's consumption. Second, it takes 10 percent of the orchard—10 trees—which is 10 percent of Alex's saving. If this is all the government did, there would be no double taxation of saving. If, however, the income tax is also levied in the following year, Alex will be taxed on the income generated from the fruit produced by the 90 trees that he owns. If the income tax is levied in the year after that, Alex will again be taxed on the income generated, and so on. The income tax is thus taxing Alex's saving twice. It taxes the initial saving *plus* all the future income generated from the saving. To avoid the double taxation of saving, either the original saving of 100 trees should not be taxed or the income generated from the after-tax number of trees (namely 90) should not be taxed.

The same logic can be applied to cash saving. Suppose that the income tax rate is 25 percent and that you earn $20,000. Out of the $20,000 you consume $16,000 and save $4000. When you earn it, you owe the government 25 percent of your total income, or $5000. You can think of that as a tax of 25 percent on consumption ($4000) and 25 percent on savings ($1000). Why, then, do we say that the income tax is a double tax on saving? To understand the argument you have to think about the $4000 that is saved.

If you save $4000, you will no doubt put it to some use. Safe possibilities include putting it in an interest-bearing account or buying a bond with it. If you do either of these, you will earn interest that you can consume in future years. In fact, what we are doing when we save and earn interest is spreading some of our present earnings over future years of consumption. Just as the orchard yields future fruit, so the bond yields future interest, which is considered income in the year it is earned, and as such is taxed. Now the only way that you can earn that future interest income is if you leave your money tied up in the bond or the account. You can consume the $4000 today *or* you can have the future flow of interest; you can't have both. Yet both are taxed. In fact, the value of the bond you buy with today's saving is the present discounted value of the future flow of interest to which you are entitled. (If this sounds unfamiliar, review Chapter 11.

Suppose that the interest rate is 10 percent. If you save $4000 and put it into a long-term bond that pays 10-percent annual interest, you have converted your $4000 into a flow of $400.00 per year. That flow will be taxed at 25 percent, or $100.00 per year. Thus your saving is taxed both when you earn it *and* as you consume it in the future, and many people think this is unfair.

It is also inefficient. As we mentioned earlier, and as you will see in more detail later, a tax that distorts economic choices creates *excess burdens*. By double-taxing saving, an income tax distorts the choice between consumption and saving, which is really the choice between present consumption and future consumption. This also tends to reduce the saving rate and the rate of investment—and ultimately of economic growth.

Income as the Best Tax Base   Your ability to pay is your ability to command resources, and your income is the best measure of your capacity to command resources today. According to proponents of income as a tax base, you should be taxed not on what you actually draw out of Hobbes's pot, but on the basis of your *ability*, or *power*, to draw from the pot. In other words, your decision to save or consume is no different from your decision to buy apples, to go out for dinner, or to give money to your mother. It is your *income* that enables you to do all those things, and that is what should be taxed, regardless of its sources and regardless of how you use it. Saving is just another use of income.

If income is the best measure of ability to pay, the double taxation argument doesn't hold water. An income tax taxes savings twice only if consumption is the measure used to gauge a person's ability to pay. It does not do so if income is the measure used. Acquisition of the orchard enhances your ability to pay today; a bountiful crop of fruit enhances your ability to pay when it is produced. Taxing both is thus indeed fair.

Wealth as the Best Tax Base   Still others argue that the real power to command resources comes not from any single year's income but from accumulated wealth. Aggregate net worth in the United States is many times larger than aggregate income.

If two people have identical annual incomes of $10,000, but one also has an accumulated net worth of $1 million held in a safe deposit box, is it reasonable to argue that these two people have the same ability to pay, or that they should pay equal taxes? Most people would answer no. Those who favor income taxation, however, argue that net wealth comes from *after-tax income* that has been saved. An income tax taxes consumption and saving correctly, they say. To subsequently take part of what has been saved would be an unfair second hit—or *real* double taxation.

No Simple Answer   As you can see, the "best-base" debate has a number of sides. Before the 1970s, most tax economists favored a comprehensive income base. Today a very significant group of economists favor a comprehensive personal consumption tax. Part of the reason for the increasing popularity of consumption taxes is a growing concern with the low saving rate in the United States. Since 1978 there has been concern with productivity growth, and many point to the inadequacy of saving as the culprit. As we saw in earlier chapters, household saving provides resources for firms to invest in capital that raises the productivity of labor.

TAX INCIDENCE

When a government levies a tax, it writes a law assigning responsibility for payment to specific people or specific organizations—corporations, for example. To understand a tax, however, we must look beyond those named in the law as the initial taxpayers.

First, remember the cardinal principle of tax analysis: the burden of a tax is ultimately borne by individuals or households; institutions have no real taxpaying capacity. Second, even if a tax is levied directly on households, its burden is not always borne by those initially responsible for paying it. Directly or indirectly, tax burdens are often shifted to others. When we speak of the **incidence of a tax**, we are referring to the ultimate distribution of its burden.

The simultaneous reactions of many households and/or firms to the presence of a tax may cause relative prices to change, and price changes affect the well-being of households. The well-being of an individual household depends on both input and output prices. Stated another way, households may feel the impact of a tax on the sources side or on the uses side of the income equation. On the **sources side**, a household is hurt if the net wages or profits that it receives fall; on the **uses side**, a household is hurt if the prices of the things that it buys rise. If your wages remain the same but the price of every item that you buy doubles, you are in the same position you would have been in if your wages had been cut by 50 percent and prices hadn't changed.

To rephrase the point, the imposition of a tax or a change in a tax can *change behavior*. Changes in behavior can affect supply and demand in markets and cause prices to change. When prices in input or output markets change, some households are made better off and some are made worse off. These final changes determine the ultimate burden of the tax.

Tax incidence   When we speak of the incidence of a tax, we are speaking of the ultimate distribution of its burden.

Sources side/uses side   The impact of a tax may be felt on one or the other or both sides of the income equation. A tax may cause net income to fall (damage on the sources side) or it may cause prices of goods and services to rise so that income buys less (damage on the uses side).

Tax shifting *Occurs when tax burdens are transfered from those upon whom taxes are initially levied to others.*

Tax shifting takes place when households can alter their behavior and do something to avoid paying a tax. This is especially easy to do when only certain items are singled out for taxation. For example, suppose a heavy tax were levied on bananas. Initially the tax would make the price of bananas much higher, but there are many potential substitutes. Consumers can avoid the tax by not buying bananas, and that is exactly what many of them will do. As long as the substitutes are reasonably close, consumers are not bothered much. But, as demand drops, the market price of bananas falls and banana growers lose money. Thus the tax shifts from consumers to the growers, at least in the short run.

On the other hand, a tax such as the retail sales tax, levied at the same rate on *all* consumer goods, is harder to avoid. The only thing that consumers can do to avoid such a tax is to consume less of everything. If consumers do this, saving will increase, but otherwise there are fewer opportunities for tax avoidance and therefore for tax shifting. The general principle here is that broad-based taxes are less likely to be shifted and more likely to "stick" where they are levied than "partial taxes" are.

The Incidence of Payroll Taxes

In 1987, over 38 percent of federal revenues came from social insurance taxes, also called "payroll taxes." The revenues from the various payroll taxes go to support social security, unemployment compensation, and other health and disability benefits for workers. As you saw earlier in the chapter, some of these taxes are levied on employers as a percentage of payroll, and some are levied on workers as a percentage of wages or salaries earned.

To analyze the payroll tax, let us take a tax of T per unit of labor levied on *employers* and briefly sketch the reactions that are likely to follow. When the tax is first levied, firms find that the price of labor is higher. Where before they paid W per hour, they now must pay $W + T$. Firms may react in two ways. First, they may substitute capital for the now-more-expensive labor. Second, they may cut production, owing to higher costs and lower profits. Both reactions mean a lower demand for labor. Lower demand for labor, in turn, reduces wages, and part of the tax is passed on, *or shifted to*, the workers, who end up earning less. As you will see, however, the extent to which the tax is shifted to workers depends on how workers react to the lower wages.

We can begin a more formal analysis of this situation with a picture of the market before the tax is levied. Figure 18.3 shows equilibrium in a hypothetical labor market with no payroll tax. Before we proceed, we should review the factors that determine the shapes of the supply and demand curves.

In competitive markets, the demand for labor depends on its productivity, and, as you saw in Chapter 10, a competitive, profit-maximizing firm will hire labor up to the point that the market wage is equal to labor's *marginal revenue product*. The shape of the demand curve for labor shows how responsive *firms* are to changes in wages. Several factors determine a firm's reactions to changes in wage rates: how easy it is to substitute capital for labor, whether labor costs are large or small relative to total costs, and how elastic the demand for the firm's product is.[3]

The shape of the supply curve shows how responsive *workers* are to changes in wages. As you saw in Chapter 6, lower wages may affect workers' behavior in two ways. First, lower wages mean that for the same amount of effort, workers will earn less

---

[3] If demand for output is highly inelastic, increases in costs from a rise in wages primarily flow through to consumers in higher prices.

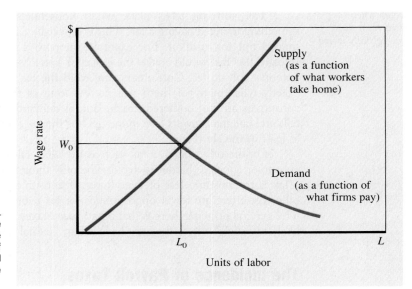

FIGURE 18.3
Equilibrium in a Competitive
Labor Market—No Taxes

With no taxes on wages, the wage
that firms pay is the same as the wage
that workers take home. At a wage of
W_0 the quantity of labor supplied and
the quantity of labor demanded are
equal.

income. They will therefore be able to buy less, and, if we think of "leisure" as a good, they will buy less of that too, by working more. Earlier, we called this the *income effect*.

Second, however, a lower wage also means that leisure is less expensive relative to other goods—an additional hour of leisure means an hour of *lost* wages, and wages are now lower. Workers "substitute" leisure for other goods by working less and buying less of other goods with the lower income. We called this the *substitution effect*. An upward-sloping labor supply curve means that, on balance, the substitution effect dominates the income effect, and that lower wages lead to less work effort. If the opposite were true, the labor supply curve would "bend back."[4]

In any event, the labor supply curve represents the reaction of workers to changes in the wage rate. Their behavior depends on the wage that they actually take home per hour of work *after taxes*. Labor demand is, of course, a function of the full amount that firms must pay per unit of labor, an amount that may include a tax if it is levied directly on payroll, as it is in our example. When it is present, such a tax drives a "wedge" between the price of labor that firms face and take-home wages.

In Figure 18.3, there were no taxes, and the wage that firms paid was the same as the wage that workers took home. At a wage of W_0, then, quantity of labor supplied and quantity of labor demanded were equal, and the labor market was in equilibrium.[5]

But now suppose that employers must pay a tax of $\$T$ per unit of labor. Figure 18.4 shows a new supply curve parallel to the old supply curve but above it by a distance, T. The new curve, S', shows labor supply as a function of what firms pay. No matter whether workers pay the tax or firms pay it, there is a difference between what firms pay and workers take home.

If the initial wage is W_0 per hour, firms will face a price of $W_0 + T$ per unit of labor immediately after the tax is levied. Workers still receive only W_0, however. The higher wage rate, that is, the higher price of labor that firms now face, reduces their demand for labor from L_0 to L_d, and they lay off workers. Workers initially still receive W_0, so the

[4]Evidence on the relative size of the income and substitution effects is presented in Chapter 19.
[5]Although the supply curve has a positive slope here, that slope implies nothing about the actual shape of the labor supply curve in the United States. Empirical estimates of supply elasticities are more fully treated in Chapter 19.

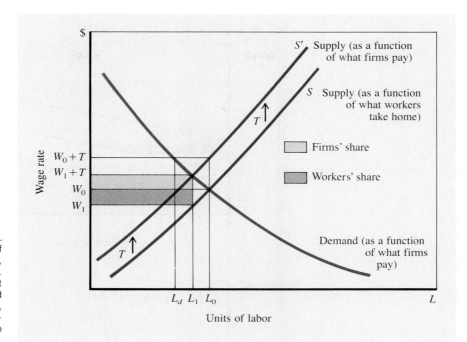

FIGURE 18.4

Incidence of a Per Unit Payroll Tax in a Competitive Labor Market

With a tax on firms of $T per unit of labor hired, the market will adjust, shifting the tax partially to workers. When the tax is levied, firms must at first pay W_0+T. That reduces demand to L_d. The result is excess supply, pushing wages down to W_1 and passing some of the burden of the tax on to workers.

amount of labor supplied does not change, and the result is an excess supply of labor equal to $(L_0 - L_d)$.

The excess supply puts downward pressure on the market wage, and wages fall, shifting some of the tax burden onto workers. The issue, of course, is How far will wages fall? Figure 18.4 shows that a new equilibrium is achieved at W_1, with firms paying $W_1 + T$. When workers take home W_1, they will *supply* L_1 units of labor; if firms must pay $W_1 + T$, *they will also demand* L_1 units of labor, and the market clears.

Thus the burden of the payroll tax is shared by employers and employees. Initially, firms paid W_0; after the tax, they pay $W_1 + T$. Initially, workers received W_0; after the tax, they end up with W_1. Total tax collections by the government are equal to $T \times L_1$; geometrically, they are equal to the whole shaded area in Figure 18.4. The workers' share is the lower portion, $(W_0 - W_1) \cdot L_1$; the firms' share is the upper portion, $((W_1 + T) - W_0)) \cdot L_1$.

Figure 18.5 parts a and b show that the ultimate burden of a payroll tax depends, at least in part, on the *elasticity of labor supply*. If labor supply is very elastic, that is to say, responsive to price, take-home wages do not fall very much, and workers bear only a small portion of the tax. But if labor supply is inelastic, or unresponsive to price, *most* of the burden is borne by workers. Empirical studies of labor supply behavior in the United States suggest that for most of the work force, the elasticity of labor supply is close to zero. This leads to the conclusion that most of the payroll tax in this country is probably borne by workers.

An interesting conclusion is that the result is exactly the same if the tax is initially levied on workers rather than on firms. To see this, suppose we go back to the equilibrium in Figure 18.5, with wages at W_0, but now the tax of $T per hour is levied on workers rather than firms. The burden will end up being shared by firms and workers in the *exact same proportions*. Initially, take-home wages will fall to $W_0 - T$. Workers will supply less labor, creating excess demand and pushing market wages up. That shifts part of the burden back to employers. The "story" is different, but the result is just the same.

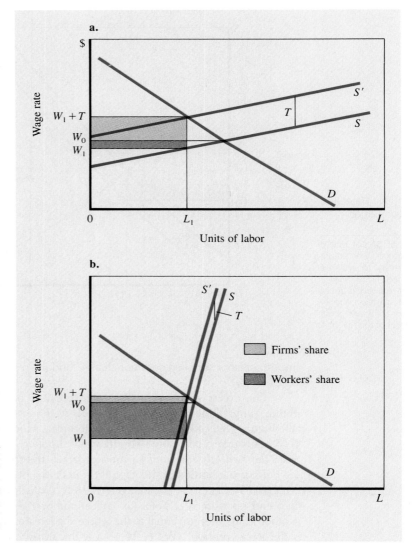

FIGURE 18.5

Payroll Tax with Elastic (a) and
Inelastic (b) Labor Supply

The ultimate burden of a payroll tax
depends on the elasticities of labor
supply and labor demand. For example, if supply is relatively elastic, as in
part a, the burden falls largely on
employers; if the supply is relatively
inelastic, as in part b, the burden falls
largely on workers.

In Table 18.4, you see an estimate of the incidence of payroll taxes in the U.S. in 1985. This estimate assumes that both the employers' share and employees' share are ultimately *borne by employees*. The payroll tax turns out to be regressive for two reasons. First, in 1985 the tax did not apply to wages and salaries in excess of $39,600; those who made more paid no tax on wage and salary income in excess of that amount. Second, wages and salaries fall as a percentage of total income as we move up the income scale. That is, those with higher incomes earn a larger portion of their incomes from profits, dividends, rents, and so forth, and these kinds of income are not subject to the payroll tax.

Some economists dispute the conclusion that the payroll tax is borne entirely by wage earners. Even if labor supply is inelastic, some wages are set in the process of collective bargaining between unions and large firms. If the payroll tax results in a higher gross wage in the bargaining process, firms may find themselves faced with higher costs. Higher costs, in turn, either reduce profits to owners or are passed through to consumers in higher product prices.

TABLE 18.4

Estimated Incidence of Payroll Taxes in the United States in 1985

If we assume that workers bear the full burden of the payroll tax (both employees' and employers' shares), then it is regressive. First, only salaries and wages up to $39,000 were taxed in 1985. Second, wages and salaries fall as a portion of total income as income rises.

Population ranked by income	Tax as a percentage of total income
Bottom 10%	9.4
Second	8.7
Third	7.9
Fourth	7.9
Fifth	7.8
Sixth	7.5
Seventh	7.2
Eighth	7.0
Ninth	6.4
Top 10%	3.6
Top 5%	2.6
Top 1%	1.4

Source: Joseph Pechman, *Who Paid the Taxes, 1966–1985?* (Brookings Institution, 1985).

But as you will see in Chapter 19, a smaller and smaller portion of the labor force is unionized; less than 18 percent of those employed currently belong to unions. In spite of arguments to the contrary, then, to the extent that markets are competitive, the burden of the payroll tax does fall heavily on employees.

The Incidence of Corporation Profits Taxes

Another tax that requires careful analysis is the corporate profits tax levied by the federal government, as well as by most states. The *corporate profits tax*, or *corporation income tax*, is a tax on the profits of firms that are organized as corporations. Partnerships and proprietorships do not pay this tax. Rather, the owners report the income from their firms directly on their individual income tax returns.

Thus we can think of the corporate tax as a tax on capital income, or profits, in one sector of the economy. As we set out to examine this tax, for the sake of simplicity we will assume that there are only two sectors of the economy, corporate and noncorporate, and only two factors of production, labor and capital. Owners of capital receive profits, and workers are paid a wage.

Like the payroll tax, the corporate tax may affect households on the *sources* or the *uses* side of the income equation. The tax may affect profits earned by owners of capital, wages earned by workers, or prices of corporate and noncorporate products. And, once again, the key question is how large these changes are likely to be.

When the tax is first imposed, it initially reduces net, or after-tax, profits in the corporate sector. Assuming that the economy was in long-run equilibrium before the tax was levied, firms in both the corporate and noncorporate sectors were earning a "normal rate of return," and flows of investment were in rough balance; there was no reason to expect higher profits in one sector than in the other. All of a sudden, firms in the corporate sector become significantly less profitable. (To illustrate how much less profitable, the tax rate applicable to most firms up through 1986 approached 46 percent.)

In response, capital investment begins to favor the nontaxed sector because after-tax profits are higher there. Firms in the taxed sector contract in size or, in some cases, go out of business, while firms in the nontaxed sector expand, and new firms enter its various industries. As this happens, the flow of capital from the taxed to the nontaxed sector reduces the profit rate in the nontaxed sector; more competition springs up, and this in turn drives down product prices. Some of the tax burden now shifts to capital income earners in the noncorporate sector, because they end up earning lower profits.

As capital flows out of the corporate sector in response to lower after-tax profits, the profit rate in that sector rises somewhat because fewer firms means less supply, which means higher prices, and so forth. Presumably, capital will continue to favor the nontaxed sector until the *after-tax profit rates equalize* in the two sectors. Thus even though the tax is imposed on just one sector, it eventually depresses profits in all sectors equally.

Already we see that product prices may change. Under these circumstances, the products of corporations will probably become more expensive, and products of proprietorships and partnerships will probably become less expensive. But because almost everyone buys both corporate and noncorporate products, these "excise effects" are likely to have a minimal impact on the distribution of the burden; in essence they cancel each other out.

Finally, what about labor? Labor can be affected in a number of ways. Given that we have a contracting sector and an expanding sector, if the contracting sector were the more labor intensive, that is, if it used more labor relative to capital, wages might fall even though employment remained full in the economy as a whole. If the expanding sector were the more labor intensive, however, wages might actually be driven up. Furthermore, because the corporate profits tax essentially taxes the use of capital, firms might be pushed to *substitute* more labor-intensive methods of production. That would increase the demand for labor and reduce the demand for capital, raising wage rates relative to returns from capital.

The ultimate burden of the corporate tax appears to depend on several factors: the relative capital/labor intensity of the two sectors, the ease with which capital and labor can be substituted in the two sectors, and elasticities of demand for the products of each sector. In 1962 Arnold Harberger, of the University of Chicago, analyzed this problem rigorously and concluded that owners of corporations, proprietorships, and partnerships all bear the burden of the tax in rough proportion to profits, even though it is directly levied only on corporations. He also found that wage effects of the corporate tax were small and that excise effects, that is, effects on the prices of products, were roughly neutral.[6]

Although most economists generally accept Harberger's view of the corporate tax, there are arguments against it. For example, a profits tax on a monopoly firm earning above-normal profits is *not* shifted to other sectors unless the tax actually drives profits below the competitive level.

You might be tempted to conclude that because monopolists can control market price, they will simply pass on the profits tax in higher prices to consumers of monopoly products. But theory predicts just the opposite: that the tax burden will remain with the monopolist.

Remember that monopolists are constrained by market demand. That is, they choose the combination of price and output consistent with market demand that maximizes profit. If a proportion of that profit is taxed, the choice of price and quantity will not change. Why not? Quite simply, if you behave so as to maximize profit, and then I come and take some fixed proportion of it, such as half, you maximize your half by maximizing the whole, which is exactly what you would do in the absence of the tax. Thus your price and output do not change, the tax is not shifted, and you end up paying

[6]Arnold Harberger, "The Incidence of the Corporate Income Tax," *Journal of Political Economy*, Vol. LXX (June 1962).

TABLE 18.5

Estimated Burden of the United States Corporation Income Tax in 1985

Assuming that half of the burden falls on owners of corporations and that the other half is shared equally by all those who earn capital income, the burden of the corporate tax is quite progressive. Only the top twenty percent are estimated to pay over one percent of their incomes in tax.

Population ranked by income	Corporate tax burden as a percentage of total income
Bottom 10 percent	0.5
Second	0.5
Third	0.6
Fourth	0.6
Fifth	0.7
Sixth	0.8
Seventh	0.8
Eight	0.9
Ninth	1.2
Top 10 percent	3.6
Top 5 percent	4.5
Top 1 percent	5.7

Source: Pechman, *Taxes?*

the tax. In the long run, capital will not leave the taxed monopoly sector, as it did in the competitive case, because even with the tax, the monopolist is earning higher profits than are possible elsewhere.

The fact that there is so much room for debate about who the corporate tax hurts illustrates the advantage of broad-based direct taxes over narrow-based indirect taxes. Because it is levied on an institution, the corporate tax is indirect, and therefore it is always shifted. Furthermore, it taxes only one factor, capital, in only one part of the economy, the corporate sector. The income tax, on the other hand, taxes all forms of income in all sectors of the economy, and it is virtually impossible to shift—we know who pays it. It is difficult to argue that a tax is a good tax if we can't be sure who ultimately ends up paying it.

Table 18.5 presents an estimate of the actual incidence of the U.S. Corporation Income Tax in 1985. These figures have been arrived at on the basis of compromise assumptions—that is, half of the burden is assumed to fall fully on owners of corporations, as in the monopoly model, and half of the burden is assumed to be shared equally by all those who earn capital income, as in the competitive model. None of the burden is assumed to fall on consumers or wage earners. Under such assumptions, the burden of the corporate income tax is clearly progressive, because profits and capital income make up a much bigger part of the incomes of high-income households.

The Overall Incidence of Taxes in the United States

A complete treatment of tax incidence, one that included an analysis of each individual tax, would take more space than we have here. Many researchers have done complete analyses under varying assumptions about incidence, and in most cases their results agree. State and local taxes, with sales taxes playing a big role, seem as a group to be mildly regressive. Federal taxes, dominated by the individual income tax but increasingly affected by the regressive payroll tax, are mildly progressive. The overall system is mildly progressive.

Figure 18.6 shows an estimate of the overall burden in 1985. It is based on a set of assumptions that the author of the study finds to be the "most reasonable." Overall, the

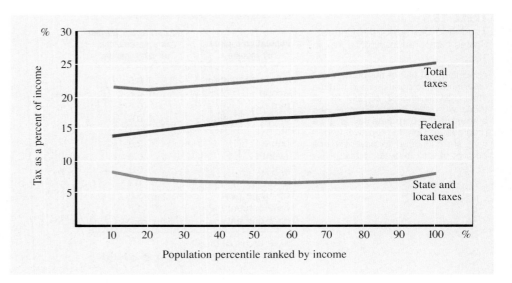

FIGURE 18.6
Federal, State, and Local Taxes as a Percentage of Total Income by Population Decile, 1985

Under the most reasonable set of assumptions, state and local taxes are mildly regressive at the bottom and mildly progressive at the top. Federal taxes are progressive, and the overall tax burden is mildly progressive. Taxes have very little impact on the distribution of income.
Source: Pechman, *Taxes?*

study concludes that the system is mildly progressive: higher-income households pay a slightly larger portion of their income in tax. The tax burden rises from 22 percent of total income at the bottom to 25 percent at the top.

It is important to note, as we said in the previous chapter, that a *proportional* tax system has very little impact on the distribution of income. The relative income shares going to each income group remain about the same after taxes as they were before taxes. Thus what redistribution does take place in the United States is not done on the income side of the government's budget but on the expenditure side.

EXCESS BURDENS: THE PRINCIPLE OF TAX NEUTRALITY

You have seen that when households and firms make decisions in the presence of a tax that differ from those they would make in its absence, the burdens of the tax can be shifted from those for whom it was originally intended. Now we can take the same logic one step further. *When taxes distort economic decisions, they impose burdens on society that in aggregate exceed the revenue collected by the government.* The amount by which the burden of a tax exceeds the revenue collected by the government is called the **excess burden** of the tax. (Excess burdens are also sometimes called "dead weight losses.") Because excess burdens are a form of waste, or lost value, tax policy should be written with an eye toward minimizing them.

In practice, all taxes change behavior. A product-specific excise tax raises the price of the taxed item, and people can avoid the tax by buying substitutes. An income tax distorts the choice between present and future consumption and between work and leisure. The corporate tax influences investment and production decisions—investment is diverted away from the corporate sector, and firms may be induced to substitute labor for capital.

Excess burden   Often the full burden of a tax to society exceeds the total amount of revenue collected by the tax. The excess burden of a tax is the amount by which its full burden exceeds the total revenue collected. Also called "deadweight losses."

How Do Excess Burdens Arise?

The idea that a tax can impose an extra cost, or excess burden, by distorting choices can be seen clearly with a simple numerical example. Consider a competitive industry that produces an output, X, using the technology shown in Figure 18.7. Using technology A, firms can produce a unit of output with seven units of capital (K) and three units of labor (L). Using technology B, a unit of output requires four units of capital and seven units of labor. A is thus the more capital-intensive technology.

If we assume that labor and capital each cost $2.00 per unit, it costs $20.00 to produce each unit of output with technology A and $22.00 with technology B. Thus firms will choose technology A. Because we assume competition, output price will be driven to cost of production, and the price of output will in the long run be driven to $20.00 per unit.

To narrow our focus to the distortion of technological choice alone, we assume that demand for the good in question is perfectly inelastic at 1000 units of output. That is, regardless of price, households will buy 1000 units of product. At a price of $20.00 per unit, that means consumers pay a total of $20,000 for 1000 units of X.

Now along comes the government and levies a tax of 50 percent on capital. That has the effect of raising the price of capital, P_K, to $3.00 = $2.00 (1 + t) where t = .5. Figure 18.8 shows what would happen to unit cost of production. With capital now more expensive, the firm switches to the more labor-intensive technology B. With the tax in place, X can be produced at a unit cost of $27.00 per unit using technology A but for $26.00 per unit using technology B.

If we assume that demand is inelastic, buyers continue to buy 1000 units of X regardless of its price. (We shall ignore any distortions of consumer choices that might result from this.) Recall that the tax is 50 percent, or $1.00 per unit of capital used. Because it takes four units of capital for each unit of output, firms now using technology B

FIGURE 18.7

Firms Choose the Technology that Minimizes the Cost of Production

If the industry is competitive, output price will be $20.00 per unit. If 1000 units of output are sold, consumers will pay a total of $20,000 for the good.

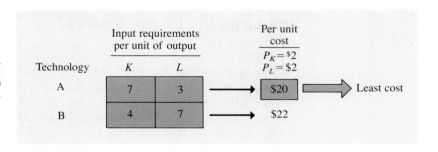

FIGURE 18.8

Imposition of a Tax on Capital Distorts the Choice of Technology.

If the industry is competitive, output price will be $26.00 per unit. The tax is $1.00 per unit of capital. If technology B is used, and if we assume that total sales remain at 1000 units, total tax collections will be 1000 x 4 x $1.00 = $4000. But consumers will pay a total of $26,000 for the good—$6000 more than before. Thus there is an excess burden of $2000.

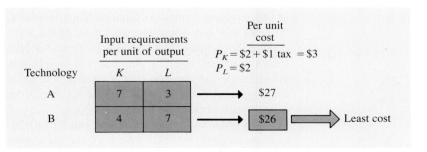

will pay a total tax to the government of $4.00 per unit of output produced. With 1000 units of output sold, total tax collections amount to $4000.

But if you look carefully, you will see that the burden of the tax exceeds $4000. After the tax, consumers will be paying $26.00 per unit for the good. Twenty-six dollars is now the unit cost of producing the good using the best available technology in the presence of the capital tax. Thus consumers will pay $26,000 for 1000 units of the good. This represents an increase of $6000 over the previous total of $20,000. The revenue raised from the tax is $4000, but its total burden is $6000. Thus there is an *excess burden* of $2000.

How did this excess burden arise? Look back at Figure 18.7. You can see that technology B is less efficient than technology A (unit costs of production are $2.00 higher per unit using technology B). But now the tax on capital has induced firms to switch to this less efficient, labor-intensive mode of production. Thus, there is a waste of $2.00 per unit of output. The *total* burden of the tax is equal to the revenue collected plus the loss due to the wasteful choice of technology, and the *excess* burden is $2.00 per unit times 1000 units, or $2000.

The same principle holds for taxes that distort consumption decisions. If I prefer to consume bundle X rather than bundle Y when there is no tax, but I choose bundle Y with a tax in place, not only do I pay the tax, I also end up with a bundle of goods that is worth less than the bundle I would have chosen without the tax. Again, we have the burden of an extra cost.

In general, the larger the distortion that a tax causes in behavior, the larger the excess burden of the tax. Taxes levied on broad bases tend to distort choices less and impose smaller excess burdens than taxes on more sharply defined bases. The more partial the tax, the easier it is to avoid. An important part of the logic behind the tax reforms of 1986 was that broader bases and lower rates reduce the distorting effects of the tax system and minimize excess burdens.[7]

How Large Are Excess Burdens?

It is possible to approximate the size of excess burdens if we know something about how people respond to price changes. Look at the demand curve in Figure 18.9. The product originally sold for a price, P_0, equal to marginal cost which, for the sake of simplicity, we assumed was constant. As you recall, when input prices are determined in competitive markets, marginal cost reflects the real value of the resources used in producing the product. Wages, for example, reflect the marginal revenue product of labor; the cost of capital reflects the marginal revenue product of capital. That means that if $25.00 worth of resources flow out of the sector represented in Figure 18.9, they will end up being used in other sectors to produce final products worth just $25.00 to consumers.

P_0 is a very good approximation of the value to society of one marginal unit of product X. Anyone who values it more highly has already bought it at P_0; anyone who values it at less than P_0 per unit will simply not buy it. But now along comes the government and imposes a tax at a rate t. The price of the product to consumers rises in the long run to $P_0(1+t)=P_1$. The higher price drives demanders to seek substitutes, and quantity demanded falls from X_0 to X_1.

In order to measure the total burden of the tax we need to recall the notion of *consumer surplus* from Chapter 6. At any price, some people pay less for a product than it

[7]Charles McClure, "Rationale Underlying the Treasury Proposals," *Economic Consequences of Tax Simplification*, Federal Reserve Bank of Boston (1986).

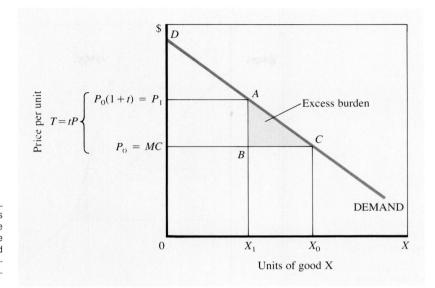

FIGURE 18.9

The Excess Burden of a Distorting Excise Tax

A tax that alters economic decisions imposes a burden that exceeds the amount of taxes collected. An excise tax that raises the price of a good above marginal cost drives some consumers to buy less desirable substitutes, reducing consumer surplus.

is worth to them. All we reveal when we buy a product is that it is worth at least the price being charged. For example, if only one unit of product X were auctioned, someone would pay a price close to D in Figure 18.9. By paying only P_0, that person got a "surplus" equal to $(D - P_0)$. The next demander is willing to pay a bit less, but that person still gets a significant "surplus" that is only slightly less than $(D - P_0)$. Moving down the demand curve, the person sitting on the demand curve at P_1 gets a surplus equal to $(P_1 - P_0)$ when the price is P_0. If we were to continue, we would discover that the total consumer surplus from the production of good X for sale at P_0 is just equal to the area of the large triangle DCP_0.

At the higher price, P_1, consumer surplus is reduced to DAP_1. The government collects revenues equal to tP_0 per unit times X_1 units, or the area P_1ABP_0, and there is a net loss to consumers equal to the area of ABC. To understand this, consider what happens if we begin at P_0 and slowly raise the price artificially. Quantity demanded declines as higher prices drive consumers to substitutes, and we move from X_0 down toward X_1. Resources—capital, land, and labor—are shifted out of the production of this good and into the production of other, *less desirable*, goods. As we move up the demand curve from C to A, the actual value of X to marginal buyers increases, as does the lost welfare per unit. The shaded triangle represents the cumulative loss in value to those consumers who would have bought more of X at the lower price.

Another way to see this "excess burden" is to divide consumers into just two groups: those who continue to buy X at the higher price, P_1, and those who shift to substitutes. Those who continue to buy X at the higher price lose surplus, but it goes to the government as the tax. The revenue to the government is exactly equal to the losses imposed on those who value X more highly than P_1. Those who shift away from X pay no tax, but they do bear losses, because they end up buying less desirable substitutes. Therefore, the total loss exceeds the revenue collected.

Excess Burdens and the Degree of Distortion   The size of the excess burden that results from a decision-distorting tax depends on the degree to which decisions change in response to it. In the case of an excise tax, consumer behavior is reflected in elasticity of demand. The more elastic the demand curve, the greater is the distortion caused by any

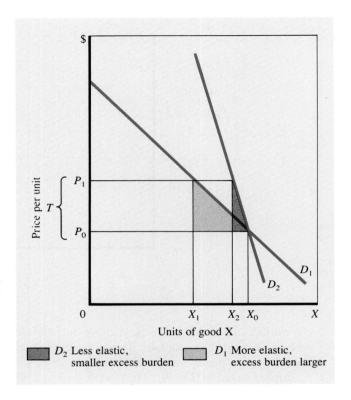

FIGURE 18.10

The Size of the Excess Burden of a Distorting Excise Tax Depends on the Elasticity of Demand

The size of the excess burden from a nonneutral tax depends on the degree to which decisions or behaviors change in response to it. For an excise tax, relevant consumer behavior is reflected in the elasticity of demand. An estimate of demand elasticity permits us to measure the rough size of the excess burden.

Principle of second best The fact that a tax distorts an economic decision does not always imply that such a tax imposes an excess burden. If previously existing distortions exist, such a tax may actually improve efficiency.

given tax rate. Figure 18.10 shows this effect clearly. The same tax, T, causes demand to drop less along demand curve D_2, and the resulting excess burden is smaller.

If demand were perfectly inelastic, no distortion would occur, and there would be no excess burden. The tax would simply extract part of the surplus being earned by consumers. That is why some economists favor uniform land taxes over other taxes. Land is in perfectly inelastic supply, and a uniform tax on all uses distorts economic decisions less than taxes levied on other factors of production that are in variable supply.

The Principle of Second Best   Now that we have established the connection between taxes that distort decisions and excess burdens, we have to go back and say *"but not always."* Nonneutral taxation is sometimes actually desirable when other distortions already exist in the economy. This is called the **principle of second best.** At least two kinds of circumstances favor nonneutral taxes: the presence of *externalities* and the presence of *other distorting taxes*.

We have already examined the case of externalities at some length in Chapter 16. If some activity by a firm or household imposes costs on society that are not considered by decision makers, then the households are likely to make bad, economically inefficient choices. Pollution is the classic example of an externality, but there are thousands of others. An efficient allocation of resources can be restored if a tax is imposed on the externality-generating activity that is exactly equal to the value of the damages caused by it. Such a tax forces the decision maker to consider the *full* economic cost of the decision.

Because taxing for externalities changes decisions that would otherwise be made, it does in a sense "distort" economic decisions. But its *purpose* is to force decision makers to consider real costs that they would otherwise ignore. In the case of pollution, for example, the distortion caused by a tax is desirable—it improves economic welfare. Instead of causing an excess burden, it results in a gain of efficiency.

A distorting tax can also improve welfare when there are other taxes present that already distort decisions. Suppose, for example, that there were only three goods, X, Y and Z. Suppose further that there was a 5 percent excise tax on both Y and Z. The taxes on Y and Z distort consumer decisions away from those goods and toward X. Imposing a similar tax on X reduces the distortion of the existing *system* of taxes. When consumers face equal taxes on all goods, they cannot avoid the tax by changing what they buy. Thus the distortion caused by imposing a tax on X corrects for a *preexisting distortion*—the taxes on Y and Z. Here, again, a nonneutral tax can improve economic welfare.

To see this, go back to the example described in Figures 18.7 and 18.8. Imposing the tax of 50 percent on the use of capital generated revenues of $4000 but imposed a burden of $6000 on consumers. But now a distortion exists. Consider what would happen if you now imposed a tax of 50 percent, or $1.00 per unit, on labor with the capital tax already in place. Such a tax would push our firms back toward the more efficient technology A. If you work it out, in fact, the new tax will generate a total revenue of $6000, but the added burden to consumers would be only $4000.

Optimal Taxation   The idea that taxes work together to affect behavior has led tax theorists to search for optimal taxation systems. Knowing how people will respond to taxes would allow us to design a system that would *minimize the overall excess burden*. For example, if we know the elasticity of demand for all traded goods, we can devise an optimal system of excise taxes that are heaviest on those goods with relatively inelastic demands and lightest on those goods with relatively elastic demands.

The information required to implement the optimal tax systems that have been suggested, however, makes them impractical. This point brings us full circle, and we end up where we started, with the principle of neutrality.

Principle of neutrality   A tax that distorts economic decisions for no good reason is less efficient than a tax that is more neutral.

The Principle of Neutrality   Taxes that affect economic decisions *for no good reason* impose burdens on society that exceed the revenues collected by the tax. The size of the excess burden imposed by a tax depends on the degree to which decisions change in response to it. Taxes that adhere to the **principle of neutrality**, that is, that are neutral with respect to economic decisions, are preferred on grounds of efficiency. Broad-based taxes are more difficult to avoid than narrow-based taxes, and low rates distort less than high rates.

BEYOND THIS CHAPTER

With this chapter, we complete our picture of the role of government in a market economy. One chapter can do nothing but introduce the basic subject matter of public finance and present a sampling of the issues that it deals with. The field is very broad. Thousands of books and journal articles have been written on the economics of taxation. This chapter is also the first of several that survey some of the special fields of applied microeconomics. We turn next to the specialty of labor economics.

SUMMARY

1. Public finance is one of the major subfields of applied economics. A major interest within this subfield is the economics of taxation.
2. Taxes are paid by people. Taxes may be imposed on transactions, institutions, property, and all kinds of other things, but in the final analysis, taxes are paid by individuals or households.
3. The base of a tax is the measure, or value, upon which the tax is levied. The rate structure of a tax determines the portion of the base that must be paid in tax.
4. If the burden of a tax rises as a percentage of income as income rises, the tax is said to be progressive. If the burden of a tax falls as a percentage of income as income rises, the tax is called regressive.
5. There is much disagreement over what constitutes a fair tax system. One theory contends that people should bear tax burdens in proportion to the benefits that they receive from government expenditures. Another contends that people should bear tax burdens in line with their ability to pay.
6. The three leading candidates for best tax base are income, consumption, and wealth.
7. As a result of behavioral changes and market adjustments, tax burdens are often not borne by those initially responsible for paying them. When we speak of the incidence of a tax, we are referring to the ultimate distribution of its burden.
8. Taxes change behavior, and changes in behavior can affect supply and demand in markets, causing prices to adjust. When prices change in input markets or in output markets, some people may be made better off and some may be made worse off.
9. Most economists conclude that most of the payroll tax in this country is probably borne by workers. Under this assumption, payroll taxes are regressive.
10. The ultimate burden of the corporate tax appears to depend on several factors. One generally accepted study shows that the owners of corporations, proprietorships, and partnerships all bear the burden of the tax in rough proportion to profits, even though it is directly levied only on corporations; that wage effects are small; and that excise effects are roughly neutral. However, there is much room for debate about who the corporate tax hurts.
11. Taken together under a reasonable set of assumptions about tax shifting, federal, state, and local taxes in the United States are either roughly proportional or very mildly progressive.
12. When taxes distort economic decisions, they impose burdens that in aggregate exceed the revenue collected by the government. The amount by which the burden of a tax exceeds the revenue collected by the government is called the excess burden. The size of excess burdens depends on the degree to which economic decisions are changed by the tax. The most efficient taxes are broad-based, relatively neutral taxes.
13. If previous distortions, such as externalities exist, properly designed taxes, taken by themselves, may impose less burden than they generate in revenues, because they correct for an existing inefficiency.

REVIEW CONCEPTS

tax base   434
rate structure   435
proportional   435
progressive   435
regressive   435
benefits-received principle   438
ability-to-pay principle   438

incidence of a tax   442
sources side/uses side   442
tax shifting   443
excess burden   450
principle of second best   454
principle of neutrality   455

REVIEW QUESTIONS

1. Lester Thurow, Dean of the Sloan School of Management at MIT, once proposed that the best tax system would be a combination of a personal consumption tax and a wealth tax. Such a combination avoids double taxation but gets at accumulated ability to pay. Either defend or rebut his position.

2. A citizens group in the Pacific Northwest has the following statement in its charter:

Our goal is to insure that large, powerful corporations pay their fair share of taxes in this country.

To implement this goal, they have recommended and lobbied for an increase in the corporation income tax and a reduction in the individual income tax. Would you support such a petition? Explain your logic.

3. For each of the following say whether you agree or disagree and why:

a. "An income tax is a double tax on saving, but an income tax and a wealth tax combined is a triple tax on saving."

b. "Economic theory predicts unequivocally that a payroll tax reduction will increase the supply of labor."

c. "Corporation income taxes levied on a monopolist are likely to be regressive, because the monopoly can simply pass on their burden to consumers."

4. In calculating total faculty compensation, the administration of Doughnut University includes payroll taxes (social security taxes) paid as a *benefit* to faculty. After all, those tax payments are earning future entitlements for the faculty under social security. The American Association of University Professors, however, has argued that, far from being a benefit, the employer's contribution is simply a tax, and that its burden actually falls on the faculty, even though it is paid by the university. Discuss both sides of this debate.

5. Suppose that the Federated Perkland Islands had only a single tax, a stiff tax on entertainment and recreation including restaurant meals, disco dances, concerts, country club memberships, health clubs, and the like. Would such a tax impose an excess burden? Explain your answer carefully.

A Perki senator has proposed replacing the single tax with a broad-based retail sales tax on all goods and services. Would you support such a move? Why or why not?

6. What reforms would you suggest in the current structure of taxes in the United States?

APPENDIX TO CHAPTER 18
The Tax Reform Act of 1986

On August 18, 1986, a House-Senate Conference Committee gave final approval to a bill that would later that fall be enacted as the Tax Reform Act of 1986. This legislation contained the most sweeping reforms to the U.S. tax system ever enacted. This appendix will describe its major provisions and some of the economic arguments for and against them. The act made changes in both the individual income tax and the corporation income tax. Before we discuss specific changes, we need to describe these taxes in a bit more detail than we have so far.

The Individual Income Tax

Every spring, Americans go through a ritual. People who earn wages or salaries receive a W-2 form from their employers, interest earners receive 1099s from their banks. Most of us collect our papers and sit down to fill out our tax returns for the Internal Revenue Service. Due on April 15th, the tax return (Form 1040 or 1040EZ) reports all the income subject to the tax that we have earned during the previous calendar year and tells the IRS how much total tax we owe. Because taxes are withheld from wages during the year and sent to the IRS by employers, most people actually pay only a small amount or get a refund on April 15.

The *tax code* is a set of rules that are built into the forms that you must fill out for the IRS. These rules in essence determine how much you end up paying. The tax code actually runs to several thousand pages, and highly trained tax lawyers frankly admit that neither they nor anyone else fully understands all of it.

Many of the specific rules establish the kinds of income to be taxed. These rules define the "base" of the tax. While most forms of income are included and subject to tax, many are not. In 1984 total personal income in the United States was $3.11 trillion. Of that amount, $2.23 trillion was reported to the IRS on tax returns. Many forms of income do not have to be reported at all. Taxable income in 1984 was $1.70 billion. Thus only about 54 percent of total personal income was actually taxed.

Between total income and taxable income, a number of items get subtracted off. There are four major categories: exclusions, adjustments, exemptions, and deductions. Exclusions are forms of income that are simply not subject to the tax and are often not even reported. Two important examples of exclusions are interest earned on state and local bonds and employers' contributions to pension funds.

Adjustments to income include contributions that you make to special accounts called Individual Retirement Accounts. Before the act, there were other adjustments, including one for married couples with two earners, another for moving expenses and for other expenses that you might have to make in connection with your work. If you are a salesperson, for example, you may have to travel around a lot and pay for it out of your pocket.

Exemptions are a flat dollar amount that you subtract from your income. Everybody gets one. Married couples get two. You also get an additional one for each dependent child, if you are blind, or if you are over 65. As of 1989, for each exemption you can subtract $2000 from your income before the tax rates are applied.

Deductions are next. Taxpayers are entitled to subtract a standard deduction, or they can itemize certain expenses and subtract the total from income if it is greater than the standard deduction. Itemized deductions include extraordinary health care expenses, most state and local taxes paid, including income and property taxes, interest expenses paid on mortgages, charitable contributions, and other specific items. In 1988 the standard deduction was $3000 for individuals and $5000 for married couples. This amount will be indexed upward with inflation every year.

One other way that households have reduced their incomes for tax purposes is to participate in "tax shelters." A tax shelter is an enterprise that may earn a cash profit, but which on paper looks as if it is earning losses. Those losses can be subtracted from income when you figure your taxes. There is nothing illegal about this at all. The rules were actually designed to encourage people to engage in the shelter activities.

Most shelters earn paper losses because of the way capital costs are accounted for. The way a firm, whether a proprietorship, a partnership, or a corporation, calculates its profits is to add up revenues and then subtract costs. When a firm buys a capital asset such as a machine or building, the cost must be taken over a number of years, presumably as it wears out or loses value. These capital cost deductions are called *depreciation expenses*. Ideally, a machine that wears out and loses its value in three years will be depreciated over three years. While equipment actually does wear out and lose its value, buildings often do not. In fact, many real estate investments actually increase in value over the years. Nonetheless, owners are allowed to subtract depreciation expenses, even if they are not occurring. These are often large, and they make the enterprise look as if it is suffering losses. These losses "shelter" other forms of income, because they are subtracted before taxes are calculated.

Once everything is subtracted—exclusions, adjustments, exemptions, and deductions—what remains is called *taxable income*. Taxable income is subjected to progressive marginal rates, and the results are sent to the IRS. (We discuss the rate structure below.)

Individual Income Tax Changes in the 1986 Act

The basic idea of the recent tax reform was threefold: (1) to simplify the system so that people can understand it better, (2) to reduce the marginal rates to increase the incentive to work, save, and invest, and (3) to make more income subject to the tax in order to compensate for the revenue loss from the lower rates and reduce the distortion of economic decisions. Some of these objectives were achieved, while debates about others will continue for years to come. The approach was to try to broaden the base by cutting the number of things that people can subtract. With fewer things to subtract, the law is simpler, and revenue goals can be achieved with lower rates.

Many people felt the act would never pass because of the politically powerful special interests that benefited from the prereform provisions. For example, the law contains some severe restrictions on tax shelters, and the real estate industry opposed these provisions with a huge lobbying campaign. To the surprise of many people, Representative Dan Rostenkowski and Senator Eugene Packwood produced a bill that actually cut deeply into many, but certainly not all, of the special privileges built into the system.

Here are a few of the major changes.

1. A significant increase was made in the standard deduction and the personal exemption. These reduce taxes significantly at the very bottom of the income distribution. For example, in 1986 the personal exemption was only $1050 and the standard deduction was $2300 for a single person. Thus the tax rates began to bite in at just over $3000 of income for a single person. The personal exemption and standard deduction now total $5000, and because of some other less important provisions, the income where an individual would begin to pay taxes is a bit higher than that. Estimates are that these provisions removed 4.8 million poor people from the tax roles.

2. Marginal tax rates were drastically reduced. In 1978 there were 26 marginal income brackets. The first $1000 dollars of taxable income was taxed at 14 percent for all taxpayers, regardless of income. Income over $200,000 was taxed at 70 percent. Rate reduction began with the 1978 tax act, which cut the number of brackets to 16. The Economic Recovery Tax Act of 1981 kept the 16 brackets but cut the rates. The top rate, for example, was reduced to 50 percent. The 1986 act reduced the 16 brackets to two, and the rates to 15 percent on the first $17,850 for single persons ($29,750 for married couples) and 28 percent on income over that amount. (Table 18.2 described this.) (Actually, there is also a hidden bracket of 33 percent for incomes over $89,560 for single persons and over $149,250 for married couples.)

3. A number of provisions broadened the base. The ability to deduct losses from tax shelters was greatly reduced. Income from realized capital gains (for example, your profits when you sell a share of stock for more than you paid for it) is now taxed as ordinary income; before the act, 60 percent of any profit was simply excluded. All unemployment benefits are now subject to the tax. Sales taxes paid are no longer deductible. The category of "other itemized deductions" has been limited to the extent that they exceed 2 percent of income. Deductions for consumer interest paid was phased out. Scholarship and fellowship income previously excluded is now taxable. The two-earner deduction was eliminated. And the list goes on. Many other provisions also had the same base-broadening effect.

Overall, these provisions led to a decrease in revenue from the income tax. Because the overall bill was meant to be revenue neutral, these lost revenues had to be made up somewhere. The place they found was the corporate income tax.

Changes in the Corporate Income Tax

After all the changes are phased in, the act will have increased corporate taxes by about $120 billion and reduced individual income taxes by about the same amount. While average corporate rates have increased as a result of the new law, marginal corporate tax rates were cut. Although corporate rates are progressive, most corporate income is subject to the top rate. In 1986 the top corporate rate was 46 percent. The top corporate rate as of 1989: 34 percent.

If rates were cut, how did corporate tax receipts increase? Two major provisions account for most of the increase. First was the repeal of the investment tax credit(ITC). Prior to 1987, corporations (and proprietorships and partnerships as well) were permitted to take up to 10 percent of the total amount of every investment that they made and subtract it from their tax liability. Suppose, for example, that a firm was considering a $10 million new branch plant. With the ITC, such a firm, under the old law, could reduce the taxes it owed the government by $1 million dollars. Thus the ITC effectively reduced the "price" of capital by up to 10 percent. This measure was introduced by the Kennedy administration in the early 1960s to stimulate investment.

Another major provision of the 1986 law that led to increased corporate taxes was to lengthen substantially the period over which capital assets can be depreciated. Longer depreciation periods mean that the expenses taken for capital depreciation in any given period are lower, and thus profits on the books are higher. Also, corporations, like individuals, now have to pay taxes on capital gains as if they were ordinary income.

Was the Tax Reform Act Good or Bad for the Economy?

As with any major piece of legislation, there is some good news and some bad news. Some economists are wildly enthusiastic about the act, hailing it as the best piece of tax legislation in history. Others would have voted against it.

Most economists agree that the lower tax rates are good for incentives. Recall from our discussion of behavior earlier in this chapter that it is marginal rates that affect decisions that people make. Lower rates should encourage people to enter the labor force and work longer hours, because the lower rates effectively increase the after-tax marginal wage rate. Similarly, lower taxes should increase the incentive to save, because income from savings will be subject to lower taxes. And by eliminating consumer interest from the base, consumers are discouraged from borrowing.

There is some disagreement about whether the new tax system is more or less progressive than the old. Certainly the personal income tax rates are far less progressive than they were. Offsetting that, however, is the fact that the increase in the standard deduction and personal exemption removed 4.8 million poor from the rolls. Besides, many of the base-expanding provisions—the restriction of tax shelter income, for example, will have their biggest impacts on the rich. Thus, although the rich get lower rates, they must pay on a larger portion of their incomes. Overall, over 81 percent of the population will pay less income tax.

The progressivity issue, however, is further complicated by the increase in the corporation tax. If we accept the view that the burden of the corporation tax falls on capital income, then the $120 billion increase in the corporation tax falls largely on higher incomes. This would make the whole package look quite progressive. Not all tax economists are willing to make this assumption, however.

Another plus is that base broadening and elimination of shelters makes the tax system more neutral with respect to economic decisions. The broader the base, the fewer the avenues that people have down which to escape taxes. The ability to shelter income with losses generated by overly generous depreciation rules meant that many major investments were made, not because they were likely to be profitable but rather because of the tax losses that they promised to generate. Shopping centers, office buildings, and even hotels sit with very high vacancy rates in part because of this.

One major criticism of the act is that its provisions substantially reduced the incentive to invest. The repeal of the investment tax credit, the nonpreferential treatment of capital gains, and the new depreciation rules cut the return to investment sharply. Lower investment will reduce the rate of growth in the longer run. Defenders of the act reply that the old system *over*subsidized capital investment, and that the new law is less of an interference than the old. Critics rejoin that capital accumulation *should* be subsidized in the name of economic growth.

Finally, almost everyone agrees that the law does little to simplify the code. It is still a difficult exercise for most families to file an accurate income tax return. Final judgment about the effects of the act will wait until we see how people and businesses respond to it.

19 The Economics of Labor Markets and Labor Unions

In 1987, 114.2 million people in the United States, out of a labor force of 121.6 million, held jobs. Somehow 114.2 million people sort themselves out into thousands of different occupations and particular jobs, performing an enormous variety of tasks in exchange for wages that range from a few dollars an hour to millions of dollars a year. Some have little or no formal education, while others have invested many years and thousands of dollars in education and training. Some work only part time, while others hold more than one job. Some large employers hire hundreds of people each year into well-defined jobs with specific job descriptions. Small firms, on the other hand, may hire only one or two people every few years for very loosely defined jobs. And of course many people work for themselves.

This chapter explores the sorting process. The second of several chapters designed to survey some of the subfields of applied economics, this chapter is about "labor economics," and it addresses a number of important questions. How do people and jobs get matched? How are wage rates determined? Under what circumstances do people get trained? When do firms hire? What happens when people lose their jobs?

These questions, by and large, are answered in what we refer to collectively as "the labor market," but in fact there are many labor markets. There is a market for professional basketball players, a market for lawyers, a market for carpenters, and a market for unskilled workers. Each market operates under a different set of rules and through a different set of institutions, but the basic forces that drive all of them are the same.

Several earlier chapters have touched on the economics of labor markets. In Chapter 6 we looked at some of the decisions that lie behind the labor supply curve; in Chapter 10 we discussed the factors that determine the demand for labor; in Chapter 17 we listed several reasons for the inequality of wages. After a quick review, this chapter discusses the workings of labor markets in a more systematic fashion.

In the last part of the chapter, we take up *labor unions*. Labor unions have existed for about two hundred years now, and their effects are the subject of considerable controversy. Do they succeed in raising wages? Do they create unemployment? What is their impact on productivity? Almost everyone has a strong opinion about unions. Some say they are responsible for all of our economic woes; others believe that they are the only hope for economic justice.

COMPETITIVE LABOR MARKETS: A REVIEW

A brief review of a few key concepts should set up our examination of how labor markets function in theory.

The Demand for Labor   Remember that firms make several decisions simultaneously: they decide how much to produce, they choose among alternative techniques of production, and they decide how much of each input to demand. If they have market power, they also decide what price to charge. In making these decisions, they use information from product markets, from input markets, and from their knowledge of technology.

The concept of *marginal revenue product* (MRP) is central to an understanding of the demand for labor. The **marginal revenue product of labor** (MRP_L) is the additional revenue that a firm would take in by hiring one additional unit of labor, *ceteris paribus*. Because labor is presumably productive, hiring more yields more product. The product produced by one marginal unit of labor is called the *marginal physical product of labor* or simply *marginal product of labor*. To turn that product into revenue, it must, of course, be sold. Product prices, as you know, are determined in output markets, and purely competitive firms take them as given. Thus the added revenue from hiring one more unit of labor is the marginal product of labor (MP_L) times the price of output: $MP_L \times P_X$.[1]

Figure 19.1 graphs a firm's decision to hire in a competitive labor market. The market-determined wage rate is W^*, and the firm can hire all the labor it wants at that

Marginal revenue product of labor   *The additional revenue that a firm will take in by hiring an additional unit of labor. An added hour of labor will, presumably, lead to additional output which will be sold in the market. Marginal revenue product is equal to the marginal physical product of labor times the price of output.*

FIGURE 19.1
Demand for Labor in Competitive Markets Depends on Labor's Productivity

Competitive firms will hire labor as long as marginal revenue product of labor ($MRP_L = MP_L \times P_X$) exceeds the market wage. With only one variable factor of production, the marginal revenue product curve *is* the demand curve for labor.

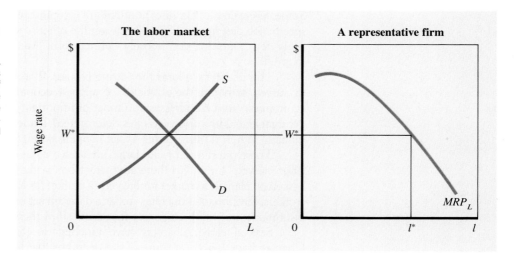

[1]For firms in imperfect markets where output price is set by the firm, marginal revenue product is equal to marginal physical product times marginal revenue—$MRP_L = MP_L \times MR$. MRP is still the revenue gained by hiring an added unit of labor.

wage. Thus we can think of W^* as the marginal cost of a unit of labor. Firms will hire as long as the marginal gains in revenue from hiring additional units of labor (MRP_L) exceed W^*. When labor is the only variable input, the MRP curve is the firm's demand curve for labor. When more than one factor of production can vary, the demand curve is more complicated, but essentially still the same. (This is explained in Chapter 10).

The point is that demand for labor depends on what labor can produce *and* how much its product sells for in output markets. The *physical* product of labor is technologically determined. Given the state of technology, the machinery and other equipment available, and the level of effort required to produce something, there is a limit to what one unit of labor can produce. But the *revenue* product of labor depends on the *market value* of its product; if no one wants to buy what it produces, what it produces has no market value.

The Supply of Labor Households supply labor. In any given labor market, the supply of labor depends on some factors that households do control and some that they do not.

First, each household member must decide whether to work. The alternatives to working for a wage are either working for no pay or enjoying one's leisure. In this regard, households face a trade-off. Working yields a wage as well as some nonpecuniary rewards and/or costs—you may like the working environment and get a lot of satisfaction from being creative or productive, or you may hate your job because it is dull, or even dangerous. The opportunity cost of working, however, is either the value of what can be produced using the same time *or* the value of leisure. If you are not in the labor force working for a wage, you can paint your house or sleep in the sun. Both of these alternatives have a value that you must weigh in a decision to take a job.

Beyond this basic decision to work or not to work, a more complicated set of choices and constraints comes into play. Not everyone can supply his or her labor in every market. A 110-pound man would probably not offer his services to the National Football League as a player. A carpenter with no medical training would be breaking the law if she sold herself as a surgeon. Each market requires its own set of skills that workers are either born with or that they must acquire.

Human capital   The stock of knowledge, skills, and talents that people possess; it can be inherited or acquired through education and training.

Human Capital The stock of knowledge, skills, and talents that human beings possess by nature or by nurture is called **human capital**. When people who have special skills or knowledge earn higher wages, a part of their wage can be thought of as a return on human capital. Human capital can be inborn or acquired.

Both households and firms invest in human capital. The principal form of *human capital investment* financed primarily by *households* is **education**. When parents send their children to school, they are investing in human capital that they hope will pay dividends later on. The principal form of human capital investment primarily financed by *firms* is **on-the-job training**. Presumably, training workers raises their productivity and yields dividends to the firms that provide such training.

On the job training   The principle form of human capital investment undertaken by firms.

Governments also invest in human capital. Federal and state governments have sponsored and subsidized numerous training programs over the years. Local governments are responsible for public elementary and secondary education, state governments have built great state university systems, and the federal government provides billions in student financial aid. Some argue that public health expenditures are also essentially human capital investment. A healthy labor force is a prerequisite for a productive labor force.

The Equilibrium Wage Wage rates in competitive markets are determined by supply and demand. As in any other market, if quantity demanded exceeds quantity supplied, wages should rise until the quantity demanded and the quantity supplied are equal. The

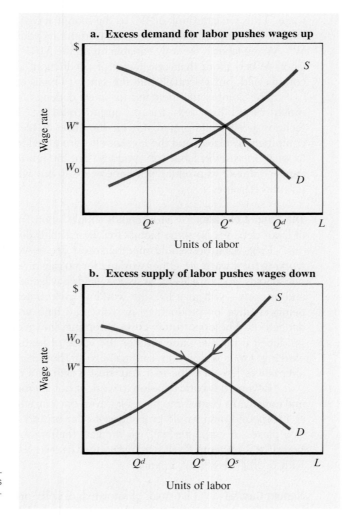

FIGURE 19.2
Excess Demand and Supply in
Labor Markets

When excess demand exists, wages
will generally rise. When excess supply exists, wages will generally fall.

higher wages that result should then both reduce the quantity demanded and stimulate
the quantity supplied. Part of Figure 19.2 shows excess demand for labor, and here, as
you see, the initial wage of W_0 rises until the market clears at W^*.

When there is an excess supply of labor, we would expect to see market wages fall.
At W_0 in part 6 of Figure 19.2, quantity supplied exceeds quantity demanded, and this
creates a downward pressure on wages. If wages fall, quantity demanded will increase, and
quantity supplied will fall until an equilibrium is restored at W^*.

Disequilibria sometimes persist, however. Minimum wage laws may prevent wages
from falling in response to a surplus. Union contracts may hold wages up beyond where
they would settle in the absence of a union. Even in competitive markets, some prices are
slow to adjust in response to surpluses. Downwardly inflexible, or "sticky," wages have
been a puzzle since John Maynard Keynes called attention to the problem in the 1930s. If
you stop and think about it for a minute, you will see that involuntary unemployment
would not exist if wages adjusted completely whenever there was an excess supply of
labor. This is a very important topic in macroeconomics, as you will see.

THE LABOR MARKET IN ACTION

So far we have dealt with the labor market in the abstract. A better way to grasp the basic economic logic of labor markets, however, is to work through a number of concrete examples of the theory as it applies in typical everyday decisions.

Should I Go to School?   Cathy graduated from Liberty State College with an Associate Degree in June two years ago. Currently she works as a technical assistant in a small firm that trains people to work with personal computers. She likes the job, but she feels stuck; there isn't any room for her to move up in the company without more training. In her present job, she makes $7.50 per hour.

A technical school located near her home is offering a one-year program leading to a certificate of proficiency in two computer languages. With this training, which would move her up a notch in the labor market, she is all but assured of a job paying $9.50 per hour. But tuition at the school is $5000, and students must attend full time. If going to school full time for a year means that Cathy must give up her job, she will incur an opportunity cost of $12,000 in take-home pay ($15,000 less taxes of $3000) in addition to the $5000 tuition. If the books and materials that she needs for the program come to $1000, the full cost of a year's training is $18,000. Cathy must decide if the investment is worth making.

Cathy is considering an investment in *human capital*. The training will increase her productivity and thus her wages in the future. Table 19.1 shows some simple calculations. If we assume that Cathy works 40 hours per week and 50 weeks per year, her wages will increase by $4000 each year. To get a net return, we must remember to subtract taxes. At her income level, the *marginal tax rate*, that is, the rate applicable to marginal dollars of income, is about 25 percent.[2] This figure includes social security (7.51%), federal income

TABLE 19.1

Analysis of a Decision to Attend a Training Program for One Year

Annual return to investment
   Wage rate with no training = $7.50 per hour
   Wage rate with training   = $9.50 per hour

Assuming 40 hours per week, 50 weeks per year		
Annual pay with no training ($7.50×40×50)	= $15,000	
Annual pay with training ($9.50×40×50)	= 19,000	
Gross increase ($2.00×40×50)	= +$4,000	
Marginal tax rate = .25		
Tax on increase	$1,000	
Net annual increase in pay	$3,000	

Cost of training
   Tuition   5,000
   Books and materials   1,000
   Forgone wages, one year $12,000
    (After taxes: total taxes = $3000)
    Total Cost $18,000

Annual return on investment   3,000

$$\frac{3,000}{\$18,000} = 16.7\%$$

---

[2]Notice that her *average tax rate* is only 20 percent. She is currently paying a total of $3000 in taxes on an income of $15,000. What matters when we calculate her gains from the new job *at the margin* is her *marginal tax rate*, which is 25 percent.

taxes (15 percent), and a city income tax (2.5%). (There are no state income taxes in her state.) After taxes, then, Cathy's income will be $3000 a year higher if she gets the training.

If we simplify and assume that these flows will continue into the future—that is, that they will stay the same in "real," or inflation-adjusted, dollars—then her investment will yield 16.7% per year in real terms. Whether that is a "good" return depends on the market. In 1987 long-term bonds yielded only 9 percent *before* taking inflation into account. Cathy's expected return is certainly better than that on a savings account.

But there is more to Cathy's situation than this. For one thing, we have only counted costs and benefits measured in actual dollars. When individuals make such decisions, they usually add other costs and benefits into their calculations. Some people hate school and can't stand to study; that adds to the cost of the investment. At school, however, they might make valuable contacts, and at least they can use the school's placement service to get new job interviews. And the higher-paying job might offer intangible psychological rewards and nicer people to work with. All of these benefits would add to the yield of the investment.

Often these "utility" gains and losses dominate the pecuniary costs and benefits. Someone might decide to pursue a Ph.D. in classics even if the probability of landing a good faculty position in the field was very low. The yield on such an investment would lie entirely in psychological rewards.

For another thing, this simple example shows that *taxes* and *financial aid* affect the yields of different courses of action and have an impact on decisions. If, for example, Cathy received a $5000 tuition scholarship, even without any extra money for room and board, it would reduce the cost of her investment considerably—to $13,000. This raises the yield on the investment to 23 percent ($3000/$13,000), and that might well tip the balance in favor of school.

A cut in taxes would have the conflicting effects of increasing the cost of the training while increasing the net benefits. Cathy would sacrifice more take-home pay to attend school, but she would get to keep more of the $4000 annual wage increase in the foreseeable future. The net effect will probably be to increase the return on an investment made now. See if you can show that reducing both average and marginal tax rates to 15 percent would increase the yield to 18.1%.

What Does McDonald's Pay?   At two locations about 40 minutes apart in the Boston area, McDonald's hires workers at very different wage rates. At one franchise, a small sign on the counter reads "Help wanted, full or part time." If you ask about a job, however, you will find that they have only one part-time opening, and that the wage rate offered is the minimum wage, $3.35 per hour. At the other location, a large sign says "Full-time or part-time positions available, day or night shifts, excellent benefits and $7.00 per hour." This location has six openings.

Why would one restaurant pay wages nearly twice as high as an identical place with identical jobs in the same metropolitan area? The franchise owner simply finds that she has no applicants at lower wages, and even at the higher wage rates, she has a very difficult time keeping her available positions filled.

Clearly the two restaurants are buying labor in different labor markets. If people could move at no cost from one point to another, such wage differences would disappear. But there are costs. Neither of these restaurants is accessible by public transportation. Thus to take a job at one of them, you must live nearby or have a car. Restaurants such as McDonald's draw much of their labor from the supply of high-school students who want to work part time. Most of them don't have cars. The high-wage franchise is on a major highway at some distance from local high schools and residential areas; the low-wage franchise is in the center of a town.

Other factors as well probably affect the available labor supplies at the two locations. The median income of the four towns surrounding the high-wage franchise is 50 percent higher than the median income of the four towns surrounding the low-wage franchise. To the extent that the labor supply is made up of students, parents' income may well have an effect. Higher-income families may spend some of their money buying leisure for their children. Many lower-income families expect older children to contribute to the family income.

The data support this argument. In one of the lower-income towns, 82 percent of all high-school students held at least one part-time job during the school year. In one of the high-income towns, only 24 percent of high-school students held part-time jobs.

In the high-wage area, the demand for labor in general is also higher. A number of major employers relatively close by pay high wages and hire part-time workers. In addition, workers, whether or not they are students, are more likely to have cars in the high-wage area. Cars give them the ability to search for work over a wider geographical area.

This example illustrates at least three important points. First, labor supply depends on a number of factors including wage rates, nonlabor income, and wealth. Second, individual firms have very little control over the market wage; firms are forced to pay the wage that is determined by the market. Finally, because people cannot be moved free of charge, and because people do not reside at their work places—as capital does—there is an important spatial dimension to labor markets. Different supply and demand conditions can and do prevail at different geographical locations. This is true across regions as well as within cities. Labor markets in different regions of the country—Northeast, South, and so forth—are very different.

Should I Stay In or Drop Out?   David was a highly paid young lawyer with a major Chicago firm. Three years ago he made partner, and his share of the firm's earnings last year was over $150,000. This year he resigned, sold his North Side condominium, and moved to Jackson, Wyoming, where he bought a small restaurant and a cabin near the edge of the Grand Teton National Park. The best he can hope to earn from the restaurant is about $20,000 per year, and even that is an optimistic forecast.

Was this an irrational thing for David to do? If you add up the dollars and calculate the pecuniary gains and losses, as we did for Cathy, he is giving up a great deal. Economic theory, however, in no way suggests that such a decision is irrational. David made his decision to accept a lower pecuniary income in exchange for a number of things from which he derives utility. No two people have the same set of preferences. The hectic life of a big city may have been a significant cost to him. The beauty of Wyoming and the climate may be invaluable benefits. He may like to ski, or he might have simply wanted to buy more leisure time.

The critical point is that preferences play a very important role in the decisions we make about labor supply, as well as in the decisions we make about what to consume. As you saw at the beginning of this chapter, there are 111 million jobholders in the United States. Every one of them has a unique set of talents and preferences. Every one of them has made a different set of decisions about investing in human capital. Those differences help to explain the way people end up being sorted out across jobs.

A Word of Caution   Do not assume, however, that the importance of individual preferences and choices makes generalization about labor market behavior impossible. An enormous amount of empirical work has documented that labor behaves in predictable ways in response to incentives. The manager of the McDonald's franchise in the high-wage area got a response by *raising* wages, not by *lowering* them. People with high nonwage incomes supply less labor than people with low nonwage incomes.

The fact that labor does respond to incentives is important for public policy. In fact, one of the central themes in the "supply side" economic policies of the Reagan administration was that workers would respond to higher after-tax wages by supplying more labor and working harder.

Let us now turn to a more detailed discussion of several important public policy issues that involve the labor market.

LABOR MARKETS AND PUBLIC POLICY

One of the basic beliefs of the Reagan administration from the very beginning in 1981 was that high rates of taxation were at the root of the economic problems faced by the United States during the 1970s. High tax rates had reduced the incentive to work, save, and invest, it was said. If only tax rates went down, increasing take-home pay, more people would go to work, people already working would work harder, and more investment and capital formation would take place. All of this would expand the *supply* of goods and services and that, in turn, would help reduce unemployment and inflation simultaneously.

Taxes and Labor Supply

Theoretical Effects of Taxes on Labor Supply   These principles were subsequently embodied in the Economic Recovery Tax Act passed by Congress in 1981. This act cut individual income tax rates across the board and changed a number of important provisions of the corporation income tax that substantially reduced the burden of taxes on corporations. The same argument underlay the continuing tax reform debates that climaxed in the substantial changes to the tax code enacted in 1986. (These changes were described in the appendix to Chapter 18.) The President's reform proposals in May of 1985 put the logic of this thinking explicitly: "By taxing workers' earnings at excessively high rates . . . [the current system] . . . discourages work . . . and prevents workers from reaching their full potential."[3]

The tax cuts proposed for individuals and families were designed to increase the supply of labor. But careful thought shows that tax cuts could increase *or decrease* labor supply. Nobody disagrees with the fact that reducing taxes on income increases the "net wage." The debatable issue is, instead, What is the likely impact of higher net wages on the supply of labor?

As you recall from Chapter 6, higher wages have both a **substitution effect** and an **income effect**. Higher net wages increase the *price of leisure*. Increasing the price, or opportunity cost, of leisure unambiguously leads to additional work effort as people find an incentive to substitute other goods, bought with income from working, for leisure. But higher net wages also make people better off. By working the same number of hours, workers can earn more income. That added income can be spent on any combination of goods, *including leisure*. That is, because I have a higher income, I may decide to consume more leisure, with the effect that I actually work less.

Thus the income and substitution effects work in opposite directions. If the income effect is larger, higher net wages will actually *reduce* the supply of labor.

Substitution effect of higher wages   Consuming an additional hour of leisure means sacrificing the wages that would be earned by working. Thus, when the wage rate rises leisure becomes a more expensive commodity, and households may "buy" less of it. This means working more.

Income effect of higher wages   When wages rise, people are better off. If leisure is a normal good, they may decide to consume more of it and to work less. This is the income effect of the wage increase.

[3] "The President's Tax Proposals to the Congress for Fairness, Growth, and Simplicity" (May 1985).

Evidence of the Effects of Taxes on Labor Supply   Many studies have attempted to measure the effect of changes in net wages on labor supply. A recent survey looks at 28 studies of the behavior of adult males and 22 studies of the behavior of adult females.

Twenty of the 28 studies of men's labor-force behavior—over 70 percent—find that the overall wage elasticity is negative but small. A negative wage elasticity means that an *increase* in wages actually *reduces* labor supply, that is, the supply of labor curve for adult males seems to bend back (see Figure 19.3). The negative income effect is therefore larger than the positive substitution effect. All but two of the studies reported finding positive substitution effects and negative income effects.

Table 19.2 summarizes the results of the general survey. The overall average of wage elasticities for men is −.06. In other words, a net wage increase of 10 percent would reduce the supply of labor by 0.6%. Thus the tax cuts of the 1980s probably had a tiny negative effect on the supply of adult male labor.

The evidence shows the opposite effect for women, however. Of the 22 studies, all but two find a positive overall wage elasticity. This suggests that for women, the substitution effect of a wage increase dominates the income effect. The average of all 22 studies is +.94. In other words, an increase in net wages of 10 percent would *increase* the supply of adult female labor by a full 9.4%. All but one study of women finds a negative income effect, while all the studies surveyed that report substitution elasticities found them to be positive.

FIGURE 19.3

A Backward-Bending Labor Supply Curve

Above point *A*, higher wages actually reduce labor supply. Higher wages lead to higher incomes, and that can lead to additional consumption of leisure.

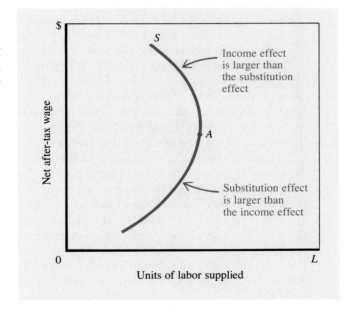

TABLE 19.2

Survey of Labor Supply Elasticity Studies

Evidence suggests that men's labor supply does not respond very much to changes in wage rates. In fact, higher wages actually seem to reduce men's labor supply slightly. Women seem to be much more responsive and, in contrast to men, work more when net wages rise.

	Total wage elasticity	Income elasticity	Substitution elasticity
Men (28 studies)	−.06	−.16	+.12
Women (22 studies)	+.94	−.17	+.80
Overall median	+.10	−.15	+.25
Upper quarter	+.38	−.03	
Lower quarter	−.07	−.27	

Source: Ingemar Hanson and Charles Stuart, "Tax Revenue and the Marginal Cost of Public Funds," *Journal of Public Economics* (August 1985).

The tax reforms of 1986 were designed, among other things, to have a maximum effect on the labor supply by *cutting marginal rates* but *expanding the tax base* at the same time. (Remember that the income tax base is the amount of income that is subject to taxation.) Suppose, for example, that your income is $200.00, you are allowed to deduct $100.00, and your tax rate is 10 percent. In this case your tax would be $10.00 (10 percent of $100.00), and you would take home $190.00. Now suppose that your tax rate was cut to 5 percent, but all your deductions were disallowed. You would still pay $10.00 in tax (5 percent of $200.00) and take home $190.00, but *marginal* dollars would be taxed at only 5 percent. If, for example, you decided to work overtime and earn $50.00 more, the new tax would take only $2.50, while the old tax would have taken $5.00.

Such a change in the tax system makes leisure more expensive relative to other goods, but it does not provide households with more income to buy leisure. Thus there is a substitution effect but no income effect to counteract it.

Welfare and Labor Supply

Every person makes two decisions which, taken together, determine the amount of labor that is supplied. First, everybody must decide whether to work. Those who do not work and are not looking for work are considered out of the labor force. Second, all those who do opt to participate in the labor force must decide how many hours to work. There has always been some worry that, by providing a "guaranteed" minimum standard of living, welfare programs available to those at the bottom of the income distribution give potential workers a disincentive to enter the labor force and go to work.

When we looked at the incentive effects of taxes, we discovered that income and substitution effects worked in opposite directions. Imposing a tax reduces income; if we think of leisure as a good, people will choose to buy less of it and will instead tend to work *more*. But it is also true that imposing a tax or increasing marginal tax rates reduces the opportunity cost, or price, of leisure. With leisure less expensive at the margin, people will tend to buy more of it and work *less*. Because the two effects counteract each other, theory cannot tell us a priori whether taxes will increase or decrease the supply of labor.

Income maintenance programs, however, produce income and substitution effects that work in the *same* direction. Theory predicts that both effects will reduce work effort and labor supply. Nearly all "income maintenance" programs are targeted on households with low incomes. Because households with higher incomes are ineligible, if a household increases its income by working, it will *lose* some or all of its income-maintenance benefits. The system, then, imposes an *implicit tax* on income from labor earned by those that are eligible for welfare.

Because of the number of income-tested programs, such as food stamps and public housing, this implicit tax on earnings can be quite high. If you earned $3000 and lost $2000 worth of benefits, your implicit tax rate would be 66 percent. For some people, the loss of benefits has been estimated at over 100 percent of marginal income earned.

If we think of loss of benefits as an implicit tax, we are led to the conclusion that income and substitution effects no longer offset each other. Comparing a world with an income maintenance program and a world with none, labor supply is likely to be lower in the presence of the program. Income maintenance programs obviously provide income, some of which is undoubtedly "spent" on leisure. Withdrawing benefits as income rises reduces the opportunity cost of leisure. Suppose, for example, that for every dollar of income I earn, I lose $.50 in benefits. If the hourly wage available is $4.00, then consuming an extra hour of leisure would cost me only $2.00; I give up $4.00 in income, but retain $2.00 in benefits. Thus the substitution effect also leads to a decrease in labor supply.

The question for policy makers is how much of a reduction in labor supply actually results from the programs that exist today. A major review of studies done in 1981 estimates that overall labor supply is 4.8% lower than it would be if all transfer programs were eliminated.[4] A more recent paper by two Harvard Professors concludes:

> There are undoubtedly some reductions in labor supply by female family heads induced by the current program. But, studies suggest that AFDC has had a modest effect in reducing work. Welfare mothers do not seem to be very sensitive to work incentives. Most recently, changes have been made in the AFDC program which essentially eliminate all work incentives. After four months, benefits are reduced at least one dollar for each dollar the woman earns over $30. Yet there apparently has been little change in the work of single mothers.[5]

This is an important conclusion. Budget cuts during the early 1980s indeed increased the rate at which benefits are withdrawn from welfare recipients. As a result, effective implicit tax rates are very high, and in many cases over 100 percent. If people continue to work in spite of such a large disincentive, there must be nonpecuniary rewards. It just may be that the work ethic is alive and in better health than many people seem to think.

Matching Jobs and Workers: The Costs, Benefits, and Mechanics of Search

One important fact about the labor market is that the flow of workers into and out of the labor force is continuous. Some enter school, some graduate, others are promoted, and as the population ages, some retire. Some people quit jobs, some are fired, and some take leaves or temporarily drop out of the labor force. At the same time, some firms expand and must hire new workers, changes in technology generate needs for new skills and make others obsolete, and some firms fall on hard times and must lay people off.

This constant flux results in a continuous process of sorting available workers among available jobs. New entrants expend time and effort searching for the best possible jobs; firms send out recruiters to schools or raid competing firms, often bringing in candidates from long distances. All of this works fairly imperfectly, however, and no matter how well it works, the distribution of skills and abilities among the available work force never corresponds exactly to the skills and abilities currently in demand.

Some people find it puzzling that the newspaper is full of available job listings while the headlines of the same paper lament very high unemployment rates. In the fall of 1982, when over 12 million people were unemployed, the daily papers carried pages and pages of available jobs. The problem is that the skills and abilities of available job seekers often do not match the needs of firms. And, of course, unemployment also has a regional dimension. Not only do the skills demanded not always match the skills supplied, the location of jobs (labor demand) does not always correspond to the location of job seekers. In 1987 just under 15 percent of the labor force in Louisiana was out of work, while in Massachusetts the unemployment rate was below three percent.

A person who is entering the labor force for the first time or who is considering a job change must carefully sift out the set of jobs that might be available given his or her skills,

[4]Sheldon Danziger, Robert Haveman, and Robert Plotnick, "How Income Transfer Programs Affect Work, Savings and the Income Distribution: A Critical Review," *Journal of Economic Literature* (September 1981).

[5]David Ellwood and Lawrence Summers, "Poverty in America: Is Welfare the Answer or the Problem?" National Bureau of Economic Research, working paper 1171 (October 1985).

experience, ability, and choice of location. People, even those without highly specialized skills, might have hundreds of possibilities open to them. The problem is finding out about them. Job searching is a process of gathering data.[6] By making phone calls, applying, being rejected, or perhaps even turning down job offers, job hunters find out about what is available and what they can expect. The **job search** is thus an extended process of "sampling."

> **Job search** *The process of gathering information about job availability and job characteristics.*

Thinking about the process of job search as information gathering is revealing. We all want the best available job, the one that matches our abilities and aspirations and pays the highest possible wage. For many people, there are readily available jobs that are not desirable; every college graduate could get a job working the counter at Burger Baby's, but most have higher expectations.

In theory, job hunting by an individual should continue as long as the expected gains from continuing the search exceed the costs of doing so. The *costs* of search are those things that are lost by continuing, the most important of which are *forgone earnings* and one's *time*. Other costs include such things as transportation, dressing for interviews, paper, postage, and telephone bills. The potential benefits from continued search depend on the job seeker's expectations. As the person gathers more and more information, expectations should become more and more accurate.

Public policy can affect the process of searching for a job in several ways, and it certainly has an impact on the efficiency of the economy. Consider, for example, the *unemployment insurance* program. Being laid off or spending an extended period of time unemployed—that is, actively looking for a job—can be a devastating experience. During periods of unemployment the suicide rate increases, the crime rate increases, and other indications of "pain" appear in the economy. To alleviate some of this pain, we have an unemployment compensation system that pays benefits to workers who lose their jobs. Although rules are set state by state, most states pay benefits for 20 weeks.

Unemployment benefits reduce the cost of the job search, and some researchers have argued that this results in *inefficiency*. Until recently, unemployment benefits were not taxable, and for some people they make up as much as 80 percent of lost wages. With the costs of looking for a job reduced in this fashion, people have an incentive to prolong the process. Prolonged job search drains tax revenues, artificially increases the unemployment rate, and keeps productive workers off the job.

Here is another clear example of a trade-off between efficiency and equity. The primary justification for the unemployment insurance program is *fairness*. It is designed to alleviate the pain of the unemployed and to ease their transition into a new job. It should also lead to *efficiency*. After all, society gains if people are matched with the right jobs. But because unemployment benefits lead to significantly reduced search costs, they may lead to extended search and waste as well.

Both the government and the marketplace have responded to this problem of providing information to job hunters. In recent years, employment agencies have become more and more in evidence. Many employers are making more frequent use of "headhunters," specialized firms that quietly and confidentially gather information from people interested in senior positions, people who are currently employed and do not want it known that they are looking around. This keeps costs low, both to the potential applicant and to society. Acutely aware of the unemployment problem, the government also sponsors a number of programs to help match jobs and workers. Most state

[6]The Bureau of Labor Statistics classifies as "unemployed" only those people who are actively searching for jobs. Those who stop searching are considered "out of the labor force."

unemployment agencies have job banks, and in many states unemployment recipients are required to check in and take job referrals.

One can think of job information as a *public good*. Having it produced and made available centrally is clearly a more efficient use of society resources than having thousands or even millions of workers out gathering the same information independently.

This brief discussion should give you an idea of the policy issues that labor economists concern themselves with. It is just a sampling, however. Note, for example, that we have not even mentioned labor unions. (We do describe them in the last part of this chapter.) The labor market is large and complex, and because the commodity being supplied and demanded is human energy, it has always been of central concern to policy makers.

OCCUPATIONS AND WAGES IN THE UNITED STATES

We have already said that the labor market is not one market—it is made up of many separate, but often closely related, markets. Computer programmers sell their labor in a separate market from high school math teachers, but some overlap exists between the two markets. When there is excess demand for computer programmers, for example, wages rise, and many high-school math teachers with computer skills may be attracted out of the teaching profession and into programming.

Nonetheless, a general sorting process is always going on. As a result, different occupational groups end up earning wages that differ, and the distribution of income reflects these differences. As you recall from Chapter 17, wages differ across jobs for two basic reasons: differences in jobs and differences in workers.

For example, in competitive markets, equilibrium wages are equal to the productivity of the marginal worker. And the product of a highly skilled machine operator is clearly worth more than that of an unskilled laborer. An unskilled laborer working on a routine set of tasks adds little to the final value of a product compared to the value added by a skilled machinist working with complex capital equipment. Workers who supply their labor in markets that demand unusual or highly developed skills should be expected to earn higher wages, *ceteris paribus*.

But wages are determined by the forces of supply *and* demand. At most major American universities, you must have a Ph.D. to be appointed to the faculty in Greek and Latin. The training and skills required are quite high. But because there are very few positions relative to the number of qualified applicants, wages for Greek and Latin professors have remained quite low. By the same token, during the 1970s, when plenty of qualified people were going into teaching at the elementary and high-school levels, wages fell substantially in real terms, that is, relative to inflation. In the last few years, however, many school systems have had difficulty filling open positions, particularly in math and science, and teachers' salaries have increased significantly.

Compensating differentials
Differences in wages that result from differences in working conditions. Risky jobs usually pay higher wages, and highly desirable jobs usually pay lower wages.

Some jobs are more desirable than others. Some jobs, like those in coal mining or heavy construction, involve higher levels of risk than others. Table 19.3 shows the number of lost workdays per one hundred employees for several industries. Coal miners lose nearly 100 days for every one lost by stockbrokers. Jobs that are more desirable and less risky tend to pay less than jobs that are less desirable and more risky. These wage differences are called **compensating differentials**.

TABLE 19.3

Lost Workdays Per Year Due to Occupational Injury or Illness Per 100 Fulltime Employees, 1980

One of the reasons that some jobs pay more than others is that they subject workers to risks.

Occupation	Workdays lost per year (per 100 employees)
Anthracite (coal) mining	276.7
Trucking and warehousing	187.9
Heavy construction contractors	117.6
Air transportation	105.0
Textile manufacturing	62.8
Retail trade	44.5
Services	35.8
Banking	8.1
Security, commodity brokers	3.1

Source: Statistical Abstract of the United States, 1986.

Recent Trends in Labor Force Behavior and Wages

Tables 19.4, 19.5, and 19.6 present some data on trends in the U.S. labor market and on actual wage rate and income differentials. During the last three decades, the labor-force behavior of men and women has changed in some significant ways. For example, in 1960 only 36.5% of all white women were in the labor force. This figure is now well over 50 percent. Nearly 50 percent of black women were in the labor force as early as 1960. It is also worth noting that male labor-force participation has dropped for both races, with a very sharp drop for black men during the early 1970s.

Table 19.5 shows that average hourly earnings vary extensively across industries. Average earnings in the telecommunications industry are nearly three time as high as wages in eating and drinking places. Earnings in banking are significantly lower than earnings in advertising.

Table 19.6 gives a very rough breakdown of occupations in the United States. A look at the number of workers gives evidence of **occupational segregation** by sex. About 48 percent of all employed women are in the categories of administrative support (including clerical support) and service workers, while only 16 percent of all men work at jobs in these categories. The executive, administrative, and management category includes roughly twice as many men as women. Women also earn substantially lower wages than men in virtually every category, and the overall median income of women is nearly 50 percent lower than that of men.

Occupational segregation   The fact that men and women seem to be concentrated in certain occupations. For example, most secretaries and nurses are women and most college professors are men.

TABLE 19.4

Labor-Force Participation Rates for Those 16 Years of Age and Over

Labor force participation by black and white men has fallen, while more and more women are entering the work force.

	WHITE		BLACK	
	Men	Women	Men	Women
1960	83.4	36.5	83.0	48.2
1970	80.0	42.6	76.5	49.5
1975	78.7	45.9	71.0	48.9
1980	78.2	51.2	70.6	53.2
1986	76.9	55.0	71.2	56.9

Source: Statistical Abstract of the United States, various editions.

TABLE 19.5
Average Hourly Earnings in
Several Industries, 1986

Differences in wages reflect differences in jobs and workers. Wages are ultimately determined by the forces of supply and demand, market by market.

Industry	Average hourly earnings of production workers (Feb. 1986)
Pipe lines, except natural gas	$15.12
Telephone communication	$12.75
Computer and data processing	$11.37
Advertising	$11.26
Legal services	$11.11
Sanitary services	$9.63
Auto dealers and service stations	$7.46
Banking	$7.08
Nursing and personal-care facilities	$5.77
Variety store	$4.70
Eating and drinking places	$4.40

Source: Bureau of Labor Statistics, Employment Earnings (May 1986).

TABLE 19.6
Income Differences by Sex and
Occupation, 1984

Income earned varies extensively across occupations. Women are disproportionately represented in the administrative support, clerical, and service worker categories. Women appear to earn substantially less than men in all categories.

Occupation	WOMEN		MEN		RATIO OF WOMEN TO MEN	
	Number	Median	Number	Median	Number	Income
Total	55,226	$ 8,675	66,454	$17,026	.83	.51
Executive, administrative, management	4,616	16,083	8,174	29,980	.56	.54
Professional specialty	7,400	16,106	7,152	28,363	1.03	.57
Sales	7,354	5,212	6,967	18,208	1.06	.29
Administrative support, including secretarial	15,574	10,870	3,823	17,296	4.07	.63
Machine operators, assemblers, and operators	4,012	8,674	5,116	15,929	.78	.54
Service workers	11,176	3,833	7,031	7,507	1.59	.51

Source: U.S. Bureau of the Census, "Money Income and Poverty Status of Families in the U.S.," Current Population Survey, no. 149, p. 60.

Discrimination, Crowding, and Wage Differentials

These data make it clear that women and men are not randomly distributed across occupations. It also shows that women, on average, earn significantly less than men. One explanation for these observations is *gender discrimination* in the labor market.

Labor market **discrimination** occurs when one group of workers receives inferior treatment from employers because of some characteristic irrelevant to job performance. Inferior treatment may involve being systematically barred from certain occupations, receiving lower wages, or inability to win promotion or obtain training.

Suppose that women (the same argument can be made for blacks and other minorities) were systematically barred from a number of occupations. To make it simple, let's call the occupations reserved for men (or whites) sector X, and the rest of the economy sector Y. Since women (or blacks) are excluded from X, the supply of labor in

Discrimination   The inferior treatment of an identifiable group, often drawn along racial, ethnic, or gender lines, by employers because of some characteristic irrelevant to job performance.

sector X is reduced, and wages are higher than they would otherwise be. On the other hand, women (blacks) must *crowd* into the occupations reserved for them. That increases the supply of labor in sector Y and pushes wages down. Thus occupational segregation resulting from discrimination against women (blacks) is sufficient to cause a wage differential if the number of restricted jobs is large relative to the size of the population discriminated against.

But there is more to the story than wage differentials. Occupational discrimination also results in a net loss of welfare in the economy. To understand this argument, you need to recall that the demand for labor depends on the productivity of that labor. When extra workers are crowded into sector Y, wages fall. Because wages are lower, more workers will be hired. (Recall that workers will be hired as long as the value of their product at the margin exceeds the going wage.) With more workers working at a lower wage, the *marginal* product of workers in Y will end up lower than it otherwise would be.

The reverse occurs in sector X. With fewer workers supplying their labor in the reserved sector, wages remain high. The marginal product of workers in X, then, remains high. Now consider transferring one worker at a time from sector Y to sector X. If we assume that the discrimination was unrelated to job qualifications, workers will be moving from a sector in which their productivity was low at the margin to a sector where it is high. Thus the value of the product gained in sector X is greater than the value of the product lost in sector Y. There is thus a net gain in value. *Ending discrimination, then, should increase national income.*

The logic behind this is simple. If workers vary in their talents in ways unrelated to gender or race, rules or behaviors that force one group into specific occupations are clearly inefficient. It is exactly the same as the logic of an earlier example. If Ohio land is more productive in corn than in wheat, a law that restricts its use to wheat production is clearly wasteful.

Critics of this discrimination story argue that competition should force the walls of discrimination down rather quickly. If women (or blacks) were more productive than the current wage would suggest, some firms would hire them into the restricted occupations, driving those who persist in their discrimination out of business.

Those who defend the discrimination and crowding theory rejoin that the pure-competition story is naive. They argue that the link between productivity and wages is difficult to establish, and that those in positions of power, usually white men, have both the incentive and the ability to maintain discriminatory practices over long periods.

A lively and, needless to say, emotional debate continues back and forth among labor economists. One particular piece of the debate that has ended up in the courts in recent years is the controversy over *comparable worth*. The argument is that women are systematically paid less for work of equal, or at least comparable, value. This controversy was discussed in a box in Chapter 17.

LABOR UNIONS AND COLLECTIVE BARGAINING

So far we have focused on the behavior of firms and workers in labor markets that are competitive. This is by no means the whole story, however. For many years, a substantial number of workers have been and still are employed under contracts negotiated between their employers and their labor unions. In 1985 just under 17 million workers, about 18 percent of all people employed in the United States, belonged to unions. Needless to say, the bargaining that takes place between parties acting on behalf of firms and of workers does not necessarily produce the same outcome as the operation of an unregulated, competitive labor market.

Nearly all eligible workers in a number of major industries, including automobiles, mining, and steel, belong to unions. But workers in other industries, perhaps the most significant today being the high-tech industries, have not been unionized. While unions are still a major force in the economy and in American society, they do not enjoy the influence and power that they once did. Union membership has fallen dramatically as a percentage of all those employed. In absolute numbers, union membership is about the same as it was in 1954, but the number of jobs has nearly doubled. In 1954 nearly 35 percent of workers were in unions. The current figure, as we just said, now stands at under 18 percent.

Figure 19.4 chronicles the rise and fall of the labor movement in the United States. There are three important periods. Between 1937 and 1945, union membership went from under 14 percent of the employed to over 35 percent. From 1947 to 1960, union membership remained constant at about 33 percent. But since 1960, the figure has declined in every year but two, and it now stands at its lowest level since 1937.

We begin this discussion of labor unions and collective bargaining with a brief history of the labor movement in the United States. We then turn to economic theory and an analysis of the potential effects of an organized labor force. When we finally present what is known about the actual effects of unions, we will find significant disagreement among researchers.

FIGURE 19.4

Union Membership as a Percent of Those Employed

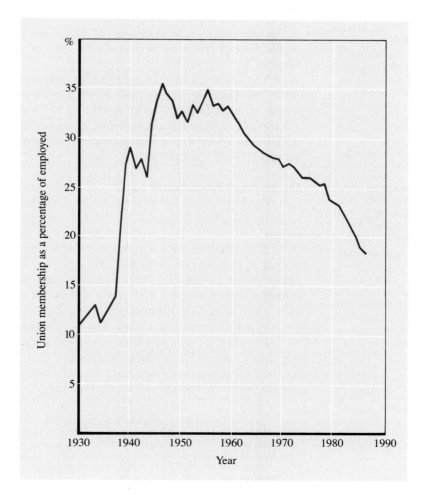

The Labor Movement in the United States

Some scholars have associated unions with the medieval craft guilds, but the guild members were master craftsmen who owned capital and often employed workers. Actually, unions as we know them first appeared in Great Britain and the United States in the late eighteenth and early nineteenth centuries as associations of workers with similar skills.

At that time, workers as individuals had no control over the conditions of their working lives; political and economic power was concentrated in the hands of owners. Workers found, however, that there was strength in uniting. From their earliest years, union objectives have been *higher wages* and *improved working conditions*.

Employers resisted, of course. They used the law, coercion, and brute force in an effort to stop union organizing and activity. Union members were fired, workers were forced to sign **"yellow-dog contracts"** in which they promised not to join a union, and companies hired strikebreakers, thugs, and even gunmen to intimidate organizers. Without laws on their side, the unions had no hope of success. Because changes in existing law and passage of new law follow only from political power, that power became an important union goal, and politics remains at the heart of the labor movement today.

One of the earliest successful labor organizations in the United States was the **Knights of Labor**, founded in 1869. The Knights, which included both skilled and unskilled workers, attempted to organize all workers into one great union. After it successfully struck the Wabash railroad, owned by "robber baron" Jay Gould in 1885, its popularity and power grew dramatically, and in 1886 the Knights claimed 700,000 members.

The decline of the Knights of Labor, however, came quickly. Although allegations of its association with the 1886 Haymarket bombing in Chicago that killed seven policemen were false, the strike against Gould was gradually broken, and their radical positions on social issues cost them public support. In the end, a lack of unanimity, as well as the rapid inflow of unskilled immigrants, weakened the union's economic power, and the organization gradually disintegrated.

The American Federation of Labor   Founded in 1881, the **American Federation of Labor (AFL)** was to be a practical, nonideological movement. While its goal was to improve the lot of skilled workers, it fully accepted the existing social *and economic* system.[7]

The AFL evolved in a mold largely set by Samuel Gompers, a cigar maker who was elected its president in 1886, and who served in that capacity until his death in 1924. Made up of independent organizations, each given exclusive jurisdiction over its particular craft or area, the AFL was a "federal" union. Between 1900 and the beginning of World War I, its membership grew from about half a million to about two million, and by 1920 it had doubled again to nearly four million.

During the 1920s, the labor movement stagnated. A major antiunion offensive by employers, widespread antilabor sentiments, conservative U.S. presidents, and hostile courts all contributed to a significant drop in union membership. Gompers died in 1924, and the AFL was left without strong leadership.

Yellow-dog contracts   Contracts forced on labor by management which prohibit workers from joining unions.

Knights of Labor   One of the earliest successful labor organizations in the United States, it recruited both skilled and unskilled laborers. Founded in 1869, the power of the Knights of Labor declined after the Chicago Hay Market bombing in 1886.

American Federation of Labor   Founded in 1881, the AFL was successfully led by Samuel Gompers from 1886 until 1924. A practical, nonideological union, the AFL existed as a "confederation" of individual craft unions representing skilled workers, each with an independent organization and an exclusive jurisdiction. Now merged with the CIO, the AFL maintains a preeminent position among unions today.

[7]Many critics of the capitalist system find the fact that this principle has characterized the American labor movement from the beginning an anathema. The Marxist critique of capitalism argues that workers are inevitably exploited to the point that they rise up and overthrow the capitalist system, replacing it with a socialist or communist state. To a Marxist, the labor union is the instrument of revolt. In Western Europe, union ideology has always been much closer to that envisioned by Marx than in the United States. For example, this country has never seen a more committed anticommunist than George Meany, who served as president of the AFL-CIO for many years.

Decline in Unionization: Some Recent Evidence

Trade union membership has declined precipitously in the United States in the last 15 years. Union members made up about 25 percent of those employed in the private, nonagricultural sector of the economy in 1973. By 1985, that figure had dropped to 14 percent.

In a recent paper, Professor Henry Farber of MIT and the National Bureau of Economic Research shows two reasons for this decline. One reason is increased employer hostility and resistance toward unions and union organizing activity. The second explanation is a decreased desire for unionization by nonunion workers who are becoming more satisfied with their jobs and have less faith that a union would be able to improve their wages and working conditions. Shifts in the demographic, industrial, and occupational composition of employment do not seem to explain this decrease in unionization.

Farber's data come from the "Quality of Employment Survey" conducted by a University of Michigan group in 1977, and from a 1984 Harris poll. Both of these surveys asked nonmanagerial, nonunion workers if they would vote for union representation on their current jobs if a secret ballot election were held. Farber estimates that the demand for union representation among nonunion workers declined from about 40 percent in 1977 to 32 percent in 1984, while the total demand for union representation fell from nearly 60 percent in 1977 to 47 percent in 1984. By his calculations, there was an 11 percent decline in actual unionization among those surveyed. Farber figures that six percentage points of this decline represent reduced demand for union representation and five points come from a drop in the supply of union jobs relative to demand.

Why have managers become more antiunion? Farber argues that it is likely because of an increase in the costs of unionization for employers. There has been a major increase in the level of foreign competition over the past decade, particularly in the manufacturing sector that has formed the heart of the union movement in the United States. In 1958, only about 3 percent of manufacturing sales in the United States were imports. This rose to about 7 percent by 1977 and to 11 percent by 1984. "In the past, with no significant foreign competition . . . American firms could afford to accommodate higher costs associated with labor unions by sharing some of the gains of a relatively closed economy with their workers," Farber writes. "However, the increased openness of the American economy may make it prohibitively expensive to bear these higher costs because higher product prices will not be borne by consumers who have attractive foreign alternatives."

As for employees, the two surveys show a dramatic improvement between 1977 and 1984 in nonunion workers' satisfaction with their jobs. Relatively more pleased with pay, job security, and other elements of their work, these workers are less likely to demand union representation. Because there was a decline in real earnings in this period, the general increase in worker satisfaction with pay suggests that the standards against which workers judge their wages fell during the economic and competitive dislocations of the late 1970s and early 1980s. Although a majority of nonunion workers still believe that unions improve the wages and working conditions of workers, the size of that majority fell substantially from 1977 to 1984. Farber concludes that if unions are to recoup their losses, they need to convince relatively satisfied workers that unions provide real value in the current competitive environment.

With a changed political and social climate in the nation, employers are calling into serious question the role of trade unions in American society and the economy for the first time since that role was defined in the 1930s, Farber suggests. "With the economic recessions of the 1970s and 1980s, more overt antiunion behavior became socially and politically acceptable, turning what had been a stagnation of the union movement into a virtual rout."

Source: From the NBER Digest, National Bureau of Economic Research, Cambridge, MA., August 1987.

The Depression and the New Deal   The Great Depression began in 1929, and with it came a new start for unions. In 1932 Congress passed the Norris-LaGuardia Act, which stopped the use of court-ordered injunctions to prevent strikes. Franklin Roosevelt was elected in 1932, and prolabor legislation was a major part of his New Deal.

The most important piece of New Deal labor legislation came in 1935. The Wagner Act, also called the National Labor Relations Act, guaranteed workers the right to join unions. It also required management to engage in *collective bargaining* if a majority of its employees so desired. To enforce the law, the act set up the **National Labor Relations Board (NLRB)**. In 1938 the Fair Labor Standards Act established the "minimum wage," which rose from $.25 an hour in 1938 to $3.35 an hour in 1987.

The Congress of Industrial Organizations   The AFL was an association of craft unions representing skilled workers. Prior to the 1930s, no real attempt had been made to

National Labor Relations Board   A watchdog board established by the Wagner Act in 1935 whose duties include ensuring that all workers are guaranteed the right to join unions and that firm managers participate fairly in collective bargaining if so requested by a majority of their employees.

organize the growing numbers of semiskilled workers in mass production industries, such as steel and automobiles.

John L. Lewis, president of the United Mine Workers, and a number of other unions within the AFL independently tried to organize the steel, automobile, rubber, and chemical industries. In 1935, when the AFL decided not to endorse his plan, Lewis founded the Committee for Industrial Organization which became the **Congress of Industrial Organizations (CIO)**. The AFL subsequently expelled the unions involved in the rebellion. The new competition led to organization drives that pushed total union membership up rapidly in the late 1930s and early 1940s. By the end of World War II in 1945, membership had hit nearly 15 million, over 35 percent of all workers.

Not surprisingly, the rapid rise in union power triggered some reaction. The Smith-Connally Act of 1943 and the Taft-Hartley Act of 1947 introduced new government controls over unions. Any strike that was deemed to "imperil the national health or safety" could be suspended by the courts through an injunction for an 80-day "cooling off period." President Reagan used such an injunction to stop a railroad strike in 1986. The Taft-Hartley Act also gave states the right to pass "right-to-work" laws. Such laws, currently enforced in 20 states, make illegal union shop agreements requiring workers to join unions. Right-to-work laws have seriously hampered union organizing in the states that have them.

The Merger of the AFL and the CIO   The AFL and CIO coexisted independently twenty years until they merged in 1955 under the leadership of two men who would dominate the movement for many years, Walter Reuther and George Meany. In 1968 Reuther's United Automobile Workers left the AFL-CIO and joined the International Brotherhood of Teamsters, the truck drivers' union that the AFL-CIO had earlier expelled for corrupt practices.

Recent History and Continued Decline   The 1980s have not been kind to the labor movement. First, in 1981 President Reagan "broke" a national strike of air traffic controllers. Public employees do not have the same right to strike as workers in other industries, and when Reagan fired 11,400 controllers, their union went bankrupt. The traveling public had been greatly inconvenienced by the strike, and the union did not receive a great deal of public sympathy.

Second, the labor movement moved decisively in 1984 to throw all its political muscle behind the Democratic presidential candidate, Walter Mondale. Partly because of intense early union organizing, Mondale received the nomination, but he was over-whelmingly defeated by Ronald Reagan in November. Many people felt that Mondale was simply too closely associated with unions at a time when they were falling from favor with the voting public. Mondale's overwhelming defeat certainly contributed to the difficulties faced by union organizers.

Third, international competition for U.S. markets as well as for markets around the world has increased tremendously. The American steel and automobile industries, for example, have found themselves losing markets rapidly to Japanese and European producers. Justifiable fear of foreign competition has weighed in powerfully on the side of firms when contracts come up for negotiation. In the last few years, major unions, including the United Automobile Workers, have signed contracts calling for major *reductions* in wages to make various industries more competitive.

Finally, deregulation and increased domestic competition have reduced the power of unions in several key industries. For example, the airline industry was deregulated in 1978. Since then a number of new firms have entered the industry, offering low fares by

Congress of Industrial Organizations (CIO)   *Founded by John L. Lewis, president of the United Mine Workers, after the AFL rejected his plan to organize the steel, rubber, automobile, and chemical industries in 1935, the CIO was the first union to organize semiskilled laborers in the mass production industries. After 20 years of independence, it merged with the AFL in 1955.*

employing only nonunion employees at much lower salaries. Airline pilots at nonunion airlines make between half and two thirds the salaries of their union counterparts. Increased competition also threatens the power of unions in trucking and telecommunications.

The Effects of Unions and Bargaining

One way to analyze union power is to think of a union as a monopolistic seller of labor in a market. If there were many buyers, the union's situation would be very similar to that of a pure monopolist selling in output markets: the union would restrict the supply of labor and charge a wage rate above the competitive equilibrium. But wages may not be the only concern of unions. Other objectives might include keeping all of its members employed or improving working conditions.

Unions as Monopolies   Let us assume for a moment that a union is the only seller of labor in some market. Unlike monopolistic firms in output markets, however, unions usually have more than one objective, and multiple objectives can conflict with each other. Further suppose that, as an initial condition, union membership is less than the number of workers that would be employed if the market were competitively organized and that the objective is to maximize its members' wages and keep them all employed. In Figure 19.5, if L_u is the number of union members, the union would set a wage W_u. At that wage rate, there would be an excess supply of workers, or unemployment, in this market equal to the difference between L_s and L_u, but the unemployed would all be nonunion workers.

Now in order for this wage to hold, the union would have to restrict membership, and unions do. Some simply refuse to admit new members; many have long apprenticeship programs that must be completed before a worker is admitted. Unions have also been accused of using racial and gender barriers to restrict membership, and, as a matter of policy, they usually favor strict controls on immigration.

FIGURE 19.5

A Competitive Labor Market and a Monopoly Union

If the union imposes a wage of W_u, demand for labor will be limited to L_u. But there will be a labor supply of L_s. Thus, many will not be able to find jobs. But if union membership was L_u, all the unemployed would be nonunion workers.

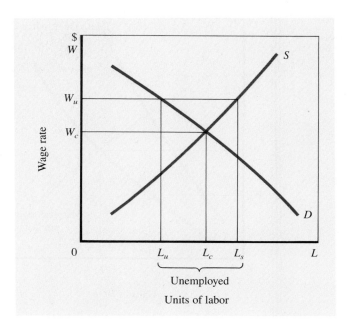

You can see the trade-off from the diagram. If wages were set lower, more workers would be employed. If union membership were greater than L_u, the leadership would have to make a tough decision. They could get more members into jobs, but only by accepting a lower wage for everyone or by somehow increasing demand for the services of their members.

Over the years, unions have shown great concern for keeping members in jobs. Clearly the preferred route has been to increase demand for workers rather than to take pay cuts. Unions have used many techniques for shifting the demand curve to the right. Union contracts now include provisions for job security, especially for those with seniority. Some contracts have clauses that preserve jobs even when it is inefficient to do so. The most often-cited example of this widely used and widely criticized policy, called **featherbedding**, involves the coal shovelers that trains had to carry for years after they were all powered by diesel engines rather than by coal.

Unions have actively sought protective trade measures such as tariffs and quotas to prevent foreign producers from cutting into the demand for domestic, union-made goods. Parking your new Toyota in the parking lot of a General Motors plant in Detroit would not be a popular thing to do. Some unions have gone so far as to advertise union-produced products. The International Ladies Garment Workers for many years ran an ad accompanied by a popular jingle that told you to "look for the union label."

Union Power versus Monopsony Power   In Chapter 13, we examined a market structure in which there is just one buyer. To maximize profits, a single buyer of labor—a monopsonist—that could control part of the labor market would lower wages and hire fewer workers.

Figure 19.6 shows a monopsonist facing a competitive labor supply, S. We have defined marginal resource cost (MRC) as the additional cost of hiring one additional unit of labor at the margin (see Chapter 13). To a monopsonist, marginal resource cost (MRC) is higher than the current wage. In order to attract additional workers, the

FIGURE 19.6
A Profit-Maximizing Monopsonist

A profit-maximizing monopsonist would pay a wage, W_m, below the competitive level, W_c.

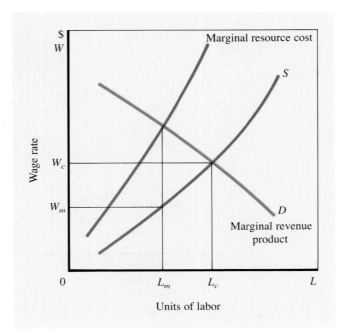

monopsonist must increase the wage. If we assume that all workers in this market are paid the same wage, then MRC has two components: the wage paid to the marginal unit of labor itself and the additional wages that must be paid to all workers because the marginal worker must be attracted into the work force. Thus the monopsonist will hire only up to the point that MRC is equal to labor's marginal revenue product (MRP), and that will be at a lower wage and a lower level of employment than would prevail under competition.

When a monopsonist faces a monopolistic *seller* of labor such as a union, it is a different story. The union, of course, tries to impose a wage rate above the going cost of wages, W_c. The monopsonist wants to pay a wage below W_c. The final result depends on the relative bargaining strengths of the union and the firm. In a sense, the union in this model exists to resist and exercise **countervailing power** on the buying side of the labor market. Indeed, many of the most highly unionized markets are in concentrated monopsonist-like industries such as steel and automobiles.

To summarize, union power in a competitive labor market is likely to be inefficient. Pushing up wages reduces labor demand and can actually cause unemployment and restrictions on union membership. In markets where the buying side is highly concentrated, however, unions may actually drive wages closer to their efficient levels.

Do Unions Actually Raise Wages?   The answer to this question, not surprisingly, is yes. An overwhelming number of studies using very different sets of data and techniques have found that unions *have succeeded in raising wages*. An early and well-known study by H. Gregg Lewis surveyed the existing literature in 1963 and found that unions succeeded in increasing wages by 10 to 15 percent.[8]

Modern cross-sectional studies using more sophisticated econometric techniques to control for characteristics of union and nonunion workers found union wage increases on the order of 20 to 30 percent.[9]

Other Effects of Unions and Some Evidence   The picture of unions that has emerged from this discussion so far is not very pretty. The monopoly model leads us to the same unflattering conclusions. First, unions raise wages above the competitive level, and this leads to unemployment and the underuse of labor. Second, union work rules and featherbedding reduce productivity. Third, unions create inequities by forcing wage differentials between similar workers. And finally, unions may discriminate to limit membership and hold down labor supply.

Another view has recently been put forth by two Harvard economists, Richard Freeman and James Medoff. They argue that unions in fact have a *positive* effect on the allocation of resources. According to Freeman and Medoff, unions actually raise productivity. Union members, they say, have lower quit rates, remain more loyal to the firm, maintain a higher morale, and are more likely to cooperate on the job. By communicating with management, they help put efficient policies into effect. They collect information on workers' preferences that leads to more efficient design of benefits packages and better personnel administration.[10]

Freeman and Medoff present a very convincing argument supported with a great deal of data. Their conclusions have been debated, however, and they are far from becoming "conventional wisdom."

[8]H. Gregg Lewis, *Unionism and Relative Wages* (Chicago: University of Chicago Press, 1963).
[9]See Richard Freeman and James Medoff, *What Do Unions Do?* (New York: Basic Books, 1984), Chapter 2, "The Union Wage Effect."
[10]Freeman and Medoff, *Unions.*

Are Unions Good or Bad?

At the beginning of the chapter, we said that everyone has an opinion about labor unions. Some view them as a major imperfection in the labor market. According to this view, higher wages distort the decisions of firms and make the United States less competitive in world markets. Unions reduce productivity by imposing inefficient work rules. To Freeman and Medoff, unions have raised productivity by providing a channel through which union members can communicate with management, develop loyalties, and achieve a better degree of cooperation. Marxist thinkers, of course, see unions as the instrument through which workers will ultimately rise up and throw off the shackles of capitalism.

No real consensus is possible. The truth is probably that unions have done some good and some ill. What is clear is that they have lost a great deal of power and influence in recent years. Whether the future holds continued decline or rebirth remains to be seen.

SUMMARY

1. Demand for labor in competitive markets depends on labor's productivity. Firms will hire labor as long as its marginal revenue product exceeds the market wage.

2. Households supply labor. The supply of labor depends on some factors that households control and some that they do not. The alternatives to working for a wage are working for no pay or enjoying one's leisure. Labor supply decisions depend to a large extent on preferences for work and leisure.

3. The stock of knowledge, skills, and talents that human beings possess by nature or by nurture is called human capital. The principle form of human capital investment financed primarily by households is education. The principle form of human capital investment financed primarily by firms is on-the-job training. Governments invest heavily in human capital.

4. When a surplus exists in a labor market, we would expect to see wages fall, but sometimes disequilibria persist. Downwardly inflexible, or "sticky," wages have always been a puzzle since John Maynard Keynes called attention to the problem in the 1930s. If wages adjusted quickly to a surplus of labor, there would be no such thing as involuntary unemployment.

5. Labor supply depends on a number of factors including wage rates, nonlabor income, and wealth. Individual firms have very little control over the market wage; firms are forced to pay the wage that is determined by the market. Because people cannot be moved free of charge and because people do not reside at their work places—as capital does—there is an important spacial dimension to labor markets.

6. A large amount of empirical work has documented that labor reacts in predictable ways in response to incentives.

7. Careful thought shows that tax cuts could increase or decrease labor supply.

8. Evidence suggests that men's labor supply does not respond very much to changes in wage rates. In fact, higher net wages actually seem to reduce slightly the labor that men supply. Women seem to be more responsive, and, in contrast to men, women work more when net wages rise.

9. Recent changes in the welfare system, specifically in the Aid to Families with Dependent Children program, have virtually eliminated incentives for eligible recipients to work. Benefits are reduced by at least a dollar for every dollar of earned income. But there seems to have been little change in the labor supply of eligible mothers.

10. Job searching is a process of gathering data. In theory, job hunting should continue as long as the expected gains from continuing to search exceed the costs of doing so.

11. Labor market discrimination occurs when one group of workers receives inferior treatment from employers because of some characteristic irrelevant to job performance. Inferior treatment may involve being systematically barred from certain occupations, receiving lower wages, or being unable to win promotion or obtain training.

12. If workers have similar levels of productivity, rules or behaviors that force one group into specific occupations are inefficient.

13. While unions are still a major force in the economy and in American society, they do not enjoy the power or the

influence that they once did. As a percentage of those employed, union membership stands at its lowest level since 1937.

14. Some economists view unions as an imperfection in the labor market. They argue that higher union wages distort the decisions of firms and make the U.S. less competitive in world markets. They point to work rules that reduce productivity. Others argue that unions are an essential response to market power on the buying side of the labor market. Some also contend that unions actually increase productivity.

REVIEW CONCEPTS

marginal revenue product of labor (*MRP*)   464
human capital   465
education   465
on-the-job training   465
substitution effect   470
income effect   470
job search   474
compensating differentials   475
occupational segregation   476

discrimination   477
yellow-dog contracts   480
Knights of Labor   480
American Federation of Labor (AFL)   480
National Labor Relations Board (NLRB)   481
Congress of Industrial Organizations (CIO)   482
featherbedding   484
countervailing power   485

REVIEW QUESTIONS

1. Jane is considering returning to school to get an MBA. She currently makes $30,000 and pays $9000 in taxes (30%). Tuition at the school of her choice is $15,000 per year, and the program runs for two years. She must attend full time and would receive no financial aid.
   a. What is the total cost of acquiring an MBA?
   b. What other information might you need to get a better picture of the full cost? (*Hint*: What about summers?)
   c. If the degree would raise her expected wage by $5000 per year in real terms after taxes for a long time, what is the rate of return on investment in an MBA for Jane? What if the increase were $15,000?
   d. To make a final judgment, what other factors might Jane want to consider?
2. Some people have suggested that the Department of Labor should establish a computerized national and regional job bank to provide people with listings of available jobs, updated daily. Is this a good idea, or is it an unwarranted intrusion of the government into the private sector? Explain your answer.
3. Explain how the functioning of income-tested programs such as welfare acts as a tax on the poor that can have an effect on their work effort.

4. Explain how unemployment insurance could actually lead to unemployment. If evidence were found to support this claim, we should abandon the unemployment compensation system immediately. Agree or disagree? Explain your answer.
5. If you had to drop out of school and fully support yourself and your mother, how would you begin the task of searching for a job? Who would you talk to first? Second? Write a plan for finding and getting the best possible job.
6. The American Brotherhood of Widget Makers has 15,000 members. Today all are employed, and the wage rate is $15.00 per hour. The union, however, is considering a push to raise wages by $1.50 per hour. A union economist has pointed out that evidence for the industry suggests a labor demand elasticity of −1. What is the potential cost of a new wage contract that accepts the 10-percent hike? What further contract provisions might you suggest to reduce or eliminate these potential losses?
7. You are a journalist assigned by your managing editor the task of writing an article on whether unions raise productivity or reduce productivity. You have two months to collect evidence. What information would you need to draw your conclusions? Design a research project to answer your editor's question.

20 The Location of Economic Activty: Cities and Regions

Since Chapter 4, we have been discussing the economic decisions made by individual firms and households, including how much to produce, what to produce, which technology to use, how much of each input to demand, what to consume, and how much to save, but we have not yet touched on one equally important decision—*where to locate*. Every household must live somewhere, and every firm must locate its facilities. In a very real sense, our world has been shaped by the collective location decisions of millions of households and firms. For example, the collection of factories, office buildings, roads, houses, apartment buildings, stores, museums, schools, and so forth that we know as a city exists only because people once decided that those things needed to be close together.

Location decisions are no different from other decisions made by firms and households. For households, they depend on preferences, incomes, and relative prices. A graduate of Ohio State University who decides to look for a job in Cincinnati may like the Cincinnati area, but she is also likely to be influenced by factors such as job opportunities, wage rates, and the cost of living. For firms, decisions depend on potential revenues, costs, and profits. Digital Equipment Corporation opened a production facility in Ireland because it seemed profitable to do so. Anthony Athenas opened a seafood restaurant on a pier in Boston because he thought it would be a potentially profitable location.

Our exploration of the economics of locational choices begins with a look at the economic forces behind the urbanization process that began for the Western world around the middle of the eighteenth century. We then turn to the microeconomics of locational choice. Location is determined in the market for land. In theory, land use is determined by a market that allocates space to its most productive use. But land markets are highly regulated. In many areas, land use is carefully planned and enforced with zoning rules and regulations.

Finally, we discuss some of the social consequences of past locational choices: the high concentrations of poor people and minorities in cities while high-income families live in separate suburban jurisdictions; the struggles of central cities to maintain schools and essential public services on declining revenue bases; and the problem of some regions with the flight of jobs, high unemployment, and poverty.

URBANIZATION AND THE INDUSTRIAL REVOLUTION

Industrial Revolution   The rapid economic growth that began around the mid-eighteenth century in England. It was fueled by increasing agricultural productivity, technological advances, and new, efficient forms of transportation and it resulted in the factory system and massive urbanization.

The world before the eighteenth century was primarily rural, and most people were engaged in agriculture. In 1700, about three quarters of the population of England lived in rural areas or on farms. The largest cities on the European continent had only about 50,000 inhabitants. But sometime around the middle of the eighteenth century, a rapid change began to transform the character of life, first in England and later all across Europe and in the United States. This change came to be known as the **Industrial Revolution**. Increasing agricultural productivity, technical advances in manufacturing, and new efficient forms of transportation all contributed to a period of rapid economic growth. One of the consequences was a rapid, massive urbanization of the population. As early as 1812, only about one quarter of the population of England was still engaged in agriculture.

Changes both in the cities and in agriculture contributed to this urbanization. In the early part of the eighteenth century, England was largely populated by a class of small peasant farmers, cotters, and squatters who lived off "common lands" open for anyone's use. Later in the century, Parliament began passing "acts of enclosure" that locked most of the common land into private holdings to facilitate the application of large-scale farming techniques.

At the same time, factories were being built in the cities, and jobs were becoming available there. Historians disagree about why the cities filled up with people. Some argue that the rise of the factory and the availability of jobs and reasonable wages attracted peasants to the city. Others contend that the enclosure movement forced peasants off the common lands leaving them with no place else to go but the cities. This large pool of cheap labor, then, may have stimulated the rise of the factory. Whatever the cause, a rural society was transformed into an urban one, people jammed into the cities, and the modern industrial society was born.

A similar process occurred in the United States two centuries later. Table 20.1 chronicles urbanization in the United States since the turn of the twentieth century. In

TABLE 20.1
Urban and Rural Population of the United States, 1900–1980

In 1900 a majority of Americans lived in rural areas. By 1980 nearly three fourths lived in urban areas.

	Urban (millions)	Percentage of total	Rural* (millions)	Percentage of total
1900	30.2	39.7	45.8	60.3
1920	54.2	51.2	51.6	48.8
1940	74.4	56.5	57.2	43.5
1960	125.3	69.9	54.0	30.1
1970	149.3	73.5	53.9	26.5
1980	167.1	73.7	59.5	26.3

*The census definition of rural is places with less than 2500 persons.

Source: Historical Statistics of the United States and Statistical Abstract of the United States, various editions.

1900 over 60 percent of the population lived in "rural" areas. Between 1940 and 1960, the urban population increased by 51 million to nearly 70 percent of the total, while the rural population fell by more than three million. Between 1970 and 1980, rural areas saw a resurgence of population growth, but nearly three quarters of the population remained urban.

WHY DO WE HAVE CITIES?

Cities are what they are because individual firms and households decided to build, to expand, to move, and to invest there. Governments also decided to build ports, roads, buildings, communications systems, power facilities, and the like. The question is, What forces influenced these decisions and led to the large agglomerations, or concentrations, of people, buildings, and activities that we know as cities?

Economic Forces that Foster Urbanization

Transaction-Cost Economies   Societies in which most people live close to subsistence and in which most families produce only for themselves have little need for markets. As economic growth occurs and agricultural productivity rises, people have the time to produce other things, and exchange becomes necessary and desirable. With the seemingly infinite number of different goods and services produced in a modern industrial society, we engage in many exchanges daily; if you do errands in the morning, go shopping in the afternoon, and go out at night, you can spend *all day* making such exchanges.

Engaging in exchange is not costless. Buyers and sellers need information on prices, on availability of alternatives, on quality, and so forth. Goods need to be transported from where they are produced to where they are sold and finally to where they are consumed. Although modern technology is introducing new ways of shopping at home, via catalogue, computer terminal, and TV, most exchanges take place face-to-face. We still go to the market, and we still bear **transaction costs**.

Transaction costs   All the time and money costs, other than production costs and final prices, that are involved in buying and selling: dissemination of product information, advertising, transportation to and from market, and so forth.

Clearly the cost of engaging in transactions is minimized when a buyer can engage in many transactions at a single location. In medieval Europe, towns grew up around markets where sellers met buyers at a common point to display their wares, and buyers went to get those wares or to choose among them. If a buyer needs 10 items, it is clearly more efficient to get them in one trip to a common marketplace than to go to 10 different places for them. It is also advantageous if a seller can go to one location and be exposed to thousands of potential buyers.

To convince yourself that transaction costs matter, imagine a world in which they were zero. That is, imagine that it cost nothing in either money or time to move people or goods from place to place. In such a world, economic activity would spread itself uniformly, and there would be no agglomerations, or cities.

Competition   Competition for markets leads naturally to concentration of economic activity. A simple story told by Harold Hotelling many years ago about competition along a strip of beach nicely illustrates this point.[1]

Imagine two hot dog carts, A and B, competing for business on a beach along which bathers are spread out evenly. In Figure 20.1, carts A and B are at first randomly located.

[1]Harold Hotelling, "Stability in Competition," *Economic Journal*, 39 (March 1929), 41–57.

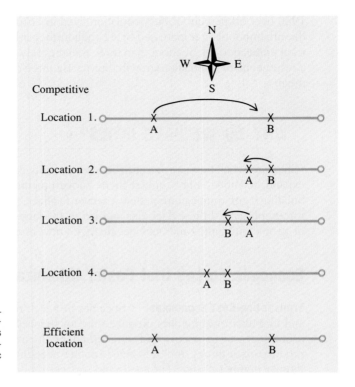

FIGURE 20.1
Competition for Space Along a Beach

Competitive sellers would locate together at the center of a beach. This simple model illustrates how competition can lead to inefficient geographic concentration of economic activity.

Assume that the hot dogs at each cart are of equal quality and that each cart owner wants to sell as many hot dogs as possible. Given the competitive nature of the situation and given B's location, the optimal place for A is just west of B (location 1 in Figure 20.1). At that point, A would get all the customers along the beach to the left, and B would get all the customers along the beach to the right. With A now in place, B would hop around to the other side (location 2). A would then hop west of B (location 3). The process would end with the two locating together at the center and splitting the market down the middle (location 4).

Interestingly enough, even in such a simple world competition does not necessarily result in the best or most efficient location from the point of view of the bathers or, if we generalize, of the members of society. When competition has pushed A and B to the center of the beach, people at either end must walk half its length to get a hot dog. If the carts had instead located separately, with A one fourth of the way down the beach and B three fourths of the way down the beach, no one would have to walk more than one fourth the length of the beach to get a hot dog. If A and B would locate this way (see Figure 20.1, bottom), transaction costs for society would be minimized.

Economies of Scale in Transportation   In antiquity, as in the present, large ships carried goods at lower average cost than small ships. In other words, the larger the load, the lower the transportation cost per unit. Large ships had to be unloaded, of course, and that led to the development of port cities. With the development of the railroad, which could move large quantities of goods quickly between points, it made no sense to stop a freight train every five miles. In other words, the longer the run between stops, the lower the cost per mile. Scale economies of both kinds led to large railheads and the development of cities to service them.

While the reasons that large cities grow up around important ports or railheads seem obvious, there are also many ideal sites for shipping that never develop, and there are many major ports in inferior locations. Neither Los Angeles nor Houston has a natural port, for example, while Sag Harbor, at the eastern end of Long Island, and Rockport, Maine, have magnificent natural harbor sites. Obviously it takes more than natural endowments to assure a city's commercial viability.

Economies of Scale in Production Technology

For many industries, large-scale, capital-intensive techniques are the most efficient method of production. This means that large numbers of people must work together in a single plant or at a single location.

During the Industrial Revolution in England, the first industry to register extraordinary gains was textiles. The cotton textile industry had always been a "cottage" industry before 1750. Most of the spinning and weaving was done in individual cottages by workers, mostly women, working part time to supplement the family income. Raw materials were "put out," and final goods were collected by the owners. The development of new spinning and weaving technologies in the late 1700s meant that economies of scale could be achieved if many people worked together in a factory. As more and more complex products required more and more steps in fabrication and finishing, and, in some cases, as products became larger and larger, economies of scale required that increasingly larger numbers of people work cooperatively in production.

Some claim that the rise of the factory did not depend on technological advances alone. According to one thesis, as families earned more income in the nineteenth century, they worked fewer hours. (Remember the income and substitution effects and the possibility of a backward bend in the labor supply curve). When this happened, owners of textile-producing firms had difficulty securing enough labor. By moving their work out of the cottage and into the factory and giving workers the choice of working ten hours every day or not at all, owners were able to increase the supply of labor enough to meet their needs.

Whether its causes lay in economies of scale and increasing complexity of production or simply the forcible extraction of more hours of work out of labor, the result was the factory—a place where many people worked in close physical proximity.

Linked and Population-Serving Industries

The establishment of a port or a railhead meant (and still means) the employment of people. Those people require service, and thus **population-service industries** arise. Housing gets built, and many different firms are established: food stores, taverns, restaurants, hotels, gas stations, theatres, professional sports teams, and the like. These establishments, in turn, employ people, and the process continues.

Businesses themselves buy services from other businesses. Connected to the growth of basic businesses in an area are service industries that is, **linked industries**, such as banking, insurance, accounting, computing, and brokerage firms, all of which, in turn, employ more people whose requirements serve to expand population-serving industries.

Economists at the Department of Commerce estimate what they call "employment multipliers." An **employment multiplier** is an estimate of the number of total jobs created for every new job that moves into an area. If a new firm moves into an area bringing with it, say, 1000 jobs, employment in the area may well expand by more than twice that number. This is because linked industries and population-serving establishments are likely to grow up around the new firm.

The Increase in Specialization

Certain industries produce highly specialized goods and services that do not have a mass market. In order to find enough customers to ensure

Population-serving industry An industry that grows up to serve the needs of the people living or working in an area.

Linked industry An industry that grows up to serve the business needs of firms in an area.

Employment multiplier A figure used to estimate the total number of jobs in an area created by the introduction of one new job to the area.

their success, such industries need to reach a very large market. The more specialized a product, the smaller the percentage of the population that it will appeal to. To obtain sufficient business, the specialized producer naturally must locate near a lot of people. The more specialized the firm, the less likely it is to be found outside of a major metropolitan area. Large cities have dozens of surgeons who specialize in the reconstruction of hands, while many rural areas have no physicians at all. A major city may have ten restaurants specializing in Vietnamese food. Try to find one in a rural county in Illinois.

A *feedback effect* here is undeniable. Large concentrations of people are likely to attract specialized businesses, but the availability of a wide variety of goods and services is also something that makes living near a big city attractive to many people. Small metropolitan areas have less variety than large ones, and variety diminishes sharply when you move away from metropolitan areas.

Economies of Large Complex-Factor Markets   Availability of trained labor at many skill levels is essential to the smooth operation of firms with complex production processes, and people with specialized skills are not everywhere to be found. Just as households looking for specialized products tend to live near big cities, so firms requiring skilled labor of many kinds may have no choice but to locate near a major population center.

Random Historical Events that Foster Urbanization

Taken together, the economic factors we have just itemized explain to some extent why we have the agglomerations of economic activity that we call cities. They do not, however, completely explain why cities are where they are:

> Cities are not ordained. . . . To say that a city grew "because" it was located at a good site for trading is, in view of what we can see about the world, absurd.[2]

There are some cities that started because settlers landed at a random spot on the coast or because they got tired of traveling on the way west. Others were the result of careful economic planning. Today location decisions are made every day by firms and households, and those decisions continue to shape the landscape. Some of those decisions are the result of precise economic calculations, and others are the result of seemingly random, idiosyncratic choices.

There is a bit more to history than this, but that is the subject of many other courses and thousands of volumes. With that acknowledgement, we now turn to a more detailed look at location decisions of firms and households.

THE LOCATION OF BUSINESS FIRMS

No topic is of greater concern for state governors than employment, and employment in a state or a region depends upon location decisions made by business firms. Just as presidents rise and fall with the national economy, governors rise and fall with the economies of their states. Most states have development departments charged with the responsibility of attracting new firms and encouraging established firms to stay and expand. Within the last ten years, many states have established tax reform commissions. A

[2]Jane Jacobs, *The Economy of Cities* (New York: Random House, 1969).

Silicon Valley

Silicon Valley, stretching northwest from San Jose to Palo Alto, California, is home to many of the world's most important computer manufacturers. Why are so many high technology firms located in this one part of California?

Because Silicon Valley is near Stanford University, it attracts talented people—a mix of first-rate scientists, university researchers, even Nobel Prize winners. These people provide the research and development efforts that fuel the success of these computer firms. Silicon Valley also boasts over one-third of the largest venture capital companies in the country, companies to which computer firms turn when they need start-up and expansion funds. The balmy California weather is yet another attraction to offer prospective employees.

Companies normally locate their operations near the natural resources needed in their business. For example, steel mills are located near iron ore deposits. The natural resource that makes the computer industry tick is silicon, which gives its name to Silicon Valley. But computer manufacturers do not flock to California for access to this *physical* resource. The resources that they are after are the intelligent minds and money found in this area.

Steven Jobs and Stephan Wozniak are two of the intelligent minds who helped change the face of computing. The two founders of Apple Computer manufactured their first computer because they didn't have enough money to go out and buy one. The Apple I was put together with a random assortment of parts "liberated" from Hewlett-Packard and Atari, where the two men worked. The computer was an instant success. Jobs sold his Volkswagen and Wozniak his calculator to buy enough parts to put together 100 computers. A local store requested 50 computers, and the two men, working in a garage at the home of Jobs' parents, put together the machines.

Jobs and Wozniak recognized that there was a market for a microcomputer. They approached their supervisors at Hewlett-Packard and Atari to suggest that one of the companies produce the Apple I. Both firms turned them down. So the two men established their own company in 1976. A local venture capitalist helped them put together a business plan, get a $250,000 line of credit, and raise $600,000. Apple Computer was in business. During 1977, the company's sales reached $2.5 million. In 1978, sales hit $15 million. In 1979, they jumped to $70 million. By 1982, sales had reached an amazing $583 million.

However, Apple Computer might never have come into existence were it not for Intel. To make their first computers Jobs and Wozniak used a microprocessor invented at Intel by another brilliant young man, Ted Hoff. Hoff's invention was a major breakthrough for Intel, a company started by Dr. Robert Noyce in 1968. Noyce had developed the integrated circuit while working at Fairchild Camera and Instrument Company. His work was so admired in Silicon Valley that he had no trouble finding the capital to start his own firm. A venture capitalist spent only a half hour on the phone to line up the $2.5 million that Noyce and a partner needed to start Intel.

Many other computer companies had start-ups similar to Apple's and Intel's. Intelligent people with new ideas knew that Silicon Valley offered the venture capital and the brilliant minds that would help their companies break new ground and prosper. This high-tech region was such a success that it spawned imitators around the country. Boston's Route 128 is home to such computer giants as Wang Laboratories, Digital Equipment Corp., and Data General. In North Carolina, Research Triangle Park contains 40 private and government research and development organizations in such fields as electronics and pharmaceuticals.

Other "Silicon Valleys" are springing up in Salt Lake City, upstate New York, Colorado Springs, and elsewhere. Companies are attracted to these high-tech corridors because they find a concentration of talented minds there. They are hoping to find the two young people who, like Jobs and Wozniak, will design the next Apple computer.

Sources: Dirk Hanson, *The New Alchemists*, Boston: Little, Brown 1982; Everett M. Rogers and Judith K. Larsen, *Silicon Valley Fever*, New York: Basic Books, 1984.

top item on the agenda of practically every one of them has been a study of the impact of state taxes on industrial location decisions.

The single most important thing to understand about business location decisions is that they are complicated. The easiest way to see just how complicated they are is to look at the profit function of a single firm. *Profits* are the difference between total revenue and total cost of production:

$$\text{profit} = TR - TC = P \times Q - (P_1 X_1 + P_2 X_2 + \ldots P_n X_n).$$

Total revenue is the price of output times the quantity sold. *Total cost* is the total cost of all the inputs required. In the equation we have n inputs which we presume include various kinds of labor, capital, land, transport costs, and so forth. P_1 is the price of the first input, X_1 is the quantity of the first input used, and so forth.

Before we added in the question of location to our analysis of profit-maximizing firms, we assumed that each firm knew the price of output, the price of each input required, and the technologies of production available. That information was used to pick one profit-maximizing level of output. The addition of the location question brings with it a significant complication. The fact is that *every single variable in that profit function may change from location to location*. In other words, when a firm shops around for a location, it must think about the price it can charge, the amount it might sell, the costs of transportation, wage rates, rent levels, the taxes it must pay, and so forth *at every possible location*. Once it calculates these factors, presumably the firm will pick the location where its profit will be highest.

Location and Profits

Locational Variation in Revenues   For a perfectly competitive firm selling a homogeneous product to a national market, revenues depend on market price alone, and the market price will be almost the same wherever the firm is located. For all other firms, revenues depend, to some extent, on location.

But let us back up for a minute. As you have seen, revenues depend on demand, but, more specifically, they depend on price (P) and how much the firm can sell (Q). A gas station located on a deserted country road would not sell much gasoline. A store that sells deep-sea fishing equipment exclusively would probably not last long in Nebraska. Clearly a retail outlet that sells goods or services directly to people would find that it must be accessible to its customers. Many firms comfortably located along major state and U.S. highways found themselves in deep trouble when the interstate highway system diverted traffic away from them.

The price that a firm can charge for its product may also vary with location. Take, for example, the corner convenience store. Everyone knows that small neighborhood grocery and drug stores charge higher prices than the big supermarkets and chain drug stores. They can do so and not go out of business because they are convenient. There is a cost associated with getting in the car and driving the two or three miles to the supermarket, and when I need only one or two things, it is worth the extra charge just to run down to the corner.

Location can also work to keep prices down. Most college towns, for example, have several stores that sell tapes and records to students. In such places, this business is quite competitive—these items are heavily discounted, and any store that charges a higher price than another store for popular albums will lose most of its business. But if you want to buy a record album in a relatively isolated suburban community with only one small store that sells records among other things, you will probably pay a substantially higher price. By the same token, the lowest gasoline prices are found along roads that are well traveled by local residents and where there are several gas stations. When competitors are not very accessible, prices tend to be higher; you encounter the highest gas prices of all in remote areas, in the centers of large cities, and at rest stops along interstate highways.

Locational Variation in Costs   Some costs that firms incur vary from location to location and some do not. For many firms, the cost of transporting inputs to the point of production and outputs to the point of sale make up a large component of final cost. Clearly transport costs depend upon what needs to be transported where.

Automobiles are a prime example. Components must be produced, then assembled, and the final product must be shipped to dealers all over the world. Many of an automobile's component parts are produced from steel and aluminum. Moving iron ore, bauxite, coal, and whatever else is necessary to the sites of aluminum and steel production, transporting the raw materials to production facilities, moving finished parts to assembly plants, and shipping assembled automobiles to dealers is an enormously complex set of tasks. The costs of all this clearly depend on the sites of ore sources, production facilities, assembly plants, and dealers.

Other costs also vary with location. For one thing, wage rates vary significantly across the country. The highest average wages are in the Pacific Northwest, in Oregon and Washington, for example, and in the north central industrial states of Michigan, Ohio, Indiana, and Iowa. The lowest-priced labor is found in the deep South and in northern New England. Average wage rates in 1987 ranged from a low of $7.59 in Mississippi to a high of $12.90 in Michigan. Energy costs have also assumed a more important role in location decisions since the run-up of energy prices in 1973. Firms that locate in the warmer climates of the Southeast and Southwest, of course, don't have to spend as much on heating costs.

Firms that employ people to work in offices face wide variations in the cost of office space, both within and across metropolitan areas. The rental price of floor space in office buildings is normally quoted in terms of dollars per square foot per year. High-quality accessible office space in New York City and Boston was renting for over $100.00 per foot per year in 1986. In the same cities, firms could find reasonable office space in less attractive locations for under $10.00 per square foot. In cities experiencing economic downturns—Houston, for example—vacancy rates as high as 20 percent led building owners to cut rents sharply and to offer longer-than-normal leases.

As we saw in Chapter 13, the cost of capital to a firm depends to a great extent on the cost of financing. Neither the cost of borrowing nor the cost of raising funds through bond or stock offerings varies significantly across cities and regions, because the banking industry is highly integrated. If interest rates in Phoenix increase, Phoenix banks can obtain funds from outside the region, or firms themselves may turn directly to credit markets outside the area. Money can thus move quickly from low-demand regions to high-demand regions. The stock market and the bond market are national markets. A household in Columbus, Ohio, may save and deposit some of its income in a local brokerage account, with the proceeds going to finance a new wing on a fiberglass plant near San Diego.

Location and Public Policy   Public officials have sought for decades to influence the locational choices that firms make. Both tax and expenditure policies have been continued to encourage businesses. Several years ago, New York State had a number of provisions in its Corporate Franchise Tax designed to promote the expansion of firms within the state. The "jobs-incentive-credit" program, for example, gave firms a tax reduction if they expanded their employment in the state by a minimum of one percent during the year.

Before the tax reforms of 1986, the federal government provided states with another "tool" for attracting business. For many years, the interest earned on most bonds purchased from state and local governments or their agencies has not been subject to federal income taxation. This, in turn, meant that state and local governments did not have to pay as much interest as they otherwise would have in order to borrow money; because the interest was tax free, states and localities were able to sell bonds bearing a lower interest rate. As a result, the interest rate on state and local bonds has always been significantly below the corporate borrowing rate. Before the Tax Reform Act of 1986, state and local governments could also pick out industries that they thought would produce broad social benefits and then issue "industrial revenue bonds" to the public at tax-free interest rates. The proceeds from the sale of the bonds were passed on to the firms, and the firms ended up paying lower interest rates than they would have paid if they had borrowed on their own.

Some states and cities negotiate property tax rates with new firms, offering juicy abatements and other perquisites. Others build access roads or new freeway interchanges to benefit new firms at taxpayer expense. During the days when urban renewal was seen as the salvation of run-down inner cities, city governments paid for most of the land and site-improvement costs before developments began.

For years, economists have debated whether state tax and expenditure policies have a significant effect on business location decisions. The evidence is mixed. Those who find no effect argue that state and local taxes represent a very small portion of total costs for most firms, and tax rates vary less across states than most people think. When decision makers are asked in surveys which factors played a key role in their location decisions, taxes and other special incentives do not score high. Most, but not all statistical studies that try to identify the factors that seem to have influenced actual location decisions find that state and local taxes and expenditure policies are insignificant. The factors that do seem to play a major role include the availability of a trained labor force, wage rates, and transport costs. But the view that state taxes and expenditures have little or no effect on location decisions is not universally held by economists. Some studies have found statistical evidence that site choice *is* sensitive to tax rates. Others point to specific examples of firms that claim to have been influenced by incentives.

Whether or not incentives work, it is not at all clear from the standpoint of national policy that intense competition among state governments for employment is a good thing. Firms are naturally drawn to the locations that best suit their own circumstances, and when a firm is able to move from one state to another and reduce real costs, the nation as a whole benefits. If state policies succeed in changing those decisions, the result is inefficient. And if many states compete by throwing money at firms to attract them, one state's gain is another state's loss—it is a "zero sum game." Suppose, for example, an automobile company decides to build a new plant in state X for cost reasons. The company then tells states W, X, Y, and Z that they are all in the running. The resulting competition ultimately forces state X into offering a substantial subsidy that wastes state tax dollars and has no effect on the firm's decision.

Land Costs and Density of Development   One of the most important factors, that shows a significant variation within a city or a metropolitan area, is land costs. If you think about a city or metropolitan area as a series of concentric rings around the city center, land area increases significantly as you move out from the center.[3] Space near the center is also the most accessible. It is not surprising, then, that in nearly all cities, land value decreases with its distance from the city center.

As you recall from the discussion of factor prices and technological choice in Chapter 7, most firms can produce their output in a number of alternative ways, using a number of different combinations of inputs. They may be able to substitute capital for labor, labor for capital, capital for land, and so forth. The substitutability of capital for land is of particular importance to the discussion of industrial location.

A firm that spreads out in a sprawling one-story plant complex is using a lot of land relative to capital. A firm that builds a skyscraper, on the other hand, uses a lot of capital

---

[3]If you recall the formula for the area of a circle, area increases with the *square* of the distance from the center: area $= \pi r^2$. Thus, the *supply* of developable land increases with the square of the distance from the city center.

relative to land. Near the center of a city, where land is very expensive, we would expect firms to substitute capital for land, and, indeed, we see tall buildings near the center of cities and sprawling one-story plants near the periphery.

The possibility of substituting capital for land has implications for the kinds of firms that locate downtown and the kinds that locate out in the suburban ring. Firms whose employees work in offices find it relatively easy to operate efficiently in tall buildings. These include firms in industries such as business services, finance, insurance, and real estate. Manufacturing firms, which must move materials through many stages of production, find it impractical, and in many cases impossible, to produce in a multistory plant. Imagine assembling a car in a 20-story building. In other words, manufacturing firms find it very difficult to substitute capital for land and as a consequence manufacturing plants locate farther and farther away from the city center on less expensive land. At the same time, corporate headquarters, law firms, accounting firms, insurance companies, and the like are more likely to locate in the center city on more expensive land.

This is not to say that there are no office-based firms on the periphery and no manufacturing firms in the central city. Many firms that occupy office buildings are in business to serve people and to serve other firms. Insurance companies, banks, brokerage houses, and the like find it important to locate in or near suburban residential areas, and major manufacturing firms located in the suburbs require the services of lawyers, accountants, consultants, and so on. As a consequence, many office buildings have sprung up in suburban rings around major cities. At the same time, many manufacturing plants are still located in or near central cities.

The Complexity of Business Location Decisions

We have already said that the economics of location decisions is extremely complicated. Choosing the optimal level of output when input and output prices are known with certainty is hard enough. When you then allow all prices to vary from location to location, the decision becomes much more complex. Because of this complexity, it is difficult to generalize about, and to predict, industrial location patterns. It is even more difficult to design public policies that significantly change patterns of economic development to benefit a particular state or region. Such policies are expensive and they generally fail.

THE LOCATION OF HOUSEHOLDS

Everyone needs some place to live. Furthermore, at least one person in almost every household is employed. This means that residential location depends to a large extent on work place locations. Because of the costs associated with getting from home to work and back, the natural tendency is for households to cluster around areas of high employment.

Monocentric City Models

The earliest models constructed to analyze residential location made the assumption that all employment was located at the center of the city and that households bid against each other for the locations accessible to the central city. Most models also assumed that land and capital were substitutable in the production of housing.

The story embodied in those models says that because their commute is shorter, those who end up living close to the center city bear lower transportation costs, and this desirability of location is reflected in their bids for land. But as people move away from the center, their transportation costs increase. Location therefore becomes less desirable and bids for housing fall. An equilibrium can exist only where the land prices just offset the lower transport costs closer to the center. If, at current land prices, a household on the periphery could increase its welfare by moving closer to the center, it would bid the closer land away from its current occupant.

With higher land prices at the center, theory predicts that we will find substitution of capital for land. And, indeed, high-rise apartment buildings do appear most frequently in downtown areas, while garden apartments and single-family homes are usually found farther out. Despite the simplicity of the assumptions, the **monocentric,** or "single-center," **models** that assume central employment are a good way to begin to understand the process of residential location.

Clearly job location is not the only factor that affects residential location decisions. Housing is an enormously complicated "product." It has many different dimensions, and people have different preferences, which also shift over time. Some families have a taste for space, others feel lost in it; some love urban living, while others are afraid of crime. Some want to be near water; others prefer mountains. Many people never leave their home towns; others can't wait to get away. Some people have high incomes and others are poor. This heterogeneity of tastes and incomes is reflected in the heterogeneity of the housing stock in the United States from huge, single-family country estates to million-dollar downtown condominiums, from urban ghetto apartments to rural shacks.

Discrimination in the Housing Market

Bidding for accessible locations tells only a small part of the residential location story. Census data reveal that black and white Americans still live, by and large, in separate neighborhoods, both in urban and rural parts of the country. The South has many rural blacks, and there is virtually complete segregation in its small towns. In the North, black people live in the cities. While more mixed neighborhoods exist today than existed 20 years ago, they are few and far between.

Many theories to explain why blacks and whites live separately have been offered. Blacks earn lower incomes on average. Income differences, however, explain only a small fraction of actual segregation. The hypothesis that blacks live separately by choice and do not want access to predominantly white neighborhoods is not supported by evidence. Ample evidence does support a third hypothesis, however—that blacks are denied equal access to the housing market through *discrimination.*

Racial covenants Provisions spelled out in deeds to property that prohibited sale of that property to members of specific racial or ethnic groups.

Racial discrimination in the housing market has been documented in many forms. Until recent years, many property deeds carried provisions that restricted an owner's ability to sell to blacks. These "**racial covenants**" were actually enforceable until the 1950s, when the courts threw them out. Even with no formal agreements, however, owners and real estate agents in all white neighborhoods often do everything possible to prevent selling or renting to blacks and those who belong to ethnic groups that form the underclass peculiar to a given region.

During the 1950s and 1960s, many black people moved from the rural South to the urban North. When they arrived, they found their access to the housing market limited. Certain neighborhoods were designated for black occupancy, and for them to buy or rent elsewhere was difficult. Adding in all the costs, including the potential risks they would

Ghetto premium   *Evidence suggests that during the 1960's and 1970's housing in sections of U.S. cities inhabited predominantly by blacks was more expensive than comparable housing in white areas. The price difference came to be called a ghetto premium.*

face, it was an expensive proposition for a black to buy, or try to buy, in a white neighborhood. As demand pressure for housing increased in the designated black areas, prices there rose. Dozens of studies during the 1960s and early 1970s documented the existence of **ghetto premiums**. Blacks were paying more to live in the ghetto than whites of comparable means were paying to live in virtually identical housing in white areas.

While the ghetto premiums seemed to disappear during the 1970s, this was probably more because blacks stopped moving to the city in great new waves than it was because discrimination had ended. A number of very recent studies have shown that racial and ethnic discrimination in housing continues to be widespread today, despite decades of efforts to stop it. One study using matched pairs of "auditors," one black and one white, revealed among other things that blacks seeking apartments are invited to inspect 36.3% fewer units than their white counterparts.[4]

Table 20.2 shows how the black population is distributed in the United States. In 1980 the 26.4 million blacks in the U.S. made up 11.7% of the population. Of that total, 21.7 million, or 82 percent, lived in metropolitan areas; of those in metropolitan areas, 73 percent (60 percent of the total) lived in the center of cities. Data on selected metropolitan areas in Table 20.3 show the extent to which blacks were concentrated in central cities in 1980.

TABLE 20.2

Distribution of White and Black Population Between Central Cities, Metropolitan Areas and Nonmetropolitan Areas, 1980

Blacks are more likely to live in central cities than whites.

	Black (in percent)	White (in percent)
In central cities	60	27
In metropolitan areas outside central cities	22	47
Total in metropolitan areas	82	74
Outside metropolitan areas	18	26
Total	100	100

Source: U.S Bureau of the Census

TABLE 20.3

Concentrations of Blacks in Cities and Metropolitan Areas in 1980

Blacks are concentrated in the central parts of U.S. metropolitan areas.

	Central city population that is black (percentage)	Metropolitan area population outside of central city that is black (percentage)
Atlanta	66.5	13.4
Boston	22.5	1.6
Chicago	39.8	5.6
Dallas	29.3	7.4
Los Angeles	17.0	9.7
New York City	25.3	7.5
St. Louis	45.5	10.6
United States	21.7	5.9

Source: U.S. Bureau of the Census

[4]See John Yinger, "Measuring Racial Discrimination with Fair Housing Audits: Caught in the Act," *American Economic Review* (December 1986).

TABLE 20.4
Poverty in United States Metropolitan Areas and Central Cities, 1980

The urban poor in the United States are concentrated in central cities.

	CENTRAL CITY			METROPOLITAN AREA (SMSA) OUTSIDE OF THE CENTRAL CITY		
	Population (thousands)	Poor	Percentage	Population (thousands)	Poor	Percentage
Atlanta	425	113	26.6	1604	124	7.7
Boston	562	107	19.0	2201	172	7.8
Chicago	3005	601	20.0	4098	278	6.8
Dallas	904	126	13.9	2070	167	8.1
Los Angeles	2967	478	16.1	4510	477	10.6
New York	7072	1392	19.7	2048	171	8.3
St. Louis	453	97	21.4	1903	143	7.5

Source: United States Bureau of the Census, "Estimates of Social, Economic and Housing Characteristics." PHCBO-S1-1 State and Selected Metropolitan Areas; County and City Data Book (1983).

The Filtering Process and Housing for the Poor

Most poor people today live in old housing once occupied by higher-income people, housing that has declined in quality and value over the years. Virtually all unsubsidized new housing in the United States is built for those at the upper- and middle-income levels. As rich people buy the new homes, their old homes become available to those in lower income brackets.

Filtering   The process wherein the newest and best housing goes to the wealthy, their former housing passes down to those of middle income, their former housing passes down to those of low income, and the oldest housing passes finally to the poor. Thus, housing "filters down" the income-distribution ladder.

As housing "filters" down the income-distribution ladder, it depreciates. The cheapest housing, the housing available to poor people, is often housing that is the oldest, or that has depreciated the fastest from lack of upkeep. The theory is that by encouraging new construction with tax breaks and subsidies, the **filtering** process will work faster than the deterioration of older housing stock, and everyone will end up in better housing.

The central parts of cities are usually the oldest parts. Because the oldest housing falls to the poorest people, low-income housing has in many places become concentrated in the inner city. Table 20.4 presents data on people below the poverty line in 1980 in seven metropolitan areas. The poor are much more likely to live in the central city than in the metropolitan area outside of it.

THE LAND MARKET, RENT, AND LOCATION

Before you can understand where economic activity is finally located and how it is arranged in space, you need to understand the land market. Land is the ticket to location. In the absence of restrictions, you would expect to see locations going to the user who is willing to pay the most. A small commercial space in Harvard Square might end up occupied by a restaurant, a clothing store, a copy center, or some other kind of firm. Under ordinary circumstances, the firm that ends up in the space should be the one that is willing to pay the most for it.

Rent as a Function of Location

The amount that a firm is willing to pay for a location depends on how profitable it can be at that particular location. A restaurant at a popular, accessible downtown location will sell more meals than a comparable restaurant in a dangerous neighborhood. It will probably be able to charge higher prices, as well. The owners would probably earn large profits at the popular location, but they would also have to pay a much higher rent if they did not own the land—there is no such thing as a free lunch. The land—that is, location—is the critical factor, and the owner of the land will not give it away.

Suppose I own a lot beside a new interchange that is just being built on an interstate highway. The land had previously been farmed, but now I want to sell or rent it. What is it worth? It is worth exactly what some person or some firm is willing to pay for it. The best use of the land will probably turn out to be a gas station, a fast food restaurant, or a motel. What such an establishment is willing to pay depends on how much business it expects to get at that location. If my lot is inaccessible, say 10 miles from the highway in the middle of a soybean field, no matter how little I ask for it, no firm will locate there. Cheap land doesn't do a retail or a service firm any good if it can't get customers to come there.

To see how the land market operates, let us take a small vacant lot near a popular square in a major metropolitan area. Suppose that the lot has two potential uses, a suite of offices and four small apartments. Table 20.5 gives revenue and cost estimates for these two projects. At what rent level would a rational investor decide that the project was simply not worth it? If you were the landowner, how much could you charge, and who would end up with the land? To get at pure land value, it is important to think of the landowner and developer as two people, although they are often the same person.[5]

First, each of the two projects will require a *capital investment*: a structure must be built. Constructing the office suite will cost a flat $100,000, while building a set of four small apartments costs $150,000. Notice that these are *capital expenditures*. When a firm (the developer) invests $100,000 in a new piece of capital, it acquires an asset, but it does not incur a cost—at least not as an accountant or an economist would define a cost. We

TABLE 20.5

Hypothetical Revenue, Cost, and Profit Calculations for Competing Uses of a Building Lot

	Offices	Four studio apartments
Capital investment required	$100,000	$150,000
Expected annual revenues	50,000	28,000
Expected annual costs (excluding rent and capital cost)	− 30,000	− 8,000
Accounting profit (before rent and capital cost)	$20,000	$20,000
Normal return to capital (10 percent yield)*	− 10,000	− 15,000
Potential bid rent	$10,000	$5,000

*This figure could also be thought of as the annual cost of borrowing at 10 percent to finance the capital investment required.

[5]Throughout the discussion that follows, we assume that the landowner and the person who owns the business (and the capital stock of the business) are separate people. Many businesses, of course, own the land on which they are located, but this does not change the story.

If I operate a business on land that I own, and another firm would earn more profits on my land than I do, I should consider renting it and moving my business to a different location. If I stay, I give up the rent that I could have earned. The *potential* rent on the land I own is an *opportunity cost* that I must consider. If other firms in my industry produce on less expensive land than I, they can undersell me and force me to move to a less costly location. It is easiest to understand how the land market works, however, when we think of the landowner's decisions as distinct from the business owner's decisions.

assume that the building maintains its value over time as long as it is maintained, and as long as it maintains its value, the buyer has really not incurred a cost—he can always sell. The same is true for the apartments. In both cases, the cost of maintaining the structure's value is included in the expected annual costs.

If the offices generate a stream of $50,000 per year in revenues against costs of $30,000, that leaves a cash profit before rent and capital costs of $20,000. The initial capital expenditure required for the offices is $100,000, and, let us assume, the normal rate of return is 10 percent—that is, to get an investor (developer) interested in making the $100,000 investment, he or she must get a return of at least 10 percent, or $10,000 per year. (In other words, that is the cost of the use of the capital, or *capital cost*.) If our developer were to borrow the money from a bank at a cost of 10 percent or to use his or her own money at an opportunity cost of 10 percent, then that $10,000 per year of the $20,000 profit from the building would go back to the developer as a normal return on investment.

With capital cost subtracted from cash profits, the office building yields a flow of $10,000 per year. Thus the office project developer could *theoretically* be pushed to pay up to $10,000 per year in rent to the landowner. At any higher rent, however, it would not earn sufficient revenues to cover basic costs, including capital costs.

What about the apartment complex? The apartments would rent for $583 per month each, yielding a total of $28,000 per year in rental income. Maintenance and other costs are only $8000. The cash income before land rent and capital costs is $20,000, the same as for the offices. But the capital costs are higher. The initial capital expenditure required is $150,000, or, at an interest rate of 10 percent, $15,000 a year. This means that the potential apartment developer could not pay a rent of more than $5000. Thus the apartment developer would lose interest and drop out of the bidding if rent at the location went over $5000.

The office building would win the location because it would get a greater net flow of profit from the location, and its developer would be willing to bid the most. Assuming that these numbers are right, the best use of the location, from the landowner's point of view, is to provide office space. That is also true from society's point of view, because using the land as office space would create more value. Any rational landlord would want to charge a rent closer to $10,000 per year. Thus you can see that rents are determined by the amount that potential users of a location are willing to pay for it, and that amount, in turn, depends on the likely profits of locating at the site in question.

This insight also helps us to explain a seeming paradox. There are many locations at which profits seem to be high, and yet the firms that occupy them go out of business. Why should this be so? If the high profits are the result of a prime location, the rent on that location is also likely to be very high. The landowner, or perhaps we should say the location owner, is not likely to sell the benefits of what he or she owns cheap. But what makes sense for the location owner may squeeze the occupying firm's profits. Thus even at prime locations, new investors (or firms) cannot expect to make much over a normal rate of profit because they need to buy the ticket to the location—they must rent the land.

Restraints on a Free Land Market: Zoning and Planning

Land-use planning   A *regulatory system, generally overseen by local zoning boards, that stipulates what kinds of industries, businesses, and housing may locate in an area, and under what conditions.*

So far we have been discussing the market for land as if it were a free, unregulated market. But land markets are rarely free. Generally they are regulated by *zoning boards*, locally appointed bodies that are responsible for what is sometimes called **land use planning**.

Zoning   *The designation of certain areas for industry, commerce, and housing. Often these categories are broken down into subcategories which specify the kind of business allowed, the number of families allowed within a single residential building, how much land a residence must have around it, and so on.*

Towns, understandably, will not let a steel mill locate next to a residential neighborhood. Building a house or locating a business next to, or near, other homes and businesses obviously has a number of external effects. These effects may be costs, or they may be benefits; either way, they can be insignificant or they can be huge. A new business could cause traffic congestion or generate sight, air, or noise pollution, particularly if it moved into an area that was already highly congested. A run-down abandoned mansion in a residential area could, on the other hand, be converted into a beautifully landscaped and well-maintained conference center.

Nearly all cities and towns are **zoned**, that is, specific areas are dedicated to commercial activities, industrial activities, residences, and so on. Within the residential zone category, many cities and towns have specific subzones for multifamily housing and for single-family housing. Some towns have been accused of using zoning powers to restrict development to exclude all but the very wealthy. A town that sets a rule that only single-family houses can be built and that each must be built on a minimum of five acres of land, for example, is probably leaning in this direction. Local governments also issue *building permits*, and some towns have limited the number of building permits that may be issued in order to slow population growth. Such procedures, however, have been challenged successfully in the courts.

Zoning can certainly affect the value of a location, and it can change its use as well (which may amount to the same thing). Suppose, for example, that the town board zoned the location we have been describing (see Table 20.5) for residential use only. The owner of the land could only rent it to the developer that wanted to build the apartments. Instead of earning a rent of $10,000 per year as an office location, the property could earn only $5000 per year at most, and the offices would be forced to look for a second-best place to locate.

Is it most efficient not to regulate the land market and to let locations go to the highest bidder? In the absence of regulations, the office building, which is willing to pay the most for the location, would get the location. The goal of the market is to channel resources to their best use, and this, in one sense, is a best use. There may, however, be *externalities*. The use of the land in question for offices might lead to congestion, people coming and going from the neighborhood, loss of privacy, a possible increase in crime, and so forth. If these external costs exceed $5000 per year, the apartments, not the offices, would be a more efficient use of the space.

Many cities go beyond basic zoning and have planning boards. The function of a local planning board is to identify all the costs and benefits of various arrangements and to maximize the total net value to the community. Many universities have departments of city planning and teach courses on land use planning. The arrangement of economic activity within cities is thus determined by a combination of market forces and decisions of regulatory bodies.

REGIONAL GROWTH AND CHANGE

As you saw early in the chapter, one of the primary concerns of the states and their governors is jobs. A major goal of most state-level policy makers is to attract industry and increase employment in the state. But states are part of regions, and regions are part of the country. No governor of an individual state could in any way influence, much less stop, the major recession of 1982. National recessions do not respect geographical boundaries; although some states did better than others, all states suffered during that downturn.

Neither can any state governor stop major shifts that take place within and among regions. For example, during the years after World War II, the New England economy was heavily based in traditional manufacturing. Particularly important industries were textiles; leather goods, especially shoes; and furniture. During the 1960s and 1970s those industries began to decline. Low-cost labor in the South and abroad in Hong Kong, Korea, Taiwan, and elsewhere led textile mills to shift their operations out of the New England region. Region-wide declines were also registered in leather and furniture. With the loss of these firms, unemployment rose sharply. By the mid 1970s, the unemployment rate in New England was higher than for any region in the country except the Pacific Northwest. While many pointed to high taxes as a factor, the simple fact was that other regions and countries were better places for those industries to locate.

In fact, population and employment have been shifting toward the South and West for many decades. Table 20.6 presents some data on the share of population in each of four large regions and Census Bureau projections for 1990 and 2000. There is every reason to expect that the trends observed through 1986 will continue.

Recent employment trends resemble population trends. Table 20.7 shows changes in employment by region between 1977 and 1987. Once again the largest gains were in the West and South, while the Mid-Atlantic and North Central region grew much more slowly.

Sometime in the mid 1970s, New England's fortunes began to turn around. While traditional industries continued to close down and move out, a different group of new industries were born, grew, and began to prosper. A number of firms producing high technology products experienced enormous growth. In Massachusetts alone, the Digital

TABLE 20.6

U.S. Resident Population by Region, 1950–1986 and Projections

There has been a gradual movement of population out of the Northeast and Midwest toward the South and West.

	1950	1960	1970	1980	1986	1990	2000
Northeast	26.1	24.9	24.1	21.7	20.7	20.2	19.4
Midwest	29.4	28.8	27.8	26.0	24.6	23.9	22.3
South	31.2	30.7	30.9	33.3	34.4	34.9	36.2
West	13.3	15.6	17.1	19.1	20.2	20.9	22.2

Source: Statistical Abstract of the United States, various editions

TABLE 20.7

Employment by Region, 1977 and 1987

	1977 Employment (thousands) and percentage of total	1987 Employment (thousands) and percentage of total	Change (percentage)
New England	4,983 (6.0)	6,386 (6.3)	+28.2
Mid-Atlantic	14,258 (17.2)	16,578 (16.3)	+16.3
South Atlantic	13,015 (15.7)	17,954 (17.6)	+37.9
East North Central	16,239 (19.6)	17,501 (17.2)	+7.8
East South Central	4,831 (5.8)	5,666 (5.6)	+17.3
West North Central	6,450 (7.8)	7,373 (7.2)	+14.3
West South Central	7,938 (9.6)	9,973 (9.8)	+25.6
Pacific Northwest	3,211 (3.9)	3,946 (3.9)	+22.9
Pacific Southwest	12,039 (14.5)	16,551 (16.2)	+37.5
United States total:	82,964 (100)	101,928 (100)	+22.9

Source: Data Resources, Inc.

Equipment Corporation and Wang Laboratories, both very small companies in 1970, employed well over 100,000 sixteen years later. At the same time, thousands of smaller high-tech companies started operations. By the mid 1980s, the New England region had the lowest unemployment of any region in the country. With steady employment growth and a turnaround in population declines, housing prices rose more quickly in the Northeast than in any other part of the country.

During the same period, the West South Central states of Texas, Oklahoma, and Louisiana have seen a major recession due mainly to the huge drop in energy prices after 1983. The drop in crude oil prices meant that producers had lower incomes and that exploration was less attractive. The economies of those states depend heavily on oil and gas production and exploration. Incomes have fallen, unemployment is high, and housing values have dropped.

These major trends are the result of naturally occurring economic events that had absolutely nothing to do with state economic policies. The modern "industrial revolution" in New England happened because of a nationwide explosion in the demand for new products made possible by technological advances. And the decline of more traditional manufacturing sectors in the Midwest and the East is due to cost differentials that grew up over a long period of time as well as a strong dollar and international competition during most of the 1980s.

THE ECONOMICS OF URBAN DECLINE AND RECOVERY

Many large American cities endured a host of troubles during the 1960s and 1970s. Firms moved to the suburbs, creating unemployment in the central cities. Buildings were abandoned, crime rates rose. City governments found themselves with a declining tax base at the same time that the demand for public services was increasing. Many cities in addition to New York faced serious fiscal crises: many lost their bond ratings and came close to defaulting on their debts.

Urban decline results directly from lack of investment. In one sense, we can see a city as a huge agglomeration of capital: factories, houses, office buildings, warehouses, government buildings, roads, water and sewer systems, bridges and so forth. Some of this is private capital, some of it is public capital. But all capital depreciates, and unless it is maintained, repaired, and periodically replaced, it deteriorates in the most physically real way.

Urban decline   The deterioration of the private and social capital stock of a city which results from the lack of investment by both private and public sectors.

Abandoned housing is simply housing that has not been maintained. Roofs need to be replaced every ten years or so, walls must be painted, and plumbing systems and heating systems need to be repaired and replaced. When owners stop investing, deterioration accelerates, and soon the building is ready for the scrap dealer and the rats.

Run-down buildings often have a positive value. Unfortunately, it is sometimes advantageous to walk away from a property, not when its value is zero but when its value has fallen lower than the obligations of the owners. Building owners, for example, must pay property taxes in addition to their maintenance costs, and they usually have heavy mortgages. If I owe $100,000 to a bank on a mortgage for any apartment building, but I have allowed the building to deteriorate to a point where it is worth only $40,000, I am better off defaulting on the mortgage and letting the bank take the building. If I have not paid my property taxes for 10 years, and the bill for back taxes plus penalties exceeds $40,000, I may as well let the building go rather than pay.

Social capital also decays if governments do not continuously invest. In many cities, water systems, sewer systems, roads and bridges, and transit systems are in a very bad state of repair. The task of maintaining public capital stocks is staggering. The New York subway system, which carries 1.1 billion passengers per year, consists of 231 miles of track, 461 stations, and 6700 cars. The New York water system contains 6150 miles of main water lines; 95 percent is old cast iron pipe of various ages, strengths, and sizes. Anyone who has driven in New York knows what the streets are like. One 1979 estimate put the costs of needed replacement and repair to New York's streets, water systems, and subways, at nearly $12 billion.[6] That figure is undoubtedly much higher now.

Urban economists point to a number of factors that explain the lack of investment during the last quarter century. Since the end of World War II, firms have been gradually moving out of the central cities and into the suburban ring. Improvement in both transportation and communications technology has made the suburbs a more attractive location. As a result of this, among many other factors, population followed. Suburban housing investment boomed, while inner city housing began to decay. Then during the 1950s and 1960s, poor rural blacks moved to northern cities in record numbers. Discrimination limited their housing choices, and they became concentrated in central cities. Because very little low-income family housing, subsidized or unsubsidized, is located in the suburbs of America, the urban poor have little choice but to live in central cities.

All of this had a devastating effect on city budgets. First the tax base declined. Business firms were moving to the suburbs. Inner-city housing filtered down the depreciation ladder, property values fell, and some properties came off the tax rolls altogether. Lower-income families are less able to pay taxes than higher-income families. Second, the expenditures required to run city government increased. Old, poorly maintained, buildings are more likely to catch fire, increasing the need for fire protection. Crime rates are higher in poor areas than in high-income areas, necessitating more police and courts. In addition, poor and homeless people need more services.

With the squeeze on city budgets, it is not surprising that the social capital stock in many cities is inadequately maintained. Roads, water systems, government buildings are all in a state of disrepair.

Taxes, Public Services, and Segregation by Income

Property tax finance, coupled with local responsibility for public services, education, and a substantial portion of the social welfare system, have together led to increasing segregation by income and have exacerbated the problem of urban decay.

For many years, state governments and local governments shared responsibility equally for public welfare programs to aid the very poor in the United States. In 1960, in fact, localities accounted for 49.5% and states accounted for 50.5% of total state and local public welfare expenditures. Since then this responsibility has gradually been shifted to the states. By 1980 the local share was down to 27 percent and the state share was up to 73 percent. Of course, local government has always been responsible for elementary and secondary education and for the provision of most local public services, such as police and fire protection. Nationally, about three quarters of all local tax receipts come from the *property tax*, which is a proportional tax on the assessed value of all property.

[6]David Grossman, *The Future of New York City's Capital Plant* (Washington, D.C.: The Urban Institute, 1979).

Consider two towns, A and B. Let A be the older town with a depreciating housing stock occupied by poor people. With a high proportion of poor, social welfare expenditures and the need for social services will be high in A. Also, low-income families have more school-age children on average. Those needed services put added pressure on the tax system. If at the same time property *values* are lower in A, the tax *rates* required to support the higher level of service may be extraordinary.

The arithmetic is simple. Suppose the average house in A is valued at $30,000 and the average house in B is valued at $120,000. Suppose also that citizens of both towns A and B have an average of one school-age child per household. A property tax rate of 2 percent in town A would yield enough to finance $600 per student per year, while in B the same rate would yield $2400 per student per year. In many American cities, suburban school districts boast much lower tax rates *and* higher expenditures for education.[7]

When you add it all up, a higher tax rate and lower quality of education and public services put added pressure on those who can afford it to get out and move to the suburbs. The increased income segregation that results then further exacerbates the problem of decline. In the extreme, if all the poor lived together and all the rich lived together, no redistribution of income could take place through local governments, and public services would be produced only in proportion to income.

Urban Decline and Public Policy

The first major federal program designed to deal with the problem of urban decay was the **urban renewal** program enacted in 1949. By the mid 1960s, billions of dollars had been spent in hundreds of cities to clear slums and bring investment back into the city. The federal government provided the money, and local governments evicted the people, cleared the land, and sold it to private developers—usually at a price that amounted to about 30 percent of the cost of clearing.

By the mid 1960s, it was clear that the urban renewal program was not the answer to the nation's urban woes. It was true that many projects increased the local tax base, but severe costs went uncounted. Many poor and middle-income families were uprooted and displaced, and a great deal of useful capital was destroyed. Renewal projects often cleared stable lower-middle-income neighborhoods because developers did not want to locate in the worst parts of town. Regardless of where they were undertaken, renewal projects reduced the supply of low- and moderate-income housing and drove up house prices and rents. Some urban "blight" was cleared, but it simply moved to other locations.

During the 1970s, the urban renewal program was all but abandoned: it had treated the symptoms and not the disease, and it had had severe side effects. To replace it, policy makers began a search for other programs to slow or reverse urban decline without destroying valuable capital and displacing people.

One way to help the situation would be to relieve some of the pressure on local governments by shifting responsibility for financing some local public services to higher levels of government or simply by sharing federal and state revenues with localities. It can be argued that all of society benefits from reinvestment in our cities. Many people, of

---

[7]The system of financing education using local property tax revenues has been challenged in the courts on numerous occasions. The best known cases were *Serrano v. Priest* in the California Supreme Court in 1971 and the *San Antonio Independent School District v. Rodriguez*, which went to the U.S. Supreme Court in 1972. In 1987 the same issue was raised in New Jersey when Camden, a relatively poor, declining city, brought suit against the state, pointing to nearby Cherry Hill, where property tax rates were lower and school expenditures higher.

course, work in the cities and enjoy the night life but retreat to the suburbs when work and play are finished. Those people certainly enjoy the benefits of police and fire protection, and they use public facilities.

Between 1960 and 1980 the percentage of local expenditures financed with local sources of revenue declined steadily from just under 70 percent to 55.9%. In 1980, 44.1% of local expenditures were financed with grants from the federal government and from state governments.[8] Since 1980, however, the trend has been reversed as the Reagan administration made progressive, significant cuts in federal aid to states and localities.

In addition to reducing tax burdens and improving public services, literally hundreds of different "urban development" programs emerged from the dust of the urban renewal program: urban development block grants and action grants, enterprise zones, Section 8 housing, urban homesteading, neighborhood housing services, low-interest loans to small business, and so forth. But while all of these programs have had some impact, the fundamental economic forces that led to decay in so many of our central cities have not changed. There are poor people in the United States, and they have become increasingly concentrated in the cities. People with low incomes cannot pay high rents, and they generate a disproportionate demand for local public services.

During the past five years, a number of cities that were in serious trouble in the 1970s have experienced a resurgence of investment. Warehouses, fishing piers, factories, and other eighteenth- and nineteenth-century structures have been rehabilitated and converted into popular downtown shopping areas, sometimes with spectacular results. The Cannery in San Francisco, Seattle's Waterfront, Boston's Faneuil Hall Market Place, and many other restorations have been tremendously successful. Many cities have experienced a boom in the construction of hotels and office buildings. Even New York City, on the edge of bankruptcy only 10 years ago, has become relatively prosperous, and one no longer hears any serious talk of default on its bonds.

Whether this signals the revitalization of the city, and whether it will happen in many more cities remains to be seen. It has not been a painless process. Many of the jobs in the new high-rise office buildings are white-collar jobs in finance, insurance, real estate, and service firms. Often the people who hold those jobs are not residents of the city but of the suburbs. In addition, many new young urban professionals are moving back into the city, and the housing market is feeling pressure from added demand.

BEYOND THIS CHAPTER

This chapter exposed you to another decision that must be made by every firm and every household: where to locate. It has also introduced another field of applied microeconomics: *urban economics*. The location decisions of millions of economic agents have given us the physical environment in which we live. Cities grew up in the first place because of economic forces; cities have become what they are today because of economic forces. To understand urban problems and to formulate rational urban policy, it is essential to understand markets, how they operate, and how they are likely to respond to various kinds of public policies.

Almost by definition, the urban decline of recent years is the result of disinvestment, both public and private. The increasing concentration of poor people in central cities has led to private disinvestment in central-city housing. Improved transport technology and high land prices have caused the decentralization of manufacturing jobs. Eroding tax bases and increased demand for services have put enormous pressure on local government

[8]Tax Foundation, *Facts and Figures on Government Finance* (1983).

finances. The result has been a low level of maintenance of city roads, water systems, public transit systems, and so forth.

If cities as we have known them are to make a comeback, both the public and private sectors will have to invest in them, and it is unclear whether this will happen. If cities are to change in some important ways, if they are to become largely nonresidential, for example, the same analysis holds, of course. Whether urban problems are old or new, the further study of urban economics may be one of the most exciting enterprises you can undertake.

SUMMARY

1. Our world has been shaped by the location decisions of millions of households and firms.
2. Sometime around the middle of the eighteenth century, a period of rapid change, the Industrial Revolution, began to transform the character of life, first in England, later all across Europe and the United States. One of the changes involved the massive urbanization of the population.
3. Behind the rise of cities were economic forces. Some important ones are transaction costs, competition for markets, transportation costs, economies of scale in production, the rise of linked and population-serving industries, and increased specialization in both product and labor markets. All of these factors lead, to some extent, to agglomeration of economic activity.
4. Firm location decisions are complex because costs and revenues are likely to be different at every potential location.
5. Public officials have sought for decades to influence the locational choices that firms make. Unfortunately, there is mixed evidence, at best, on the effectiveness of such efforts.
6. Because of the costs associated with traveling between home and work, the natural tendency is for households to cluster around areas of high employment. If employment is concentrated at the center of a city, land rents and population density should decline with distance from the center.
7. Black and white Americans still live, by and large, in separate neighborhoods, in part because discrimination has denied blacks equal access to the housing market.
8. The location of economic activity is determined by the functioning of land markets. The activity that ends up occupying a given space is the one that is willing to pay the most for it. The amount that a firm is willing to pay for a location depends on how profitable it is likely to be at that location.
9. Land use is generally regulated by town zoning or planning boards. The function of a local planning board is to identify all the costs and benefits of various arrangements and to maximize the total net value to the community.
10. Many large cities in the United States experienced decline and decay during the 1960s and 1970s. Urban decay results directly from lack of investment, both public and private. Housing stocks have deteriorated, businesses have moved to the suburbs, and social capital—roads, bridges, transit systems—have fallen into disrepair.
11. Property tax finance, coupled with local responsibility for public services, education, and a substantial portion of the social welfare system, have together led to increasing segregation by income and have exacerbated the problem of urban decay.
12. Public policies to stimulate investment in cities have been somewhat effective, but the fundamental forces that led to decay in many of our central cities have not changed.

REVIEW CONCEPTS

Industrial Revolution   490
transaction costs   491
population-serving industries   493
linked industries   493
employment multiplier   493
monocentric model   500
racial covenants   500

ghetto premiums   501
filtering   502
land-use planning   504
zoning   505
urban decline   507
urban renewal   509

REVIEW QUESTIONS

1. Recently retired from academic life, Emily has decided to open a gas station. Her research suggests the following:

   Gasoline sells for $1.10 at all locations (assume there is only one grade of gasoline)

   Gasoline can be purchased from wholesalers for $1.00 per gallon.

   It would cost $300,000 to build a gasoline station, regardless of location

   Annual costs of running a station are $50,000, regardless of how much gasoline is sold—this includes maintenance and full upkeep on the building

   The interest rate is 10 percent

   She is considering two locations, A and B; each is a one-acre lot:

	Location A	Location B
Expected annual sales	1 million gallons	2 million gallons
Price of lot	$250,000	$1,000,000

   Would you advise her to go into business? If so, where should she locate?

2. The largest single federal housing subsidy is the provision of the individual income tax that allows homeowners to deduct property taxes and mortgage interest payments from their income for tax purposes. Describe in detail how a subsidy that accrues almost exclusively to middle- and upper-income families might raise the quality of housing occupied by lower-income families. (*Hint*: recall the filtering process.) What specific assumptions would one have to make in order to predict such a result?

3. In 1973 and 1974, gasoline was in short supply, and energy prices, including gasoline prices, rose dramatically. How would you expect such an increase to affect the spatial arrangement of economic activity—households and firms—if those prices remained high?

4. Some cities in the United States have experienced renewed development in their central business districts. High-rise office buildings were built at a record pace in the early 1980s in some of our older cities that had earlier experienced decline. That growth has been denounced by some community leaders on the grounds that the benefits do not accrue to city residents, but rather to suburban residents. Make a list of all the benefits and costs you can think of that might result from a modern office tower in an older city. What groups benefit? What groups lose out? Be sure to include some discussion of the housing market.

III INTERNATIONAL ECONOMICS

21 International Trade and the Theory of Comparative Advantage

One of the great lessons of the 1970s was that all economies, even large ones like that of the United States, depend to some extent on other economies and are affected by events outside their borders. The oil embargo imposed on the United States by the Arab oil producing nations in 1973–1974 has had a major effect on economic events ever since. Ask anyone in Iowa about the impact of foreign trade on farm prices and therefore on the well-being of American farmers. Drivers of Hondas and Toyotas are not very popular in Detroit. Steel workers in Pittsburgh and in Youngstown know very well what cheap German and Japanese steel has done to the economies of those towns.

The United States economy is by no means "closed." We trade with hundreds of different countries. In 1987 we sold $29.9 billion worth of agricultural products to foreign buyers; from them we bought $42.3 billion worth of petroleum and petroleum products. Overall, we imported $547 billion worth of goods and services, which is more than 12.2% of our GNP.

This chapter discusses the economics of international trade. After a brief overview of U.S. foreign trade during this century, we turn to economic theory and explore the basic logic of international trade, considering the question Why should we engage in trade at all? Finally, we address the emotional issue of protection. Should we protect certain industries from international competition, and if so, which ones? With strong arguments for and against it, protection has been debated for centuries, and the debate may well continue for centuries to come.

THINKING OF THE ECONOMY AS OPEN OR CLOSED

Recall that in a closed economy, equilibrium is reached when planned aggregate expenditure and aggregate output are equal. The three components of planned aggregate expenditure that we discussed are consumption spending by households (C), planned investment spending by business firms (I), and government purchases of goods and services (G). In our models so far, the basic equilibrium condition is

$$Y = C + I + G.$$

National output, or income (Y), increases or decreases when there is a disequilibrium. If G falls, for example, thus leaving planned aggregate expenditure less than aggregate output, inventories of firms will build up and firms will respond by reducing production.

Opening the economy to foreign trade adds a fourth component to planned aggregate expenditure—exports of goods and services, which we denote X. Exports represent foreign purchases of goods and services produced in the United States. At the same time, opening up the economy also means that U.S. consumers and businesses have more choice. Instead of spending our entire income on American produced products, we can turn to foreign producers for consumer goods, raw materials, and capital goods.

From an accounting standpoint, consumption (C), planned investment (I), and government purchases (G) all include expenditures on goods produced abroad. Thus we can write $C = C_D + C_F$, $I = I_D + I_F$, and $G = G_D + G_F$ where C_D is consumption of domestically produced goods and services and C_F is consumption of foreign produced goods and services, and so forth. The total level of imports (M) is thus the sum of $C_F + I_F + G_F$. The correct expression for planned aggregate expenditure on *domestically* produced goods and services is

$$AE \equiv C_D + I_D + G_D + X.$$

Since we know that $C_D = C - C_F$, $I_D = I - I_F$, and $G_D = G - G_F$, we can write

$$AE \equiv C + I + G + X - (C_F + I_F + G_F),$$

or, since $C_F + I_F + G_F = M$,

$$AE \equiv C + I + G + (X - M).$$

The expression $(X - M)$ is referred to as "net exports."

With this in mind, you can see that increases or decreases in either imports or exports can throw the economy out of equilibrium and cause national income to change. A big decrease in exports, ceteris paribus, for example, would mean a drop in spending on domestically produced goods and services. Inventories would rise and output would fall.

IMPORTS AND EXPORTS IN THE UNITED STATES

Prior to 1970, imports and exports of goods and services accounted for a relatively small and stable fraction of GNP in the United States. Table 21.1 shows imports and exports for selected years since 1915. In all but a few years between 1915 and 1970, imports accounted for only somewhere between four percent and six percent of GNP. During the Depression and immediately following World War II, the figure dropped below four percent, but never did it rise above six percent.

Beginning in 1970, the volume of international trade increased quite significantly. Imports and exports doubled as a percentage of GNP during the 1970s, reaching over 12 percent by 1980. While exports dropped to 9.5% of GNP by 1987, imports dipped and then rebounded back to 12.2%.

The Composition of U.S. Trade

Table 21.2 breaks down merchandise imported and exported in 1987. Perhaps the most surprising observation about these lists is their tremendous diversity.

Although no single category dominates either list, the largest category—more than a third of our exports and one fifth of our imports—is capital goods except automotive, a very broad category that includes many very specialized and diverse products. This diversity in part explains the large volume of cross trading. The United States has

TABLE 21.1
U.S. Imports and Exports of Goods and Services, 1915–1987

Between 1960 and 1980, imports and exports increased steadily in relation to GNP. Between 1980 and 1987, imports stayed roughly constant while exports fell.

	EXPORTS OF GOODS AND SERVICES		IMPORTS OF GOODS AND SERVICES	
	Billions of dollars	Percentage of GNP	Billions of dollars	Percentage of GNP
1915	4	9.9	2	5.5
1925	6	6.5	5	5.6
1935	3	4.5	3	4.3
1945	16	7.7	10	4.8
1955	20	5.0	18	4.5
1960	27	5.4	23	4.6
1965	39	5.7	32	4.7
1970	63	6.3	59	6.0
1974	147	10.3	138	9.6
1976	172	10.0	162	9.4
1978	220	10.2	230	10.6
1979	287	11.9	282	11.7
1980	342	12.5	333	12.2
1981	376	12.3	362	11.9
1982	349	11.0	349	11.0
1983	333	9.8	370	10.9
1984	360	9.6	454	12.1
1985	358	9.0	461	11.5
1986	376	8.9	482	11.4
1987	427	9.5	547	12.2

Source: 1915–1970, *Historical Statistics of the United States*; 1970–1987, *Survey of Current Business*.

TABLE 21.2
Major Categories of Merchandise
Imports and Exports by the
United States, 1987

Exports	Billions of Dollars	Percentage of Total
Agricultural products	29.5	11.8
Nonagricultural products	221.3	88.2
Total	250.8	100.0
Food, feeds, and beverages	24.4	9.7
Industrial supplies and materials	69.2	27.6
Capital goods except automotive (machinery, aircraft, etc.)	89.2	35.6
Automobiles, vehicles, parts, and engines	26.6	10.6
Consumer goods except automotive	17.9	7.1
All other	23.6	9.4
Total	250.8	100.0

Imports	Billions of dollars	Percentage of Total
Petroleum and petroleum products	42.3	10.3
Nonpetroleum products	367.7	89.7
Total	410.0	100.0
Food, feeds, and beverages	24.3	5.9
Industrial supplies and materials	113.1	27.6
Capital goods except automotive (machinery, aircraft, etc.)	87.7	21.4
Automobiles, vehicles, parts, and engines	85.3	20.8
Consumer goods except automotive	87.2	21.3
All other	12.4	3.0
Total	410.0	100.0

Source: Survey of Current Business (March 1988), Table 3, p. 44.

developed a highly competitive computer and office equipment industry; the Japanese and others have done very well producing telecommunications equipment. The second most important category of U.S. exports is industrial supplies and materials—$69.2 billion in 1987. Further behind we find automobiles and food.

Prior to 1970, imports of petroleum and petroleum products never amounted to more than $3 billion and were never more than 10 percent of total imports. The rapid run-up in oil prices in 1973–1974 changed all that. Table 21.3 chronicles the rise and fall of crude petroleum as a major import. In 1980 crude oil accounted for more than one quarter of all merchandise imports. By 1985 that number was less than one tenth.

Two other important categories of imports that have received a great deal of attention because of their impact on major U.S. industries are automobiles and iron and steel. In 1985 imports of automobiles and parts totaled $46.6 billion, and imports of iron and steel amounted to $10.3 billion.

TABLE 21.3

U.S. Imports of Crude Petroleum, 1970–1987

Crude petroleum became a major import item in the 1970s. By 1980 oil imports accounted for nearly one fourth of total imports. In the 1980s the ratio of imports of crude petroleum to total merchandise imports fell to around 10 percent.

	Billions of dollars	Percentage of total merchandise imports
1970	2.8	7.0
1973	4.2	10.5
1975	18.3	19.0
1978	32.1	18.6
1979	46.1	21.9
1980	62.0	25.3
1981	61.9	23.7
1982	45.9	18.8
1983	36.8	14.3
1984	36.5	11.2
1985	33.0	9.6
1986	33.8	9.2
1987	42.3	10.3

Source: *Statistical Abstract of the United States, 1987; Survey of Current Business.*

Surpluses, Deficits, and the Call for Protection

Trade surplus, trade deficit   Trade surplus: *The situation when a country exports more than it imports.* Trade deficit: *The situation when a country imports more than it exports.*

Until the 1970s, the United States always exported more than it imported. When a country exports more than it imports, it runs what is called a **trade surplus**, and before 1970 the United States ran a trade surplus for goods and services as a whole, as well as for merchandise. Table 21.4 shows the U.S. balance of trade for merchandise and total goods and services for selected years since 1915.

TABLE 21.4

U.S. Balance of Trade (Exports minus Imports) 1915–1987 (billions of dollars)

After the 1975 recession, the United States began running increasingly large merchandise trade deficits.

	Merchandise	Goods and Services
1915	+1.1	+1.7
1925	+0.9	+1.1
1935	−1.8	+0.1
1945	+5.8	+6.0
1955	+4.0	+2.2
1960	+4.6	+4.1
1965	+5.3	+7.1
1970	+2.7	+5.8
1974	−5.5	+9.4
1976	−9.5	+9.5
1978	−33.9	−9.9
1979	−27.5	+5.1
1980	−25.5	+9.5
1981	−28.0	+13.8
1982	−36.4	−.2
1983	−67.1	−37.1
1984	−112.5	−94.3
1985	−122.1	−102.7
1986	−144.3	−127.7
1987	−159.2	−147.2

Source: 1915–1970, *Historical Statistics of the United States*; 1974–1987, *Statistical Abstract of the United States* and *Survey of Current Business* (March 1988) Table 1.2.

Once again, the 1970s marked a turning point. After 1970 the United States began to import more merchandise than it exported. When a country's imports exceed exports, it runs a **trade deficit**. Merchandise deficits climbed steadily through 1987, reaching over $150 billion. The overall goods-and-services deficit shows much more variation, but it is also quite large from 1984 on.

The large trade deficits that continued into the early and middle 1980s touched off a big political controversy. Foreign competition hit U.S. markets hard. Less expensive foreign goods—among them steel, textiles, and automobiles—began driving U.S. manufacturers out of business at an alarming rate, and thousands of jobs were lost in important industries. Cities such as Pittsburgh, Youngstown, and Detroit found themselves with major unemployment problems.

The natural reaction here was to call for protection. That is, many people wanted the President and Congress to impose tariffs and import restrictions that would make foreign goods less available and more expensive, a situation that, in turn, would protect American jobs. As you might guess, this argument was nothing new. For hundreds of years, industries have petitioned governments for protection, and societies have debated the pros and cons of free and open trade. For the last century and a half, the principal argument used against protection has been the theory of comparative advantage.

THE LOGIC OF FREE TRADE: THE THEORY OF COMPARATIVE ADVANTAGE

Corn Laws *The tariffs, subsidies, and restrictions enacted by the British Parliament in the early nineteenth century designed to discourage imports and encourage exports of grain.*

Perhaps the best-known debate on the issue of free trade took place in the British Parliament during the early years of the nineteenth century. At the time, the landed gentry—that is, the landowners—controlled Parliament. For a number of years, imports and exports of grain had been subject to a set of tariffs, subsidies, and outright restrictions collectively called the **Corn Laws**. Designed to discourage imports of grain and encourage exports, the Corn Laws' purpose was to keep the price of food high. The landlords' incomes, of course, depended on the prices they got for what their land produced. The Corn Laws thus clearly worked to the advantage of those in power.

Another group in British society had begun to gather strength, however. With the Industrial Revolution, a class of wealthy industrial capitalists emerged. The industrial sector had to pay workers at least enough to live on, and a living wage depended to a great extent on the price of food. Tariffs on grain imports and export subsidies that kept grain and food prices up increased the wages that capitalists had to pay, and these high wage payments cut into their profits. The political battle raged for years. But as time went by the power of the landowners in the House of Lords was significantly reduced, and when the conflict was finally over, in 1848, the Corn Laws were repealed.

Theory of comparative advantage *Ricardo's theory that specialization and free trade will benefit all trading partners (real wages will rise), even those that may be absolutely less efficient producers.*

Participating in this battle on the side of repeal was David Ricardo, a businessman, economist, member of Parliament, and one of the fathers of modern economics. Ricardo's principal work, *Principles of Political Economy and Taxation*, was published in 1817, two years before he entered Parliament. Ricardo's **theory of comparative advantage** claimed that trade enables countries to specialize in producing the products that they produce best. According to the theory, *specialization and free trade will benefit all trading partners (real wages will rise), even those that may be absolutely less efficient producers.*

This basic logic remains at the heart of free trade debates even today. It was invoked numerous times by President Reagan over the last few years of his administration as he wrestled with Congress over various pieces of protectionist legislation.

Specialization and Trade: The Two-Person Case

Perhaps the easiest way to grasp the theory of comparative advantage is to examine a simple two-person society. For example, recall Bill and Colleen stuck on a deserted island. Suppose that they have only two basic tasks to accomplish each week: gathering food and cutting logs to be used in constructing a house. If Colleen could cut more logs than Bill in a day and Bill could gather more berries and fruits, it would be clear that specialization would benefit both of them.

But suppose that Bill is slow and somewhat clumsy and that Colleen is better at both cutting logs *and* gathering food. Ricardo's point is that it still pays for them to specialize. They can produce more in total by specializing than they can sharing the work equally.

Suppose, for example, that Colleen can gather 10 bushels of food in a day and that Bill can gather only eight. Further suppose that Colleen can cut 10 logs in a day, but that Bill can cut only four. Now most of their time is spent on food production, but a couple of days a week they can work on the house. When Colleen gives up a day of food gathering to do this, she produces 10 logs and they give up 10 bushels of food. In order for Bill to produce 10 logs, he would have to work for two and one half days. The sacrifice in terms of food would be 20 bushels ($2\frac{1}{2} \times 8$), or twice as much. Thus even though Colleen is absolutely a better food gatherer, Bill should specialize in food gathering and Colleen should work on the house.

In this example, Colleen has an advantage over Bill in cutting wood because when she cuts, each log costs less in terms of food. The opportunity cost of logs is lower if Colleen cuts them. As you will see from the formal definitions of absolute and comparative advantage below, Bill enjoys a comparative advantage in food production and Colleen enjoys a comparative advantage in log cutting, even though Colleen is absolutely better at producing both goods.

These ideas explain a good deal of what goes on around us. Why does a novelist who types 100 words per minute hire a typist who types only 75? Can't the author get the work done faster by typing it herself? The answer of course is yes, but her time is better spent writing. The cost is too great in terms of something else—writing—that she can do with her time. The same logic applies to countries.

Absolute Advantage versus Comparative Advantage

Absolute advantage, comparative advantage   Absolute advantage: *The advantage in the production of a product enjoyed by one country over another when it uses fewer resources to produce that product than the other country does.* Comparative advantage: *The advantage in the production of a product enjoyed by one country over another when that product can be produced at lower cost than in the other country in terms of other goods.*

A country is said to enjoy an **absolute advantage** over another country in the production of a product if it uses fewer resources to produce that product than the other country does. For example, suppose country A and country B produce wheat, but that A's climate is more suited to wheat and its labor is more productive. Country A will therefore produce more wheat per acre than country B and use less labor in growing it and bringing it to market. Country A thus enjoys an absolute advantage in the production of wheat.

A country enjoys a **comparative advantage** in the production of a good if that good can be produced at lower cost *in terms of other goods.* Consider again countries A and B. Now suppose that both A and B produce wheat and corn and further that A enjoys an absolute advantage in the production of both—that is, A's climate is better than B's, and fewer of A's resources are needed to produce a given quantity of *both* wheat and corn. Now A and B must each choose between planting land in wheat and corn. To produce more wheat, either country must transfer land from corn production; to produce more corn, either country must transfer land from wheat production. Thus the cost of wheat *in each country* can be measured in bushels of corn, and the cost of corn can be measured in bushels of wheat.

Suppose that in country A, a bushel of wheat has an opportunity cost of two bushels of corn—that is, to produce an additional bushel of wheat, A must give up two bushels of corn. At the same time, suppose that producing a bushel of wheat in country B requires the sacrifice of only one bushel of corn. Even though A has an *absolute* advantage in the production of both products, B enjoys a *comparative* advantage in the production of wheat. In a very important sense, wheat can be produced at "lower cost" in country B. Under these circumstances, Ricardo claims, B can benefit from trade if it specializes in the production of wheat.

Mutual Absolute Advantage

To illustrate Ricardo's logic, let's start with a very simple case. Suppose that Australia and New Zealand each have a fixed amount of land and are isolated from the rest of the world. Suppose further that there are only two goods—wheat, used to produce bread, and cotton, used to produce clothing. This two-country/two-good world does not exist, of course, but its operations can be generalized to many countries and many goods.

Before we proceed, we have to make some assumptions about the preferences of the people living in New Zealand and those living in Australia. If the citizens of both countries go around naked, there is no need to produce cotton at all; all the land can be used to produce wheat. For the sake of simplicity, however, let us assume that people in both countries have similar preferences with respect to food and clothing: both populations use both. We will further assume that preferences for food and clothing are such that they imply equal consumption of bushels of wheat and bales of cotton.

Finally, we shall assume that each country has only 100 acres of land for planting and that land yields are those given in Table 21.5. Notice that New Zealand can produce three times the wheat that Australia can on one acre of land, and Australia can produce three times the cotton that New Zealand can in the same space. New Zealand thus has an absolute advantage in the production of wheat, and Australia has an absolute advantage in the production of cotton. In cases like this, we say they have **mutual absolute advantage**.

If there is no trade and each country divides up its land to obtain equal units of cotton and wheat production, each country produces 150 bushels of wheat and 150 bales of cotton. New Zealand puts 75 acres into cotton but only 25 acres into wheat, while Australia does the reverse. The results appear in Table 21.6.

TABLE 21.5
Yield Per Acre of Wheat and Cotton

	New Zealand	Australia
Wheat	6 bushels	2 bushels
Cotton	2 bales	6 bales

TABLE 21.6
Total Production of Wheat and Cotton Assuming No Trade and Mutual Absolute Advantage

	New Zealand	Australia
Wheat	25 acres × 6 bu/acre 150 bushels	75 acres × 2 bu/acres 150 bushels
Cotton	75 acres × 2 bales/acre 150 bales	25 acres × 6 bales/acre 150 bales

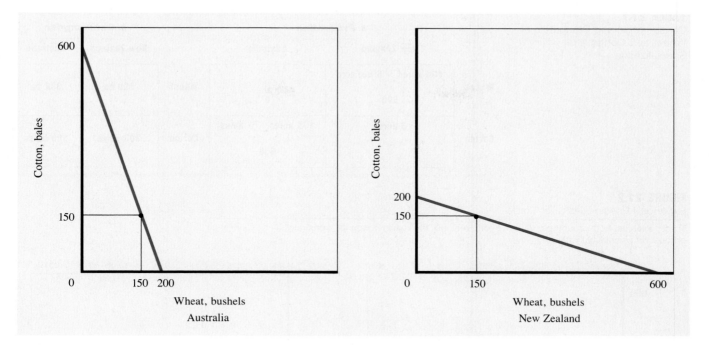

FIGURE 21.1

Production Possibility Frontiers for Australia and New Zealand

Absent trade, countries are constrained by their own resources and productivity.

We can organize the same information in a somewhat different way if we construct separate production possibilities frontiers for each country. In Figure 21.2, which presents the positions of the two countries before trade, each country is constrained by its own resources and productivity. If Australia put all its land into cotton, it would produce 600 bales of cotton and no wheat; if it put all its land into wheat, it would produce 200 bushels of wheat and no cotton. The opposite is true for New Zealand. Note that each country is constrained to pick a point along its own production possibilities curve.

Because both countries have an absolute advantage in the production of one product, it is reasonable to expect that specialization and trade will benefit both countries. Clearly Australia should produce cotton and New Zealand should produce wheat. Transferring all land to wheat production in New Zealand yields a total of 600 bushels; transferring all land to cotton production in Australia yields 600 bales. An agreement to trade 300 bushels of wheat for 300 bales of cotton would double both wheat and cotton consumption in both countries. Final production and trade figures are given in Table 21.7 and Figure 21.7. Trade enables both countries to move out beyond what their previous resource and productivity constraints permitted.

In the case where New Zealand was technically superior in wheat and Australia technically superior in cotton, this should not be surprising. Now, however, let us turn to the case where one country has an absolute advantage in the production of *both* goods. You can already hear protectionists in the low-productivity country crying, "But how can we compete with a country that is more efficient in the production of everything?" And if the low-productivity country has lower wages, protectionists from the high-productivity country will indignantly inquire, "How can we be expected to compete when they have such cheap labor?"

TABLE 21.7
Consumption and Production of
Wheat and Cotton after
Specialization

| | a. **Production** | | | b. **Consumption** | |
	New Zealand	Australia		New Zealand	Australia
Wheat	100 acres × 6 bu/acre 600	0	Wheat	300 bu	300 bu
Cotton	0 acres 0	100 acres × 6 bales 600	Cotton	300 bales	300 bales

FIGURE 21.2
Expanded Possibilities after Trade

Trade enables both countries to move out beyond their own resource constraints—beyond their
production possibility frontiers.

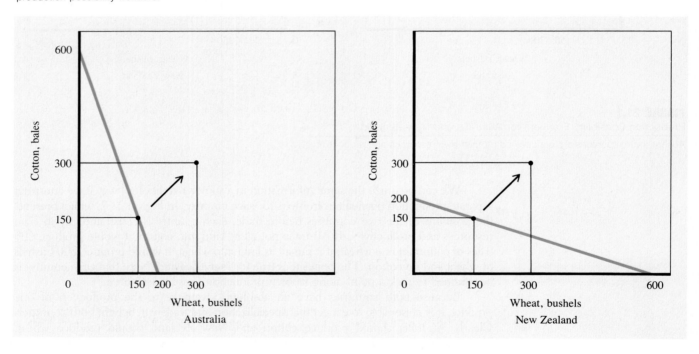

Australia

New Zealand

Gains from Comparative Advantage Alone

Table 21.8 contains some different production coefficients for New Zealand and
Australia. In this new case, New Zealand has a considerable absolute advantage in the
production of both cotton and wheat, with one acre of land yielding six times as much
wheat and twice as much cotton as in Australia. Ricardo would argue that *specialization
and trade are still mutually beneficial.*

Assume again that preferences for food and clothing imply consumption of equal
units of cotton and wheat in both countries. New Zealand would split up its 100 available
acres evenly, or 50:50, between the two crops. The result would be 300 bales of cotton
and 300 bushels of wheat. Australia would again split its land 75:25. Table 21.9 shows

TABLE 21.8

Yield Per Acre of Wheat and Cotton

In this case New Zealand has an absolute advantage in the production of both goods.

	New Zealand	Australia
Wheat	6 bushels	1 bushel
Cotton	6 bales	3 bales

TABLE 21.9

Total Production of Wheat and Cotton—Assuming No Trade

Even though they have the same amount of land, the climate is much better in New Zealand. Thus, New Zealand has an absolute advantage in producing both goods.

	New Zealand	Australia
Wheat	50 acres × 6 bu/acre 300 bu	75 acres × 1 bu/acre 75 bu
Cotton	50 acres × 6 bales/acre 300 bales	25 acres × 3 bales/acre 75 bales

that final production in Australia would be 75 bales of cotton and 75 bushels of wheat. Once again, before any trade takes place each country is constrained by its own domestic production possibilities curve.

Now imagine that we are at a meeting of trade representatives of both countries. As a special adviser, David Ricardo is asked to demonstrate that trade can benefit both countries. The professor divides his demonstration into three stages, which you can follow in Table 21.10.

In stage 1, Australia transfers all its land into cotton production. When it does, it will have no wheat at all and 300 bales of cotton. New Zealand cannot completely specialize, because it will not be able to get enough cotton from Australia, but in stage 2, it does

TABLE 21.10

Realizing a Gain from Trade when One Country Has a Double Absolute Advantage

In this case New Zealand has a comparative advantage in wheat production and Australia has a comparative advantage in cotton. Specializing increases consumption in both countries.

	Stage 1			Stage 2	
	New Zealand	Australia		New Zealand	Australia
Wheat	50 acres × 6 bu 300 bu	0 acres 0	Wheat	75 acres × 6 bu 450 bu	0 acres 0 bu
Cotton	50 acres × 6 bales 300 bales	100 acres × 3 bales 300 bales	Cotton	25 acres × 6 bales 150 bales	100 acres × 3 bales 300 bales

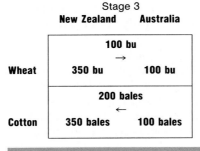

	Stage 3	
	New Zealand	Australia
Wheat	100 bu → 350 bu	100 bu
Cotton	200 bales ← 350 bales	100 bales

transfer 25 acres out of cotton and into wheat. Now New Zealand has 25 acres in cotton that produce 150 bales and 75 acres in wheat that produce 450 bushels.

Finally, they trade. We assume that New Zealand ships 100 bushels of wheat to Australia in exchange for 200 bales of cotton. After the trade, New Zealand has 350 bales of cotton and 350 bushels of wheat; Australia has 100 bales of cotton and 100 bushels of wheat. Both countries are better off, and both have moved beyond their own production possibilities frontiers.

Why Does Ricardo's Plan Work?

The reason that Ricardo's scheme works is quite simple. To understand it, let us go back to the definition of comparative advantage.

The real cost of producing cotton is the wheat that must be sacrificed in order to produce it. *When we think of cost this way, it is less costly to produce cotton in Australia than to produce it in New Zealand, even though it takes more land.* In terms of opportunity cost, a bale of cotton in New Zealand costs one bushel of wheat; in Australia it only costs one third of a bushel of wheat. Because three bales are produced by one acre of land, to get a single bale an Australian need transfer one third acre of land. And because an acre of land produces a bushel of wheat, losing one third acre to wheat implies the loss of one third bushel of wheat. Thus *Australia has a comparative advantage in cotton production.*

Conversely, New Zealand has a comparative advantage in wheat production. A unit of wheat in New Zealand *costs* one unit of cotton; a unit of wheat in Australia *costs* three units of cotton. When countries specialize in producing those goods in which they have a comparative advantage, they maximize their combined output and allocate their resources more efficiently.

Terms of Trade

Ricardo might suggest a number of deals to the trading partners. The one you just examined benefited both partners; in percentage terms, Australia made out slightly better. Other deals might have been more advantageous to New Zealand.

Terms of trade   *The ratio at which a country can trade domestic products for imported products.*

The ratio at which a country can trade domestic products for imported products is called the **terms of trade**. The terms of the trade determine how the gains from trade are distributed among the trading partners. In the case we just considered, the agreed-upon terms of trade were that one bushel of wheat would exchange for two bales of cotton. Such terms of trade benefit New Zealand, because it can now get two bales of cotton for each bushel of wheat; if it were to transfer its own land, it would get only one. The same terms of trade benefit Australia, because it can get one bushel of wheat for two bales of cotton, whereas a direct transfer of land use forces it to give up three bales of cotton to get a bushel of wheat.

If the terms of trade changed to three bales of cotton for every bushel of wheat, that would favor New Zealand. In fact, at those terms of trade *all* the gains from trade flow to New Zealand. Notice that such terms do not benefit Australia at all because the opportunity cost of producing wheat domestically is exactly the same as the trade cost: a bushel of wheat costs three bales of cotton. If the terms of trade went the other way, changing to one bale of cotton for each bushel of wheat, only Australia would benefit.

New Zealand gains nothing, because it can already substitute cotton for wheat at that ratio. To get a bushel of wheat domestically, however, Australia must give up three bales of cotton, and one-for-one terms of trade would make wheat much less costly.

Clearly both parties must have something to gain for trade to take place. In this case, you can see that both Australia and New Zealand will gain when the terms of trade are set between 1:1 and 3:1, cotton to wheat.

Comparative Advantage and Exchange Rates   These examples have all shown that trade can result in gains to both parties. But these deals were arranged by omniscient planners, and unfortunately omniscient planners are in short supply in the real world. In fact, when trade is free, patterns of trade and trade flows result from the independent decisions of thousands of importers and exporters and millions of private households and firms. Private households decide whether to buy Toyotas or Chevrolets, and private firms decide whether to buy machine tools made in the United States or machine tools made in Taiwan, raw steel produced in West Germany or raw steel produced in Pittsburgh.

Before a citizen of one country can buy a product made in, or sold by, someone in another country, a currency swap must take place. Consider Shane, who buys a Volkswagen from a dealer in Boston. He pays in dollars, but the German workers who made the car receive their salaries in deutsche marks. Somewhere between the buyer of the car and the producer, a currency exchange must be made. Probably the regional distributor takes payment in dollars and converts them into marks before remitting the proceeds back to Germany.

To buy a foreign-produced good, then, I have to buy foreign currency. The price of Shane's Volkswagen in dollars depends on both the price of the car stated in deutsche marks and the price of deutsche marks. You know this very well if you have ever travelled in another country. In May of 1988, a dollar exchanged for 5.71 French francs, making each franc worth $0.175. Now suppose that you are in France, and you see a nice bottle of Bordeaux wine for 120 francs. How can you figure out whether you want to buy it? You know what dollars will buy you in the U.S., so you have to convert the price into dollars. Since each franc will cost you $0.175, 120 francs is worth 120 × 0.175, or $21.00.

Exchange rate   The ratio at which two currencies are traded one for the other.

The relative attractiveness of foreign goods to American buyers, and of American goods to foreign buyers, depends in part on **exchange rates**. If the rate at which dollars could be converted into francs suddenly jumped to 10:1, that is, 10 francs to every dollar, that same bottle of wine would cost only $12.00.

Thus, to understand the patterns of trade that result from the actions of thousands of independent buyers and sellers—households and firms—we must know something about the factors that determine exchange rates. While we do not formally analyze the determinants of exchange rates until the next chapter, we can demonstrate two things here: first, that for any pair of countries, there is a range of exchange rates that will lead automatically to both countries realizing the gains from specialization and comparative advantage, and second, that within that range, the exchange rate will determine which country gains the most from trade—that is, exchange rates determine the terms of trade.

Trade and Exchange Rates in a Two-Country/Two-Good World   Consider first a simple two-country/two-good model. Suppose that both the United States and West Germany produced two goods—rolled steel and raw timber. Table 21.11 gives the current prices of both goods as domestic buyers see them. That is, in Germany timber is priced at three deutsche marks (DM) per log foot, and steel is priced at four DM per rolled meter. In the United States, timber costs $1.00 a foot and steel costs $2.00 per meter.

TABLE 21.11
Domestic Prices of Timber (per foot) and Rolled Steel (per meter) in the United States and West Germany

	UNITED STATES	WEST GERMANY
Timber	$1	3 DM
Rolled steel	$2	4 DM

Now American and German buyers have the option of buying at home or importing to meet their needs. Which of these options they choose will depend on what the exchange rate turns out to be. For the time being, we will ignore transportation costs and we will assume that German and American products are of equal quality.

Let us start with the assumption that the exchange rate is $1.00 = 1 DM. From the standpoint of American buyers, neither German steel nor German timber is competitive at this exchange rate. A dollar buys a foot of timber in the United States, but if converted into a mark, it will buy only one third of a foot. The price of German timber to an American is $3.00 because it will take $3.00 to buy the necessary three DM. Similarly, $2.00 buys a meter of rolled steel in the United States, but the same $2.00 buys only one half a meter of German steel. The price of German steel to an American is $4.00, twice as much as domestically produced steel.

On the other hand, at that exchange rate the Germans find that U.S.-produced steel and timber are both less expensive than steel and timber produced in Germany. Timber at home costs three DM, but three DM buys $3.00, and that buys three times as much timber in the United States. Similarly, steel costs four DM at home, but four DM buys $4.00, and that buys twice as much American-made steel. Thus, at an exchange rate of $1.00 = 1 DM, Germany will import steel and timber and the United States will import nothing. As you will see in the next chapter, this exchange rate is not likely to persist for very long.

At the other extreme, suppose that the exchange rate is 1 DM = $0.25. We could thus say that the "price" of a DM is $0.25. That means that a dollar buys four DM. At this exchange rate, the Germans buy at home and the Americans import. Now Americans must pay a dollar for a foot of timber, but the same foot can be had in Germany for $0.75. Since one DM costs $0.25, three DM can be purchased for $0.75. Similarly, timber which costs $2.00 in the U.S. costs an American half as much in Germany, since $2.00 buys eight DM, which buys two feet there. At the same time, Germans are not interested in importing, because both goods are cheaper when purchased from a German producer. In this case, the United States imports both goods and Germany imports nothing. Again, this exchange rate is not likely to persist.

So far, we can see that at exchange rates of $1.00 = 1 DM and $1.00 = 4 DM we get trade flowing in only one direction. Let us now try $1.00 = 2 DM, or 1 DM = $0.50. First, notice that Germans will buy timber in the United States. German timber costs three DM per foot, but three DM buys $1.50, or enough to buy one and one-half feet of timber in the United States. American buyers will find German timber too expensive, hence Germany will import timber from the United States at that exchange rate. At $1.00 = 2 DM, however, both German and American buyers will be indifferent between German and American steel. To U.S. buyers, domestically produced steel costs $2.00. Since $2.00 buys four DM, a meter of imported steel also costs $2.00. German buyers also find that steel costs four DM, whether domestically produced or imported. Thus there is likely to be no trade in steel.

But now look what happens if the exchange rate rises so that $1.00 buys 2.1 DM instead of just two. While American timber is still cheaper to both Germans and Americans, all of a sudden German steel begins to look good to U.S. buyers. Steel

TABLE 21.12

Trade Flows Determined by
Exchange Rates

With the prices given in Table 21.11,
trade will flow in both directions between countries only if the price of DM
is between $0.33 and $0.50

EXCHANGE RATE	PRICE OF DM
$1 = 1 DM	$ 1 Germany imports timber and steel
$1 = 2 DM	$.50 Germany imports timber
$1 = 2.1 DM	$.48 Germany imports timber; United States imports steel
$1 = 2.9 CM	$.34 Germany imports timber; United States imports steel
$1 = 3 DM	$.33 United States imports steel
$1 = 4 DM	$.25 United States imports timber and steel

produced at home costs $2.00 per meter, but $2.00 buys 4.2 DM, and that buys more than a meter of steel in Germany. Thus when the exchange rate rises above $1.00 = 2 DM, trade begins to go in both directions. That is, Germany will import timber and the United States will import steel.

If you look at Table 21.12 carefully, you will see that in fact trade goes in both directions as long as the exchange rate settles between $1.00 = 2 DM and $1.00 = 3 DM. Stated the other way around, if the price of a DM is between $0.33 and $0.50, trade will go in both directions.

Exchange Rates and Comparative Advantage   What is interesting is that if the foreign exchange market drives the exchange rate anywhere in this range, the countries will automatically adjust and comparative advantage will be realized. Here is the story. If the exchange rate is between two and three DM per dollar, American buyers begin buying all their steel in Germany. The American steel industry finds itself in trouble. Plants close, and American workers begin to lobby for tariff protection. At the same time, the timber industry does well, fueled by strong export demand from Germany. Thus the timber-producing sector expands. Resources, including capital and labor, are attracted into timber production.

The opposite occurs in Germany. The German timber industry suffers losses as export demand dries up and Germans turn to cheaper American imports. In Germany lumbermen turn to the government and ask for protection from cheap American timber. But steel producers are happy in Germany. Not only are they supplying 100 percent of the domestically demanded steel, but they are selling to American buyers as well. Thus the steel industry expands, and the timber industry contracts. Resources, including labor, flow into steel.

With this expansion-and-contraction story in mind, let us look again at our original definition of comparative advantage. If we assume that prices reflect resource use and that resources can be transferred from sector to sector, we can calculate the opportunity cost of steel/timber in both countries. In the United States, a meter of rolled steel consumes twice the resources that a foot of timber consumes. Assuming resources can be transferred (labor can be retrained and so forth) the opportunity cost of a meter of steel is two feet of timber. In Germany, however, a meter of steel uses resources costing four DM, while a unit of timber costs three DM. Thus to produce a meter of steel means the sacrifice of only one and one-third feet of timber. Because the opportunity cost of a meter of steel is lower in Germany, we say that Germany has a comparative advantage in steel production.

Conversely, consider the opportunity cost of timber in the two countries. Increasing timber production in the United States requires the sacrifice of half a meter of steel for every foot of timber—producing a meter of steel uses $2.00 worth of resources, while producing a foot of timber requires only $1.00 worth of resources. But each foot of timber production in Germany requires the sacrifice of three fourths of a meter of steel. The opportunity cost of timber is lower in the United States, and therefore the United States has a comparative advantage in the production of timber.

As you can see, if exchange rates end up being in the right range, the free market will drive each country to shift resources into those sectors in which it enjoys a comparative advantage. Only those products in which a country has a comparative advantage will be competitive on world markets.

How the Exchange Rate Determines the Terms of Trade   Recall now the exchange rate between U.S. dollars and deutsche marks as shown in Table 21.12. We saw there that only when the exchange rate was between $1.00 = 2 DM and $1.00 = 3 DM will trade flow in both directions. Within the band bounded by these two ratios, both countries benefit, but which country benefits more depends upon whether the final exchange rate is closer to 1:2 or 1:3.

Obviously, if Americans get more *DM* per dollar, they get more German goods per unit of American goods. With the exchange rate close to $1.00 = 3 DM, the terms of trade favor the United States. Notice that at $1.00 = 2.9 DM (1 DM = $0.34), even though trade goes both ways, the gains to Americans are high and the gains to Germans are low. Americans continue to buy American timber at the same price, but they find German steel, at only $1.36, much cheaper. Germans, however, gain little. They buy steel at home for the same four DM, and although American timber, at 2.9 DM is cheaper, it is not very much cheaper than German timber at three DM.

Exchange rates closer to $1.00 = 2 DM swing the terms of trade in favor of Germany, since Germans then get more dollars for their DM. At $1.00 = 2.1 DM, German buyers gain a substantial advantage. They have to pay only 2.1 DM for a foot of American timber, almost 30 percent less than they would pay if there were no trade. At this same exchange rate, Americans have to pay $1.92 for German steel, only a four-percent saving over the no-trade case.

THE THEORY OF COMPARATIVE ADVANTAGE AND OBSERVED TRADE FLOWS

You have now seen that specialization and trade can benefit all trading partners, even those that may be inefficient producers in an absolute sense. If markets are competitive, and if foreign exchange markets are linked to goods-and-services exchange, countries will indeed specialize in producing those products in which they have a comparative advantage, as our two-country/two-good model showed.

So far, however, we have said nothing about the sources of comparative advantage. What determines whether a country has a comparative advantage in heavy manufacturing or in agriculture? What explains actual trade flows observed around the world? In fact, various theories and empirical work on international trade have provided a number of partial answers to these questions. First, most economists look to **factor endowments**, that is, to the quantity and quality of labor, land, and natural resources, as the principal source of comparative advantage. Second, factor endowments seem to explain a significant portion of actual world trade patterns.

Factor endowments   The quantity and quality of labor, land, and natural resources of a country.

The Heckscher-Ohlin Theorem

Heckscher-Ohlin theorem   *A theory explaining the existence of a comparative advantage by a country's factor endowments: a country has a comparative advantage in the production of a product if that country is relatively well endowed with inputs used intensively in the production of that product.*

Eli Heckscher and Bertil Ohlin, Swedish economists writing in the first half of this century, expanded and elaborated on the theory of comparative advantage. The **Heckscher-Ohlin theorem** ties the theory of comparative advantage to factor endowments. It assumes that products can be produced using differing proportions of inputs and that inputs are mobile between sectors in each economy, but that factors are not mobile *between* economies. A country has a comparative advantage in the production of a product, then, *if that country is relatively well endowed with inputs used intensively in the production of that product.*

The idea is fairly simple. A country with lots of good fertile land is likely to have a comparative advantage in agriculture. A country with a large amount of accumulated capital and, perhaps, a high saving rate is likely to have a comparative advantage in heavy manufacturing. A country with lots of human capital is likely to have a comparative advantage in highly technical goods.

After an extensive study, Edward Leamer of UCLA has concluded that a relatively short list of factors accounts for a surprisingly large portion of world trade patterns. Natural resources, knowledge capital, physical capital, land, and skilled and unskilled labor. Leamer believes, explain "a large amount of the variability of net exports across countries."[1]

Other Explanations for Trade

Comparative advantage is not the only reason that countries trade, of course. Comparative advantage does not explain why many countries both import and export the same goods. The United States, for example, both exports and imports automobiles.

Another explanation for international trade argues that just as industries within a country differentiate their products in order to capture a domestic market, so they also differentiate their products to please the wide variety of tastes that exists worldwide. The Japanese automobile industry began producing small, fuel-efficient cars before U.S. automobile makers did, for example. As they did so, they developed expertise in creating products that attracted a devoted following and that elicited considerable brand loyalty. BMW's, made only in Germany, or Volvos, made only in Sweden, also have their champions in many countries. Just as product differentiation is a natural response to diverse preferences within an economy, it is also a natural response to diverse preferences among economies.

This idea is not entirely inconsistent with the theory of comparative advantage, however. If the Japanese have developed skills and knowledge that gave them an edge in the production of fuel-efficient cars, that knowledge can be thought of as a very specific kind of capital not currently available to other producers. The Volvo company invested in a form of intangible capital that we call "goodwill." That goodwill, which resides in Sweden as the company does, is the source of the comparative advantage that keeps Volvos selling on the international market. Some economists distinguish between gains from **"acquired" comparative advantages** and **"natural" comparative advantages**.

Another explanation for international trade holds that some economies of scale may be exploited by producing for a world market that would not be available when producing only for a more limited domestic market. But the evidence suggests that economies of scale are exhausted at relatively small size in most industries, and so it is hard to believe that they constitute a very important explanation for world trade.

[1]Edward E. Leamer, *Sources of International Comparative Advantage: Theory and Evidence* (Cambridge, Mass: MIT Press, 1984), p. 187.

TARIFFS, QUOTAS, AND FREE TRADE

Tariff   *A tax on imports.*

A **tariff** is a tax on imports. The average tariff on imports into the United States is now about five percent, although certain protected items have much higher tariffs. For example, the tariff rate on concentrated orange juice is a flat $0.35 per gallon, on rubber footwear it varies from 20 percent to 48 percent, and on canned tuna it is 35 percent.

Quota   *A limit on the quantity of imports.*

A **quota** is a limit on the quantity of imports. Quotas can be mandatory or voluntary, and they may be legislated or negotiated with foreign governments. The best-known voluntary quota, or "voluntary restraint," was negotiated with the Japanese government in 1981. Japan agreed to reduce the number of automobiles it exported to the United States by 7.7%, from the 1980 level of 1.82 million units to 1.68 million units. In 1985, when President Reagan decided not to ask Japan to continue its restraints, auto imports jumped to 2.3 million units, nearly 20 percent of the U.S. market. Quotas currently apply to products as diverse as mushrooms, heavy motorcycles, and color television sets.

Most tariffs today were not enacted on the floor of Congress. The 1974 Trade Act contained an "escape clause" that qualifies an industry for protection if it has been injured by foreign competition. Injury occurs when imports increase and domestic employment, output, and profits fall.

Smoot-Hawley tariff   *The U.S. tariff law of the 1930s, which set the highest tariffs in U.S. history (60 percent); it set off an international trade war and caused the decline in trade, which is often pointed to as a cause of the worldwide depression of the 1930s.*

The United States has always been a high-tariff nation, with average tariffs of over 50 percent for much of its history. The highest tariffs were in effect during the depression following enactment of the **Smoot-Hawley tariff**, which pushed the average tariff rate to 60 percent in 1930. The Smoot-Hawley tariff set off an international trade war when our trading partners retaliated with tariffs of their own. Many economists point to the decline in trade that followed as one of the causes of the worldwide depression of the 1930s.[2] In 1974 the United States, along with 22 other nations, signed an agreement to reduce barriers to trade and to keep them down. It also established an organization to promote liberalization of foreign trade. The **General Agreement on Tariffs and Trade (GATT)**, first considered an interim arrangement, continues to work today, and it has been quite effective.

Every president since the General Agreement has argued for free trade policies, yet each one during his term used his powers to protect one sector or another. Eisenhower and Kennedy worked for restraints on Japanese exports of textiles; Johnson restricted meat imports; Nixon restrained imports of steel and tightened restrictions on textiles; Carter protected steel, textiles, and footwear; Reagan added sugar and automobiles.

Protection   *The shielding of some sector of the economy from foreign competition through the use of tariffs or quotas.*

Despite these cases, the general movement in the United States has been away from tariffs and quotas. Several successful rounds of tariff-reduction negotiations have reduced trade barriers to their lowest levels ever. Many, however, feel that today the world is perilously close to a major trade war. The issue of **protection** was a major issue in the 1988 presidential election, beginning with early debates between Democratic candidates Governor Michael Dukakis and Senator Richard Gephardt.

The Case for Free Trade

In a very real sense, the theory of comparative advantage *is* the case for free trade. Trade potentially benefits all nations, and the hypothetical case of the United States and Germany we just examined lays out the basic logic behind this statement. A good is not

---

[2]See especially Charles Kindleberger, *The World in Depression 1929–1939* (London: Allen Lane, 1973).

imported unless its net price to buyers is below that of the domestically produced alternative. When the Germans found U.S. timber less expensive than their own, they bought it, yet they continued to pay the same price for homemade steel. Americans bought less expensive German steel, but continued to buy domestic timber at the same lower price. Under these conditions, *both Americans and Germans ended up paying less and consuming more.*

In that story, resources, including labor, move out of steel production and into timber production in the United States. In Germany, resources, including labor, move out of timber production and into steel production. Thus the resources in both countries are more efficiently used. Tariffs and quotas, which interfere with the free movement of goods and services around the world, reduce or eliminate those gains.

Supply and demand curves illustrate the same point. Suppose that panel a. of Figure 21.4 shows domestic supply and demand for textiles. In the absence of trade, the market clears at price of P_d. Q' units of textiles are produced and consumed. P_w is the world price of textiles stated in dollars—that is, the price on world markets allowing for the fact that dollars must be converted into foreign currency. (Recall that we worked out several such conversions in the steel-and-timber example to support the argument that trade takes place when the exchange rate makes imported steel less expensive in *dollars* than domestic-made steel.)

Assuming that imported textiles are less expensive than domestic textiles, Americans buy them at price P_w. At P_w, domestic producers are undercut and domestic production falls from Q' to Q_d. At this point, resources move out of textiles into other sectors of the economy, presumably those sectors in which *we* enjoy a comparative advantage.

FIGURE 21.3

The Gains From Trade and Losses from the Imposition of a Tariff

A tariff of t increases the market price facing consumers from P_w to P_w+t. The government collects revenues equal to the shaded area. On balance, there is a loss of consumer surplus (X) and a loss of efficiency in production (Y).

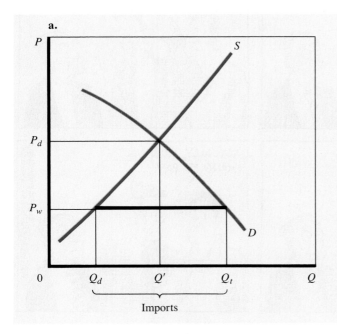
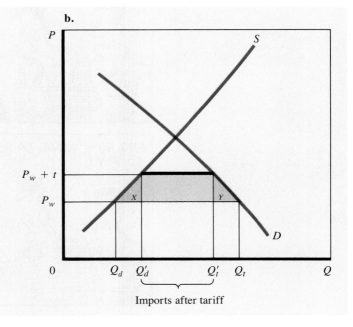

Consumers get textiles at a lower price and thus they buy more. Consumers are better off, and resources are more efficiently employed.

Panel 2 of Figure 21.4 shows what happens when a tariff at a rate of t per unit is imposed. The tariff does several things. First, it increases the market price that consumers pay for the good. Second, the higher price generates more domestic supply, and, as domestic output rises from Q_d to Q_d' some textile workers get their jobs back. Third, imports decrease. There are some revenues from the tariff, which are equal to the shaded area in the diagram, but they are smaller than the loss of efficiency and the losses to consumers.

These two sources of "loss" to the economy are both shown in the diagram. First, at a world price of P_w, resources are drawn into production only to Q_d. At a domestic price of $(P_w + t)$ domestic production expands, drawing in the required resources needed. The upward-sloping supply curve, which reflects production costs, shows that unit costs rise as output expands. We thus end up producing textiles at a higher cost per unit. The loss from this inefficiency is roughly equal to the area of triangle X.

In addition, consumers end up paying a higher price for textiles than they would have. For those who continue to buy at the higher price, the additional payment goes to the government as revenue, the shaded area in panel 2 of Figure 21.4. Some consumers reduce their consumption or stop buying the good altogether, and they lose a consumer surplus equal to triangle Y. The net loss to society from the tariff is approximately equal to the sum of triangles X and Y.

Trade barriers, then, prevent us from reaping the benefits of specialization, push us to adopt relatively inefficient production techniques, and force consumers to pay higher prices for protected products than they would otherwise pay.

The Case for Protection

A case can also be made in favor of tariffs and quotas, of course. Over the span of U.S. history, it has been made so many times by so many industries before so many Congressional committees that it almost seems that all pleas for protection share the same testimony. The box below presents testimony offered on behalf of the shears and scissors industry, for example.

It Saves Jobs   The main argument for protection is that foreign competition costs Americans their jobs. When we buy Toyotas, American cars go unsold. This leads to layoffs in the domestic auto industry. When we buy Japanese or German steel, steelworkers in Pittsburgh lose their jobs. When we buy shoes or textiles from Korea or Taiwan, the millworkers in Maine and Massachusetts, as well as South Carolina and Georgia, lose their jobs.

It is true that when we buy goods from foreign producers, domestic producers in those sectors of the American economy do suffer. But there is no reason to believe that the workers laid off in the contracting sectors will not be ultimately reemployed in other expanding sectors. In the New Zealand/Australia story, land in Australia went out of wheat production after trade began because New Zealand could produce it better. But that land did not stand idle; it moved into cotton production. In the United States/Germany story, U.S. labor was indeed laid off in the steel industry, but it was reabsorbed in the expanding timber industry.

Foreign competition in textiles, for example, has clearly cost American jobs in that industry. Many thousands of textile workers in New England fell victim as the textile mills there closed down over the last third of a century. But with the tremendous expansion of high-tech industries, the unemployment rate in Massachusetts fell to one of the lowest in the country in the mid 1980s, and New Hampshire, Vermont, and Maine also boomed. Over time the United States lost its comparative advantage in textiles to countries with larger unskilled labor pools, but other new industries have grown up in which we do have a comparative advantage.

While all of this is true, the adjustment process is far from costless. The knowledge that some other industry, perhaps in some other part of the country, may be expanding is of little comfort to the person whose skills become obsolete or whose pension benefits are lost when her company abruptly closes a plant or goes bankrupt. Whenever sectors contract, whether because of foreign competition or simply economic change at home, the human costs are large.

The history of the American economy is a history of growth and change. As new technologies develop and old ones die out, new jobs are created and old skills become obsolete. Some sectors expand and others contract. One reason for contraction at home is that foreign countries often grow and develop a comparative advantage. The resource endowment of Taiwan, for example, may simply make it possible for that country to produce textiles as good as ours, if not better, at a lower cost. We can save jobs by protecting the industry, but the consequent rise in the price of textiles adversely affects everyone, including those whose jobs have been preserved.

There is no reason that a country cannot *engage in significant foreign trade and have full employment at home as well*. We do have transition problems, however. Clearly an unemployed steel worker does not take kindly to being called a "transition problem." Waiting until one can be "absorbed in another sector" is neither comfortable nor, in some cases, possible. The social and personal problems brought about by industry-specific unemployment, obsolete skills, and bankruptcy as a result of foreign competition are very real, both socially and personally.

The Never-Ending Plea for Protection

**TRADE EXPANSION ACT OF 1962
STATEMENT OF B. C. DEUSCHLE
IN HEARINGS BEFORE THE
EIGHTY-SEVENTH CONGRESS, SECOND SESSION
COMMITTEE ON WAYS AND MEANS, HOUSE OF REPRESENTATIVES**

MR. KEOGH (presiding). You are recognized, Mr. Deuschle.

MR. DEUSCHLE. Thank you, Mr. Chairman.

Mr. Chairman and members of the Committee on Ways and Means, my name is B. C. Deuschle.

I am vice president of the Acme Shear Co., located in Bridgeport, Conn. I appear before this committee as president of the Shears, Scissors & Manicure Implement Manufacturers Association, the only national trade association of domestic manufacturers of scissors and shears.

The scissors and shears industry is a distinct industry and should not be confused with the larger industry and flatware industries.

The association respectfully wishes to record with this committee its strong opposition to H.R. 9900 in its present form. This bill could destroy industries such as ours and add to the unemployment problem.

During the past 15 years representatives of our association have appeared before this committee and other congressional committees, the Committee for Reciprocity Information and the Tariff Commission, to present our views on the impact of imported scissors and shears on our domestic industry.

We have never requested or suggested that a complete embargo be placed on the import of scissors and shears. All that we have asked for and desire is a fair competitive opportunity, not an advantage. . . .

The workers in the domestic scissor and shear industry do not want to become wards of the State; they want to use their skills, which have taken years to develop. These workers are not interested in retraining; over many years they have developed a skill they are proud of and want to continue the work they are happy doing.

If the scissors and shears imported during 1961 had been manufactured in the United States, it would have provided over 2 million man-hours of factory work, or full-time employment for over 1,000 American employees.

Domestic manufacturers of scissors and shears have modernized and automated their operations in an effort to meet foreign competition. But foreign manufacturers also have modern equipment and with their lower wage rates are underselling domestic firms in the U.S. market at today's rate of duty.

H.R. 9900 would give the President unrestricted authority to reduce duties and thereby further reduce the cost of imported scissors and shears in our market. Under the provisions of this bill, scissors and shears would be buried in a category with many other items and the duty cut 50 percent.

This would mean a reduction of at least 20 cents per pair at the retail level for scissors and shears now being retailed at $1 to $1.29 per pair. . . . manufacturers would be forced to close

their doors and discharge their employees. The United States would then become wholly dependent on imported scissors and shears.

We cannot understand how it could be in the national interest to permit such a loss. We would lose the skills of the employees and management of the industry as well as the capital investment in production equipment. In the event of a national emergency and imports cut off, the United States would be without a source of scissors and shears, basic tools for many industries and trades essential to our defense.

The scissor and shear industry is one of the oldest in the world. The skill was brought to the United States from Germany at a time when the United States needed new industry and a scissor and shear industry in particular.

Scissors and shears of all sizes and types are used in every school, retail establishment, office, factory, hospital, and home in the United States. Scissors cannot be classified as a luxury, gimmick, or novelty.

Scissors are used to separate us from our mothers at birth; to cut our toenails; to trim the leather in our shoes; to cut and trim the materials used in every piece of clothing that we wear.

They are used to cut our fingernails, to trim our mustaches, the hair in our ears and nose, and to cut the hair on our heads—even down to the end of the road when our best suit or dress is cut down the back so that the undertaker can dress us for the last ride. Scissors are truly used from birth to death. They are essential to our health, education, and general welfare.

I ask you gentlemen, is this an industry that should be permitted to become extinct in this country? . . .

MR. KNOX. Then, in your opinion, and in many other people's opinion, the industry, itself, would be unable to operate in competition if the duty was cut by 50 percent?

MR. DEUSCHLE. Yes, sir. . . .

If this does not happen, it looks as though the administration will force American industry to become competitive on an international basis. There is only one way that it can become competitive on an international basis, and that is if we can reduce our cost to a point where we are competitive.

How do you do that? You have to reduce your cost by automation, mechanization, elimination of labor. This is a wonderful concept, but the large labor unions in this country do not favor this sort of program.

They would like to see wages increased. Unless the administration stops inflation in other quarters, how in the world can they expect American industry to cut costs and automate and get their costs down to a point where they can compete with foreign countries.

These problems can be dealt with in one of two ways. We can ban imports and give up on the gains from free trade, acknowledging that we are willing to pay premium prices to save domestic jobs in industries that can produce more efficiently abroad. Or we can aid the victims of free trade in a constructive way, helping them retrain for jobs with a future. In some instances, programs to relocate people in expanding regions may be in order. Such programs deal directly with the transition without forgoing the gains from trade.

Cheap Foreign Labor Makes Competition Unfair   Let us say that the Koreans gained their "comparative advantage" by paying their workers low wages. How can U.S. automobile companies compete with companies that pay wages that are less than a quarter of what we pay?

First of all, wages in a competitive economy reflect productivity. American workers make higher wages because they are more productive. We have more capital per worker, and our workers are better trained. Second, trade flows not according to *absolute* advantage but according to *comparative* advantage: all countries benefit, even if one country can produce everything more cheaply.

It Protects the National Security   Beyond simply saving jobs, certain sectors of the economy may appeal for protection for other reasons. The steel industry has argued for years with some success that it is vital to our national defense. In a war, we would not want to depend on foreign countries for products as vital as steel. Thus even if we acknowledge another country's comparative advantage, we may want to protect our own resources.

No industry has ever asked for protection without invoking the national defense argument. The testimony on behalf of the scissors and shears industry argued that "in the event of a national emergency and imports cutoff, the United States would be without a source of scissors and shears, basic tools for many industries and trades essential to our national defense." The question, then, lies not in the merit of the argument but in just how serious it can be if every industry uses it with equal vociferousness.

It Encourages Dependency   Closely related to the national defense argument is the claim that countries, particularly small or Third World countries, may come to rely too heavily on one or more trading partners for many items. If Lilliput comes to rely on a major power for food or energy or some important raw material in which the large nation has a comparative advantage, it may be difficult for the smaller nation to remain politically neutral. Some critics of free trade say that the superpowers have consciously engaged in trade with smaller countries to create just such dependencies.

Therefore, the argument goes, small independent countries should consciously avoid trading relationships that might lead to political dependence. This may involve developing domestic industries in areas where a country has a comparative disadvantage. To do this would mean protecting that industry from international competition.

It Protects Infant Industries   Young industries in a given country may have a difficult time competing with established industries in other countries. And in a dynamic world, a protected **infant industry** might mature into a strong one worldwide because of an acquired, but real, comparative advantage. If such an industry is undercut and driven out of world markets from the beginning, that comparative advantage might never develop.

It is interesting to note that young industries are usually not the ones asking for protection. For example, the high-tech industries that seem to have a real comparative advantage in the United States today have by and large resisted asking for help. Most action in Washington has been on behalf of old, declining industries that are losing their comparative advantage.

Infant industry   A young industry of a country which may need temporary protection from competition from the established industries of other countries in order to develop an acquired comparative advantage.

It Provides Protection during Temporary Currency Overvaluations   In 1983 and 1984, many people argued that the dollar was artificially strong—that is, it bought more yen, DM, and francs than it should. An overvalued dollar makes U.S. goods look undesirable to foreigners, who have to pay more to get dollars, and it makes foreign goods look cheap to Americans.

When such a situation arises, whether artificially or normally but *temporarily*, protection might be required to tide over certain industries. It is extremely difficult, however, to decide just what the "proper" exchange rate should be. This problem is explored in the next chapter, where we examine in more detail the factors that determine exchange rates.

FREE TRADE AND FULL EMPLOYMENT

Before this chapter, this text has been describing a closed economy. Now we have opened up our discussion by admitting the rest of the world. You now know something about what and how much the United States imports and exports, as well as something about how import demand and export production fit into the structure of a simple economy.

This has brought us to the important debate between freetraders and protectionists. On one side is the rationale of comparative advantage, formalized by David Ricardo in the early part of the nineteenth century. According to this view, all countries benefit from specialization and trade. The gains from trade are real, and they can be large; free international trade raises real incomes and improves the standard of living.

On the other side, the protectionists point to the loss of jobs and argue for the protection of workers from foreign competition. Indeed, while foreign competition can cause job loss in specific sectors, it is unlikely to cause net job loss in an economy, and workers will over time be absorbed in expanding sectors.

Foreign trade and full employment can be pursued simultaneously. Although economists disagree about many things, the vast majority of them favor free trade.

SUMMARY

1. All economies, even large economies like that of the United States, are affected by events outside their borders.
2. In an economy open to trade, exports of goods and services add a fourth component to planned aggregate expenditure. Consumers and businesses in open economies have more choices—instead of spending exclusively on domestically produced products, they can turn to foreign producers for consumer goods, capital goods, and raw materials.
3. Beginning in the early 1970s, the volume of imports and exports increased sharply as a percentage of GNP in the United States. In 1980 exports peaked at 12.2% of GNP. In 1987 merchandise imports exceeded exports by nearly $159.2 billion.
4. The theory of comparative advantage, dating to the writings of David Ricardo in the nineteenth century,

holds that trade enables countries to specialize in producing the products that they produce best. According to the theory, specialization and free trade will benefit all trading partners, even those who may be absolutely less efficient producers.
5. A country is said to enjoy an absolute advantage over another country in the production of a product if it uses fewer resources to produce that product. A country has a comparative advantage in the production of a product if that product can be produced at a lower cost in terms of other goods.
6. Trade enables countries to move out beyond what their previous resource and productivity constraints permitted.
7. When trade is free, patterns of trade and trade flows result from the independent decisions of thousands of importers and exporters and millions of private households and

firms.

8. The relative attractiveness of foreign goods to American buyers and of American goods to foreign buyers depends in part on exchange rates.

9. For any pair of countries there is a range of exchange rates that will lead automatically to both countries realizing the gains from specialization and comparative advantage. Within that range, the exchange rate will determine which country gains the most from trade—that is, exchange rates determine the terms of trade.

10. The Heckscher-Ohlin theory looks to relative factor endowments to explain comparative advantage and trade flows. A country has a comparative advantage in the production of a product, according to Heckscher-Ohlin, if that country is relatively well endowed with the inputs that are used intensively in producing it.

11. A relatively short list of inputs explains a surprisingly large portion of world trade patterns. But the simple version of the theory of comparative advantage cannot explain why many countries import and export the same goods.

12. Other theories argue that comparative advantage can be acquired. Just as industries within a country differentiate their products in order to capture a domestic market, so they also differentiate their products to please the wide variety of tastes that exists world wide. Many countries, for example, are successfully competing for a share of the world demand for automobiles.

13. In a very real sense, the theory of comparative advantage is the case for free trade. Trade barriers prevent us from reaping the benefits of specialization, push us to adopt relatively inefficient production techniques, and force consumers to pay higher prices for protected products than they would otherwise pay.

14. The case for protection rests on the proposition that foreign competition results in a loss of American jobs. But there is no reason to believe that the workers laid off in the contracting sectors will not be ultimately reemployed in other expanding sectors, though this adjustment process is far from costless.

15. Some argue that foreign competition is unfair because of cheap labor in some countries with which we compete. But currency prices on foreign exchange markets should adjust to low wages to make the goods of high wage countries competitive in world markets.

REVIEW CONCEPTS

trade surplus and trade deficit   897
Corn Laws   898
theory of comparative advantage   898
absolute advantage and comparative advantage   899
mutual absolute advantage   900
terms of trade   904
exchange rate   905
factor endowments   908
Heckscher-Ohlin theorem   909

acquired comparative advantage and natural comparative advantage   909
tariff   910
quota   910
Smoot-Hawley tariff   910
General Agreement on Tariffs and Trade (GATT)   910
protection   910
infant industries   915

REVIEW QUESTIONS

1. The following table gives 1984 figures for yield per acre in Ohio and Kansas:

	Wheat	Soybeans
Ohio	44	36.5
Kansas	39	17.5

Source: U.S. Dept. of Agriculture, *Crop Production*, 1985.

a. If we assume that farmers in Kansas and Ohio use the same amount of labor, capital, and fertilizer, which state has an absolute advantage in wheat production? Soybean production?

b. If we transfer land out of wheat into soybeans, how many bushels of wheat do we give up in Ohio per additional bushel of soybeans produced? In Kansas?

c. Which state has a comparative advantage in wheat production? In soybean production?

The following table gives the distribution of land planted for each state in millions of acres:

	Total acres under till	Wheat	Soybeans
Kansas	21.3	11.2	1.6
		(52.6%)	(7.5%)
Ohio	10.6	1.1	3.8
		(10.3%)	(35.8%)

Are these data consistent with your answer to part c? Explain.

2. The United States imported $18.6 billion of "food and live animals" in 1985 and exported $19.3 billion.

    Name some of the imported items that you are aware of in this category. Some of the exported items.

    The United States is said to have a comparative advantage in the production of agricultural goods. How would you go about testing that proposition? What data would you need?

    Are the numbers above consistent with the theory of comparative advantage? Suppose you had a more detailed breakdown of which items we import and which we export. What would you look for?

    What other theories of international trade might explain why the same goods are imported and exported?

3. Export subsidies have been proposed to prop up food prices and help struggling family farmers. Would you favor such subsidies? Write a letter to your congressman or congresswoman explaining why.

4. Germany and France produce white and red wines. Current domestic prices for each are given in the following table:

	Germany	France
white wine	5 DM	10 francs
red wine	10 DM	15 francs

Say that the exchange rate is 1 deutsche mark = 1 franc.

  a. If the price ratios within each country reflect resource use, which country has a comparative advantage in the production of red wine? white wine?

  b. Assume that there are no other trading partners and that the only motive for holding foreign currency is to buy foreign goods. Will the current exchange rate lead to trade flows in both directions between the two countries?

  c. What adjustments might you expect in the exchange rate? Be specific.

  d. What would you predict about trade flows between Germany and France in the long run?

22 Economic Growth in Developing Nations

Our primary focus in this text has been on issues facing the United States. Rent control in New York City, the Reagan tax cut of 1981, and antitrust action against AT&T are familiar to us as Americans. But the economics you have been studying applies equally well to other countries: Parisians may face rent-control programs, Mrs. Thatcher's government in the United Kingdom could institute tax reductions, and the Japanese might decide to break up some of their domestic monopolies. We can analyze these and other issues in Britain, France, and Japan fairly confidently, because these countries have so much in common with the United States. In spite of differences in languages and cultures, all these countries have modern industrialized economies that rely heavily on markets to allocate resources. What about the economic problems facing Ethiopia, or Haiti, or China, however? When we look at these poor, less-developed nations, can we apply the same economic principles?

In short, the answer is yes. All economic analysis deals with the basic problem of making choices under conditions of scarcity, and the problem of satisfying their citizens' wants and needs is certainly as real for Ethiopia and Haiti and China as it is for France, England, and the United States. The universality of scarcity is what makes economic analysis relevant to all nations, regardless of their level of material well-being or ruling political ideology.

The basic tools of supply and demand, theories about consumers and firms, and theories about the structure of markets all contribute to an understanding of the economic problems confronting the world's developing nations. However, these nations often face economic problems quite different from those seen by richer, developed countries. For the developing nations, the economist may have to worry about chronic food shortages, explosive population growth, and hyperinflations that reach triple, and even quadruple,

541

digits. The United States and other industrialized economies rarely encounter such difficulties any more.

The instruments of economic management also vary across nations. While the United States can control its money supply through the purchase or sale of government securities in a well developed financial market, the financial markets of many developing countries are so limited that markets for government securities may not even exist. Control of the money supply can therefore boil down to a question of whether to print money. And while the United States can use progressive income taxes to redistribute income, the poorest nations of the world may have no meaningful personal income taxation system to which to turn.

While economic problems and the policy instruments available to tackle them vary across nations, economic thinking about these problems can be transferred from one setting to another. Let us now turn to some of the economic problems specific to developing nations in an attempt to capture some of the insights that economic analysis can offer.

HOW "THE OTHER THREE FOURTHS" LIVE

Sometime during the 1980s the population of the world will reach five billion people. Most of the roughly 190 different nations belong to the developing world, in which about three fourths of the world's population live.

In the early 1960s, the nations of the world could be assigned rather easily to categories: the *developed countries* included most of Europe, North America, Japan, Australia, and New Zealand; the *developing countries* included the rest of the world. The developing nations were often referred to as the "Third World," to distinguish them from the Western industrialized nations (the "First World") and the Socialist bloc of Eastern European nations (the "Second World").

In the late 1980s, however, the world does not divide into three parts as neatly or as appropriately as it once did. Rapid economic progress has brought some developing nations closer to the developed economies. Countries such as Brazil and Korea, while still considered to be "developing," are often referred to as middle-income, or newly industrialized, countries. In addition, the great wealth of some oil exporting nations, such as Kuwait and Saudi Arabia, distinguishes them from other developing nations. Meanwhile, still other countries have stagnated and fallen so far behind the economic advances of the rest of the world that a new designation, the "Fourth World," has been coined to describe them. Such nations include much of sub-Saharan Africa and some of South Asia.

While the countries of the developing world exhibit considerable diversity, both in their standards of living and in their particular experiences of growth, marked differences still separate the developing from the developed nations. To begin with, the developed countries have a higher average level of material well-being. By material well-being, we mean the amounts of food, clothing, shelter, and other commodities an average person consumes. Comparisons of gross national product (GNP) per capita—that is, of the value of goods and services produced per person in an economy—are often used as a crude index of the level of material well-being across nations. As you can see from Table 22.1, GNP per capita in the industrial market economies significantly exceeds that of both the low- and middle-income developing economies.

In addition to the growth of income per person, other characteristics of economic development include improvements in basic health and education. The degree of political and economic freedoms enjoyed by individual citizens might also be part of a

TABLE 22.1 Indicators of Economic Development

Country group	GNP per capita, 1983 (dollars)	Life expectancy, 1983 (years)	Infant mortality, 1983 (deaths before age one per 1000 births)	Secondary-school enrollment, 1982 (number enrolled as percentage of population aged 12–17	Percentage of labor force in agriculture, 1981
Low-income (e.g., China, Ethiopia, Haiti, India)	260	59	75	30	73
Lower middle-income (e.g., Indonesia, Nicaragua, Turkey, Zimbabwe)	750	57	87	35	54
Upper middle-income (e.g., Korea, Mexico, Portugal, Syria)	2,050	65	59	51	30
High-income oil exporters (e.g., Libya, Saudi Arabia)	12,370	59	90	44	46
Industrial market economies (e.g., Japan, Germany, New Zealand, United States)	11,060	76	10	87	6
East European nonmarket economies (eg., USSR, Poland, East Germany)	(NA)	70	30	90	17

Source: World Development Report, 1985 World Bank. Note that all numbers refer to weighted averages for each country group, where the weights equal the populations of each nation in a specific country group.

comprehensive definition of what it means to be a developed nation. Some of these criteria are easier to quantify than others, and Table 22.1 presents data for different types of economies according to some of the more easily measured indices of development. As you can quickly see, the industrial market economies enjoy higher standards of living according to whatever indicator of development is chosen.

Behind these statistics lies the reality of the very difficult life facing the people of the developing world. For most, meager incomes permit only the basic necessities. Most meals are the same, consisting of the food staple—typically rice, wheat, or corn—of the region. Shelter is primitive. Many people share a small room, usually with an earthen floor and no sanitary facilities. Eighty percent of the population live in rural areas where agricultural work is hard and extremely time-consuming. Productivity (output produced per worker) is low, because household plots are small, and only the crudest of farm implements are available. Low productivity means that farm output per person is at levels barely sufficient to feed a farmer's own family, with nothing left over to sell to others. School-age children may receive some formal education, but illiteracy remains a chronic problem for young and old alike. Infant mortality runs seven times higher than in the United States. Typically, while parasitic infections are common and debilitating, there is only one physician per 5000 people, so the opportunity to obtain medical care is minimal.

Life in the developing nations is a continual struggle against the circumstances of poverty, and prospects for dramatic improvements in living standards for most people are dim. However, as with all generalizations, there are important exceptions. Some nations are better off than others, and in any given nation, an elite group always lives in considerable luxury. Just as in any advanced economy, income is distributed in a fashion that allows a small percentage of households to consume a disproportionately large share of national income. Income distribution in developing countries is often so skewed that the richest households of very poor nations surpass the living standards of many high-income families in the advanced economies.

In sum, however, poverty, not affluence, dominates the developing world. In absolute terms, recent studies suggest that 40 percent of the population of the developing nations has an annual income insufficient to provide for adequate nutrition. While the developed nations account for only about one quarter of the world's population, they are estimated to consume three quarters of the world's output. This leaves the developing countries with about three fourths of the world's people, but only one fourth of world income. The simple result is that most of our planet's population is poor.

FACTORS THAT DETERMINE ECONOMIC ADVANCE

Why Some Nations Are Rich and Some Poor

Economists have been trying to understand the process of economic growth and development since the days of Adam Smith and David Ricardo in the eighteenth and nineteenth centuries, but the study of development economics as it applies to the Third World has a far shorter history. The geopolitical struggles after World War II brought increasing attention to developing nations and their economic problems. During this period, a central question of the new field of development economics was simply Why are some nations poor and others rich? If economists could understand what barriers to economic growth prevented nations from developing and what prerequisites would enable them to develop, then they could prescribe suitable strategies for achieving that goal.

While a general theory of economic development applicable to all nations has not emerged and probably never will, some basic factors that limit a poor nation's economic advance have been suggested. These include insufficient capital formation, a shortage of human resources, a lack of social overhead capital, and the constraints imposed by dependency on the already developed nations.

Capital Formation   You have already encountered the concept of a production function as it applies to a firm's conversion of inputs into outputs. The same principle applies to a nation, where the inputs of labor, land, natural resources, and physical capital combine to produce national output. One explanation for low levels of output in developing nations is the absence of sufficient quantities of necessary inputs. Developing nations have diverse resource endowments—Zaire, for instance, is abundant in natural resources, whereas Bangladesh is resource poor. Almost all developing nations have a scarcity of physical capital relative to other resources, especially relative to labor. The small stock of physical capital, including factories, machinery, farm equipment, and other types of productive capital, constrains labor's productivity and, in turn, national output.

Vicious-circle-of-poverty   The hypothesis that suggests that poverty is self-perpetuating since poor nations are unable to save and invest enough to accumulate the capital stock which would help them grow.

But to cite capital shortages as the cause of economic backwardness does not really explain much. After all, why is capital in such short supply in developing countries? Many explanations have been offered. One, known as the **"vicious-circle-of-poverty"** hypothesis, suggests that a poor nation must consume most of its income just to maintain its already low standard of living. Just as a poor *family* does, a poor *nation* finds that the opportunity cost of forgoing current consumption (that is, by saving instead of consuming output) is too high. Consuming most of national income implies limited saving, and this, in turn, implies low levels of investment. Without investment, the capital stock does not grow, income remains low, and the vicious circle is complete. Poverty becomes self-perpetuating.

The difficulty with the vicious-circle argument is that if it were true, no nation could ever develop. For example, Japanese GNP per capita at the turn of the century was well below that of many of today's developing nations. If the vicious-circle explanation were correct, Japan could never have grown into the industrial power it is today. The vicious-circle argument fails to recognize that every nation has *some* surplus above consumption needs that is available for investment. Often this surplus is most visible in the conspicuous-consumption habits of the nation's richest families. In any case, poverty alone cannot explain capital shortages, nor is poverty necessarily self-perpetuating.

In a developing economy, scarcity of capital may have more to do with a lack of incentives for citizens to save and invest productively than it has to do with any absolute scarcity of income available for capital accumulation. The inherent riskiness and uncertainty that surround a developing nation's economy and its political system tend to reduce incentives to invest in any activity, especially those that require long periods of time to yield a return. Many of the rich in developing countries take their savings and invest them in Europe or in the United States rather than risk holding them in what is often an unstable political climate. Savings transferred to the United States do not lead to physical capital growth in the Third World. The lack of a strong work ethic or the nature of the class structure may also explain the tendency toward conspicuous consumption and away from saving by many of the Third World's richer households. Finally, a range of government policies including price ceilings, import controls, and even outright appropriation of private property tend to discourage investment activity.

Whatever the causes of capital shortages, the absence of productive capital does prevent income from rising in any economy. The availability of capital, however, is a necessary, but not a *sufficient*, condition for economic growth. The Third World landscape is littered with idle factories and abandoned machinery. Clearly other ingredients are required to achieve economic progress.

Human Resources   Capital is not the only factor of production required to produce output. Labor is an equally important input. But the quantity of available labor rarely constrains a developing economy. In most developing nations, rapid population growth for several decades has resulted in rapidly expanding labor supplies. If the quantity of labor is not a problem, however, the *quality* of available labor may pose a constraint on the growth of income. Or, to put it another way, the shortage of **human capital**—the stock of knowledge and skill embodied in the work force—may act as a barrier to economic growth.

Human capital   *The stock of knowledge and skill embodied in the work force.*

Human capital may go undeveloped for a number of reasons. Among the poorest members of the developing nations, malnutrition and the lack of basic health care can substantially reduce labor productivity. Programs to improve nutrition and health represent one kind of human capital investment that can lead to increased productivity and higher incomes. The more familiar forms of human capital investment, including formal education and on-the-job training, may also play an important role. Basic literacy, as well as specialized training in farm management, for example, can yield a high return to both the individual worker and the economy. Education has grown to become the largest category of government expenditure in many developing nations, in part because of the belief that human resources are the ultimate determinant of economic advance.

Another frequently cited barrier to economic development is the apparent shortage of entrepreneurial activity in developing nations. Innovative entrepreneurs who are willing to take risks are indeed an essential human resource in any economy. In a developing nation, new techniques of production rarely need to be invented, since they can usually be adapted from the available technology of the already developed nations. But entrepreneurs who are willing and able to organize and carry out economic activity do appear to be in short supply in much of the Third World. Family and political ties often seem to be more important than ability when it comes to securing positions of authority. Whatever the explanation, development cannot proceed without human resources capable of initiating and managing economic activity.

Social Overhead Capital   Anyone who has spent time in a developing nation knows how difficult it can be to send a letter, make a local phone call, or travel within the country itself. Add to this list of obstacles problems with water supplies, frequent electrical power outages—in the few areas where electricity is available at all—and often ineffective mosquito and pest control, and you soon realize how deficient even the simplest, most basic of government-provided goods and services can be.

Social overhead capital Basic infrastructure projects such as roads, power generation, and irrigation systems.

As in any economy, the government has considerable opportunity and responsibility for involvement where conditions encourage natural monopoly (as in the utilities industries), where public goods (such as health care or education) must be provided, and where there are externalities (neighborhood effects such as pollution or congestion). In a developing economy, the government must place particular emphasis on creating a basic infrastructure—roads, power generation, irrigation systems. There are often good reasons why such projects, referred to as **social overhead capital**, cannot successfully be undertaken by the private sector. Many of these projects operate with economies of scale, which means that they can be efficient only if they are very large. But in that case, they may be simply too large for any private company, or even a group of such companies, to carry out. Such projects include dams, roads, and power grids.

Finally, many socially useful projects can not be economically undertaken by the private sector because there is no way for private agents to capture enough of the returns to make such projects profitable. This so-called **"free-rider problem"** is well known in the economics of the developed world. (For a full discussion of this problem, See Chapter 16). Consider national defense, for example. Since everyone in a country benefits from national defense, whether or not that person has paid for it, anyone who attempted to go into the private business of providing national defense would quickly go broke. Why should I buy any national defense at all if *your* purchase of defense will also protect me? Why should you buy any, if *my* purchase will also protect you? Problems of free riders are widespread throughout the developing world.

Governments in the Third World can do important and useful things to encourage development, but many such efforts must lie in areas that the private sector would never touch. If government action in these realms is not forthcoming, economic development may be curtailed by a lack of social overhead capital.

Dependency theory The theory that the poverty of the Third World is due to the "dependence" of the developing world on nations that are already developed; it suggests that even after the end of colonialism, this dependence is maintained because developed countries are able to use their economic power to determine to their own advantage—and the disadvantage of others—the relative prices and conditions under which the international exchange of goods takes place.

Dependency Theories   Radical economists take an entirely different approach to understanding why some nations are rich and others poor. Some find the explanation within the developing nations themselves. In advanced industrial economies, the merchant classes were responsible for breaking down traditional feudalism and replacing it with a capitalist economy oriented toward growth and development. In the developing nations, however, the class that could foster capitalism, has not followed the same path, perhaps out of fear of a socialist takeover. In the view of some analysts, potential capitalists have not transformed traditional societies but have instead acted to maintain the status quo and have thus retarded economic advance.

Another radical position, called **dependency theory**, is that the poverty of the Third World is due to the "dependence" of the developing world on nations that are already developed. (A dependent country is one whose *economy* is conditional on the development and expansion of another economy.) During the colonial period, European powers dominated much of the political and economic life of what is today the developing world. Colonial powers sometimes directly destroyed local industries, either by prohibiting certain economic activities or by flooding the colony's markets with manufactured goods from the mother country. Furthermore, by not developing basic physical infrastructure or local human capital, and by draining mineral wealth from the colonized country, colonialism created economies that were helpless and economically dependent by the time political independence was achieved.

Radical economists also contend that economic dependency is today maintained, even though colonialism is long past, through the structure of international trade relations. Developed economies provide important markets for the exports of developing nations and often are their only sources of critical inputs. Industrialized economies also influence world interest rates, capital flows, and exchange rates. Through their economic power, it is argued, industrialized nations often determine to their own advantage—and the disadvantage of others—the relative prices and conditions under which the international exchange of goods takes place.

Dependency theorists argue that the unequal relationship between rich and poor nations in world markets works to the detriment of the developing world. This view has lead many Third World leaders to call for a **"new international economic order"** (**NIEO**). Such an arrangement would require agreements between developed and developing nations that would increase the gains that accrue to the developing world from international exchange. Plans for such a set of agreements have been widely discussed in the Third World. But there has been virtually no progress in reaching any sort of accord, because of divisions among the developing nations and a lack of cooperation from most developed countries.

Strategies for Economic Development

Just as no single theory appears to explain economic backwardness, so it is unlikely that one development strategy will succeed in all nations. In fact, many alternative development strategies for the Third World have been proposed over the past 30 or 40 years. Although these strategies have taken many different tacks, they all share the recognition that a developing economy faces certain basic trade-offs. An insufficient amount of both human and physical resources dictates that choices must be made. Some of the basic trade-offs that underlie any development strategy include those between agriculture and industry, exports and import substitution, and central planning and the markets.

Agriculture or Industry?   Third World countries began to gain their independence in the period just after World War II. The tradition of promoting industrialization as the solution to the problem of the developing world dates from this time. The early five-year development plans of India called for promoting manufacturing, while the current Marxist government in Ethiopia has similar intentions. Industry has several apparent attractions over agriculture. First, if it is true that capital shortages constrain economic growth, then the building of factories is an obvious mechanism for increasing a nation's stock of capital. Second, and perhaps most important, one of the prime characteristics of more developed economies is their structural transformation away from agriculture and toward manufacturing and modern services. As Table 22.2 shows, agriculture's share in GNP declines substantially as per capita incomes increase. The share of manufacturing and modern services increases correspondingly, especially in the early phases of economic development.

TABLE 22.2
The Structure of Production in
Developed and Developing
Economies, 1983

| | **SHARE OF GROSS DOMESTIC PRODUCT (PERCENTAGE)** | | | |
| | | **Industry** | | |
COUNTRY GROUP	Agriculture	**Manufacturing Only**	Total	Services
Low-income	37	14	34	29
Lower middle-income	22	16	35	42
Upper middle-income	11	24	37	52
High-income oil exporters	2	6	65	33
Industrial market economies	3	24	35	62

Source: *World Development Report, 1985*, World Bank.

Many economies have pursued industry at the expense of agriculture. Since the early 1970s, however, the agricultural sector has received considerably more attention than it had previously been paid. In many countries, industrialization has been either unsuccessful or disappointing—that is, it did not bring the benefits that were expected. Experience suggests that simply trying to replicate the structure of developed economies does not in itself guarantee, or even promote, successful development.

By comparison, agricultural strategies have numerous benefits. While some agricultural projects, such as the building of major dams and irrigation networks, are very capital intensive, many others, such as extension services to help teach better farming techniques, or small-scale fertilizer programs, have low capital and import requirements. Programs like these can affect large numbers of households, and because their benefits are directed at the rural areas, they are most likely to help a country's poorest families.

Both industrialization and agricultural strategies have their disadvantages. Experience over the last three decades suggests, however, that some balance between these approaches leads to the best outcome. The Chinese have referred to this dual approach to development as "walking on two legs"—that is, it is important and effective to pay attention to both industry and agriculture.

Exports or Import Substitution?   As developing nations expand their industrial activities, they must decide what type of trade strategy to pursue. The choice usually boils down to one of two major alternatives: export promotion or import substitution.

Import substitution An
industrial trade strategy that favors
developing local industries that can
manufacture goods that replace
imports.

The term **import substitution** refers to an industrial trade strategy that favors developing local industries that can manufacture goods that replace imports. For example, if fertilizer is currently imported, import substitution calls for establishment of a domestic fertilizer industry to produce replacements for those imports. This strategy gained prominence throughout South America in the 1950s. At that time, most developing nations exported agricultural and mineral products, goods that faced uncertain and often unstable international markets. Furthermore, the **terms of trade** for these nations—the ratio of export to import prices—seemed to be on a long-run decline.[1] A decline in a country's terms of trade means that its imports of manufactured goods become relatively expensive, while its exports—mostly primary goods such as rubber and wheat and oil—become relatively inexpensive.

[1]It now appears that the terms of trade for Third World countries as a group were not actually on a long-run decline. Of course, the prices of commodities have changed, with some (such as oil until recently) doing very well, and others (such as wool) doing quite poorly. During the 1950s, however, many policy makers came to believe that the purchasing power of developing-country exports was undergoing a permanent slump.

Under these conditions, the call for import-substitution policies was understandable. Special government actions, including tariff and quota protection and subsidized imports of machinery, were set up to encourage new domestic industries. Multinational corporations were also invited to begin domestic operations.

The current view of import-substitution strategies is that they have failed almost everywhere they have been tried. With domestic industries sheltered from international competition by high tariffs (often as high as 200 percent), major economic inefficiencies were created. For example, Peru has a population of less than 20 million, only a tiny fraction of whom could ever afford to buy an automobile. Yet at one time the country had five or six different automobile manufacturers, each of which produced only a few thousand cars per year. Since there are substantial economies of scale in automobile production, the cost per car was much higher than it needed to be, and valuable resources were squandered producing cars when they could have been devoted to another, much more productive, activity.

Policies designed to promote import substitution often encouraged capital-intensive production methods, which limited the creation of jobs. Finally, import-substitution policies hurt export activities. Obviously, a country like Peru could not export automobiles, since it could only produce them at a cost far greater than their price on the world market. Worse still, import-substitution policies encouraged the use of expensive domestic products, such as tractors and fertilizer, instead of lower-cost imports. These policies thus served to tax the very sectors that might have successfully competed in world markets. To the extent that the Peruvian sugar industry had to rely on domestically produced, high-cost fertilizer, for example, its ability to compete in international markets was reduced, because its production costs were artificially raised. Paradoxically, import-substitution policies designed to conserve scarce earnings of foreign currency ended up exacerbating foreign exchange shortages and precipitating recurrent balance-of-payments crises.

Export promotion An *outward-looking trade policy which is designed to encourage the production of exports through measures such as maintaining favorable exchange rates and subsidies to export industries.*

As an alternative to import substitution, some nations have pursued strategies of **export promotion**. As an industrial market economy, Japan holds out to the developing world a striking example of the economic success that exports can provide. With an average annual per capita real GNP growth rate of roughly six percent per year since 1960, Japan's achievements are in part based on industrial production oriented toward foreign consumers.

Japan's success has not gone unnoticed in the developing world. Starting around 1970, Hong Kong, Singapore, Korea, and Taiwan all began to pursue export promotion of manufactured goods. Their growth rates have surpassed even Japan's. Other nations, including Brazil, Colombia, and Turkey, have also had some success at pursuing a more outward-looking trade policy. Government support of export promotion has often taken the form of maintaining an exchange rate that is favorable enough to permit exports to compete with products manufactured in developed economies. Governments also have provided subsidies to export industries.

While export promotion has generally succeeded during the 1970s and 1980s, growing protectionism in the industrial market economies may limit the gains that developing nations can expect in the years ahead. If the industrialized nations can set increasing limits on their imports of manufactured products from the Third World, one of the more successful development strategies we know of will be fundamentally weakened.

Planning or the Marketplace?   As part of its strategy for achieving economic development, a nation must decide how its economy will be directed. Its basic choices lie between a market-oriented economic system and a centrally planned one.

In the 1950s and into the 1960s, development strategies that called for national planning commanded wide support. The rapid economic growth of the Soviet Union, a centrally planned economy, provided a historical example of the speed with which a backward agrarian nation could be transformed into a modern industrial power. (The often appalling costs of this strategy were less widely known.) Furthermore, the poor development of many commodity and asset markets in the Third World led many experts to believe that market forces could not direct an economy reliably and that major government intervention was therefore necessary. Even the United States, with its commitment to free enterprise in the marketplace, supported early central planning efforts in many developing nations.

Today planning takes many forms in the Third World. In some settings, central planning replaces market-based outcomes with direct, administratively determined controls over such economic variables as prices, output, and employment. In other situations, national planning amounts to little more than the formulation of general five- or ten-year goals that serve as rough blueprints for a nation's economic future.

The economic appeal of planning lies in its ability to channel savings into productive investment and to coordinate economic activities that private actors in the economy might not otherwise undertake. The reality of central planning is that it is technically difficult, highly politicized, and a nightmare to administer. Given the scarcity of human resources and the unstable political environment in most developing nations, planning itself, let alone the enactment of the plan, becomes a formidable task.

The failure of many planning efforts has brought increasing calls from outside experts for less government intervention and more market orientation in developing economies. The elimination of price controls, movement toward a freer determination of the exchange rate, privatization of state-run enterprises, and reductions in import restraints are examples of market-oriented reforms that are frequently recommended by such international agencies as the International Monetary Fund and the World Bank. Throughout the developing world, a recognition of the value of market forces in determining the allocation of scarce resources appears to be increasing. Nonetheless, government intervention still has a major role to play. In the decades ahead, developing nations will continue to determine those situations where planning is superior to the market and those where the market is superior to planning.

Growth or Development: Are They Alternatives?

Until now, we have used the words "growth" and "development" as if they meant essentially the same thing. But it is not at all clear that this is so. One can easily imagine instances in which a country has achieved higher levels of income (growth) with little or no benefit accruing to most of its citizens. Thus one central question in evaluating alternative strategies for achieving economic development is whether promoting growth in the economy necessarily achieves development.

In the past, most development strategies aimed at increasing the growth rate of income per capita. Many still do, based on the expectation that by increasing the size of national income, the benefits of economic growth will "trickle down" to all members of society. If this is what happens, then growth should promote development.

By the early 1970s, however, the relationship between growth and development was increasingly being called into question. A major study by the World Bank in 1974 concluded that it is now clear that more than a decade of rapid growth in underdeveloped countries has been of little or no benefit to perhaps a third of their population. . . . Paradoxically, while growth policies have succeeded beyond the expectations of the first development decade, the very idea of aggregate growth as a social objective has increasingly been called into question.

The World Bank study indicated that increases in GNP per capita did not guarantee significant improvements in development indicators such as nutrition, health, and education. Although GNP per capita may indeed have risen, its benefits trickled down to only a small minority of the population. This realization prompted the call for new development strategies that would directly address the circumstances of poverty. Such new strategies favored agriculture over industry, called for domestic redistribution of income and wealth—especially land, and encouraged programs to satisfy basic needs such as food and shelter.

By 1980 the international macroeconomic crises of skyrocketing oil prices, worldwide recession, and Third World debt had forced attention away from programs designed to eliminate poverty directly. Nonetheless, the lesson remains that economic growth does not guarantee economic development and that concerted efforts may be required to transform growing output capacity into economic benefits that reach most of a nation's people.

SPECIFIC DEVELOPMENT ISSUES

Every individual developing nation has a cultural, political, and economic history all its own and therefore confronts a unique set of problems. Still, it is possible to talk usefully about common economic issues that each nation must face in its own particular way. These issues include rapid population growth, food shortages, and the Third World debt problem.

Population Growth

The populations of the developing nations are estimated to be growing at about two percent per year. This compares with a population growth rate of only 0.6% per year for the industrial market economies. If the Third World's population growth rate remains at two percent, it will take only 34 years to double. From its 1987 level of 3.8 billion it will reach over 7.5 billion by the end of year 2020. Meanwhile, it will take the industrialized nations 122 years to double their populations. This gives new meaning to the old saying that "the rich get richer and the poor get children." What is so immediately alarming about these numbers is that given all of the current economic problems the developing nations have now, it is hard to imagine how they can possibly absorb so many more people in such a relatively short period.

Concern over population growth is not new to the world. Thomas Malthus expressed his fears about the population increases he observed around 200 years ago. Malthus believed that while populations grow geometrically, food supplies grow much more slowly because of the **diminishing marginal productivity of land.**[2] Taken

[2]The law of diminishing marginal productivity says that with a fixed amount of some resource (land), additions of more and more of a variable resource (labor) will produce smaller and smaller gains in output.

together, these two phenomena led Malthus to predict the increasing impoverishment of most of the world's people unless population growth could be checked.

Malthus's fears for Europe and America proved unfounded, because he did not anticipate either the technological changes that revolutionized agricultural productivity or the eventual decrease in population growth rates in Europe and North America. But Malthus may have been right, only premature. Does the developing world now fit his predictions? While some contemporary observers believe that the Malthusian view is correct and that the earth's population will eventually outstrip its resources, others argue that technological change and demographic transitions (to slower population growth rates) will permit further increases in global welfare.

Is Rapid Population Growth Bad?   Surprisingly, we know far less about the economic consequences of rapid population growth than you might expect. Conventional wisdom warns of dire economic consequences from the Third World's "population explosion," but these predictions are difficult to substantiate with available evidence. The rapid economic growth of the United States, for example, was accompanied by relatively rapid population growth by historical standards. Nor has any slowing of population growth been necessary for the economic progress achieved by many of the newly industrialized countries. Nonetheless, population expansion in many of today's poorest nations is of a magnitude unprecedented in world history, as Figure 22.1 clearly shows. From the year A.D. 1 until the mid 1600s, populations grew slowly, at rates of only about 0.04% per year. Since then, and especially since 1950, rates have skyrocketed. Today populations are generally growing at rates of 1.5% to 4.0% per year throughout the Third World.

Growth rates like these have never occurred before, and no one really knows what impact they will have on economic development. But a basic economic concern is that such rapid population growth may limit investment and that this, in turn, will restrain

FIGURE 22.1

The Growth of World Production, Projected to 2020 A.D.

For thousands of years, population grew modestly. From 1 A.D. until the mid 1600s, population grew at about .04% per year. Since the industrial revolution, population growth has occurred at an unprecedented rate.

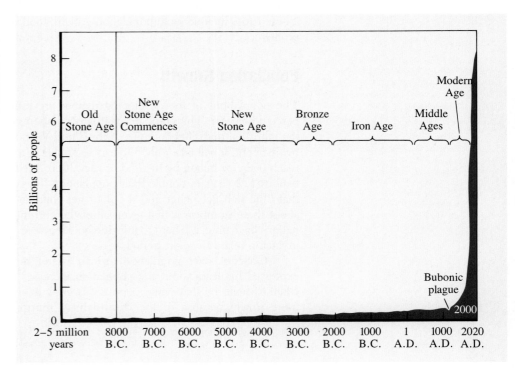

increases in labor productivity and income. Rapid population growth changes the age composition of a population, generating many dependent children relative to the number of productive working adults. Such a situation may diminish saving rates, and hence investment, as the immediate consumption needs of the young take priority over saving for the future.

Furthermore, even if, as some authorities contend, low saving is not a necessary consequence of rapid population growth, other economic problems remain. The ability to improve human capital through a broad range of programs, from infant nutrition through formal secondary education, may be severely limited if populations simply explode. Such programs are most often the responsibility of the state, and governments that are already weak cannot be expected to improve their services under the burden of population pressures that rapidly increase demands for all kinds of public goods and services.

Kenya, for example, at a population growth rate of 4.2%, has one of the highest rates in the world. It is likely to see its 1986 population of over 20 million people grow to almost 40 million by the turn of the century. This is a daunting prospect, and it is hard even to imagine how in so few years Kenya will be able to provide its population with the physical and human capital needed to maintain, let alone improve, already low standards of living.

Causes of Rapid Population Growth   Population growth is determined by the relationship between births and deaths—that is, between rates of **fertility** and **mortality**.[3] In fact, the **natural rate of population increase** (excluding migration) is defined as the difference between the birth rate and the death rate. So, if the birth rate is four percent, for example, and the death rate is three percent, the population is growing at one percent per year.

Historically, low rates of population growth were maintained because of high mortality rates despite high levels of fertility. That is, families had many children, but average life expectancies were low, and many children (and adults) died young. In Europe and North America, improvements in nutrition, in public health programs (especially those concerned with clean drinking water and sanitation services), and in modern medical practices led to a fall in the death rate and hence to more rapid population growth. Eventually fertility rates also fell, returning population growth to a low and stable rate, as you can see in Figure 22.2.

The figure also shows that in the developing nations, public health interventions and improved nutrition over the past 30 years have brought about precipitous declines in mortality rates. Fertility declines have not quickly followed, however, and this has led to high rates of population growth. Reduced population growth, of course, rests on decreased birth rates, but attempts in this direction must take account of how different peoples feel and behave with regard to fertility.

Fertility   *The fertility rate, or the birth rate, is equal to the number of births per year divided by the average population and then multiplied by 100.*

Mortality   *The mortality rate, or the death rate, is equal to the number of deaths per year divided by the average population and then multiplied by 100.*

Natural rate of population increase   *Defined as the difference between the birth rate and the death rate (it excludes migration).*

---

[3]There are many complex and sophisticated measures for analyzing births and deaths in a community. The simplest measures are the crude birth and death rates. We can define the crude birth rate as

$$B = \frac{\text{Number of births during a year}}{\text{Average or midyear population}} \times 100$$

Similarly, the crude death rate is

$$D = \frac{\text{Number of deaths during a year}}{\text{Average or midyear population}} \times 100$$

Given the birth and death rates, we can define the crude rate of natural increase (population growth rate) as

$$P = B - D.$$

More sophisticated measures are explained in any standard textbook on demography.

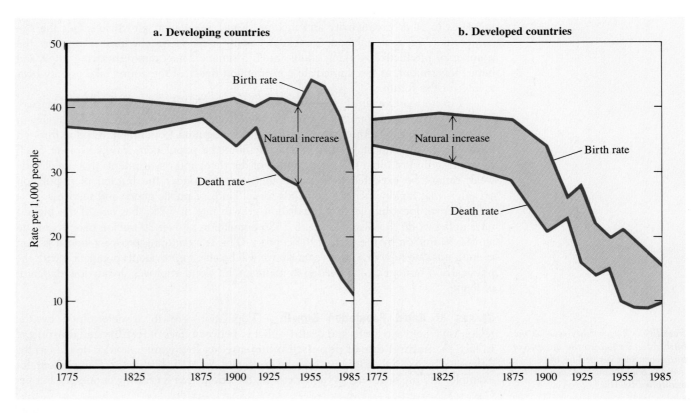

FIGURE 22.2
The Natural Increase in Population, 1775–1985

Family planning and modern forms of birth control may be important mechanisms for decreasing fertility, but by themselves such programs have had rather limited success in most countries where they have been tried. If family planning strategies are to be successful, they must make sense to the people who are supposed to benefit from them. Therefore the planners of such strategies must understand why families in developing nations have so many children.

To a great extent, Third World peoples want large families because they believe they need them. Economists have attempted to understand fertility patterns in the Third World by focusing on the determinants of the demand for children. In agrarian societies, children are important sources of farm labor, and they may thus make significant contributions to household income. Without public systems of old-age support, such as social security, children may also provide a vital source of income for parents who are too old to support themselves. With the high value of children enhanced by high rates of infant mortality, it is no wonder that families try to have many children to insure that a sufficient number will survive childhood.

Cultural and religious values also affect the number of children families want to have, but the economic incentives to have large families are extremely powerful. Only when the relationship between the costs and benefits of having children changes will fertility rates decline. Expanding the opportunities for women in an economy increases the opportunity costs of child rearing (by giving women a more highly valued alternative to raising children) and often leads to lower birth rates. Government incentives for smaller families, such as subsidized education for families with fewer than three children, can have a similar effect. In general, rising incomes appear to decrease fertility rates, indicating that economic development itself reduces population growth rates.

Economic theories of population growth suggest that fertility decisions made by poor and not-so-poor families should not be viewed as uninformed and uncontrolled. An individual family may well find that having many children is a rational strategy for economic survival given the conditions in which it finds itself. This does not mean, however, that having many children is a net benefit to society as a whole. When a family decides to have a large number of children, it imposes costs on the rest of society; the children must be educated, their health provided for, and so forth. In other words, what makes sense for an individual household may create negative externalities for the nation as a whole.[4] Thus any nation that wants to slow its rate of population growth will probably find it necessary to have in place economic incentives for fewer children as well as family planning programs.

Food Shortages: Acts of Nature or Human Mistakes?

Television footage portraying victims of the famine in Ethiopia burned indelible images of starving people into the minds of most Americans. No other event in recent memory so forcefully dramatized the Third World's ongoing food crisis. Severe famines like that in Ethiopia have occurred throughout recorded history, but they no longer plague the advanced nations. In the past ten years, the famines that have struck various parts of Africa and Asia represent the most acute form of food shortage confronting the developing nations. Chronic food shortages afflict almost every developing country, however, and account for widespread caloric and protein deficiencies, especially among Third World children.

Pictures of the parched Ethiopian countryside might lead a casual observer to conclude that famines are ultimately acts of nature. After all, if the rains do not come or the locusts do, human beings can do little but wait. This simplistic view of food shortages fails to recognize the extent to which contemporary food crises are often very much the result of human behavior. Even such natural events as severe flooding can often be traced to the overharvesting of firewood, which denudes the landscape, increases soil erosion, and exacerbates spring floods.

Human behavior is very much behind the inadequate distribution of available food to those who need it. India now grows enough grains to feed its vast population, for example, but malnutrition remains widespread because many people cannot afford to feed themselves. Globally, it has been estimated that redistributing only two percent of world food supplies between developed and developing nations could eliminate world hunger. Part of the distribution problem involves failures to stockpile adequate food reserves in years of good harvests. Other problems include transportation and communication barriers that prevent supplies from reaching those in need. Beyond technical obstacles, world and domestic politics also heavily influence where, how, and whether food is available. During the second Ethiopian famine, in 1988, for example, the government blocked relief agencies from delivering food and medical supplies to the famine area because a civil war was being waged there.

---

[4]An *externality* occurs whenever one agent's behavior effects the welfare of others. A firm may find it rational to dump its waste into a nearby river, but in so doing it may ruin the river for fisherman and bathers downstream. This is an example of a negative externality.

While food shortages are recognized chronic problems, developing nations often pursue farm policies that actually discourage agricultural production. Agricultural production in sub-Saharan Africa today is lower than it was 20 years ago. Economists believe that misguided agricultural policies are responsible for much of this decline.

Pricing Policies and Agricultural Output

Few governments in either industrialized or developing nations have permitted market forces alone to determine agricultural prices. In the United States and much of Europe, farm subsidies often encourage production and result in food surpluses rather than shortages. In developing nations, a few countries follow similar policies, maintaining high farm prices both to increase agricultural production and to maintain farm incomes. However, many developing nations follow a different route, offering farmers low prices for their output.

Produce-marketing boards   The structures through which some Third World governments both buy farm output and sell it to urban residents at government controlled prices.

In order to appreciate the motives behind different pricing policies, you need to understand several things about the structure of agricultural markets in many developing nations. Often the government is the primary purchaser of both basic foodstuffs and export crops. Through **produce-marketing boards,** Third World governments both buy farm output and sell it to urban residents at government-controlled prices. By setting the prices they pay to farmers at low levels, the government can afford to sell basic foodstuffs to urban consumers at low prices. Governments often find this an attractive course of action because the direct political influence of the relatively small urban population typically far outweighs the influence of the majority who live in the countryside. Because most city dwellers spend about half their incomes on food, low consumer prices bolster the real incomes of the urban population and help keep it content. Urban food riots have been common in developing nations over the years, and the very existence of a government may hinge on its food-pricing strategy.

While we can easily appreciate the political motives behind food pricing, policies that set artificially low prices have significant pitfalls. Farmers react to these prices—often set so low that farmers cannot cover their production costs—by reducing the amount of output they produce. Back in the city, meanwhile, excess demand for food at the artificially low ceiling prices imposed by the government may promote the emergence of black markets.

Many developing economies that have followed low agricultural pricing policies have experienced exactly this set of outcomes. Until recently, for example, Mexico kept corn prices low in order to hold down the price of tortillas, the basic item in the diet of much of Mexico's urban population. As a result, corn production fell as farmers switched to crops whose prices the government did not control. Domestic corn shortages became widespread, and corn had to be imported in order to sustain urban demand.

Agricultural Output: The Supply Side   In 1980 a single American farmer could provide enough food to feed 75 people. In most developing economies, a single farmer can barely provide food to feed his or her own family. While differences in agricultural pricing policies account for some of this gap, other factors are also at work. Traditionally, low agricultural productivity in the developing world was blamed on the ignorance and laziness of peasant farmers. A more enlightened view today traces the problem to shortage of inputs, including land, fertilizer, irrigation, machinery, new seed varieties, and agricultural extension services, which provide credit and technical advice to farmers.

Green Revolution   *The agricultural breakthroughs of modern science such as the development of new, high-yield crop varieties.*

Modern agricultural science has created a so-called **"Green Revolution"** based on new, high-yield varieties of wheat, rice, and other crops. Using new, faster-growing varieties instead of the single-crop plants they have relied upon for centuries, some farmers can grow three crops of rice a year. In Mexico, under ideal conditions, "miracle" wheat has produced 105 bushels of grain per acre, compared with traditional varieties that yield only 11.5 bushels.

If the Green Revolution suggests that science can, in principle, solve world food shortages, the often disappointing history of Third World experiments with scientific agriculture offers a less optimistic story. Economic factors have greatly limited the adoption of Green Revolution techniques. New seeds are expensive, and their cultivation absolutely requires the presence of many complementary inputs, including fertilizers and irrigation. With poorly developed rural credit markets, farmers often face interest rates so high that new technologies, regardless of their promise in terms of higher yields, are out of reach or unprofitable. The failure of peasant farmers to adopt new agricultural techniques has often been blamed on superstition or lack of education. Upon closer examination, however, such decisions typically reflect a rational choice. Given the costs and benefits of new inputs and the inherent riskiness to the farmer of any new method of cultivation, it is not surprising that it has often been difficult to get Third World farmers to accept the Green Revolution.

Peasant farmers are also constrained by the amount of land they have to work. In some nations, high population density in the rural areas requires highly labor-intensive cultivation. In other countries, maldistribution of land decreases agricultural output. Throughout Latin America, for example, it is estimated that less than 2 percent of all land owners control almost 75 percent of the land under cultivation. Improved crop yields often follow land reforms that redistribute holdings, because owner households are often more productive than tenant farmers. Land reform has had positive effects on output in countries with economic systems as diverse as those of Korea and the People's Republic of China.

In conclusion, while acts of nature will always threaten agricultural production, human actions, especially policies designed to support the agricultural sector, can have a major impact on reducing the food problems of the developing world.

Third World Debt

In the 1970s, development experts worried about many crises facing the developing world, but the debt crisis was not among them. Within a decade, this situation changed dramatically. The financial plight of nations such as Brazil, Mexico, and the Philippines has become front-page news. What alarmed those familiar with the debt situation was not only its potential impact on the developing nations, but a belief that it threatened the economic well-being of the advanced nations as well.

Between 1970 and 1984, developing nations borrowed so much money from foreigners that their combined debt increased by 1000 percent, to almost $700 billion. Three nations alone—Brazil, Mexico, and Venezuela—had outstanding loans to three major U.S. banks (Citibank, Chase-Manhattan, and Manufacturer's Hanover) that were more than double the net worth of those financial institutions. As recession took hold in the advanced countries during the early 1980s, growth in the exports of the debtor countries slowed, and many found they could no longer pay back the money they owed. The prospect of loan defaults by Third World nations threatened the entire international financial system and transformed the debt crisis into a global problem.

The Evolution of the Debt Crisis

International financial crises, including threatened and actual defaults on foreign obligations, have a long history that extends well back into the nineteenth century. But the roots of the current debt crisis go back only as far as the early 1970s. A simple analysis of the supply and demand for credit explains much of the present situation.

With domestic capital scarce and increased saving obtainable only with great difficulty, developing nations often wish to secure foreign capital. Outright grants in the form of foreign aid from friendly governments are the most desirable form of such assistance from a developing country's point of view, because they do not require any repayment. But such aid is usually small, and it has grown smaller over time. Thus developing nations have come to rely on borrowing from abroad. The lower the price of capital and the greater the expected return, the greater the quantity they will wish to borrow. Meanwhile, suppliers of capital are willing to lend to developing nations if the interest rate they can charge for loans is high enough to offset the relatively greater risks of lending overseas.

The recent debt crisis began soon after the first OPEC oil price increase in 1973. Many OPEC members suddenly found themselves awash in dollars, money they literally could not spend fast enough to keep up with the funds flowing into their coffers.[5] Rather than spending these "petrodollars," many OPEC countries ended up with large capital account surpluses on their balance of payments (just as your checking or savings account balances would go up if you earned a lot more than you spent in the course of a year). These vast sums had to end up somewhere, and they naturally found their way into the international banking system. Banks were of course eager to recycle these funds by loaning them out to countries that wanted to borrow. Because funds were in such abundant supply, they were often available at interest rates that were extremely low, or even negative after allowing for inflation.

Banks in the developed nations also noted the recent and rapid growth in many developing economies and concluded that profitable investments were available and that Third World growth prospects were encouraging. Meanwhile, oil price hikes increased the demand for foreign capital in non-OPEC developing countries: nations such as Brazil found that their oil import bills had suddenly soared as a result of the OPEC price rise. With no corresponding increases in export revenues to pay for the extra imports, borrowing from abroad became even more attractive. Taken together, all these forces propelled the borrowing of Third World countries to new heights.

A second oil price shock occurred in 1979, and soon the international financial situation changed abruptly. Advanced economies, especially the United States, responded to escalating inflation with a tight monetary policy. Interest rates rose sharply, increasing the interest payments on Third World loans, most of which had variable interest rate provisions. An appreciating U.S. dollar also increased the burden of Third World debt repayment, since most loans were denominated in U.S. dollars. As obligations to Western banks increased, the developing nations' ability to pay fell. With the recession in the industrial market economies, demand for Third World exports declined. Export volumes and prices dropped, and growing protectionism in the United States and Europe worsened the situation for developing-country borrowers.

---

[5]Many OPEC countries embarked on vast and ambitious development plans, building new cities, roads, universities, and so on. Even so, their small populations and underdeveloped economies simply could not absorb the funds they received from their oil exports.

Unable to find the export earnings needed to pay back their foreign obligations, developing nations could meet their payments either by decreasing imports or by borrowing even more from abroad. Different countries adopted different approaches. Decreasing imports threatened economic growth at home, because imports of oil and machinery are vital to the functioning of most Third World economies.

The only alternative to decreasing imports is to borrow more from abroad, but this at best only forestalls inevitable adjustments. The worsening situation was revealed by growing **debt service ratios**, which measure the amount of debt service—repayment of loan principal plus interest payments—as a percentage of export revenues. In some extreme cases, these ratios approached 100 percent, meaning that all of a debtor nation's export revenues would be required just to satisfy debt repayment, with little, if any, foreign exchange left over to pay for imports.

As the situation deteriorated, another option appeared: debtor nations might simply repudiate their debts outright and **default** on their outstanding loans. Default is not an attractive option, either to lenders or borrowers. Bankers never favor default, but when it occurs with domestic loans, some collateral is usually available to cover all or part of the remaining debt. For loans to another country, however, such collateral is virtually impossible to secure. Given their extensive involvement with Third World borrowers, Western banks did not want to set in motion a pattern of international default. Nor did borrowers want to default. Third World leaders recognized that to default might result in the denial of access to developed-country banking facilities and to markets in the industrial countries. Such results would pose major obstacles to further development efforts.

Various countries **rescheduled their debt** as an interim solution. Under a rescheduling agreement, banks and borrowers negotiate a new schedule for the repayment of existing debt, often with some of the debt written off and with repayment periods extended. In return, borrowing countries are expected to sign an agreement with the International Monetary Fund to revamp their economic policies so as to provide incentives for higher export earnings and lower imports. This kind of agreement is often referred to as a **stabilization program**, and it usually requires painful austerity measures such as currency devaluations, a reduction in government expenditures, and an increase in tax revenues.

After the Debt Crisis: An Epilogue

By 1988 the debt crisis was not over but it had moderated, largely as a result of recent macroeconomic events leading to reduced interest rates and a depreciated U.S. dollar. The international economy has all but revived, helping some nations' export earnings. Other nations have benefited from new domestic policies. Still other countries, including Mexico, Panama, and many African nations, however, continue to face debt burdens that are unmanageable in the short run.

Of the lessons of the last ten years, one is that although foreign capital still has a valuable role to play in the developing world, proper management of that capital is essential. Much foreign borrowing was wasted on projects that had little chance of generating the returns necessary to pay back their initial costs. In other cases, domestic policies that used debt as a substitute for adjusting to new economic circumstances proved to be harmful in the long run. Overall, much of the optimism over the prospects of the developing economies was inappropriate. Whatever else may have been learned from these mistakes, the debt crisis underscored the growing interdependence of all economies —rich and poor.

Debt service ratio   *The repayment amount of loan principal plus interest payments as a percentage of export revenues.*

Debt rescheduling   *An agreement between banks and borrowers where a new schedule of repayments of the debt is negotiated; often some of the debt is written off and the repayment period is extended.*

Stabilization program   *An agreement between a borrower country and the International Monetary Fund where the country agrees to revamp its economic policies so as to provide incentives for higher export earnings and lower imports.*

SUMMARY

1. The economic problems of the developing countries in large part differ from those confronting industrialized nations. The policy options available to governments may also differ. Nonetheless, the tools of economic analysis are as useful in understanding Third World economies as they are in understanding the United States economy.

2. The central reality of life in the developing countries is poverty. Although some countries have done well over the past 40 years, and although there is considerable diversity across the Third World, most of the people in most developing countries are extremely poor by U.S. standards.

3. While a general theory of economic development applicable to all nations has not emerged and probably never will, some basic factors that limit a poor nation's economic advance have been suggested.

4. Almost all developing nations have a scarcity of physical capital relative to other resources, especially relative to labor. The vicious-circle hypothesis argues that poor countries cannot escape from poverty because they cannot afford to postpone consumption (that is, to save) in order to make investments. In its crude form, the hypothesis is clearly wrong inasmuch as some prosperous countries, such as Japan, were at one time poorer than many Third World countries are today. However, it is often difficult to mobilize savings efficiently in many developing nations.

5. Human capital—the education and skills acquired by the work force—plays a vital role in development.

6. Third World countries are often burdened by inadequate social overhead capital, ranging from poor public health and sanitation facilities to inadequate roads, telephones, court systems, and so on. Such social overhead capital is important, but often expensive to provide, and many governments are simply not in a position to undertake many useful projects because they are too costly.

7. So-called "dependency theories" argue that the reason for the poverty of the Third World is the relationship between the advanced industrial nations and the developing countries, a relationship designed by the former to work to their own advantage at the expense of the latter.

8. Because advanced or developed economies are characterized by the large share of output and employment in the industrial sector, many developing countries seem to have believed that development and industrialization were synonymous. In many cases, developing countries have pursued industry at the expense of agriculture.

9. Import substitution policies, an industrial trade strategy that favors developing local industries that can manufacture goods that replace imports, were once widely practiced in the Third World. In general, such policies have not succeeded as well as those promoting open, export-oriented economies.

10. In the past, most development strategies aimed at increasing the growth rate of income. Many still do, based on the expectation that by increasing the size of national income the benefits of economic growth will trickle down to all members of society. By the early 1970s, however, the relationship between growth and development was increasingly being called into question, and there was a call for new development strategies that would directly address the circumstances of poverty.

11. Rapid population growth is characteristic of many Third World countries. The reasons for this phenomenon vary from country to country and from culture to culture, but it is clear that families respond to economic incentives in deciding how many children they wish to have. Large families can be economically rational for parents who need support in their old age, or because children offer an important source of labor on the family farm or in the family business.

12. Just because parents find it in their interests to have large families, this does not mean that having many children is a net benefit to society as a whole. Rapid population growth can put a strain on already overburdened public services, such as education and health.

13. Food shortages in developing countries are not simply the result of bad weather. Public policies that depress the prices of agricultural goods, thereby lowering farmers' incentives to produce, are common throughout the Third World, and human behavior is very much behind the inadequate distribution of available food to those who need it. While acts of nature will always threaten agriculture production, human actions, especially policies designed to support the agricultural sector, can have a major impact on reducing the food problems of the developing world.

14. Since 1970 the debts of Third World countries have grown tenfold. As recession took hold in the advanced countries during the early 1980s, growth in the exports of the debtor countries slowed, and many found they could no longer pay back money they owed. The prospect of loan defaults by Third World nations threatened the entire international financial system and transformed the dept crisis into a global problem.

REVIEW CONCEPTS

vicious-circle-of-poverty   544
human capital   545
social overhead capital   546
free-rider problem   546
dependency theory   546
new international economic order (NIEO)   547
import substitution   548
terms of trade   548
export promotion   549
diminishing marginal productivity of land   551

fertility   553
mortality   553
natural rate of population increase   553
produce-marketing boards   556
green revolution   557
debt service ratio   559
default   559
debt rescheduling   559
stabilization programs   559

REVIEW QUESTIONS

1. In what ways that you can think of are Third World, or developing, countries different from industrialized, or developed, countries? In what ways are they similar?
2. "The main reason developing countries are poor is that they don't have enough capital. If we give them machinery, or build factories for them, therefore, we can greatly improve their situation." Comment.
3. "Poor countries are trapped in a vicious circle of poverty. In order for output to grow, they must accumulate capital. In order to accumulate capital, they must save (consume less than they produce). But because they are poor, they have little or no extra output available for savings—it must all go to feed and clothe the present generation. Thus they are doomed to stay poor forever." Comment on each step in this argument.
4. Explain the meaning of the term "human capital," and assess its relevance in economic development.
5. It is sometimes said that in advanced countries, people invest in the quality of their children, whereas in the Third World, families prefer to have a large *quantity* of children. Why do you think this might be so? Focus on economic, as opposed to cultural, reasons.

6. If you were in charge of economic policy for a Third World country, and wanted to promote rapid economic growth, would you choose to favor industry over agriculture? What about exports versus import substitution? In each case, briefly explain your reasoning. How do you explain the fact that many countries chose industry and a protectionist import-substitution policy for many years?
7. "All we need to do is to promote rapid growth of per capita incomes in the Third World and the poverty problems will then take care of themselves." Comment.
8. Why are population growth rates so high in developing countries? (Focus on birth and death rates.) Should we be concerned that rapid population growth is detrimental to the economic progress of the developing world? If so, what would you do if you wanted to lower the birth rate in, say, Honduras or Indonesia?
9. "Famines are acts of God, resulting from bad weather or other natural disasters. There is nothing we can do about them except to send food relief after they occur." Explain why this position is inaccurate, concentrating on agricultural pricing policies and distributional issues.

23 Alternative Economic Systems

As everybody knows, a powerful rivalry exists between the Soviet Union and the United States. For over twenty years, the People's Republic of China was virtually a closed country, and relations between the United States and China were extremely hostile. In Europe, an Iron Curtain separates East and West. In Africa and Latin America, revolutionary movements continuously challenge established governments for power.

Because these and most other international conflicts today involve rivalry among economic systems, you cannot begin to understand international relations without some knowledge of how economic systems differ. This chapter discusses those differences, explores their roots in economic theory, and describes the structure and performance of several specific economies, including the United States, the Soviet Union, China, and Japan.

Every society has both a political system and an economic system, of course, but the political and economic dimensions of a society are often confused in everyday language. This chapter compares and contrasts the theory, the institutional structure, and performance of *economic systems* only. Of the two major alternative systems, a *socialist economy* is one in which most capital—factories, equipment, building, railroads, and so on—is owned by the government rather than by private citizens. A *capitalist economy* is one in which most capital is privately owned. The terms "socialism" and "capitalism" refer to *economic* systems. The terms "democracy" and "dictatorship," on the other hand, refer to *political* systems.

Whether particular kinds of political systems tend to be associated with particular kinds of economic systems is hotly debated. The United States and Japan are examples of countries with essentially capitalist economic systems and essentially democratic political institutions. The Soviet Union and Poland have basically socialist economies, and political power is highly concentrated in a single political party. But these observations do not imply that *all* capitalist countries have democratic political institutions or that *all* socialist countries are subject to totalitarian party rule.

563

Many countries—Chile and Taiwan, for example—have basically capitalist economies without having democratic political institutions. Korea was another until 1987, when it began a dramatic transition to democracy. And many countries have economies that are much closer to the socialist end of the economic spectrum than the United States while maintaining strong democratic traditions. France voted in the socialist government of Francois Mitterrand in 1981, and that government promptly nationalized several major industries. Great Britain and Sweden are other examples, among many, of democratic countries that support certain strong socialist institutions.

But do certain kinds of economic systems lead to repressive governments? Austrian economist Friedrich Hayek argues that the answer is yes:

> Economic reforms and government coercion are the road to serfdom. . . . Personal and economic freedoms are inseparable. Once you start down the road to government regulation and planning of the economy, the freedom to speak minds and select political leaders will be jeopardized.[1]

Others counter with the claim that social reform and active government involvement in the economy are the only ways to *prevent* the rise of a totalitarian state. They argue that free and unregulated markets lead to inequality and the accumulation of economic power. Accumulated economic power, in turn, leads to political power that is inevitably used in the interests of the wealthy few and not in the interests of all.

This chapter describes and analyzes the characteristics of several economic systems and begs the question of whether they necessarily lead to particular political institutions. The discussion is both descriptive and normative: we *describe* how various systems determine the allocation of resources, and we *evaluate* some of the strengths and weaknesses of each system. We open our analysis with the assumption that economic systems can be distinguished along two basic dimensions: (1) the degree to which capital is owned by private citizens instead of by the government, and (2) the extent to which economic decisions are made by central planners rather than by private firms and households in markets.

SOCIAL VERSUS PRIVATE OWNERSHIP OF CAPITAL: SOCIALISM VERSUS CAPITALISM

Capitalist   *An economy in which private firms and households own the "means of production," which include both capital and land.*

A **capitalist** economy is one in which private firms and households own the "means of production," which include both capital and land. In a **socialist** economy, ownership of capital and land lies with the government, presumably on behalf of the people. *Social ownership* is another term that is often used to describe this system.

Socialist   *An economy where ownership of capital and land lies with the government, presumably on behalf of the people; also called social ownership.*

There are no pure socialist economies and no pure capitalist economies. Even the Soviet Union has a large private sector. Fully one fourth of agricultural output in the USSR is legally produced on private plots and sold, and in a large and growing "second economy," private citizens provide goods and services to each other, sometimes in violation of the law. The United States, on the other hand, supports many government enterprises, including the postal system. The government itself employs about 17 percent of the total American labor force.

But public ownership is the exception in the United States, and private ownership is the exception in the Soviet Union. Other countries with basically socialist economies include China, the East European Soviet bloc countries (Poland, Hungary, and East

[1]Friedrich Hayek, *The Road to Serfdom* (Chicago: The University of Chicago Press, 1944).

Germany, among others), Cuba and Nicaragua in the Western hemisphere and Ethiopia and Tanzania in Africa. Besides the United States, countries with basically capitalist economies include West Germany, Japan, and Korea.

Central Planning versus the Market

Market-socialist economy   An economy such as that of Yugoslavia which combines government ownership with market allocation.

Economic systems also differ significantly in the extent to which economic decisions are made through **central planning** rather than through a **market system.** In some socialist economies, the allocation of resources, the mix of output, and the distribution of output are determined centrally according to a *plan*. The Soviet Union, for example, generates five-year plans and one-year plans. The latter lay out very specific production targets in virtually every sector of the economy. In other economies, decisions are made independently by buyers and sellers responding to market signals. Producers produce only what they expect to sell. Labor is attracted into and out of various occupations by wages determined by the forces of supply and demand.

Just as there are no pure capitalist and no pure socialist economies, there are no pure market economies and no pure planned economies. Even in the Soviet Union markets exist and determine to a large extent the allocation of resources. Production targets in the United States are set by many agencies, including the Pentagon. And planning also goes on in huge corporations.

Generally, socialist economies, in which the government owns the means of production, favor central planning over market allocation, and capitalist economies rely to a much greater extent on the market. Nonetheless, some variety persists. Yugoslavia, for example, is a socialist country that makes extensive use of the market. While ownership rests with the government, individual firms determine their own output levels and prices and make their own investment plans. Yugoslavian firms borrow from banks in order to finance investments and pay interest on their loans. The system in Yugoslavia is often referred to as a **market-socialist economy**.

What Is the Best System?

The conflict between economic systems in today's world takes place on two levels. On one hand, there are alternative economic theories that lead to dramatically different conclusions about the relative merits of market-capitalist and planned socialist systems. On the other hand, there is the actual performance of these differently organized economies. We first examine the theoretical underpinnings of the two major economic systems that compete for influence today.

ALTERNATIVE ECONOMIC THEORIES

Karl Marx and Marxian Economics

Perhaps no single modern thinker has had a greater impact on the world in the twentieth century than Karl Marx. Today about one third of the world's population lives in countries that point to Marx's work as the basis of their economic systems. Bluntly put, Marxian theory concludes that the capitalist system is morally wrong and ultimately doomed to failure.

The biggest general misconception about Marx's work is that it contains a blueprint for the operation of a socialist or communist economy. In fact, Marx did not write much about socialism; he wrote about capitalism. Published largely after his death in 1883, his major work, the three-volume *Das Kapital*, is an extensive analysis of how capitalist economies function and how they are likely to develop over time. *The Communist Manifesto*, published with Friedrich Engels in 1848, and his other writings contain only a rough sketch of the character of the socialist and communist societies that Marx predicted would ultimately replace capitalism.

Marx's economic theories lie at the root of his interpretation of history. In examining his work, let us begin with what might be called "Marxian microeconomics" and then turn to the macroeconomic conclusions that emerge from it.

The Labor Theory of Value   The centerpiece of Marx's economic theories is the **labor theory of value**. Marx argues that the value of a commodity depends exclusively upon the amount of labor required to produce it. Commodities are the physical embodiment of the labor that produced them:

> A commodity has value, because it is a crystallization of social labor. The greatness of its value, of its relative value, depends upon the greater or less amount of that social substance contained in it. . . . The relative values of commodities are, therefore, determined by the respective quantities or amounts of labor, worked up, realized, fixed in them.[2]

Labor theory of value   Marx's theory that the value of a commodity depends exclusively upon the amount of labor required to produce it; that is, commodities are the physical embodiment of the labor that produced them.

The **labor theory of value**, of course, had to address the nature and uses of capital. Goods can be produced with a variety of combinations of capital and labor. Are goods that are produced with a lot of capital and little labor worth less? Capital, according to Marx, is the physical embodiment of the **past labor** that was used to produce it. When used in production, capital contributes value by passing that past labor through to the final product. A machine that took 100 hours to build contributes 100 hours of value to final products over its lifetime. The value of a commodity is the sum of the values contributed by present labor and past labor, that is to say, capital.

Notice we have been talking about the *value* of commodities, not *prices*. Actual market prices, according to Marx, are driven to "values" (determined by labor input) by the forces of supply and demand. (The mechanism that Marx envisioned is very much like the perfectly competitive system that we described in Chapters 1 through 10 of this book.)

Means of production   Marx's term for capital and land.

Value of labor power   The wage rate; it depends on the amount of clothing, shelter, basic education, medical care, and so on required to produce and sustain labor power.

The Nature of Profit to Marx   If commodity values depend only on labor's contribution, where does profit come in? Capitalists own the **means of production**, Marx's term for land and capital. They hire individual workers who have no way to make a living except by selling their *labor power*. Capitalists make a profit by paying workers a daily wage, a wage that is less than the value that workers contribute to final products in a day.

The wage rate is the "**value of labor power**," and it is determined just as is the value of any other commodity. That is, the value of labor power depends on the amount of labor required to "produce" it. To produce and sustain labor power requires food, clothing, shelter, basic education, medical care, and so forth. The value of labor power, then, is determined by the amount of labor it takes to produce those things necessary to sustain a worker and his or her family. In essence, Marx was proposing a *subsistence theory of wages*.

[2]Karl Marx, *Wages, Price and Profit*, (Peking: Foreign Languages Press, 1975), pp. 34–35.

Let's suppose that it takes four hours to produce everything necessary to sustain a worker for a day. A day's wage paid by capitalists will be the equivalent of four hours worth of value. If a worker is employed for 12 hours, the capitalist ends up with a final product containing 12 hours of value but only needs to give four hours worth of value—or wages—to the worker. The difference is profit, which Marx called **surplus value**.

Surplus value   *The profit a capitalist expropriates by paying workers less than the value that they produce.*

Profit is thus value created by workers but expropriated by capitalists. Capitalists are able to expropriate surplus value because they own the means of production and thus control access to it. Profit is not a reward for any productive activity, it is merely extracted by virtue of ownership. Marx referred to the ratio of surplus value to the value of labor power as the "**rate of exploitation.**"

Rate of exploitation   *The ratio of surplus value to the value of labor power.*

The Nature of Profit in Neoclassical Economics

The bulk of this text has presented mainstream, or neoclassical, economic theory, with its deep roots in nineteenth-century philosophy. At this point we should reflect briefly on the nature of profit in that model, because it is so different from the Marxian notion of surplus value.

Neoclassical economics views capital as a productive factor of production just as labor is a productive factor. If you have one worker digging a hole and you want a bigger hole faster, you can get one by hiring a second worker *or* by giving the first worker a better shovel. Add labor, you get more product; add capital, you also get more product. According to neoclassical theory, in a competitive market economy every factor of production ends up being paid in accordance with the market value of its product. Profit-maximizing firms hire labor *and* capital as long as both contribute more to the final value of a product than they cost.

Orthodox theory views profit as the legitimate return to capital, a productive factor of production. To Marx profit was value created by labor that was unjustly expropriated by nonproductive capitalists who were able to exploit labor by virtue of their ownership of the means of production.

The Dynamic Laws: Marx's Predictions

The labor theory of value led Marx to conclude that capitalism as a system was doomed. The essence of his argument is that the rate of profit has a natural tendency to fall over time. With the rate of profits falling, capitalists increase the rate of exploitation, pushing workers deeper and deeper into misery. At the same time, the ups and downs of business cycles become more and more extreme. Ultimately workers are pushed to the point that they rise up and overthrow the repressive capitalist system.

Marx came to the surprising conclusion that the falling rate of profit *results from* the accumulation of capital. He had observed that over time processes of production tend to become more capital intensive. As technology changes and capitalists become wealthy, new machines are introduced and factories grow bigger. This process of capital accumulation Marx saw as a natural result of capitalists' search for more and more profit.

But this process of capital accumulation contains a trap. Remember that, in Marxian theory, capital is the embodiment of past labor which is simply passed through into the value of final commodities. If a capitalist buys a machine produced with 100 hours of labor, 100 hours of value must be paid to acquire it. The machine, in turn, ultimately adds 100 hours worth of value to final product, but *only 100 hours and nothing more.* In other words, there is no profit or surplus value in past labor. Surplus value comes only from paying *present* labor less that the amount of value that it produces.

If the ratio of past labor to present labor embodied in a product rises, profit as a percentage of product value must fall. Suppose that past labor contributes one fourth of a product's value, and present labor contributes three fourths. Further, suppose that the rate of exploitation is one third. That is, of the value created by present workers, a third goes to capitalists and two thirds is paid to workers as wages. Profit, or surplus value, is thus 25 percent of the value of product (one third of three quarters). But if past labor accounted for half of final product value instead of only a quarter, the same rate of exploitation would produce a profit equal to only one sixth of product value (one third of a half). Thus *capital accumulation actually causes the rate of profit to fall.*

To counteract this **falling rate of profit**, Marx argued, capitalists are forced to increase the rate of exploitation. One way to increase the rate of exploitation is to lengthen the working day. That is, if a worker puts in 14 hours instead of 12, but still receives the same daily wage, profits will rise. Wages, of course, can only be cut to subsistence.

Another way to counteract the falling rate of profit is to seek higher profits abroad. The establishment of colonies opens up new investment opportunities from which surplus value can be milked. Thus capitalist countries not only exploit their own workers, they ultimately become **imperialists**, exploiting workers around the world.

Marx's Theory of History: Historical Materialism　The view that capitalism would ultimately collapse under its own weight was part of a longer view of history. Capitalism had emerged naturally from a previous stage, *feudalism*, which had emerged from an even earlier stage, *ancient slavery*, and so forth. In this evolutionary view, capitalism would come to be replaced by socialism, which, ultimately would be replaced by communism.

At each stage, Marx says, a set of rules called the **social relations of production** define the economic system. Contradictions and conflicts inevitably arise at each stage, and these problems are ultimately resolved in the establishment of a new set of social relations. The conflicts in capitalism include alienation, increasing exploitation, and misery (or as he called it, "emiserization"), and deeper and deeper business cycles.

It is clear that Marx was eager for the demise of capitalism. He advocated strong and powerful labor unions for two reasons. First, unions would push up wages above subsistence and transfer some of the surplus value back to workers. Second, unions were a way of raising the consciousness of workers about their condition. Only through class consciousness would workers be empowered to throw off the shackles of capitalism, in a revolution that would inevitably be bloody.

Actual Performance May Not Matter　These are powerful ideas. They argue that private ownership and profit are unfair and unethical. Even if it could be demonstrated that the incentives provided by the institution of private property result in faster economic growth or improved living standards, anyone who accepts Marx's interpretation of capitalism has to reject its institutions on moral grounds, on ideological grounds, or on both.

The Neoclassical View

It should already be clear that the argument in this text rests on mainstream **neoclassical economic theory**. Its proponents argue that neoclassical economics provides a set of tools that can be used to analyze how economic systems function without a priori value judgments about the outcomes.

Neoclassical theory assumes that an economic system exists to produce what people want. The members of a given society are the only true judges of how successfully that goal is fulfilled, but the theory does provide some assumptions about what those judgments are likely to be. One is that "more is better than less." For example, if by using a more efficient technology, a product can be produced at lower cost, then adoption of that technology is unambiguously good, because now more can be produced in total, and that will, at least potentially, improve the well-being of someone.

Outcomes, of course, can only be judged on the basis of clearly stated criteria. In Chapter 1, we defined four such criteria that have been used over and over again in subsequent analyses: (1) *efficiency*, (2) *equity*, or *fairness*, (3) *growth rate*, and (4) *stability*. A new look at these criteria may help us toward some insights into the relative merits of alternative economic systems. As we apply these four criteria one by one, we shall be looking to see whether mainstream economics leads us to conclude that a private ownership/market system is preferable to a social ownership/centrally planned system a priori. At the end of the chapter, we turn to the actual performance of several economies.

At this point, you already know one thing: mainstream economics leads neither to the conclusion that private ownership and profit are immoral or unfair nor to the conclusion that private ownership and free market allocation are unambiguously good. Free markets do some things very well, and, as in the case of naturally occurring market failure, some things rather poorly.

Efficiency   An *efficient* economy is one that produces what people want and does so at least cost. A change is said to be efficient if it at least potentially improves the well-being of some without harming others. It can be shown—and if you have taken microeconomics you have already seen—that if the market system in which resources are allocated is perfectly competitive, the result is efficient. Firms will only produce products that people want, because if people do not want a product, they will not buy it. The welfare of individual producers depends on profits. To maximize profits, they must minimize cost, and that requires efficient production. If they do not produce efficiently, other producers will drive them out of business.

It also turns out that social ownership and collective organization can lead to inefficiency. The logic can be found in what has come to be called the "**tragedy of commons.**" Suppose an agricultural community had 10,000 acres of grazing land. If the land were held in common so that all farmers had unlimited rights to graze their animals, each farmer would have a clear incentive to overgraze: he or she could reap the full benefits of grazing an additional calf while the costs would be borne collectively. The system provides no incentive to conserve. Dividing the land up into private plots prevents the tragedy of commons because each farmer now bears the full costs of grazing and then takes care not to overgraze.

As we shall see later in the chapter, this insight aptly describes some of the tensions in Soviet and Chinese agriculture. In both the Soviet Union and China, most agriculture is organized collectively, but some production takes place for the market on private farm plots. On collectively run farms, individuals share the costs and benefits of productive enterprise. If all but a small fraction of my extra work benefits others and if all but a small fraction of any costs I impose by being lazy or inefficient falls on others, what incentive do I have to work hard and conserve? On a private plot, the owner reaps all the rewards of efficient operation and hard work and bears all of the costs of his own inefficiency.

The rejoinder, of course, is that members of collectives have a *social* responsibility to work hard and to conserve. Inevitably, then, the argument turns to private versus social incentives. Indeed, if people are motivated as much by their concern for the public good as they are by their own self-interest, the tragedy of commons is not a tragedy. Orthodox economics assumes that individuals act in their own self-interest. In that sense, it supports private ownership as an efficient institution.

Tragedy of commons The idea that collective ownership may not provide the proper private incentives because individuals do not bear the full costs of their own decisions while they do enjoy the full benefits.

Another theoretical argument in favor of private ownership and market decision making has to do with the amount of information required to do national economic planning. In a private-market setting, each decision maker need consider only the private costs and benefits of the decision. Private producers need understand only the techniques used to produce their own products. The decisions of even small private firms generally require reasonably sophisticated analysis and lots of information. Firms must analyze projected sales, alternative technologies, location of production facilities and sales offices, labor and capital requirements and costs, and so on. Even the owner of the corner gas station uses a personal computer now. To run the *entire economy* efficiently through a central plan requires an almost incomprehensible amount of information. Every sector must be coordinated with every other sector. Quantities, prices, transportation, and so forth all must be simultaneously determined or the system will not function smoothly.

The conclusion that private ownership and competitive markets are efficient, however, rests heavily on a set of very restrictive assumptions. There must be perfect information available to consumers on product quality, price, and availability. All markets must have many buyers and many sellers, and no individual firm can exercise any control over product price. All products in a given market must be identical: there can be no product differentiation. There can be no external costs or benefits. And the list of conditions describing a perfectly competitive market goes on and on. But, you may ask, what about the real world?

Although the competitive market model that we describe in Chapters 1–10 represents only a very small part of any real economy, you learned about it for two reasons. For one thing, it does describe some market forces that exist in all markets reasonably well. For another, it is simple, and thus it makes a good place to start studying the way markets function.

Why, then, do markets fail to operate efficiently? One reason is that private firms have no incentive to produce goods whose benefits are collective. Such goods, of which national defense is the classic example, are called **public goods** (they are described in detail in Chapter 16.) With public goods, anyone can enjoy their benefits, whether they pay for them or not. **Private goods** can be withheld for nonpayment—McDonald's makes a profit selling hamburgers because you don't get to eat a hamburger until you pay for it—and the market thus forces people to reveal their preferences for private goods. There is no mechanism that forces people to reveal how much they are willing to pay for public goods.

Public goods must therefore be produced through some form of collective action. In other words, there must be planning. Someone must decide how much to produce and how to finance it. One of the functions of government in all societies is to provide people with certain services that would not otherwise be produced. Public goods theory is mainstream neoclassical economics, and it demonstrates clearly that some central economic planning is necessary in all societies.

Another source of market inefficiency lies in the fact that private production and/or private consumption often generate social costs and benefits that are not considered by private decision makers. These costs and benefits are called **externalities** (which are also discussed in Chapter 16). The most often-cited example of an externality is pollution. Firms that dumped toxic wastes into the ground many years ago (or even recently) were not held responsible for the damage that might result from their actions. Nor, until recently, have firms that polluted the air and water borne any responsibility for the costs their actions imposed on society.

But for society to achieve an efficient allocation of resources, decision makers *must* consider the costs involved in externalities. Once again, the unregulated market fails, and some collective action is required. Because the market system provides no mechanism for evaluating the damages that result from the self-interested actions of firms, someone, presumably a branch of government, such as the Environmental Protection Agency, must do it, and that involves planning.

Still another source of inefficiency that often leads to public control is the existence of what are called **natural monopolies**. It sometimes happens that in order to take advantage of cost savings, firms must be very large. Huge firms, however, if left unregulated have an incentive to raise prices and cut output. Public utilities, such as electric companies, are often cited as examples. All states have public utility commissions that completely regulate the activities of such firms. PUC's set prices and profit rates and often supervise day-to-day operations. Once again, we see the need for planning.

The natural monopoly case provides a nice example of the tension between private ownership and social control. Consider again the tragedy of commons that occurred when farmers let their cattle out to graze on collectively owned acreage. One way to prevent overgrazing was to divide up the land and let private landowners make decisions for themselves. Suppose, however, that raising cattle efficiently requires a minimum of 10,000 acres. With that amount of space, grass and hay to feed the cattle can be planted and harvested using big machines. This would mean that separate farmers acting independently could not take advantage of the best technology. What, then, is the solution? One is to allow for the farmers to work together and plan production in order to maximize yield and profit jointly. But that is exactly the same solution as keeping social/public ownership and regulating and planning production as a society.

To summarize the argument thus far, in the perfectly competitive model, private firms have an incentive to produce what people want and to do so at least cost—that is, to behave efficiently. With collective or public ownership, everyone bears the costs and benefits of individual actions. If individuals act in their own self-interest without regulation, the result is inefficient—the tragedy of commons. In addition, private ownership and market organization mean that the amount of information required of any one firm or individual for efficient decision making is relatively small. Central planning requires an enormous volume of information.

But in terms of efficiency, mainstream economic theory does *not* conclude that laissez-faire capitalism is completely successful. For example, in such a system public goods would not be produced, externalities would not be considered, and unregulated monopolies would very likely underproduce and overprice.

Equity: Private Ownership and Income Inequality   Mainstream neoclassical economics views capital, labor, and land as equally important inputs that earn returns based on what they contribute to production. On this basis, then, interest, profit, and rent as returns to capital and land are conceptually no different from, and no less justified than, wages as returns to labor. In fact, without a proper return, there would be no incentive for capital accumulation, and therefore there would be an insufficient amount of it.

This is not to say, however, that unregulated market operations lead to a distribution of income that is just. The private enterprise system can, and does, lead to massive personal fortunes. Those who start up private firms that make it big can end up being very rich, and these fortunes are handed down to their children and their children's children. In a socialist economy, the "profits" from enterprise accrue to the state and, in essence, these benefits are divided up equally among the people.

The argument in favor of permitting the winners to get and keep large rewards is that such rewards lead to risk taking, innovation, new products, better production techniques, and other "good things." Indeed, some argue that the hope of making a killing is what keeps the heart of a capitalist system pumping and its blood flowing. Entrepreneurs are gamblers. By taking risks, trying new products, starting new firms, they keep the economy dynamic. Without the possibility of a big win, they would not take such risks.

Once again, theory provides no clear right answer. Capital income *is* unequally distributed. Whether the inequalities that result are fair or unfair, and whether the incentives that result from those inequalities are sufficient to justify their existence—the answers depend on the ethics of the society in question.

Growth   The rate of growth in a market economy depends on several factors: the rate of capital accumulation, the amount of education and training—that is, of human capital formation, and the rate of technological advance, to mention just a few. In market economies, these factors depend on private decisions. Capital formation takes place when private firms invest. In order to invest, firms must have access to household savings. For technology to advance, firms need to engage in research and development, and basic research must be undertaken by someone. Most of these decisions about when, whether, and how much to invest are private, and thus the growth rate is the end result of millions of private choices.

In a planned economy, the portion of GNP devoted to capital goods is set by the planners. To increase growth, all that needs to be done is to shift resources into capital production. Similarly, the plan specifies how much research and development will be undertaken, and in what areas. One would think, therefore, that planned economies could grow at a much greater rate than market economies.

In fact, however, the picture turns out to be quite mixed. During the Stalinist era in the Soviet Union, a very large portion of GNP was devoted to capital production, and the result was indeed rapid growth. But every ruble spent on capital was a ruble not spent on consumption goods. Standards of living were kept low. A planned economy could devote 100 percent of its national product to capital formation, but if it did, its people would not eat.

Even though planned economies have the potential to grow faster than market economies, a trade-off clearly exists. In addition, as we shall later see, the recent record of actual economic growth among socialist economic systems is as mixed as it is among capitalist economic systems.

Stability   Macro stability is undoubtedly a lesser problem in a centrally planned economy than in a market economy. Prices are centrally set, and that builds in protection against inflation. In the same manner, programming the number of jobs to match the number of people in the labor force can keep the unemployment rate at very low levels.

Prices and employment levels are not generally controlled in market economies. Excess demand, external shocks, and changing expectations can lead to price inflation, and periodic slowdowns can lead to high rates of unemployment. Proponents of market systems acknowledge this instability, but, they argue, the efficiency gains from market allocation justify the cost.

The debate over how much stability is necessary and desirable surfaces during periods of inflation. In the 1970s and early 1980s, the U.S. economy experienced two periods of severe inflation followed by deep recessions. In part, the recessions were the "price" that we paid to get rid of inflation, and some economists argued that the price was

Oscar Lange: Efficient Socialist Planning

In a series of articles written over many years, Oscar Lange has argued that it is at least conceivable to design an efficient system of social ownership and partial central planning.* In Lange's model, prices of consumer goods and labor are set by supply and demand forces in the market. Producer-goods prices are set by a central planning board through trial and error. Socialist producers are required to minimize costs and set output at the level that equates price and marginal cost. If you have studied microeconomics, you know that this is what would occur in competitive private markets.

In his early work, Lange concluded that information requirements and the complexity of the mathematical problems involved in planning made heavy reliance on the market and trial-and-error pricing necessary. In his later work, Lange was more optimistic about "pure" planning because of the advent of high-speed computers:

> . . . so what's the trouble? Let us put the simultaneous equations on an electronic computer and we shall obtain the solution in less than a second. The market process with its cumbersome tatonnements** appears old-fashioned. Indeed it may be considered a computing device of the preelectronic age.†

*Oscar Lange, "On the Economic Theory of Socialism," *Review of Economic Studies*, 4, no. 1 (October 1936), 53–71.
**Tatonnements* is a French word used by early economic writers to refer to the interactions among suppliers and demanders as prices adjust to equilibrium. Formally the word means "fumblings or gropings." The French verb *tatonnen* means "to feel one's way."
†Oscar Lange, "The Computer and the Market," *Socialism, Capitalism and Economic Growth: Essays Presented to Maurice Dobb*, ed. C.H. Feinstein (Cambridge: Cambridge University Press, 1967).

too high. The only serious alternative to controlling inflation by monetary and fiscal measures alone is to impose *wage and price controls*, or **incomes policies**. The United States has imposed strict controls on wages and prices several times in recent history, first during World War II, next for a short time during the Korean War, and then again in August of 1971. In 1971–1972, true controls were in place for only six months. There have been several other periods when the federal government used wage/price *guidelines*, but they had no real teeth.

When controls are in place, the market allocation mechanism breaks down, and the result is a de facto system of national economic planning. The government in effect answers such questions as Which prices should be allowed to rise and What sectors are causing bottlenecks? During periods when controls are in place, wage/price administrations act very much like central planning boards.

Does Theory Provide an Answer?

The first part of this chapter has summoned two bodies of theory, Marxian and orthodox neoclassical, to see if either gives us any a priori reason to prefer a private ownership/ market system to a centrally planned socialist system. Does theory provide any answers? Some believe that it does. If you accept the basic logic of Marxian analysis, you need go no further. To a Marxist, the actual performance of the economy is not as important as the basic morality of the system by which it operates. On the other hand, if you agree with Hayek that central planning inevitably leads to repression, then it is better to stay with the market even though it may not lead to efficient or fair results in the short run.

Neither mainstream economic theory nor socialist theory establishes beyond doubt that markets work better than economic planning or that socialism is better than capitalism. Without a compelling theoretical argument on one side or the other, we must turn to practice and the actual performance of a number of systems.

ALTERNATIVE ECONOMIC SYSTEMS: STRUCTURE AND PERFORMANCE

The Soviet Union

The History of the Soviet Economy   Marx envisioned socialist revolution as occurring in *advanced* capitalist states where a repressive industrial society had already pushed workers to unite and rise up against their industrialist masters. The Russian nation in 1913 had experienced the beginnings of modern economic growth, but it could hardly have been called an advanced capitalist system. Table 23.1 shows that although its relative position in terms of per capita income had improved in the half century prior to 1913, it still lagged far behind the other industrial countries of the world.

When the Bolsheviks took power after the October Revolution in 1917, they found themselves without the advanced industrial base that Marx had envisioned and with no real blueprint for running a socialist or communist state. Marx's writings provided only the broad brush strokes. Undaunted, the new government immediately abolished private land ownership and ordered that the land be distributed to those who worked on it. It also established worker control of industry and nationalized the banks. Sweeping nationalization of industry began in June 1918. The use of money, private trade, and any differentials in wages were abolished. All decisions were made centrally.

The headlong rush into uncharted waters proved too much, and between 1921 and 1928, there was a retreat from the initial hard line back toward a market orientation. The **New Economic Policy** of the period was characterized by decentralization. Most smaller industrial enterprises were denationalized, although the peasants remained in control of agriculture. State control of production was replaced by market links between consumers and industry and between industry and agriculture.

The experience of these two periods, 1917–1921 and 1921–1928, was debated at length. Finally, in 1928, the Soviet Union settled on a structure that remains essentially intact today: comprehensive central planning and collectivization of agriculture. In that year, under the leadership of Joseph Stalin, the first of many "five-year plans" was approved. The emphasis of the plan was rapid industrialization and the production of industrial capital; in fact, the plan called for a *doubling* of the fixed capital stock of the

New Economic Policy   *The Soviet economic policy in effect between 1921 and 1928 which was characterized by decentralization and a retreat back toward a market orientation.*

TABLE 23.1
Per Capita Income (Rubles)

	1861	1913
Russia	71	119
U.K.	323	580
France	150	303
Germany	175	374
U.S.	450	1033
Netherlands	—	366
Norway	166	659
Sweden	112	340
Italy	183	261
Spain	—	199
Austria-Hungary	—	190

Source: Paul Gregory and Robert Stuart, *Soviet Economic Structure and Performance*, 2nd ed., (New York: Harper & Row, 1981), p. 20.

Soviet Union *in five years*. Consumer goods were to be produced only when all other needs of the new industrial structure had been met.

The industrialization program depended on a steady flow of food and agricultural raw materials from the countryside, and that did not come easily. Stalin was forced to rely more and more on coercion, and in 1929 he ordered the wholesale collectivization of agriculture. The land holdings of the peasants were organized into collective farms that were obligated to deliver state-ordered quotas of farm products. Repression was severe, and countless numbers of peasants perished.[3]

No real debate about economic matters took place in the Soviet Union until after Stalin's death in 1953. In 1965 official reforms were introduced by the government of Alexei Kosygin. Most recently, Mikhail Gorbachev announced a series of reforms in 1986 and more dramatic reforms in 1987, but so far the essential structure of the economy has remained unchanged.

The Structure of the Soviet Economy

The Soviet economy is a centrally planned socialist economy. Virtually all of its productive assets, including most land and capital, are owned by the state. There is no formal private business sector, there is no market for capital goods, and there is virtually no income from property. The labor market is the only factor market that exists. Outside of money made from illegal activities and yields from private farm plots, the only incomes to households are wages and transfer payments from the government. State-owned enterprises may earn "socialist profits," but they accrue to the state, which uses them for a variety of purposes.

The State Productive Enterprise

State productive enterprise   The fundamental functional unit in the industrial sector of the Soviet economy; each enterprise is run by a state-appointed director who is in full charge of its operations but who is also bound by constraints imposed by plans and laws.

The fundamental functional unit in the industrial sector of the Soviet economy is the **state productive enterprise**. Each enterprise is run by a state-appointed director who is in full charge of its operations but who is also bound by constraints imposed by plans and laws. The assets—the land, buildings, equipment, and inventories—of the enterprise are owned by the state and are provided free of charge.

Each enterprise director is charged with fulfilling a set of targets contained in the enterprise's annual operational plan. Once approved, these detailed plans are regarded as law. While the reforms of 1965 introduced a number of new "indicators" that included profitability and improvement in labor productivity, the principal measure of success remains meeting the output targets that are laid out in the plan.

Within each enterprise, there are incentive funds out of which bonuses are paid to managers and workers for superior performance. The balances in these funds are accumulated out of the profits of the enterprise. Most enterprises classify workers into six grades. On top of a basic wage, workers may receive bonuses, overtime pay, regional supplements, and hardship allowances. The ratio of highest grade wages to lowest grade wages, including hardship allowances, was 3.29 in 1975.[4]

The Planning Process: A System of Material Balances

Five year and annual plans   Five-year plans: Plans developed in the Soviet Union by the State Committee for Planning which provided general guidelines and directions for the next five years. Annual plans: Plans developed by the same agency which contain the particular output targets, prices, materials, requirements, investment plans, and financial flows down to the monthly level.

The agency responsible for preparing the central economic plan in the USSR is the State Committee for Planning, or *Gosplan*. **Five-year plans** provide general guidelines and directions, but they do not provide operational instructions or spell out specific goals. **Annual plans** contain the particular output targets, prices, materials requirements, investment plans, and financial flows down to the monthly level. A "**system of material balances**" lies at the heart of the plan and coordinates the production targets of producer-goods enterprises with the

[3]George Orwell's novel *Animal Farm* is a parable of this period in Soviet history.

[4]Kanji Haitani, *Comparative Economic Systems: Organizational and Managerial Perspectives*, (Englewood Cliffs, N.J. Prentice-Hall, Inc. 1986), p. 124.

requirements of final-goods enterprises. Of course, the plan must take account of the availability and location of labor and natural resources, as well as the distribution of skills.

Although supply and price of consumer goods in the Soviet Union are managed, demand for consumer goods is left essentially free. The real trick is to insure that there is a reasonable balance between supply and demand, both in the aggregate and in specific sectors. Aggregate expenditure is managed on the income side with an income tax. But the most important tool for balancing both individual markets and the macroeconomy is the **turnover tax**. The turnover tax is simply a sales tax levied on consumer goods at a different rate in each market. Figure 23.1 presents a simple flow diagram of the Soviet economy in 1977, a scheme that remains essentially unchanged today. There you can see how income taxes and turnover taxes are used to equate the production and sales of consumer goods with income after taxes and saving.

Turnover tax   A Soviet sales tax levied on consumer goods at a different rate in each market; these taxes are used along with income taxes to equate the production and sales of consumer goods with income after taxes and saving.

At the market level, prices are set to provide individual enterprises enough to cover costs and generate some profit. The turnover tax is used to mark price up or down to equate estimated demand with the output that has been targeted. Figure 23.2 shows how it works. The enterprise is assigned a target output of Q^*, and a price P_e is set to cover costs. If planners have estimated demand to be D, a turnover tax of T is levied on consumers. For some goods, a subsidy is used to push price below cost. Meat and milk prices, for example, are set far below cost, with the retail price of beef at less than half what it costs the state to produce it.

The Labor Market   Although the state controls supply in Soviet output markets, leaving demand essentially unmanaged, the opposite is true in the labor market. The state takes the supply of labor and the distribution of skills as fixed in the short run. Just as consumers are essentially free to choose among outputs in the marketplace, workers are essentially

FIGURE 23.1

A Simple Model of Financial Flows in the Soviet Union, 1977
Source: M. Elizabeth Denton, "Soviet Consumer Policy: Trends and Prospects." In U.S. Congress, Joint Economic Committee, Soviet Economy in a Time of Change, vol. 1, 96th Cong., 1st sess., 1979 (Washington, D.C.: U.S. Government Printing Office, 1979), pp. 766, 785, and 188; USSR Facts and Figures Annual, 2 (1978), 215. Reproduced in Haitani op. cit. pg. 139.

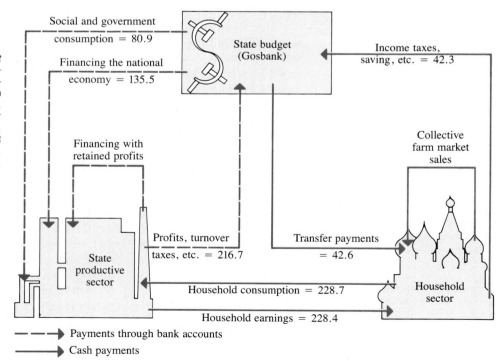

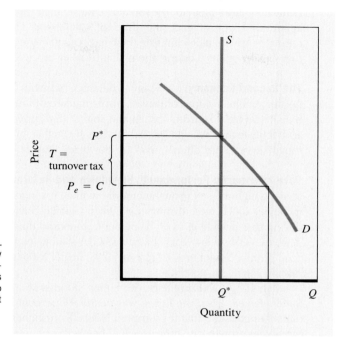

FIGURE 23.2
Setting Prices, Output, and Taxes to Balance Supply and Demand

In the USSR, prices are set to allow enterprises to cover costs and generate some profits; the turnover tax is used to push prices up or down to equate estimated demand and target supply.

free to choose their occupations and their places of work. Wages are set to clear the labor market and to attract workers into undesirable occupations and regions of the country.

In the long run, the government can influence the supply of labor and skills, as well. A close relationship is maintained between educational planners and economic planners to insure that the system is producing workers with the right skills. Graduates of secondary and vocational schools and discharged military personnel are placed in local enterprises or are directed to jobs by local authorities. Trainees do not appear to be forced to accept any particular assigned job, although college graduates are obligated to work where the state assigns them for three years.

When wage differentials fail to attract workers into difficult jobs and isolated regions, there is prisoner labor to fall back on. Although some claim that these estimates are not accurate, the Central Intelligence Agency estimates that there are over four million prisoners in penal work camps in the Soviet Union.[5]

Agriculture   The agricultural sector in the Soviet Union has three parts: state farms, collective farms, and private plots. State farms are organized and run exactly like state productive enterprises. Directors are appointed by the government, and farm workers are treated no differently from workers in any other sector.

In theory collective farms differ somewhat from state farms. They are owned by members, who elect the managers. Official statistics classify collective farmers as peasants, not workers. But in practice there is very little difference. Both state and collective farms are given quotas to fulfill. The state effectively controls the election of the managers. Before 1966 collective farmers were paid a share of the farm profits, not a wage. Now collective farmers are guaranteed a wage at the rate paid by state farms.

There are also some 34 million private plots on which rural households raise crops and some livestock. Although these plots account for only about 3 percent of the

[5]"A New Report: Soviets' Record on Slave Labor," *U.S. News and World Report*, November 22, 1982, p. 31.

cultivated land area in the Soviet Union, they produce roughly 25 percent of total agricultural output and one third of total meat and milk output.[6] The government regulates private plots, limiting their size, usually to an acre or less, and the portion of time that can be spent working them. Cultivation of these plots is extremely productive.

The Second Economy   Many productive activities in which Soviet citizens engage are not legal. The volume of private unplanned economic activity is quite significant. Goods may be brought in from abroad and sold at high prices; service providers such as doctors and dentists may sell specialized services for higher prices on the side; auto parts and auto repair services are often traded on the black market.

Soviet Economic Performance: Slowdown and Reform   The Stalinist/Soviet strategy to achieve high rates of growth certainly worked for many years. The highest rates of growth in Soviet GNP were during the 1950s. Official Soviet statistics put the real growth rate during that decade at over 10 percent, an extraordinary rate, at which real output would double every seven years. Even the CIA's more conservative estimates shown in Table 23.2 put the Soviet growth rate at 5.7%, nearly 80 percent above the U.S. average for the decade.

In 1957 GNP in the Soviet Union stood at about 39 percent of GNP in the United States. A year later, the figure was nearly 44 percent. The Soviets were catching up at a rate so remarkable that it prompted Nikita Khrushchev's promise, "We will bury you!" If the Soviet growth rate estimates had been correct, and if both countries had continued to grow at the same rates that they did during the 1950s, Soviet GNP would have surpassed U.S. GNP by 1970.

The primary engine of Soviet growth was clearly capital accumulation. During the 1950s, the capital stock of the USSR grew at 9.5% annually; in the United States, the figure was only 3.6%. Through 1975 Soviet capital stocks grew at twice the rate of capital accumulation in the United States But these growth rates did not continue, and during the 1970s they slowed down. Between 1975 and 1985, even the slowly growing U.S. economy outperformed the Soviet Union. In 1975 per capita GNP in the Soviet

TABLE 23.2

Economic Growth and Investment in the Soviet Union and the United States, 1950–1984

	USSR net material product (USSR, official figures)	USSR real GNP (CIA)	USA real GNP	USSR capital stock	USA Capital stock
		ANNUAL AVERAGE RATE OF GROWTH			
1950–1960	10.3	5.7	3.2	9.5	3.6
1960–1970	7.1	5.1	4.0	8.0	4.0
1970–1975	5.7	3.7	2.6	7.9	4.0
1975–1980	4.3	2.7	3.7	6.8	3.9
1980–1984	—	2.6	2.7	6.3*	3.6
1984–1987	—	1.8	3.9	NA	NA

Sources: Abram Bergson, "Gorbachev calls for Intensive Growth," *Challenge*, Nov/Dec, 1985. For the United States, *Statistical Abstract of the United States, 1986*, *Historical Statistics of the United States*, and Economic Report of the President, 1988
*1980–1983

[6]Haitani, *Comparative Economic Systems*, p. 118.

Union stood at 48.2% of per capita GNP in the United States. In 1985 the figure was 48.1%. Between 1984 and 1987, the U.S. economy grew twice as fast as the Soviet economy.

Part of the reason for the slowdown has been the sluggishness of Soviet agriculture. Despite the fact that Russia once served as the "breadbasket of Europe," the Soviet Union has in recent years been unable to meet its own basic food needs. The grain harvest, perhaps the key indicator of agricultural productivity, has fallen. According to one estimate, the average annual harvest for the years 1979–1982 was 15 percent below the average annual harvest for the years 1973–1978. Imports during the later period amounted to nearly 20 percent of total domestic production.[7]

Another cause of concern has been low labor productivity. In his 1976 book *The Russians*, Hedrick Smith claimed that absenteeism among blue-collar workers had reached disastrous proportions, and there are still widespread reports of alcoholism and loafing.[8] This view was expressed forcefully in speeches by Mikhail Gorbachev in June of 1987 in which he introduced dramatic reforms (see the box on the following pages). Whatever the cause, labor productivity increased very slowly in the late 1970s.

The lackluster performance of the Soviet economy during recent decades has spurred a series of *reforms*. The first, and until 1987 the most significant, was the package announced in 1965 by Premier Alexei Kosygin. The Kosygin plan focused on enterprise managers, reducing the controls placed on them by the central system and encouraging them to respond spontaneously to changing conditions as reflected in profits, sales, and worker performance. The number of targets was reduced significantly, and enterprise profits received more emphasis. A system of investment finance was established, and enterprises assumed a larger role in investment planning. Enterprise managers were also given more freedom to control an expanded incentive bonus system for workers.

The period from 1965 to 1978 saw a gradual retreat from earlier reforms. Strict controls were placed on the size and distribution of enterprise incentive funds. Managerial bonuses were tied to the fulfillment of targets, and the number of targets was expanded. By the late 1970s, the Soviet system was very much as it had been in the early 1960s, with output, prices, and investment centrally planned and administered.

Then, in July of 1979, with great fanfare the Soviet Union announced another "sweeping" set of reforms. But observers agree that the changes did nothing but reinforce the traditional features of the system and, if anything, they increased the rigidity of the central planning system.

The focus of reform shifted to the performance of agriculture in 1986. In that year, Mikhail Gorbachev announced a major restructuring of the agricultural sector that gave local units and the peasantry significant new freedoms. Local units, for example, can now use the market to dispose of any surplus over five-year plan levels. Payments to state and collective farm workers are tied to productivity and profits. Local directors have been given much more authority over management and investment decisions. But the best was yet to come.

The Reforms of 1987   In June of 1987, Gorbachev announced a series of reforms that if fully implemented would, according to *The New York Times*, "constitute the most extensive restructuring of the Soviet economy since Stalin forged the present system in the 1930s." The reforms were accepted unanimously by the 1500-member Supreme Soviet a few days after they were announced.

---

[7]See Marshall I. Goldman, *USSR in Crisis: The Failure of an Economic System* (New York: Norton, 1983), p. 65.
[8]See Hedrick Smith, *The Russians*, (New York: Quadrangle/the New York Times Book Company, 1976), pp. 296–97.

Gorbachev's Proposed Reforms, 1987

On June 25, 1987, Mikhail Gorbachev gave a speech to the Communist Party's Central Committee outlining his plans for the Soviet economy. The extent of the reforms proposed was shocking, even to the most seasoned of Soviet watchers. The following are excerpts from the 111-page speech:

Let us begin with the development of the national economy. The political bureau had drawn attention in due time to the complexity and responsibility of this year's tasks. It would seem that this was understandable to all. But serious miscalculations were made already in the first months of the year, leading to malfunction in many sectors of the economy. Both the political bureau and the Government had to take urgent measures to righten the situation, and although it is normalizing, considerable losses have been sustained.

But what had happened at the beginning of the year could have been foreseen and prevented. But this was not done, and those primarily responsible for this are the U.S.S.R. State Planning Committee (Comrade N. V. Talyzin) and the U.S.S.R. State Committee for Material and Technical Supply (Comrade L. A. Voronin).

ENTHUSIASM HAS FLAGGED

It is a fact that in many places the enthusiasm has flagged, and work is being conducted in an extremely languid manner. Instances of drunkenness have become frequent again. Loafers, spongers and pilferers—people who live at the expense of others—again feel at ease.

The causes as a rule turn out to be the same: lack of discipline, negligence, mismanagement and irresponsibility. The same is also evidenced by the violation of Soviet airspace by the West German sports plane and its landing in Moscow. This is an unprecedented occurence from all points of view.

SHORTAGES OF CONSUMER GOODS

Some ministries treat the manufacture of consumer goods formally as a secondary matter. In some places it is viewed only as a burden.

We cannot put up with the lag in community and consumer services, with an unsatisfactory situation in passenger transport, communications, tourism, physical training and sport. Can the situation be considered normal when repairs of housing, household appliances, the making of footwear and clothes both in the city and countryside become a great problem.

It is not accidental that a "shadow economy" of sorts has emerged in that sphere. Consider the following figure: Decisions of the Central Statistical Administration report that, according to their estimates, the population annually pays for these services about 1.5 billion rubles to private individuals.

REORGANIZATION: THE PLAN

It is essential to change over from predominantly administrative to predominantly economic methods of management at every level, to broad democratization in administration and to activating the human factor in every way.

This changeover involves:

Firstly, a drastic extension of the margins of independence for amalgamations and factories, their conversion to full-scale profit-and-loss accounting and self-financing, increased responsibility for achieving the highest end results, fulfillment of obligations to clients, a direct linkage of the collector's income level to its work performance and extensive use of the team contract in labor relations.

The package included some surprising changes. First, price subsidies are to be drastically reduced or eliminated, even on such politically untouchable items as meat, bread, dairy products, and housing. Second, all limits on what workers may earn are to be removed, and salaries are to be directly tied to performance. Third, the decision-making authority of the farms and enterprises are to be greatly expanded. Each of these entities is expected to make a profit, and the central plan will contain far less detail than in previous years. At the same time, Gorbachev called for sharp increases in small-scale family farming and for a "competitive atmosphere" among enterprises to insure that goods are sold to consumers at the lowest possible prices that will still cover costs of production.

Perhaps the most radical of the reforms, however, was that job security, a sacred tenet of the Soviet system, would be reduced. For the first time, enterprises can actually fire lazy workers, and unproductive enterprises will be shut down.

The extent to which these reforms will be implemented, and whether they will have a significant effect on Soviet economic performance, may not be known for many years. But there is no question that Gorbachev has, at least on paper, turned the economy of the Soviet Union sharply back toward the market, with the hope of increased efficiency, productivity, and growth.

Secondly, radically transforming centralized economic management, raising its qualitative level and focusing it on the main issues determining the strategy, quality, pace and proportion of development of the national economy as a whole and its balance, while at the same time decisively relieving the center of interference in the day-to-day activities of subordinate economic bodies.

Thirdly, a cardinal reform in planning, pricing, financing and crediting, transition to wholesale trade in productive goods and reorganized management of scientific and technological progress, foreign economic activities, labor and social processes.

Fifthly, going over from the excessively centralized, command system of management to a democratic one, promoting self-administration, creating a mechanism for activating the individual's potential, clearly delineating the functions and fundamentally changing the style and methods of work of party, local government and economic bodies.

The main thing we should achieve by adopting the new mechanism is giving broad rights to factories and insuring their real economic independence based on full-scale profit-and-loss accounting.

CHANGING THE PRICING SYSTEM

A radical reform of the pricing system is a most important part of the economic overhaul. Without it, a complete transition to the new mechanism is impossible.

Those who manufacture products whose prices are unjustifiably understated have no incentive for the increase of output, and those who, because of excessive prices, get surplus profits have no incentive to lower outlays, to enhance effectiveness. In this situation normal economic relations in the national economy are simply impossible.

The ministries should really become the scientific, technological, planning and economic headquarters of their industries, should account to the country for meeting the requirements of the national economy in the produces of their industries, be responsible for bringing production and its quality to world levels, and vigorously go about improving their sectors structurally and promoting specialized and cooperative production arrangements, should work out economic norms, levers and stimuli.

We must realize that the time when management consisted of orders, bans and calls has gone. It is now clear to everybody that such methods can no longer be employed, for they are simply ineffective. To create a powerful system of motives and stimuli encouraging all workers to fully reveal their capability, work fruitfully, use production resources most effectively—such is the requirement of the times.

WAGES AND UNEMPLOYMENT

The system of pay and labor incentives must be arranged in a new way. The law on enterprise guarantees enterprises the right to raise wage rates and wages, to establish bonuses. The possibilities of effective stimulation are dramatically expanded. But it is particularly important that actual pay of every worker be closely linked to his personal contribution to the end result, and that no limit be set on it. There is only one criterion of justice: whether or not it is earned.

The People's Republic of China

Compared with both the Soviet Union and the United States, the People's Republic of China is very large and very poor. Its population is over one billion, and per capita income is about one twentieth of what it is in the United States. The history of the People's Republic, established after the revolution of 1949, has been marked by wild gyrations of policy and some extraordinary economic experiments.

Great Leap Forward   The new strategy in the People's Republic of China which began in 1958 where they departed from the Soviet model and shifted from large-scale capital-intensive industry to small-scale labor-intensive industry scattered across the countryside. In addition, material incentives were reduced and replaced by the motivating power of revolutionary ideology and inspiration.

Socialization After the Revolution   Soon after gaining power, the Chinese Communists became involved in the Korean War and found themselves heavily dependent on the Soviet Union. Not surprisingly, the early structure of the economic system was built on the Soviet-Stalinist model. The first five-year plan, from 1953 to 1957, focused on capital-intensive heavy industries. Agriculture was collectivized, household farming was eliminated, and compulsory output quotas were put in place.

In 1958 the Chinese departed sharply from the Soviet model and launched a new strategy called the **Great Leap Forward**. The focus of production shifted from large-scale capital-intensive industry to small-scale labor-intensive industry scattered across the countryside. In addition, material incentives were reduced and replaced by the motivating power of revolutionary ideology and inspiration. Although initially successful, the strategy quickly failed, and in the early 1960s, output fell below 1958 levels. Between 1961 and 1965, material incentives were restored and the period was relatively calm.

During the 1960s and 1970s, economic development in China suffered a heavy blow from the **Great Proletarian Cultural Revolution** that began in 1966. For almost a decade, the rule was ideological purity. The faithful, which included almost everyone, denounced those who favored material incentives and reform, and scientists, engineers, managers, and scholars were sent to the countryside to work in the fields. The universities were essentially closed down. Untrained revolutionary cadres replaced trained specialists in almost all jobs, and the economy suffered terribly. Most estimates place per capita income and consumption in the late 1970s at levels only slightly above the levels of 1956–1957.[9]

The Reforms of Deng Xiaoping   Chairman Mao died in September of 1976, and the Cultural Revolution formally ended with the arrest of the "Gang of Four" only a few months later. At the same time, China watched as her once poor neighbors, Japan, South Korea, Taiwan, and Singapore enjoyed extraordinary growth and prosperity.

In December of 1978, the Chinese Central Committee, under the leadership of Deng Xiaoping, announced sweeping reforms. These early reforms focused on agriculture, and they signaled the beginning of profound changes in the character of the Chinese economy that would continue over the next ten years.

Prior to 1978, each commune shared the harvest equally among its members. Incentives were purely collective, and everything was done for the glory of the revolution. In addition, the cadres often overstated harvests. When this happened, the state raised local delivery quotas, leaving the peasants with barely enough to go around. The new system begun under Deng Xiaoping gave individual families, through a 15-year family contract, formal rights to the land that they worked. Families were also given the rights to dispose of any surpluses and to hire out part of the family labor force to enterprises outside the family plot. Deng gave the Chinese peasants permission to enrich themselves, and they have.

The results have been extraordinary. Output of grain and other basic necessities, such as cotton, has increased substantially. More important, rural industry burgeoned, employing over 20 percent of the rural labor force by 1985. From 1978 through 1983, wheat production increased at an annual rate of 8.6%, rice at 4.3%, and cotton at 16.4%. From 1981 to 1984, the growth rate of all agricultural output reached 11.0% annually. In 1984 China actually became an exporter of food, despite a population of over a billion. Peasant income has more than doubled in less than a decade, and private consumption and housing construction are up sharply.[10]

In order to improve their lot the peasants on the farms had to be able to increase their consumption, not just of food but of other things as well. Increased production of consumer goods, construction materials for improved housing, and the expanded need for small-scale agricultural implements called for a shift from heavy to light industry. The quality of peasant housing also increased dramatically.

Similar reforms were implemented in Chinese industry on an experimental basis in 1978. Initially enterprises were able to retain 15 to 25 percent of any profits over and

---

[9]See Nicholas Lardy, "Agricultural Reform," *The Journal of International Affairs*, Winter, 1986.

[10]"China: Economic Performance in 1985, A Report to the Subcommittee on Economic Resources, Competitiveness and Security of the Joint Economic Committee." The Central Intelligence Agency, Washington, D.C.: March 17, 1986, (mimeo) p. 2.

above those in the plan. By 1984 Chinese enterprises across the country were retaining over 85 percent of increased profits. The goals of both industrial and agricultural reform have been to increase the role of the producing unit, to increase individual incentives, and to reduce the role of the state and the central planners.

The most significant thrust of all these reforms is the movement by the Chinese government to support the expansion of enterprise rights. Very much in the spirit of the Soviet New Economic Policy of the 1920s, the Chinese are actively encouraging small private trade and manufacturing. There is an increasingly important private sector actually competing with state stores in style, service, quality, and even price. By 1986, 480,000 "new economic associations" had 4.2 million employees.[11] China is also now encouraging foreign investment. Initially only joint ventures with the government were permitted, but now foreigners retain 100-percent ownership in several projects. There is even a Chinese stock market!

What is going on in China today is a remarkable experiment. A centrally planned socialist state is shifting dramatically away from the Soviet model and is embracing many elements of both private ownership and the market. For now, the Chinese have abandoned strict ideology. It is clear that they are concerned with economic performance, and the early returns suggest that they are getting it.

But the vote is not all in. China has reversed its path dramatically a number of times over recent decades. Deng was 84 years old in 1988. There are harsh critics, within the government and outside, who argue that the reforms have gone too far and are undermining both traditional society and the fundamental ideology of the state, which remains Marxist-Leninist. The story, in other words, is still unfolding, as it is in the Soviet Union.

Japan

No discussion of alternative economic systems would be complete without a few words on Japan. No country in history has accomplished what the Japanese economy has during the post-World-War-II period. It is, with good reason, called the "Japanese economic miracle."

Since 1950 per capita GNP in Japan has grown from less than 20 percent of the U.S. figure to over 70 percent. Between 1951 and 1973, real GNP in Japan grew at an average annual rate of over 10 percent—in just over two decades, a seven-and-a-half-fold increase. Since the mid 1970s, economic growth in Japan has slowed, but it has still significantly outperformed the U.S. economy. Table 38.3 presents real growth rates for both economies between 1975 and 1985.

What led to the Japanese "miracle?" Was it simply a matter of culture? Japan is a very disciplined society with a strong work ethic and a long tradition of cooperation. But while cultural differences may be part of the story, there is far more to it than that.

Structurally, Japan's is essentially a free market capitalist economy. No industrialized country in the world has a smaller public sector, and none has a more "pro-business" government. To a very large extent, the private decisions of households and firms produced the miracle.

To explain Japan's success more specifically, analysts point to four major factors: (1) very high rates of saving and investment, (2) a highly trained labor force, (3) rapid absorption and effective utilization of technology, much of it imported, and (4) a

[11]*Beijing Review*, no. 25, June 23, 1986.

progrowth government policy.[12] Of these, perhaps the single most important cause of Japan's growth right up to the present has been her incredible rate of investment. Between 1951 and 1973, the capital stock of Japan grew at more than 9 percent per year, and for a substantial period investment approached 40 percent of GNP. Between 1960 and 1980, the capital stock in the U.S. increased at about 4 percent per year, while gross investment fluctuated between 15 and 17 percent per year. Virtually all of Japan's investment was financed with domestic saving. Japan's rate of saving by households has been the highest in the world.

Until recent years, rates of return on new investment in Japan have been high. But today Japan faces a new problem. Its high rates of investment have virtually exhausted the investment opportunities in the nation and pushed rates of return on saving to very low levels. The saving rate has stayed high, however, and this has led many Japanese to look abroad for a place to put their savings. A significant part of those savings has been flowing to the United States during the 1980s. Real interest rates are much higher in the U.S. than in Japan, and a considerable number of all new U.S. government bonds are now being sold to the Japanese. The Japanese are also investing dollars in common stocks and real estate by the billions.

The second factor contributing to Japan's economic success is the quality of the Japanese labor force. As early as 1950, Japan had an education level comparable to that of the United States, despite a much lower level of economic development, and most workers were employed in jobs that demanded extremely low productivity relative to the education and training of those holding them. As the capital stock grew, workers moved easily into higher-productivity jobs. In other growing countries, low labor skills have slowed the adoption of modern, capital-intensive production techniques.

Japan also consciously adopted the most advanced industrial technologies in the world. Much of the knowledge necessary to do this was available in technical journals or obtainable in American graduate schools, and some came embodied in machinery and equipment imported into Japan. The Japanese were extremely effective at improving upon and commercializing what they imported, and until the last few years, they devoted a smaller portion of their GNP to research and development than did the United States.

Ministry of Trade and Industry (MITI)   *The agency of the Japanese government responsible for industrial policy, it uses tariffs and subsidies to protect and subsidize key industries and helps some sectors plan orderly reductions in capacity.*

The role of government in the Japanese economy is certainly different from what it is in the United States. There is disagreement among economists about the importance of government as an instrument of growth in Japan. It is clear that the main source of growth has been in the private sector but that the government has played a supportive role. For example, after World War II, the government, through the **Ministry of Trade and Industry (MITI)**, used tariffs and quotas to protect and subsidize a number of key industries including coal, steel, electric power, and shipbuilding. During the 1960s, the emphasis shifted to include chemicals and machinery. In the mid 1980s, the government and the private sector launched a partnership designed to develop and market the next generation of computers. MITI also helped and continues to help as some sectors plan orderly reductions in capacity. In short, the Japanese government is actively involved in the allocation process and has much to say about which industries will grow and which will not.

A number of economists have suggested that the U.S. adopt an "industrial policy" similar to Japan's. Others counter with the argument that private capital markets do a much better job than any potential government agency of deciding which industries will grow and which will not.

---

[12]This discussion owes much to an excellent paper by Hugh Patrick and Henry Rosovsky, "Japan's Economic Performance: An Overview" in *Asia's New Giant*, Patrick and Henry Rosovsky, eds., (The Brookings Institution, 1976).

CONCLUSION

This section has introduced very briefly the institutions, history, and performance of three very different economic systems. So brief a description, we acknowledge, must be superficial—and somewhat frustrating. Many volumes, after all, have been written on single aspects of each of these three systems. But a study of basic economics without such a "tour," however hasty, would be incomplete.

Concluding on this note is, we hope, an enticement to further study. This is an exciting time in economics. Never before have systems changed so dramatically in such a short period of time. Many believe that the reforms in the Soviet Union and China have brought competing systems much closer together and that the time is ripe for a significant reduction in world *political* tensions. That can occur, however, only if we develop a mutual understanding of how our different systems work and why they are structured the way they are.

SUMMARY

1. Any comprehension of international relations today rests on some understanding of how alternative economic system differ.

2. Economic systems can be distinguished along two basic dimensions: (1) the degree to which capital is owned by private citizens or by the government, and (2) the extent to which economic decisions are made by central planners rather than by private firms and households in markets.

3. A capitalist economy is one in which private firms and households own the means of production—capital and land. In a socialist economy, ownership of capital and land lies with the government, presumably on behalf of the people. There are no pure socialist or capitalist economies.

4. Generally, socialist economies favor central planning over market allocation and capitalist economies rely to a much greater extent on the market. Nonetheless, there are markets in all societies, and planning takes place in all economies.

5. According to Marxian thought, private ownership and profit are unfair and unethical. Profit is value created by labor that is unjustly expropriated by nonproductive capitalists who were able to exploit labor by virtue of their ownership of the means of production.

6. In orthodox neoclassical economics, profit is a return to a productive factor, capital, just as wages are paid to another productive factor, labor.

7. Marx predicted that falling rates of profit, increasing exploitation, and more exaggerated business cycles would eventually cause capitalism to collapse under its own weight.

8. A number of arguments that seem to favor market organization and private property can be found in orthodox economics, but mainstream theory does not conclude that laissez-faire capitalism is completely efficient or fair.

9. The Soviet economy is a centrally planned socialist economy. Virtually all of its productive assets, including most land and capital, are owned by the state. The fundamental functional unit in the industrial sector of the Soviet economy is the state productive enterprise. Each enterprise is run by a state-appointed director who is in full charge of its operations but who is also bound by constraints imposed by plans and laws.

10. In 1987 Mikhail Gorbachev announced the most extensive restructuring of the Soviet economy since the 1930s. The reforms include increased reliance on the price mechanism, reduced job security, and a removal of limits on what workers can earn.

11. In 1978 there were sweeping reforms in the organization of the Chinese economy, particularly in the agricultural sector. The Chinese have shifted dramatically away from the Soviet model and have embraced many elements of both private ownership and the market. Early returns suggest that these reforms have improved the performance of the Chinese economy.

12. Analysts point to four major factors to explain Japan's success: (1) very high rates of saving and investment, (2) a highly trained labor force, (3) rapid absorption and effective utilizatation of technology, much of it imported, and (4) a progrowth government policy.

REVIEW CONCEPTS

capitalist   564
socialist   564
central planning   565
market system   565
market-socialist economy   565
labor theory of value   566
past labor   566
means of production   566
value of labor power   566
surplus value   567
rate of exploitation   567
falling rate of profit   568
imperialism   568
social relations of production   568

neoclassical economic theory   568
tragedy of commons   569
public goods and private goods   570
externalities   570
natural monopolies   571
incomes policies   573
New Economic Policy   574
state productive enterprise   575
five-year and annual plans   575
system of material balances   575
turnover tax   576
Great Leap Forward   581
Great Proletarian Cultural Revolution   582
Ministry of Trade and Industry (MITI)   584

REVIEW QUESTIONS

1. "The difference between the United States and the Soviet Union is that we have a capitalist economic system and they have a totalitarian government." Explain how this comparison confuses the economic and political aspects of the two societies. What words describe the economic system of the Soviet Union?
2. What is the "tragedy of commons?" Suppose that all workers in a factory were paid the same wage and had no chance of being fired. Use the logic of the "tragedy of commons" to predict the result. How would you expect workers to behave? Do the 1987 Gorbachev reforms address this potential problem? If so, how? If not, why not?
3. A perfectly competitive market system would produce an efficient allocation of resources, but the world is not like the perfectly competitive model. Name three assumptions of the model that do not hold in the real world and explain why government, even in a capitalist economy, may become involved.
4. The distribution of income in a capitalist economy is likely to be more unequal that it is in a socialist economy. Why is this so? Is there a tension between the goal of limiting inequality and the goal of motivating risk taking and hard work? Explain your answer in detail.
5. What do the reforms in China and the Soviet Union have in common?
6. "There is no doubt that a centrally planned socialist system has the potential to grow faster than a market-oriented capitalist system." Do you agree or disagree? What are some of the trade-offs facing socialist planners who set target growth rates?

Glossary

Ability-to-pay principle *A basis for taxation which stipulates that citizens should bear tax burdens in line with their ability to pay taxes.*

Absolute advantage, comparative advantage *Absolute advantage: The advantage in the production of a product enjoyed by one country over another when it uses fewer resources to produce that product than the other country does. Comparative advantage: The advantage in the production of a product enjoyed by one country over another when that product can be produced at lower cost than in the other country in terms of other goods.*

Accelerated depreciation *A provision of tax law that allows firms to write off against profits the full cost of a piece of equipment or a new building according to a certain formula within a period that is shorter than the actual useful life of that equipment or building.*

Accommodation *A monetary policy whereby the Fed allows the money supply to grow at a rate sufficient to take into account inflation and real growth.*

Accrual basis *A way of reporting revenues and expenses in which revenues are recognized when they are earned (not when actually received) and obligations are recognized when they are incurred (not when actually paid).*

Adjustment costs *The costs that a firm suffers when it changes its production level: the costs of selling machinery or buying new machines and the costs of letting people go or of hiring and training new employees, for example.*

Aggregate *The sum or total across individuals in a given category: consumption, investment, and so forth.*

Aggregate demand curve *A curve showing the relationship between the level of output in the economy and the price level.*

Aggregate income *The total income received by all factors of production during a given period.*

Aggregate output *The total quantity of real goods and services produced (or supplied) by all factors of production during a given period.*

Aggregate output (income) (Y) *The combined term used to remind you of the exact equality between aggregate output and aggregate income.*

Aggregate production function *The mathematical representation of the technological relationship between inputs and national output, or gross national product.*

American Federation of Labor *Founded in 1881, the AFL was successfully led by Samuel Gompers from 1886 until 1924. A practical, nonideological union, the AFL existed as a "confederation" of individual craft unions representing skilled workers, each with an independent organization and an exclusive jurisdiction. Now merged with the CIO, the AFL maintains a preeminent position among unions today.*

Antitrust Division (of the Justice Department) *One of two federal agencies empowered to act against those in violation of antitrust laws. It initiates action against those who violate antitrust laws and decides which civil cases to prosecute and against whom to bring criminal charges.*

Assets *All the property of a firm or organization. Tangible assets have a physical reality: cash, land, equipment, buildings. Intangible assets exist only in law or in people's minds: patents, franchises, copyrights, good will, trademarks. Current assets are cash or can be converted into cash within one year. Long-term assets are not easily converted into cash: property, buildings, plant equipment, intangible assets and so forth.*

Automatic stabilizers *Revenues and expenditure items in the federal budget that automatically change with the state of the economy: tax revenues that rise during an expansion, for example, and expenditures for transfers that fall.*

Average fixed costs (AFC) *Total fixed cost divided by the number of units of output; a per unit cost measure.*

Average propensity to consume (APC) *The proportion of income households spend on consumption. Determined by dividing consumption (C) by income (Y).*

Average total cost (ATC) *Total cost divided by the number of units of outputs, a per unit cost measure.*

Average variable cost (AVC)

Average-cost pricing *Setting price to cover average cost per unit including a "fair return"; the policy most often applied in regulating monopoly pricing.*

Averch-Johnson effect *The observed tendency for regulated monopolies to build more capital than they need. This usually occurs when allowed rates of return are set by a regulatory agency at some percent of fixed capital stocks.*

Balance of payments *The record of a country's transactions in goods, services, and assets with the rest of the world; also the record of a country's sources (supply) and uses (demand) of foreign exchange.*

Balance of trade *The merchandise trade balance or a country's merchandise exports minus its merchandise imports.*

Balance on capital account *The sum of the following (measured for a given period): the change in private U.S. assets abroad, the change in foreign private assets in the United States, the change in U.S. government assets abroad, and the change in foreign official assets in the United States.*

Balance on current account
Net exports of goods and services plus the category "Net transfer payments and other."

Balance sheet   An overall account of an organization's financial status, showing what it has, what it owes, and what it is worth at any given point in time.

Balanced-budget multiplier   The multiple by which the equilibrium level of output (income) changes for every dollar of change in government spending that is balanced by a dollar change in taxes so as not to create any deficit. This multiplier is equal to one: the change in Y resulting from the change in G and the equal change in T is exactly the same size as the initial change itself.

Bank reserves   The deposits that a bank has at the Federal Reserve bank, as well as its cash on hand.

Barrier to entry   One of a number of ways to prevent new firms from entering and competing in monopolistic industries: Barriers include licensing or other explicit government policies, patents, huge start-up costs, hostile actions, etc.

Barter   The direct exchange of goods and services for other goods and services.

Benefits-received principle   A theory of fairness, dating back to Adam Smith and before, which holds that taxpayers should contribute to government (in the form of taxes) in proportion to the benefits that they receive from government spending.

Bond   An I.O.U. A promise to pay some specific amount at some specific time in the future. Usually bonds specify a flow of payments to the owner that is determined by a specific annual interest rate applied to a specified face value. A 10 year 8% $1000 bond, for example, is a promise to pay the holder $1000 in 10 years and $80 each year in the interim.

Bretton Woods   The site in New Hampshire where a group of experts from 44 countries met in 1944 and agreed on a new international monetary system of fixed exchange rates.

Budget constraint   The limits imposed on household choices by income, wealth, and product prices. A line which separates those bundles of goods that are available to a household from those that are not.

Capacity output   The maximum amount of output that a firm can produce in the short run.

Capital   Anything that is produced by the economic system which is used subsequently as an input in the production of future goods and services.

Capital accumulation   The rate at which capital is added to the already existing capital stock.

Capital gain   An increase in the value of something owned (such as a share of stock or a piece of real estate) over the price initially paid for it.

Capital inflow and outflow
Capital inflow: The situation when foreigners buy U.S. IOU's, such as Treasury bills and give up some of their currency in exchange for dollars. Capital outflow: The situation when Americans buy IOU's of other countries and give up dollars in exchange for other currencies.

Capital markets   The input, or resource, markets in which households supply their savings, for interest or for claims to future profits, to firms who demand funds in order to invest in capital.

Capitalist   An economy in which private firms and households own the "means of production," which include both capital and land.

Cartel   A group of firms that get together and make joint price and output decisions.

Ceteris paribus   Literally, "all else being equal." Used to analyze the relationship between two variables while the values of other variables are held unchanged.

Change in business inventories   Another kind of gross private investment: the amount by which the stocks of inventories of firms change during a period, or the goods that firms produce now for sale later.

Clayton Act   Passed by Congress in 1914, it clarified the "rule of reason" and outlawed specific monopoly behaviors such as tying contracts, unlimited mergers, and price discrimination.

Clearing interbank payments   One of the functions of the Fed. Allows member banks to trade ownership of deposits among themselves and thus to shift money around almost instantaneously.

Closed versus open economy   Closed economy: An economy which is entirely self-contained and does not carry on any type of exchange with the rest of the world. Open economy: An economy which does engage in trade or which is opened up to the rest of the world.

Coase theorem   The proposition that if bargains were reached costlessly, then externalities would not result in an inefficient allocation of resources. Through bargaining and negotiations, private parties can and will arrive at the efficient solution when externalities are present without government involvement.

Collusion   The act of joining with other producers in an effort to limit competition and increase joint profits.

Collusion and tacit collusion   Collusion occurs when price- and quantity-fixing agreements among producers are explicit. Tacit collusion occurs when such agreements are implicit.

Command economy   An economy in which the state makes most economic decisions. That is, the central government decides what gets produced, when, and for whom.

Commodity money   Items used as money that also have intrinsic value on their own.

Compensating differentials Differences in wages that result from differences in working conditions. Risky jobs usually pay higher wages, and highly desirable jobs usually pay lower wages.

Complementary and substituteable inputs   Factors of production are used together to enhance each other and can also be used in place of each other.

Complements   Goods for which an increase in the price of one decreases the demand for the other.

Congress of Industrial Organizations (CIO)   Founded by John L. Lewis, president of the United Mine Workers, after the AFL rejected his plan to organize the steel, rubber, automobile, and chemical industries in 1935, the CIO was the first union to organize semiskilled laborers in the mass production industries. After 20 years of independence, it merged with the AFL in 1955.

Consent decrees   Formal agreements on remedies drawn before, during, or after litigation among all parties to an antitrust case.

Constant returns to scale   When an increase in scale of production has no effect on average costs per unit produced.

Constant-cost industry   An industry that shows no economies or diseconomies of scale as the industry grows. Such industries have flat, or horizontal, long-run supply curves.

Consumer price index (CPI)   A price

index computed each month by the Bureau of Labor Statistics using a consumption bundle that is meant to represent the "market basket" purchased monthly by the typical urban consumer.

Consumer sovereignty   The idea that consumers ultimately dictate what will be produced (or not produced) by choosing what to purchase (and what not to purchase).

Consumer surplus   The difference between the maximum amount a person is willing to pay for a good and its current market price.

Consumption function   The relationship between consumption and income. "Function" refers to a relationship between variables.

Contraction, recession, or slump   The period in the business cycle from a peak down to a trough, during which output and employment fall.

Corn Laws   The tariffs, subsidies, and restrictions enacted by the British Parliament in the early nineteenth century designed to discourage imports and encourage exports of grain.

Corporate bonds   Promissory notes, or written promises, issued by corporations to pay back borrowed money at the end of a specified period of time and to provide a stream of interest income at a specified rate on the principal amount in the meantime. How corporations raise money to finance new projects, among other things.

Corporate income tax   Assessments levied on the profits (or net incomes) of corporations. (Profits from proprietorships and partnerships are taxed as ordinary personal income of the owners.)

Corporate profits   Another income component of GNP; the income of corporate businesses.

Corporation   A form of business organization resting on a legal charter that establishes the corporation as an entity separate from its owners. Owners hold shares and are liable for the firm's debts only up to the limit of their investment, or share in the firm.

Cost-of-living adjustments (COLAs)   Contract provisions which tie wages to changes in the cost-of-living.

Cross-price elasticity of demand   A measure of the response in demand for one good to a change in the price of another good.

Crowding out   The decline in planned investment spending induced by a higher interest rate when that increase in the interest rate is caused by rising output and income (and therefore increased money demand) accompanied by no expansion in the money supply.

Currency debasement   The fall in the value of money that occurs when its supply is expanded rapidly.

Current dollars   The actual prices that one pays for goods and services.

Cyclical unemployment   The unemployment that occurs when the economy slows down or goes into a recession.

Debt rescheduling   An agreement between banks and borrowers where a new schedule of repayments of the debt is negotiated; often some of the debt is written off and the repayment period is extended.

Debt service ratio   The repayment amount of loan principal plus interest payments as a percentage of export revenues.

Decreasing returns to scale, or diseconomies of scale   When an increase in scale of production leads to higher average cost per unit produced.

Decreasing-cost industry   An industry that shows external economies of scale—that is, its average costs decrease as the industry grows. The long-run supply curve for such an industry has a negative slope.

Deficit sensitivity index (DSI)   The amount by which the deficit changes with a one dollar change in GNP.

Deflation   A decrease in the overall price level.

Demand curve   A graph illustrating the data in a demand schedule—that is, how much households will buy of a good or service at different prices.

Demand determined   When a good is in fixed supply, its price is determined exclusively by what firms or households are willing to pay for it. When a good is in fixed supply we say that its price is demand determined.

Demand schedule   A table showing how much of a given product households will buy at different prices.

Dependency theory   The theory that the poverty of the Third World is due to the "dependence" of the developing world on nations that are already developed; it suggests that even after the end of colonialism, this dependence is maintained because developed countries are able to use their economic power to determine to their own advantage—and the disadvantage of others—the relative prices and conditions under which the international exchange of goods takes place.

Depreciation   The fall in value of one currency relative to another.

Depreciation, or capital consumption allowances   The amount of capital that is "consumed," or "used up," within a given period.

Depression   A severe, prolonged recession. The precise definitions of "severe" and "prolonged" are arguable.

Desired, or optimal, level of inventories   The level at which the extra cost (in lost sales) from lowering inventories by a small amount is just equal to the extra gain (in interest revenue and decreased storage costs).

Diminishing marginal utility   The decrease in satisfaction found in a single unit of a product as more and more of it is consumed.

Diminishing returns   The idea that, in the presence of a fixed factor of production, firms eventually find the return to increasing other inputs diminishes. Implies that within its current scale of plant, a firm's marginal cost eventually rises.

Discount rate   The interest rate that member banks pay when they borrow from the Fed.

Discouraged worker effect   The decline in the measured unemployment rate that results when people who want to work but cannot find work grow discouraged and stop looking for jobs, dropping out of the ranks of the unemployed, the labor force, and the statistics.

Discrimination   The inferior treatment of an identifiable group, often drawn along racial, ethnic, or gender lines, by employers because of some characteristic irrelevant to job performance.

Disposable, or after-tax, personal income   Personal income minus personal income taxes. The amount that households actually have to spend or save.

Dividends   The profits of a corporation that the firm pays out each period to shareholders. Also called "distributed profits."

Double coincidence of wants   The condition necessary for successful barter:

both parties to an exchange must want what the other has.

Drop-in-the-bucket problem   Another problem intrinsic to public goods: the service is usually so costly that the level of its provision does not depend on whether or not any single person pays or not.

Durable goods, nonduraable goods, and services   The three main categories of consumer expenditures. Durable goods are those that last a relatively long time, such as cars and household appliances. Nonduraable goods are those that are used up fairly quickly, such as food and clothing. Services are the things we buy that do not involve the production of physical things, such as legal services and education.

Economic costs   The full costs of production including (1) a normal rate of return on investment, and (2) the opportunity cost of each factor of production.

Economic growth   An increase in the total output of an economy. Often the term is used to refer to increases in output per capita.

Economic income   The amount of money a household can spend during a given time period without increasing or decreasing its net assets. Wages, salaries, dividends, interest income, cash and noncash transfer payments, rents, and so forth are sources of economic income.

Economic profits, or excess profits   Profits over and above the normal rate of return on investment; anything greater than the normal opportunity cost of investing.

Economic theory   A general statement or set of statements about cause and effect in economic life.

Economics   The study of how human beings and societies choose to use the scarce resources that nature and previous generations have provided.

Efficiency   When applied to economics, the condition in which the system is producing what people want at the least cost. More formally, a condition in which no one can be made better off without making someone else worse off.

Elastic; unitary elasticity   Elastic describes a demand relationship in which the percentage change in quantity demanded is larger in absolute value than the percentage change in price. Unitary

elasticity describes a demand relationship in which the percentage change in quantity of a product demanded is the same as the percentage change in price (a demand elasticity of -1).

Elasticity   Responsiveness. Used to quantify the response in one variable when another variable changes. The elasticity of A with respect to B is the percentage change in A divided by the percentage change in B.

Elasticity of Labor Supply   A measure of the response of labor supplied to a change in the price of labor. Can be positive or negative.

Elasticity of supply   A measure of the response of quantity of a good supplied to a change in price of that good. Likely to be positive in output markets.

Empirical economics   An approach to economics that uses observation to test theories.

Employed   The description of any person 16 years old or older (1) who works for pay, either for someone else or in his or her own business for one or more hours a week, (2) who works without pay for 15 or more hours a week in a family enterprise, or (3) who has a job but has been temporarily absent, with or without pay.

Employee compensation   The largest income component of GNP, includes wages, salaries, and various supplements—employee contributions to social insurance and pension funds, for example—paid to households by firms and the government.

Employment multiplier   A figure used to estimate the total number of jobs in an area created by the introduction of one new job to the area.

Equilibrium   The condition in which quantity supplied and quantity demanded are equal. The price at which this happens is the equilibrium price.

Equity   "Fairness." One criterion for judging the final distribution of what society produces.

Excess burden   Often the full burden of a tax to society exceeds the total amount of revenue collected by the tax. The excess burden of a tax is the amount by which its full burden exceeds the total revenue collected. Also called "deadweight losses."

Excess demand   The condition in which quantity demanded exceeds quantity supplied at the current price.

Excess labor, excess capital   Labor and capital that the firm is holding that are not needed to produce the current level of output.

Excess reserves   The difference between a bank's actual reserves and its required reserves.

Excess supply   The condition in which quantity supplied exceeds quantity demanded at the current price.

Exchange rate   The price of one country's currency in terms of another country's currency.

Expansion, or boom   The period in the business cycle from a trough to a peak, during which output and employment rise.

Expectations effect on prices   The process of a firm's raising its prices because it believes its competitors are going to raise their prices thus shifting out the demand curve for the firm's product. If rival firms are doing the same thing, then all firms will be raising prices because they expect prices to be raised.

Expectations errors   Another explanation for unemployment based on the idea that firms may not know the market clearing wage and that therefore the firms simply set wages wrong some of the time.

Expenditure approach, income approach   Two ways of computing GNP. The expenditure approach measures the amount spent on all final goods during a given period. The income approach measures the income—wages, rents, interest, and profits—received by all factors of production in producing final goods.

Export promotion   An outward-looking trade policy which is designed to encourage the production of exports through measures such as maintaining favorable exchange rates and subsidies to export industries.

External economies and diseconomies of scale   If industry growth results in a decrease of long-run average costs, that means there are external economies of scale; if industry growth results in an increase of long-run average costs, that means there are external diseconomies of scale.

Externality   A cost or benefit resulting from some activity or transaction that is imposed or bestowed upon parties external to the activity or transaction. Sometimes called spillovers or third-party effects. Often externalities are in the form of public goods, falling collectively on many people.

Factor endowments   The quantity and quality of labor, land, and natural resources of a country.

Federal Open Market Committee (FOMC)   A group composed of the seven members of the Board of Governors of the Federal Reserve System, the president of the New York Federal Reserve Bank, and four of the Fed district bank presidents on a rotating basis; it sets goals for the money supply and interest rates and directs the operation of the Open Market Desk in New York.

Federal Reserve System (the Fed)   The central banking system in the United States.

Federal Trade Commission (FTC)   A federal regulatory group created by Congress in 1914 to investigate the structure and behavior of firms engaging in interstate commerce, to determine what was unlawful "unfair" behavior, and to issue "cease-and-desist" orders to those found breaking the law.

Fertility   The fertility rate, or the birth rate, is equal to the number of births per year divided by the average population and then multiplied by 100.

Fiat, or token, money   Items designated as money that have no other intrinsic value.

Filtering   The process wherein the newest and best housing goes to the wealthy, their former housing passes down to those of middle income, their former housing passes down to those of low income, and the oldest housing passes finally to the poor. Thus, housing "filters down" the income-distribution ladder.

Final goods   Those products that are not resold to someone else.

Financial capital markets   A set of institutions that together channel household saving into productive capital investment projects by firms.

Financial intermediaries   Banks and other institutions that make available money from those who have money to lend to those who want to borrow money.

Financial net worth   Financial assets minus financial liabilities.

Financial saving   The difference between the income a sector receives and the expenditures it pays out in a given period of time.

Fine tuning   Interventions in the macroeconomy by the government by means of taxing, spending, and influencing the interest rate and the money supply in order to (1) accomplish specific output, employment, and inflation goals, (2) stabilize the economy.

Firm   An organization that comes into being when someone or some group decides to transform resources (inputs) into products (outputs) for sale in the market. Firms are the primary producing units in a market economy.

Fiscal drag   The negative effect on the economy that results when average tax rates increase because taxpayers have moved into higher income brackets during an expansion, or an inflation.

Fiscal policy   The taxing and spending tools that the government can use to influence the macroeconomy, specifically: tax rates, government purchases of goods and services, and transfer payments. Using these tools, the government attempts to influence the level of output, the composition of output, the price level, the unemployment rate, and so on.

Five year and annual plans   Five-year plans: Plans developed in the Soviet Union by the State Committee for Planning which provided general guidelines and directions for the next five years. Annual plans: Plans developed by the same agency which contain the particular output targets, prices, materials, requirements, investment plans, and financial flows down to the monthly level.

Fixed cost   Any cost that a firm bears in the short run that does not depend on its level of output. These costs are incurred even if the firm is producing nothing. There are no fixed costs in the long run.

Fixed proportions, variable proportions   A fixed proportions production function is one in which the same ratio of capital to labor is always required to produce a unit of output. A variable proportions production function is one in which different amounts of labor and capital can be substituted for one another in different combinations to produce a unit of output.

Flow-of-funds accounts (FFA)   Data collected and published by the government describing total values of household and corporate wealth, government debt, and so on.

Food stamps   Vouchers issued to low-income families and individuals by the government that can be used to purchase food.

Foreign exchange   All currencies other than the domestic currency of a given country.

Free entry and exit   The condition in which no barriers prevent new firms seeking profits from entering and producing in a market and in which existing firms seeking to cut losses can stop production and leave a market. An assumption of perfect competition.

Free-rider problem   A problem intrinsic to public goods: because people can enjoy the benefits of public goods whether or not they pay for them, everyone is disinclined to pay for them. Consumption is not contingent upon payment.

Frictional and structural unemployment   The unemployment occurring even when the economy is at or near full capacity because the economy is always changing and because people are entering the labor force, changing careers, and so forth.

Full employment budget   An economist's construction of what the budget would be if the economy were producing at a full employment level of output.

Full employment regime   A theoretical situation in which no households are constrained from working as much as they want to work at current wage rates.

Fundamental accounting identity   The basic equation around which the balance sheet is organized:

Game theory   Analyzes oligopolistic behavior as a complex series of strategic moves and reactive countermoves among rival firms. In game theory firms are assumed to anticipate rival reactions.

General equilibrium   The condition in which equilibrium prevails simultaneously in all markets in an economy.

Generally accepted accounting principles (GAAP)   The rules established by precedent or current authoritative ruling that govern the measurement and reporting of the flow of resources throughout the economy.

Ghetto premium   Evidence suggests that during the 1960's and 1970's housing in sections of U.S. cities inhabited predominantly by blacks was more expensive than comparable housing in *white areas. The price difference came to be called a ghetto premium.*

Gini coefficient   *A commonly used measure of inequality of income derived from a Lorenz curve. It can range from zero to a maximum of one.*

GNP deflator   *The ratio of nominal GNP to real GNP multiplied by 100. An overall measure of prices.*

Government debt   *The total amount of outstanding government securities held by the public.*

Government purchases of goods and services   *A category of government spending that includes the portion of national output that the government buys within a given period—F14s for the Navy, memo pads for the FBI, salaries for mail sorters.*

Government spending multiplier   *The multiple by which the equilibrium level of output (income) increases (decreases) for every dollar of an increase (decrease) in government spending.*

Gramm-Rudman-Hollings Bill   *The law passed by the U.S. Congress and signed by President Reagan, which set a target for the federal deficit each year. If the targets were not met, the law called for automatic spending cuts.*

Great Leap Forward   *The new strategy in the People's Republic of China which began in 1958 where they departed from the Soviet model and shifted from large-scale capital-intensive industry to small-scale labor-intensive industry scattered across the countryside. In addition, material incentives were reduced and replaced by the motivating power of revolutionary ideology and inspiration.*

Green Revolution   *The agricultural breakthroughs of modern science such as the development of new, high-yield crop varieties.*

Gross domestic product (GDP)   *The total market value of all final goods and services produced within a given period of time by factors of production located within the country regardless of who owns them.*

Gross investment, net investment   *Gross investment is the total amount of investment made during a given period without regard to depreciation and replacement costs. Net investment is gross investment minus depreciation.*

Gross margin, or gross profit   *Net sales revenues minus the cost of goods sold.*

Gross national product (GNP)   *The total market value of all final goods and services produced within a given period by factors of production owned by the country's citizens.*

Gross private investment   *Total investment—that is, the purchase of plants, equipment, and inventory—by the private (or nongovernment) sector. Measured for a given period of time.*

Heckscher-Ohlin theorem   *A theory explaining the existence of a comparative advantage by a country's factor endowments: a country has a comparative advantage in the production of a product if that country is relatively well endowed with inputs used intensively in the production of that product.*

Herfindahl-Hirshman index   *A mathematical calculation using existing firm market share figures that is currently used by the Antitrust Division of the Justice Department to determine whether a proposed merger is in the public interest.*

Historical cost   *Cost at the time of purchase; establishes the value of an asset on the books of a firm.*

Homogeneous products   *Undifferentiated outputs: products that are identical to, or indistinguishable from one another and perfectly substitutable for each other—such as wheat from two different farms.*

Household   *The consuming units in the economy.*

Human capital   *A form of intangible capital that includes the skills and other knowledge that workers have or acquire through education and training and which yields valuable services to a firm over time.*

Identity   *Something that is always true.*

Imperfectly competitive industry   *An industry in which single firms exercise some degree of market power. A firm exercises market power when it is able to raise the price of its product without losing all of its demand.*

Implementation lags   *The time that it takes to put the desired policy into effect once economists and policy makers recognize that the economy is in a slump or a boom.*

Import substitution   *An industrial trade strategy that favors developing local industries that can manufacture goods that replace imports.*

Impossibility theorem   *A proposition demonstrated by Kenneth Arrow which shows that no system of aggregating individual preferences into social decisions will always yield consistent, non-arbitrary results.*

Income effect of higher wages   *When wages rise, people are better off. If leisure is a normal good, they may decide to consume more of it and to work less. This is the income effect of the wage increase.*

Income elasticity of demand   *Measures the responsiveness of quantity demanded to a change in income.*

Income statement, statement of earnings   *A statement of an organization's revenues and costs from its activities over an operating cycle, usually a year.*

Increasing returns to scale, or economies of scale   *When an increase in scale of production leads to lower average costs per unit produced.*

Increasing-cost industry   *An industry that shows external diseconomies of scale—that is, its average costs increase as the industry grows. The long-run supply curve for such an industry slopes up.*

Industrial policy   *Government involvement in the allocation of capital across manufacturing sectors.*

Industrial Revolution   *The rapid economic growth that began around the mid-eighteenth century in England. It was fueled by increasing agricultural productivity, technological advances, and new, efficient forms of transportation and it resulted in the factory system and massive urbanization.*

Industry   *All the firms that produce a similar product. The boundaries of a "product" can be drawn more widely—"agricultural products"—less widely—"dairy products"—or very narrowly—"cheese." The term "industry" can be used interchangeably with the term "market."*

Industry supply curve (in the short run)   *The sum of marginal cost curves (above AVC) of all firms in an industry.*

Infant industry   *A young industry of a country which may need temporary protection from competition from the established industries of other countries in order to develop an acquired comparative advantage.*

Inferior good   *A good for which demand goes down when income goes up.*

Inflation   *A general increase in prices and wages.*

Injunction   A court order forbidding the continuation of behavior that leads to damages.

Innovation   The use of new knowledge to produce a new product or to produce an existing product more efficiently.

Input choices   The decisions that firms make about what goods and services to buy and how much of them to buy in order to produce their output.

Input markets   The markets in which the resources used to produce products are demanded by firms and supplied by households.

Intangible capital   Invisible, nonmaterial things that contribute to the output of future goods and services, such as reputation and good will.

Interest rate   The "price" that borrowers pay to lenders for the use of money; it provides a link between the money market and the goods market.

Interest sensitivity or insensitivity of planned investment   Interest sensitivity occurs when planned investment spending changes a lot in response to small changes in the interest rate; interest insensitivity occurs when little or no change in planned investment occurs as a result of a change in the interest rate.

Intermediate goods   Those products that are produced by one firm for use in further processing by another firm.

Interstate Commerce Commission (ICC)   A federal regulatory group created by Congress in 1887 to oversee and correct abuses of the railroad industry.

Invention   An advance in knowledge.

Inventory investment   A firm's production of more output than it sells within a given period. Also an addition to the capital stock.

Investment   Purchase by firms of the new buildings, equipment, and inventories that add to their capital stock.

Investment tax credit   Another provision of tax law that allows firms to deduct a certain percentage of the cost of a new investment from their tax liability in the year that the investment is made.

J-curve effect   The idea that following a currency depreciation, a country's balance of payments may get worse before it gets better.

Job search   The process of gathering information about job availability and job characteristics.

Kinked demand curve model   A model in which the demand curve facing each individual firm has a "kink" in it. The kink follows from the assumption that competitive firms will follow suit if a single firm cuts price but will not follow suit if a single firm raises price.

Knights of Labor   One of the earliest successful labor organizations in the United States, it recruited both skilled and unskilled laborers. Founded in 1869, the power of the Knights of Labor declined after the Chicago Hay Market bombing in 1886.

Labor force   The number of people employed plus all those who are unemployed.

Labor force participation rate   The ratio of the labor force to the total population 16 years old or older.

Labor markets   The input, or resource, markets in which households supply work for wages to firms that demand labor.

Labor productivity   The ratio of output to employment, or how much output on average each worker produces. If firms are holding excess labor, this figure can be misleading.

Labor theory of value   Marx's theory that the value of a commodity depends exclusively upon the amount of labor required to produce it; that is, commodities are the physical embodiment of the labor that produced them.

Labor-intensive, capital-intensive   Labor-intensive production methods use much labor but few and/or relatively inexpensive machines. Capital-intensive production methods use many and/or relatively expensive machines but less labor.

Laffer curve   The graph, named after Arthur Laffer, with the tax rate on the vertical axis and tax revenue on the horizontal axis, assumes that there is some tax rate beyond which the supply response is large enough to lead to a fall in tax revenue for further increases in the tax rate.

Laissez-faire economy   Literally from the French: "allow them to do." An economy in which individual people and firms pursue their own self-interests without any interference or direction by government. The free market operates entirely without restraint.

Land-use planning   A regulatory system, generally overseen by local zoning boards, that stipulates what kinds of industries, businesses, and housing may locate in an area, and under what conditions.

Law of diminishing returns   The observation that when additional units of a variable input are added to fixed inputs after a certain point, the additional product of a unit of the added variable input declines.

Law of one price   The theory that if the costs of transportation are small, the price of the same good in different countries should be roughly the same.

Legal tender   Money that a government has legally required to be accepted in payment of debts.

Lender of last resort   One of the functions of the Fed. It may provide funds to a bank in trouble.

Liability rules   Legally enforced requirements that those who do damage must compensate those who can establish the fact of and the degree of damage.

Liabliities   All the short- and long-term debts of an organization. Current liabilities are owed within one year. Long-term liabilities are debts that are owed in more than one year.

Life-cycle model   The theory that households make lifetime consumption decisions based on their expectations of lifetime income.

Linked industry   An industry that grows up to serve the business needs of firms in an area.

Liquidity   A property of money that makes it a good medium of exchange as well as a store of value: it is readily accepted and thus easy to exchange for goods.

Loaned up   The condition of a bank when it has no excess reserves, when the ratio of its reserves to its deposits is exactly equal to the required reserve ratio. When a bank is fully loaned up, it can make no more loans.

Long run   That period of time for which there are no fixed factors of production. Firms can increase or decrease scale of operation and new firms can enter and existing firms can exit the industry.

Long-run competitive equilibrium   When P = SRMC = SRAC = LRAC and economic profits are zero.

Lorenz curve   A widely used graph of the distribution of income, with cumulative "percent of families" plotted along the *horizontal axis and cumulative "percent of income" plotted along the vertical axis.*

Lucas supply function   *The supply function, originated by Robert Lucas, that embodies the idea that output (Y) depends on the difference between the actual price level and the expected price level, or the price surprise.*

Luxury goods   *Goods for which income elasticity is positive and greater than one.*

Macroeconometric model   *A set of equations, which are estimated from data, designed to explain the behavior of the economy or some part of the economy.*

Macroeconomics   *The branch of economics that examines the economic behavior of aggregates—income, employment, output, and so on—on a national scale.*

Marginal costs (MC)   *An increase in total cost that results from producing one additional unit of output; a per unit cost measure.*

Marginal damage cost (MDC)   *The additional harm done by increasing the level of an externality producing activity by one unit. If producing product x pollutes the water in a river, MDC is the additional cost imposed on residents by the added pollution that results from increasing output by one unit of x per period.*

Marginal efficiency of investment (MEI) schedule   *An "investment demand curve" showing a negative relationship between investment and the interest rate.*

Marginal factor cost (MFC)   *The additional cost of adding one more unit of a given factor of production, such as labor.*

Marginal product   *The additional output that can be produced by adding one more unit of a specific input ceteris paribus.*

Marginal propensity to consume (MPC)   *That fraction of a change in income that is consumed, or spent.*

Marginal propensity to import   *The change in imports caused by a $1.00 change in income.*

Marginal propensity to save (MPS)   *That fraction of a change in income that is saved.*

Marginal rate of substitution   *The rate at which a person is willing to substitute X for Y. More formally, the ratio of the marginal utility derived from consuming good X to the marginal utility*

derived from consuming good Y.

Marginal rate of transformation (MRT)   *The numerical value of the slope of the production possibilities frontier. The number of units of one kind of good you can get by giving up one unit of another kind of good.*

Marginal revenue   *The additional revenue that a firm would earn by raising its level of output by one unit.*

Marginal revenue product (MRP)   *The additional revenue gained by producing and selling one more unit of output. In competition, P × MR.*

Marginal revenue product of labor   *The additional revenue that a firm earns by hiring one more unit of labor.*

Marginal social cost (MSC)   *The total cost to society of producing an additional unit of a good or service. MSC is equal to the sum of marginal resource costs and marginal damage costs.*

Marginal utility   *The additional satisfaction gained by the consumption or use of one more unit of something.*

Market   *The institution through which buyers and sellers interact and engage in exchange.*

Market demand   *The sum of all the quantities of a good or service demanded by all the households buying in the market for that good or service.*

Market failure   *What happens when some malfunction in the market mechanism results in a misallocation or unproductive use of resources, that is, in inefficiency.*

Market organization   *The way an industry is structured. Structure is defined by how many firms there are in an industry, whether products are differentiated or are virtually the same, whether or not firms in the industry can control prices or wages, and whether or not competing firms can enter and leave the industry freely.*

Market supply   *The sum of all the quantities of a good or service supplied by all the firms producing in the market for that good.*

Market-socialist economy   *An economy such as that of Yugoslavia which combines government ownership with market allocation.*

Matching principle   *An accountant's practice of recognizing expenses and the revenues they generate at the same time in order to match the two.*

Means of production   *Marx's term for*

capital and land.

Medicare and Medicaid   *In-kind government transfer programs that provide health and hospitalization benefits, Medicare to the aged and their survivors and to certain of the disabled, regardless of income, and Medicaid to people with low incomes.*

Medium of exchange or means of payment   *A function of money; it is exchanged for goods and services when people want to buy things and goods and services are exchanged for it when people want to sell things.*

Microeconomics   *The branch of economics that deals with the functioning of individual industries and the behavior of individual decision-making units—single business firms and households.*

Minimum wage laws   *Laws which set a floor for wage rates.*

Ministry of Trade and Industry (MITI)   *The agency of the Japanese government responsible for industrial policy, it uses tariffs and subsidies to protect and subsidize key industries and helps some sectors plan orderly reductions in capacity.*

Model   *The formal statement of a theory. Usually a mathematical statement, or series of such statements, of a relationship between two or more variables.*

Modern economic growth   *The period of rapid and sustained increase in real output per capita that began in the Western World with the Industrial Revolution.*

Monetary policy   *The tools that the Federal Reserve Bank uses to influence the money market by expanding and contracting the money supply, which in turn affects the interest rate, which in turn affects the goods market and output (income) (Y).*

Money illusion   *The term used to describe any change in the amount of labor supplied or in the amount of consumption based only on a change in nominal wages (rather than real wages). It may appear in the very short term due to lack of information but it is generally incompatible with the microeconomic theory of consumer behavior.*

Money income   *The measure of income used by the Census Bureau. Because it excludes noncash transfer payments, capital gains income, and a few other items, it is significantly less inclusive than* "economic income."

Money multiplier   The multiple by which deposits can increase for every dollar increase in reserves; basically, one divided by the required reserve ratio provided there is no leakage out of the system.

Monopolistic competition   An industry structure (or market organization) in which many firms compete, producing similar but slightly differentiated products. There are close substitutes for the product of any given firm. Monopolistic competitors have some control over price. Price and quality competition follow from product differentiation. Entry and exit are relatively easy, and success invites new competitors.

Monopoly   An industry structure (or market organization) in which there is only one large firm that produces a product for which there are no close substitutes. Monopolists can set prices although they are subject to some market discipline. For a monopoly to continue to exist something must prevent potential competitors from entering and competing for profits.

Monopsony   A market in which there is only one buyer for a good or service.

Moral suasion   The pressure exerted by the Fed on member banks to discourage them from borrowing heavily from it.

Mortality   The mortality rate, or the death rate, is equal to the number of deaths per year divided by the average population and then multiplied by 100.

Movement along a demand curve   What happens when a change in price, up or down, causes quantity demanded to change.

Multiplier   The multiple by which the equilibrium level of output increases or decreases when some variable, such as planned investment, changes.

M1, transactions money   Cash and cash substitutes that can be used for actual transactions: bills, coins, and checking account balances.

M2, broad money   M1 plus near monies that can be easily converted into cash—or transferred into checking accounts, savings accounts and money market accounts.

National income   Net national product minus indirect taxes less subsidies, or the total amount earned by factors of production in the economy.

National income accounts (NIA)   Data collected and published by the government describing the various components of national income in the economy.

National Labor Relations board   A watchdog board established by the Wagner Act in 1935 whose duties include ensuring that all workers are guaranteed the right to join unions and that firm managers participate fairly in collective bargaining if so requested by a majority of their employees.

Natural monopoly   An industry which realizes such large economies of scale in producing its product that single-firm production of that good or service is most efficient. An industry with a continuously declining average cost curve.

Natural rate of population increase   Defined as the difference between the birth rate and the death rate (it excludes migration).

Natural rate of unemployment   The unemployment that occurs "naturally" in practice. Although "natural" is hard to define, the phrase is usually taken to be frictional unemployment plus structural unemployment.

Near monies   Funds that are relatively close substitutes for transactions money, such as savings account balances and money market accounts.

Net exports   The difference between exports (sales to foreigners of U.S.-produced goods and services) and imports (purchases of goods and services from abroad.) The figure can be positive or negative.

Net income   That which is left after costs are deducted from revenues; the profits of a firm.

Net interest   Another income component of GNP; the interest paid by businesses to the households that made the loans.

Net national product   Gross national product minus depreciation; a nation's total product less what is required to maintain the value of its capital stock.

Net operating income   The gross margin minus other operating expenses.

Net taxes (T)   All the taxes collected by the government minus all the transfer payments the government makes during a given period.

New Economic Policy   The Soviet economic policy in effect between 1921 and 1928 which was characterized by decentralization and a retreat back toward a market orientation.

Nominal GNP   Gross national product measured in current dollars.

Nominal wage rates, real wage rates   The nominal, or money, wage rate is the wage rate measured in current dollars. The real wage rate is the wage rate measured in the goods and services those dollars can buy—that is, the nominal wage rate adjusted over time for changes in the price level. It is the real wage rate that affects consumption and labor supply decisions.

Nonexcludable   Another characteristic of most public goods: their benefits fall on all members of a group or a society and no one can be excluded from enjoying those benefits once the good is produced.

Nonlabor income channel   The way in which a change in government spending affects the economy through its effect on nonlabor income such as dividends.

Nonlabor, or nonwage, income   Any income that is received from sources other than working—inheritances, dividends, interest, rents, transfer payments and so on.

Nonresidential investment   One kind of gross private investment: expenditures by firms on final goods such as machines, tools, buildings, and so on.

Nonrival in consumption   A characteristic of public goods: one person's enjoyment of the benefits of a public good does not detract from another's enjoyment of them.

Nonsynchronization of income and spending   The mismatch between the timing of money inflow to the household (usually once a month) and the timing of money outflow for household expenses (usually all through the month.)

Normal good   A good for which demand goes up when income is higher and for which demand goes down when income is lower.

Normal rate of profit, or return   A rate of profit that is just sufficient to keep owners and investors satisfied; for relatively risk-free firms it should be the same as the interest rate on risk-free government bonds.

Normative economics   An approach to economics that analyzes outcomes of economic behavior, evaluates them as good or bad, and may suggest improvements.

Occupational segregation   The fact that men and women seem to be concentrated in certain occupations. For *example, most secretaries and nurses are women and most college professors are men.*

Okun's law   *The law which predicted that the unemployment rate decreased about one percentage point for every three-percent increase in GNP. As with the Phillips Curve, Okun's law has not turned out to show a stable relationship.*

Oligopoly   *An industry structure (or market organization) with a small number of (usually) large firms producing products that range from highly differentiated (automobiles) to standardized (steel). One huge firm may dominate or a few large firms may share market power. Firm behavior in an oligopoly varies from monopolistic to highly competitive. In general, entry of new firms into an oligopolistic industry is difficult but possible.*

On the job training   *The principle form of human capital investment undertaken by firms.*

Open Market Desk   *The office in the New York Federal Reserve Bank from which government securities are bought and sold by the Fed.*

Open market operations   *The purchase and sale by the Fed of government securities in the open market; a tool to expand or contract the amount of reserves in the system and hence the money supply.*

Opportunity cost   *What we give up, or forgo, when we choose one thing over another.*

Opportunity cost of leisure   *The market goods and services one gives up by not working for a wage.*

Opportunity set or choice set   *The options among which a household may choose in the market after considering the limitations imposed by its budget constraint. The set of all commodity bundles available to a household given its income, wealth, and current prices.*

Out of the labor force   *The description of a person who is not employed and has not made an active effort to look for work during the most recent four weeks.*

Paradox of thrift   *The observation that increased saving can have an effect opposite to its intent: decreased consumption by households results in decreased output, which in turn results in decreased income so that households are less well off than they were when they*

began to save. This does not happen if there are channels through which increased saving can be converted into increased investment.

Pareto efficiency, or optimality   *A condition in which no change is possible that will make some member of society better off without making some other member of society worse off.*

Partnership   *A form of business organization in which there is more than one proprietor. The owners are responsible jointly and separately for the firm's obligations.*

Per capita GNP   *GNP divided by the population of the country.*

Perfect competition   *An industry structure (or market organization) in which there are many firms, each small relative to the industry, producing virtually identical products and in which no firm has any control over prices but takes price as given. In perfectly competitive industries, new competitors can freely enter and exit the market.*

Perfectly contestable market   *A market in which entry and exit are costless. If capital were fully mobile, a firm could enter a market, compete for profits, and leave without incurring start-up or shut-down costs.*

Perfectly elastic demand   *A horizontal demand curve. If price is increased, quantity demanded drops to zero.*

Permanent income   *Expected long-run future income.*

Personal consumption expenditures   *A major component of GNP: expenditures by consumers on goods and services.*

Personal income   *The total income of households—that is, national income minus retained corporate profits and minus social insurance tax payments made to the government and plus interest income received by households and transfer payments to households. The income received by households after paying social insurance taxes but before paying personal income taxes.*

Personal saving   *The amount that households have per period that is left over after they have spent whatever they are going to spend in that period.*

Personal saving rate   *The percentage of personal disposable income that is saved. If low, demand is high and households are spending a lot relative to their incomes; if high, demand is low and households are*

spending cautiously.

Phillips Curve   *A graph with either the rate of wage inflation or the rate of price inflation on the vertical axis and some measure of demand pressure, such as the unemployment rate, on the horizontal axis. The curve implies a trade-off between inflation and unemployment, a trade-off which broke down in the 1970s and 1980s.*

Physical, or tangible, capital   *Material things used as inputs in the production of future goods and services, such as buildings, machinery, and inventories.*

Planned aggregate expenditure $[AE \equiv C + I]$ *The total planned expenditure for newly produced goods and services during a given period.*

Planned, or desired, investment, actual investment   *Planned investment refers to those additions to capital stock and inventory planned by firms; actual investment is the actual amount of investment that takes place; it includes items such as unplanned changes in inventories.*

Plant and equipment investment   *A firm's purchase of additional machines or factories or buildings within a given period. An addition to the capital stock.*

Policy mix   *The shifting combination of fiscal and monetary strategies that policy makers use to influence the level and composition of income and output and the level of the interest rate at any given time.*

Political business cycle   *A business cycle generated by policy makers for the purpose of maximizing their chances of being reelected.*

Population-serving industry   *An industry that grows up to serve the needs of the people living or working in an area.*

Positive economics   *An approach to economics that seeks to understand behavior and the operation of systems without making judgments. It describes what is and how it works.*

Post hoc, ergo propter hoc   *Literally, "after this (in time), therefore because of this." A common error made in thinking about causation: if Event A happens before Event B happens, you cannot infer that A caused B.*

Poverty line   *The officially established income level that distinguishes the poor from the non-poor. It is set at three times the cost of the Department of Agriculture's minimum food budget.*

Present discounted value   *The present*

discounted value of R dollars to be paid t years in the future is the amount you need to put aside today, at current interest rates, to insure that you end up with R dollars t years from now. It is the current market value of a contract to deliver R dollars in t years.

Price ceiling A maximum price per unit above which producers of a good or service may not legally charge; usually imposed by government regulation.

Price discrimination What happens when a firm charges different buyers different prices for the same product. Such strategies are illegal if they drive out competition.

Price elasticity of demand The ratio of the percentage change in quantity demanded to the percentage change in price.

Price leadership The result when one firm that dominates an oligopoly sets prices and all the smaller firms in the industry follow its pricing policy.

Price surprise The actual price level minus the expected price level.

Price-expectations effect on wages The effect that expectations about the rate of inflation in the future will have on nominal wages if both firms and workers think about wage rates in real terms.

Principle of neutrality A tax that distorts economic decisions for no good reason is less efficient than a tax that is more neutral.

Principle of second best The fact that a tax distorts an economic decision does not always imply that such a tax imposes an excess burden. If previously existing distortions exist, such a tax may actually improve efficiency.

Private sector Includes all independently owned profit-making firms, nonprofit organizations, and households; all the decision-making units in the economy that are not the government.

Produce-marketing boards The structures through which some Third World governments both buy farm output and sell it to urban residents at government controlled prices.

Producer price indices A measure of prices that producers receive for products at all stages in the production process.

Producers Any person or group of people, whether private or public, who transform resources into usable output.

Product differentiation One strategy

that firms use to achieve market power. Accomplished by producing truly different products and by creating differentiated product images by means of advertising.

Product, or output, markets The markets in which final goods and services are exchanged.

Production The process through which firms combine and transform inputs into outputs.

Production function The relationship between output and inputs—that is, how much output can be produced given a variety of combinations of capital and labor and other inputs.

Production possibility frontier (ppf) A graph that shows all the combinations of goods and services that can be produced given the resources of a society and the existing state of technology.

Production technology The relationship between inputs and outputs.

Productivity, or labor productivity Output per worker hour; total output divided by the number of hours worked in the economy.

Progressive tax A tax whose burden, expressed as a percentage of income, increases as income increases.

Property income Income from the ownership of real property and financial holdings. It takes the form of profits, interest, dividends, and rents.

Proportional tax A tax whose burden is the same proportion of income for all households.

Proprietors' income Another income component of GNP; the income of unincorporated businesses.

Proprietorship A form of business organization in which a person simply sets up to provide goods or services at a profit. In a proprietorship, the proprietor, or owner, is the firm. The assets and liabilities of the firm are the owner's assets and liabilities without limit.

Protection The shielding of some sector of the economy from foreign competition through the use of tariffs or quotas.

Public assistance, or "welfare" Government transfer programs that provide cash benefits to (1) families with dependent children whose incomes and assets fall below a very low line and (2) the very poor regardless of whether or not they have children.

Public choice theory An approach to economic theory which proceeds on the

assumption that the elected and nonelected public officials who set economic policies and regulate the players act in their own self interest (just as firms do).

Public goods Goods or services that bestow collective benefits on members of society; they are, in a sense, collectively consumed. Generally, since benefits are collective, one cannot be excluded from enjoying them once they are produced. The classic example is national defense.

Public sector Includes all agencies at all levels of government federal, state, and local.

Pure monopoly An industry made up of only one firm that produces a product for which there are no close substitutes and in which significant barriers exist to prevent new firms from entering the industry.

Pure rent The return to any factor of production that is in fixed supply.

Quantity demanded The amount of a product that a household would buy in a given period if it could buy all it wanted at the current price.

Quantity theory of money The theory based on the identity $M \cdot V \equiv P \cdot Y$ and the assumption that the velocity of money (V) is constant (or virtually constant).

Queuing A nonprice-rationing mechanism which uses waiting in line as a means of allocating goods and services.

Quota A limit on the quantity of imports.

Racial covenants Provisions spelled out in deeds to property that prohibited sale of that property to members of specific racial or ethnic groups.

Rate of exploitation The ratio of surplus value to the value of labor power.

Rational-expectations hypothesis The hypothesis that people know the "true model" of the economy and that they use this model to form their expectations of the future.

Real GNP Gross national product measured in the dollars of a fixed, or base, year.

Real interest rate The interest rate minus the rate of inflation.

Receivables and payables Receivables are revenues earned but not yet collected; payables are obligations incurred but not yet paid.

Recession Formally, a period in which real GNP declines for at least two consecutive quarters. Marked by falling output and rising unemployment.

Recognition lags   The time it takes for policy makers to recognize the existence of a boom or slump.

Regressive tax   A tax whose burden, expressed as a percentage of income, falls as income increases.

Relative-wage explanation for unemployment   An explanation for sticky wages (and therefore unemployment): if workers are concerned about their wages relative to other workers in other firms and industries, they may not be willing to accept a wage cut unless they know that all other workers are receiving similar cuts.

Rent seeking   Actions taken by firms or households to preserve extranormal profits. For example, a monopolist might lobby the government for an exclusive license that would prevent competition.

Rental income   Another income component of GNP; the income received as rent by property owners.

Required reserve ratio   The percentage of its total deposits that a bank must keep as reserves.

Residential investment   Another kind of gross private investment: expenditures by households and firms on new houses and apartment buildings.

Resources   Anything provided by nature or previous generations that can be used directly or indirectly to satisfy human wants.

Response lags   The time that it takes for the economy to adjust to the new conditions after a new policy is implemented; the lags that occur because of the operation of the economy itself.

Retained earnings   The profits that a corporation keeps, usually for investment purposes, rather than paying them out to shareholders. Also called "undistributed profits."

Return, or yield, on investment   The profits that flow from an investment over time.

Revenue, total revenue   Receipts from the sale of product. P x Q.

Rule of reason   The criterion introduced by the Supreme Court in 1911 and used to determine whether a particular action was illegal ("unreasonable") or legal ("reasonable") within the terms of the Sherman Act.

Run on a bank   What happens when those who have claims on a bank (deposits) present them (withdraw their deposits) all at the same time.

Saving   That part of household income that a household does not consume during a given period.

Shares of stock   Financial instruments that give to the holder a share in the ownership of a firm and therefore the right to share in the profits of the firm.

Sherman Act   Passed by Congress in 1890, the Act declares every contract or conspiracy to restrain trade among states or nations illegal and declares any attempt at monopoly, successful or not, a misdemeanor. Interpretation of what specific behaviors were illegal fell to the courts.

Shift of a demand curve   What happens when a new relationship between quantity demanded of a good and the price of that good is brought about by a change in something that had previously been held constant, like tastes or income.

Short run   The period of time for which two conditions hold; the firm is operating under a fixed scale (fixed factor) of production and firms can neither enter nor exit an industry.

Shut-down point   The lowest point on the average variable cost curve. When price falls below AVC, total revenue is insufficient to cover variable costs and the firm will shut down and bear losses equal to fixed costs.

Smoot-Hawley tariff   The U.S. tariff law of the 1930s, which set the highest tariffs in U.S. history (60 percent); it set off an international trade war and caused the decline in trade, which is often pointed to as a cause of the worldwide depression of the 1930s.

Social capital or infrastructure   A form of tangible capital, produced largely by governments but in some cases also by private firms, that renders services that contribute to the public good. Roads, highways, bridges, water and sewer systems, public utilities, transportation systems, telecommunications networks, and so forth are a few examples.

Social choice   The problem of deciding what societies want. The process of somehow aggregating or adding up individual preferences to make a choice for the whole.

Social insurance, or payroll tax   Assessments figured as a percentage of wages and salaries levied on employees and employers. Proceeds support various government-administrated social-benefit programs. The largest of these is the social security system, which issues various cash and health benefits to retirees, the disabled, and survivors of workers who paid into the system; another program is the unemployment compensation system administered by the states.

Social overhead capital   Basic infrastructure projects such as roads, power generation, and irrigation systems.

Social security system   The federal system of social insurance programs. It includes three separate programs that are financed through separate trust funds: an old age and survivors insurance program, a disability insurance program, and a health insurance program for the elderly.

Social-contract explanation for unemployment   Another explanation for sticky wages: firms enter into a "social contract" with workers not to cut nominal wages.

Socialist   An economy where ownership of capital and land lies with the government, presumably on behalf of the people; also called social ownership.

Sources side/uses side   The impact of a tax may be felt on one or the other or both sides of the income equation. A tax may cause net income to fall (damage on the sources side) or it may cause prices of goods and services to rise so that income buys less (damage on the uses side).

Spreading overhead   The process of dividing total fixed costs by more units of output. What happens is that average fixed cost declines as Q rises.

Stability   A condition in which output is steady or growing with low inflation and full employment of resources. Refers to stability of output and prices.

Stabilization program   An agreement between a borrower country and the International Monetary Fund where the country agrees to revamp its economic policies so as to provide incentives for higher export earnings and lower imports.

Stagflation   The persistence of high unemployment (stagnation) at the same time that the price level is rising rapidly (inflation).

State productive enterprise   The fundamental functional unit in the industrial sector of the Soviet economy; each enterprise is run by a state-appointed director who is in full charge of its operations but who is also bound by constraints imposed by plans and laws.

Sticky wages The downward rigidity of wages as an explanation of unemployment.

Stock variables, flow variables Stock variables *have values measured at a given point in time. Flow variables have values measured over a given period of time.*

Store of value *Another function of money: it transports purchasing power from one time and place to another.*

Structural deficit, cyclical deficit A structural deficit *occurs because of the structure of government taxing and spending programs and may exist whether or not there is full employment. A* cyclical deficit *occurs because the economy is in a downturn of the business cycle; by definition, the cyclical deficit of the full employment budget is zero.*

Structural unemployment *The long-run unemployment problems that result when rapid changes in the structure of the economy result in significant losses of jobs in certain industries and in the availability of other jobs for which enough people are not trained.*

Substitutes *Goods that can serve as a replacement one for the other; when the price of one increases, demand for the other goes up.*

Substitution effect of a wage change *What happens when a wage increase leads to a substitution of labor for leisure because leisure now has a higher opportunity cost (or a wage decrease leads to a substitution of leisure for labor since leisure has a lower opportunity cost.)*

Sunk costs *Another name for fixed costs (or total fixed costs) in the short run because firms have no choice but to pay them.*

Supply curve *A graph illustrating the data in a supply schedule—that is, the quantity of a product that firms will supply at different prices.*

Supply schedule *A table showing how much of a product firms will supply at different prices.*

Surplus, deficit A surplus *results when the government takes in more than it spends during a given period; revenues minus expenditures is a positive number. A* deficit *results when the government spends more than it takes in during a given period; revenues minus expenditures is a negative number.*

Surplus value *The profit a capitalist*

expropriates by paying workers less than the value that they produce.

Tariff A tax on imports.

Tax base *The measure or value upon which a tax is levied. Examples include income, sales, and home value.*

Tax incidence *When we speak of the incidence of a tax, we are speaking of the ultimate distribution of its burden.*

Tax multiplier *The multiple by which the equilibrium level of output (income) increases (decreases) for every dollar of a decrease (increase) in taxes.*

Tax rate *The percentage of a tax base that must be paid in taxes—15 percent of income, for example.*

Tax shifting *What happens when the person or institution on which a tax is initially levied does not bear its entire burden. The burden of a tax can be shifted when markets and prices adjust to its presence.*

Terms of trade *The ratio at which a country can trade domestic products for imported products.*

The business cycle *A period during which an economy expands and contracts.*

The Cournot model *A model of a two firm industry (duopoly) in which each firm fails to properly anticipate the reaction of its competitor to its own output and pricing decisions.*

The goods market *The market in which goods and services are exchanged and in which the equilibrium level of output is determined.*

The Great Depression *The period of bank failures, severe economic contraction, and high unemployment that began with the collapse of stock prices in October 1929 and continued throughout the 1930s.*

The incidence of a tax *Refers to the ultimate distribution of the burden of the tax among households.*

The money market *The market in which financial instruments are exchanged and in which the equilibrium level of the interest rate is determined.*

The three basic questions *The questions that all societies answer by means of their economic organization: (1) What gets produced? (2) How does it get produced? (3) Who gets what is produced?*

Theory of comparative advantage *Ricardo's theory that specialization and free trade will benefit all trading partners (real wages will rise),*

even those that may be absolutely less efficient producers.

Time lags *Delays in the response of the economy to stabilization policies.*

Total cost (TC) *The sum of total fixed and total variable costs.*

Total revenue (TR) *The product of price per unit and the quantity of output the firm decides to produce* $(P \times Q)$.

Trade surplus, trade deficit Trade surplus: *The situation when a country exports more than it imports.* Trade deficit: *The situation when a country imports more than it exports.*

Tragedy of commons *The idea that collective ownership may not provide the proper private incentives because individuals do not bear the full costs of their own decisions while they do enjoy the full benefits.*

Transaction costs *All the time and money costs, other than production costs and final prices, that are involved in buying and selling: dissemination of product information, advertising, transportation to and from market, and so forth.*

Transaction motive *The main reason that we hold money—to buy things.*

Transfer payments *Payments by the government, such as social security, veterans benefits, and welfare, to people who do not supply current goods, services, or labor in exchange for these payments.*

Treasury bonds, notes, and bills *Promissory notes, that is, written promises, issued by the government to pay back borrowed money at the end of a specified period of time and to provide a stream of interest income at a specified rate on the principal amount in the meantime. How the government raises money to finance its deficit.*

Turnover tax *A Soviet sales tax levied on consumer goods at a different rate in each market; taxes are used along with income taxes to equate the production and sales of consumer goods with income after taxes and saving.*

Unconstrained supply of labor, constrained supply of labor *The* unconstrained labor supply *is the amount a household would like to work within a given period at current wage rates if it could find the work. The* constrained labor supply *is the amount a household actually works within a given period at current wage rates.*

Underground economy   That part of the economy in which transactions take place and in which income is generated that is unreported for various reasons and therefore not counted in GNP.

Unemployed   The description of a person 16 years old or older who is not working, is available for work, and has made specific efforts to find work during the previous four weeks.

Unemployment rate   The percentage of the labor force that is unemployed.

Unemployment regime   A theoretical situation in which some households are constrained from working as much as they want to work at current wage rates.

Unit of account   Another function of money: its use as a standard unit provides a consistent way to quote prices.

Urban decline   The deterioration of the private and social capital stock of a city which results from the lack of investment by both private and public sectors.

Utilitarian justice   The idea that a dollar in the hand of a rich person buys "less" than a dollar in the hand of a poor person. If the marginal utility of income declines with income, transferring income from the rich to the poor will increase total utility.

Utility   The basis of choice. The satisfaction, or reward, a product yields. The intangible "worth" we find in things

that enables us to compare and rank unlike things.

Utility possibility frontier   A graphical representation of a two person world that shows all points at which A's utility can only be increased if B's utility is decreased. That is, it represents all Pareto efficient points at which A can be made better off only by making B worse off.

Value added   The difference between the value of goods when they leave a production stage and the cost of the goods when they entered that stage.

Value of labor power   The wage rate; it depends on the amount of clothing, shelter, basic education, medical care, and so on required to produce and sustain labor power.

Variable cost   Any cost that a firm bears as a result of production and which depends on the level of production chosen.

Velocity of money   The number of times a dollar bill changes hands, on average, during the course of a year; the ratio of nominal GNP to the stock of money.

Vicious-circle-of-poverty   The hypothesis that suggests that poverty is self-perpetuating since poor nations are unable to save and invest enough to accumulate the capital stock which would

help them grow.

Voting paradox   A simple demonstration of how majority rule voting can lead to seemingly contradictory and inconsistent results. A commonly cited illustration of the kind of inconsistency described in the impossibility theorem.

Wage rate   The most important influence on the choice between working (supplying labor) and not working: the amount you are paid if you work.

Wage-expectations effect on wages   The process that causes a firm to increase its own wage rate because it expects other firms to raise their wage rates.

Wealth channel   The way in which a change in government spending affects the economy through its effect on wealth.

Yellow-dog contracts   Contracts forced on labor by management which prohibit workers from joining unions.

Zoning   The designation of certain areas for industry, commerce, and housing. Often these categories are broken down into subcategories which specify the kind of business allowed, the number of families allowed within a single residential building, how much land a residence must have around it, and so on.

Index